Defenseless Under the Night

Defenseless Under the Night

The Roosevelt Years and the Origins of Homeland Security

MATTHEW DALLEK

OXFORD
UNIVERSITY PRESS

OXFORD

UNIVERSITY PRESS

Oxford University Press is a department of the University of Oxford. It furthers
the University's objective of excellence in research, scholarship, and education
by publishing worldwide. Oxford is a registered trade mark of Oxford University
Press in the UK and certain other countries.

Published in the United States of America by Oxford University Press
198 Madison Avenue, New York, NY 10016, United States of America.

Library of Congress Cataloging-in-Publication Data
Names: Dallek, Matthew, 1969- author.
Title: Defenseless under the night : the Roosevelt years and the origins of Homeland Security / Matthew Dallek.
Other titles: Roosevelt years and the origins of Homeland Security
Description: New York City : Oxford University Press, [2016] | Includes index.
Identifiers: LCCN 2015048180 (print) | LCCN 2015048979 (ebook) | ISBN 978–0–19–974312–4
(hardcover : alk. paper) | ISBN 978–0–19–046953–5 (Updf) | ISBN 978–0–19–046954–2 (Epub)
Subjects: LCSH: United States. Office of Civilian Defense—History. | Civil defense—United States—
History—20th century. | World War, 1939–1945—United States. | World War, 1939–1945—War work—
United States. | Landis, James McCauley, 1899–1964. | Roosevelt, Eleanor, 1884–1962—Influence. | Civil
defense—United States—Citizen participation. | United States—Defenses—History—20th century.
Classification: LCC UA927 .D36 2016 (print) | LCC UA927 (ebook) | DDC 363.350973/09044—dc23
LC record available at http://lccn.loc.gov/2015048180

1 3 5 7 9 8 6 4 2
Printed by Sheridan Books, Inc., United States of America

To Tara,
Sammy, and Eli

I sit in one of the dives
On Fifty-second Street
Uncertain and afraid
As the clever hopes expire
Of a low dishonest decade:
Waves of anger and fear
Circulate over the bright
And darkened lands of the earth,
Obsessing our private lives;
The unmentionable odour of death
Offends the September night.

. . . Defenceless under the night
Our world in stupor lies;
Yet, dotted everywhere,
Ironic points of light
Flash out wherever the Just
Exchange their messages:
May I, composed like them
Of Eros and of dust,
Beleaguered by the same
Negation and despair,
Show an affirming flame.
    —W. H. Auden, "September 1, 1939"

CONTENTS

Acknowledgments   xi

Introduction: Guns and Butter   1

1. Ultimate Armageddon   17

2. No Pact, Treaty, Symbol, or Person   35

3. Two Fronts   51

4. The Problem of Home Defense   69

5. An American Plan   85

6. London Burning   103

7. A Sweeping Conflagration of Insanity   119

8. Heart and Soul   153

9. We Can't All Run to Central Pk   169

10. A Man Must Be Protected   185

11. Fair Game   205

12. The Liberal Approach   223

13. All These Rights Spell Security   245

Conclusion: National Security Liberalism   259

Notes   265
Index   327

ACKNOWLEDGMENTS

This book probably would never have seen the light of day were it not for the generous support of the Woodrow Wilson International Center for Scholars. The Wilson Center provided a fellowship that enabled me to launch my research. My appointment as a public policy scholar there enabled me to start writing the manuscript. The terrific staff and fellows along with the collegial atmosphere made for a wonderful academic home. I am particularly indebted to Lindsay Collins, Louisa Clark, Krishna Aniel, Kim Conner, Philippa Strum, Arlyn Charles, Lucy Jilka, Robert Litwak, Mike Van Dusen, and librarians Janet Spikes, Dagne Gizaw, and Michelle Kamalich for their support for this book. In addition, I am grateful to the Alicia M. Patterson Foundation for awarding me an initial grant that helped me get this project off the ground.

Several archivists provided critical assistance as I sought to navigate a set of collections that were richer and more complex than I had originally imagined. Archivists at the Franklin D. Roosevelt Library—especially Bob Clark and Virginia H. Lewick—helped guide me in the Franklin and Eleanor Roosevelt papers while making my visits there more enjoyable. The FDR Library also awarded me a timely research grant that facilitated my work in its holdings. The Library of Congress's Jeffrey M. Flannery helped me figure out how to search the James M. Landis papers and other collections in the Manuscript Division, while archivists at the National Archives in College Park, Maryland, oriented me in the Office of Civilian Defense records. And the New York City Municipal Archives' staff aided my research in Fiorello H. La Guardia's papers with patience and professionalism.

My research was also supported in ways small and large by my colleagues. At the University of California Washington Center (UCDC), political scientist Bruce Cain was not only my supervisor but he also became my mentor. He provided financial and moral support that enabled me to make progress on my research and was a key backer who helped sustain my scholarship during his time at UCDC and beyond. He is a model of what it means to be a teacher, scholar, and mentor, and I am grateful to him for all that he has done to help me in my career and professional development. My UCDC colleagues Chantal Quintero, Alfreda Brock, Marc Sandalow, James Desveaux, Amy Bridges, Peter Ryan, Phil Wolgin, John Lawrence, Preeti Piplani, Janou Gordon, and Melanie DuPuis were among those who provided thoughts on the book and welcome companionship. My colleagues at George Washington's Graduate School of Political Management were equally instrumental, and I especially wish to thank director Mark Kennedy, program director Lara Brown, and chief of staff Sarah Gunel for their support for my research, as well as for a timely late-stage research grant that helped me complete the manuscript.

Several research assistants contributed to the publication of this book, and I don't know where I'd be without their commitment to this project. Lindsay Petersen, Ben Arnett, and Kevin Lerner helped me track down an array of hard-to-find books, articles, and archival documents. Laurel Sallack-Macupa provided superb research assistance during the intensive research phase and as I was preparing the manuscript for publication. Laurel helped edit and fact-check the entire manuscript. A first-rate historian in her own right, she brought her intelligence, sharp eye for detail, and judicious good sense to this project, helping to bring it to fruition.

My agent John Wright gave me constructive feedback on the manuscript and has been a friend and wise counselor throughout this process. My editor Susan Ferber is simply a great editor whose patience and belief in this book breathed life into its pages. She read and edited every chapter, helped me sharpen my arguments, and served as a vital sounding board. Thank you, Susan. Thanks as well go to the production editor Rob Wilkinson and copyeditor Karen Jameson for shepherding the book so ably through to its completion. And the Journal of Policy History helpfully published a book excerpt.

Numerous friends and colleagues provided terrific insights that strengthened the manuscript, while their historical and political expertise enhanced my research and writing in ways that are deeply appreciated. Above all, I am grateful to a group of great friends and extremely talented scholars who formed what we have come to call "Red-Line Group" (so named because we all lived on Washington's Red line metro) in which we read and comment on each other's books. Wendy Williams, Mary Ellen Curtin, Marie Therese-Connolly, Robyn Muncy, and Philippa Strum (our fearless leader) read and graced every page with their sage edits, passionate ideas, and historical knowledge. Individually and collectively, they helped me sharpen the book's themes, deepen the book's ideas, and infused the isolated process of research and writing with intellectual rigor, warm friendship, lively conversations over many pizza dinners, and much joy. Thanks, as well, to historians Salim Yaqub, Deirdre Moloney, and Patricia Sullivan for their comments on the manuscript along the way.

My friends David Greenberg, Michael Signer, Mark Feldstein, and Vincent Cannato helped improve the book's prose and themes through their excellent edits and nuanced suggestions. Other friends, including Jeff Shesol, Mark Brilliant, Warren Bass, David Karol, and Joseph Crespino, offered their insights on the Roosevelt years, the shifting character of American liberalism, and historical scholarship in general. All of these friends are models of what it means to be a researcher, writer, and scholar, and they continue to inspire my own work. Another dear friend Gary Tell provided encouraging words on the book and offered perceptive commentary when he explained how civil defense had made a lasting imprint on his hometown of Pittsburgh. He is deeply, deeply missed. Early conversations with Christopher Capozzola sharpened my thinking. Family friend Jeff Kelman generously read the manuscript and forced me to refine the book's concepts. At a host of academic institutions, from George Washington to Georgetown, Carnegie Mellon, the University of California, and Virginia Tech, faculty and graduate students gave me the chance to discuss my research, and I appreciate their constructive suggestions. In addition, I was fortunate to receive extremely knowledgeable feedback from anonymous readers who evaluated the proposal and the manuscript at the request of Oxford University Press.

Finally, I wish to thank my family for their love and unstinting support, without which this book simply would not have existed. My sister Rebecca Dallek and brother-in-law Mike Bender are not just relatives but much-loved friends and neighbors. My parents Robert and Geraldine Dallek were kind enough to read and edit the entire manuscript, and their savvy suggestions were only surpassed by their invaluable love and support. They are wonderful parents who remain models for me, professionally and personally, in more ways than they know. This book was ultimately brought into being because of my wife, Tara Sarathy's love, support, and partnership. While this book was being hatched, researched, written, and revised, Tara and I married, bought a house together, and had two wonderful boys. Through it all she cheered me on and helped me find the time to write while fulfilling the roles of mother and partner with her characteristic good cheer, love, and wonderful sense of humor and concern for others. Sammy, four, and Eli, two, were also inspiring to me as I worked on this book. One day out of the blue, Sammy declared that he was going upstairs to write his own book in his "work office." From the time he could talk, Eli has insisted that he have books read to him "on the rocking chair." Their love of stories were among the many joys that they have brought into our lives, and this book is dedicated to all three of them.

Defenseless Under the Night

Introduction

Guns and Butter

At the start of 1938, President Franklin Roosevelt feared that a majority of Americans were indifferent to Adolf Hitler's aggressive intentions. The events of October 30, 1938, however, changed this impression. One month earlier, British Prime Minister Neville Chamberlain had ceded Czechoslovakia to Hitler as part of the Munich Agreement. On the streets of Prague, throngs of men, hearing that the Sudetenland had been handed to the Nazis, screamed, clenched their fists, and wept. Across the Atlantic, on the night of October 30, on the eve of Halloween, six million Americans listened in the security of their homes to the sounds of the Ramon Raquello Orchestra performing on CBS radio. Shortly after the music began, an announcer interrupted the show with breaking news.[1]

Scientists had recorded "incandescent gas explosions" coming from Mars; seismic activity was reported in Princeton. Then the report became grim. In nearby Grover's Mill, New Jersey, a meteor lay "half buried in a vast pit." Aliens had begun to exit what turned out to be a spaceship. U.S. soldiers toting machine guns had come to the site to investigate, but the aliens used heat rays to incinerate the Americans in "one of the most startling defeats ever suffered by an army in modern times." Aliens were invading the East Coast. The announcer described a group of New Yorkers running toward the East River and jumping into the river as if they were rats. Black smoke enveloped Times Square.[2]

According to newspaper accounts, tens of thousands of those who listened to the broadcast believed that this massacre—the "War of the Worlds"—was real. Some of them began to panic. While the scope of the panic was likely exaggerated, the fear that enveloped the American public was genuine. In the days following the broadcast, Americans read news stories about how their fellow citizens who had heard Welles's broadcast had reacted to the show.[3]

Readers learned that the hysteria, which began on the East Coast, spread through telephone calls and old-fashioned word-of-mouth. In New Jersey, the madness was said to have moved swiftly across the cities and suburbs. Newark residents, their faces etched with "hysteria," ran from their homes with wet towels and handkerchiefs wrapped around their heads as protection from the gas. Doctors, nurses, and ambulances rushed to aid victims of the attack. An area hospital treated fifteen people for shock with sedatives and psychological counseling.[4]

The panic, Americans also learned, was uncontrollable. Columnist Walter Winchell assured his radio listeners that "America has not fallen." New York City police said the show was "no cause for alarm." Yet the voices of calm were not heard. Switchboards lit up with calls, spreading fears that America was being bombed. One man called to tell his uncle that an invasion was underway. The uncle fled his apartment on Manhattan's Riverside Drive. Relatives of audience members phoned managers at a New York theater. When the managers learned that aliens were bombing the East Coast, they announced the news to the crowd. People stood up and evacuated. Public officials were rendered impotent against the force of such rumors.[5]

Newspapers reported that the urban public looked to police to help them live through the attacks. One New Yorker phoned a police station in Washington Heights and reported that "enemy planes were crossing the Hudson." A man in Harlem told police that he had just heard President Franklin Roosevelt issue an order to "pack up and go north." New Yorkers visited police stations with their suitcases in hand and urged officers to help them evacuate from the city. The confusion extended along the Atlantic Seaboard. People in Providence, Rhode Island; and Fayetteville, North Carolina, reportedly wept when they learned that New York City had been destroyed. In Birmingham, Alabama, some residents began praying. The Midwest was not immune, either. Two residents of Tulsa, Oklahoma, had heart attacks and one person had a stroke amid the mass flight. An Ohio man phoned the *New York Times* switchboard to ask if the world was coming to an end. On the West Coast, too, Americans injured themselves in their panic or frantically called the police.[6]

The question Americans raised in the days after the broadcast was this: how could a fake radio show reap so much chaos? After all, not since the British burned the Capitol in the War of 1812 had the United States experienced a land invasion. The Atlantic and Pacific Oceans remained vast buffers, walling off Americans from Europe and Asia. Plus, FDR had supposedly dealt fear a blow with the New Deal. Having survived the worst of the Great Depression, the United States had an intact democracy and a strong president who had saved capitalism from itself. So, experts mused, what had caused so many people to panic?

Experts faulted the power of radio, and the explanation, though hardly sufficient, had a grain of truth. The "War of the Worlds" sparked an anguished debate about radio's dark side. The president of the National Association of Broadcasters expressed "regret" that this new medium had spread so much fear across the country. CBS, for its part, announced a ban on any programming that could possibly alarm its listeners. A Democratic senator offered his proposal to quash any show that inflamed public hysteria. Federal Communications Commission Chairman Frank McNinch said he welcomed any idea that promised to curb radio's ability to sow panic.[7]

Other critics blamed the artistry of Orson Welles. This explanation, too, had some merit. In Welles's masterly hands, the "War of the Worlds" carried the aura of authenticity. The aliens touched down in New Jersey, midway between New York, America's commercial capital; and Washington, the nation's political capital. A fictional Secretary of the Interior came on the air, giving the broadcast another layer of truth. The pre-Halloween twist was a devious touch. And the entire broadcast was done like a news report—not a typical radio drama. The news anchor was becoming a voice of authority, and to have the news anchor break in to a program with a bulletin was another ingenious stroke that created an eerie sense of verisimilitude.[8]

Finally, a few experts pointed to a popular dread in the body politic that in late 1938 consumed American culture and defined people's state of mind. Hitler's military aggression, coupled with his sheer capacity for evil, had conditioned some Americans to fear for their lives even though they remained thousands of miles from any actual battlefield. Americans had become jittery, dispirited, and scared. The *Washington Post* argued that "the mere thought of invasion from the air" was enough to incite a mass panic. Rabbi Edgar Magnin of the Wilshire Boulevard Temple in Los Angeles said in a sermon in November 1938 that "our nerves are cracked." He argued that modern superstitions had replaced ancient ones and that new conspiracies and fantasies were ascendant. The antifascist columnist Dorothy Thompson called the panic a result of "primeval fears lying under the thinnest surface of the so-called civilized man."[9]

The prospect of a European conflagration strained the American people's psyches. The idea of a "European Armageddon" had "badly spooked" Americans, *Time* magazine reported. And "the impending menace of a disastrous war" had led Americans to feel a "state of terror," according to the *New York Times*. Spain's 1936 Civil War and Japan's 1937 Rape of Nanking raised "horrible questions" about modern life, making real the idea of terror inflicted on women and children living in communities long regarded as safe havens.[10]

Radio dramas had set the stage for the late-October crisis of national confidence. Playwright Archibald MacLeish's "Fall of the City," broadcast in April 1937 and narrated by Orson Welles, told the story of a dictator who brazenly destroyed a city. In "They Fly Through the Air with the Greatest of Ease," playwright Norman Corwin dramatized how pilots gunned down civilians and lauded their own efforts as "a budding rose" unfolding before their eyes.

Just a week before Welles's "War of the Worlds" broadcast, another MacLeish play, "Air Raid," debuted on the radio, reinforcing the horror of air war. The show started with children at play. Sirens whined. Bombs whizzed through the air. Children screamed. The *Christian Science Monitor* called "Air Raid" more "appalling" than anything Welles had done with "War of the Worlds." MacLeish's "Air Raid" resembled the reality of modern combat, whereas "War" was a work of science fiction. All of these radio dramas, coupled with real-world signs that Europe stood on the brink of a catastrophe, created a mood within the United States that made tales of mass panic so believable. In the days that followed, Americans raised still deeper questions about what the future held. People wondered how rational thought would survive when millions of citizens felt besieged with a dread of modern life. Americans asked how democracy would withstand the unprecedented power of Hitler's military might and the fascist appeal.[11]

From the Oval Office to City Halls and city streets, they had few good answers.

Three years later, in the hours after bombs rained on Pearl Harbor, Washington's leaders still harbored doubts about democracy's staying power. But they were loath to convey them to the American people. On December 8, 1941, First Lady Eleanor Roosevelt traveled the brief distance from the White House to Capitol Hill and listened to President Franklin D. Roosevelt deliver an emergency speech to a joint session of Congress about Japan's surprise attack on Pearl Harbor. Thousands of sailors and civilians had died on U.S. soil, and the United States had finally become a belligerent. ER had long thought that such an attack was coming, and in the hours afterwards she felt with FDR almost a sense of relief because now they knew what they and their fellow Americans had to face. "The die was cast," she later wrote.[12]

ER had a larger role to play than simply serving as presidential spouse, however. As assistant director of the Office of Civilian Defense (OCD), she had to move swiftly to mobilize the American people to defend the home front from expected enemy air raids. After FDR rallied the nation with his address ("A date which will live in infamy," he declared), Eleanor Roosevelt returned to the White House to prepare for an overnight flight to Los Angeles. Rumors abounded that a Japanese invasion of the West Coast was a distinct possibility. Her ally in this home-defense campaign was another prominent national figure—the bombastic New York mayor, Fiorello La Guardia, the OCD's director. La Guardia had been preparing to respond to a Pearl Harbor-style attack for months. He viewed the bombing as evidence of his own prescience. In 1941, he had crisscrossed the United States, telling civilians that their cities could soon come under attack. He implored the public to participate in emergency drills, learn how to take shelter, and get involved in home defense activities. When Pearl Harbor seemed to vindicate his warnings, La Guardia sanctimoniously announced, "Hell, this isn't a pinochle party we're having. It's war."[13]

The plane trip was harrowing. Once La Guardia and ER were airborne, the mayor fell asleep, and she awoke him with a start. The pilot had given her a news report that Japan had attacked the city of San Francisco. La Guardia parted the curtains and pressed his face against a plane window. He scanned the skyline for signs of a city in flames. He found none. The report, it turned out, was mistaken; instead of making an emergency landing in San Francisco, La Guardia ordered the pilot to continue toward its original destination. They were heading into the unknown, straight toward a sprawling city on the Pacific Coast, widely regarded as the nation's most defenseless region.[14]

The collective fears that the home front would be attacked—that enemies were lurking in the shadows of American society—were rooted in larger concerns about military, geopolitical, and technological developments during the mid- and late 1930s. The fears found expression on the nation's news radio shows, in newspaper headlines, and in comments by elected officials at all levels of government. Journalists chronicled the horrors of fascist military movements in Europe and Asia. Americans had access to harrowing firsthand accounts of Germany's aerial bombardment of the Spanish town of Guernica (later memorialized in Pablo Picasso's painting) and learned about the state-sponsored terrorism that Adolf Hitler had inflicted during his conquest of Czechoslovakia. In June 1940, France's defeat shook America's confidence. The U.S. ambassador in Paris, William C. Bullitt, warned Americans that they should feel the danger that the Nazis posed to the territorial integrity of the United States, lest they suffer the same fate as Europe. Later that year, Edward R. Murrow's eyewitness accounts from London's rooftops of the Nazis' "Blitz" deepened the dread that was spreading across the United States. Murrow's vivid descriptions of a city under physical siege and psychological torment resonated with millions. Approximately 43,000 British civilians died in the Blitz, and 140,000 more were injured. Murrow communicated to the Americans the awesome firepower of Germany's Luftwaffe, as it rained bombs on London week after week, month after bloody month.[15]

In response to these warnings, city officials in the United States directed their attention to a relatively new aspect of war in an age when there no longer seemed to be any front. This novel development was sometimes popularly termed "home defense." England became the model for America's leaders. New York's politicians and police and fire officials sent a delegation to London to study home defense planning in the hopes of developing a comparable strategy for New York. Eleanor Roosevelt began to correspond with Lady Stella Reading, who led England's Women's Royal Voluntary Service. The first lady wanted to learn how British leaders such as Reading had maintained civilian morale, provided social services, and created opportunities for Londoners to volunteer in wartime. In February 1941, Reading assured ER that she took comfort from the first lady's moral and political aid "so that some of us may survive to carry on the tradition for which all of us are ready to die."[16]

The pressure built. In early 1941, the U.S. Conference of Mayors adopted a resolution urging the president to establish a federal agency to promote civilian mobilization and strengthen civilian protection. In May 1941, the president took action. His executive order established the Office of Civilian Defense to protect American lives from foreign and domestic threats alike. La Guardia, who had flown combat planes in World War I, had taken a keen interest in home defense planning. As a strong New Dealer (despite his Republican affiliation) and the elected leader of one of America's most vulnerable cities, the mayor appeared to be a perfect fit for the new director's position. After FDR appointed him, La Guardia began work as head of the OCD with a near-maniacal commitment to preparing the public for enemy incursions onto U.S. soil, even while he remained as mayor. Working seven days a week, shuttling between New York and Washington, "the little firebrand," as the *New York Times* called him, developed an obsession with distributing fire-fighting equipment to the nation's cities and states. He encouraged civilians to parade in quasi-military formation and vowed to distribute 50 million gas masks to states on both the West and East Coasts in case of a chemical weapons attack.[17]

La Guardia was less a home defense theorist than he was a true believer in action, even if the steps he undertook were disorganized and frenetic. As a fervent adherent to a federal government that intervened in citizens' lives in order to keep them safe, he concluded that civilian protection and mass mobilization went hand-in-hand. His organizing principle of home defense was volunteer participation led by robust federal action devoted to protecting lives. While the federal government would assume an important leadership role, La Guardia wanted to organize Americans at the grassroots, which he believed would save the most lives if the United States were attacked. He regarded citizens not as passive recipients of government protection, but rather as partners with Washington who had an obligation to organize in their own self-defense. As head of home defense, he encouraged Americans to work as fire and air raid wardens, patrol their streets, and participate in blackout drills. He wanted boys to clean backyards and basements so they could reduce the risk of fire to homes caused by incendiary bombs. His OCD sought to coordinate emergency medical teams, prepare hospitals for mass casualties, station guards at industrial plants and water sources, and teach civilians how to become first responders. Though he did not label it as such, his leadership helped forge national security liberalism, a philosophy that used the federal government to prioritize military security ahead of social protections— with long-term consequences for the postwar world. Ironically, one of America's leading urban reformers temporarily pushed the New Deal in a novel direction as he fought to use the federal government to organize home defense activities in states and cities and to maximize civilians' physical safety.[18]

His efforts also led to the erection of a quasi-military civilian army. His movement inspired a war psychology among millions of his fellow citizens, helping to diminish isolationism before and after Pearl Harbor. His campaign on behalf of self-defense ultimately deepened a war mindset that prepared the country for military intervention. In the aftermath of Japan's attack in December 1941, the home defense program made the idea of fighting more palatable to the American public.

While the OCD had been established in order to unite prewar America, however, La Guardia also provoked dissent and stirred acrimonious political debate. He adopted controversial positions that roiled civilians and government officials alike. He endorsed spying on citizens considered subversive and clashed with J. Edgar Hoover's FBI over training the nation's police. He launched a "Freedom Sunday" campaign to propagandize about home defense in churches and temples, infuriating priests and rabbis. La Guardia even estimated the odds (3 percent; 6 percent—his numbers varied) that New Yorkers would be bombed, sowing fear in an already jittery nation.[19]

While they shared New York City as a hometown and a devotion to aiding the working class and poor, La Guardia and Eleanor Roosevelt had distinct styles and attitudes and came across as unlikely partners in the home defense movement. A first-generation Italian American, La Guardia was rotund, five-feet-two-inches tall, and with his trademark black Stetson hat perched atop his head, he cut a charismatic political figure. As mayor, he used to race across New York City's streets to help firemen battle fires and aid commuters in the wake of subway derailments, a "fiery little man with the black hat and angry tongue," as one obituary put it, in touch with his constituents' innermost fears and their most basic struggles.[20]

At five feet ten inches, ER towered over the diminutive mayor, and she hailed from upper-crust Protestant origins. Her Uncle Theodore, the nation's twenty-sixth president, gave her away to FDR at their New York wedding on March 17, 1905. Eleanor Roosevelt's family wealth, surname, and deep roots in the United States connoted an American version of aristocracy, while La Guardia's immigrant identity bespoke the mindset of a relentless up-from-nothing striver. Their tenures at home defense also had distinct thrusts and were animated by clashing concepts of what national security meant in the context of total war. While the mayor worked to militarize the home front during his time running home defense, ER sought to establish a wartime New Deal that would boost morale, advance military production, and secure a better life for all citizens, making democracy a concrete, cherished force in the lives of every American.[21]

Both reacted to the fascist threat by recasting the meaning of "defense" and New Deal liberalism in a democracy under siege from fascism. The inter-war years challenged and upended the first lady's notion of the purpose of war itself. In January 1919, she and FDR, then serving as assistant secretary of the Navy, visited Paris. She toured hospitals, reviewed battlefields, and reflected that "What the men who fought there lived through is inconceivable." From these experiences and her encounters with women who had lost loved ones, she concluded that World War I had proven that pacifism was the only sane path for the twentieth century.[22]

By 1938, however, she had done an about-face. She had become an antifascist who viewed defending America with arms as a fundamental responsibility of American government. When she and FDR listened to Hitler's radio address in which he threatened the invasion of the Sudetenland in Czechoslovakia, she declared that Hitler "makes me sick." Hitler's militarism and bluster; his antipathy for God; and his utterly cavalier attitude toward human life appalled her.

Nearly two decades after watching progressive dreams of a postwar peace fizzle at the end of World War I, Eleanor Roosevelt was rethinking the connection between national security, the role of government, and democracy. She regarded Hitler as a growing menace to the United States who had to be stopped militarily.[23]

Eleanor Roosevelt is typically described as the conscience of social domestic liberalism. The most common images of her are as a social settlement house worker; advocate for the poor; and architect of the UN's Declaration of Human Rights. She donated her own money to assist refugees and pushed for social justice through federal programs. Her life is often told as the story of the awkward, shy girl who used the pain of her upbringing (her father and uncles were alcoholics, and her parents both died before she was eleven) and her marriage (she found letters revealing FDR's affair with his secretary Lucy Mercer in 1918) to become one of the century's leading champions of equal rights. During the early New Deal, she fought for the National Youth Administration (NYA) to give jobs to youth and the National Labor Relations Act to give rights to workers. She advocated for slum clearance to aid the poor and helped win passage of the Federal Art Project to assist struggling artists. Visiting coal mines and sharecroppers' homes, she drew attention to the plight of forgotten men and women. In 1939, when the Daughters of the American Revolution denied a request to have African American singer Marian Anderson perform in its Constitution Hall in Washington, D.C., Eleanor Roosevelt resigned from the organization. She had the unique ability to empathize with the misfortune of others and focus the nation's attention on unmet human needs. She also had a direct line to the Oval Office. Rexford Tugwell, a member of FDR's brain trust, recalled watching ER telling the president such things as "Franklin, I think you should . . . " or

"Franklin, surely you will not . . . ." Her determination and political savvy helped push the New Deal in countless "new directions," he marveled.[24]

These images, though apt, are hardly complete. They fail to capture her impact on the debate about the direction, tenor, and fate of New Deal liberalism during the war years. From roughly 1936 to 1945, Eleanor Roosevelt forged an approach that influenced FDR, the debate about democracy, and postwar debates about government's proper role in society. Her New Deal liberalism was based on fighting a government-led and citizen-powered war on two equally vital and interrelated fronts. First, from 1938 to 1941, while most Democrats shared FDR's desire to aid Britain and prepare for war, she challenged isolationists both on the antiwar Republican right including America First (the nation's most powerful isolationist group) and on the antiwar liberal left. She argued that the federal government must prioritize military defense and send aid to the Allies and expand America's Armed Forces. She amplified FDR's warning in 1939 that new weapons of attack and new methods of warfare had shrunk time and distance and made the Pacific and Atlantic Oceans much easier for the nation's enemies to cross. The president warned that the U.S. interior, not just the coasts, was for the first time a battle zone. Eleanor Roosevelt assured that in future wars all civilians would find themselves targets of enemy attacks and that "Gases and airplanes . . . may be used for the breaking of morale in the opposing nation."[25]

By the late 1930s, the first lady argued that without a government-backed arms expansion, the New Deal and even American democracy could no longer endure. She worked assiduously to bring the antiwar left into the military preparedness camp. ER told one pacifist youth group in 1940 that while "I don't want to go to war" and "you don't want to go to war," "war may come to us." She warned 1,000 African American congregants at a Washington, D.C., church that "Every time word goes back to Germany that" we are divided on the arms buildup "we are nailing one more nail in our coffin." She likened isolationists in the United States to Nazi appeasers. After the 1940 presidential campaign, she argued that if Wendell Willkie had defeated her husband, democracy would have suffered enormously due to the Republican affinity for isolationism.[26]

Her pro-government views toward the international crisis also flowed from her convictions about the military's role in a democratic society in the age of total war. Her sons volunteered for service and were in danger because they wore the uniform. She saw the military as a repository of citizen action in democracy's defense. She toured sprawling Army bases where "young America's" patriotism, faith in liberty, and readiness to sacrifice inspired and impressed her. She supported new military spending and intervention as guarantors of the nation's physical security. Her faith in preparedness sent liberals a signal that a military buildup might not spell the end of the New Deal after all, as some liberals then feared, but rather that the war might be a way to deepen, justify, and transform the liberal project. She helped make it permissible for some on the antiwar left to rally behind the administration's defense plans and insisted that only robust federal action could provide for the nation's physical security.

Her liberalism rested on a second and equally important front that she and her allies referred to as "social defense." While she pulled the antiwar left into the preparedness camp, she also strove to draw liberal hawks into the New Deal camp. She called on government to put social defense on a par with military preparedness. "Government" ought to be "as much interested today in seeing [Americans] well housed, well clothed and well fed, obtaining needed medical care and recreation" as government is committed to military defense, she argued. In November 1941, she stated that World War II "will bring us more education in the knowledge of what community needs really are, and better organization within our communities to make every place in this country a better place in which to live, and therefore more worth defending."[27]

For Eleanor Roosevelt, the war was a fight to secure a better postwar future, which meant an expanded New Deal updated to meet wartime social needs. Thus, she called on government to work with citizens to set up day care centers near defense plants, teach citizens about nutrition and consumer rights, and build decent housing for newly relocated war workers. In order to prevail, citizen morale had to be maintained. In the battle for hearts around the globe, American democracy, she argued, had to show that it was a superior system of government over fascism. Finally, social defense was going to improve the health of the population, equip more Americans to qualify for military service, and make defense workers more productive.

In January 1941, dozens of the nation's most influential women came to the White House to hear ER and her allies unveil a plan for what they called the American Social Defense Administration. Under their plan, the government would provide volunteer roles for virtually every American woman who would work to better people's lives and advance the war effort. Volunteers were going to improve the education system, sanitation, public health, housing, and train women in skills so they could find good-paying jobs. FDR, however, blocked this plan because his priority was securing aid for Great Britain and he saw her idea as too radical and too ambitious.[28]

Yet Eleanor Roosevelt succeeded in casting the war as a struggle to ensure a government as concerned with people's welfare as it was with warfare. Her efforts through the social defense enterprise helped defend Social Security, labor rights, banking regulations, aid to the poor, and other New Deal programs, which lasted into the Cold War and beyond. Her influence, admittedly, is hard to quantify. She wasn't president, senator, or governor; she held no veto pen and cast no votes. But the first lady outlined her vision in her six-day-a-week nationally syndicated column, "My Day." She delivered a weekly radio address, gave countless talks to liberal and civic groups, aired her ideas in popular magazines, effectively lobbied FDR on a host of issues, and replied to tens of thousands of letters she received from leading liberals and ordinary citizens alike, stitching them into a loose coalition of like-minded social defense advocates. Liberals such as Florence Kerr, Joseph Lash, and Elinor Morgenthau put their faith in her leadership even more than they did in the president's. By 1940, two-thirds of the public approved of the first lady's performance. During the war years, she prodded FDR to defend the New Deal's gains and through her force of will and position in government secured appointments for her allies in the wartime administration. In 1941, when FDR announced his vision of "freedom from want" and "fear" (in his four freedoms address) and then in 1944 when he issued his call for an Economic Bill of Rights including the right to a good job and enough income to provide for "adequate food and clothing and recreation," he was channeling Eleanor Roosevelt's notion that social and military defense constituted the war's two fronts.[29]

When FDR appointed her as assistant director of the Office of Civilian Defense in September 1941, she also became the first wife of the country's chief executive to hold an official post in her husband's administration. She led a program that ultimately recruited more than ten million volunteers, including an estimated three million who performed some type of social defense role. Citizens working through their government fed women and children, provided medical and child care, trained defense plant workers, led salvage campaigns, improved transit systems, planted victory gardens, and helped women learn about nutritious diets. Her political vision helped make it acceptable for liberals to champion big government both in terms of military affairs and social experimentation, a government devoted to both guns and butter. She advanced the tradition of projecting American values abroad by using government to ensure that America reflected its own founding principles, building on the progressive legacy during World War I.[30]

The war did not yield all that the first lady wanted, of course. Social defense took a back seat to military security. After 1938, FDR refused to support health care reform. His 1940 budget cut social spending and raised defense spending. In 1943, the Civilian Conservation Corps (CCC), National Youth Administration, and Works Progress Administration (WPA), all emblems of the New Deal, died. He had not completely given up on social liberalism, but fighting the war took precedence over expanding the New Deal.

Moreover, the first lady's home defense mission foundered. By early 1942, divisions between the competing visions of La Guardia and ER were beginning to harden; his national security liberalism clashed with her wartime beliefs. In ER's eyes, La Guardia was no longer the decisive commander she had once seen;

she found him arrogant, vindictive, unfocused on the voluntary features of her social agenda, and ignorant of the need to bolster morale. She complained to FDR about La Guardia's faltering leadership. La Guardia was sharing his concerns about the first lady with the president as well. FDR, preoccupied with fighting in the Pacific, began to fume. "I can't take Eleanor and La Guardia. Each one comes with a story; each one is right . . . I cannot cope with it and I want you to try and keep them away from me and reconcile their differences," he told an aide. Their differences were not, in fact, reconcilable, and La Guardia and Eleanor Roosevelt had become political liabilities to his wartime administration. In February, his patience dissipating, FDR pressured each of them to resign from the Office of Civilian Defense.[31]

ER's involvement with the home defense movement thus highlights the limits of social-defense liberalism in the age of total war; human security, a term then in use, was subordinated to military defense, or national security liberalism, as international threats to the United States intensified. Anti–New Deal critics attacked ER's ideas as totalitarian and her programs as a boondoggle, and their work retarded liberal momentum. While her role in home defense has typically been cast as a low point in her life, her leadership of the social defense movement illuminates the shifting character of New Deal liberalism, underscoring its gains, its political appeal, and, ultimately, its transformation. Her ideas, politics, and arguments in the war years shed light on the fate of social reform during national security crises and the tensions that roiled wartime liberalism.[32]

With his thin face, protruding ears, and hawk-eyed gaze, New Deal administrator and Harvard-trained lawyer James Landis was brought in by the president to pick up the pieces, and he looked every bit like a harried wartime general. Though he was less of a household name than either of his predecessors, Landis had an impressive résumé: Supreme Court clerk to Justice Louis Brandeis; Harvard Law School dean; chairman of the Securities and Exchange Commission; regional director of home defense for New England. Through it all, Landis was a New Deal loyalist. When FDR appointed him to run home defense, Landis built on the infrastructure put in place by his predecessors and helped transform the OCD into a semi-military apparatus. Landis's tenure showed that home defense could acquire a wide following in a democracy and underscored the depth of militarization that occurred on the home front during the war. He adopted La Guardia's national security liberalism, without ever discarding ER's notion of social defense. He had an expansive notion of government's responsibilities in wartime. As head of the OCD, he seized upon the war as an opportunity to strengthen a government–citizen partnership that defended communities nationwide from nonmilitary threats. Under Landis's OCD, natural disasters, for example, were deemed important threats to the home front, even in the midst of a global war. Home defense volunteers fixed roads, delivered supplies, and saved victims from floods on the Potomac and Shenandoah Rivers in late 1942 and in Tulsa, Oklahoma, in 1943. Landis's OCD cast a wide net: the agency's Civil Air Patrol not only bombed German submarines, but also delivered food to Americans in remote areas, battled forest fires, and searched for crews aboard ships lost at sea.

Above all, though, Landis strained to militarize civilians. He trafficked in a message of fear. Addressing thousands of Americans at pro-war rallies, he urged civilians to "think war, sleep war, and eat war" as they prepared for the bombing that he warned was coming to their cities. Echoing La Guardia's inflammatory rhetoric, Landis appeared in newsreels warning civilians about the dangers that lurked within. His name appeared on millions of pieces of literature that stoked concerns about the imminent threat of attacks on American soil. Landis's militarism won some converts, but other Americans chafed under federal mandates about how to behave. Landis ultimately adopted a form of national security liberalism that prioritized the home front's military needs ahead of social defense liberalism.[33]

In his 1933 fireside chat about the banking crisis, Franklin D. Roosevelt urged Americans to "unite in banishing fear." Roosevelt's faith that Americans could vanquish fear gave hope that citizens could survive the Great Depression and preserve their nation's democracy. In January 1941, the president described his wartime goal as "freedom from fear." This theme—conquering fear—has often defined his presidency, leadership, and legacy. The Roosevelt years are often recalled as the moment when FDR overcame the nation's paralytic fears by averting an economic collapse and preventing fascists from destroying democracy. Although this book draws on such themes, it also focuses on a less well-known set of fears that roiled Americans between 1938 and 1944—fears that the home front had become vulnerable to attack due to the rise of unprecedented international threats. Americans feared that Hitler's air force might bomb their cities; that fifth columnists were capable of toppling their government; and that gas and biological weapons in the hands of madmen would kill civilians en masse, fueling hysteria that would lead to a dictatorship being established in the United States.[34]

In spite of his vow to become "Dr. Win-the-War," FDR's attitude toward the New Deal waxed and waned. After 1938, he harvested his political capital for military mobilization, his top priority. Yet as an architect of the New Deal who was committed to assisting the poor and working class through federal action, he felt some measure of sympathy for ER's social defense ideals. Roosevelt knew that the war preparations required a larger purpose, buoyed by democratic aspirations that would unite 130 million Americans. In addition, the president had long opposed conservative critics who wanted to use the war to abolish his social reforms. Plus, he saw political advantages in maintaining the support of his domestic liberal allies. A wartime New Deal, liberals believed, could decisively end the Great Depression and make social defense a permanent fixture in communities nationwide, and FDR, at times, did not dispute that theory.

La Guardia's vision of militarization strongly appealed to the president, as well. FDR saw a self-defense program as a means of preparing the country to fight a war. He and La Guardia openly challenged the decades-old national consensus that America's ocean barriers would protect the country from foreign invaders. They argued that the world had "grown so small," FDR's words, and that total war had put all civilians in harm's way. They found evidence for their assertion in fascist victories, which seemed to pose a direct threat to national security. Military commanders, journalists, veterans, and civic activists echoed their warnings, advancing the notion that civilians were in the sights of fascist militaries. Although many Republicans and some antiwar Democrats insisted that Americans were immune from the threat, FDR and La Guardia used the debate about home defense to tarnish isolationist assumptions as hackneyed and antiquated. Their argument that the war eventually would reach America's shores made millions of Americans more receptive to aiding the Allies and preparing for war.[35]

The idea of American civil defense is typically dated to the Cold War, but it actually had its origins in the Roosevelt administration's home defense program during World War II. During the late 1930s and early '40s, liberals directly addressed the growing sense that America was vulnerable to air raids and other threats as the nation entered the age of total war. Although home defense during World War II had numerous shortcomings, its flaws were markedly different from those of its Cold War successor. While Cold War liberals promoted the illusion that evacuation, "duck and cover," and shelter construction might protect Americans from a Soviet nuclear attack, and while in most instances these leaders were fully aware that their campaign was based on public deception, World War II liberals genuinely believed that home defense was necessary and would yield tangible results. Certainly, Roosevelt justified his policy of aiding the Allies and rebuilding the U.S. military by highlighting the unprecedented ways in which the home front was vulnerable to Nazi aggression. He gained political and strategic advantage from his home defense arguments. But, pointing to examples of air power in Europe and Asia, he and America's defense establishment concluded that home defense in fact would keep Americans safe from air raids, sabotage, naval shelling, germs, gas, and even invasion. It would also prop up morale and hedge against the possibilities of panic, prerequisites to a strong defense. National security officials led by FDR and La Guardia worked to convince the public that civilian lives were on the line.[36]

For the most part, they succeeded. By 1942, the home defense program had mobilized almost 10 percent of the population—one of the largest volunteer, government-backed programs of the Roosevelt years. Americans registered for service because they believed that fifty million citizens living in target zones that spanned 300 miles inland along the West and East Coasts and parts of the South (zones defined by U.S. Army planners) were within striking distance of Axis bombers. They also participated because they believed that volunteering at the local level constituted a defense of individual liberties and formed a striking contrast with regimented fascist programs. Citizens lobbied Washington to create roles for them in keeping the country safe. Millions of Americans joined home defense to fulfill ER's vision of defense as a function of human security and economic opportunity.[37]

The home defense mission also accelerated the friction between Americans who looked to the federal government for their physical and social protection and those who feared the expansion of federal power as an assault on individual rights and local prerogatives. The split was not simply a partisan one. Mayors of various stripes argued that the Roosevelt administration was the only institution capable of defending lives, homes, and infrastructure. Although big city mayors were willing to cede their power and rely on federal control, numerous state, town, and rural officials opposed federal authority as trampling on the rights of their constituents and denounced federal home defense orders as a backdoor to dictatorship. Unsurprisingly, the isolationist Midwest was less receptive than the West and East Coasts. Paradoxically, as the federal government made its presence felt in communities nationwide, some Americans welcomed it as the ultimate in public safety, while others saw it as the unwanted apotheosis of patriarchal New Deal reforms and national security orders.[38]

The debate about homeland security in the 9/11 world echoes some of the debates that erupted over home defense throughout World War II. During the Roosevelt years, the politics of home defense emerged as a flashpoint nationally for the first time and rippled across society as Americans experienced physical vulnerability as a significant source of concern. Washington made its initial foray into protecting the American people from harm at the hands of ruthless foreign enemies. Originating in the years leading up to World War II, the fear of foreign attack has now become a permanent fixture of American life, underscored by Pearl Harbor, the shadow of nuclear war, 9/11, and the Boston Marathon bombing. Americans battled in World War II over how America's besieged democracy should respond to the threat of new technologies, unscrupulous foes, and unparalleled international forces that had raised concerns about whether democracies could survive in the modern era. This Roosevelt-era debate highlights the quintessentially American argument about government's role in keeping civilians safe, improving people's lives at home, and finding the proper balance between defending individuals' liberty and providing for citizens' physical safety and social well-being. These questions remain as pertinent in our own times as they were more than seventy-five years ago when Orson Welles interrupted the Ramon Raquello Orchestra's dance music "to bring you a special bulletin" that America was being invaded .[39]

1

Ultimate Armageddon

Better the occasional faults of a government that lives in a spirit of charity than the consistent omissions of a government frozen in the ice of
its own indifference.
— Franklin Delano Roosevelt, 1936

In January 1939, Eleanor Roosevelt coined an axiom about fear that was different
from FDR's famous formulation—"the only thing we have to fear is fear itself."
In an article called "Keepers of Democracy" in the *Virginia Quarterly Review*, she
wondered why hundreds of thousands of Americans had panicked after listening to "The War of the Worlds" broadcast. She answered that Americans had
acquired a so-called fear complex. She argued that "a sane people, living in an
atmosphere of fearlessness, does not suddenly become hysterical at the threat
of invasion, even from more credible sources, let alone by the Martians from
another planet." Some reactionaries inside the United States had launched a hunt
for subversives, she asserted, referring to congressional committees investigating
suspected fascists and communists during the 1930s. Their theories—"Negroes
are all Communists"; public schools "are all under the influence of Jewish teachers"—had created a climate of fear that made the overreaction to a radio fiction
possible, ER posited.[1]

Running for the hills was not the legacy that the nation's founders had
bequeathed, she added. The Founding Fathers had braved moral threats and
overcome physical hazards during the American Revolution, while in the late
1930s, ER wrote, Americans had to prepare to "meet present-day dangers with
more courage than we seem to have." Six years after FDR sought to stamp out
fear, ER suggested something else—that fear still sullied the landscape; that "a
growing wave . . . of fear, and of intolerance which springs from fear" had to be
arrested. She argued that "unless we learn to live together as individuals and as
groups, and to find ways of settling our difficulties without showing fear of each
other and resorting to force, we cannot hope to see our democracy successful . . .

We face," she warned, "an ultimate Armageddon, unless at the same time an effort to find some other solution is never abandoned."[2]

FDR and ER both had Armageddon on their minds during the late 1930s. The president feared that Nazi bombers could destroy American cities; the first lady fretted that the war ahead would halt social progress at home. FDR worried about crafting an internationalist foreign policy that did not alienate American isolationists; the first lady thought that the German-American Bund and strident anti-communists on Martin Dies's House Un-American Activities Committee (HUAC), established in 1938 to ferret out the nation's internal enemies, tarred the New Deal with the brush of communism and threatened civil liberties. FDR struggled with the prospect of running for a third term during an international crisis and defending the New Deal from his critics; the first lady contemplated a wartime New Deal that could show the world how democracy was the wisest, most humane form of government.[3]

How ER defined freedom in this prewar moment has not been fully understood. She came to regard social defense—a wartime push to strengthen democracy through domestic reforms—as the solid foundational rock on which national defense would ultimately have to sit. She began to view the coming war as a chance to launch a fresh New Deal—a program as ambitious as the flurry of reforms passed in 1933 and 1935. While FDR said time was running short to build planes and assemble an Army, ER argued that the window for bettering the lives of other Americans was also shutting. The New Deal thus far, she said in 1938, had "bought us time to think"; so much more remained to be accomplished. Nazism represented not only a military threat to the United States but also an existential problem for American democracy. The answer was to build a progressive coalition at home whose social program would highlight the benefits that flowed from democratic government and showcase the flaws inherent in the fascist "slave" ideology that abridged racial, religious, and economic freedoms— enabling Western liberals to win a victory in the battle for the minds of men and women raging around the globe.[4]

When Eleanor Roosevelt arrived in Washington in the fall of 1913 at the age of twenty-nine, she viewed herself as the shy wife of the new assistant secretary of the Navy. World War I would indelibly shape her view of herself in public life and show her that she could lead through times of crisis. It would also persuade her that military mobilization must not push to the sideline the national struggle to promote social and economic justice. Her initial tasks were satisfying, if hardly groundbreaking. She knocked on the doors of the wives of young officers and asked them if she could assist them in any way. Traditional notions of gender roles shaped her view of her responsibilities. She was "the wife of a public official," she recalled, who "had nothing to offer of an individual nature."

She concentrated on child-rearing and hosting dinners, and she became one of the "slaves of the Washington social system." She felt appalled that Martha Peters and Alice Roosevelt Longworth, the wives of congressmen, had displayed so much independence and considered it her duty to keep to her place as the wife of a public servant.[5]

FDR's position opened up new opportunities to her. Traveling with her husband on his first official naval tour, she visited New Orleans; Biloxi; Pensacola; and Brunswick, Georgia. She endured endless dinners (in Brunswick, FDR ate "several kinds of possum"), logged long hours on trains, listened to her husband's speeches, and accompanied him on a Navy yard inspection. She found the travel "feats of endurance," but she realized that she had the "ability to stand things" and that confidence "has stood me in good stead throughout the rest of my life."[6]

When war erupted in Europe in the summer of 1914, ER sided with the anti-war attitudes of Secretary of State William Jennings Bryan. She became a pacifist. She recalled that Bryan was handing out "miniature plowshares made from old guns," and she concurred that modern arms had to become tools that would lift up the lives of other humans. But her views were also shifting. In response to Germany's unrestricted submarine warfare in the Atlantic in February 1917, President Woodrow Wilson announced that the United States was breaking off diplomatic relations with Germany. ER contemplated what going to war actually meant for the United States. She naively decided that U.S. financial and naval power would be the only instruments needed. After German U-boats sank U.S. ships and killed American citizens and an intercepted telegram revealed that Germany had urged Mexico to attack the United States, Wilson appeared before Congress on April 2 and called for a declaration of war on Germany. Eleanor Roosevelt had learned that Wilson was going to address Congress, and FDR "got me a seat" in the chamber. As she exited the Capitol after hearing Wilson's speech, she recalled "the world rocking all around us" and felt "half dazed by the sense of impending change."[7]

America's entry in the war on April 6, 1917, altered her universe. Her faith in "my ability to meet emergencies" deepened. She helped set up the Navy Red Cross, used her home to distribute free wool and knitted garments, and worked two to three shifts each week in the Red Cross canteen located in Washington's railroad yards. In the summer of 1918, she dropped off her children in Hyde Park, the Roosevelt home on the Hudson River—there was always plenty of household help—and returned to Washington. In July, she worked from 9 a.m. until 1 or 2 a.m. in a blistering tin shack that served as the canteen's kitchen. When young men passed through on their way to Europe, she helped them gain access to hot showers, cigarettes, candy, postcards, and other small comforts. Working alongside other women, she felt the camaraderie of war work, and even when a bread-cutting machine gashed her "finger almost to the bone," she applied handkerchiefs to stop the bleeding and kept working. Other encounters revealed the horrors of modern war. Visiting the naval unit of St. Elizabeth's, the country's lone federal hospital for the mentally ill, she saw young men who were so disturbed they were locked in padded cells. She met a fair-haired young boy who constantly mumbled to himself orders he had received after undergoing the terror of air war in Dunkirk. The "poor demented creatures with apparently very little attention being paid them, gazing from behind bars or walking up and down on enclosed porches," she reflected, stayed with her decades later.[8]

The conditions galled her, and she lobbied Secretary of the Interior Franklin Lane, under whose jurisdiction the hospital fell, to investigate. Lane ultimately helped secure the funding that would make St. Elizabeth's a model of "what every Federal institution in Washington should be." She took direct action to assist the needy in other ways. When she met a mother whose son had been gassed, she ensured that a nurse would accompany the son out West where he would have a better chance to recover. (Despite her best efforts, the son died.) She had the Red Cross construct a recreation center for wounded soldiers and raised $500 in support of occupational therapy. The war made her, she recalled, "more determined to try for certain ultimate objectives"—a forceful voice in the public arena.[9]

The dislocations stemming from the war became imprinted on her mind. In the fall of 1918, she saw Washington as an overcrowded city that lacked the housing to cope with the influx of workers. When a flu pandemic struck, she realized that the city was short of hospitals. She delivered food to patients at Red Cross temporary hospitals and tried to nurse her husband and their five children, all sick, back to health.[10]

The end of the war proved to be a bitter ordeal, dashing her hopes that Wilson would succeed in establishing an international order based on national self-determination and an end to war. On February 4, 1919, she sat on a train with FDR traveling from Paris to Brest. A correspondent for the *New York Times* handed them a copy of the charter of the League of Nations. ER believed that war would become a thing of the past and eagerly absorbed the document that envisioned a future of peace. Wilson impressed her. Large French crowds lined the railroad tracks to get a glimpse of the American president. The French called him their savior. "Little did we dream at that time what the future held," she recounted.[11]

Inside the United States, war liberalism had sown divisions among some progressives who believed that the state was being used to stifle antiwar dissent and trample on people's civil liberties. The administration's suppression of antiwar speech; the mass mobilization of anti-German thought that led to physical violence against some ethnic Americans; Woodrow Wilson's endorsement of racial segregation despite the clear demonstration of African American patriotism and military valor; and the "Palmer Raids," named after Attorney General Mitchell

A. Palmer, in which immigrants, union members, and radicals were rounded up, jailed, and occasionally deported stirred some deep concerns in the progressive community that wartime government was violating the very democratic principles it was fighting to uphold overseas. In the eyes of many progressives, the expansion of state power had big downsides as well as upsides, and at least some progressives turned to a more explicit class-based politics promoting workers' economic interests in the post-Armistice period.[12]

In addition, World War I had turned many progressives into pacifists. When the postwar disappointments—the Senate's refusal to ratify the League, the punitive Armistice, millions of lives destroyed—became clear, Eleanor Roosevelt became a foe of all wars. Indeed, by the early and mid-1930s, ER argued that World War I had proven that war was an utter waste. "It does not matter very much which side you fight on in any war" because "the effects are just the same whether you win or whether you lose," she wrote in an essay for *Why Wars Must Cease*. World War I had failed to secure a lasting peace, and the consequences of that bloodshed "proved for the first time in our history that the war idea is obsolete." She argued that, "far from preventing future wars, the settlements arrived at have simply fostered hostilities." She championed the antiwar cause with vigor and intelligence. In 1935, she hosted a White House dinner attended by leaders of the National Committee on the Cause and Cure of War, and she compared war to antiquated practices including colonial-era witch trials and nineteenth-century pistol duels. Just as those traditions were odious and unacceptable to modern habits of mind, the practice of total war was absurd and equally nihilistic. It achieved nothing. The first lady endorsed the Emergency Peace Committee and joined the advisory board of the Quaker-led American Friends Service Committee, another antiwar organization.[13]

When her *Virginia Quarterly* article was published in January 1939, the New Dealers seemed to be on the defensive. In 1936, FDR had won a landslide reelection. By 1937, the country had plunged into a recession, and the president's bold (some said reckless) plan to pack the Supreme Court with liberal justices had foundered amid congressional and media opposition. In 1938, the president's proposal to reorganize the government to make Washington more efficient also failed. FDR's critics claimed that his court-packing and reorganization schemes constituted dictatorial steps. Congressman Charles Eaton spoke for many when he huffed that "the advance guard of totalitarianism has enthroned itself in the Government in Washington." One bill, the Fair Labor Standards Act, became law in 1938, but some liberals saw it as only a partial victory. While the legislation achieved a ban on child labor and raised workers' wages from 25 cents to 40 cents an hour over the course of several years, its provisions had also omitted four out of five American workers from coverage.[14]

Election Day 1938 brought unwelcome news to the White House. The Democratic Party lost 8 Senate and nearly 100 House seats. FDR's approval rating stood at around 55 percent—still strong, but less than the 60-plus percent rating he held in 1936; fewer than half of all adults now identified themselves as Democrats. Although FDR's Democratic Party retained healthy majorities in both chambers of Congress, Southern Democrats had joined conservative Republicans to form an anti-New Deal voting bloc, and in January 1939 its members set their sights on reversing as much of the New Deal as possible. The political momentum was at the conservatives' backs. They cut relief programs, abolished the Federal Theatre Project, and tarred both of the Roosevelts with the brush of socialist dictatorship. The White House had empowered the federal bureaucracy, critics claimed, and trampled individual rights while eviscerating the nation's free market philosophy.[15]

Still, the 1938 midterm election results did not lead to the dismantling of the New Deal. The New Deal's foes had not been able to topple the pillars of Social Security, collective bargaining rights, and the Civilian Conservation Corps and National Youth Administration, among other relief and recovery programs. Yet, as the fascist threat grew in 1938 and 1939, FDR was forced into a campaign for military preparedness and had to distance himself from his domestic agenda. The war's rumblings undercut liberal hopes that a new round of social reform was possible.[16]

Eleanor Roosevelt was fifty-three years old in 1938 and in her sixth year in the White House. Her visibility, policy ideas, lobbying, and intellectual interests had arguably already had more of an impact than the majority of her predecessors, combined. She had not completely abandoned the traditional role of first lady: in the late 1930s, she hosted White House dinners, published articles on good manners, and professed her desire to keep silent at events where her husband was speaking. Nonetheless, the muted public role expected of first ladies then was anathema to ER's intellectual commitments, political ideals, and moral compass. "Fearful that she would lose the independence she worked so hard to achieve and that her goals would be subsumed into her husband's agenda, ER wanted a job of her own—a job in which she could be an actor, not just a hostess," one historian wrote of ER's early White House days. By 1938, she still hoped for her own position in the administration. Above all, she set her sights on making a positive contribution to the lives of millions of Americans as they faced the rise of international fascism.[17]

Before she could make that contribution, however, she needed to relinquish her long-held antiwar positions. Military conditions from China to Spain began to force her to rethink her pacifist sympathies. In the late 1930s, events abroad were sufficiently shocking to move the first lady onto a pro-intervention path. Like FDR, she accepted the idea that modern science and technological achievements could bring death and destruction in wartime to unprecedented levels. While isolationists such as the famed aviator Charles Lindbergh downplayed the fascist threat in the mid-thirties, ER predicted as early as January 1936 that "this country still feels very much detached from the rest of the world because of its size and distance, but that will not last forever." She added that the next war would be unlike World War I because "future wars will have no fronts. What we hear of Spain and China makes this seem very probable. Gases and airplanes will not be directed only against armed forces, or military centers, they may be used for the breaking of morale in the opposing nation. That will mean shelling of unfortified cities, towns and villages, and the killing of women and children. In fact this means the participation in war of entire populations."[18]

ER's declining faith in pacifism was also hastened by developments suggesting that total war was a fact of life. During World War I, European leaders fretted over the possibility of a collapse in a country's morale. Although the casualties were relatively light, Germany's use of primitive Zeppelin planes to bomb Londoners set off a debate about maintaining morale amid the stress of wartime. In 1920, Sigmund Freud raised the idea that the mere dread of bombing might prove so traumatic that civilians would become paralyzed and surrender. A year later, Italian theorist Giulio Douhet argued in his groundbreaking book *The Command of the Air* that civilians and factories in enemy nations offered a legitimate military target to belligerents. Wars, he predicted, were destined to turn into clashes between entire peoples in which each side sought to destroy the other's popular will. Fears of total war and its effects on civilians metastasized. A combination of factors—fascist targeting civilians, rapid technological advances, the growing role of industrial production in prosecuting wars—made morale a preoccupation for military planners and political leaders alike. Eleanor Roosevelt was concerned.[19]

In 1935, Italy used its air force to gas Ethiopians, and Emperor Haile Selassie warned that Mussolini's strategy of "carrying . . . terror into the most densely populated parts of the territory" was a way of spreading fear and murdering civilians in cold blood. During the 1930s, British experts were forecasting that in two months of any air war waged by Germany, 600,000 civilians would die, 1.2 million would be injured, and morale would plummet. Before Britain entered World War II, the Ministry of Information began to keep tabs on national morale, assessing whether civilians appeared calm or ill-at-ease, whether they were more likely to endure the strain of bombing or flee in fear for their lives.[20]

This debate preoccupied the first lady, too. As the international crisis deepened, she abandoned her claim that war had to be avoided at all costs. By early 1938, she was publicly breaking with her antiwar allies and implicitly criticizing isolationists who wanted America to stay out of Europe's conflicts. "Force is the only voice which carries conviction and weight with certain groups," she declared in February. She urged Americans to support "better equipment for self defense," adding, "we must maintain our own forces." A combination of factors led her to change her views on national defense, which, in turn, forced her to champion social defense as an antidote to wartime dislocations and totalitarian ideology.[21]

When Japan invaded China, "the most peace-loving nation in the world," ER, having observed years of Japan's aggression, concluded that simply wishing away one's enemies bordered on foreign policy malpractice. "Unpreparedness and an unwillingness to fight have not succeeded in keeping people at peace," she reminded her readers. The atrocities of Francisco Franco's fighters in Spain's Civil War—and the potent accounts of them in the international news media—shocked her into becoming an impassioned antifascist. She declared in 1937 that "what is happening in Spain might happen anywhere." An air raid on the coastal city of Valencia demonstrated to her that war made people "senseless and cruel and needlessly destructive." The bombardment of women and children was particularly appalling to ER, and when Franco's bombers launched air raids on Bilbao and Madrid, she asked FDR's State Department to pressure Franco to provide safe passage for children so they could escape the war zone.[22]

She led a campaign within the White House to lift an arms embargo and supply weapons to Spain's antifascist Loyalist government. "I am not neutral in feeling," she defiantly wrote one critic. "I believe in Democracy and the right of a people to choose their own government without having it imposed on them by Hitler and Mussolini." When Franco's victory appeared imminent, ER told sympathetic administration aide Leon Henderson that the United States' refusal to assist Spain was, in hindsight, a "tragic error." "We were . . . too weak" to assist the antifascists, she lamented, likely referring to the administration's refusal to challenge the Neutrality Acts that had handcuffed it militarily.[23]

Her former antiwar allies came across by the late 1930s as naïve about the nature of fascism. During the spring of 1938, one of ER's acquaintances explained to her that her plan for ensuring peace in the United States was to abolish its Navy, reduce its Army, and strengthen its coastal fortifications. The country would be protected from invaders, the acquaintance thought, and the savings realized by the slimmed-down military could be used to advance social gains at home.

While the first lady found her friend's vision to address the "social needs of the day" appealing, she believed it was a fantasy. Putting more guns along the coastlines would be very costly, she reasoned. There were too "many miles of borders to defend"—and in any case, modern ships and planes could cross such vast distances that America's coastal defenses would be easily wiped out.

ER's views became more hawkish as news from Europe grew bleaker. If the United States refused to keep a strong Navy, she declared, then "an attacking enemy could come unmolested fairly near to our shores" or "land in a nearby country which might be friendly to them, without any interference on our part." The Navy had better be capable of intercepting enemy ships many miles off American shores, while the Army, she added, was "the first line of defense in case somebody does land on our borders, or attempts to approach us by land through a neighboring country."

"In a world which is arming all around us, it is necessary to keep a certain parity" with America's enemies, she continued. Pacifists and isolationists had failed to understand that the Atlantic and Pacific Oceans no longer offered the protective buffers they used to provide, she concluded.[24]

The German novelist Thomas Mann's *The Coming Victory of Democracy* further challenged her earlier view that all wars were nihilistic exercises in mass destruction. In order to defend democracy, Mann said, the world's democracies needed to use force to stop Hitler's aggression. She studied Mann's arguments carefully. By September 1938 she was questioning whether men and women who had wedded themselves to "certain [democratic] ideas" had the "moral right" to avoid the use of force when those ideas were under threat.[25]

ER's hatred of Hitler and Nazism informed her views on national defense and deepened her desire to revive social defense in America to show why democracy was the best antidote to totalitarian regimes. The Munich Conference was a wake-up call. On September 12, 1938, ER and FDR were visiting their son James, who was being treated for ulcers at the Mayo Clinic in Rochester, Minnesota, when Hitler delivered a speech on the radio. The Roosevelts boarded a nearby train car and listened to Hitler's radio talk. The Fuhrer charged that the Czechs had trampled on the rights of Germans living in the Sudetenland under Czech control. He threatened to grab the Sudetenland in order to defend the rights of his fellow citizens. In London, anti-aircraft batteries were set up, air raid trenches were being dug in Hyde Park, and the government was distributing gas masks to civilians.

To Eleanor Roosevelt, Hitler's self-regard and martial bluster was an appalling spectacle. Hitler, she said, "makes me sick." He was, she added, "a mad man" with enormous military power at his fingertips. Appeasement was a failed strategy. She said that when the British caved to Hitler's demands during the Munich Conference, they gave him "all he wanted"—a grievous error in judgment. Hitler would never stop; he would just take more and more. Appeasing him was equivalent to a sham foreign policy: it either would merely have the effect of postponing an inevitable war with the Nazis or enable a fascist takeover of all of Europe. When Hitler's tanks rumbled into Czechoslovakia in September, she criticized the weakness of the British and French response and sympathized with "the poor Czechs!"[26]

During Hitler's invasion of Czechoslovakia, the East Coast experienced the most powerful hurricane since 1815. Houses were ruined, neighborhoods ripped apart. Some of the first lady's close friends had homes in the hurricane's path. One-hundred-mile-per-hour winds left 380 Rhode Islanders dead and more than 60,000 East Coast residents homeless. Yet all she could think about was the conflict in Europe; war became a preoccupation, even an obsession. "No one can think of much else these days," she admitted. In late 1938 and early 1939, she waited for the moment when Europe would burst completely into flames. Dread was a constant companion, as she scanned the newspapers each day for news of greater horrors. Her radio habits before going to sleep became an evening drama in which she waited for news that Europe had plunged completely into a war from which there would be no exit.[27]

At the same time, Hitler's persecution of Europe's Jews affronted ER's commitment to religious tolerance and human rights. Hitler's anti-Semitism helped convince her that the war against Nazi fascism was a Manichean battle and that arming for war was the right thing to do. She recoiled at the Nazi seizures of Jewish homes, the burning of Jewish temples, and Kristallnacht—when Hitler's storm troopers pillaged Jewish neighborhoods in November 1938. ER did not shy from expressing her support for European Jewry. She endorsed establishing Jewish refugee colonies in Palestine. She lobbied the Roosevelt administration to lift its restrictions on Jewish immigration. She battled against a largely anti-Semitic State Department and urged fellow citizens through "thought and example" to show why their democracy was superior to fascism in its treatment of minorities. And she praised the idea of a global campaign to eliminate prejudice, even as she sometimes spread the anti-Semitic view that, as she wrote a German friend in 1939, "the ascendancy of the Jewish people" should be curbed.[28]

Other moments hardened her antifascist views. Having hosted the crown princes and princesses from the Nordic countries at the White House, ER grew more sympathetic to the plight of democracies in Western Europe. Prior to a visit from King George and Queen Elizabeth, the U.S. Ambassador to France, William Bullitt, sent ER a secret memo urging her to ensure that every detail—from the furniture in the royal couple's rooms to what to put in their bathrooms—was just right so that the diplomatic mission would be unblemished. Having attended the Allenswood Academy in England from 1899 to 1902 and studied under her beloved French tutor and mentor Marie Souvestre, ER long ago developed an affinity for the British and the enlightenment principles she had learned from Europeans.[29]

A shrinking world shaped her attitudes. By 1938, she was convinced that nations had grown closely interdependent on each other. In the modern world, it was impossible to go it alone or wall off America from the chaos afflicting other continents. To strive just to "save our own skins" would backfire, she feared. If Hitler were to win the war, Americans could not "escape the conditions which will undoubtedly exist in other parts of the world and which will react against us," she argued. Modern arms, coupled with the fascist philosophy of force, haunted her thoughts. Even if some peace settlement were to be achieved, "we may, of course, be wiped off the face of the earth before" that accord took effect, she warned.[30]

At the same time that she was rethinking her views on war and the fascist threat, ER was also searching for ways to recast America's democratic traditions. She began to adopt a more robust communitarian vision—democracy from the bottom-up—than she had since becoming first lady. ER had often defined "security" in expansive terms. At the height of the Great Depression, she concluded that being secure involved more than simply being safe from physical harms. In November 1933, she emphasized that *"our country as a whole and each one of us as an individual cannot be secure until we have taken care of our less fortunate brothers and sisters."* Yet the threat of total war—where American civilians might be on the front lines, where national morale mattered a great deal, where the victors would determine fundamental questions about human liberty and human dignity—sharpened her definition of what real security entailed. The combined power of fascist military force, the prospect of enemy bombers destroying civilian morale, worries that Americans were running scared and feeling insecure about their way of life, and her rising fear that American democracy was undergoing retrenchment and decaying under the assault of reactionaries who viewed all government programs as a form of totalitarianism—all these things shaped her desire to launch a massive experiment in social defense—a wartime New Deal. Addressing the Southern Conference for Human Welfare in late November 1938, ER said the war storm raised an existential challenge to American liberals. The looming prospect of Hitler's global dominance forced liberal activists to focus as much on the home front as on the military build-up. Progressives, she argued, "must prove to the world that democracy is possible and capable of living up to the principles upon which it was founded." If democracy were to falter in America, then in her view it would be sure to fail across the world.[31]

National defense, then, was unworthy of the name if it did not feature a sustained national effort borne by all Americans to improve democracy in countless communities. Her nascent philosophy was as generous in spirit as it was expansive in scope—and it found expression in countless acts, large and small. She would come to champion causes—civic engagement, civil liberties, and economic justice. Ordinary citizens needed to take an informed, thoughtful approach to improving their communities. She insisted that "as individuals we will live cooperatively, and to the best of our ability, serve the community in which we live." America's ethnic, racial, and religious culture was strong because it was diverse, and so by honoring that diversity and promoting tolerance for all peoples, American democracy would become a counterweight to the fascist appeal to the masses' darkest impulses. The pursuit of happiness was just as vital a value to cultivate as the constitutional rights to "life" and "liberty." The coming war, Eleanor Roosevelt believed, was an extended moment of grave danger and an extended opportunity to create "a new way of living."[32]

Her emerging public philosophy was not simply an exercise in soft-headed idealism. The first lady was accustomed to getting things done, and her pragmatism would inform her approach to the national mobilization. Any reform program, she felt, actually had to "equalize educational opportunities," assist the unemployed, boost old age pensions, help young people find good jobs, and invest in recreation and the arts, which she said were as much of "a necessity to the average human being" as food, shelter, and health care. Americans had to begin in the late 1930s to "set our national house in order," resolve conflicts between social groups at home, bolster the country's "mental and spiritual forces," and wage a complete war against the Axis enemy and all that Hitler embodied. Human security at home, she concluded, would enable American democracy to win the battle for global minds that would need to be waged during and after the war.[33]

She also feared that the New Deal spirit had waned and worried that anti-New Deal conservatives were routing American liberals through their sustained attacks on FDR's domestic programs. When she addressed the February 1939 meeting of the American Youth Congress, she praised "the things that have been done" to provide a social safety net during the prolonged economic crisis, but the New Deal had yet to "solve the fundamental problems." While government did not have the entire solution, it had a positive role to play, and the administration's social program thus far had merely "bought us time to think." The stakes for democracy were as vital in the late 1930s as they were during the economic emergency when her husband took the oath of office in March 1933. "If we hope to see the preservation of our civilization, if we believe that there is anything worthy of perpetuation in what we have built thus far, then our people must turn to brotherly love, not as a doctrine but as a way of living."[34]

Even though New Deal liberals were on the defensive in the late 1930s, Eleanor Roosevelt found hope in numerous sources of democratic inspiration that would form the vanguard of a revived New Deal agenda. For starters, there were the young people. When she attended the World Youth Congress in August 1938 at Vassar College near the Roosevelts' estate in Hyde Park, she praised the delegates as "the best agents for peace" and found hope in harmonious exchanges among youth whose governments were then engaged in armed conflict. Young people were able to rise above the worst aspects of humanity. They embodied the hope of a peaceful, more enlightened world. When delegates from Japan and China bonded over their shared experiences as members of the Young Women's Christian Association, the first lady was heartened. When she saw young citizens from warring countries posing together for a picture, holding in their hands a copy of the *New York Times* featuring a headline about Japan's bombing of China, she considered it an inspiring antiwar statement. "Many groups heard their countries criticized without hissing or leaving, really a lesson," she argued, for warring leaders that dialogue and reason could trump fear and recriminations. She also applauded the "Vassar Pact" approved by the delegates. The pact urged nations to reduce their armed forces, end the practice of air raids on civilians, defend human rights, and promote democratic suffrage.[35]

If she saw youth as the vanguard of progressivism, she also began to frame the American struggle for racial justice in the context of Hitler's fear-mongering. Just as she sought to open doors to Jewish refugees fleeing Hitler's persecution, so too she fought for African American rights in order to blunt the ways in which the United States echoed fascism in its own social practices. To ER, Jim Crow stained American democracy, undercutting the claim that democracies were superior to totalitarian regimes. Her speeches to civil rights audiences and defiance of white supremacists during a meeting of civil rights leaders in Birmingham came in the context of fascist oppression overseas. Then, on February 28, 1939, she announced in her syndicated column that she was resigning from the Daughters of the American Revolution. Howard University had invited African American singer Marian Anderson to give a concert in DAR's Constitution Hall but the DAR refused to let a black singer perform there. ER's resignation was major news. She later had Anderson perform at the White House for the British king and queen during their June visit—a poignant antifascist statement.[36]

Her interpretation of the fascist threat shaped her wartime liberalism. Pitted against diplomats including Ambassadors Joseph Kennedy in London and William Bullitt in Paris, men who were unsympathetic to the plight of European Jews, ER cast immigration policy as a moral question—a chance to show democracy at its most humane. Abner Larned, who headed Michigan's WPA, had a seat next to the first lady at a White House dinner during the mid-1930s. Her interest in immigrant reform left a deep impression. Larned subsequently wrote a letter to ER proposing that the WPA run the nation's new "program of registering and finger-printing aliens" and use its personnel and classes to help Americanize immigrants. The WPA, he explained, would build "understanding and sympathy" into an otherwise unfeeling program. Larned praised immigrants as law-abiding citizens and claimed that friendly classes would show them that

America's new immigration laws were "not intended to spy on them or list them as subversive elements." Larned's proposal was, the first lady replied, excellent.[37]

In 1939, as part of the effort to revive the stalled New Deal, she cultivated and deepened her ties to an array of administration officials. When the Senate Appropriations Committee threatened to cut the budget of the WPA, ER asked Colonel Francis C. Harrington, WPA's administrator, to describe the impact of earlier cuts on relief recipients. Preparing for a lecture tour in March, she offered to endorse WPA programs in the cities and towns she visited. On January 26, one WPA official wrote the first lady that her assistance would be invaluable. "I can point to many places in the Midwest where the program began to be recognized only after you had put your hands upon it," the colleague assured ER. "Often the effect was electrifying."[38]

The missives about defending liberalism did not slow even as the war came closer to America's shores. In the face of Hitler's military victories and conservatives' attack on New Deal programs at home, ER was irrepressible and unbending—a one-woman force for the causes she held dear. In 1939, she lobbied the WPA to investigate the hard-luck case of a Georgia woman who had asked ER to help clothe her nine-year-old girl and five-year-old boy. ER said that if the WPA was unable to assist the Georgia woman's children, the first lady wanted to know it, implying that she might handle the problem through her own informal channels. The requests for assistance from Americans to the first lady piled up, and ER's requests to her liberal allies did, too. She continued to press for information, sympathy, and aid for thousands of Americans who had come to her for advice and assistance.[39]

Campaigning to assist the underprivileged, ER became increasingly frustrated with the lack of national solutions to social problems. Virtually every letter to one WPA leader from Eleanor Roosevelt contained a request for information or a suggestion for taking action. ER's correspondence was so voluminous that the WPA had to send the first lady summary reports "covering the handling of your mail during the period February 1st through March 31st 1939." The first lady had forwarded to WPA officials 1,439 letters in that two-month span—all of the letters "written by women or . . . concerned with women's problems"; most of the letters included specific requests for federal assistance. Eight hundred and fifty of the letters were about the issue of finding jobs. (State and regional WPA staff were asked to take action on job-related requests.) Hundreds of women felt a personal connection to the first lady, and their letters contained requests for relief, questions about hospitalization, how to find access to affordable housing, and pleas for direct donations from ER in the form of money, clothes, "hope chests," and advice "concerning broken homes."[40]

The letters were notable for another reason: they brimmed with enthusiasm for ER's agenda. And they hinted at their faith in democratic activism that ER seemed to embody. One African American woman from Atlanta said, "Even though I may never have word of any sort from you, I wish to thank you for showing those of us who are coming along the way in these bewildering times, how fine a woman can be." Progressive non-governmental organizations worked with ER to assist some of her correspondents. The YWCA, for example, helped find an apartment for a widow after she had informed the first lady that she was homeless. ER's office aggressively kept track of individuals who had sought White House assistance.[41]

Just as she promoted civil rights for black Americans, so, too, did the first lady fight to carve out a large role for American women in the national mobilization. She had fought to appoint women to office since 1933. The cause of women's equality, which had long been one of her priorities, intensified as the totalitarian shadow crept over the world. She sought to further women's rights and elevate women to high-level posts whenever possible. When the head of the WPA in Pennsylvania left her job, ER had one request: "appoint a woman as her successor." The suggestion hinted at what would become a staple of her wartime New Deal: New Deal women would be in the forefront of that effort, forming a little-known coalition to install social defense at the center of the national defense program.[42]

As the first lady's views about fascist aggression and democratic reforms solidified, she had her share of allies—but it was hard for her to read her own husband. While FDR was sympathetic to ER's reform ideas, he began to reserve his political capital for military mobilization. At the same time, the president's vision for national defense also featured nonmilitary aims akin to his wife's—propping up civilian morale, engaging citizens in civic causes, curbing conflicts between labor and business. If Washington failed to redress the nation's unsolved social problems, he predicted, America's enemies would exploit those rifts and sow social instability at a time when national unity was vital.

FDR refused to let such wounds fester on the body politic. His social and economic reforms were as important as armaments, he declared in 1938. Human security, he argued, was a pillar of national security. Americans needed access to good jobs at good pay, and in the late 1930s he endorsed the activities of social-action organizations such as the Mobilization for Human Needs. He also campaigned—sometimes coordinating with the first lady, more often on his own initiative and through other channels—to push the New Deal in wartime directions. Speaking to the National Convention of Townsend Clubs, an organization dedicated to the establishment of a government-sponsored old age pension plan, he pledged that while Washington mobilized industry to meet military needs, his administration had "no intention of neglecting the other phase of preparedness"—shoring up the "social, economic and moral structures of American life."[43]

White House aides and administration officials heeded FDR's message. In May 1939, the War Department's Louis Johnson suggested that once a Federal Security Agency (FSA) had been established (it was to promote economic security, administer Social Security, and protect the food supply among other functions), the War Department should have a "Liaison Officer" on the FSA administrator's staff so social services and military requirements could be coordinated. In 1939, under Eleanor Roosevelt's leadership, a significant push to revive the New Deal sprang to life within the administration. Civic groups and administration liberals battled for input over the pre-Pearl Harbor New Deal.[44]

Leading New Deal women were potent voices in the debate about the organization and character of the new FSA—and would be even more influential in any wartime New Deal. The textile workers union urged the administration not to allow the American Medical Association to block the appointment of progressive activist Josephine Roche to run the FSA.[45]

In 1939, FDR ultimately tapped Paul McNutt, the former democratic governor of Indiana, to run the agency; he was a strong political ally, anti-union, and a champion of the militaristic American Legion. Despite the disappointment among some liberals, the FSA had the ambitious goal of enacting the president's "human needs" reform agenda. The agency, a clearinghouse for social programs, included the CCC, NYA, Office of Education, Social Security Board, Public Health Service, and an American Printing House for the Blind. FDR and McNutt collaborated on a variety of social projects. The president ordered McNutt to establish a secret committee of liberals to recommend new forms of training for CCC leaders, to counter the loss of reserve officers who were now leaving in order to enter the U.S. Army. The Corps' purpose was "to take unemployed young men off the streets of towns and cities and give them useful work under conditions which would contribute to their physical and moral health." While that effort had been largely successful, New Dealers sought to make the Corps permanent and provide "an important segment of the population the mechanical skills and the high morale needed in times like these." While Eleanor Roosevelt had long faulted the CCC for failing to provide youth with a comprehensive introduction to civic engagement, this new debate about reforming the CCC was consistent with her effort to find fresh strategies, programs, and ideas to improve Americans' lives and cope with wartime dislocations.[46]

Although McNutt continued to affront some New Dealers, he did work to further FDR's liberal wartime agenda. He suggested language for FDR to use in his message to Congress on unemployment compensation. His proposal was a window into the New Deal mindset circa 1939. McNutt cast the 1935 Social Security Act "as a development toward a goal rather than a finished product," and he urged FDR to declare: "Today we are engaged in a mighty national defense effort to make our country and its chosen way of life secure against all present and potential threats. This effort, however, cannot be evaluated solely in terms of armament production or mere mathematical increase in the number of our armed forces. Behind the guardians of our defense must stand a united people whose spiritual and moral values have not diminished through hunger, want or fear or insecurity. Thus, an ever-widening and ever more effective Social Security program is an essential ingredient in our preparations for national defense." Eleanor Roosevelt couldn't have agreed more.[47]

Reform-themed memos and letters, filled with suggestions for coping with mobilization, began to pour into the Oval Office. In September 1939, Democratic Senator Elbert Thomas asked FDR to investigate the impact of "the war upon health, education, business in general, and maritime shipping." FDR asked McNutt and his secretaries of Labor and Agriculture to draft a reply. While a lot of New Dealers were depressed about the future of programs they had championed, FDR made at least token efforts to view social welfare as an element in national defense. New Dealers had in no way given up on a new round of reforms, partly as a means of shoring up the people's faith in the capacity of their democracy to resolve their most basic problems of access to jobs, food, shelter, and dignity. In 1939, they passed an amendment to Social Security's old age insurance program. Senator Robert Wagner had proposed a plan to give more Americans access to health care, and in early 1940 FDR even gave his support for federal aid to build community hospitals. Liberals such as Frances Perkins, Harold Ickes, Josephine Roche, and Senators Robert Wagner and Robert La Follette Jr. pushed hard to breathe life into the New Deal, propping up the people's morale in case the United States had to enter the war.[48]

While the conversation about a wartime New Deal continued, news from Europe became bleaker by the day. At 5 a.m. on September 1, 1939, FDR called Eleanor Roosevelt and gave her the news: Germany had invaded Poland. England and France would soon declare war on Germany. ER turned on her radio to listen to Hitler's address to the Reichstag. She understood enough German to decipher Hitler's remarks, and she acidly pointed out that Hitler "never mentioned that there was a God whom we are supposed to love, nor did he show the slightest sympathy for the people whom he had plunged into the war." On October 3rd, she told one antiwar activist that she "would rather die than submit to rule by Hitler."[49]

She felt the United States had no choice but to arm itself and prepare to fight. She took comfort from knowing that "New Deal social objectives . . . had fostered the spirit that would make it possible for us to fight this war." The coming war would be fought for control of land, sea lanes, and air space—she knew that.

She also believed that World War II would come down to a battle of ideas, pitting fascist regimentation against social democratic experimentation. Americans had better be prepared "to fight with our minds," as she put it, or else the gains that the New Deal had started to deliver would be lost. The Nazi agenda in all of its brutality, she thought, would end Americans' last hope for building a humane future.[50]

2

No Pact, Treaty, Symbol, or Person

> Long-distance guns, aerial bombardments and poisonous gases will
> recognize no pact, treaty, symbol or person.
> —Fiorello La Guardia, 1930

New York Mayor Fiorello La Guardia had a vision of democracy much like
Eleanor Roosevelt's. He believed that democracies had an obligation to aid the
poor, provide services to workers and shopkeepers, and help immigrants gain
access to economic opportunity. During the late 1930s, he also argued that
Hitler threatened the future of American democracy. But where ER supported
social defense (a wartime New Deal) combined with military mobilization,
La Guardia worried primarily about the air threat facing the nation's big cities.
He dreaded the prospect that enemy bombs would incinerate New York's apartment buildings and urban landmarks. Little terrified him more than the thought
that air raids would sow even more panic than was created by Orson Welles's
"War of the Worlds."

And, like Eleanor Roosevelt, La Guardia's view of the issue of war mobilization evolved over time. He had served as a combat pilot in Italy during World
War I, giving him a firsthand brush with air power. Like many progressives,
La Guardia became a pacifist during the 1920s. Yet, as mayor during the 1930s,
he came to regard Hitler as a direct threat and wanted to expand the nation's
military might.

Public safety became a preoccupation of his during his time in City Hall. He
concluded that a breakdown in the civic order could undermine social progress.
Fearing that residents could be made to feel unsafe in their homes, he thought
that any kind of military attack could collapse the entire edifice—city government and public faith in their leaders—upon which stability in the city had
been built. Impelled by this conviction, he began to lobby for a joint federal–
municipal home defense plan to protect civilians.

Rotund, five-feet-two-inches tall, and bristling with kinetic energy, the mayor
was an ally of President Roosevelt and, although a Republican, a champion of

the New Deal. Earlier in the decade, he had joined hands with FDR to construct bridges, tunnels, and airports to improve the lives of New Yorkers. La Guardia made City Hall less corrupt and more accountable, and he found a reliable ally in the White House. However, during the late 1930s, "the Little Flower"—Fiorello means "little flower" in Italian—worried increasingly that America's cities had become vulnerable to German and Japanese air fleets that had already attacked Spain, China, and Czechoslovakia. La Guardia shifted his near-singled-minded focus away from reforms improving civilians' lives at home toward a form of liberalism that prioritized the protection of civilians from enemy attacks—recasting New Deal liberalism as a national security philosophy.

Around 1938, La Guardia and FDR started to forge a different sort of alliance resting on their shared hatred of Hitlerism. They made a formidable national security team. Leading a coalition of internationalists, they devoted their efforts to military mobilization and campaigned to persuade citizens that fascist threats had put American lives at risk.[1]

Isolationism had sunk deep roots in the politics and culture of post-World War I America—forming a wall of opposition to FDR's and La Guardia's approach. Isolationists insisted that Americans would be naive to fight a second war in Europe, where so many citizens had died during World War I for no apparent reason. Initially, FDR spent little political capital challenging the isolationist creed. He saw foreign affairs as a means to help the United States cope with the economic emergency. He called on the world to achieve "peace by disarmament" and pursued a policy of friendship toward Latin America, declaring in his first inaugural address that "In the field of world policy, I would dedicate this nation to the policy of the good neighbor." During his first term, Roosevelt subscribed to the Monroe Doctrine's conceit issued by President James Monroe in 1823 that the greatest threats to the United States would only emerge from within the hemisphere.[2]

During much of his second term, the politics of isolationism remained ascendant and nettlesome. Between 1935 and 1939, Congress passed a succession of Neutrality Acts that prohibited the president from supplying arms to foreign governments, and FDR reluctantly signed these acts into law. A grassroots movement in the United States was promoting pacifism, shaping the conduct of U.S. foreign policy. The isolationist impulse remained strong throughout the 1930s, despite news accounts that told of the triumphs of fascist militaries. Italian dictator Benito Mussolini invaded Ethiopia, while Spain's fascist leader Francisco Franco waged a civil war for control of Spain. In the meantime, 50,000 American veterans marched in Washington in opposition to calls for United States intervention in Europe's wars. In February 1937, a Gallup Poll found that 95 percent of the American public thought that the United States should stay out of any European war. Sears Roebuck chairman Robert Wood spoke for antiwar business leaders when he predicted that U.S. intervention in Europe's conflicts would destroy capitalism. Isolationist Democratic Senator Burton Wheeler warned that U.S. participation in any European war would needlessly slaughter millions of Americans. Aviation hero Charles Lindbergh defined isolationist thought when he claimed that the United States still only needed "the Atlantic Ocean on the east and the Pacific on the West" for its protection and added that "an ocean is a formidable barrier, even for modern aircraft."[3]

By the late 1930s, however, there were hints that the isolationist mood was starting to shift as Hitler began to demonstrate the full force of German military might. Franklin Roosevelt and La Guardia responded accordingly, focusing especially on the airplane. These leaders insisted that technological advances had upset cherished notions of geographic security, and they described how shifts in military doctrine had altered how wars were fought and won. La Guardia was particularly enthusiastic. On a sweltering day in July 1938, he hosted at City Hall a special celebration of aviator Howard Hughes, who had recently flown around the world. At a city council meeting, La Guardia personally strode to the back of the chamber to open the double doors for Hughes, as a large crowd looked on. Then, standing before a gaggle of microphones, the mayor said that air power was a reflection of the best and worst in the human condition. He predicted that soon he would be able to fly to Moscow and call his wife to explain that he was visiting Russia for the weekend. (He imagined her reply: "Oh, no. You'd better make it Bucharest. You might want to run for office again some day.") The airplane could knit diverse peoples into a peaceful world community, he argued. But air power had a dark side. He knew that fascists used it as a weapon of terror, a tool to break civilians' will to fight. Air power, La Guardia concluded, had become a danger to the existence of democratic civilization and had already retarded the quest to achieve progress on a global scale. Roosevelt agreed. Both men began to regard home defense as a major new problem confronting the United States. Together, they sought to move liberals toward a philosophy that prioritized physical safety ahead of economic reforms and social gains during the late 1930s. Under their leadership, New Deal liberalism began to concern itself more with national protection from military harms rather than with resolving such problems as mass unemployment, poverty, and labor rights. FDR and La Guardia argued that Americans had to rethink their national defense policies in order to ensure that the United States remained a beacon that lit the way for democracy during what poet W. H. Auden had called a "low, dishonest decade."[4]

La Guardia's passion for home defense can be traced back to experiences early in his life. Born on December 11, 1882, in a Greenwich Village apartment to Italian and Austrian immigrants, he acquired a taste for military culture as a young boy.

His father, Achille, served as a musician in the Army, and La Guardia's family settled at Whipple Barracks in the town of Prescott, then part of the Arizona Territory. At age seven, soldiers taught La Guardia how to fire a gun. He grew up in a virtual war zone where Native Americans and settlers battled one another and where bandits, cowboys, and ambushes were commonplace. During the Spanish-American War, his family's fortunes turned for the worse. Achille ate rotten meat, contracted hepatitis, and was unable to serve with his unit in Cuba. He moved his family to Trieste, Italy, where his wife had been raised. At age eighteen, La Guardia found a job working as a clerk at the American consulate in Budapest.

His rise through the ranks was swift and notable. He learned five languages and used his skills as a translator to become a consular officer in Fiume, Italy. Soon, however, he tired of the diplomatic life. At twenty-three, he returned to New York, attended NYU law school at night, and found a job as a Civil Service interpreter on Ellis Island. He translated Italian, German, and Croatian for officials interviewing immigrants who were seeking to enter the United States and acquired a firsthand view of the flaws in the immigration system. He discovered that city aldermen were taking bribes from immigrants in exchange for marriage licenses, and he found the city's judiciary equally corrupt. La Guardia joined New York's Republican Club. Eager to reform the way business was done in the city, he ran for Congress in 1916 as a candidate who championed cleaner government, and in November he won the first of seven terms.[5]

Soon after arriving in Washington, he took a step that won him national acclaim. In July 1917, as a sitting Congressman, he entered Washington's Southern Railway Building, strode into the Aviation Section of the Signal Corps, and applied to serve as a pilot in the U.S. Army Air Service. He had acquired a taste for the burgeoning field of aviation. After graduating from law school in 1910, he had had an aircraft manufacturer as a client of his law practice. He took flight lessons at the company's Long Island training school and became fascinated with airplanes. He told the major interviewing him that "so long as I could fly," he would accept any rank. So he was made a First Lieutenant in the Army. Based in Fiume while simultaneously serving in Congress, La Guardia showed those "grousing about Congressmen sending others to wars" that at least one House member had the courage of his convictions. He used his role in the military to shed his hyphenated status as a first-generation immigrant and burnish his reputation as a patriot who defended democracy with passionate intensity.[6]

World War I helped give birth to his belief that conditions in Europe directly affected the lives of civilians in the United States. The war in Europe was killing America's young men, and La Guardia came to see it as a struggle over the future of democracy itself. During the war, La Guardia trained U.S. and Italian pilots, flew combat missions, battled malaria that ravaged his base, and provided his men with edible food. As he flew with Italian pilots in a Caproni plane, La Guardia survived near misses, and his feelings about the impact of air power intensified. On one mission, La Guardia's plane strafed Austrian enemy trenches, and two enemy fighters riddled his plane with bullets. On a different occasion, his plane crashed in high winds, and La Guardia suffered a lifelong back injury. His reputation at home soared. He was being feted as "the Flying Congressman." The *New York Times* called him a "gallant aviator" while the Italian government awarded him the Flying Cross, given to men for courage in combat.[7]

La Guardia's war years persuaded him that airplanes had enormous potential for good and ill—promoting commerce and cultural exchanges as well as killing innocent people. His fear deepened when La Guardia waged a campaign against an Italian manufacturer whose planes had broken apart midair, killing American pilots. In January 1918, he began to serve as the Army's liaison to a committee that was studying the effects of air power on the war. (He also served in diplomatic roles for the United States, assuring the Italian people and their government that the United States was a firm ally and would not abandon them.) In the process, he developed a lifelong interest in military and foreign affairs.[8]

When the Armistice was signed, La Guardia returned home to find the American public out of step with his progressive brand of politics. A bumptious insurgent campaigning on behalf of the underprivileged, La Guardia defied the conservative bent of the 1920s and championed a set of unpopular causes such as expanding rights for women, workers, immigrants, and African Americans. At the same time, he planted himself firmly in the foreign policy mainstream.

Following the currents of postwar thought, he had become a pacifist. He argued that in any new war "the civilian population in large and industrial centers and distant from the battle line [would] suffer more than the military forces in actual conflict." He fretted that "long-distance guns, aerial bombardments and poisonous gases will recognize no pact, treaty, symbol or person." And he endorsed the goal of achieving universal peace, proposed restricting the size of the U.S. military, and urged world leaders to seek a new era based on harmonious relations and diplomatic negotiations.[9]

But La Guardia above all focused on reforming New York City's government. In 1934, he swept into City Hall by campaigning as a reformer who would improve the slums, strengthen mass transit, provide efficient government—and end the reign of Tammany Hall and the corruption that the Democratic bosses had overseen. He became an architect of Roosevelt's reform agenda, promoting the New Deal as a way to address poverty, blight, education, and public health.[10]

Yet he also emphasized the importance of keeping New Yorkers safe during all kinds of civic crises. A hands-on mayor who had a penchant for public displays of bravura, La Guardia rushed to the scene when buildings were ablaze, barked orders at his firefighters, and helped rescue at least one fireman who had been caught under a beam battling a fire. He assured New Yorkers that their government would save their lives and maintain public order in the aftermath of natural and man-made calamities. The mayor helped clear debris after subway crashes. In January 1937, when the Mississippi River flooded, La Guardia put his city's police force at the call of the U.S. Army and vowed to use his government's resources to ensure that people in affected areas had access to potable water.[11]

La Guardia found a national base for pursuing urban reform in the U.S. Conference of Mayors. His partnership with big-city mayors solidified his view that city halls were on the front lines of keeping their residents physically safe. Maintaining public order in a metropolis teeming with seven million people was more than a passing concern of his. His fears that the Great Depression of the early 1930s would lead to riots were consistent with his subsequent fears that even a modest air raid on New York City would turn his city into a cauldron of despair and chaos.

The conference's early agenda was fundamentally shaped by the Great Depression, and the alliance between Fiorello La Guardia and Franklin Roosevelt was formed in their work on it. Established in 1933, the conference had 189 members who governed cities of at least 50,000 people. The conference sought to make cities more efficient and helped coordinate the work of the municipal governments with the Roosevelt administration's New Deal programs. Promoting the economic and social interests of their constituents, conference members also offered their input to Washington and forced New Dealers to focus on city problems. Its second president, Boston Mayor James Curley, lobbied the White House to create jobs for the unemployed and a safety net for the urban poor.[12]

In 1935, La Guardia became president and developed a set of national recommendations to promote prosperity in urban areas. He helped bring 200,000 WPA jobs to New York City, and Washington gave him unprecedented leeway to manage federal relief funds as he saw fit. FDR lauded the conference for embedding the New Deal in the nation's big cities. Roosevelt believed that he and La Guardia had tackled the most difficult domestic questions of their day, including public housing, mass unemployment, and old-age insurance. In addition to building the infrastructure of New York City, they worked together to curb pollution and served as cohosts for foreign leaders who were visiting New York.

Their alliance was rooted in their shared commitment to the New Deal, and in 1936 La Guardia was eager to help the president defend the WPA from its critics. He sent Roosevelt a conference report that denounced the "promiscuous and misinformed talk" that the WPA was a government boondoggle. "We are anxious to put a true picture before the American people as to what has been accomplished through the WPA program," La Guardia wrote, arguing that the cities had significant unmet needs and that the WPA's "work principle in giving relief assistance" was far better than relying on "the dole, based upon idleness and groceries, [which] has no place in our American scheme of society." La Guardia's report described the WPA as a model of integrity and innovation that required no apology from the liberals who had championed it.[13]

FDR likewise paid tribute to La Guardia's leadership and New Deal vision. The president wrote the mayor that their partnership would enable them to find "additional matters which serve to bring the local governments and the Federal Government into more intimate dealings with each other." FDR added that the mayors' "joint cooperation with the National Government on our common problems" was a source of democratic pride and distinction. Days after his landslide 1936 reelection victory, FDR told a meeting of the conference that the mayors must continue to make common cause with him and pursue their shared goals. "You have a lot of problems and I am glad that Fiorello . . . mentioned the fact that there is sympathy for them in the White House," the president said. "I want to keep in touch with what you do." During the late 1930s, the alliance pivoted. FDR and La Guardia not only kept in touch but also focused liberal government on defending America from foreign threats, as society became awash in fears that enemies endangered citizens across the United States.[14]

Several forces in the culture began to shape the popular view that air power in particular represented a growing scourge that could no longer be safely ignored. Newspapers and radio broadcasts underscored the scope of the menace while also chronicling the deteriorating conditions that had pushed Europe to the brink of a Second World War. Such coverage helped persuade La Guardia and FDR that advances in air power meant that the Atlantic Ocean no longer afforded Americans the protections that they had long enjoyed. While the nation was still overwhelmingly isolationist, some liberal leaders began to argue that isolationism was a recipe for national catastrophe, and their claims slowly began to resonate. During a press conference held just days after the "War of the Worlds" aired, FDR revealed the shifting character of his approach to foreign affairs, suggesting that he was rethinking liberalism itself. He tutored reporters on air power, calling it a revolution powered by technology that directly affected the lives of all Americans. The rise of aviation, FDR explained, had changed "the whole orientation of this country in relation to the continent on which we live" so that now, "from Canada to Terra del Fuego . . . , any possible attack has been brought infinitely closer than it was five years or twenty years or fifty years ago." The days when civilians could rely on the Pacific and Atlantic Oceans to guarantee their security had disappeared, Roosevelt added. When a reporter asked the president to explain how he became convinced of this fact, FDR replied that he had merely "read the newspapers for the past five years."[15]

Historian Michael Sherry has observed in his history of airpower that "the practical limitations [of aviation technology] imposed sharp restraints on the translation of ideas into action," but that "statesmen or warriors" did not initially know that such limits existed. Few historians, however, have traced the intensity, ubiquity, and even paranoia that suffused the coverage of the air menace in the run up to World War II. It was the media's coverage that helped fire the imaginations of liberal leaders such as FDR and La Guardia as well as ordinary citizens. Airplanes back then lacked the capability to depart from Germany or Japan, cross the ocean, and bomb American targets. There is no evidence that Germany possessed aircraft carriers and air bases within easy range of launching attacks on East Coast targets. But some Americans assumed otherwise. The media's growing obsession with super bombers and advanced aviation technologies made many Americans believe that air raids on U.S. soil were possible. Reporters and columnists argued that scientific advances had initiated a revolution in military affairs, and the effect on the public mind was as profound as MacLeish's "Air Raid" and Welles's "War of the Worlds" broadcasts. The reporting, even though overwrought, began to agitate people's collective anxieties about how vulnerable Americans were in an age of total war.[16]

Some feared that even a single bomb dropped on an American city could prompt citizens to flee their homes and riot in the streets as elected leaders, policemen, and soldiers were rendered impotent. These fears were rooted in the nation's history and culture, too. Even before the Wright Brother invented one of the first planes at Kitty Hawk in 1903, Europeans and Americans fantasized about machines reaping destruction on the populace from the skies. Mark Twain's 1889 *A Connecticut Yankee in King Arthur's Court* described a "vast fountain of dazzling lances of fire" that produced an apocalyptic eclipse of the sun. Ignatius Donnelly's 1890 novel *Caesar's Column* depicted cities as "only fit for temporary purposes—to see the play and the shops and the mob—and to wear one's life out in nothingness." Such novels, Michael Sherry writes, tended to "cast war as a civil conflict harnessing dreadful new weapons to internal passions." Reality and fantasy became indistinguishable from one another. As early as 1898, a Polish military expert predicted that "very soon balloons will be used to drop explosive substances" on civilians during wartime.

The elements of an "air war" panic were coming into sharper focus by the early twentieth century. Sporadic use of primitive airplanes during World War I elevated the terrible prospect of air raids fomenting urban unrest. First with Germany's "Zeppelin" raids on London, and then with the "Gotha" raids across Britain, scores of English civilians were killed. One British paper editorialized that the government had better protect civilians from bombs falling from the skies in order to avoid mass panic. After one air raid, hundreds of Britons ransacked suspected German homes and businesses. The Kaiser's high command used air raids, one British paper speculated, to inflict a "moral effect on the London mob," and when Londoners carried on with their lives, some journalists praised the public for keeping calm under fire.[17]

In the United States, fears of the air menace began to percolate in the media long before the "War of the Worlds" was broadcast to a national audience. In September 1937, the *New York Times* published "The Fear of Flying Death Darkens," which reported that in the next war air fleets could destroy civilization and turn European cities into "half-emptied husks of shattered buildings." Reporters stressed how madmen possessed new tools to inflict death on innocents on a mass scale and were within reach of their goal of achieving world domination. In February 1938, the *Washington Post* announced that in any new war, Germany would drop more tonnage of bombs on London in one day than it had rained on England during all of World War I. The *Post* described two air raids as the equivalent of the 1906 earthquake that had flattened much of San Francisco. A German air assault on London, the *Post* also estimated, was going to kill 10,000 civilians; injure 30,000; light hundreds of fires; leave giant holes in the streets; and destroy buildings, pipes, and sewers and cause floods in subways and basements, yielding "the most horrible slaughter of civilians the world has ever seen."[18]

Americans shuddered when they read accounts of actual fascist air raids that were occurring in the mid to late 1930s. In Barcelona, the *Post* reported, Franco had used bombers to destroy public buildings and kill thousands of civilians. A columnist pointed out that fascists had deployed air power to kill more than 1,100 civilians in Alicante and Granoliers, Spain, and killed thousands of innocents in Canton, China, in a single week. Picasso's 1937 painting *Guernica* depicted the horror that bombing had inflicted on Spanish women and children, stirring global outrage.[19]

The terror of air war seeped into the public discourse. A variety of media outlets reported in late September 1938 that Germany might be preparing to drop bombs on England and Czechoslovakia. Novelist Virginia Woolf watched as Londoners dug air raid trenches in a park and listened to loudspeakers telling civilians to "go and fit your gas masks," while governments across Western Europe began distributing masks to their peoples on a vast scale.[20]

With the threat of raids hanging over much of Europe, newspapers and magazines began to describe the ways in which Americans could experience the nightmare of aerial bombardment. Citizens read an account in the *New York Times* in April 1937 that a German major had taunted Americans that they were likely to panic during any raids on their cities, while Nazis had steeled the German people to withstand such onslaughts. The *Los Angeles Times* reported in June 1937 that a "Gas Attack on America," made more plausible by the rise of super bombers capable of carrying two thousand pounds of bombs and flying vast distances, could become reality and kill countless civilians. Pictures of "lethal gases descending from the sky and choking noncombatants in the streets" appeared in the *Washington Post*, with a caption saying chemical war "strikes at elemental fears." The *Post* also warned readers that germ war was a real possibility for which they had to be prepared. While the reports did not immediately influence public opinion, it softened it up and made Americans more receptive to FDR's and La Guardia's pro-intervention arguments.[21]

Liberal and conservative columnists detailed the tactics and strategies Nazis would employ to turn Americans into victims of modern war. The nation's most famous liberal columnist Walter Lippmann, for example, argued that German military bases on Gibraltar, the African Coast, and the Straits of Dover in Portugal had heightened the vulnerability of Americans to foreign threats. Dorothy Thompson added her view that if the Nazis were able to seize control of military bases in Iceland, Mexico, Greenland, the Bahamas, or the Danish Faroe Islands, they would be able to target the continental United States. The rising consensus included not just liberal writers but also conservative foes of the New Deal such as Westbrook Pegler. In one column, Pegler argued that American citizens had a right to know how military leaders intended to defend them from foreign enemy attacks.[22]

The U.S. military added to the public's impression that the air threat was no mere fantasy of reporters' overactive imaginations. While one Army major argued in 1937 that the United States could stop enemy bombers and urged Americans not to succumb to a bad case of the "airplane jitters," his peers believed that the air raids occurring in Europe were indeed plausible scenarios in the United States. A lieutenant colonel who visited Germany and Austria to study air raid defense returned home with clips from *Die Sirene*, the magazine of the Nazis' Civilian Air Defense Society, to include in his report about civil defense in Central Europe. In 1937, Major General Frank Andrews, Chief of the Army's General Headquarters Air Force, warned that enemy planes were nearly impossible to intercept and that super bombers were merely small prototypes of the type of planes that nations would soon have in their air forces. He predicted that these new planes would make the Atlantic look like the size of the English Channel.[23]

The military's assessment of the air threat shaped its policies, as well. To counter the prospect of a fascist invasion, the Army proposed putting air bases in Tampa, Florida; Hawaii; Alaska; and Puerto Rico. In May 1938, Army leaders held the first large air raid drill of the decade, part of its effort to persuade the American public that the contagion of European war could spread to communities long thought safe from such microbes. The public was simultaneously intrigued and frightened by these demonstrations in their backyards. In Farmingdale, Long Island, approximately fifty thousand people lined the roads to look up at war planes racing through the skies, and nine mock enemy bombers reached their destinations, bombing, in theory, a local airport and two aircraft factories. A housewife who watched the drill was reminded of the children in Spain and China who had lost their lives in the bombing, and a taxi driver took stock of the drill and declared that America was not ready for war on its own soil. A second drill, just weeks before the broadcast of the "War of the Worlds," involved two thousand farmers, housewives, and shopkeepers stationed at more than three hundred watch posts along the Atlantic seaboard, while a dozen planes buzzed hills and treetops before reaching their intended targets. Enemy planes coming to bomb America under the cloak of night posed an almost unstoppable danger to the public, warned a reporter for the *New York Times*. All of the uncertainties associated with modern war, coupled with a lack of proper civilian defense training, were unsettling for people to ponder.[24]

The military also raised concerns that the Nazis might use Latin America as a staging ground for a U.S. invasion. Military leaders warned administration officials that the Nazis had made inroads into the region's economy and culture, and Army historians later described the Army's goal as preventing "the establishment of any hostile air base in the Western Hemisphere from which the continental area or the Panama Canal might be bombed or from which a surface attack or invasion might be supported." In the eyes of military commanders, the danger to the United States was hardly restricted to air power alone.[25]

The pressures on FDR to respond to the air threat grew acute as members of Congress and some interest groups urged him to take steps to defend the borders and the nation's airspace. As early as 1936, Rep. Jennings Randolph wrote FDR that he should relocate aircraft factories inland because, he reasoned, "a hostile airplane carrier perhaps hundreds of miles at sea" could send planes to destroy the factories that were near the coasts, and that within an hour of take-off, fast airplanes could bomb Pratt and Whitney Aircraft in Hartford, Connecticut, and Wright Aeronautical in Paterson, New Jersey. The Air Defense League, a group of World War I veterans, chastised FDR for failing to take aggressive steps to combat the growing air threat.[26]

FDR's aides subscribed to the consensus that air war had a direct bearing on U.S. national security, upsetting past dogmas and jeopardizing the future of democracy. During a meeting in the White House, Major Alexander de Seversky, a leading theorist of air power who later wrote the bestselling *Victory Through Air Power*, told Harold Ickes, the Secretary of the Interior, that within two or three years they would see "much heavier bombers . . . capable of flying across the Atlantic, dropping their load of bombs and returning to their bases on one load of gasoline." Seversky also warned Ickes that a new fleet of bombers would be able to "fly so fast that it will be difficult to cope with them and so high that ships and anti-aircraft guns will be ineffective." Seversky then gave a copy of a forthcoming *American Mercury* article on air power to Ickes, which Ickes urged FDR to read. FDR hardly needed much persuading. Attorney General Robert Jackson wrote in his diaries that the president was a careful student of the role of air power in coming military conflicts. The president, he reflected, "knew that [modern aviation] opened a new chapter and called for new techniques. He was interested in the most minute developments of new weapons and new strategies, even new tactics."[27]

By 1938, FDR and La Guardia had begun to sound the alarm about air power. They argued that the Nazis would soon be able to advance on the United States. La Guardia came up with ideas for defending the hemisphere from attacks and lobbied Congress, business, labor, and farm groups to adopt his plans. Like many internationalists, La Guardia insisted that keeping the Nazis out of the hemisphere was paramount. He sent FDR a speech on hemispheric defense and in a cover note called the speech his "bed-time story for the President." Nazism, La Guardia warned delegates to the Pan American Congress of Municipalities in Havana, was more menacing than the bubonic plague. FDR did not dispute it.[28]

La Guardia agreed with FDR not only that Hitler was a madman but also that his war machine gave him the tools to achieve world conquest. Both men increasingly viewed his threat to the Americas in serious terms, though the mayor was also prone to taunting the Führer. Having denounced him as "a perverted maniac" in 1933, he later likened him to New York City's street trash. By 1938, he had endorsed FDR's view that neutrality was a disastrous policy that had to be repealed. La Guardia echoed the president when he declared that "the wide Atlantic has not isolated us from a world crisis" and described the Nazis' "highly elaborate and vicious system of propaganda" as a danger in Latin America. Like FDR, La Guardia agreed that fascism had become a "growing sore on the soil of the Western Hemisphere."[29]

FDR's thoughts on air power amplified La Guardia's. He articulated them in his annual message to Congress in January 1938. The president announced that the nation's coasts and even "communities far removed from the coast" were vulnerable to the threat of air raids for the first time. He declared that the years when the United States only needed to worry about defense on "one ocean and one coast" (the East Coast during World War I) were no more, and he called on Congress to appropriate nearly $9 million so the country could build its arsenal of anti-aircraft guns.[30]

As his White House began to focus more intently on the problem of home defense, FDR urged Americans to "be prepared to resist attack" while calling for production of ten thousand planes annually to counter the growing threat from overseas. In his January message to Congress in 1939, he depicted the air menace in the most vivid terms yet, painting a stark picture of what the future held in store. He warned the American people of the possibility of a "sudden attack against strategic positions and key facilities" at home and declared that the militaries of foreign enemies had acquired "a new range and speed." "The world," he warned, "has grown so small and weapons of attack so swift" that "the distant points from which attacks may be launched are completely different from what they were 20 years ago." The weapons had become more advanced and more sinister.[31]

La Guardia's intensifying fears about the Axis threat to the home front began to trump his desire to enact economic and social reforms in his city. During a meeting of the Conference of Mayors in Washington in the summer of 1939, La Guardia illustrated this shift when he focused the meeting's agenda on analyzing the threat of fifth columns and Nazi propaganda, and successfully pushed for a resolution supporting the president's foreign policy. La Guardia offered to help the administration handle the crisis overseas. He wrote Secretary of State Cordell Hull that in these "anxious moments . . . one wants to do everything to shorten and end the terrible situation." He met with FDR to explain why he wanted to conduct a "Good-will Tour to South America." After another meeting with the president on the world crisis, La Guardia half-jokingly wrote FDR that he had "many sleepless nights and nightmares" after their conversation, as the sounds of "bugles calling and drums beating and cannon shots" continued to make him tense. La Guardia, FDR replied, did not need to "stay awake nights thinking of drums and bombs" and should not worry so much because "the Navy program is having an excellent effect in Berlin, Rome and Tokyo."[32]

The nature of the threat was hardly uniform in the eyes of liberal internationalists. Hull described it as originating within Latin America, while White House aides fretted that Nazis were subverting that region's economy, installing puppet regimes, and establishing military bases as preludes to attacks against the United States. FDR's intelligence officials figured that more than three thousand Nazi planes departing from West Africa could land in northeastern Brazil, and that Nazis could then set up air bases in the city of Natal. Nazi capture of Easter Island near Chile or the Galapagos Islands would, they feared, pose a direct peril to U.S. civilians. One pro-Roosevelt organization, the Committee to Defend America by Aiding the Allies, captured the emerging consensus among liberal internationalists with a map of the hemisphere depicting swastikas on British and French territorial possessions including Martinique and Bermuda and estimates of flight times from Nazi-held lands to Miami and New York City. The White House and its supporters saw an array of threats that would likely not be confined to the European and Asian continents.[33]

During the spring and summer of 1939, military conditions overseas deteriorated, confirming, so it seemed, La Guardia and FDR's most dire forecasts. Franco had prevailed in Spain's civil war. Benito Mussolini, Italy's Il Duce, had seized control of Albania. Hitler's SS troops had the run of Czechoslovakia. In the late summer, FDR declared that Nazi bombing of women and children "has profoundly shocked the conscience of humanity," and he urged the world's powers to avoid targeting "civilian populations or . . . unfortified cities." The British thanked FDR for his moving appeal, but the president's words failed to alter the path along which Europe's powers were racing.[34]

The mood in the White House was grim. In a meeting with members of Congress, FDR put the odds of a Nazi victory over France and Britain at fifty-fifty, and he said that if the Allies were defeated then Congressmen must know that "we would find ourselves surrounded by hostile states." Looking at England, La Guardia and FDR saw a key ally under siege as officials there began planning for mass evacuations from London to rural areas. FDR announced that the defense of the Western Hemisphere was his top priority.[35]

On September 1, America's streets and living rooms echoed the eerie mood during the "War of the Worlds" broadcast as civilians gathered around radios in parked cars and their homes to hear the news that Hitler's Wehrmacht had stormed across the Polish Corridor and his Luftwaffe had begun to bomb the Polish people. One radio reporter based in southeastern Poland described entire families "huddl[ing] in fear from air attacks" and said that this was a war that had shown that it can indeed strike anywhere. In response to the Nazi attack on Poland, Britain and France declared war on Germany on September 3.[36]

In his fireside chat that day, FDR emphasized that the outbreak of war in Europe had a direct effect on every home in the United States. "It is easy for you and for me," he reasoned, "to shrug our shoulders and to say that conflicts taking place thousands of miles from the continental United States . . . do not seriously affect the Americas—and that all the United States has to do is to ignore them and go about its own business." But in this age of total war, "we are forced to realize that every word that comes through the air, every ship that sails the sea, every battle that is fought, does affect the Americana future. . . . We seek to keep war from our own firesides by keeping war from coming to the Americas. For that we have historic precedent that goes back to the days of the Administration of President George Washington. . . ." But the nature of total war, he concluded, meant that every American was in the war's path. "It is our national duty to use every effort to keep them out of the Americas."[37]

FDR shifted his military planning into high gear. He sent planes to Panama, tripled the military presence in Puerto Rico, and stepped up U.S. naval patrols in the Atlantic. La Guardia put his city on a state of alert, while isolationists cast the president and his loyalists as eager to enter a war that had no impact on the American people. Charles Lindbergh promised that "as long as we maintain an Army, a Navy, and an Air Force worthy of the name . . . we need fear no invasion of our country." FDR, charged antiwar Republican Rep. Hamilton Fish, should largely be held "responsible for the fear that pervades the Nation." La Guardia could have been counted as a chief abettor.[38]

The president and mayor began to entertain seriously at least some type of formal action to prepare the American people to handle the threat of air raids, invasion, and sabotage. A congressional committee traveled fourteen thousand miles studying the country's air defenses and issued its report that the country had to have more cannons, rifles, anti-aircraft guns, and better training for those manning the guns. La Guardia and FDR also came up with their own notions of the proper response to most of Europe being embroiled in a Second World War. La Guardia began to look to the example of England to try to find ideas for defensive measures applicable to his city. FDR wrote E. R. Stettinius Jr., his advisor on Industrial Materials, that areas such as Carlsbad Cavern and "the valley of Virginia" with its abundance of natural caves might be appropriate storage sites for "octane gasoline and other essential destructible materials." Stettinius and a committee of engineers studied FDR's idea, but they ultimately argued that it was dangerous to stash explosive mixtures inside caves and that these areas were too far removed from the places where the military needed to have access to such materials. Stettinius instead proposed that FDR consider using tanks buried in the ground covered with "a 9 inch concrete slab" as the best defense "against incendiaries and bomb fragments."[39]

The public was torn and confused. As an October 1939 Gallup poll indicated, 46 percent of the country said that Americans would likely be dragged into the war by forces outside of their control. Nearly half of the population agreed that the modern world made it "impossible . . . to keep isolated." While roughly half of the people thought that a war involving the United States was likely, and were thus more inclined to endorse preparedness, the rest of the country remained deeply skeptical that intervention offered a solution. Many Americans still believed that the oceans would protect them and that they should stay out of Europe and Asia. Still, the notion that Americans really were in some danger from foreign powers was starting to erode the public's isolationist mood that had shaped the conduct of U.S. foreign policy since the end of World War I.[40]

La Guardia and FDR still had much work to do. They had to persuade the public that preparedness was the right strategy. *Time* captured the blasé attitude that at least some Americans had felt toward the outbreak of a new European war. The magazine, quoting a Florida newspaper, described a "gay holiday crowd" that flocked to a dock in Florida to watch a British cruiser as it chased a German freighter off coastal waters. The spectators appeared to be rapt and news photographers raced to snap pictures, as if the chase was a source of entertainment and titillation. Thus, popular fears for the American future vied with public complacency, pitting the alarmists against the nonchalant. Such lax attitudes, FDR and La Guardia insisted, had to be challenged and discredited. Americans, they believed, had to become more alert, engaged, and vigilant if the president and the mayor had any chance of mobilizing citizens, defending lives, and confronting head-on the true threat to the home front that they thought was getting closer to their shores with the passing of every day.[41]

3

Two Fronts

Every individual in this country must be convinced that the
Government is as much interested today in seeing them well housed,
well clothed, and well fed, obtaining needed medical care and recreation, as they are concerned that arms are necessary for defense in the
world as it is today. Unless the two convictions go hand in hand, some-
where the unity of the nation will break. Wake up every one of you to
the two fronts on which our defense must be built!
—Eleanor Roosevelt, May 1940

Eleanor Roosevelt never abandoned the role of traditional first lady as the war
inched closer to America in 1940. When *You* magazine asked if she had any
advice to women whose husbands had entered public life, she replied, "His
career always comes first." When editors asked her to submit her favorite picture
of herself, she refused, saying, "I do not like any of them."[1]

Despite her poor self-image, she had grown confident that she had the skills
to fight for the causes that she considered essential to national defense. Without
human security, a term then in use to convey the need to protect people from
starvation, unemployment, and homelessness, she grew convinced that military
mobilization alone would be insufficient to defend Americans from the Axis
powers or prepare them to fight a total war. But in order to persuade the country that social and military defense were both requirements, she had to merge
national security liberals and wartime New Dealers into a single camp. Her effort
to do so has been largely overlooked. The first lady led a group of strong public women who sought to update the New Deal to meet war needs. She fought
to persuade Americans that it was better to arm the country than to remain
defenseless. Historian Susan Ware has written that during the 1930s New Deal
women cultivated "a 'network' of friendship and cooperation" that "maximized
their influence in politics and government." That network and its influence was
even more robust during the 1940 debate about guns and butter than it was during the New Deal's heyday. ER remained this movement's undisputed leader.
She sought a grand synthesis in which the public would come to regard both

militarization and social reforms as interrelated tools in defeating fascism and achieving a just postwar world and a lasting peace.[2]

Thirteen months after raising the prospect that an "ultimate Armageddon" was coming to the United States, Eleanor Roosevelt declared that "fear is the enemy." In February 1940, she argued in *The Nation* that the state-sponsored fear rife in Nazi Germany had been transported into the minds of those Americans who chose autocracy over democracy. Elsewhere, she warned that war "breeds intolerance everywhere," urging readers "to decide what Democracy means to them" and to worship democracy "as fervently as . . . their personal religion."[3]

To the first lady, the stakes in the struggle against fascism could hardly have been higher. The New Deal had failed to provide "the permanent solution to our problems," she announced. While it had given people hope for a better, more enlightened democracy, she argued that it needed to be revised to meet the demands of a society undergoing wrenching dislocations and facing an existential fight with totalitarian faiths. As America headed toward war, ER knew that human security had to be one of two pillars (along with military mobilization) upon which American democracy rested. Without that pillar, American democracy would be vulnerable to dictatorial solutions to the economic and social problems that plagued the country.[4]

In early 1940, ER's vision was ill defined. She urged Americans to acquire "a greater sense of social responsibility" and find the "spring which flows for all humanity." "Make life more worth living for everyone," she commanded. When La Guardia permitted the German-American Bund, a group of Nazi sympathizers, to hold a meeting in his city, ER defended his decision as a stand that demonstrated "the kind of tolerance that recalls the statement attributed to Voltaire: 'I disapprove of what you say, but I will defend to the death your right to say it.'" Even as a hardened antifascist, she believed in free speech as a way to expose and refute ideas inimical to democracy. But beyond her sympathy for the downtrodden and her belief in the right to dissent, it was not entirely clear what she wanted a wartime New Deal to achieve or how it would even be enacted.[5]

ER lobbied on behalf of the hungry, the unemployed, and the average worker. She sympathized with their plights and felt a sense of noblesse oblige. Having worked in the Rivington Street Settlement House during the Progressive era, she drew inspiration from the settlement-house movement where middle-class and upper-class women provided services and care for poor immigrants in many major American cities. She took hope from cooperatives such as Arthurdale, the New Deal community set up by the federal government during FDR's first term as a farming cooperative for displaced miners. Gradually, her belief that freewheeling capitalism had given short shrift to the common man, and her devotion to meeting the vast social, financial, and spiritual needs of the public, cohered in her 1940 campaign to enlist progressives in a fight for social reform. To her, New Deal liberalism was a tenet of "war" mobilization.[6]

By the start of the decade, liberalism had split into two rough camps. One favored military mobilization above all; the other endorsed domestic reforms to complete the New Deal's unfinished business. Eleanor Roosevelt tried to bridge the two sides, urging New Dealers to support military preparedness and national security liberals to back domestic social reforms. She aimed to build an army of progressives who could help her make the spirit of the New Deal permanent.

Her "My Day" columns offered a window into her view of the duty that citizens had to participate in their democratic government during an international emergency. Her ideal citizens were engaged in civic affairs. They were well read, curious about the world, and eager to learn about the big issues roiling the public square. They should be committed, she felt, to improving the lives of their fellow citizens. Her columns championed the rights of artists to express themselves, promoted the preservation of wilderness areas, defended the National Youth Administration and other "alphabet" agencies as enriching the lives of ordinary citizens, recommended books and articles she thought worth discussing, and denounced the sources (economic and intellectual) of fascism. Her columns urged individuals to participate fully in government affairs, taking ownership of their communities. She also insisted that the federal government needed to promote human security in the lives of all Americans.

She was increasingly outspoken in voicing her views in the political arena. Never reticent on this score, she sensed even more urgency as she saw elements of the New Deal—and her husband's support for it—slipping away. In her "My Day" column on January 4, 1940, she denounced Republicans in Congress for applauding a recent decision by FDR to accept cuts to social spending programs. Republicans were putting partisanship ahead of the national interest, demonstrating their "blindness," "ignorance," and "indifference" to human needs, including the peoples' right to health care, unemployment insurance, and spiritual morale.[7]

ER realized that to unify the two camps, she would have to act swiftly. In the spring of 1940, the war in Europe confirmed her greatest fears. On April 9, Hitler's Wehrmacht breached the borders of Denmark and overwhelmed its army. With his "blitzkrieg," or lightning attacks, Hitler seized control of Norway's ports and stormed across the nation's south. His troops overran the country and installed Nazi agent Vidkun Quisling as head of a vassal state. On April 23, ER wrote that "the news from abroad" was "disheartening to the extreme." The reports from Europe turned more terrifying in the days ahead. On May 10, Neville Chamberlain's government, beset by political woes and helpless to stop Hitler, collapsed.[8]

The new prime minister, Winston Churchill, made it clear as he entered 10 Downing Street that he rejected any appeasement of the Nazis. His defiance hardly mattered. Hitler's Panzer Divisions, the Luftwaffe, and airborne troops invaded Luxembourg, Holland, and Belgium and conquered all three countries in a matter of days. ER observed that the world faced a crucial moment. "One has but to read the record of what happened to Holland's Army—one-fourth wiped out—to realize why we must have modern weapons of war," she argued. Americans looked to France and England as their last lines of defense.[9]

As the weeks passed, conditions became bleaker. In June, the British evacuated more than 300,000 soldiers from the French port of Dunkirk across the English Channel. Thousands of British rifles, trucks, and other tools of war lay on the beaches of France, separating the British Army from its weapons and supplies. Following the British retreat, the Wehrmacht bypassed the vaunted Maginot Line and began to roll across the French countryside.

On June 22, Hitler talked to his chief of naval operations about invading Britain. At 3:15 p.m., he arrived in a black Mercedes at the same place in the Compiegne forest where Germany had surrendered in World War I. Using binoculars to get a close-up look at the Führer, journalist William Shirer reported that Hitler's face was an emblem of "scorn, anger, hate, revenge, [and] triumph." In London, Churchill and his aides studied defense plans that had been drafted in case of a Nazi invasion.[10]

Eleanor Roosevelt responded to the crisis in Europe with actions—private and public—that signaled her desire to side with the British and offer some form of resistance, however inadequate, to Hitler's aggression. Horrified by the thought of child refugees, she supported the Red Cross's refugee assistance efforts in Europe. She helped establish the U.S. Committee for the Care of European Children and persuaded an ally to run the committee. She urged the State Department and FDR to admit more refugees to the United States and helped secure entrance visas for some. She continued to work tirelessly in defense of the New Deal and military mobilization. Her columns, speeches, correspondence, and never-ending meetings testified to the intensity of her campaign to advance liberal unity. In mid-1940, she urged liberals to support military preparedness as a prerequisite to persuading the country to adopt a program of human security. Only a military capable of destroying Nazism would enable liberals to pursue policies after the war to end "the disadvantages . . . brought about by economic insecurity," she argued in *Collier's* magazine that spring. If American democracy was destroyed by fascism, then the progress toward economic and social equality made since the Progressive era would be arrested.[11]

Segregationist Democrats in Congress ensured that New Deal reforms codified the entrenched racist practices of the Deep South during the 1930s. In response, ER fought to put racial justice at the center of debate about any wartime New Deal. In mid-May, she tried to enlist African Americans in her mobilization and human security campaign, addressing one thousand black congregants at Washington, D.C.'s Zion Baptist Church. The pews were so crowded that some people listened to her talk over loudspeakers set up in the basement. She argued that the District of Columbia should be given a vote in Congress and that Congress had to address the economic plight of African Americans. At the same time, she asserted, the black community had a responsibility to endorse President Roosevelt's defense buildup, bluntly warning: "You're facing a sinister power—with no scruples—that is not held back by ethical standards. I don't mean that I think we face an invasion tomorrow. But every time we are not united, every time word goes back to Germany that we do not mean what we say . . . we are nailing one more nail in our coffin." Presenting a united front against Hitler would give them a chance, moreover, to advance civil rights, she reasoned, because democracy rather than fascism was the best antidote to the forces propping up the system of racial injustice. The reaction to her talk was muted. Speakers attacked FDR's White House for devoting millions of dollars to building weapons while refusing to address African Americans' economic needs. One labor leader was not persuaded by the first lady's arguments, telling the *Washington Post* that while Eleanor Roosevelt was focused on the hardships in Europe, 25,000 Washingtonians faced starvation that summer.[12]

Pacifists were also icy. That spring, some on the left felt that the country faced an epic choice of either advancing human security or building up its munitions of war—but that both goals were simply unattainable. ER sought to convince these pacifists otherwise. In New York City in late May, she addressed 1,100 delegates to the American Youth Conference, a group that had denounced FDR's arms buildup as a step toward war. ER informed the delegates that they had misinterpreted the international situation. She told them, "You don't want to go to war" and "I don't want to go to war," but in reality, the "war may come to us." Americans, therefore, had no choice but to arm themselves at the same time that they fought to achieve full employment, adequate public housing, and expanded economic opportunity. Her speech garnered tepid applause. When Rep. Vito Marcantonio, the lone member of the American Labor Party in the U.S. House of Representatives and the only vote in opposition to a recent defense spending bill, described military appropriations as a backdoor ploy to raise the value of "the American dollar and the British pound," and line the pockets of the richest Americans, he received a standing ovation.[13]

The first lady summed up her message about guns and butter—and the need for liberals in each camp to unite in pursuit of both goals: "When force not only rules in certain countries, but is as menacing to all the world, as it is today, one cannot live in a Utopia which prays for different conditions and ignores those which exist. One has to face the world as it is and, without discarding one's ideals, meet the realities of the day and keep on working for what one hopes will be a better future." Addressing a meeting of five hundred delegates of the Institute of Human Relations, another organization with pacifist sympathies, she declared that despite their distance from European battlefields, burying their collective heads in the sand would lead the United States to "find itself in the situation of Munich." Defenseless citizens would have to acquiesce to Hitler when they were forced to look at the barrel of a loaded gun.[14]

ER maintained at least a bit of hope that FDR sympathized with her cause of waging a two front guns-and-butter campaign. She thought that as liberals grew increasingly supportive of his call for military defense, he would reward them with renewed attention to expanding the New Deal. As he campaigned for a third term in 1940, the president, ER realized, could not simply discard key elements of his New Deal coalition. He needed her support almost as much as she needed his. The president gave some signs that he was open to her arguments, that he was prepared to lead a coalition of national security and social defense liberals. On June 10, FDR argued before students from the University of Virginia that critics who claimed that America could "safely . . . become a lone island . . . in a world dominated by the philosophy of force" harbored an "obvious delusion" that imperiled America's future. He warned that the defeat of England would thrust the United States into "a helpless nightmare," turning Americans into "a people lodged in prison, handcuffed, hungry, and fed through the bars from day to day by the contemptuous, unpitying masters of other continents." But he also defended the idea of social reform in his address, giving hope to some liberals that both goals were feasible.[15]

As FDR wrote in a note to King George VI, the postwar democracies had to concern themselves with ensuring adequate supplies of food and clothing for all peoples, meeting human needs once the crisis had passed. FDR also argued that tax rates ought to be fixed at a rate "in accordance with ability to pay," a quintessentially liberal position. In 1940 he supported the establishment of a National Nutrition Committee. He wanted to expand public housing, raise wages for the poor, make more free school lunch programs available, and preserve a food stamp program that had raised farmers' incomes. The president ordered New Deal agencies to improve housing for defense workers in Vallejo, California; and Charleston, South Carolina, and argued that in defense plants receiving federal largesse, hiring the unemployed should be the highest priority.[16]

At the same time, FDR had made arming for war his main goal, and ER remained unsure whether the president would be willing to spend political capital on a new program of butter to improve national life. Like so many of her contemporaries, ER regarded her husband as sphinxlike; she had trouble reading his intentions. In 1939, Secretary of Labor Frances Perkins told the first lady that "Franklin is really a very simple Christian." ER replied, "Yes, a *very simple* Christian." According to one interpretation of her wry comment, the first lady meant that her husband was too simplistic in his approach to good and evil and unable to comprehend the far-reaching, nonmilitary dimensions of the Nazi threat. It was vital, she felt, to pressure her husband to do the right thing and endorse social defense liberalism.[17]

ER sent FDR countless handwritten notes about appointments and issues that she deemed important, and she was among the most persistent and effective presidential advisors. Holding forth at women-only press conferences, the first lady covered such topics as the role of Federal Works Agency (FWA) writers and artists, camps that provided jobs to single women, National Youth Administration projects, unions, and war and peace.

Though she occasionally contradicted or challenged the administration's policies, her husband saw her as a powerful weapon for rallying liberals of varying stripes, mobilizing activists in support of relief programs, and amplifying his folksy communications with millions of ordinary Americans, bringing citizens closer to their government, and their government closer to them. In the run-up to the war, the president was eager to prevent conservatives from rolling back the gains made during the New Deal, but how he would do this, while also mobilizing the country militarily, remained an unanswered question. Eleanor thus realized that by enlisting her own network to lobby Franklin to expand the New Deal, she would keep butter at the fore of the debate alongside the push for guns.[18]

In a letter to ER, Agnes Reynolds, college secretary of the liberal American Student Union organization, captured the dilemma facing New Dealers who supported expanded domestic reform in 1940. Reynolds wrote that faced with the specter of all-out war, liberals had to keep democracy moving forward by teaching the public about "the meaning and value of the social legislation that we have," erecting internal defense. She praised FDR's Charlottesville speech and informed the first lady that FDR and Harry Hopkins had assured Reynolds in a meeting of their commitment to New Deal reforms. She argued that fears of economic collapse had been the basis for New Deal experimentation in the thirties, and that fears of international fascism would be the basis for New Deal experimentation in the forties. In a letter to the first lady, journalist and future ER biographer Joseph Lash described the New Deal "as basic [to defense] as armaments themselves."[19]

New Deal agencies provided ER with tailor-made organizations filled with allies eager to lobby the White House to expand domestic reforms. One acquaintance of the first family argued that the NYA was flirting with cuts to programs that assisted young women in order to spend money on military projects. He warned NYA administrator Aubrey Williams that if young women lacked access to jobs, "fifth columnists will find fertile fields in idle hands and idle minds." ER sent the letter to FDR, writing that if the government failed to use defense money to pay for social services, "a great hardship and injustice is being done."[20]

Eleanor Roosevelt also used the hardships faced by Americans, especially women, African Americans, and other underrepresented groups, to argue that letting the New Deal atrophy would be folly in wartime. In 1933, she had urged citizens to write to her and describe the "problems which puzzle or sadden you." By 1940, according to one estimate, she was receiving six hundred to seven hundred letters daily. This correspondence enabled her to remind fellow liberals that the economic crisis was far from over and that a wartime democracy that neglected its citizens would be guilty of transgressing its own values. For example, she urged La Guardia to move on an application for a job from an African American man that had languished in the Sanitary Department in Queens, as well as to end the discrimination against a disabled man who had been prevented from finding a job in the New York City school system. The first lady prevailed on New Deal agency employees to use their powers to aid forgotten men and women as well. In just one example among many, she pressed the WPA office in San Francisco to help a woman in Oakland who was desperate to find work, reminding New Dealers that the machinery in place had to be used to shore up social democracy.[21]

Wedded to the notion of a national community in which all Americans cared for one another and aided the peoples of Allied nations, her list of personal contributions to charities ran to four single-spaced pages in 1940. The groups included the American Red Cross, the American Friends Service Committee, and the U.S. Committee for the Care of European Children. One of her secretaries reported that ER gave away much of her yearly income to charities. ER felt that conditions in the United States were still dire for many citizens and that human defense was a cause that she had to embody in her daily life in order to inspire political allies to follow her lead.[22]

The first lady also linked the practice of social defense to the mission of military protection. She argued that if Americans made an investment in the public's health, the armed forces would have access to more recruits, defense factories would produce more tanks and planes, and Americans would feel more devoted to defending their way of life. She sought to enlist progressives in the public health field in her cause. In May, she led three days of meetings on setting up a national fitness program for the American people, asking her allies to lobby the president to back what a New York University professor called a "plan of cooperation for wholesome living."

ER's allies in government, who held influential positions in New Deal agencies, worked with her to enlist Americans in a national campaign to bolster public health. Federal Works Agency administrator John Carmody reported that thirty-seven thousand trained workers from his agency were leading recreation programs in all forty-eight states and more than eight thousand communities, while more than ten thousand volunteers were working to open access to citizens to sports, music, dance, theater, and other forms of recreation and entertainment to boost morale and better individuals' health. The first lady also sought to make herself a model for the rest of the country, making a point of walking, hiking, getting fresh air, and advertising her own activities so Americans felt inspired to do the same.[23]

In addition to enlisting liberals in the administration, universities, and activist organizations in her two-front campaign, Eleanor Roosevelt increasingly stressed that citizens had to take an active part in defense of their democracy. Without the participation of every member of the community, she argued, it was going to be hard to do all of the things that would be necessary to aid the Allies and prepare the country to fight the fascists, if necessary. One of her most controversial proposals of 1940 was for Congress to pass New Deal-style legislation that mandated national service for all young Americans. Defying FDR (she joked that if she kept pushing this idea, "Mrs. Roosevelt's head will come off"), she argued that mandating national service would enlist citizens as social soldiers fighting "to preserve our democracy" and giving "whatever is asked of them." She envisioned millions of young people acquiring new skills, doing work that benefited their communities, and knitting people together in a common cause. "We have too long taken our freedom and liberties for granted and have given nothing in return," she explained, and a mandatory program would ensure that the poor and working class reaped the fruits of national service. Right-wing critics denounced her plan for regimenting America's youth and imposing totalitarianism on freedom-loving Americans, while left-wing critics faulted the plan as "compulsory military training" on the home front akin to Hitlerism.[24]

Her proposal had no chance in Congress, but her campaign both stoked and reflected the grassroots disquiet in which citizens clamored for still-to-be-determined roles in national defense. As poet and Librarian of Congress Archibald MacLeish informed Harry Hopkins, FDR's federal relief administrator and ER's ally, Americans from "all walks . . . are chewing through their nails through lack of some practical outlet for their growing fear and will to resist the bloody processes of Hitlerism." Liberals were hardly in agreement on the kind of outlet citizens would have, or the roles government would give them, but ER's campaign was at least partially responsible for the growing challenge to national security liberals who wanted to subordinate social programs to military needs. MacLeish recommended that the Roosevelt administration establish a "Coordinator of Civilian Volunteer Activities for Defense" to help conserve food, aid famine victims abroad, assist defense areas, and take other ER-friendly steps that would make America, as it mobilized for war, "calmer and more united." Hopkins liked MacLeish's idea—he, too, had received hundreds of letters from people who yearned to volunteer. Hopkins joked that if they passed a plan housewives would not have to arm themselves "with machine guns." On June 29, Hopkins asked Lowell Mellett, director of the Office of Government Reports, to explore avenues for enacting MacLeish's program.[25]

The first lady also worked through liberal media outlets to define security as the combination of arms and social services being built in tandem. At the behest of ER, Selden Rodman, the editor of *Common Sense*, a liberal magazine, published an article by the first lady about the challenge of meeting the promise of democracy "domestically, through the Defense program." Based on the positive reaction to ER's article, Rodman enthused to her, the New Deal clearly "*is going on!*" Politically astute women who had received appointments in the administration in unprecedented numbers provided another source of support for ER's two-front campaign. In May, FDR, using the 1916 National Defense Act, established a seven-person National Defense Advisory Commission that in addition to military-related goals was going to promote health, employment, worker safety, consumer rights, and combat discrimination based on age, race, and gender.[26]

Five of the seven members were so-called dollar-a-year men, well-off industrial leaders—"not what the New Dealers wanted," the Republican *New York Herald Tribune* observed. Still, one of them, Harriet Elliott, ran the Division of Consumer Protection and aligned herself with the ideas and values of ER's two-front war. As Dean of Women at the University of North Carolina, Greensboro's Women's College, Elliott, according to one sympathetic administration official, was "a great liberal." Elliott defined her job, as she reported to President Roosevelt, as ensuring that democracy would not be diminished during the defense mobilization. Elliott endorsed ideas for keeping inflation under control, stabilizing living costs for average citizens, and ensuring "a healthy and effective population" through better diets for the American people. She assured Eleanor Roosevelt that they shared the same goals and that the nascent field of "civilian defense [had to form] an integral part of the defense program rather than an isolated unit." ER was so taken with her ally's mission that she instructed Elliott to send her any memos or reports going to the president's desk so she could make sure FDR did not neglect them. The two women formed a productive team, as they searched for ways to raise living standards and mobilize America's women to engage not in "knitting and parades" (a veiled reference to

World War I) but in a campaign to secure "the human element in the defense program."[27]

Elliott made her mission explicit when she informed the president that her goal was to stitch "human defense" into "the total defense picture." Seeking support from consumer organizations, manufacturers, and retail stores, she and ER announced that mobilization had to address the needs of forty-five million citizens who were "living below the [social] safety line" because they lacked access to adequate diets, and Elliott called for an *"experiment in democratic planning,"* or "real democratic defense," providing health and food security to every American. They proposed establishing a Women's Volunteer Defense Committee ("to hold the home line front in local communities"), and Elliott invoked ER's ideas when she wrote the first lady that strengthening community life was by definition "a defense measure" that would demonstrate how democracy was effective at solving social problems.[28]

The first lady never succeeded in allying New Deal proponents with national security liberals in a vast, cohesive coalition with a shared vision of guns and butter. The ideological gap was sufficiently vast that she could never fully bridge it. FDR, reluctant to put his full weight behind her causes, often gave her less than what she wanted. Ultimately, home defense was not the best vehicle for her to pursue her reforms. The concept encompassed so many elements of national defense that her vision of social liberalism got diluted and could not gain the necessary political traction, especially as it had to compete for attention with other concerns including fears of home front attacks and unprecedented military mobilization.

Nonetheless, her leadership put social defense liberalism at the center of public debate, and in the process, she was able to mobilize a coalition of women, youth, workers, and some African Americans in support of her ideals. In particular, she drew hundreds of women to her cause, including members of the League of Women Voters, the National Association of Colored Women's Clubs, and the American Association of University Women. Ellen Woodward, who led the administration's Social Security Board, informed ER that at an upcoming conference on unemployment "national women leaders (big names in the news)" had to be recruited to lead the charge to make democracy work within their communities.[29]

In 1940 ER persuaded FDR that subordinating human needs in the defense mobilization was equivalent to jettisoning the New Deal. He agreed to let her and her allies explore the possibilities of social defense within the national security program. During a White House meeting with FDR, regional WPA supervisors described the ways in which volunteers in their program had aided public health campaigns, provided children with nutritious meals, and trained women in skills enabling them to find good-paying jobs. As the meeting broke

up, the president asked ER's supporter Florence Kerr, an assistant administrator in the WPA, to draft a plan to give roles to women volunteers. ER had
forced human security onto the presidential agenda, cracking open the door to
a wartime New Deal of still unknown dimensions.[30]

Kerr, a veteran New Dealer, was first and foremost loyal to Eleanor Roosevelt.
"Come on into Washington. I want to talk to you," Harry Hopkins told Kerr
by phone in 1935. Hopkins had befriended Kerr at Grinnell College, a small,
progressive school in rural Iowa where Kerr went on to teach English and
became active in the movement to aid the state's unemployed during the Great
Depression. Kerr accepted Hopkins's invitation. Hopkins hired her to serve as
regional director of the Works Progress Administration's Division of Women's
and Professional Projects. The WPA was a strong New Deal agency that helped
employ Americans who had lost their jobs; Kerr helped run the Chicago office,
which included thirteen states in the Midwest, and in 1938 she was promoted to
assistant administrator of the WPA.

Kerr was drawn into the first lady's orbit. Hopkins told her that anybody who had to report both to the president and the first lady was caught
"between the two blades of the scissors." Kerr never forgot the observation,
but she had come to admire ER's vision, determination, and focus on wom-
en's rights. The first lady demanded all of Kerr's energy in fighting for the
New Deal amid the tide of war drawing the country away from domestic
social activism.[31]

Kerr saw the WPA as a "great instrument of practical democracy." In August
1940, she praised two million WPA workers as an "inner line of defense," and
pledged that her allies were prepared to aid the nation during the international
crisis. Kerr, said one person who introduced her at an event in 1940, had "more
people [working under her] than any other woman in the world."[32]

Mass mobilization—inchoate as a concept—was becoming more popular as
a way for ER to unite liberals, and all Americans, under the defense banner, and
a way to sell reform to conservatives, some of whom were skeptical about any
social experimentation but might agree to it if it had a military purpose. The
idea took root in the culture at large. The Washington Post, for example, editorialized that the government had to teach women such skills as "nursing, motor
repairing, agriculture, signaling, flying, mechanics, [and] marksmanship" as part
of a defense mobilization that covered human needs and military requirements.
New Deal women leaders also spoke in favor of mounting a "total defense" in the
face of total war, making expansive concepts of defense part of the lingua franca
of wartime liberalism. They used the war crisis as an argument in support of
social defense. For example, Dr. Martha Eliot, chief of FDR's Children's Bureau,
made plans in 1940 to train Americans in assisting children, mothers, and pregnant women during the war emergency and sought presidential approval for her

ideas. Eliot would eventually visit England to study the welfare of children who had been evacuated to the countryside during the Blitz.[33]

Women liberal leaders were not the only New Dealers eager to graft social defense onto military mobilization. Hopkins gave his tacit endorsement to a human security agenda, and Roosevelt aides Louis Brownlow and William McReynolds argued that the White House should include programs to meet human needs in the arms buildup. Running for a third term, the president announced in a campaign speech in Boston that "unprecedented dangers require unprecedented action to guard the peace of America against unprecedented threats." He signed a law that would draft American "boys" into the armed forces for a period of twelve months, the first peacetime draft in U.S. history. But he assured mothers and fathers that "your boys are not going to be sent into any foreign wars." He was also concerned with job growth and the housing and nutrition needs of "your boys," assuring mothers and fathers that their sons in military training camps were not going hungry and would have good shelter. FDR was masterful at balancing the forces of war, reelection, and the New Deal, all of which came together in his campaign. The president championed Lend-Lease, his destroyer-for-bases deal, loaning aging destroyers to the British in exchange for leases on their bases in strategic areas. He highlighted the social and economic gains achieved by the New Deal and ridiculed Republicans for having opposed his efforts to build America's Army, Navy, and air forces.[34]

His campaign for a third term presented ER with an opportunity to increase pressure on the president. She seized it. The first lady's address to the Democratic National Convention in Chicago electrified liberals and rallied the party behind the president's campaign. Calling for mobilization and unity, she urged "all good men and women to give every bit of service and strength to their country that they have to give . . . . This is the time when it is the United States that we fight for, the domestic policies that we have established as a party that we must believe in, that we must carry forward." The reelection effort became a vehicle for ER and her allies to remind the country of the New Deal's benefits and build grass-roots expectations that reforms would not suddenly be sacrificed to military programs. The selection of Henry Wallace, a strong progressive, as FDR's running mate was a victory for Eleanor Roosevelt.[35]

President Roosevelt also reached out to wartime New Dealers; he, too, wanted to pull them into his preparedness camp and reassemble the New Deal coalition, even though he made no promises of big reforms in a third term. In 1940, he went out of his way to assure the liberals attending a White House Conference on Children in a Democracy that he was still the New Deal's quarterback, still the same man who once served on the New York Milk Committee that delivered milk to poor children. The country, he announced, must not be allowed to "stop and rest on our rather meager laurels." At other times during the campaign, he

proposed establishing more hospitals to serve the rural poor and a hour limit
on the workweek for hospital employees, and warned against any "cancellation
of . . . the great social gains which we have made in these past years. . . . There
is nothing in our present emergency to justify a retreat from any of our social
objectives—conservation of resources, assistance to agriculture, housing and
help to the underprivileged." He even told members of his Cabinet that recreation and education reforms would bolster the national defense.[36]

This was not mere lip service. Nor was the president's rhetoric a simple-
minded paean to the efficacy of central planning as the sole solution to economic
crisis. He was searching for ways to keep the New Deal's objectives at the center of American politics, even as he had no idea how such a wartime feat could
be accomplished. On balance, however, FDR, committed though he was to the
New Deal, was less optimistic than ER about his ability to achieve both butter
and guns simultaneously. He paid tribute to the former, but he knew that he had
to put his political capital behind pursuing the latter. His victory on Election
Day, narrower than in 1932 and 1936, was still a landslide. He trounced Wendell
Willkie, the utilities-executive-turned-Republican nominee, carrying 38 states,
winning 449 Electoral College votes (to 82 for Willkie). He only lost one region,
the isolationist Midwest.

If FDR had won a mandate, it was to arm the nation and keep the war away
from its shores. But ER had her own ideas of what a third term should yield. She
believed that she had another four years in which to build her own alliances,
win support for the New Deal, and unify liberals in an antifascist program.
Democracy, she wrote back in May, should become "something for which every
citizen will feel he will willingly die." "Wake up every one of you to the two fronts
on which our defense must be built!," she exclaimed.[37]

Looking ahead, FDR's aides (such as Murray Latimer and Wayne Coy) waxed
confident that the New Deal was not dead and that it could be expanded as a
part of national defense. In this, they reflected the president's own commitment
to social and economic reforms as well as their own faith that butter must not
be completely ignored in the rush toward mobilization. The president asked
them to suggest ideas for his January address to Congress defining his third-term
vision. His aides sent him memos brimming with bold ideas for reforms that
enhanced the New Deal. They argued that the government had to take action in
response to social dislocations arising from war mobilization.

On December 2, FDR's economic advisor Lauchlin Currie sent him a pile
of material that highlighted the need for additional social reforms. The memos
covered such issues as unemployment, the youth problem, a pension for the
aged, and the human security question. Advisor Murray Latimer wanted FDR to
increase unemployment benefits by expanding the eligibility period, eliminating

variations among the states, and qualifying more Americans to receive benefits. Other advisors set their sights higher: they wanted to achieve full employment in the president's third term. They urged him to expand pension programs and youth training and to spend more on public works. Currie said that the NYA must provide jobs to every youth who wanted a private-sector job but had failed to find one. His plan would nearly double—from 800,000 to 1.5 million—the number of young people receiving job assistance from the government. Currie predicted that the eight million unemployed in December 1940 would fall to two million jobless in 1943. He envisioned the nation's $75 billion income soaring past $107 billion by 1943, partly due to these programs.[38]

Aides suggested specific language on human security for FDR to include in his State of the Union address. "Nothing must divert our minds and our hearts from the things which must be done to make America safe from foreign attack," one draft stated. The truth was that "men do not fight with armaments alone." Echoing Eleanor Roosevelt, the draft said that Americans "must have . . . a passionate belief in the way of life which they are helping to defend." After eight years of steady social and economic progress, the draft of the statement continued, the American people must push ahead in the fight against economic insecurity and the forces of fear that had plagued the country since the onset of the Great Depression. This draft had FDR announcing his support for additional college assistance to the poor, more youth job training programs, and guaranteeing a "minimum income for Americans older than 65." Aides wanted the address to say that FDR's wartime New Deal would feature "security for the aged and disabled" beyond that achieved in 1935 with the passage of Social Security and a strengthened safety net for millions of the unemployed. By enacting an updated New Deal sensitive to the needs of mobilization, the administration would strengthen the home front in the fight against fascism and in the long-range battle for a lasting peace. Declare "minimum security for all our people" as a focus of the third term, Frederic Delano, the chairman of the National Resources Planning Board, suggested. Expand Social Security to include the previously excluded domestic and agricultural workers, he also recommended, adding that providing these services to the poor was a litmus test of any responsible democracy.[39]

Some of FDR's aides went even further—offering suggestions in the starkest of ideological terms—justifying a wartime New Deal by framing the fight as a battle of democratic individualism against totalitarian regimentation. Presidential assistant Wayne Coy repeated ER's argument when he told FDR that military and human defense must be seen as "twin guardians of the public interest" and "not . . . enemies in a death grip for control of the public purse." "Progress and human dignity" had to be preserved by building up the nation's military defenses, and social defense had to be an element of any preparedness program, he added. Such ideas had echoes from the time in World War I when progressives cast the fight as a battle to advance liberty and equality on the home front rather than simply to achieve military victory over the Kaiser and defend the principle of self-determination overseas. During the height of the Great Depression, both Roosevelts defined the economic emergency as a war on deprivation and despair. While the notion that these goals—social and military defense—were complementary and not contradictory was hardly ER's alone, she became one of its most effective exponents during the 1940 campaign and its aftermath.[40]

Coy cautioned that the "Doubting Thomases" on FDR's political right sought to kill the New Deal in the name of bolstering military might, while FDR's left-wing critics believed that a stronger welfare state was the only defense needed against the threat of fascism. Conservatives would starve "the very democratic values we seek to preserve," Coy warned the president, whereas some on the left had a recipe for committing suicide by refusing to prepare the country militarily. FDR's task in his speech was to find the middle ground and reconcile these competing priorities into a more unified whole, Coy suggested. Coy argued point-blank that FDR's speech to Congress should endorse a dual campaign to defend America militarily and secure its general economic health and social vitality. FDR had to save the United States from the fate that had befallen "Czechoslovakia, Norway, Denmark, and France" and repudiate the totalitarian "assumption that the individual is important only as he contributes to the purposes of the state," Coy added. Further, he pointed out that the advocates for public welfare had a greater stake than anybody in ensuring that the country was prepared to wage war against the Nazis.[41]

Administrator of the Federal Security Agency Paul McNutt affirmed Coy's ideas in his suggestions to Roosevelt. "National security must include social security," McNutt, the conservative former Indiana governor, wrote to FDR on January 3. Social Security had helped more than two million of the aged, 850,000 dependent children, almost 50,000 blind people, and millions of the unemployed. McNutt reasoned that "if war-torn Britain finds it possible and necessary to improve and extend her social security system surely we can and should do so." FDR's leadership, he argued, should give all Americans a "minimum basic security" rooted in "life, liberty, and the pursuit of happiness."[42]

The first lady embraced the post-election advice that White House aides were urging on the president. In the days following his reelection victory, she continued to make the case for social defense. On December 10, she said it was unfair to ask labor to "make sacrifices of labor and hours" due to defense needs without asking for equal sacrifices from "manufacturers and business concerns and the general public." ER's vision of social defense encompassed all Americans, including minorities. In December, she talked to Coy about how Howard University, the historically African American institution, needed new buildings

for its Engineering School and dentistry program. In a handwritten note to FDR
she encouraged him to submit a funding request to the Budget Bureau for these
programs. ER and her troops also renewed their call on New Deal agencies to
meet human needs as part of the military buildup. Ellen Woodward, for example, informed the first lady that the WPA's "social defense program" had taken
steps to address the nation's human needs, and warned that if WPA workers were
redirected to military projects, social defense would suffer.[43]

The crafting of FDR's congressional message showed that Eleanor Roosevelt
and other reform advocates achieved at least a partial victory. One night, FDR,
his speechwriter Samuel Rosenman, Robert Sherwood, and Hopkins gathered in
the White House study. They were going to review the third draft of the address
and make their revisions. FDR wanted to figure out an ending for his speech. The
president "leaned far back in his swivel chair" and stared at the ceiling for a long
time, Rosenman recalled in his memoirs. FDR then leaned forward and began
to tell his aides what he wanted to say in his peroration. Gripping a yellow pad of
paper in his lap, Rosenman began to take notes.

On January 6, FDR delivered one of the most memorable speeches of the
twentieth century. Known as the "Four Freedoms" address, it was grounded in
the ideals, politics, and arguments of the post-election, wartime moment. He
argued "that the democratic way of life is . . . being directly assailed in every part
of the world . . . . This assault has blotted out the whole pattern of democratic life
in an appalling number of independent nations." In the last third of the speech,
he shifted his focus, declaring that Americans needed to understand the essential truth that "men . . . do not fight by armaments alone."

He said that "those who man our defenses, and those behind them who build
our defenses, must have the stamina and courage which come from unshakable
belief in the manner of life which they are defending. The mighty action that we
are calling for cannot be based on a disregard of all things worth fighting for. The
Nation takes great satisfaction and much strength from the things which have
been done to make its people conscious of their individual stake in the preservation of democratic life in America."

Because "social and economic problems . . . are the root cause of the social
revolution which is today a supreme factor in the world," "this is no time for any
of us to stop thinking about" these woes. The United States must build "the foundations of a healthy and strong democracy," he announced. His address went on
to include a plea for the programs so passionately championed by Coy, Currie,
and Eleanor Roosevelt. He called on the nation to achieve full employment,
provide social "security for those who need it," expand unemployment and pension programs, ensure equal opportunity for youth, improve access to medical
care, promote the goal of "a wider and constantly rising standard of living," and
defend the rights of citizens to engage in free speech. He asserted that the blood

spilling on the battlefields of Europe and Asia was a war to determine whether "four essential human freedoms" would endure. The arms buildup, then, had as its larger goal the preservation of "freedom of speech," "freedom of religion," and two other freedoms reminiscent of Eleanor Roosevelt's arguments: "freedom from want"—and, most relevant of all to the coming debate about setting up a home defense program, "freedom from fear."[44]

In 1940, La Guardia pondered how Americans would liberate themselves from fear. His answers bore only a passing resemblance to Eleanor Roosevelt's.

4

The Problem of Home Defense

The brutal force of modern offensive war has been loosed in all its
horror.
—Franklin Delano Roosevelt, 1940

In the spring of 1940, as Hitler's Army rumbled across Western Europe, Roosevelt administration officials; mayors; journalists; and some civilians, especially those living on the coasts, felt a growing concern for the safety of their country. They concluded that Americans had become more vulnerable to attack. Interest in the concept of home defense rose to new heights as the year unfolded. Scattered defense efforts proliferated in neighborhoods, cities, and states, but these activities lacked federal coordination and became an array of functions that lacked even a semblance of cohesion and efficiency. Meanwhile, White House aides disagreed about the scope and purpose of home defense. Some of them argued that home defense should register millions of volunteers, while others said that upholding public morale should be the focus of any effort to defend the home front from foreign enemy threats. In brief, confusion reigned.[1]

Some anti-New Deal conservatives argued that the president was doing too little to address the nation's home defense needs. Thomas Dewey, the New York district attorney who was seeking the Republican nomination for president, told two thousand people at a rally in Vermont that any home defense program had to feature "hard work and guns" as opposed to just "words and social amenities." Dewey denounced Roosevelt's idea that home defense should be led by "communists and fellow travelers," as Dewey scathingly put it, adding that FDR had also refused to stop a rally held in celebration of Hitler that had occurred in New Jersey, a sign of presidential weakness.[2]

Amidst this debate, Fiorello La Guardia launched his campaign to pressure Roosevelt to enact home defense nationwide. He led fellow mayors, police chiefs, municipal employees, and national security officials toward the shared goal of militarizing the public to protect cities from foreign enemy attack. He envisioned a disciplined civilian army that could defend lives and property, strengthening every American's physical safety. He sought to create a war mind-set among the public and establish a program unequivocally led by the federal government, while advocating a form of national security liberalism at odds with Eleanor Roosevelt's conception of what national defense should mean and do.

In the spring of 1940, fantasy and reality collided in the popular culture on the question of home defense. Increasingly focused on the likelihood of an enemy attack, the media chronicled the fighting in Europe in terms that related it to the lives of average Americans. The media's message was that Hitler's blitzkrieg attacks were a prelude to what Americans were going to experience firsthand on their own soil. *Time* magazine pointed out that newspaper headlines in the United States described news from the war in ways that felt to readers like a "seven-day Orson Welles broadcast of an invasion from Mars." Pundits declared that the balance of power in Europe had shifted toward the dictators, arguing that since Napoleon's day the United States had never been as endangered as it was in 1940. One columnist observed that Nazis were preparing to invade South America, while some publications in the Midwest warned that Canada could become a gateway for any invasion that eventually touched the nation's interior. Walter Lippmann contended that the Monroe Doctrine was under greater strain than at any time since the British burned the capital in the War of 1812.[3]

Conservative isolationists engaged in a war of words with their liberal opponents. Charles Lindbergh, for example, dismissed administration warnings of imminent danger as the noxious pro-war "chatter of calamity and invasion." The public was hardly in favor of going to war in 1940, and FDR tailored his reelection campaign accordingly. But the antiwar mood that had taken hold in the country during the mid-1930s was beginning to slacken. In early June, the Gallup Poll found that more than 80 percent of the American public believed that the United States was unprepared "to defend its own borders," while only 15 percent said America was safe from enemy attacks—figures that suggested an erosion in isolationist opinion. Anecdotes had a way of feeding on themselves, spreading fear across the country. One news report said that people in Seattle and New York City had committed suicide after hearing that Hitler had overrun nations in Western Europe, while a Pennsylvania gun club had reportedly started instructing its members in techniques for downing Nazi parachutists.[4]

The popular worry about the threat of fifth columnists intensified, finding an audience more receptive in the United States than at any time since the Red Scare had turned subversion into a major national issue, in 1919. Anti-New Deal conservatives tended to stress the danger of communist subversion in the United States, while pro-FDR liberals concerned themselves with fascist inroads in U.S. cities, labor unions, defense plants, and the administration itself. FDR warned the public that "new methods of attack" include "The Trojan Horse

[and] The Fifth Column that [betray] a nation unprepared for treachery, Spies, saboteurs and traitors." That spring, the *Oregonian* newspaper also warned that "adroit apologists" were plotting to assist foreign militaries by identifying the optimal places to start an invasion and where the enemy should drop his bombs. One veterans' organization notified White House officials that three hundred armed men could slaughter many civilians and take control of a city of twenty thousand residents.[5]

In hindsight, it is easy to say that military realities—Americans remained far from the front lines, after all—made such fears of internal attack mere cant and hype, which Roosevelt and his supporters exploited in order to persuade the public to mobilize for war. But in mid-1940 it was hardly irrational for at least some Americans to conclude that Nazi advances imperiled the lives and homes of civilians living thousands of miles away from Europe. Despite the hyperbolic warnings that subversives posed imminent danger to American lives (there is scant evidence that Nazi efforts to propagandize to Americans, steal military secrets, and sabotage the defense program ever posed a major threat to the pre-paredness program), Hitler's lightning-quick victories over the "low countries" were nonetheless shocking enough to Americans; democracies appeared to be falling like dominoes. Moreover, at least some Americans knew that Hitler viewed them as a degenerate people and that he had targeted them as part of his grandiose, yet seemingly plausible, plans for global military conquest. His preparations, begun in the late 1930s, included what one historian has described as "trans-Atlantic naval and air warfare with ships and planes capable of attacking the United States."[6]

Newspapers and opinion leaders continued to voice their concerns that Germany and Japan were slowly encroaching upon American territory. The *New York Times*, for example, reported that Nazis, posing as tourists, salesmen, and refugees, had made inroads into Mexico's army and government and that they would soon seize landing fields close enough to launch air raids on the Panama Canal. The *Times* added that Japanese fishing vessels had been surveying waters off the coast of California, which, the paper of record implied, was an ominous sign for coastal residents.[7]

In the spring of 1940, there was a growing conviction that inroads made by Hitler in Europe and Latin America imperiled Americans on an unprecedented scale, in ways that were still hard to fathom yet also deeply alarming. The fears of both the activities of "fifth columnists" as well as a potential military inva-sion spread throughout the highest levels of the federal government. Nelson Rockefeller, who was serving as coordinator of Commercial and Cultural Relations Between the American Republics, warned President Roosevelt that newspapers in South America found evidence that the Nazis had violated a security perimeter that had been established in the Hemisphere, and that Hitler might use Peru as a staging ground to invade the United States. Worried that spies and saboteurs would infiltrate the United States and assist an invasion, the president and his men ratcheted up their actions to protect the country from espionage. FDR asked a judge to track anti-American propaganda on the Virgin Islands, while the administration investigated a report that a Nazi spy was seen photographing Fort Benning and Fort McPherson. The president ordered an official in the Interior Department to assist the Federal Bureau of Investigation and the Army with any investigation of fifth column activity they were conducting. He ordered Federal Power Commission Chairman Leland Olds to station military guards to defend transmission lines and power plants and replied to a letter about the threat of spies from red-baiting Rep. Martin Dies, the chair of the House Committee on Un-American Activities, that the country should not underestimate the fifth column problem that was then surfacing. Growing fears of fifth columns were also reflected in public opinion polls; Gallup reported that almost half of the American people believed that spies were living among them.[8]

During the spring of 1940, FDR issued his most forthright appeal to the public that the threat to the security of the home front was soaring. Using the idea of a foreign enemy attack to advance his larger thesis that the country needed to mobilize militarily right away, the president delivered a special address to a joint session of Congress on May 16 in which he declared that the Nazis' victories over much of Western Europe had rightly concerned the American people, and that Hitler's novel approach to waging war had required every neutral country "to look to its defenses in the light of new factors." He warned that "no attack [was] so unlikely or impossible that it may be ignored" and announced that "the brutal force of modern offensive war had been loosed in all its horror." America's longtime natural fortifications had crumbled before everybody's eyes. He explained how:

> The Atlantic and Pacific Oceans were reasonably adequate defensive barriers when fleets under sail could move at an average speed of 5 miles an hour. Even then by a sudden foray it was possible for an opponent actually to burn our National Capitol. Later, the oceans still gave strength to our defense when fleets and convoys propelled by steam could sail the oceans at 15 or 20 miles an hour. But the new element—air navigation—steps up the speed of possible attack to 200, to 300 miles an hour. Furthermore, it brings the new possibilities of the use of nearer bases from which an attack or attacks on the American Continents could be made. From the fiords of Greenland it is 4 hours by air to Newfoundland; 5 hours to Nova Scotia, New Brunswick, and Quebec; and only 6 hours to New England. The Azores are only 2,000 miles from parts of our eastern seaboard, and if Bermuda fell into hostile

hands it is a matter of less than 3 hours for modern bombers to reach our shores. From a base in the outer West Indies, the coast of Florida could be reached in 200 minutes. The islands off the west coast of Africa are only 1,500 miles from Brazil. Modern planes starting from the Cape Verde Islands can be over Brazil in 7 hours. And Para, Brazil, is but 4 flying hours to Caracas, Venezuela; and Venezuela but 2 1/2 hours to Cuba and the Canal Zone; and Cuba and the Canal Zone are 2 1/4 hours to Tampico, Mexico; and Tampico is 2 1/4 hours to St. Louis, Kansas City, and Omaha. On the other side of the continent, Alaska, with a white population of only 30,000 people, is within 4 or 5 hours of flying distance to Vancouver, Seattle, Tacoma, and Portland. The islands of the southern Pacific are not too far removed from the west coast of South America to prevent them from becoming bases of enormous strategic advantage to attacking forces . . . . We have had the lesson before us over and over again—nations that were not ready and were unable to get ready found themselves overrun by the enemy. So-called impregnable fortifications no longer exist.[9]

His Democratic liberal allies ratified and extended the president's arguments in the public sphere. Florida Senator Claude Pepper declared that the "fortresses, canals, rivers, forests, everything that responsible statesmen and experienced soldiers have counted upon to save their countries and their peoples [in Europe had] collapsed almost like matchboxes." Now the time had come to "save our country and our people from the iron heel of Hitlerism," Pepper said.[10]

Speaking for a lot of liberal internationalists, Pepper and the president argued that both England and France, America's great allies, were at risk of falling to the Nazis. If that happened, American lives would be in imminent peril. FDR's Attorney General Robert Jackson confided to his diary that the president felt unnerved by the combined power of Germany's air, land, and sea forces, and that Winston Churchill was facing a terrible dilemma in the president's estimation. Churchill, FDR reasoned, had the option of using Royal Air Force planes in defense of France, leaving Britain defenseless against Nazi air power; alternatively, Churchill could hold his planes in reserve but if France were to be defeated Churchill would be accused of having doomed Britain's last major ally on the Continent. "*We* may have to face [a similar situation] if things continue as they are going now," the president warned Jackson.[11]

As conditions on the ground in Europe continued to deteriorate in spring 1940, FDR grew even more concerned about the problem of American home defense. After sketching a map that showed where stationary guns had been placed on the U.S. coasts, the president showed it to Harry Hopkins, one of his closest aides. Such guns, FDR lamented, were futile against the tools of modern war. As far as the home front was concerned, FDR had not yet settled upon a single, clear answer to the question of how best to defend Americans in their homes and neighborhoods, but he knew that this dilemma had become a live issue and one that he could completely ignore only at his political peril. He also realized that indefinitely delaying a decision about how he should handle home defense was not in the national interest. He did not know how much time the United States had left before the war made its way to the Americas.[12]

News of the fall of France on June 22 raced like a thunderbolt across much of the United States. Few of America's leaders had predicted a fascist triumph in France coming in such an abject fashion. More than any other event, Hitler's conquest of France acted as a catalyst to the home defense debate, pushing the issue more toward the center of politics. It was already clear that the U.S. Army was going to be involved in home defense in some capacity. Back in March, George Marshall, the Army's chief of staff, had signed off on the concept of a home defense program, but civilians in the administration, he and fellow military leaders concluded, were best positioned to lead the campaign. The Army needed to free itself to focus on building its offensive capabilities. While the Department of War published some guidelines for civilians about how they should behave during an air raid, the Army had little interest in taking control of the home defense project.[13]

In June, the White House became ground zero in the burgeoning debate about defending America. Concerned with the threat of an invasion, the president ordered John Carmody, the Federal Works administrator, to study how best to evacuate people from cities. White House economic advisor Lauchlin Currie believed that the time had come for FDR to champion a program, and proposed that the president respond to growing popular interest in volunteer roles with a fireside chat urging every city and town to set up their own defense councils. Not only would the councils function as rifle clubs and centers for morale building; they would also become places where volunteers could build the infrastructure for war, prepare to handle evacuations, bolster housing and public health, and train for first-aid work.[14]

Currie's proposal, which elicited a tart reaction from the president's military aides, spawned a fierce debate. Secretary of War Harry Woodring argued that such a call to the country by the president "would needlessly alarm our people and would tend to create the erroneous impression that the military forces of the nation are unprepared to deal with any likely threat to our security." A presidential declaration that communities should begin to set up defense councils would also invite charges in Congress and the popular press that FDR had failed to prepare the military for national defense, warned Woodring. Instead, Woodring

counseled that FDR should continue to state that his administration was studying the home defense issue—and leave it at that.[15]

Roosevelt heeded Woodring's advice. In 1940, he had to expend his political capital on enacting the military draft, fighting for Lend-Lease, and convert-
ing peacetime industries to wartime production. In addition, he had to mount
a campaign for a third White House term. The president thought that by urging
Americans to set up defense councils, he would indeed give his critics fodder
that they could use to charge Roosevelt with whipping citizens into a pro-war
frenzy.

Thus, the White House fell largely silent on the problem of home defense,
creating a void that others swiftly filled with their own ideas. Nobody moved
into this space with more aplomb and passion than New York City Mayor
Fiorello La Guardia, who, along with mayors from across the country, called
on the White House to adopt a uniform home defense strategy that prioritized
the needs of urban areas. La Guardia believed that the federal government
had the unique ability to coordinate defense programs and meet national crises. Whether it was the economic emergency at home or the storm crashing
over Europe, La Guardia had faith that cities could partner with the Roosevelt
administration to ensure adequate security for all Americans. He thought that
almost all U.S. cities were at risk and that organizing civil defense through the
states was ineffective (states, he said, were not targets, whereas urban population and industrial centers were firmly in the Nazi sightline).

In contrast to the collaboration he had forged with Washington to further
the New Deal, La Guardia felt that Roosevelt had shunned cooperation and
shortchanged the security needs of metropolitan areas. That, he felt, had to
change. Mayors had offered to lend the administration the use of airports, vacant
buildings, and public lands, but the administration rebuffed them. Roosevelt's
aides asked the mayors to provide their views on national plans to police cities;
La Guardia saw the request as a small step. He grew frustrated with the delays
in Washington. On June 24, FDR and La Guardia discussed the home defense
question during a meeting at the White House. The mayor proposed that the
U.S. Conference of Mayors serve as the go-between between the cities and
Washington as he and FDR joined forces to set up a real protection program.
La Guardia and his chief executive at the conference, Paul Betters, proposed
that Roosevelt establish a Division of Local Cooperation to forge home defense
in cities across America. FDR asked members of his Cabinet and Defense
Commission to review their idea.[16]

Simultaneously, La Guardia and Betters mobilized the mayors behind their
campaign to build pressure on the administration to establish a federal home
defense agenda. Maury Maverick, San Antonio's pro-New Deal mayor, argued
in his three-page reply to Betters's request for input on home defense that

Washington had to give the cities resources and guidance. Maverick wanted Washington to standardize police training, take charge of Home Guards, stop outbreaks of panic, and give people roles as volunteers on the home front. Maverick disclosed that his office had been deluged with requests from his constituents to give them posts in a quasi-military civilian defense force.[17]

Maverick agreed with La Guardia and spoke for other mayors when he voiced the opinion that the hardship of France was due to an inability to coordinate national and local forces to prepare for blitzkrieg. Americans had better learn this lesson from France, he warned. Raising such issues as evacuation and the need to combat fifth columnists in San Antonio, he cited his city's proximity to Mexico and its defense plants as reasons it needed more aid from Washington.[18]

The mindset that cities were the new front in home defense and that municipal workers must join an army of civilian defenders was on vivid display during a gathering of the International Municipal Signal Association in Jacksonville, Florida. Charged with keeping lines of communications open during a crisis, the signal operators heard Paul Betters say that bombing campaigns on their cities had turned into a legitimate threat and that under such conditions communications were vital links. An FBI agent told the operators that a single enemy plane could drop one thousand incendiary bombs on one of their cities, causing a hundred fires. The agent advised them to be on the lookout for strangers who tried to gain access to central alarm stations used to alert civilians to air raids.[19]

FDR moved forward on home defense, but in ways that La Guardia and other mayors found halting and even blinkered. During his news conference in August, FDR announced that his administration was in the process of studying "the problem of home defense" and that he had no ready-made solution. He needed to figure out how to "replace the regular regiments of the National Guard for purely home defense" purposes if the Guard was called into service, and he suggested that he might build the program around "World War veterans and their organizations such as the American Legion and the United Veterans of Foreign Wars." Also in August, FDR decided to take a step in La Guardia's direction by setting up a Division of State and Local Cooperation to guide home defense activities that were then sprouting. Roosevelt named Frank Bane as the division's director. A former combat pilot who had enjoyed success as a leader of state and local public welfare agencies and had served as Roosevelt's director of the Social Security Board, Bane, at least on paper, came off as a strong pick. He blended experience as a WWI veteran with skills as a depression-era welfare leader.[20]

The barriers standing in Bane's path, however, turned out to be higher than most people had anticipated. The division lacked the ability to impose its will on city and state governments. Despite his background, Bane lacked standing and respect with mayors and governors. And his mandate—from coordinating home defense to consumer protection to public health and housing—was so broad as to muddy his mission.[21]

When Bane assumed his post, more than half of the forty-eight states had established or were establishing state defense councils, and their focus and mission covered the waterfront of activities. Set up under a variety of state and federal laws (including Section 61, an Amendment to the 1916 National Defense Act, giving states the authority to set up a home army when the National Guard was forced into federal service, and individual state laws that enabled governors to form militias in moments of crisis), the defense councils were most notable in August 1940 for the breadth of their functions and the diversity of their agendas. Massachusetts's Committee on Public Safety focused on mitigating shortages of consumer staples such as food and gas and assisting state residents whom the conversion to a war economy had displaced. Governor Culbert Olson of California had to resort to a law from the First World War to set up a state defense agency when his legislature twice rebuffed his plan to establish a defense council. As a result, Olson's agency lacked resources, had insufficient authority to coordinate the response to incendiary bomb fires, and was co-opted by California Fire Marshal Lydell Peck into a force to ferret out fifth columnists. Peck ordered firefighters to investigate employees in defense factories, digging up information about their race, their politics, and their places of birth. (Peck announced that home defenders in California were also responsible for vetting packages that were sent to defense factories and for thwarting enemy plots that sought to poison the water and food supplies and spread harmful germs among defense workers.)[22]

Instead of laboratories of democratic experimentation, the states more closely resembled leaderless classrooms all at work on a myriad of ill-defined tasks and activities with little coordination. Minnesota worked on creating a militarized home defense force to thwart attacks on the state. Wisconsin prioritized public health and air defense. New Hampshire made plans to evacuate its residents. New Jersey studied how to handle an influx of New Yorkers fleeing across the Hudson to save their own lives during an air raid, while Maine stressed the training of women as home defenders. In New York, defense leaders investigated the problem of racism in employment in defense industries. Texans worked to stop Nazi infiltration from Mexico. South Carolina's governor sought to eliminate the threat of subversives and make "America safe for Americans." Florida focused its efforts on volunteer recruitment, nutrition, and setting up 880 air raid watch posts.[23]

Bane could do little to coordinate these disparate activities and end the home defense confusion. He hoped to help prepare states to battle incendiary bomb fires, ensure an adequate supply of housing for those working in defense industries, and provide the infrastructure to educate and care for the families of workers and draftees who had relocated during the rush to mobilization. He failed at virtually all of these tasks. Governors resisted Bane's attempts to tell them how to run home defense in their states, concluding that the division's advice was meddlesome and inimical to the rights of states to determine their own policies and judge threats on their own terms.[24]

In Oregon, Governor Charles Sprague rejected Bane's advice that he set up a state defense council. Having won office in 1938 partly on a pledge to thwart the federal government's efforts to influence local affairs, Sprague asserted in 1940 that advice from Bane's office was more evidence of interference by out-of-touch liberals who had little regard for Oregonians' interests. If he were to establish a defense council, reasoned Sprague, his constituents would conclude that an attack on Oregon was imminent, and they would be more inclined to panic. Such a council, the governor insisted, would also invite charges that Sprague was seeking dictatorial powers during the international emergency. An aide to Bane informed his boss that Sprague and his advisors had no clue about a real home defense program, and the division's leaders came away from their discussions with Sprague dispirited. Sprague blasted Washington for trampling on the prerogatives of his office and the rights of his constituents, reminding Bane that as the duly elected leader of his state, only his office could legitimately serve as the "*message center and liaison between the National Defense Council, the War Department, and the State of Oregon.*" Within Oregon proper, local leaders disputed Sprague's nonchalant attitude, arguing, for example, that the statehouse had to offer a robust plan of military protection for Oregon's water reservoirs and electric grids, deter mob violence targeting minorities should air raids come, and defend arms plants from fifth columnists.[25]

In Washington State, the debate about home defense was also ideologically charged and politically divisive. When Democrat Clarence Martin held the governor's chair, the state set up a defense council, tracked enemy "aliens," and guarded natural resources. All of these things pleased division leaders in Washington, and they saw Martin as a friend and partner to the home defense project. Martin's replacement, however, was a Republican hostile to the New Deal and the Democratic Party, and he stacked his defense council with his yes-men and stripped the council of its authority. Complicating matters, the people of the state were becoming impassioned about home defense, and their efforts lacked guidance from state officials. In Spokane, six thousand people showed up at a pro home defense rally, while Tacoma's mayor bragged that his city had one of America's most formidable home defense organizations. One Home Defense Committee planned to hold a blackout drill in Seattle, while an organization devoted to training women in home defense lobbied Olympia to strengthen the moral and physiological fiber of the state's residents.[26]

Against the backdrop of Hitler's invasion of France, such poor coordination of home defense policy intensified the public's anxiety and led to an even greater sense of impending chaos. In late August, the Gallup Poll reported that 42 percent of the American public felt that if the Nazis were to rout Britain in the war, the United States would become much more vulnerable to Nazi invasion. At the same time, more Americans became concerned about foreign spies. A building manager in Washington, D.C. informed the White House of spies living in his midst, and a Texas man wrote in to say that he knew of stockpiles of Nazi guns near the U.S.–Mexico border. Popular books spoke to the anxiety rippling across communities, including such titles as *Nazi Spies in America,* a successor to World War I era publications including *My Adventures as a German Secret Agent* in which a spy chronicled his efforts to invade the United States using Mexico as his base of operations. FDR's administrative assistant, James Rowe, reported on instances of civilians undertaking vigilante actions, recalling episodes from the First World War that to some liberals at least evoked the worst kind of citizen excesses against immigrants. Liberals by and large concluded that law enforcement rather than individuals should be responsible for rounding up suspects.[27]

As the fears seemed to spin out in different directions, Bane's division was feckless and unreliable. The Roosevelt administration, the nation's mayors concluded, had prioritized the state councils at the expense of urban interests. The president had understandably focused his defense programs on other priorities, which produced a level of stalemate and gridlock that La Guardia sought to break in the fall of 1940. The New York mayor, enraged by Bane's futile efforts to cajole the states, left one meeting on home defense like "a war horse chomping on the bit," as notes of the session put it. As William McReynolds informed the president, La Guardia led the Conference of Mayors to file an objection with the White House that they saw no value in "being subordinated to State supervision."[28]

Roosevelt understood the degree of La Guardia's displeasure and he decided to send the mayor's opinions to his aides for their consideration. Roosevelt needed La Guardia that fall, just as La Guardia needed the president. The two men, longtime allies, began to forge a fresh alliance rooted less in their New Deal reform convictions than in their shared faith in internationalist politics and policy amidst the slaughter in Europe. In the fall, La Guardia made himself indispensable to FDR's foreign policy. Having broken with Midwestern progressives who continued to oppose American intervention in the war, the mayor became one of the president's strongest supporters on international affairs. He started to set the stage for his eventual appointment to the director of FDR's newest war agency responsible for home defense, in May 1941.

La Guardia insisted that FDR was a leader with the vision to see in the war a clear, growing menace to national sovereignty. He sided with Roosevelt because

he wanted to protect New Yorkers from Hitler and despised the fascist dictators. Seeing little hope for living harmoniously in the same world as Hitler and
Mussolini, the Little Flower wanted to prepare Americans to go to war and was
interested in a job in the national defense program. Appearing at the christening
of New York's newest seaplane terminal, La Guardia praised it as auguring New
York's first routine flights across the Atlantic. FDR issued a statement that was
read in front of 10,000 people who attended the ceremony. "A strong man armed
in this modern way of the air . . . is indeed one who keepeth the peace," the president announced. At the opening of the Academy of Aeronautics in Queens that
would train plane mechanics, La Guardia told 150 city and military leaders that
the academy should be seen by Hitler as a warning shot that Americans were
ready for the Nazis. FDR appreciated La Guardia's bellicosity. The mayor had a
knack for bluster that the president was not able to mimic but that helped FDR
make his case that fascist military force had to be met with democratic military preparedness. La Guardia lobbied for the repeal of the Neutrality Acts in
Congress, which were preventing the president from sending military assistance
to Britain, and he even proposed circumventing them. And La Guardia let FDR
know that he was deeply involved in the debate about defense, urging the president to consider mobilizing a "Pan American Army" and grabbing control of the
Azores and Cape Verde Islands in order to solidify hemispheric defense. FDR
saw La Guardia as a liberal loyalist who was knowledgeable on foreign affairs,
and he appointed him to serve as the U.S. chairman of the Permanent Joint
Board on Defense for the United States and Canada, which was to coordinate on
plans in case either nation was attacked.[29]

La Guardia also championed FDR's unprecedented bid for a third term. The
Republican La Guardia and Nebraska Senator George Norris cochaired the
Independent Committee for Roosevelt and Wallace (Henry Wallace, FDR's running mate). The organization symbolized independents' support for Roosevelt's
New Deal as well as for his wartime leadership. La Guardia, an ethnic New Yorker,
spoke for millions of working-class people in the cities, and Norris, who embodied the values of the heartland, helped firm up rural support for the president
during a tough reelection fight. La Guardia described Roosevelt as the person
who had taken on "a responsibility of greater importance to the future of our
country than ever before confronted any man or any candidate in our entire history." La Guardia saw in Roosevelt "a household idol," the phrase used by Robert
Jackson in his memoirs to sum up how the president's admirers regarded him in
1940. (To his critics, Jackson wrote, FDR was a "demon.")[30]

FDR profited from La Guardia's insights and advice. The mayor urged the
president during a campaign swing through New York to play down the issue
of the draft and highlight his New Deal accomplishments, including infrastructure (the Brooklyn-Battery tunnel), housing (a project in Queens), and what

La Guardia called FDR's avid pursuit of "humanity in government" (the Tri-borough Tubercular Hospital). When La Guardia urged a group of Harvard alumni to give the president their support during the international crisis, FDR expressed his gratitude to him for "restoring my speaking acquaintance with my fellow Harvard graduates."[31]

Few campaign surrogates spoke more acidly than La Guardia about the Republican presidential nominee, Wendell Willkie, a corporate lawyer and one-time utility executive. La Guardia pledged to the president that he was about to "take the war path in earnest for you"—and he delivered. At a campaign rally of 23,000 Roosevelt supporters in Chicago that October, La Guardia accused Willkie of misleading the public by tarring Roosevelt as a war-mad commander-in-chief. He reminded voters that FDR had repeatedly pledged to keep the country out of the war, and if Willkie were to defeat the president in November, La Guardia warned, the Republican would inaugu-rate a "reign of terrorized fright." "Down the utility gang," La Guardia cried. During a rally for the president in Detroit, La Guardia gave his speech for Roosevelt, and he grew so incensed with a heckler that the two men nearly came to blows.[32]

At the same time that he was championing the president's foreign policy and reelection bid, La Guardia was forging ahead with his own plans to defend New York from enemy actions. He had already communicated with the War Department about how his city and the U.S. military would react if there was "an air threat to New York City," as Woodring explained to Roosevelt. La Guardia privately talked to other mayors about the steps his city had taken to prepare itself for the day when it was bombed: he had a list compiled of New York City landmarks most in need of protection, and, among other things, he had given orders that all people in a skyscraper during an air raid had to take cover ten floors from the top of the building. The people must not, he warned, attempt to flee the building since on the streets they would be easy prey for enemy pilots searching for targets.[33]

The federal government, La Guardia argued in September, was the lone insti-tution with the resources, clout, and authority to coordinate home defense in cities across America. In his testimony before the Senate Committee on Military Affairs, he proposed that the Army take charge of home guard units on the the-ory that Europe's experience had proven that home guards were vital aspects of national defense. He called on Congress to spur the administration to strengthen protections at "waterways, water supplies, power plants, railroads, highways, bridges, docks and wharves, and strategic points of attack." He explained that the nation had so many vulnerabilities that defensive operations were going to require "real soldiering" by civilians who had received military training. One Senator echoed La Guardia's views, arguing that Washington should begin to federalize and train home guards who even now were standing watch over piers and other strategic sites.[34]

FDR slowly was coming around to La Guardia's view that in order to give Americans an adequate level of military protection, the national government had to take the lead in setting up a home defense operation. In September, Roosevelt indicated that his relationship with big-city mayors was as strong as ever, but it had shifted from the New Deal commitment to making "great social gains" to the militaristic quest to prevent fascist dictators from interfering in the affairs of the American people. FDR wrote the members of the U.S. Conference of Mayors, then meeting at the Waldorf-Astoria in New York City, that Washington with aid from the cities already had begun to ferret out fifth columnists; train more pilots in military tactics; and discuss ways to achieve "the protection and civil defense of water supplies, power stations, arteries of transportation and other key points."[35]

A wartime climate settled over the meeting. New York police closely guarded the dignitaries who entered the hotel and the mayors as they toured the city's World's Fair and attended theater productions. Instead of a tight focus on issues of human security, the conference's agenda featured talks by Robert Jackson on the constitutional requirement of elected leaders to provide for the common defense, General George Marshall on the need for collaboration between the cities and the military, and Cleveland's mayor on how once the United States was in the war cities would become "points of primary attack."[36]

La Guardia stood at the center of this shift in focus among mayors toward national security, and in the wake of FDR's reelection victory, he helped plant the idea in the minds of some Americans that he had the skills and experiences to lead a major effort in the defense program. A Baltimore-based businessman wrote the president that La Guardia's "honesty, patriotism, and tireless energy" made him the best person to lead the nation in building its munitions for war. The chairman of the Council of Personnel Administration, Fred Davenport, urged Roosevelt to find a spot for La Guardia in the defense program so he could "blast holes in resistances, governmental and extra-governmental." Roosevelt informed Davenport that his idea was "not at all . . . bad" and that he hoped he could "make it bear fruit." A civil rights official in Atlanta urged that La Guardia receive an appointment as the secretary of labor, and a former general in the Marines described La Guardia as a skilled executive with support from labor and capital who should run the White House's Defense Commission. La Guardia was led to believe that he was about to be named to the post of secretary of war, replacing Woodring, and he planned to resign from City Hall, telling Rexford Tugwell, a Roosevelt aide, "I can't stay [in New York] with the world falling to pieces." FDR, however, concluded that La Guardia's temperament was ill suited to serve in that post and that La Guardia was most effective running the nation's most populous city, which was crucial to any successful wartime mobilization.[37]

"The formative period is over," one presidential aide wrote FDR on November 26. "The great vote of confidence in you has eliminated suspense. All hands are on deck for full steam ahead." When the topic turned to national defense in general and home defense in particular, the "hands" may have mustered on deck, but they were also rowing in multiple directions at once without guidance from the captain about where the ship of state should go next. Just as Eleanor Roosevelt and her followers advised the president to back a new set of reforms leading to social gains, other White House aides counseled restraint on social spending and urged him to keep his focus fixed on building up the military defense. In December, the United States was mobilizing the National Guard for duty, and by then the draft had been signed into law, arms production was picking up, and not only did Roosevelt have a third term in which to work but he also had chipped away at some of the isolationist sentiment in the country. A Gallup Poll found that 72 percent of people who supported FDR and 65 percent of those favoring Willkie thought that the fate of Britain was going to do much to determine the safety of Americans in the years ahead.[38]

The mayors signaled in the wake of Roosevelt's victory that they were going to press the White House to adopt a strategy to defend the home front. The American Municipal Association argued in its end-of-year report that a priority for its members was resolving the problem of home defense. Modern war, the association observed, had put a set of new strains on the cities, and Washington needed to establish an advisory committee to end confusion and more closely coordinate the activities of government agencies and defense organizations. Indeed, the pace of home defense activities at all levels from state capitals to city halls was dizzying. Thirty-six states had created a defense council, with seven hundred local defense councils now functioning nationwide by year's end. In Alabama, there appeared new schools to train local police in home defense, while in Southern California, home defense volunteers could take courses in sanitation, engineering, and recreation. New York had its own set of civil defense classes available to volunteers, and the FBI was busy training police in coping with war conditions in U.S. cities. On top of the need for coordination by the federal government, the association argued that the movement should further the progressive ethos and improve life in the cities by protecting the public from outbreaks of disease, improving peacetime firefighting techniques, and making the cities more hospitable places in which to live.[39]

FDR could delay taking action on the problem of home defense, but how much longer he could wait without losing support of key constituencies was anybody's guess. The *Washington Post* announced that the chances of air raids coming to a city were high enough to warrant concrete steps to shore up home defenses. FDR's Division of State and Local Cooperation had floundered, disappointing the mayors. Governors were alternately cooperative and resistant to federal instructions on issues regarding military protection, and La Guardia had mobilized the mayors to pressure the White House to adopt home defense on a federal basis as soon as possible. The idea, however remote, that a city could be bombed or invaded, and that Americans would be ill-equipped to cope militarily and psychologically, weighed on the consciences of FDR and La Guardia. Yet by the end of 1940, the United States still was not on the verge of adopting a federal home defense policy, though a consensus was building among Roosevelt's followers that any home defense initiative had to channel this popular energy and prepare the public to meet the fate of France and England with fortitude, stoicism, and heroics. New Deal liberals had to prevent a Nazi wrecking ball from destroying an increasingly unstable social order.[40]

5

An American Plan

> In order to realize [victory in the war] all sorts of activities are set
> going, arrangements made, organizations instituted, as incidental
> means. After they have been called into being they cannot be whisked
> out of existence merely because the war has come to an end. They have
> acquired an independent being and in the long run may effect conse-
> quences more significant than those consciously desired.
> —John Dewey, "The Social Possibilities of War," 1918

The New Deal has often been depicted as a prewar program in which benefits principally flowed down from Washington, D.C., and into the nation's cities, towns, and states. Federal agencies employed the jobless, provided relief to the neediest citizens, and established an old-age insurance program named Social Security. The government hired citizens to build bridges and roads and pave trails in national parks. The Securities and Exchange Commission regulated Wall Street, while the Federal Deposit Insurance Corporation guaranteed individuals' deposits and policed the banks. The New Deal, some historians have argued, was confined to a particular period of time and saved capitalism from its own worst excesses and wove the government more deeply into the fabric of society in ways that are still deeply contentious.[1]

Those explaining the New Deal's demise often argue that FDR's failed court-packing plan, Democratic defeats in the 1938 midterm elections, and the need to prepare the country for war undercut the politics of reform. While this interpretation has much to recommend it, stressing the extent to which momentum for economic reform slowed in the post-1938 period, it also downplays the degree to which the various notions of New Deal liberalism remained viable in the eyes of progressives during the war years. This narrative shortchanges the ways in which the idea of New Deal liberalism evolved to go beyond the reforms passed at the height of the Great Depression. Some liberals had misgivings about the growing power of the federal government to intervene in people's daily lives; others turned away from economic planning and income redistribution and endorsed growth liberalism. And some progressives saw the state as the ultimate bulwark of physical security in an increasingly interdependent and perilous world order. But however they defined the idea, many of them were searching for a way to keep New Deal liberalism at home alive and relevant to wartime society. As historian Meg Jacobs has written, "rather than see the twentieth century as divided by distinct eras of political reform, we need to appreciate the continuities of a certain kind of American liberalism that transcends the chronological division of traditional political history." Missing from most accounts of twentieth-century liberalism is how Eleanor Roosevelt launched a movement composed largely of women that, in 1941, put a proposal on the president's desk to transform American life by empowering millions of women and catapulting them into the economic mainstream. Her plan was going to enable her to complete what she saw as the unfinished New Deal revolution.[2]

Under it, rather than the federal government conferring benefits on citizens, citizens were going to work through their government and their communities to confer benefits on one another. ER envisioned the government recruiting virtually all American women as volunteers in an effort to provide food, shelter, recreation, and health care to every citizen. Her plan was a promise to transform gender roles, bringing women more fully into the beating heart of the nation's economic life. Her proposal anticipated the president's 1944 "Economic Bill of Rights," arguing that the war's goals were not just victory over fascism but also a just democracy that distributed benefits more equitably to more Americans.

Eleanor Roosevelt's agenda, one of the boldest gambits of her White House years, framed the New Deal as a pillar of the nation's military mobilization. Her initiative, she said, would give the Army access to healthier soldiers, make workers in defense plants more efficient, and give citizens a greater stake in society, making them more willing to defend their way of life. It also countered the fascist approach that subordinated citizens to the state. She would fulfill the promise of democracy by helping citizens take action as individuals and work with the federal government from the bottom-up to ensure better lives for their fellow Americans.[3]

By early 1941, the first lady had lost patience with the isolationist approach to the war in Europe. She called antiwar leaders who sympathized with the Nazis appeasers, and she warned that if Wendell Willkie, who had accused the president of warmongering, had won the White House, democracy would have been dealt a grievous blow. While she had not been able to unite the preparedness and New Deal camps as she had hoped to do in 1940, by early 1941, she still wanted to create a wartime New Deal and felt she had enough people behind her to make her vision reality. She wished to "continue with the progressive social legislation as part of national defense," she wrote in January.[4]

Her vision had strong roots in the political upheavals ushered in during World War I. In 1918 liberal theorist John Dewey had found much to admire in "the social possibilities of war," observing that WW I has "brought into existence agencies for executing the supremacy of the public and social interest over the private and possessive interest." The progressive movement, he predicted, "will never go backward." For a time, the war's liberal achievements appeared to buoy Dewey's thesis. The federal government had partnered with private industry, prompting one progressive to proclaim, "Laissez-faire is dead!" Suffragists used their pro-war stances to help win ratification of the Nineteenth Amendment granting voting rights to women. The military draft provided job opportunities to white women and African Americans, while public health emerged as a key issue in national politics during the war years, as historian Robyn Muncy observed.

Despite the post-armistice setbacks that progressives encountered—the government ultimately broke labor strikes, deported immigrants, harassed radicals, and imprisoned antiwar dissidents—Dewey's description of war as an incubator of social progress never quite vanished from the American political scene. Progressive women reformers such as Children's Bureau director Julia Lathrop suggested that social woes at home were comparable to Kaiser Wilhelm II's battle-hardened soldiers in terms of the peril posed to citizens' lives and the democratic future. Indeed, Lathrop had fielded an "army of trained women," one reporter wrote, who were marching "on the households of the poor, attacking the city and village that does not insure its babies pure milk." As a forbearer to ER's approach, the Women's Committee of the Council of National Defense recruited volunteers who were trained to seek the abolition of poverty during wartime and championed reforms in such areas as child welfare; mother's pensions; improved education for all children; and better health care for mothers, pregnant women, and children. Although the post-1918 period failed to achieve these goals, the dream of a government-led and citizen-powered assault on social maladies retained its hold on the progressive imagination well into the 1920s and 1930s. Just as some women reformers had sought to breathe life into Dewey's ideals during the First World War, Eleanor Roosevelt and countless other women helped to update and embodied the reform tradition during the Second World War.[5]

In 1940, President Roosevelt had asked the WPA's Florence Kerr to draft a legislative plan that would essentially find ways to advance the New Deal during Roosevelt's third term. The plan, which was based on the ideas ER had discussed with Kerr, was on FDR's desk by January 1. While Kerr had drafted it, Eleanor Roosevelt had indelibly shaped it. The plan was partly in response to the numerous letters sent to the White House from ordinary citizens urging that the government give them roles (paid and unpaid) to serve their country in national defense. The public, ER concluded, was in front of the government on the question of service, and now was the time for the White House to catch up with the masses and meet the public's growing desire to defend their democracy. ER argued that the goal of attaining the common good was being pursued with greater vigor by more Americans each day, and that people's social needs were going to have to be met. The first lady had concluded that the interests of workers, women, youth, and African Americans "were being forgotten," her biographer Joseph Lash has observed. When Nelson Rockefeller asked her to lead a goodwill tour of Latin America, she replied that she had too much to do at home. Franklin agreed with Eleanor's priorities. He argued that she should not let such offers distract her from "the larger nation-wide group that Mrs. Kerr is about to make plans for."[6]

The plan ER and Kerr submitted on New Year's Day conveyed the deepest hopes of American liberals for 1941. Instead of preserving the New Deal's economic gains (as FDR's failed court-packing plan was supposed to accomplish), their plan was a way of turning the New Deal into a grassroots program in which an army of millions of women served in roles that benefitted wartime society through social action. The plan asked the president to go to Congress and request legislation establishing an agency called the American Social Defense Administration. The agency was going to improve the education system, sanitation, public health, housing, and train women in skills so they could find good-paying jobs. Five million women were going to cultivate gardens to feed their fellow citizens, and two million women would be trained in first aid and other emergency defense activities. Some women would police traffic in cities, while others would learn Spanish (to make them better citizens of the Hemisphere), assist immigrants, meet community needs, and teach ten-to-eighteen-year-old girls why all Americans had a responsibility to serve their country. While volunteers would comprise the bulk of this movement, some of the women would likely need to be paid, and all of the work would receive guidance (and, presumably, resources) from the Roosevelt administration.[7]

Their slogan for their new agency—"I SERVE AMERICA BECAUSE I LOVE AMERICA"—captured their vision of what they called "an American plan." In contrast to the fascist vision that forced civilians to obey the state with abject subservience, their plan relied on volunteers. Women, who were traditionally responsible for "social welfare in the home," ER and Kerr argued, were now going to be asked to bolster social justice within their local communities. By enlisting them in a range of "Health, Welfare and Cultural Services," the social defense agency, they argued, was going to "make America a better place in which to live."[8]

ER and Kerr fully intended to help America win the war militarily by making life better for people on the home front. And they believed that their agency would strengthen democracy in ways that spilled over into the postwar world.

By inculcating the idea of service in the hearts of women and by bringing social and economic benefits to poor, working-, and middle-class Americans of every race, their plan promised to make America into a more equitable country in which all of its members felt valued and all citizens worked to promote the common good. And the new agency had another benefit—connecting Americans to their government in more intimate ways. ER and Kerr pointed to "Dynamic Democracy Discussion Groups" that would illuminate for President Roosevelt both "the problems and progress of Government," providing feedback on his leadership.[9]

Before FDR could even respond to the plan, ER launched a campaign to generate support for her proposal. In a White House meeting with more than fifty of America's most politically powerful women (including Senator Hattie Caraway, Rep. Mary Norton, Rep. Margaret Chase Smith, Francis Perkins, Ellen Woodward, Katharine Lenroot, Elinor Morgenthau, and wives of other cabinet members and Supreme Court justices), ER and Kerr unveiled their proposal and urged the attendees to push for social defense legislation. While ER awkwardly joked that women were known to spill secrets, she asked them to pledge themselves to secrecy anyways. The first lady reminded them that many hundreds of women had written to her and FDR with requests for roles in national defense. The American Social Defense Administration was going to give them this opportunity, she promised. Kerr proceeded to read her seven-page proposal verbatim, as the guests listened, bored by the monotony of the exercise. The meeting ended without any concrete agreement on the steps they would next take to further the social defense cause.[10]

If their campaign began with more of a whimper than a flourish, ER and Kerr continued to channel their energy into making social defense a top priority in the White House. On January 9, they sent FDR a slightly revised proposal that renamed the agency the Home Defense Commission. This change reflected their desire to make the proposal politically palatable, shielding it from the charge that it was social engineering by the federal government. The term "home defense" covered a wider array of activities than social defense, implying both military defense and human security. The commission would now recruit men as well as women, making the program more universal and, therefore, less of an affront to mores that had prevailed in America for decades.

Still, their updated proposal remained largely unchanged from its January 1 incarnation. Millions of citizens would still conduct socially beneficial tasks, bringing progress to people in communities nationwide. The plan called on Americans to adopt a form of "military citizenship," stressing that by mobilizing millions to serve in home defense, they would do the work necessary "to make America the best place on earth." Volunteers would put government-issued pins on their lapels (close to their hearts), wear uniforms, and provide the missing ingredient in the mobilization—improving life at home while industry produced arms and the Army trained soldiers for combat. ER also suggested that FDR declare in a fireside chat in March that he wanted to establish the Home Defense Commission as part of "the most comprehensive program of participation by a people in a Democracy since the signing of the Declaration of Independence."[11]

Besides lobbying FDR to embrace their idea, ER and Kerr had to persuade Americans of the wisdom of social defense. Kerr hoped to use mass entertainment, namely, radio soap operas. She proposed enlisting scriptwriters and advertisers to reach women listeners with a message favorable to social defense activism. Inserting social defense into the soaps would put before millions of women "in a very natural way" the merits of citizen participation, as "they are dusting, sweeping, baking, and tending their homes," Kerr wrote. By glamorizing and humanizing social defense, she added, liberals would win support from the masses for their agenda. ER called Kerr's proposal a "good idea," and Kerr put the proposal into FDR's take-home reading materials. FDR was forced to acknowledge that the concept was at least worthy of serious consideration, a project of some importance. Under pressure from ER and Kerr and liberal New Deal constituencies, the president asked his aides to give him feedback on the proposal.[12]

While ER remained uncertain of where FDR stood on the question of social defense, she worried that he was being forced to abandon the New Deal to which he had so long been devoted. While eating lunch with him at their estate in Hyde Park, ER urged him to prevail on the U.S. housing coordinator to restore funding for low-income housing, which Congress had recently cut with the National Defense Housing Act. Instead of acceding to her wishes, the president said that he planned to name Charles Palmer, a well-known foe of affordable housing, as his new housing coordinator. The first lady began to attack FDR for jettisoning the poor. Listening to the conversation, ER's mother-in-law grabbed the president's wheelchair and moved him away from the table and out of the first lady's line of fire.

ER needed FDR to advance her agenda just as FDR needed ER to further his. She relied on his voice, power, and prestige to keep alive the social defense cause. He did not have the luxury of ignoring the people for whom she spoke. With war on the horizon, the president needed to hold on to the support of her admirers, the intellectuals, journalists, and artists, African Americans, youth, and women, as they were all key components of his New Deal coalition. At the same time, FDR, though he was whipsawed by social and military demands, remained attached politically and intellectually to the New Deal program. Not only did he think it crucial to preserve the social gains he had achieved (social security, collective bargaining, minimum wage, and other measures), but he also agreed with ER that if the people did not have a stake in preserving their democracy, their morale and the pace of arms production would suffer, and the country would be more vulnerable to fifth columnists and the preachments of those who claimed democracy was a false idol that could never satisfy people's most basic needs. ER saw in FDR a husband and a president who was sympathetic to what she was trying to achieve, but who was caught in tough political crosscurrents. Author of the New Deal, he was, she knew, a foe of anti-statist conservatives, and a president who understood the role of government in easing the hardships caused by the depression. In 1940, the unemployment rate was nearly 15 percent; by 1941, it was still high at almost 10 percent. FDR had no crystal ball telling him that preparedness was going to end the depression for good and meet the country's economic needs.[13]

On January 11, FDR, who still was focused on his top priority, Lend-Lease, sent a note to his secretary Pa Watson asking him to set up a meeting on home defense with ER, Kerr, Ellen Woodward, Harriet Elliott, Harold Ickes (who endorsed a morale-building program for the home front), budget director Harold Smith, and Paul McNutt, who directed the Federal Security Agency overseeing some of the New Deal's activities. The meeting decided nothing. FDR informed the press corps that the direction of home defense had not yet been determined; the only certainty was that any program had to give citizens roles in defense of their democracy. For her part, Kerr spoke publicly about home defense as a vehicle for buttressing the morale of the people. Their statements, vague and noncommittal, reflected a struggle within the administration over the direction that the program was going to take.[14]

FDR continued to engage in what Kerr feared was a "stalling technique." He appointed Kerr, McNutt, and Elliott to a subcommittee to hash out differences and recommend a strategy. Kerr informed FDR that "axe-grinders" on the subcommittee put up roadblocks to the idea of home defense. Kerr knew that FDR was prone to letting his aides "fight it out," which "was a heart-breaking thing for the people who were involved, but that was the only way he worked." Now FDR was giving Kerr a firsthand taste of his preferred approach to resolving big issues. McNutt led foes in arguing that any program was going to undermine the authority of other New Deal agencies. Moreover, McNutt argued to the president, a "federalized organization with a Federal Home Defense Secretary and staff in each State" and each county and a "Home Defense Commissioner" were likely to impede defense efforts led by state and local leaders and trample on state and local prerogatives.[15]

Kerr and ER continued to lobby the president to embrace social defense as an urgent matter of national security. Only the federal government, they claimed, could tackle the problem on the necessary scale. Any initiative was sure to spark controversy; "the possibilities of color, fire, and drama in home defense mobilization" were real, Kerr warned FDR. But liberals, she argued, should not be deterred. Kerr asked the women who attended the January 7 launch meeting to send their ideas and support a movement that would "mean so much" to all Americans. How should the United States define the threats facing it, and how should the government and the public respond to these threats? Were threats primarily military in nature? Or, was the specter of economic crisis and social dislocation, which could unravel the social fabric and bring fascists to power, even more frightening?[16]

These questions underwrote the debate about the fate of the New Deal and the obligations of citizens to democracy during the international emergency. FDR once told the future Pope Pius XII, Eugenio Pacelli, that "the great danger in America is that it will go fascist," and Kerr was convinced that if economic distress became acute enough, it was easy to see people in America "pick[ing] up the bludgeons" and becoming "perfectly capable of overthrowing the government." If enough children of men did not have any food, the men "would get wild," Kerr had concluded. Federal Works Agency director John Carmody urged FDR to understand that the federal government alone had the power and reach to unify the public and mobilize "literally millions of people" for socially useful roles. Carmody agreed with ER and Kerr that home defense was going to have a "smash promotional psychology" that would unite citizens in support of liberal internationalism.[17]

Asking liberals around the country to rally to their cause, ER and Kerr mobilized influential constituencies on behalf of social defense. When the commander of the Green Guards of America, which sought to give women defense training, informed ER that her members had been barred from conversations about "the woman's Home Defense Group," ER replied that the activists should have a voice in these meetings. The National Social Work Council offered its support for a federal–civilian partnership to bolster social democracy, while the American Public Welfare Association called for more government-led physical fitness for workers and soldiers living in defense areas. Leaders of the NYA, WPA, and CCC announced training programs to help civilians find well-paid jobs in the defense program, and the grassroots came to adopt the language used by ER to justify social defense. C. D. Jackson, who led the Council for Democracy, which had been established to counter the antiwar propaganda of the America First Committee, pledged to the first lady the support of his members for the "proposal for citizen participation in the defense program," explaining that he had worked with community groups to tackle "the unfinished jobs of democracy" rather than enlisting civilians in "pseudo-military activities." The city of Pasadena, California, Kerr assured ER, was about to launch its program to give women roles in social defense, which should, she added, "bring [ER] a smile."[18]

Kerr, especially, worked to underscore that ER was the unrivaled champion of a social defense program. She proposed organizing a dinner to "express our gratitude to Mrs. Roosevelt for . . . developing plans for, and inspiring interest in, Home Defense." Even if most of the enrollees in their program would be volunteers, ER and Kerr found inspiration for social defense in Kerr's WPA, which, Kerr reminded ER, had thousands of paid workers who had helped feed the hungry, bolster the public health, and provide aid to needy children. If thousands of government workers could achieve so much progress, Kerr reasoned, millions of government-led volunteers could make concrete contributions to communities nationwide. Kerr reminded the first lady that WPA-sponsored music concerts over lunch at the U.S. Arsenal in Springfield inspired workers to boost their productive capacity. She painted a picture for the first lady of government dance troupes lifting the spirits of soldiers stationed in Arkansas, and government-run classes developing the minds of military pilots and sailors. Such WPA activities all "related to home defense," Kerr assured the first lady, adding that the WPA was also working with the War Department on a confidential study of air raid precautions in the United States. Kerr's report on the WPA impressed ER sufficiently that she sent it to FDR with a note scribbled on the upper right-hand corner, "I think you would like to read."[19]

Few of Eleanor Roosevelt's supporters thought that a social defense program was misguided or unnecessary. Instead, the questions they posed in early 1941 regarded the scale of the program and when to push it through Congress. These issues were hardly inconsequential. Rep. Mary Norton, who chaired the House Committee on Labor, replied to a request for advice by urging ER to delay her fight in Congress until a vote could be taken on H.R. 1776, the president's Lend-Lease bill. Do not, Norton counseled, provide "any information about 'Home Defense' at this time" because critics would take potshots and help sink the concept. She argued that the start of social defense should be gradual with the knowledge that millions of mobilized civilians and "all that we hope for would come in time." ER, Norton added, still had her work cut out for her. The first lady had to teach the public about the benefits of such a program and counter the skittishness among some liberals and conservatives that a home defense commission augured a federal reign of "regimentation, socialization, [and] propagandizing." Norton reminded ER to alert women "to the fact that our country is in real danger and until we can bring to them a realization of the dangerous situation confronting them, I'm afraid they will not take the personal interest in the plan that must be taken if it is to succeed. . . . I hear on every side 'we are not at war, why become hysterical?' " FDR himself took Norton's qualms seriously enough to ask aides to read her memo "in strict confidence."[20]

The unfolding debate in the White House and the country yielded little progress on the problem of home defense in January, 1941. On January 27, Kerr wrote the first lady that FDR's subcommittee had failed to reach any consensus. McNutt continued to voice his objections, and Kerr angrily wrote in a note to ER that their "central and vital idea [behind social defense], the people back at home as volunteer workers, disappears farther and farther into the mists of incidental detail" during the subcommittee discussions. Kerr argued that the grassroots was instrumental to the success of any social defense program, and suggested that the political climate had shifted so much that they needed to assure the public that this new federal agency was not going to be a threat to individual liberty. They were proposing, Kerr explained, to assign people "useful and needed" tasks that would ultimately be the work of the people themselves. Americans, Kerr figured, wanted "practical defense work in their own communities," and she informed ER that "if our effort is to hit the target, I believe it must be definitely 'of the people,' not 'of the government.'"[21]

Despite their frustration inside the capital, ER could reasonably conclude that the American public was at least somewhat supportive of her vision. Citizens, she believed, were more enlightened than some of their elected leaders. ER found hope in the social activism sponsored by the American Red Cross and the American Women's Voluntary Services (AWVS). Washington Post reporter Katharine Graham (who later became its publisher) published an article describing ordinary women as a "huge source of [grassroots] energy." Graham revealed that twenty-five thousand women had signed up as volunteers with the capital's local Red Cross chapter in one month, while the AWVS was actively recruiting women to fight such maladies as inadequate diets, poverty, and coping with air raids. Hundreds of thousands of women, she reported, were studying the needs in their communities and preparing to meet them in order to stem the forces that could lead to chaos if social defense was delayed for too long.[22]

The grassroots network of liberal organizations and citizens who admired the first lady was making its power felt. Some five thousand organizations participated in a "National Social Hygiene Day," and Kerr addressed a meeting of participants, describing social services as a vital component of war mobilization. The president of the National League of Women Voters wanted to visit with ER to discuss home defense, while leaders of Student Defenders of Democracy asked FDR how students could defend the New Deal and its attendant social gains in wartime. Defining patriotism in terms of social mobilization, the first lady argued to leaders of the General Federation of Women's Clubs during a White House tea that her proposal was going to give communities the flexibility to address their own needs, and framed her idea as simply a way to give all citizens the chance to defend their way of life.[23]

In early 1941, Eleanor Roosevelt drew inspiration from Lady Stella Reading's leadership of Britain's Women's Voluntary Services (WVS). In May 1938, Home Secretary Sir Samuel Hoare had asked Reading, "If bombs should fall, don't you think it would be a good idea to have women instruct householders to protect themselves and the community?" The Women's Voluntary Services for Air-Raid Precautions was born, with Reading as its chairwoman. Reading acquired a reputation as a hero during the Blitz in the fall of 1940; she tapped the energy of ordinary women to do jobs in nursing, first aid, nutrition, and countless other fields necessary to propping up civilian morale and the social order.[24]

The WVS impressed the news media as a triumph of the democratic spirit worthy of emulation among the American public. By September 1939, the WVS had 47 paid officials and approximately 160,000 air raid volunteers, 368,000 transport workers, 100,000 medical workers, and 130,000 assisting with evacuations. Over a single weekend, some 200,000 women helped evacuate hospitals in London and made arrangements for alternative housing—feats the *New York Times* dubbed a "triumph." The *Sunday Times* hailed Reading's group as "the greatest single organisation of its kind in the world," ballooning to more than a million members. With a majority of British women participating in the movement, volunteers drove trucks and ambulances; fixed cars; worked as nurses, cooks, photographers, and in social services; salvaged war materials; trained in gas warfare; rebuilt bombed-out homes; treated victims suffering from shock; helped "invalids, old people, lonely people, mothers of small children" cope with air raids; and gave food and shelter to people who had lost access to these basic human needs. They even studied techniques for preventing mass panic. Dressed in green overalls; dark coats; or sometimes blouses, skirts, and felt hats or five-pound steel helmets, volunteers came to embody the defiance, pluck, and discipline that were required to make the social gains that ER was envisioning in the United States, whether or not it was ever bombed.[25]

The WVS also came to be seen as an antidote to the social instability that seemed on the verge of consuming Britain. In London, fights erupted in public shelters, much of the poor East End had been destroyed, and the smell of feces and urine wafted through Piccadilly's shelter station as the threat of epidemics worsened. Western democracies peering into the abyss became a theme in the United States, and American scholars, journalists, and liberal politicians lionized English women as disciplined heroines—"the greatest surprise of this war." Ambassador Averell Harriman and Treasury Secretary Henry Morgenthau agreed that without the active involvement of average women, the British Empire would have likely disintegrated. The *Christian Science Monitor* gave Reading a forum to discuss her achievements, while the *Washington Post* hailed her as a hero. On a tour to observe WVS activities in London, Mrs. Dwight-Davis, director of the American Red Cross, saw etched on the faces of women a "spirit which shines out like a great light" of hope for democracy.[26]

The first lady viewed the WVS as an answer to the barbaric behavior of the Nazis as well as a ringing affirmation of the New Deal's faith that government powered by citizen participation was an instrument for unprecedented social gains. In a 1941 letter to ER, Reading described a Dantesque scene outside her window: Homes were piles of rubble as anti-aircraft balloons bobbed in the sky. Reading observed that the war had become seared into the landscapes of the British city and countryside and into the psyches of the public, producing inescapable anxiety. Reading predicted that the British would withstand the Blitz of their cities. Her citizen-soldiers provided services to meet the needs of the people during air raids, giving hope to humanity.[27]

Reading's budding alliance with ER was based on a common vision of a wartime home front. Just as ER lavished praise on the British people, Reading admired Americans as a resilient people who would aid the British war effort. Her husband, the Marquess of Reading, had served as British Ambassador to Washington, but when he died in 1935, Lady Stella Reading filled his shoes. She developed an affinity for the common man in the United States. Touring America, she forsook posh hotels and stayed in cheap accommodations. She took a job washing dishes just so she could experience life as a member of the working class. As a champion of social reform in England during the 1930s, she befriended Eleanor Roosevelt, and Reading's leadership of the WVS inspired ER's mobilization agenda. Social reform, as some scholars have argued, was not the singular product of American liberal ingenuity but rather an outgrowth of ideas and movements that crossed the waters from Europe and found fertile soil in the United States.[28]

In late 1940 and early 1941, Reading updated the first lady on British progress in volunteer training and found in her the kind of ally that sustained the British spirit amid a tide of demoralizing news on the continent. "A glance at the map might be dispiriting were it not for the knowledge of the wonderful assistance and support we are getting from you," Reading wrote ER. She stoked ER's passion for social defense, explaining to the first lady how the lines segregating the old from the young, the poor from the rich, vanished as volunteers melded into a citizen-army of social equals. Reading informed ER that she was "very anxious to give" Harry Hopkins, who was on a tour of London for FDR, "additional information on W.V.S." The first lady wanted Hopkins to detail for her how the WVS had reduced the frictions among social classes. "All of us are ready to die" to uphold the tradition of democracy, Reading assured ER, and the unbreakable spirit of Anglo-American women was going to strengthen democracy in its darkest hour.[29]

In the first months of 1941, ER also learned from Reading the transformative effects that the WVS experience was having on the lives of the women who served in its ranks. Reading described to ER a meeting with ninety-six women leaders of home defense in London. "Every type must have been represented," she wrote. "Some of them were smart and well turned out, others were rather shabby looking and desperately hard working—yet our uniform was a great equalising factor and one was able to assess each Leader at her own value." Reading added that after the war "a large number of women . . . will carry on work in connection with their local government"—advancing the shared goal of building a progressive social democracy in the postwar world. Their wartime experiences would enable them to better the fields of economics and politics as women became more fundamental to British democratic governance, Reading confided.[30]

In March, the first lady informed Reading that she intended to profit from her hard-won experience, writing her that once a program had been established in the United States, she would "get all the advice I can from you." Reading offered to help in any way she could "in regard to Civil Defence," adding that "however much governmental authority works out a framework it is always necessary to have cement [the WVS] to weld together the stones of legislation and fill in the interstices which have been left empty." Reading's letters, Eleanor Roosevelt assured her ally, were a "great help to the people who are working on our civilian defense here." There was some discussion of ER visiting England, but the first lady decided that the logistics of her visit would burden a nation that was struggling just to survive, so she stayed home.[31]

Eleanor Roosevelt was hardly the lone admirer of the progressive impulse that the actions of ordinary British women had brought into sharp relief. New Deal progressives urged the White House to look to England as a model of social democracy amid the emerging terror of the practice of total war. In 1940 and early 1941, the White House sent missions to London to study social defense and learn how to apply them to the home front. Surgeon General Thomas Parran announced that on his visit to England he would study how Britain's sanitation, schools, roads, trains, hospitals, and other public services had withstood the Blitz. Parran's team, according to the *New York Times*, would likely recommend that Washington merge military and social defense into a single home defense program, and Parran praised the efficacy of Britain's movement in his talks upon his return to the United States.[32]

After touring England, Eric Biddle, a representative of the American Public Welfare Association, also argued that the United States should copy an idea from Britain: establish a Ministry of Civil Defense, which would provide ordinary Americans with a form of human security. The British had strengthened their relief, pension, and disability insurance systems, paid bombing victims, and given free health care to some evacuees, all of which Biddle praised as demonstrations of liberalism in action. In the first months of 1941, pressure mounted on FDR to provide for civil defense along the lines of the British women's volunteer program. After accompanying Churchill on a tour of bombed-out cities, presidential envoy Averell Harriman sent some advice to FDR: "the need is for home defense."[33]

After Lend-Lease passed Congress in March, the debate about the democratic character of the home front intensified. On March 6 an anonymous report circulated that said the White House had already begun its recruitment of millions of women for volunteer participation in its social defense program. Later that day, White House Press Secretary Stephen Early told reporters that the rumor was "a cockeyed lie." The White House, Early admitted, was locked on the horns of a dilemma: America's women had told the president and first lady they desired to do something in the defense setup. FDR applauded the patriotism and passion from the citizenry, but mobilizing millions of women remained "one of the most complicated . . . problems now under study." Early added the wrinkle that the administration insisted any plan had to include men as well as women.[34]

Reports that a plan was about to be hatched elicited scorn from some Republican isolationists. By early March of 1941, the battle over home defense was fully joined, spilling into the larger arena of American politics and the debate about the worth of the New Deal and the proper role and function of government in people's lives during a national security crisis. Roosevelt's critics saw evidence of his war-mongering in his words and deeds, and rumors of a government-led mass mobilization handed an opening to his New Deal critics. Conservative members of the U.S. House took firm aim at the first lady's social defense proposal, using it to discredit liberalism as a governing philosophy. Republican Rep. Everett Dirksen belittled her scheme as just her attempt to import Hitler's program of forced mobilization of women into the United States and curb the freedoms of America's citizens. Dirksen said his own district held zero interest in adopting her plan, and he also charged that Kerr had concocted the agenda with dozens of nefarious coconspirators. "The Nazi social dictator has life and death power over the comings and goings of women in that country," Dirksen cried. "They have a battalion of spies, 50,000 strong, and they call them social wardens. With this program of social defense, are we to have a battalion of social wardens, 50 or 100 thousand strong, to enter the homes of America to tell the wives and mothers and sisters how to cook and what to cook, how many children shall be born into a family, and what measures should be taken for stimulation or curtailment of the birth rate?"[35]

The isolationist drumbeat grew shriller. *Chicago Tribune* publisher Robert McCormick, an anti-New Deal critic who had imbibed George Washington's farewell warning to the nation that future generations must avoid entangling alliances, led the assault. His paper brandished ER's proposal as a blueprint of the plan copied from Frau Gertrud Scholtz Klink, described as "the Reichs-frauenfuererin of the Frauenfront, Hitler's women's organization. The hierarchy of command is in the best Nazi form." Under the headline "Mrs. Roosevelt's Frauenfront," the *Tribune* depicted social defense as a scheme in which "music, libraries and recreation" would be used to establish a "nationwide entertainment program." The paper editorialized that the proposal resembled the Lend-Lease "dictator bill."[36]

Eleanor Roosevelt and Kerr refused to let their idea die from the nicks and cuts inflicted on it by their isolationist foes in the Midwest and beyond. They rebutted such screeds by saying that social defense would build national solidarity in a time of crisis. The first lady accelerated her push for social defense. Letters continued to flow to her offices, giving her hope and steeling her will to keep fighting to enact social reform. "Our best defense for the future begins with the children," one eighteen-year-old wrote ER. Brimming with popular requests that the administration launch a social defense movement, the letters elicited a standard response. The administration, the first lady's office replied, would soon release its plan for women's roles on the home front. "When a chairman is designated, your letter will be referred for consideration," ER's aides wrote.[37]

In March, the first lady published "Social Gains & Defense" in her friend Selden Rodman's *Common Sense*, delivering one of her most explicit appeals to date that social action had to be made an integral facet of the defense program. Her piece argued that "only with equal justice, equal opportunity, and equal participation in the government can we expect to be a united country—a country that is prepared to win out in any battle, the battle of economic production and of solving our social questions, or the battle of ideas which is perhaps today that most important of all, for ideas know no barriers. . . . It is only the knowledge that you are fighting for a better future which makes life worth living." Complacency was no longer a viable option for the American public, she asserted. Living in a democracy carried responsibilities including hard work, national service, preservation of social gains, and the need to "experiment with doing something better," she argued. America still had some distance to travel "before we can even begin to feel that we are really a democracy." Progress entailed achieving for all citizens a rising level of "satisfaction in their way of life," including greater access to education, health care, and recreation. Bremerton, Washington, had no schools and 2,500 children went without an education, she pointed out. ER described one woman who wrote her that she did not care whether Hitler or Roosevelt held power because she and her children faced starvation. One young man wanted ER to explain to him why he should risk his life for his country after six years in which he felt the United States had failed to help him find a home, a school, and a steady income.[38]

By the spring of 1941, the White House had still not settled on the scope and scale of a home defense program. ER insisted that her plan would have a bracing effect on the nation's morale. She showed FDR a letter from the chairman of the Committee for National Morale, Arthur Pope, who recommended that morale building should be a feature of any undertaking to defend the home front. Kerr called Pope's idea "a real contribution" to the defense debate. Voicing the first lady's views and ideals, Kerr also told a Women's Air Corps Club that although U.S. weapons and soldiers constituted "the front rank of our outer defenses," inner defenses had to include both morale building and economic security for all citizens. "A policy of false asceticism which imagines that we can increase our national defense by needless sacrifice of our internal strength" was going to backfire on the people, she warned. The United States, she was arguing, had to have both butter and guns in order to preserve democracy and promote the American way of life.[39]

In April, Eleanor Roosevelt raised the hopes of New Dealers when she again announced that the administration was about to provide a chance for all women to participate in a social defense program. Lunching with wives of members of Congress, ER said she wanted the White House to compile a list of women across states and cities that enumerated their skills and interests in what roles they wanted to have. This list "would let anyone know, in any part of the country, in case of fire, flood or any other emergency, what was available in woman power," she explained. She recently had learned how to fire a gun, but much more important to her was that all women learn how they could work to improve the lives of other Americans. "We are one big community—citizens of the United States of America," the first lady declared. "If things are not going well in any part of the United States, it is up to us to find out why, put our shoulders to the wheel and do something about it. It is your problem, wherever you live."[40]

Eleanor was undeterred by Franklin's refusal to enact a program, and she continued her one-woman social defense movement by playing a direct role in improving the lives of the less fortunate, as she had done for years. She helped persuade government officials to forgo the use of flimsily built trailers and use sturdier prefabricated housing for 30,000 residents of Vallejo, California. One boy, John Yakasovich, confined to a sanitarium in Monrovia, California, wrote ER, asking her to send him a radio. ER's friends Helen and Melvyn Douglas sent Yakasovich the radio on behalf of the first lady. He exclaimed, "I knew Mrs. Roosevelt wouldn't forget me." The sanitarium had a small budget. Its patients lacked resources. And the delivery of a radio to one boy brought joy to a child and enabled the spread of news and information to people across the ward. Even the tiniest of gestures, coming from ER, could have a big impact on the lives of ordinary Americans. This was the kind of spirit she was hoping to embed in the culture itself. This spirit of charity, concern for humanity, had to animate every community if Americans were going to prosecute the war against fascism with the commitment and aggression that the fight required. Even if her proposal languished amid the politics of national security in wartime Washington, she felt that the people were rallying to her vision, and held out hope that soon a social defense program would come to fruition, helping to resurrect the New Deal, and transform the lives of all Americans.[41]

6

London Burning

The pupil comes to the master to learn.
—New York City Fireman, London, 1940

On the afternoon of September 7, 1940, scores of bombers, emblazoned with swastikas visible to the naked eye, appeared in the skies and flew straight toward the heart of London. As tons of high-explosive and incendiary bombs pounded the capital, the blue skies turned the color of red, and factories, dockyards, and tenements and even whole neighborhoods were incinerated. Fires raced through timber yards so violently that black ash was released into the air and smudged residents' faces and blackened their clothing. During the first 24 hours of what came to be named the Blitz of London, hundreds of civilians were killed and thousands more were injured or lost their homes. Many civilians experienced the first wave of bombings not purely with the calm of popular legend but also as if they were "animals in the jungle," as one diplomat in London recorded in his diary.

Thousands of miles away, Americans read the accounts of the air raids and became frightened that the Blitz would incite class violence, spark riots, and even launch a revolution in Britain. Some Americans lionized British firefighters as defenders of civilization, while others fretted that sustained bombing had endangered democracy's social foundations. Militaristic liberals led by Fiorello La Guardia drew inspiration from Britain's home security movement, regarding its leader Herbert Morrison and air raid services as a wake-up call for America's cities. London became an essential laboratory, in which America's leaders could study the city's failures and achievements and apply these lessons to their own urban centers. Not only FDR and La Guardia but also the FBI, the War Department, and citizen groups sent trusted teams to England to report on the British home defense system.[1]

Above all, the firebombing of London made Americans fear that their cities might be next. If the Nazis attacked New York, they would cause mass death and hysteria, undermining the social order that New Dealers had fought to keep intact from the ravages of the Great Depression. Britain's home defense program ultimately stimulated an American effort to alter the relationship between civilians and their government, militarizing the American home front and making home defense service an urgent national priority. The Blitz inspired a self-defense movement in the United States that led to the creation of the nation's first home defense agency.[2]

The origins of home defense in World War II in particular and in the twentieth century in general are traceable to the British response to the Blitz in 1940 and 1941. Security policies were portable across countries, drawing on historian Daniel Rodgers's insight that progressives found inspiration and ideas for reform in their transatlantic allies. In this case, American liberals studied the British home defense program and took their cues from British leaders, proving Rodgers's point that "the Atlantic functioned . . . less as a barrier than a connective lifeline." The bombing of London, more than any single event in World War II, planted a psychology of fear in American soil: Americans transported in their minds the terror of bombings in England to the U.S. home front, and a robust home defense program offered the country a means of surviving the dreaded fascist onslaught. While civil defense in World War II has been depicted as a pro-war propaganda organ and the policy result of irrational fears among Americans and their leaders, the U.S. program emerged organically out of the Blitz, an event that persuaded U.S. security officials and citizens that defending America in the modern world meant importing key aspects of the British program to the United States.[3]

England's devotion to home defense was rooted in the country's geography, history, and cultural traditions. When France and Spain in 1782 sided with the colonies in the Revolutionary War, the first secretary of Britain's Home Office, Lord Shelburne, commanded town leaders to muster their forces in case they had to fight off naval attacks. In the 150-plus years since that war, Britain's Home Office had taken the lead in defending England from foreign foes. By the start of the Blitz, the Home Office had two decades worth of planning to defend the country from aerial attacks. During World War I, England contended with 103 German air raids that dropped 300 tons of bombs and killed 1,413 civilians. More than 17,000 home defense volunteers rallied to the cause. Three hundred thousand civilians took shelter in London's underground subway on any given night, and some of them prayed, in the words of one British major general, "for deliverance." An additional 500,000 people slept in their cellars.[4]

In the aftermath of World War I, British planners had few doubts that civilians would suffer the brunt of future attacks. Military experts war-gamed a scenario of French bombers dropping fifteen hundred tons of bombs on England roughly every thirty days. The Air Ministry assigned the Home Office responsibility for anti-air raid planning in 1923; by decade's end, some planners said air raids could murder more than seventy-five thousand London residents. Other scenarios provided a basis for mass fear: Winston Churchill declared in 1934 that air attacks on London would force three million residents to flee. "Problems of this kind have never been faced before," he said. The next year, the Home Office set up an Air Raid Precautions Department. The Home Office hired 120 officials by the end of 1938, and one government estimate foresaw six hundred thousand civilian deaths in the first six months of sustained air raids—a clear call for government action. Neville Chamberlain's aides and European academic experts also argued that something had to be done to avert the calamity of mass panic under the strain of aerial assault. One Danish scholar theorized that modern bombing would obliterate the norms of civilization, eroding human discipline, eviscerating law and order, unleashing chaos.[5]

Civilians paid attention to these warnings. By November 1938, seven hundred thousand had registered as air raid volunteers. After England entered the war and France capitulated in June 1940, the British home defense movement gained credibility. On June 18, 1940, the day after Churchill called the British "the sole champions now in arms to defend the world cause," bombs fell on Addington, the first air raid on greater London. The Blitz unleashed more chaos than the mottoes ("Keep calm and carry on") and the lore (the gallant firefighter) have suggested. After the bombs started to fall in June, some shelters became dens of filth known to harbor "improper behaviour." One London leader told American officials that some residents of English cities had fled the bombing and spent eight to ten hours in nearby woods before they calmed down. The Blitz spurred efforts to keep people's spirits from cracking. British author John Langdon-Davies's book *Nerves versus Nazis* assured residents that if they counted to sixty after the first bombs and were still alive, they would probably survive the attack. The Home Intelligence Office took an interest in "the possibilities of panic." Between September 1940 and May 1941, forty-three thousand civilians died in the bombing, tens of thousands of people were injured, and the Luftwaffe damaged or destroyed approximately one million buildings. But civil defense workers unquestionably saved lives, rescuing civilians who were buried beneath rubble, stopping the spread of fires, and providing people with shelter during air raids. Their impact on the psyche of the British public was also immeasurable.[6]

Americans easily imagined the London Blitz as a prelude to similar attacks on the cities of the New World. London, one academic at the time observed, had nearly nine million residents living in an area that was roughly one-third the size of New York City. When incendiary bombs pounded London's center, the *American Journal of Sociology* called the area "not much larger than Chicago's Loop." London's port was the second largest behind New York City's and the County of London roughly equaled "the size of Philadelphia." The U.S. news media expressed America's fury at the aerial targeting of Europe's civilians. The *Los Angeles Times* said the Blitz and destruction of Rotterdam had showed "diseased" German leaders employing "methods of terrorism." The newspaper warned its readers that "We are in for misery."[7]

No American brought home the dangers facing the people of London more than CBS News radio correspondent Edward R. Murrow. Smoking sixty to seventy cigarettes a day, Murrow's voice was deep and matter-of-fact; his gaze intense; and his face, one obituary said, "high-domed, worried, [and] lopsided." Poet and Librarian of Congress Archibald MacLeish paid tribute to Murrow for bringing "the city of London in[to] our houses" and making Americans feel "the flames." Legions of admirers have hailed Murrow's Johnny-on-the-spot reporting as a paragon of twentieth-century journalism. Murrow lauded Britons for their stoic defiance and Odysseus-like qualities, rising out of their homes to defend their country from barbaric attacks. But he did not restrict his reporting to the theme of British bravery and rectitude. His broadcasts underscored the sense of siege that gripped the British people. The language of his reports communicated civilian terror. He called a bomb's explosion a "bestial grunt" and described London residents holding "little cheap cardboard suitcases and sometimes bulging paper shopping bags" as "all they had left." Murrow predicted that by mid-September a Nazi invasion would likely be underway. Hitler, he said, had a ten-thousand-plane secret air force. Britain would probably have to cope with a chemical gas attack; the bombings had imposed "great . . . strain." He described one explosion as having left "the largest crater I've ever seen."[8]

Murrow framed the war in terms Americans could readily grasp, as if the United States was also in harm's way. He suggested that the bombing of London presaged America's future. He likened London to "a ghost town in Nevada" and said one policeman who juggled his silver whistle within one hundred feet of an unexploded bomb reminded him of "cops at home" twirling "a night stick on a warm spring day." On New Year's Eve, Murrow invoked the familiar argument of liberal internationalists in the States, hinting that America's fate hinged on Britain's.[9]

These grim themes seeped into the U.S. media in the fall of 1940 and became features of the popular culture, creating a climate of fear that led to the establishment of the Office of Civilian Defense. The *New York Times* termed the Nazi Blitz of London "indiscriminate bombing at its zenith." American correspondent Robert Post reported watching the film *All This and Heaven Too* in a London theater. Just as the husband in the film was about to murder his wife ("No! No! No!" she screamed), a high-explosive bomb rocked the movie palace where Post was sitting. The Luftwaffe was dropping "tens of thousands of wicked little two-pound incendiaries, either raining them from planes or sending them down in

'Molotoff breadbaskets' [a series of incendiaries falling in rapid succession and causing fire over a large section of the city], which broke in the sky and showered fire on the way down."[10]

Terrified voices of British civilians also pierced America's collective conscience. America's newspapers published letters to the editor from civilians on the London front. One social worker wrote in the *Christian Science Monitor* that shrapnel from bombs had shattered shop windows on his street. Another Londoner said every person in the city was in danger.[11]

How would urban residents handle air raids on America's cities? The *Los Angeles Times* wondered if its city could withstand sustained aerial bombing. The paper insisted that while L.A. was "simply too big to be destroyed by aerial attack," city fathers and ordinary residents had better begin to beef up their air raid defenses even if raids on the city were unlikely. Citing Hitler's romp over Rotterdam because it had lacked anti-aircraft guns, the *Times*, just by raising the question of internal defense, gave new credibility to the idea that air raids could damage Los Angeles. The Associated Press wondered if citizens of democracies might succumb to "French panic" or "fear itself." "Englishmen have learned how to restrain their fears and stand up to night after night of aerial punishment," the Associated Press reported, but whether or not Americans had the same courage and resilience was unknown.[12]

U.S. diplomats who experienced the Battle of Britain firsthand sent bleak messages back to Washington—confirming that Americans must follow the British lead in setting up home defense. Nazi bombing was so intense, the damage so punishing, that England could collapse and give Hitler a clear path to launch air raids against the American people. Diplomats' eyewitness accounts of the Blitz gave Washington a bird's-eye view of the terror, spurring America's leaders to rally behind a home defense movement. At 7 p.m. on November 14, diplomat James Wilkinson spent hours on a hilltop overlooking Coventry, watching as every six minutes German planes dropped bombs on the city, one of which shook a house near where Wilkinson stood. If Germany built enough bombers, he predicted, the Nazis would destroy the industrial capacity of the British Midlands and deal a blow to England's capacity to stay in the fight. At 10 a.m. the next morning, he drove his car into the city center; over a five-mile stretch, he saw scenes out of Dante's *Inferno*: rubble in the streets, homes in ruins, the homeless, the dazed, and civilians who somehow had managed to stay calm. "If what happened at Coventry last night keeps on happening for a few weeks," then Britain would surrender, he predicted.[13]

London County Council leader Herbert Morrison inspired New York's mayor Fiorello La Guardia, the chief proponent of a militarized home defense program in the United States. La Guardia had a role model in Morrison and used Morrison's experiences to argue on behalf of an American program. In his early fifties,

Morrison was the so-called Lord of London and the home secretary in charge of defending the country against air raids. He drew comparisons to La Guardia; the two men forged an urban, transatlantic, informal security pact. Like La Guardia, Morrison was short, energetic, and aggressive. Leading the struggle to defend London from German bombs, "Morrison," one biographer later wrote, "looks like a lean La Guardia, and Fiorello, in turn, like a paunchy 'Erbert . . . . They run the world's two biggest cities, respectively; each is entrusted with the civil defense of his country, and both hanker after a place in world affairs."[14]

Contradictions defined Morrison's rise to political power. On April 27, 1939, he told a bartender, "Give me a quick drink, and may God forgive me. I've just voted for conscription." He had refused to fight in World War I. But by 1939 he had relinquished his pacifist ideals and become a hardline antifascist. Morrison also cracked down on suspected spies and imprisoned people with few pangs of conscience. He coined the motto, "Go to it," which became a familiar phrase in besieged British cities. Blind in his right eye, he was most at home with fellow residents of London in the midst of danger. Shoppers, messengers, policemen, and news salesmen saw him on the street and waved and shouted, " 'Ello, Erbert!' "[15]

Like a lot of American liberals, Morrison despised Nazis as threats to democratic government and regarded the struggle against fascism in terms of guns and butter, military force, and social melioration. He helped show American liberals that economic liberalism and international antifascism could be a workable unified philosophy. Morrison's controversial approach to home security presaged the debates that would roil America in 1941. He sought to graft the national government's priorities and resources onto a healthy respect for local autonomy and community rights. He wanted the national government to cover the lion's share of home defense costs; under the Air Raid Precautions Act, Britain's Exchequer would pay 60 percent to 75 percent of civilian defense activities, and British leaders would review air raid defense plans in some communities. Morrison consolidated his power, shrinking the number of auxiliary fire brigades from fifteen hundred to forty. He subsidized shelters for the poor, distributed helmets and gas masks to civilians, and rallied Britain's classes in the common struggle against Hitler. He also proposed national rules for shelter behavior and encouraged greater efforts to keep shelters clean. He vowed to "step over [the] heads" of local officials who had refused to tackle these tasks.[16]

At the same time, Morrison tried to foster a healthy respect for local interests. His program emphasized the importance of volunteers and promoted the idea of self-help. He had a way with symbols, linking himself with the common man and woman in the street. He stood alongside thousands of other Londoners and survived nearby blasts while taking shelter with them in the tube. He opened a fifty-foot-deep shelter for ten thousand East End residents. One and a half million British volunteers joined his home defense program. His impassioned cries for home defense and his earnest pleas for aiding the poor earned him the status of Churchill in the eyes of some Londoners.[17]

Morrison was a foe of concentrated wealth. The Blitz hardened his desire to eradicate "the twin pests of extreme riches and extreme poverty." He feared that the social order would crack unless ordinary workers felt more economically secure. He believed that the American people would endorse his combined vision of social and military defense.[18]

Morrison's agenda earned him plaudits among the widening ranks of his admirers in the United States. From some corners, he won acclaim as a defender of the democratic creed. In November 1940, Secretary of War Henry Stimson said Morrison had remade England into "an unconquerable citadel of freedom," and British political scientist Harold Laski wrote in the *Washington Post* that Morrison ranked among England's "supreme administrators." America's critics were as unsparing in their broadsides as his defenders were fulsome in their praise. After one especially destructive raid on London, his detractors said he had failed to mobilize a sufficient volunteer response. Others questioned his statist-heavy prescriptions. In January, he required every male between the ages of sixteen and sixty not in the Armed Forces to serve as a firefighter, bomb-, or fire-spotter, calling it "your duty to yourself, your neighbors and friends, your city and your country." The *Chicago Tribune* assailed his actions as harbingers of a "social revolution as far reaching as [England] has ever known," describing more British "on the government pay rolls than ever before."[19]

America's military and political leaders sent missions to draw lessons from Morrison's experiences on the assumption that those who refused to prepare long in advance would be annihilated. They concluded that from Holland to France to Poland, Hitler's triumphs were as much the fruits of national complacency as Hitler's formidable military might. FDR, La Guardia, and other leaders also assumed that Britain's defeat would make America's cities next on Hitler's target list. In the minds of these officials, terror attacks on America led by the Luftwaffe were plausible scenarios.

These overseas missions would cement the U.S. commitment to building its own home defense program modeled on Morrison's agenda. La Guardia sent two missions to England in late 1940 and early 1941 with the express purpose of preparing New York for air raids. In the fall and winter, New York Fire Department battalion chiefs Frederic Wedemeyer and Daniel Deasy and fireman George Scott conducted a two-and-a-half-month tour of Britain's air raid defenses. When La Guardia's men arrived in London, they visited the city's firefighting headquarters, where they held a news conference. Correspondents asked the American delegation why they had decided to visit wartime England. One fireman replied that the simple answer was, "The pupil comes to the master to learn." Donning steel helmets that British firefighters had given them, New York City firefighters toured the war zone. They hailed their colleagues as heroes. When they returned home, they began drafting a report based on their findings.[20]

The nation's firefighters in general concluded that they had much to learn from the British. "The fire fighters of Great Britain are carrying on the defense of that nation," George Richardson, the secretary treasurer of the International Association of Fire Fighters, told FDR a few weeks after the Blitz began. He assured the president that "fire defense for New York, Washington, Chicago, or any other city" was a national problem that local officials alone were ill equipped to handle. His association passed a resolution urging FDR to make fire protection a national priority and "protect the citizens under modern warfare."[21]

America's police drew inspiration from London's achievements. As the International Association of Chiefs of Police explained, police wanted to learn how England had kept law and order so that America could avoid "the painful process of trial and error." FBI officials visited London and studied Scotland Yard's approach, while J. Edgar Hoover's National Police Academy incorporated British lessons into its training program. From October to February, Hoover sent two assistant directors to report on Britain's home defense setup. His aides wrote more than ten reports based on their findings, addressing such topics as counterespionage, air raid protection, communications, traffic control, and law enforcement. (New York's police leaders hoped to apply Hoover's recommendations to their city.)[22]

La Guardia's second mission, led by Police Captain Donald Leonard, sought to study England's approach to maintaining social order during the Blitz. Leonard was affronted by the horrors he witnessed. During a tour of the city of Southampton, he heard about a British seaman who had had zero communications with his family while at sea. After a six-month voyage, the sailor returned to Southampton, disembarked, and headed straight for his home. His neighborhood had been destroyed. German bombs had killed his entire family. Leonard concluded that civilians were living a nightmare and that "the burden [of security] has fallen squarely on the shoulders of those in the civilian defense organisations." Touring London, Leonard found that almost half of every building in old London had suffered significant damage, and that, despite Morrison's leadership, London's home defense program had its share of woes. Agencies vied with one another for power, officials engaged in jurisdictional disputes, and the program lacked cohesion. Leonard vowed that his analysis of London's setup would assist La Guardia's civilian defense agenda in 1941 and beyond.[23]

FDR's national security advisers sent their own fact-finding expeditions to study civil defense in London. In September, U.S. military officials visited. The following month, Secretary of War Stimson sent aides to study air raid precautions. In January, the secretary of state approved the American Legion's request to visit in order to gain a firsthand analysis of civil defense in England. America's fire officials and law enforcement leaders thought hard about the implications of London for their cities. California's fire marshal Lydell Peck instructed his staff to use London's experience to figure out the best water pumps and tanks for fighting fires. In early 1941, Massachusetts governor Leverett Saltonstall sent an aide on a six-week tour of England to study its Home Guards, and the aide asked Britain's guard leader to help Massachusetts in setting up its own forces.[24]

In the first months of 1941, FDR's focus on diplomacy, winning Lend-Lease, and accelerating the pace of military production gave other national leaders a chance to mount the campaign for home defense. La Guardia quickly filled that role, fashioning himself as the nation's leading advocate for militarizing home defense and preparing civilians to endure war in their own communities. He argued that despite its distance from Europe and Asia, New York nonetheless represented the next front in modern combat, and he assured his constituents that if war came Hitler would attack their city. On January 8, he delivered a hundred-minute stem-winder, appraising New York City's readiness for war. Nazis had New York in their sights, he warned, and the time had come for the city to enact a home defense program. If "we . . . are attacked," he declared, he would need every police and firefighter ready to go to war. He proposed exempting them from the draft so they would be available in emergencies. New York urgently needed "a great deal more equipment in the Fire Department and the Police Department, in hospitals and in the health service." The Roosevelt administration, he pleaded, must send emergency equipment to all coastal cities.[25]

Behind the scenes, La Guardia lobbied FDR. On January 31, he told the president that Hitler's bombing of London had shown how a home security strategy was essential for the United States. He urged the White House to find the funds to organize air raid warning signals, a shelter-building campaign, and improvements to communications systems, and to make plans for mutual aid during national emergencies. "The loss of a city is not local but involves and injures the entire country," he announced.[26]

On February 1, La Guardia delivered to FDR a preliminary analysis with recommendations for setting up a national home defense agency—the first agency of its kind in twentieth-century America. The plan, endorsed by La Guardia's U.S. Conference of Mayors, reflected the thinking of the nation's urban leaders. La Guardia's report painted an Orson Welles vision; just as civilians had fled in fright after hearing the "War of the Worlds" radio broadcast in October 1938, they would similarly panic when the first air raid came. High-explosive bombs, each one weighing more than one hundred pounds, La Guardia predicted, would incinerate New York's buildings and "small and light" incendiary bombs would torch people's homes and offices in uncontrollable infernos. The

Germans would rain bombs filled with mustard gas, chlorine, and "arsenical compounds," and these toxic agents would turn into "a shower of liquid" that would asphyxiate or kill by other means city residents living in tightly packed quarters.[27]

La Guardia wanted a federal civil defense board to organize the defense of urban America. The mayor told FDR that his intention was not to "alarm" Americans by calling their attention to the prospect of air raids. But waiting any longer just wasn't prudent. Montreal, located "just a few minutes by air from the border of New York State," had begun to build shelters along with other cities in Canada; Americans would be foolish if they refused to set up a national plan to defend the cities that were most "vulnerable to attack." La Guardia distinguished home defense from military offense, calling it a form of "passive" defense with civilians playing key roles. He implied that the social order would crumble if the United States refused to prepare civilians to cope with the terror of bombing.[28]

His idea was militarily more ambitious than anything his predecessors had dreamed up during World War I. Established in 1916, the Council of National Defense's initial goal was to strengthen relations between business and the federal government in order to bolster wartime industrial production. But the council failed in its mission because, as historian David Kennedy underscored, its "organizational formula [operating along state and local lines] proved spectacularly irrelevant to the economic character of an industrial nation such as America was in 1917." With industries scattered across the country, organizing the economy for war "along geographic lines" ignored "the new communities of production, distribution, and consumption," and it was bound to fail. The council next assumed a different mission, helping establish approximately 180,000 local defense councils nationwide. The broad goals of these local councils were to give citizens roles in the defense program, and indeed they engaged in pro-war propaganda, harassed antiwar dissenters, rationed food, planted home gardens, and did other jobs deemed beneficial to war mobilization.[29]

The World War I experience inspired some World War II–era leaders to dwell on the threat of sabotage. California fire marshals and Army and Navy intelligence officers attended a conference in July 1940 in which organizers urged delegates to read books by World War II–era German agents such as *The Dark Invader* (about Germany's attempts to disrupt U.S. shipments of goods to Europe). Conference-goers also warned that national security threats included jerry-rigged explosives involving lead pipes, copper, picric and sulfuric acid, wax plugs, and timers, producing bombs that caused "a sheet of intense flame," destroying ship holds and docks, to name two domestic targets. Though fears of fifth columns pervaded America during the last war, home defense leaders in the run-up to America's entry in World War II settled on a far more militarized approach to civil defense than defense councils had adopted in World War I. Defending civilians from air raids became their top priority, even as sabotage, invasion, and other threats were also worrisome.[30]

Working arm in arm, the mayors and the Roosevelt administration would use La Guardia's Civil Defense Board to launch blackout drills; start a shelter-building program; station guards at defense factories; refine evacuation planning; practice firefighting and gas defense; learn how to repair buildings damaged in air strikes; and safeguard the nation's water, food, phones, mail, electric grids, and transportation systems. La Guardia's report suggested that while New Dealers had crafted an effective response to the Great Depression, they needed to improvise and mobilize the federal government and the public to defend democracy from fascism. The problem required a national solution, not a series of local Band-Aids.

He declared that Americans must turn to England for its model policy. Britons taught them that the national government was responsible in peacetime for social welfare and law and order—and in wartime its duties expanded to include defense of lives, property, and freedom from their enemies. In peacetime, governments lit street lamps, demolished aging buildings, enrolled students in school, and provided other services (heat, potable water, sanitation) that made the cities inhabitable. In wartime, democratic government had to rethink its role in the lives of citizens. Officials would need to keep city streets dark; rescue civilians "buried beneath masses of debris"; keep students out of school; and help people with no access to heat, electricity, running water, or sanitation survive for weeks. The Battle of Britain had transformed London into a city that resembled something from the early industrial age. La Guardia's report dismissed any "eleventh-hour improvisation" as foolish. The United States would have no warning that fascists were about to attack. Echoing FDR's rhetoric, La Guardia pointed out that modern "aircraft do not recognize State political boundaries any more than microbes do; and neither do bombs for that matter." The nation's forty-eight states had become "archaic geographical boundaries" and ceding too much power to the states invited a national calamity if war broke out. The cities would be the target; only the federal government had the resources and clout to assist them. Working together, the cities and Washington had no choice but to expand their authority and defend the country militarily.[31]

In a nod to the New Deal, La Guardia recommended that in addition to appointing military and police officials to the Civil Defense Board, FDR should appoint health and welfare advocates, giving it a multidimensional purpose. The board would have morale and human security in its portfolio, assist the White House in its aid of Britain, provide Americans with information on the Allies' war progress, and expand social services. Conservative isolationists lambasted La Guardia's vision of "hostile bombers, scattering gas and high explosives from the Atlantic to the Pacific," as the *Chicago Tribune* scoffed. "Omaha, Little Rock, and Reno take notice," it joked. Evoking some of the handwringing after the Orson Welles–induced panic, isolationists castigated home defense acolytes as "gophers" cowering in their shelters when they heard the blast of a horn or a cloud happened to darken the sun. La Guardia's "poison gas . . . pronunciamento" was calculated to "alarm the citizenry."[32]

The mayor brushed off his critics and depicted civilian defense as a rational step that was squarely within the national interest. In February, he told Midwestern mayors meeting in St. Louis that the odds of an enemy strike on America's cities stood at 3 percent. He warned them to avoid feeling as if they were safe. "Neither the United States Government nor any Mayor can take that 3 percent chance," he insisted. Fascists would launch an invasion of America by softening the cities with incendiary bombs, incinerating homes, businesses, and civilians. Based on his careful analysis of air raids on other cities, La Guardia reported that each U.S. mayor must spend roughly $43,000 to ensure that its fire companies had enough water-pumping equipment and other supplies. New York City actually needed $16 million and Philadelphia $3 million to build their forces. Adequate preparation required funding and national leadership from the White House.[33]

La Guardia's home defense proposal received an airing at the highest levels. FDR's trusted aide Harry Hopkins, who on January 1, 1941, arrived in Britain to report on its war needs for FDR; Secretary of the Interior Harold Ickes, and FDR's fixer Thomas "the Cork" Corcoran ("the liberals," one internal White House document dubbed them) held talks about a "LaGuardia committee," but their views of its purpose were so conflicted "that there isn't much chance of having them work together unless there is some kind of pressure from ON HIGH."[34]

FDR's aides launched a robust debate about the "home defense thing." FDR worried that the policy lacked "ideal programs" and specific goals. His concern had some basis in fact. His aides clashed about the shape of home defense— and which specific lessons they should draw from London's experience. Ickes endorsed morale building as a crucial aspect of any undertaking, and he urged that any new agency should have authority to track the activities of the administration's antiwar critics. Director of the Office of Government Reports Lowell Mellett wanted the home defense setup to build popular support for FDR's national security strategy. The president faced a quandary. When should he establish a federal home defense committee? Who should run it? What would its mission be? How much power would it wield? How would it coordinate with other agencies, states, cities, and millions of Americans?[35]

White House aides treated all of these questions seriously. When Frank Bane, director of the Division of State and Local Cooperation, and Administrative Assistant William McReynolds sought a meeting with FDR on home defense, an official scribbled on February 28 that "McReynolds + Bane OK" and under-neath it wrote "(a) Development in city of fire apparatus; (b) gas attacks; (c) Bomb shelter." Budget Director Harold Smith suggested to FDR that Bane's division be put in charge of mass mobilization of volunteers and community assistance, writing that "we are preparing a draft of an order . . . for your con-sideration." If La Guardia's role in home defense (and the program's purpose) remained in dispute in early 1941, the number of officials involved and the pace at which they worked indicated that home defense-related questions had acquired greater urgency.[36]

Communities across the United States were also pining for action, and the pressure on the White House to adopt a program intensified. Civic groups pressed local governments to take action. On January 4, Washington's Federation of Citizens' Associations adopted a resolution urging the district to acquire "steel helmets, asbestos suits and gas masks" in order to prepare for air raids. On January 21, the American Legion and the Army launched four days of air raid drills in four East Coast states with ten thousand volunteer air raid observers. Popular support for the drills showed the growing interest in home defense among veterans and other constituencies. In one simulation, enemy planes dropped four thousand-pound bombs on New York City, destroying the foundations of skyscrapers and blasting the upper floors with "aerial torpedoes." Members of the American Legion working as air raid watchers stood on the roof of the Empire State Building and other New York landmarks, bringing a taste of war to the nation's most populous city. In mid-February, another quasi-military civic group, American Defenders of Freedom, started training volunteers in air raid defense, holding widely attended classes free of charge on Manhattan's West Forty-fifth Street. Popular opinion gradually began to favor greater preparations to handle air raids on American soil. In New England and the Mid-Atlantic states, 50 percent of residents said they supported holding blackout drills for every town and city in their states. In the West, some 46 percent of the public endorsed air raid drills, and even in the isolationist Midwest approximately one-third of residents supported drilling of some kind. The country was clearly divided on questions of intervention and home defense, but to millions of Americans the prospect of German or Japanese attacks was becoming more real. Those living in rural communities and small towns often reported that they felt "too far away" from the front; they feared, instead, that blackout and air raid drills would cause "hysteria." But millions of Americans felt vulnerable.[37]

On January 15, La Guardia held a private meeting with one hundred mem-bers of his City Defense Council. He had begun to mobilize New York City in the face of federal inaction. The meeting had a wartime aura. Held in City Hall's Council Chamber, some attendees had to circumnavigate police barricades in order to enter the hall. New York's assistant fire chief summarized the lessons his colleagues had gleaned on their home defense tours of London, and the mayor and other officials debated the efficacy of using the city's subways as shelters along the lines of London's Underground. (The War Department's engineers had discovered that some stations were too close to the surface to protect New Yorkers from bombs.) La Guardia discussed the problem of mobilizing seven million residents for war defense.

As if to mark the official start of home defense in the city, the New York Tunnel Authority also issued its pamphlet "If It Comes," which described New York as the nation's "nerve center" and "a tempting target." Lest New York repeat the chaos that Welles's radio show had wrought, "If It Comes" urged New Yorkers to follow their British counterparts: "keep calm"; "walk, never run"; "do not become panicky, and above all, do not permit any one to cause fear." While the pamphlet tried to reassure residents that their lives were almost surely safe, the cover art sent an altogether different message—depicting nineteen bombers scream-ing toward the Empire State Building. In the meantime, the War Department drafted a pamphlet, instructing civilians in basic defense techniques. Military leaders asked Bane's division to publish the pamphlet as soon as possible to sate a public desperate for details about home defense. They wanted three thousand copies for their own staff education, too.[38]

The Blitz also set into motion a little-known debate about the best means of defending Americans from land invasion and Nazi spies. Administration officials examined whether the United States needed a special police force to defend Americans from fifth columnists. One official from the Public Works Administration endorsed setting up a special home police force to uproot Axis agents and stop revolutions from within America. The plan indicated the hysteria that gripped some New Deal leaders. It called on working-class recruits to wear boots, badges, "rubber coats," and "trench hats" and carry pistols, "blackjacks," and "handcuffs" in an emergency. Milwaukee mayor Daniel Hoan argued that the plan contained "political dynamite" that would stir "a tremendous reaction throughout the country which will wind up disastrously to the Administration." Nazi fascists had put a "centralized government . . . [in] control of the constabu-lary forces," and Hoan called it "nonsensical to wage war against Hitler, if we are to adopt his system of government."[39]

In April, the mayors made a final push to persuade Washington that a home security agency had to be established. On April 21, La Guardia phoned the White House. He told Edwin "Pa" Watson that he wanted to talk to the presi-dent about the mayor's upcoming visit to Canada. When he met with FDR the next day, La Guardia notified him that he had a few revisions to the home defense plan and urged the president to enter his ideas and then release it. That month, La Guardia's long-awaited firefighting report, based on his aides' visit to England, appeared in print. Published by the U.S. Conference of Mayors, the eighty-page book featured maps, photos, and drawings and billed itself as an aid to mayors seeking to protect their residents' lives when the United States became a combatant. The mayors were asked to keep the report confidential because only officials responsible for public safety deserved access to it. "Aerial warfare has placed a tremendous responsibility on the cities and their civilian populations," the report declared, citing the British experience. Other mayors agreed with La Guardia that "the fate of Europe can be the fate of America." Chicago mayor Edward Kelly recounted a British officer who described how on the eve of Hitler's invasion, Parisians partied in nightclubs "oblivious of the fate that awaited them." Americans had to avoid that mistake.[40]

April also saw the proliferation of theories about how fascists could attack America. An Army colonel wrote in the *New York Times* that fewer than ten enemy agents had the power to infiltrate a city and "seize a radio station," destroy a subway, disable a power plant, or assassinate city leaders. The colonel had another theory: enemy planes would drop leaflets on Boston and New York (presumably to encourage surrender) before seeking to destroy these cities. He admitted that his ideas elicited "a great laugh . . . in the exuberant security of a cocktail tea anywhere in Manhattan." But Americans who dismissed such theories risked their lives because "stranger things have happened in this war." *Time* magazine acknowledged that an attack on America might appear to some readers "as remote and unreal as an invasion from Mars." But the nation's military leaders knew that foreign attacks were no fantasy and concluded that "even a minor raid might cause catastrophic mass hysteria." Lest Americans forget, "sixty minutes of hokum in an Orson Welles broadcast three years ago" had given the American people "a rough idea of what could happen." By May, FDR had concluded that he needed a national agency, run by La Guardia, based on the British model, to protect lives, property, and defend against the threat of mass hysteria. The Roosevelt administration established the Office of Civilian Defense in May 1941 in reaction to the U.S. analysis of the Blitz and a concerted lobbying effort by America's mayors, police, and fire chiefs—creating for the first time in the twentieth century a federal agency responsible for protecting lives and property from foreign attacks.[41]

A Sweeping Conflagration of Insanity

I say to the Nazis: You can have your Panzer divisions. You can have
your murder of women and children. We refuse to surrender. I say,
come on, come on, come on, we're ready for you.
—Fiorello La Guardia, *"Save-Freedom Rally,"*
Philadelphia, May 28, 1941

On May 20, 1941, FDR sided with the growing liberal conviction that home
defense was no longer an option but a national necessity. He signed the executive order establishing the nation's first Office of Civilian Defense and named
Fiorello La Guardia as its director.

La Guardia had his feet planted squarely in the mainstream of liberal internationalism and appeared at first blush to be a savvy choice for the job. He agreed
with other liberals that Nazis posed a dire threat to American lives, and he saw in
home defense a means of mobilizing millions of ordinary Americans while also
preparing the big cities to cope with air raids and give civilians courage in the
face of the terror wrought by the weapons of modern armies and the strategies
of fascist dictators.

Yet, more than other antifascists of his era, he embodied the most bellicose
strain of liberal internationalism, and he envisioned a relatively new role for the
federal government. As head of the OCD, he sought to infuse military values into
domestic society, stressed that civilian discipline was needed for public safety,
and downplayed the value of individual liberty that most Americans esteemed.
In the spring and summer of 1941, under La Guardia's leadership, some liberal
Republicans and Democrats argued that physical protection trumped other
long-time liberal goals such as union rights, relief for the jobless, access to
health care, and human security for all. As head of the home defense movement,
La Guardia catalyzed the split of liberalism into two camps, in which those seeking to militarize the home front clashed with liberals who favored a robust social
defense agenda. This war within the war divided FDR's political coalition and
accelerated as La Guardia assumed his director's post.

By May of 1941, the timing was right for FDR to set up a federal home defense agency. That March, Lend-Lease had become law, and by spring, the military draft was underway, liberating the president to focus on other war-related concerns. At the top of his list was how to protect civilian lives. Several factors shaped his approach. For starters, military leaders wanted the administration to help teach civilians not to crumble psychologically under acts of enemy aggression including invasion. Army leaders, eager to build up their offensive capacities, wanted civilians to take the lead on home defense, lifting the burden from their shoulders. Navy commanders were hoping that a civilian agency would be given responsibility for defending against air raids, sabotage, and mob hysteria.[1]

Other forces were bringing the issue to a head. One of the president's advisors, Eugene Casey, pointed out to him that establishing such an agency would enable the administration to tamp down isolationist opposition to FDR's internationalism. Home defense, then, became yet another tool in FDR's arsenal for expanding the number of Americans who were comfortable with his policy of aiding the British and other Allies militarily and economically. Equally important, FDR saw air raids, fifth columnists, and other threats as legitimate dangers that could disrupt and potentially destroy the everyday lives of millions of Americans. In confidence, he informed La Guardia that the Nazis could plausibly launch air raids on the upstate New York town of Schenectady and its defense plants. Talk of Nazi threats to the United States proved hard to confirm but even tougher to contain, and such fears coursed through the administration's senior ranks. Presidential pollster Hadley Cantril told FDR that public opinion surveys showed that well-educated citizens believed that in the event of a Nazi victory over the British, the odds of Germany attacking America by the late 1940s were reasonably high. The implication of Cantril's survey was that a home defense program could appease some of the concerns among the better educated, assuring people that plans were in place to defend them in their homes in case of attack. By the same token, Cantril informed FDR that uneducated people saw the threat as less than imminent, and he urged the president to figure out some tools to teach these skeptics that Hitler in fact represented a "radical departure from the democratic way of life."[2]

Even the nation's cultural riches seemed worth defending to FDR. When Librarian of Congress Archibald MacLeish recommended a plan to store more than 500,000 books and documents in boxes in case of air raids, FDR replied that MacLeish should use good box lumber to house the materials. The president was open to MacLeish's proposal to build a tunnel connecting the library to the Supreme Court to help people escape during emergencies. Liberals' fears worsened as the months ticked by; just as they felt that economic chaos could produce riots and social upheavals during the Great Depression, now they were concerned that air raids could topple the foundations of civilization that had maintained order in the nation's cities. A home defense agency offered them a way to mitigate some of these seemingly existential threats.[3]

Finally, FDR and his advisors felt that the war's social dislocations had to be confronted by the administration head-on. After all, Army camps, some of them recently constructed, had one million male residents, with an additional one million due to arrive by December. The strains on civilians during this period were just as hard, as two million people had relocated to find jobs in defense factories, jeopardizing the receiving communities' housing, recreation facilities, sanitation systems, and general ability to care for the migrants. Thus, a home defense agency offered FDR a way to lend a modicum of stability to a society undergoing a wrenching conversion to a war economy.[4]

As if all of these reasons were not enough for FDR, his constituents had begun to apply enormous pressure on him to establish a federal home defense organization that could coordinate activity around the country. From Erie, Pennsylvania, to Crestone, Colorado, veterans, women, business owners, and leaders of civic organizations wrote letters practically begging FDR and ER to give them defined roles in support of the national defense program. Increasing numbers of uncoordinated local volunteer efforts sprouted up around the country, threatening to undermine the entire home defense movement. FDR realized that these nascent groups required more guidance than they were currently receiving. The National Home Defense Volunteers typified the problem. Though they were patriotic, its members clamored for militarized training to defend America; they were so enthusiastic that they sent their photographs and fingerprints to FBI agents in order to weed out any suspicious people from their ranks. Chicago had a home guard trained on how to react when the enemy invaded the United States. As impressive as this passion among the grassroots seemed to administration officials, it also worried them. Chaos was not exactly helpful to a coordinated defense against the awesome might of Hitler's war machine. During a news conference that spring, FDR admitted to reporters that defining home defense was nearly impossible; it "covers so many different things," he complained, and had become "one of the most difficult things to put together in administrative form that I have yet had."[5]

FDR faced a number of unanswered questions about the proposed new agency. Was it going to focus on defending the lives of civilians against military threats? Was its mission to protect public health by trying to thwart epidemics and advance the broad New Deal cause of human security for all citizens? Should its primary goal be to mount a propaganda campaign to generate popular enthusiasm for intervention in the war against the Axis? Finally, should the agency emphasize enrolling millions of men and women to serve as volunteers in home defense roles?

FDR had no answers to these questions, but he had informed his budget director Harold Smith that "we need action" on the problem of home defense. White House aides began to compete to give shape to the emerging plan. ER had long argued that social defense must form the cornerstone of any WWII-era civilian defense agency. But another liberal, Harold Ickes, said that her ideas were "cockeyed," and he feared that ER's recent meddling in setting up the Office of Defense Health and Welfare Services was a mere prelude to her interfering in the home defense setup. In April, FDR asked to see a draft of an executive order establishing a home defense agency, and he assigned William Bullitt, former ambassador to France; Wayne Coy, a White House aide; and Smith to write it. The matter drew input from a dozen senior administration officials including Frances Perkins, the Secretary of Labor; and Henry Wallace, the vice president. Having little appetite for engaging Congress in another bruising battle over yet another divisive war program, FDR and his aides opted for an executive order, following a well-traveled path of circumventing Congress, when necessary, on delicate wartime issues. Robert Jackson, the attorney general, confirmed that setting up home defense through an executive order was indeed constitutional and consistent with FDR's expansive wartime powers.[6]

Conservative isolationists sought to preemptively block the establishment of any home defense program. Believing that some pro-intervention Democrats and Republicans were dragging the nation into another disastrous European war in which America had no legitimate stake, isolationists in the U.S. House stopped legislation that would have required blackout drills to be held in the nation's capital. New York Republican Rep. Hamilton Fish mockingly argued that the threat was so dire that perhaps congressmen should carry gas masks with them, the White House should put sandbags around FDR's home, and wardens stationed atop the Washington Monument should be on the lookout for bombers.

But it was the conservative-business-friendly and liberal internationalists whose voices were ultimately louder and more persuasive in the burgeoning debate about home defense, drowning out their isolationist critics. The *Washington Post* accused Fish of diminishing the very real prospect of an aerial attack on civilians in the United States. And District of Columbia leaders defied the spirit of the congressional vote when they set up volunteer recruitment centers in forty public schools across the city.[7]

Ultimately, La Guardia's views carried the most weight inside the White House. In a four-page memo to the president, La Guardia urged FDR to establish a strong federal department to protect civilian lives that could serve as a fourth military branch. He imagined the agency teaching Americans the "new technique of civilian defense" so that they would be prepared to meet the problems created by a revolution in military affairs, fascist brutality, and the targeting of civilians from the skies. The vision that La Guardia sketched was an ambitious one. He argued that the director should have authority to establish physical protection policies nationwide, while at the same time enlisting millions of civilians into a quasi-military army and assisting the mayors and governors in their home defense planning.

The nature of this war, La Guardia insisted, was unprecedented; it could lead to a protracted national emergency. In prior wars, he asserted in his memo, women were asked to conduct such soft tasks as "community singing, sweater knitting and basket weaving." In World War II, he countered, men must be trained to handle the day when air raids came to their cities. He proposed that the administration enact policies to ensure compliance with home defense orders in all regions of the country. The memo featured a raft of additional proposals: require those rejected from the military draft to join the domestic defense forces; all civilian defenders would take an oath of office, wear designated hats and armbands, learn how to fight fires caused by incendiary bombs, and help their fellow citizens to withstand whatever the enemy was doing to sap their will to fight. La Guardia concluded by telling Roosevelt that he was ready to serve the president in any capacity that FDR desired.[8]

Administration officials showed a draft of the executive order to La Guardia, incorporated his edits to the extent possible "this side of legislation," and won his endorsement. The document, Smith apprised FDR on May 17, was ready for the president's signature. Three days later, FDR signed Executive Order 8757, establishing the Office of Civilian Defense. The order—an amalgam of wartime liberal ideas—fused the desire for military protection of the home front (La Guardia's priority) with the notion of government-led, citizen-fueled social engineering to address the needs of all civilians affected by the war's dislocations (ER's). Specifically, the order featured four disparate goals: protect civilian lives in wartime (La Guardia's chief concern); recruit and train civilian volunteers and fashion them into a home front army (La Guardia's and ER's goals); improve the popular morale by using modern communications tools deployed by the federal government (Ickes's); and provide for Americans' common welfare, shoring up the social foundations in communities with army bases, defense plants, and other places that were feeling the pressures of the conversion to wartime production in particular (ER's).[9]

FDR had taken a bold step: for the first time, the country had established a single federal department dedicated to the physical protection of 130 million Americans, providing for the explicit defense of all 48 states and U.S. territories and possessions.[10]

FDR selected La Guardia to serve as the OCD's first director, and La Guardia was the "logical man for home defense," as one admirer wrote. Nonetheless, he had plenty of detractors. Ickes complained about La Guardia's habit of "run[ning] all over the field with the ball" and questioned his ability to tackle both of his big jobs simultaneously. ER wondered how La Guardia could possibly fit his new post into his already overstuffed portfolio. At the same time, the rough consensus among administration liberals was that La Guardia was the right man at the right time to assume this responsibility. Judge Sam Rosenman, the president's speechwriter, called La Guardia "a mad genius," and FDR saw in La Guardia a blend of drama, military prowess, urban visionary, and liberal loyalist that made him such a strong choice to lead the movement. Having engaged in combat as a pilot during the First World War, La Guardia had unique insights into the perils of air power. As mayor of New York City, La Guardia had a direct stake in ensuring that home defense was a robust, effective program. He was a student of the Blitz. La Guardia, FDR also realized, retained considerable popularity among America's mayors; and he had the requisite passion for home defense, thus enabling him to bring it to fruition. He had a reputation as a leader intolerant of and able to cut through red tape, and his oratorical skills and national visibility assured the White House that home defense would garner plenty of public attention.[11]

La Guardia's would-be competitors for the job paled in comparison to the Little Flower's qualifications. Frank Bane, director of the Division of State and Local Cooperation, lacked the national political clout required to run the OCD. Wayne Coy, as he himself acknowledged, did not have the communications skills needed to handle such a post effectively. Wendell Willkie, FDR's 1940 presidential opponent, was missing the New Deal bona fides that he ultimately would have needed to lead a seemingly significant wartime agency.[12]

La Guardia was the best and boldest choice. Rumors that he was going to be selected started to swirl in the days prior to FDR's announcement of the executive order. On May 17, La Guardia walked down the steps of City Hall with his two children, heading to a Yankees game. When a reporter intercepted them and asked La Guardia if he was going to run FDR's home defense agency, the mayor waved his arms, pursed his lips, and asked if the forecast called for rain. After meeting with FDR in the White House on May 19, La Guardia was asked by a reporter on the lawn outside if he planned to step down as mayor in order to serve in home defense. "Don't you think that is something for the people to decide?," La Guardia cryptically retorted.[13]

FDR wanted to put a strong liberal in the post, and La Guardia fit that bill. The new director enjoyed the support of working-class voters, African Americans, veterans, and urban dwellers, all of them key constituencies in FDR's Democratic presidential coalition. Having built transportation infrastructure in New York City, provided aid to the unemployed, and cleared slums, La Guardia, FDR also knew, was a strong New Dealer, "a stalwart advocate of social reform," in the words of the *Washington Post*. ER did not disagree, and FDR had had his sights set on La Guardia for a federal job for quite some time, considering him for Secretary of War, and even compiling a file of letters from people urging him to put La Guardia on the Supreme Court.[14]

The two men regarded the threat of fascism in similar terms. Like FDR, La Guardia viewed Nazism as a direct menace to American lives and the future of democracy in the Western Hemisphere. La Guardia had made himself one of the more aggressive defenders of the president's interventionist approach to foreign affairs. He had testified before Congress "with all my soul" in support of the president's Lend-Lease idea, joked that Hitler deserved a spot in the World's Fair Chamber of Horrors, assigned Jewish police officers to guard a visiting German delegation, and echoed the president's argument that military technologies had led to a shrinking world in which the United States had grown vulnerable to being attacked by a foreign power.[15]

La Guardia had endeared himself to liberal internationalists with his warnings during the Port Authority's twenty-year anniversary celebration that Hitler had New York City in his sights, and that national preparedness was essential if civilians wanted to avert a calamity. "Imagine what would happen in the area . . . below City Hall if all those employed there should try to leave their skyscrapers at the same time and crowd into subways," he told New Yorkers. People "would be piled eight deep in the streets"; "panic and disorder," he speculated, "might cause more casualties than enemy fliers." He even appropriated FDR's language, urging civilians to join together in support of liberals' "campaign against fear."[16]

The men shared an approach to issues of law and order as well. Increasingly preoccupied with stabilizing society in times of distress and mortal threats, both La Guardia and FDR's law enforcement agencies collaborated in thwarting dangers to their constituents. Hoover's FBI was leading the drive to protect internal security in the United States. During the late 1930s and early 1940s, his agents tracked alleged Nazi sympathizers and built voluminous files on German and Italian immigrants whom they considered potential threats to the home front. Hoover's and La Guardia's complementary missions underscored the extent to which the New Deal administration had morphed into a blunt instrument designed to quash internal security threats. In 1939, La Guardia's police department gave tips to FDR's FBI on guarding six hundred soon-to-be-deported German sailors. The FBI repaid the favor, sending New York police information on German and Eastern European photographers who purportedly had taken pictures of military installations around the city. FDR even asked La Guardia to lend him his police chief for a while so FDR could learn more about the problem of home defense. La Guardia came off to liberals including those in the White House as a crisis manager without peer, as he zipped through the streets of New York in his black Stetson hat, directing firemen battling blazes, and rallying first-aid workers assisting the injured from train wrecks. His mayor's car was even equipped with a radio phone.[17]

La Guardia's response to FDR's offer was never in much doubt; the job appealed to him for good reasons. As the OCD's first director, he would be able to stand squarely in the middle of a great debate about national security politics and policy. The mayor of America's most populous city had a direct stake in ensuring that the home defense program actually kept his constituents safe. The OCD job gave him the chance to work closely with his fellow mayors to build a civilian army to protect America's cities. Fired with a crusader's zeal, La Guardia wanted to use this post to persuade Americans to avert the fate of France and other nations that were being crushed under the Führer's boot. He believed that the American public's ability to fight was distressingly similar to that of the French just prior to the blitzkrieg invasion that quickly overwhelmed a great democracy. Much work lay ahead of him. And it was hardly odd that La Guardia was going to retain his post as mayor while also serving as the OCD's director. Business leaders had become "dollar-a-year-men" in Roosevelt's wartime administration, serving the country in defense roles even though they were nominally functioning as volunteers rather than as full-time, salaried federal appointees. La Guardia believed that his two roles actually reinforced each other and would make him an even more effective home defender, both in New York and across the country.[18]

Upon taking the helm of the OCD, La Guardia gave the president the kind of action he desired. The director ordered more than three hundred New York City workers to participate in a program to distribute food to people during any emergency and vowed that his federal agency would run as smoothly as New York's City Hall. He worked on plans to evacuate civilians and improve defense-area housing. But his focus remained hard for commentators to pin down. Was La Guardia going to prioritize military goals such as shooting down Nazis parachuting out of airplanes? Or was he planning to bolster the public health, improve public housing, and deliver on the promise of social defense?[19]

FDR provided as much momentum to La Guardia's agency as he could muster. He told reporters that the OCD was going to protect America's defense plants and transportation infrastructure, give citizens the tools to assist in their own defense, bolster morale, and do socially useful tasks such as ensuring "that babies get proper food." FDR asked that the OCD target young men who had not been drafted for roles as volunteers, and he directed the Departments of War and Navy to assist La Guardia's mission in every possible way. The president continued to sharpen the perception in the public's mind that the war was inching closer to the continental United States. In late May, after Germany overwhelmed the Balkans with its military might, he proclaimed that America had entered a state of "unlimited national emergency" in which enemies threatened civilians with "hostile encirclement of this hemisphere" and "predatory incursion of foreign agents into our own territory and society."[20]

Not everyone was so enthusiastic about the selection of La Guardia, however. The most oft-heard criticism of the mayor was that it was impossible for him, or any human, to serve as New York City's mayor and America's home defense chief simultaneously. The jobs were simply too demanding, the roles too big. The *Montana Daily Missoulian* published a cartoon that showed three desks— City Hall, home defense, the Permanent Joint Board on Defense—piled on top of one another with the caption, "La Guardia at work." Isolationists were also displeased by FDR's choice, arguing that the new director was going to lure the country into war fighting and impose his dictatorial style of mayoral rule on the rest of the country. When La Guardia "jumps into his Federal home defense uniform, slaps on his national fire helmet, starts gesticulating with a hydrant wrench and sounds the siren of civilian preparedness," Americans had better be ready for an eruption of fear-mongering, one isolationist argued in the *Washington Post*.[21]

But in May of 1941 such critics were still relatively lonely voices. La Guardia was highly qualified to lead the home defense program, Americans concluded, because he had the gravitas, skills, and military qualifications. There was arguably as much if not more praise than condemnation for FDR's selection. A New Orleans–based news outlet called him America's "Home Defense Boss" and assured its readers that just as La Guardia had flown in combat during WWI and still managed to vote on bills pending in the House, he could do his two current jobs at the same time. He defied the "normal limits of human endurance," a Brooklyn newspaper editorialized on his behalf. The *New York Times* reverentially referred to him as "Home Defense Chief" and predicted that La Guardia might become a member of FDR's war cabinet, win authority to ration the food supply, and wield as much power as Britain's Herbert Morrison. La Guardia was variously described as a tough-as-nails fighter (the *Washington Post*), a dynamic leader (the *Los Angeles Times*), and a planner who was capable of training an army of disciplined civilians in home defense (the AP). This outpouring of support was spontaneous, a sign of populist affection for a liberal icon who had just assumed a vast new role leading a key enterprise in the fight to save democracy. Americans from every state sent La Guardia letters endorsing his appointment; one wrote, "You are worthy." His colleagues in city halls formed another source of support, as ninety-three mayors telegrammed La Guardia their congratulations. Civilians sent him letters requesting roles in his quasi-military volunteer program. Liberal leaders such as A. Philip Randolph, the head of the African- American Brotherhood of Sleeping Car Porters, praised La Guardia as a statesman who was an excellent addition to Roosevelt's war cabinet, and Florence

Kerr of the WPA hailed La Guardia as a man capable of mobilizing millions of Americans.[22]

La Guardia left himself little time to think about the OCD's direction. He was fired with the activist spirit of using government and enlisting citizens to provide for the common defense as he now defined it. He began to push the program into areas that FDR likely had never anticipated or necessarily desired. "Bubbl[ing] and sizzl[ing] like a drop of water in a hot frying pan," as *Time* described him, La Guardia depicted the question of home defense in Manichean terms, framing it as a choice between red-blooded Americans who put their faith in democracy and fascists with no moral scruples who were bent on toppling representative government. At a rally in Central Park in front of 675,000 people (reportedly the largest in city history), La Guardia declared that the only column in the United States that mattered was the American column, and that fifth columnists were going to be destroyed. Surveying the country from his new perch in OCD head-quarters, a Washington red brick mansion where Senator James G. Blaine had lived, La Guardia soon had 100 men and women working under him. The timing for the new agency could not have been more auspicious. The American Legion and hundreds of other civic-minded groups had offered to help the OCD fill its ranks with volunteers. More than 400,000 people in Newark took part in a practice blackout, revealing a mass desire to participate in the defense of their communities. La Guardia envisioned the OCD as a way to enlist 2 million vet-erans, 10 million men, and 27 million women as home defense volunteers. He began to craft a definition of civilian defense—physically protecting the home front from foreign enemies through federal action—that surpassed virtually any liberal notion of national security that had come before it.[23]

But it was the bombast of his oratory, and the radicalism of his vision, that transformed him into a firebrand of the first order. His was a voice that, in essence, argued in favor of all-out war sooner or later against the fascist menace. When he appeared at a rally in support of internationalism at Convention Hall in Philadelphia, he inserted himself squarely into the debate between FDR and the president's America First isolationist critics. On May 28, twenty-four hours prior to the holding of a "No Foreign War" rally led by Charles Lindbergh in the same hall, La Guardia went before ten thousand men and women. Rally-goers had sung "God Bless America" with Irving Berlin leading the chorus, watched nurses and veterans march across the hall's floor in a show of strength for home defense, and listened as William Bullitt thundered that the Führer had definite plans to launch a military campaign in the Western Hemisphere. La Guardia ad libbed his talk from "the bottom of [his] heart," as he put it, and he whipped the crowd into a paroxysm of war fears mixed with anti-isolationist fury. The anti-war wing in the country, he declared, had essentially said to Americans, "Let's be careful;" "We're afraid of the Nazis." La Guardia contrasted their cowardice to his own courage and the courage of true citizens. He observed that he was "no better than 130 million other Americans, and I'm not afraid of anybody." He sent a message to Hitler as bluntly and as forcefully as he could. "I say to the Nazis: You can have your Panzer divisions. You can have your murder of women and children. We refuse to surrender." He taunted them to "come on, come on, come on, we're ready for you." The roar of the audience was so deafening that some people in the hall could not even hear the rest of La Guardia's talk.[24]

Wartime liberalism, La Guardia insisted, had to give 130 million Americans the tools to cope with the hardships of a world in the midst of a total war: the habit of discipline, a militarized mindset, and psychological resiliency. Liberals, he argued, had the toughness and the can-do spirit that this moment demanded, and in building a partnership between the government and the people, the liberal philosophy could prepare the public to meet fascist aggression.

La Guardia's vision was frightening to many Americans. He predicted that Nazi bombers could very well fly over the capital soon, and he estimated 5 to 6 percent odds that the enemy would conduct air raids against U.S. soil in the near future. Though the chances might seem low to contemporary readers, they were alarmingly high to some Americans in 1941. The *Washington Post* argued that in 1939, the country had maybe a 1 percent chance of being bombed; by mid-1941, the odds had risen, and La Guardia's estimate was on the mark. The lesson, asserted the *Post*, was that Americans could not afford to risk inaction under these circumstances. To trifle with the threat of air raids was an invitation to catastrophe like nothing the American people had ever experienced. To some particularly bellicose officials, La Guardia's estimates were even too cautious; the chairman of the Bronx City Council charged that La Guardia's lowball predictions were likely to lead to more public complacency than was desirable.[25]

La Guardia's alarmism peaked when he appeared in front of New England officials in Boston in early June. La Guardia took a plane to Boston, hurried through the airport, and "rocket[ed] about his business," in the words of the *Boston Evening American*. He told a meeting of mayors that in contrast to the "singing, sweater knitting, [and] basket weaving" that Americans did during World War I, air raid defense, disciplined action, and a military mindset were the most apt response to the threats of attacks during World War II. He commanded each of his colleagues to a man to think and act as if he was "a soldier, not a mayor." He announced that if the Nazis defeated the British Navy, they would next seize bases that would put them within bombing range of cities in the United States. It was a stark picture: of fires burning out of control, of Americans getting it "real good and hot," of Hitler invoking "schrecklichkeit" in the United States, using air raids to terrorize civilian populations with the hope of breaking peoples' wills. Unlike the tame, amateurish bombs dropped during World War I, the bombs used by fascists "break in the air and . . . just literally [snow] down" on people in the cities; under such firepower Americans could easily form mobs and trample people in, for instance, the narrow, dead-end streets of Boston. Discipline, La Guardia argued, hard-nosed organization, training, and bravery were the answers to the terror that stared every American in the face. Civilians in his army had to learn how to "take orders" and do whatever they were told to do, he said. After all, this war bore no resemblance to "a clambake or pinochle party."[26]

La Guardia's version of national security liberalism featured another controversial plank: in wartime, Americans had a higher duty to act in the spirit of the common defense than in times of peace. His policy recommendations reinforced his message that collective action to assure public safety trumped the rights of individuals to act according to their own consciences. Workers in skyscrapers had to be locked into their buildings in order to prevent them from dashing into the streets in panic. (The 1911 Triangle Shirtwaist Factory Fire, in which 146 garment workers, most of whom were young women, lost their lives due to locked doors, apparently did not factor into La Guardia's thinking.) He warned his audiences in Boston, as he had in New York, that stampedes at subway entrances could leave people in rows "eight feet deep," dying in large numbers. If civilians refused to clear streets and take shelter during air raids, La Guardia declared, they should be prosecuted, fined, and jailed. He had other tips, some small, others large, all of them relying on a government–civilian partnership to militarize life at home for ordinary Americans: He proposed training big city workers as volunteer firefighters and teaching them to handle a chemical weapons attack. He recommended distributing gas masks to fifty million civilians, putting a mobile water pump on every city block, and establishing five volunteer fire brigades for every city brigade. "Pray for me," La Guardia told the *Boston Globe* when asked about the type of support he wanted from the public. He declared that if all of his goals had not been achieved by the middle of August (an impossible deadline), he would resign from the OCD.[27]

La Guardia toured the country, proselytizing with greater and greater intensity. In Baltimore, he urged city leaders to give police the power to train wardens and discussed the defense of rail lines, streets and roads, and water systems. When he arrived in Columbus, Ohio, he urged local officials to write to him with their problems, but emphasized that he had it on good authority that Ohio was within striking distance of Axis planes and that distance did not give Midwesterners much in the way of physical security. Double the size of the city's firefighting capacity, he urged, and use home defense soldiers to defend infrastructure near Columbus. Already, the city was building its nutrition and day care programs, while the state was planning to recruit more than two thousand people into the home defense program.[28]

In the summer of 1941, La Guardia began to assemble a coalition of not just liberal politicians but also military commanders, law enforcement leaders, and ordinary citizens who came to regard a government partnership with the citizenry as the answer to the problem of modern war. Far from intentionally exaggerating the threat, La Guardia believed that the threat was real, and getting worse, and that action now was the only true response if democracy was going to survive its forthcoming trial. In correspondence marked confidential, La Guardia and his colleagues in Washington debated the military situation in and around the United States as if they were military planners in pursuit of a defense strategy. La Guardia asked the Navy secretary for his views of the most imperiled areas in the United States, while one brigadier general in the Army informed La Guardia that America faced the danger of hostile encirclement, a Nazi takeover in much of Latin America, and Nazi-acquired bases for attacking Americans in "Iceland, Greenland and Newfoundland," Brazil, the Caribbean, and Northwest Africa. Japan might attack the West Coast or Alaska, the general further warned. The question of how to defend the home front constituted a terrible problem, the general wrote La Guardia.[29]

Amid these warnings, La Guardia concluded that fascists had an array of options for challenging the territorial integrity of the United States. There was no shortage of threats, in his estimation. Administration officials informed La Guardia's lieutenants in the OCD that the Mexican people were sympathetic to the Nazi regime, while La Guardia confided to Cordell Hull, the secretary of state, that Hitler might launch an invasion of the United States via Latin America. La Guardia believed that these threats were also genuine—and why not? The FBI warned him that enemies were plotting to put bombs at Niagara Falls area power plants, prompting La Guardia to dispatch an aide to conduct an investigation. A culture of militarism pervaded La Guardia's headquarters since the inception of the OCD, adding to the sense that home defense was primarily a problem of military dimensions. Active duty and retired military officers were key members of La Guardia's civil defense team. When one of them, Lorenzo Gasser, the former deputy chief of staff of the Army, entered a room of OCD officials, his colleagues rose to their feet as if they were soldiers honoring an officer of a higher rank.[30]

Reports from London that summer of the terrors visited upon the British intensified La Guardia's desire to erect a military culture of home defense within the United States that mimicked and even surpassed Britain's home security program. La Guardia's representatives in England wrote him about the ordeals of bombing, describing how repair workers had to fix phone lines in sewage up to their necks while fires raged around them. One report warned of possible Nazi plans to use typhoid germs as a weapon against civilians, while another document described bombs so potent that they destroyed homes that stood half a football field away from the site of the blast. La Guardia's bond with Herbert Morrison, his British counterpart, tightened that summer. He believed that Morrison had saved the lives of countless civilians. Morrison returned the praise, telling La Guardia of his delight to know that he was "to do my job in the United States," and that the British island and the United States shared in the challenge of defending the lives of their people from fascist brutality.[31]

That summer, La Guardia used the machinery of modern public relations to begin the hard work of building support for his program and recruiting civilians as volunteers. His PR drive was partly a defense of the administration's effort to sell the country on the likelihood that the United States would become a belligerent. He hired Anna Rosenberg, a close ally of the president who had served as the only woman regional director of FDR's Social Security Board, to handle PR, along with an editor at *Fortune* and a vice president at CBS radio. Soon, they would be distributing booklets about what civilians should do in an air raid.[32]

Eager to plumb the latest techniques in mass psychology, La Guardia consulted with psychiatrists and psychologists for insights into reaching the people with his war message. He came away deeply disappointed that they had so few constructive suggestions to offer. The psychiatrists, La Guardia wrote in a letter to Roosevelt, were "nuts," and he jokingly proposed shooting all of them within the next five years.[33]

Administration officials had few if any qualms about using La Guardia and the OCD to persuade skeptics in the Midwest of the wisdom of FDR's strategy to intervene aggressively on behalf of the Allies. Adlai Stevenson, a special assistant in the Department of the Navy, suggested that La Guardia, in his capacity as head of the OCD, help organize a series of rallies in support of FDR's foreign policy as a counterweight to the entrenched isolationism of the Midwest. Stevenson even suggested that La Guardia use clergy, union organizers, and sports celebrities to lead the rallies, casting the defenders of Roosevelt as dynamic versus the staid and hackneyed leaders of America First such as Lindbergh; Massachusetts Democratic Senator David Walsh; and General Robert Wood, the CEO of Sears Roebuck.[34]

Just as social defense liberals saw the government as an activist force operating in the spirit of charity during the Great Depression, La Guardia and his followers cast it as the lone entity that could effectively provide for the physical safety of 130 million Americans. On June 19, 1941, La Guardia drove home his vision of government action in a statement at New York City police headquarters in which he announced his plan to recruit more than 60,000 wardens using the city's 82 precincts as recruiting stations. His City Hall deployed home guards to protect the city's harbor, readied interceptor airplanes to handle enemy action, and worked with Washington to put 10,000 air raid watchers in position to observe incoming aircraft up and down the Atlantic seaboard.[35]

His hard work began to pay off, handsomely. That summer, on average, 200 New Yorkers registered to become wardens each day, and a reported 25,000 people signed themselves up for duty in a single week. By August, 64,000 wardens were enrolled in La Guardia's program, achieving his goal. La Guardia had mobilized 18,000 policemen in defense of the city, assembled teams of nurses and doctors, found 1 million cars for use during crises, and stashed away blankets and stretchers in case of attack. His use of government to organize people into a quasi-military force was hardly restricted to New York City. He urged other mayors to force their employees to join the ranks of home defense (as he had done in New York), and he recommended that during air raids all police departments be given control over civilian government, temporarily imposing a police state on major metropolitan areas. From his perch in Washington, he began to recruit military veterans, young men rejected from the draft, members of labor unions, and members of fraternal clubs. Heeding his call to arms, the Daughters of the American Revolution and the Committee to Defend America by Aiding the Allies urged their combined 175,000 members to enroll in La Guardia's program.[36]

For all his popularity, La Guardia's use of the levers of power at the federal and city level, coupled with his frenetic bombast, hardened his image as a lightning rod that summer as well. Much was expected from his new agency, but whether or not La Guardia could meet expectations remained uncertain. One government report later criticized La Guardia for neglecting crucial details of his agency's work while at the same time refusing to empower his advisors to do the tasks that needed to be completed. One public relations specialist who tried to talk to officials in the OCD carped that finding "the key to Mr. La Guardia's set-up" was impossible. La Guardia was in charge of the agency but he was also elusive and unavailable for consultation. A reporter toured three of La Guardia's information centers in New York City, but he could not find a single brochure or booklet instructing people on how to protect themselves during air raids.[37]

La Guardia moved at such a fast pace that he failed to focus on the matters right in front of him. His half-hearted attempt to enlist the help of administration official Frank Bane in the OCD was a case in point. La Guardia told Bane during a telephone call that he had heard "from some sources that there is a possibility that you might be able to help me out here for about 60 days." Bane replied that this rumor was news to him. He asked La Guardia a sensible question: "What would you want me to do, how and when?" La Guardia had no answer for Bane. He replied that he was "tied up with the Canadians now" and promised to buzz Bane back at a later date. Bane's response was noncommittal. "Fine," he said, "you call me when you are ready." There is no evidence that the call ever came.[38]

La Guardia, FDR advisor Bernard Baruch remarked, conducted himself in such a spectacular manner that he simply could not "keep his feet on the ground."

He spent most Tuesdays and Wednesdays in Washington; most Thursdays and Fridays in New York; but also traveled across the country, lobbied mayors to adopt his firefighting plans, pushed civilians to conserve war materials, and besieged members of Congress with constant requests for tens of millions of dollars in appropriations for civilian gas masks and firefighting equipment. FDR grew leery enough of La Guardia's frantic style and ceaseless demands that he asked Anna Rosenberg to act as his buffer between the Oval Office and the OCD director. As summer wore on, La Guardia also had a bigger target on his back; conservative isolationists and even some liberals castigated him as FDR's dictator, itching to usher in a needless war on foreign soil and regiment the lives of freedom-loving Americans.[39]

La Guardia brushed off such attacks from New Dealers and isolationists alike, sticking to his script that there was no such thing as overestimating the chaos and horror that attacks on the United States would reap. In August, he wrote in the *Los Angeles Times* that all Americans should realize that in the age of total war the bombs from air raids were equal to the force of "a hundred earthquakes in rapid succession joined with a cyclone and a great conflagration." When Americans came under attack, "clouds of throat-scraping dust and choking smoke" would envelop their cities; buildings would lay in heaps of rubble; a "terror-stricken" people "milling about in frantic mobs" would unnerve all observers. He envisioned civilians "trampling themselves to death in panic" and "fighting friend and neighbor for any conveyance with wheels—and dropping like flies from whistling bomb splinters and tumbling debris." He warned readers to gird themselves for the unprecedented sight of people "bleeding to death, unattended" on the streets; "of traffic, snarled to a standstill"; and "through this frenzied welter of death and devastation stalks the crafty saboteur fanning this panic of a gibbering people into a sweeping conflagration of insanity."

La Guardia believed that a disintegrating social order had ultimately led to the capitulation of Poland, Belgium, Holland, and other Allied nations. He pointed to the example of Britain as his great source of inspiration, his hope that resilience and survival were certainly feasible. The British had prepared themselves well before the bombs began to rain on them, he announced, and that "is our cue." Discipline, passion, and obedience to government authority, he implied, were the kind of wartime liberal values that people had to adopt with speed if they had any hope of keeping the flame of democracy lit, even as the shadow cast by Nazis across the world was growing darker by the day.[40]

Figure 1 Workers digging air raid trenches in St James's Park, London, 1938. As fears of another war in Europe escalated, Virginia Woolf called London "hectic and gloomy and at the same time despairing and yet cynical and calm." Topical Press Agency/Getty Images.

Figure 2 Political cartoonist Rollin Kirby captured the disquietude felt by many of America's leaders, including Eleanor Roosevelt, following reports of panic in response to the "War of the Worlds" broadcast, in late 1938. This cartoon—"What's Happened to the American Mind?"—raised the specter of social disintegration. Rollin Kirby (1875–1952) / Museum of the City of New York. By permission of the Estate of Rollin Kirby Post.

Figure 3 FDR, La Guardia, and ER laugh at a joke en route to the World's Fair in New York City, April 30, 1939. They would soon clash over the direction of home defense—and liberalism itself. Paul Popper/Popperfoto/Getty Images.

Figure 4 Secret Service agents and White House police surrounded Eleanor Roosevelt during the annual Easter Egg roll at the White House in 1940. She feared the war would tip the balance toward security and result in a loss of the kind of openness, particularly at the White House, that she prized. AP, March 25, 1940.

Figure 5 King George VI (center) and Minister of Home Security Herbert Morrison (on left, behind King, with glasses) inspected bomb damage in Coventry, England, in November 1940. During the Blitz, Morrison declared that "Britain Shall Not Burn"; his leadership inspired America's home defense movement. Fox Photos/Getty Images.

Figure 6 La Guardia at a Washington news conference shortly after taking charge as director of the Office of Civilian Defense, May 1941. A few days later, he keynoted a rally in Philadelphia where he sent a message to the Nazis: "Come on, come on, come on, we're ready for you!" Bettmann/Corbis.

Figure 7 On July, 3, 1941, La Guardia was photographed admiring this gift from Herbert Morrison, his British counterpart. La Guardia resembled a "paunchy 'Erbert," one British author observed. Bettmann/Corbis.

Figure 8 The first lady and mayor saw eye to eye on the fascist threat and the need for military mobilization, but disagreed over the value of social defense. Two weeks after this joint radio appearance, he would name her assistant director of the OCD. Bettmann/Corbis.

Figure 9 Eleanor Roosevelt championed protections for children in wartime. Child care was seen as an investment in democracy's future as well as aiding mothers who worked in defense factories. NARA.

Figure 10 In 1941, La Guardia, left, watched as air raid wardens rescued people from a "bombed building." This demo was practice for what the director believed would soon be the real thing. Fox Photos/Getty Images.

Figure 11 Using his car's two-way radio to report an "incident," La Guardia relished war games, including this one held in his city on October 22, 1941. Six weeks later, more than 2,000 Americans would die in air raids on Pearl Harbor. Bettmann/Corbis.

Figure 12 On December 7, 1941, crowds gathered at the White House hours after the bombing of Pearl Harbor. Much to Eleanor Roosevelt's chagrin, the White House would be closed to the public for the duration of the war, although "a man," she conceded, referring to her husband, "must be protected." Thomas D. McAvoy, The Life Picture Collection/Getty Images.

Figure 13 Eleanor Roosevelt, touring the West Coast following Pearl Harbor, held forth with members of a Japanese American Joint Defense Corps in Tacoma, Washington. "Give American born Japanese, and even Japanese nationals who lived in this country for years, who have children and grandchildren and who have bought defense bonds—give them every consideration," she urged. Courtesy of Tacoma Public Library, Richards Studio Collection, Series: D12299-11.

Figure 14 In the mayor's office in Tacoma, the first lady talked with local officials about home defense. Mayor Harry Cain, at right, seated, appeared to be taking copious notes. Courtesy of Tacoma Public Library, Richards Studio Collection. Series: D12299-2.

Figure 15 Civil Defense workers practice cleaning up after a chemical attack in which "liquid vesicants"—mustard gas, for example—were used against New York's civilian population. One government document warned that such agents caused burns to skin and lung tissue. NARA.

Figure 16A On the morning of December 15, 1941, home defense officials conducted an air raid drill in New York City. Above, Times Square before the alarm.

Figure 16B Times Square, five minutes later. Home defense leaders boasted that "in one of the most crowded metropolitan areas in the world, it was possible to stop all traffic, and to get all people safely indoors." Contrary to government spin, however, the drills were often marred by confusion, defiance, and chaos. NARA.

Figure 16C On the same day, in lower Manhattan, air raid wardens demonstrated how they would sweep through Union Square, battling incendiary bombs. La Guardia reportedly was watching this drill. Bettmann/Corbis.

Figure 17 On January 12, 1942, the mayor and first lady welcomed James Landis to Washington upon his arrival to take up his responsibilities as the OCD's new executive director. By the end of February, both La Guardia and ER would be gone. Library of Congress, Prints & Photographs Division, FSA/OWI Collection [Reproduction Number, LC-DIG-fsa-8e10776]. Photographer: Howard R. Hollem.

Figure 18 The first lady testifying before Congress during a hearing on the civil defense program shortly before her ouster. Underwood Archives/Getty Images.

Figure 19 Mayris Chaney, a dancer from San Francisco, with her friend Eleanor Roosevelt. Chaney had been hired by the OCD at a salary of $4,600 per year to lift children's morale by teaching them dance. News of Chaney's appointment touched off a national scandal. Smithsonian Institution Archives. Image # 2009-2477.

Figure 20 In 1942, Landis, hawk-eyed and frenetic, urged Americans to "think war, sleep war, and eat war" and equip themselves to witness firsthand "the grime and dirt and the tragedy of bombing." NARA.

Figure 21 Block captains in Chicago with arms raised in a gesture resembling the Nazis' salute. Anti-New Deal critics feared that mass mobilization under civil defense would enable Washington to trample on individuals' freedom, but the kind of mass discipline and loyalty to government authority displayed here was fully consistent with the liberals' vision. NARA.

Figure 22 Poster on civilian loss of life. Note the signature—*F. H. La Guardia*—at bottom left. The prospect of civilian deaths on U.S. soil was a common theme in the debate about the need for home defense. La Guardia also cautioned against an outbreak of an air raid panic—or, in his colorful description, "a sweeping conflagration of insanity." By permission of the Estate of Rollin Kirby Post.

Figure 23 Three OCD firewatchers on a Detroit rooftop. In a February 1942 press
conference, President Roosevelt made news when he stated that Axis bombers "can come
in and shell New York tomorrow night, under certain conditions. They can probably,
so far as that goes, drop bombs on Detroit tomorrow night, under certain conditions."
NARA.

8

Heart and Soul

If you must voluntarily risk death, the cause is important.
—Eleanor Roosevelt, May 31, 1941

In the spring and summer of 1941, Eleanor Roosevelt believed that she had also won a mandate. She was to serve as the conscience of New Deal liberalism and implement her own agenda during FDR's third term. The American people, she believed, were behind her. She drew inspiration from the masses' words of encouragement and concluded that her vision was consistent with theirs. The most vital of all the nation's values was a community in which every American promoted the commonweal and united. Otherwise, she argued, the country would tear itself apart. In 1940 she formulated her idea of New Deal liberalism and worked to assure that FDR secured a third term. In 1941 she fought to update the New Deal in the hopes of realizing her wartime vision. In September, she would have her best chance yet.

Her dispute with La Guardia over the best way to oppose fascism deepened with the establishment of the Office of Civilian Defense in May. Prizing both guns and butter, ER fought with La Guardia to create social defense roles for volunteers, and her clash with him, which was rooted in ideology, politics, and policy, intensified over the summer. In September, having tired of her criticism, La Guardia urged ER to become his assistant director for Volunteer Participation. Once she joined his team, their disagreements reached a new level of rancor. The fight was much more than just a function of rivalrous personalities. Eleanor Roosevelt had more power (even if most of it was informal) and clout than La Guardia did nationally, and her network of supporters was also more extensive than his. ER's constituents concluded that Americans wanted a government-led effort to make the benefits of freedom more than just an abstraction to the people. The political winds were blowing in fierce gusts against the first lady in mid-1941, however, and often in ways that she did not fully recognize. Congress and the White House were refusing to elevate such issues as poverty and jobs to the top of the national agenda, and the New Deal legislative program had increasingly become an unloved orphan among many presidential aides. Even FDR no longer championed it as he once had.[1]

To be sure, ER endorsed the things that were then being done to prepare Americans to fight a war. She had not changed on this score. She started to lionize the men in uniform. Eager to see the mobilization with her own eyes and honor America's soldiers (all four of her sons ultimately joined the military), she left Mobile, Alabama, at 4:45 a.m. on April 2 in a car driven by a Secret Service agent. When she arrived at Fort Bragg in Fayetteville, North Carolina, she toured the base, hailed the courage of the soldiers, and praised the entire enterprise and the spirit of patriotism that she saw vividly etched on the faces of the men in the camp.[2]

Reminding Americans that they needed to steel themselves to meet the crisis, she also was aware that the nation stood at the brink, and felt like violence was in the air as she moved around the country. In April, when she attended her son Jimmy's wedding in Los Angeles, she lamented that he had a mere forty-eight hours of leave before he had to return to his destroyer and ship out on a perilous mission. Her Secret Service detail had been beefed up on her trip due to an unspecified death threat. When she drove the coast of Maine later that year, she commented that the brilliant blue skies and billboard advertisements for lobsters hid the fear residents felt that they could be bombed at any time.[3]

While she had criticized conservative Republican and left-wing isolationists in recent years, her campaign became a more blistering assault on the tenets of their faith in mid-1941. She said that if Americans buried their heads in the sand, they would be handing the Nazis an invitation to attack. In mid-1941, she depicted Rep. Hamilton Fish as a buffoon for claiming, in essence, that the fighting in Europe had no impact on the lives of Americans. In fact, she countered, if Hitler were to destroy the British Navy, then Americans were going to have to fight the Nazis virtually alone.[4]

In June 1941, Hitler launched Operation Barbarossa and invaded the Soviet Union. In July, President Roosevelt announced that the United States was going to freeze Japanese assets, but his modest step became a total embargo on trade with Japan when administration officials misconstrued his order. Denied access to American oil, Tokyo's military leaders decided that they had to strike in oil-rich parts of Asia before they ran out of fuel and before the United States built its navy and gained naval superiority in the Pacific. ER understood that in this climate numerous liberals were fighting to mobilize the country militarily. She concluded that her best contribution to defense was to work with citizens to provide social and economic benefits to people who had been left out of the reforms achieved during the 1930s. Now, she more explicitly tied the cause of military readiness to social progress, arguing that malnutrition, venereal disease, and substandard housing threatened people's morale, the pace of industrial production, and the ability of the Army to field a combat-ready force. Hundreds of young men had already failed their military physicals and more than two-thirds of the youth she saw during a tour of a North Carolina National Youth Administration camp were undernourished, making her wonder how a people so physically debilitated could be asked to challenge the mighty armies arrayed against them.[5]

Her answers to such questions acquired new specificity in the summer, and she did her best to implement them. She proposed that defense areas establish elementary schools, recreation centers, housing, and sewers to ensure that the people's needs in these zones had been fully addressed. As demands of the war industry crowded out the debate about how to achieve a just democracy, she also searched for arguments that would make the pursuit of "butter" more politically palatable. She revived her proposal that all women must be required to perform national service, a plan, she argued, akin to Thomas Jefferson's idea of mandatory education for all children. Her program would give women the skills to make them competitive in such male-dominated professions as law and politics, and it would lift some women out of poverty, while teaching mothers simple knowledge that, for instance, they should not be feeding breakfasts of pancakes and cold coffee to their toddlers. Although critics called it a quasi-fascist proposal (her proposal went nowhere), she was able to mostly ignore her fiercest detractors. She dismissed them as reactionaries who tended to march to the beat of their hidebound worldviews.[6]

The first lady had never run for elective office, of course, yet by the spring she had developed her own political following. With constituents by her side they formed their own alternative movement that challenged the dominant strand of national security liberalism that was ascending under FDR and La Guardia. No group was more important to ER's cause than women. When she stood in the White House and shook hands with 1,750 female administration officials, she praised them as the main reason why the federal government was such a force for achieving progress in people's daily lives. Women admirers wrote her requesting that they be given roles in the defense program. One informed ER that her "man" had joined the armed forces and that she was no longer content to do "the things that I have always done" and simply stay in the home.[7]

The Executive Order establishing the OCD did not give ER the "Social Defense Administration" that she and Kerr had long desired. Still, the document, contrary to some news reports saying the New Deal was on life support, was not a death knell for social defense, either. The order called on the OCD to mobilize millions of Americans to serve as volunteers. It sanctioned the idea that human security was a vital element in national defense, giving liberals a chance to make the case for social welfare in the war program. It was up to ER to use the order's language and the OCD's machinery to implement social defense in communities nationwide.

Regarding her as a great champion of social defense, ER's allies demanded that FDR give her a formal role in the wartime agency. They hailed the first lady as an inspiration to all women who had to launch them on a crusade on behalf of democracy. Florence Kerr, for example, urged the president to give ER the job of leading "women, if not all civilians, in the Volunteer Participation Committee for Civilian Defense," and she reminded La Guardia that "no one else can inspire the women of the country as Mrs. Roosevelt can." The first lady's "activities, her devotion, and her service to communities and people everywhere [and] her continuous example" had made her the best person to assault "the problems of home defense in every community," Kerr added. Harriet Elliott, who ran consumer protection for the administration and was also close to the first lady, urged that FDR name ER to the OCD's Volunteer Participation Committee. FDR cryptically replied that Elliott should broach the idea with La Guardia.[8]

La Guardia found the level of support that ER had hard to resist. In May, he asked her to lead the OCD's effort to recruit women in volunteer roles. She declined. She wanted the OCD to have a chance to find its sea legs. She worried that if she were to join the agency, New Deal critics would be able to attack the president and denounce her for subordinating the nation's military priorities to social experimentation. For the moment, ER preferred to use her White House platform to pressure La Guardia into recruiting a civilian grassroots movement that fostered community action. She described how listening to the president at a press conference inspired her to do her duty as a citizen. The goal of liberalism, she argued, was to understand that "it is our freedom to progress that makes us all want to live and to go on" and to pursue that goal even as the country prepared for its military defense.[9]

The first lady's vision began to shape the political culture, promoting an impression that social defense was the right idea at the right time to meet democracy's war needs. Some of the first lady's admirers amplified her faith that social defense had to animate any effort to fulfill FDR's vision of a "great arsenal of democracy." *The Philadelphia Record* declared that home defense also meant social security for average families. White House Secretary H. H. McIntyre urged an acquaintance to tell La Guardia to give women key roles in home defense. Montana Rep. Jeannette Rankin asked La Guardia if he was planning to give women ample opportunities to serve in non-protective jobs. Even FDR lauded military preparedness coupled with the "spiritual, recreational, and welfare needs" of the public as twin goals of war mobilization. He sent ER a letter describing the contributions of British women to the home front and asked that she read it and then send it to La Guardia. At the same time, New Dealers in the administration such as Florence Kerr tried to frame their New Deal programs as beneficial to national security, praising ER for grasping "what the school lunch and housekeeping aide projects have meant to thousands of American families" and why social programs would stabilize society and weaken the fifth column of economic inequality during a war.[10]

La Guardia's early actions and oratory showed the first lady that he disputed her definition of home defense. She figured out that La Guardia was ignoring the most liberal aspects of FDR's executive order, shortchanging social democracy. She managed to collaborate with him and NAACP executive secretary Walter White and the president of the Brotherhood of Sleeping Car Porters A. Philip Randolph in negotiating Executive Order 8802, which established the Fair Employment Practices Committee (FEPC) banning racial discrimination by defense contractors and the federal government. The landmark measure fell short of what civil rights leaders had originally sought, including an end to segregation in the military. But the FEPC became the first federal agency set up to protect civil rights in the twentieth century. From ER's vantage point, even this modest success by La Guardia was hardly sufficient evidence that he was devoted to social defense. One of the break points for ER happened when La Guardia asked her to serve as a judge of women's uniforms for the OCD. As the models paraded past the first lady, she concluded that La Guardia had his priorities backward. She declared in one of her columns that the OCD's director should explain the kind of jobs women were going to have before he figured out what clothes they were going to wear.[11]

La Guardia appeared incapable of working with her to satisfy the pent-up demand from women seeking roles in home defense. Thus, she began to champion her vision of what the OCD should be without much coordination with La Guardia. In the capital, she and Elinor Morgenthau, the wife of the Treasury Secretary, helped register thousands of volunteers, prompting criticism from La Guardia who said he first needed to decide on their roles before they could be recruited. ER sanctioned the actions that she wanted to see instituted nationwide. She singled out home gardens, food aid to the British, consumer education, and a conservation campaign that netted fifteen million pounds of aluminum as examples of grassroots democracy at its finest. ER called herself a typical mother who worried about her sons in uniform and insisted that her anxieties were the same as those of any mother in America. Increasingly concerned about the problem of popular morale, she also saw home defense as a chance to imbue Americans with a spirit of hope to counter the anxiety precipitated by the crisis. She asked FDR to use the OCD to propagandize about the virtues of democracy to the peoples now forced to suffer under Nazi rule.[12]

Although La Guardia took tentative steps in ER's direction during the summer, the first lady remained dissatisfied with the pace of his action. In the hopes of muting her criticism, he agreed to create the OCD's Volunteer Participation

Committee and appointed her allies such as newspaper editor Jonathan Daniels and Ellen Woodward of FDR's Social Security Board. Still, she wasn't appeased. ER arranged a meeting for Participation Committee members in the White House on July 24. She had no faith that La Guardia could lead it effectively. She urged FDR to give a talk to the group in which he praised volunteer participation and endorsed social defense roles for all citizens. ER warned FDR that if he did not do this, then La Guardia "will not do much with his volunteers."[13]

The president delivered off-the-cuff remarks at the meeting in which he channeled the first lady's ideas. He told committee members that while the OCD was a significant military asset (placing sand bags to protect buildings, blowing sirens to alert civilians to danger), it was also the basis for recruiting a civilian army fundamentally democratic in character that would respond to the "amazing number of letters" the White House had received from citizens in "literally every County in the United States." The people, he said, yearned to do their part during the national emergency. The president remarked that "we can't do it all from Washington" and urged volunteer leaders to show their fellow Americans how the war overseas had a direct impact on all of their lives. La Guardia also addressed the group, paying tribute to volunteer participation and thanking ER for her leadership. Still, the first lady remained dubious. She did not think that he was committed to using civil defense to strengthen American democracy. He was, she felt, paying only lip service to her ideas.[14]

As the tensions between them rose, the volunteer program was actually beginning to gain momentum. By summer, more than 2,500 defense councils and more than 90 training programs had been established. Florida aimed to recruit 250,000 volunteers; San Francisco officials made plans to set up public feeding centers in case of emergencies. ER's allies grew bolder, stressing the benefits of social defense to national morale. Public relations expert Anna Rosenberg praised ER for seeking to improve the national spirit, while the first lady's ally Mrs. Gifford Pinchot advocated for the appointment of New Dealer Oscar Chapman (a frequent White House dinner guest during the 1930s) to run a morale project under La Guardia's agency.[15]

Liberals kept up the pressure on La Guardia. Kerr offered to assist the OCD, and she rued La Guardia's intransigence, complaining that he had refused to let her do a single thing. Some Midwesterners recommended that La Guardia stress social action over air defense as the signature priority for their region. The news media reported that La Guardia was also making scant progress in recruiting female volunteers. In August, dissatisfaction with La Guardia surfaced during one of the first lady's press conferences. Asked to give her views of the OCD, ER replied that home defense still had far to go before it met the demands of citizens clamoring for roles. The media pounced. Her comment, some claimed, was the clearest distillation yet of her growing disenchantment with La Guardia's leadership.

ER sought to stop the tempest, with little luck. She argued in a "My Day" column that even La Guardia agreed that the volunteer program should be bolstered. She also wrote a semi-apology to La Guardia, telling him that she only meant to say "that we are not fully launched on a real program" and knew "that you feel as I do, that we have a big job ahead of us and are only just getting started."[16]

The criticism of La Guardia's inaction did not abate. The *Washington Post's* Ernest Lindley reported that the first lady's remarks reflected the growing dissatisfaction with La Guardia in high administration circles. When ER criticized La Guardia during a meeting with him and youth leaders at the White House, La Guardia decided that he could no longer tolerate her incessant backbiting. After the meeting ended, he stopped ER on the front lawn of the White House. Jabbing his finger in the air, he told her, as she, the taller of the two, towered over him, that "the criticism of 134,999,999 wouldn't touch me. Yours did." He offered her a job leading the OCD's volunteer participation division and promised that he would ask the president to approve his proposal.[17]

ER had been hoping for a formal role in the administration for years. While she remained hesitant about taking the job for all of the reasons she expressed in May, she concluded that this time, she had no choice but to accept it. For months, she had voiced doubts about La Guardia's stewardship. By joining his agency, she could fill the void that La Guardia had created and do so from a position of strength within a key wartime program. She continued to worry that colleagues might take umbrage at her position of power by dint of her relationship with the man in the Oval Office. But she banked on the fact that she could focus on the work, excel in her post, galvanize the public, and blend into the burgeoning wartime bureaucracy as best she could. Even though she expected anti–New Deal critics to exploit her role to diminish the president's foreign policy, she was not going to let reactionaries dictate her efforts on politics and policy.

The terms of the offer also made it irresistible for her. La Guardia promised her that she could run her division without his interference. "Frustrated because many of the liberal programs had to be put aside," as Anna Rosenberg had put it, ER saw this job as a way to restore some liberal programs to the center of the debate about the home front. In addition, "from all sides [she] had complaints about the lack of progress" that La Guardia had made, as she wrote a friend, and felt her duty was to "push things along." FDR refused to stand in the way of the idea, deciding, for his own reasons, that the appointment was a net benefit to him and his war program. Rather than running all over the place on an array of issues, ER would be able to channel her energies into a single mission. He figured that, as a leading liberal, ER would rally her supporters behind his war policies, even if they were disenchanted with his inaction on New Deal social welfare policies.[18]

The first lady's ambitions for transforming domestic life matched La Guardia's. She hoped that civil defense would strengthen the character of American democracy. She told La Guardia that by working together they were going to achieve two goals: "the participation of every individual throughout the country in a volunteer job who is able to do so" and making "volunteer jobs useful to the communities." Her staff, she informed La Guardia, should be told that her orders were final; they did not need his seal of approval. But there was nothing very clear about her role in the OCD, and it foretold a struggle with La Guardia over what it meant to be a liberal in a time of military crisis.[19]

While playing with her grandson on September 14 in Hyde Park, ER received a phone call from Franklin, Jr. He told her that his destroyer had safely returned to its port in the United States. The next morning, however, she learned that the health of her fifty-one-year-old, alcoholic brother, Hall, who had liver disease, had worsened. Boarding a train, she headed to Washington, where Hall was hospitalized. On the train she noticed a newspaper headline announcing that La Guardia had officially appointed her to the OCD. There was no turning back. Her allies were elated. ER's California supporter, Congresswoman Helen Gahagan Douglas, wrote the first lady that word of her appointment gave her hope for American democracy. Although she was slated to start her job on September 22, Hall's deterioration and then death on September 25 caused a delay. Hall, ER mourned, "could have had much more out of life," but his disease had robbed him of that chance. She held a memorial for him in a small ceremony in the East Room of the White House. Now more than ever, her work in the OCD beckoned to her. "Probably the best thing that can happen to anyone at a time of personal loss is to be drawn back to work by a job that has to be done," she reflected, and she likened her job to a balm that would help her absorb her grief and regain a sense of purpose.[20]

On the cusp of becoming the only first lady in history to hold a formal job in a presidential administration, the reality of her appointment came into sharper focus. She worked with neither a script nor a guidebook as she approached her role; the administration sought to make her appointment as ho-hum as possible. The White House Office of Emergency Management sent the first lady an appointment letter that included information about her start date, her salary (zero), and her per-diem ($10). She was asked to sign the letter, return it, and take her oath of office when she arrived at work on her first day. On a roster of OCD employees dated September 17, the words—"Mrs. Eleanor Roosevelt," "Asst. OCD Director"—were written in hand; officials decided that she was going to be seen as simply another member of the agency's growing staff.[21]

All the attempts at normalcy could not contain her excitement at serving in the OCD or disguise the fact that a first lady was also becoming an assistant director of a wartime agency. She had "a gleam in her eye and a sparkle which has been absent for a long time" whenever she discussed her job, her son-in-law remarked. Her position, she felt, would enable her to give birth to a better democracy grounded on greater equality and economic prosperity, fulfilling progressive dreams dating back to World War I of tying war mobilization to the attainment of social progress at home. Under her leadership, what historian Richard Hofstadter called "the Age of Reform" was going to accelerate and deepen as liberals navigated the politics of military preparedness to keep progressivism moving ahead, all of its pistons firing in unison.[22]

At 3 a.m. on September 22, ER rose from bed and worked until 6 a.m., putting her goals for her new job on paper. Minimizing the obstacles confronting her, she set mid-November as a deadline by which she wanted to achieve her goals. She studied the agency's organization; pledged to recruit women, youth, and minorities to the OCD; talked to aides Jane Seaver about the role of youth and Eloise Davison about mobilizing women; and persuaded Elinor Morgenthau to become her chief aide in the Division of Volunteer Participation. She asked all employees to send her their titles, roles, and salaries. Henceforth, all drafts of letters had to be reviewed by her secretaries before the close of business. She announced that all new plans required her approval. Such procedural reforms were intended to give her the power she needed to push her wartime New Deal into every community.[23]

Staff looked forward to her arrival with a great deal of excitement. On September 27, Anna Rosenberg, La Guardia's PR aide, informed ER that social services would soon be established in southern states, volunteer efforts were going to be concentrated in impoverished regions, and liberals would be urged to achieve a better life for all. Hopeful signs seemed to surround Eleanor Roosevelt's every step. Walking to the OCD's new headquarters in Dupont Circle on her first morning, the first lady was stopped on the street by a young woman from California who told her that she had "always wanted to shake hands with you." ER shook the woman's hand. The woman beamed. ER felt that the encounter demonstrated that the public was going to be with her in this fight. Wearing a black dress and pearl necklace as she entered headquarters, she went to the ninth floor to find her office. Piles of papers and files were strewn on the floor, and she noticed that her office had two desks (one for Elinor Morgenthau, her close aide), a fireplace, and a red carpet. Some employees were hard at work at their desks. The morning brought a flurry of activity. She took the oath of office as La Guardia looked on, met with her staff, and dashed back to the White House where she held a press conference with Harriet Elliott, highlighting the public health, old-age assistance, and pre-school policy challenges that topped their shared social agendas. Lunching with her allies Eloise Davison, Wilma

Shields, and her trusted secretary Malvina Thompson, she plotted strategy for launching a program of mass mobilization and social defense, in which a citizen-powered, grassroots movement would be established and led by the Roosevelt administration.[24]

Her duties imposed new pressures on her time and energies. Leaving the OCD's offices, she carried "armfuls of mail" back to the White House, read letters late into the night, and scribbled her "hieroglyphics" in the margins that her secretaries were somehow expected to decipher in the morning. When she pulled an all-nighter, the president was informed that the first lady's office light was on all night, prompting him to question her already stretched sleeping habits. "You didn't go to bed at all last night?" he asked her. Impelled by her quest to shore up wartime morale, mobilization, and social benefits, she faced hurdles that any New Dealer would have found daunting. ER had to figure out how to have "the Washington office . . . reach down into the local communities," as she put it. She had to collaborate across agencies in a time when the wartime bureaucracy was ballooning, and she denounced self-promotion, interagency feuds, and power struggles as inimical to the nation's war objectives. Roles for volunteers had to be defined and coordinated. State leaders, who abhorred what they perceived as La Guardia's neglect of their needs, had to be appeased. And home defense officials in the nine regions into which the Army had divided home defense had to feel invested in what New England's director termed the "general up-lift aspects" of Eleanor Roosevelt's agenda. The problem, New England's leader added, was that "you people in Washington" had muddied "the lines of communication and responsibility" and failed to coordinate on social defense issues.[25]

ER also confronted the tension pitting local interests against New Deal priorities. One member of Congress informed the OCD that a member of Los Angeles's defense committee "was one of the most reactionary individuals that I have ever know[n]" and would be an obstacle to the first lady's agenda. While some states (Arizona, Pennsylvania, Florida) had found able women to run social defense programs, others (Idaho, North Dakota, Arkansas) had not, La Guardia's aide T. S. Walmsley notified the first lady.[26]

ER intended to use every available tool to overcome these stumbling blocks. She brought unparalleled visibility to her cause. With a syndicated column, a weekly radio broadcast, a weekly press conference, and her army of followers, not to mention her direct line into the Oval Office, Eleanor Roosevelt assumed her role as one of the most admired and controversial women in America. Her bully pulpit and constituency made her more politically powerful than even La Guardia. In the fall, La Guardia impressed people as a divisive figure, while ER arguably enjoyed greater popularity. As her aide Paul Kellogg cooed, the first lady had the capacity to turn the OCD into "a yeasty force" for social progress and wring "order out of a very tangled [home defense] skein." Her hires—liberals such as Hugh Jackson (former leader of New York City's Department of Public Welfare); Mary Dublin (an expert on defense communities' needs); Molly Flynn (a leading welfare advocate); and Judge Justine Polier (on leave from the court to help ER assist needy families)—reflected an eclectic team of New Dealers determined to help her realize her vision. She mobilized the Volunteer Participation Committee, urging its members to do more to recruit volunteers and pressed OCD's leaders to make the agency more efficient. She moved with such speed in so many directions that she caused consternation elsewhere in government when her office produced a nutrition chart that more or less copied one created by the Federal Security Agency. At the same time, she retained a loyal following. While La Guardia fired members of his team on mere whims, chastised aides, and was often away from headquarters and unreachable, the first lady invited OCD aides to film-viewing parties at the White House and solicited their input on the "reasons why we are all at work," lifting employees spirits.[27]

Her sense of her own power deepened, and she was unafraid to wield it. The first lady persuaded the administration to fund a program providing health care to pregnant women and children, applauded efforts across the government to step up mass mobilization, and enlisted the OCD's regional directors in her volunteer campaign. She declared that she was eager to put "little pins into that map [on her office wall] as each one of our volunteer bureaus is established," anticipating centers popping up across all nine regions. "I believe that you have to be for something if you really want to accomplish a great deal," she wrote, adding "that all the young people, as they come into civilian defense work," had to "constantly [bear] in mind the fact that they are building for the future." Her message resonated with her supporters, including thousands of women eager to serve as war volunteers. A New York State assemblyman praised the first lady for her fight to give women economic opportunity as part of home defense.[28]

By the fall of 1941, she had refined her core message, which she worked hard to put before the public. As PR counselor George Lyon wrote in a memo to her on October 2, she needed to persuade citizens that the pursuit of health and economic security was a way to "make our country strong" and that every civilian deserved to have access to volunteer roles and do the kind of "work they wish to do." To reach the masses, the administration's PR experts advised her to use films, pamphlets, and posters. She and her advisors also relied on the mainstream media to persuade millions of citizens to participate in community action.[29]

Although ER distrusted some of the news media (she saw reporters as scandal-mongers who were eager to exploit divisions among political leaders), she and Morgenthau concluded that publications could spread their message to citizens in dramatic and galvanizing ways. Morgenthau suggested that ER find three socially conscientious reporters who were willing to write articles that would underscore how mobilization disrupted life in communities and why defense areas had to have more "entertainment, recreation, housing facilities, health . . . [and] schools." Reporters were urged to write articles on the plight of single women, particularly the unemployed and those who had relocated to take jobs related to the war but had nowhere to live. Morgenthau wanted the media to "dramatize and publicize" the need to establish "communal kitchens, school lunch programs, gardens," and recreation centers, and ER agreed that by stirring the pot of popular rage, political leaders and the American people would be more willing to attack festering social woes.[30]

ER used the news media and PR stunts to disseminate her agenda to the public, and her aide Eloise Davison proposed that rallies feature music, film, and radio celebrities who would lead the audience in calisthenics, luring citizens into the volunteer program. Self-help guru Dale Carnegie was brought into the OCD's Speaker Bureau to edit speeches, demonstrating the intensity of the public relations campaign launched not just by ER but also La Guardia and their colleagues in the fall of 1941.[31]

ER increasingly considered La Guardia the greatest obstacle blocking her agenda. She saw him as bellicose, haughty, frenetic, and aloof. He was shoving the programs he disliked into her division, she decided, and his infamous characterization of social defense as "basket-weaving, dancing in the streets, and community singing" especially rankled. True, the Little Flower praised Davison for speeches highlighting the importance of recruiting women volunteers and encouraged women (regardless of race) to join the OCD's grassroots campaign. He hailed the women of England for their displays of courage. He even quoted Eleanor Roosevelt directly when the occasion suited his purposes. But their views, styles, and temperaments were too different for them to reach a mutual accommodation. Over dinner with FDR and Harry Hopkins, ER joked with them about the director's childlike fascination with firefighting, as if he were a little boy playing at war. La Guardia, she felt, pursued melodrama over substance to the detriment of morale-building, and his frantic approach grated on her nerves. While their relationship had been relatively amicable, it frayed during their time together in the OCD. From his viewpoint, home defense was not community action serving the needy but military preparedness meant to blunt Hitler's brute force.[32]

Going it on her own, the first lady campaigned to highlight the diversity and scale of the nation's social needs. She called attention to how volunteers could shore up democracy, bringing her message to a range of audiences. On a tour of a Service Men's Information and Recreation Center in Chicago, she praised the social work and volunteer recruitment efforts she witnessed there. As wet snow blanketed the ground, she toured eight elementary schools in St. Cloud, Minnesota, and was delighted to see children lining the cold streets just to get a glimpse of the first lady. She felt she had so much to do in such a short time. She was tireless. One evening, she took an overnight train from New York, break-fasted with friends after arriving at Washington's Union Station, and passed FDR in the White House without pausing for conversation because she had to head straight to the OCD's offices. Signs continued to suggest that for all of her agency's problems, she was making progress in mobilizing the masses, particularly women. Regional directors seemed open to doing more to recruit volunteers, and an estimated four million veterans were available to serve as volunteers in home defense; participation was becoming rooted in the political culture. The *Washington Post* reported that thousands of women had registered for service to bolster the well-being of the capital's residents. And once women began to join the ranks, ER tried to design insignia and uniforms for her volunteers.[33]

Her campaign's high-water mark occurred during a conference she had organized in early November attended by 67 women's organizations (representing 25 to 30 million members). She called it the most interesting one she had ever attended. It featured a call to mobilize women and enact social defense. Held in the Department of Labor's auditorium, the guests heard from the first lady, who stressed that volunteers had to bring social benefits to their communities. ER and Anna Rosenberg prevailed on La Guardia to liken "disease, bad housing, and lack of proper nutrition" to the Nazi war machine and characterize volunteer participation as "every-day jobs of seeing that our people are well housed [and] well fed." Citizens, keynoter Archibald MacLeish said, had to pursue a shared goal of achieving better nutrition, worker protections, and access to health care, designing a "secular religion of democracy." Harriet Elliott discussed consumer issues, Martha Eliot spoke on children's health, and the Secretary of Agriculture dwelt on nutritional security. And Davison, eager to protect ER politically, recommended that the first lady avoid having her photo taken with union members, "colored groups," and the American Women's Voluntary Services so New Deal critics would be deprived of ammunition that they could use to link left-wing radicalism to the civilian defense agenda. Davison called the event a clear demonstration of "women-power."[34]

Their momentum accelerated during Civilian Defense Week in mid-November, a national celebration approved by the president to recruit volunteers and sell people on the merits of home defense. ER described civilian enlistment as a campaign to liberate Americans "from want and fear." She signed up volunteers for home defense at Dunbar and Woodrow Wilson High Schools in Washington, D.C., toured a home defense exhibit, and sought to enlist 4.5 million women volunteers, including 500,000 trained nurses and 300,000 nutrition experts. She argued during the week-long pageantry that while World War I precipitated the successful passage of women's suffrage, World War II was going to enlist women in a great campaign "to make every place in this country a better place to live, and therefore more worth defending." Even the military side of home defense needed women volunteers, she wrote, including "the aircraft warning service, and the whole protection program, as drivers of automobiles, trucks and ambulances, as telephone operators in air raid patrol centers."[35]

Statistics underscored the strides that ER had made. By mid-November, every state had at least one defense council, and there were more than 5,500 local and state defense organizations nationwide. The OCD had helped train more than 800,000 Americans in military and nonmilitary fields (nursing, nutrition) and promoted the participation of African Americans in home defense (in order to promote racial equality and further the war effort). A letter illustrates how far reaching its effects were. Written to ER by a woman in the remote mountain town of Clayton, Georgia, the letter explained that on November 1, about two dozen women held a meeting, where they ate locally grown turnips, tomatoes, and potato custard and discussed ways that they could contribute to ER's grassroots defense movement. "Homemakers all over Georgia" endorsed the first lady's campaign "heart and soul," the woman from Clayton assured ER. The first lady saw in the passion of the women from Clayton evidence that her message was resonating and that volunteer participation was proving vital to the fight to defend democracy from fascism. As if she needed more evidence of her progress, celebrities joined ER's cause, too; tennis champion Alice Marble and Hollywood film stars promoted physical fitness. Moreover, four thousand garden clubs had established mobile canteens to feed the hungry and recruited 250,000 women to plant enough vegetables to feed 1 percent of the population.[36]

All of these actions lifted the first lady's spirits and motivated her to do even more to advance her agenda. On November 22, she asked Paul Kellogg, an aide, to study the impact of defense factories and Army camps on community life and ensure that existing social services were adequately meeting the public's needs. While she prepared the country to go to war, she persuaded La Guardia to send fourteen women from the OCD to England to examine how British women were serving home defense. Upon returning home the delegation would "talk with authority to new groups throughout the country who needed to be reached with the picture." ER wanted to send Davison on a bomber, which would generate "a little publicity . . . [and] be good for us," and felt that Davison would be able "to reach a great many of our groups throughout the country who need to be stirred up." Eager to learn as much as possible from the British ordeal, La Guardia approved ER's requests, including an estimated $1,000–$1,500 to cover the costs of Davison's flights. ER wanted Americans to know how "the 'little people'" in England were faring and how they had bolstered democratic society during an existential crisis.[37]

Although La Guardia acceded to some of ER's requests, the two remained locked in conflict about the shape, focus, and direction of the home defense agenda. ER asked the director to approve a $6,000 budget to promote volunteer participation on the radio. La Guardia declined, describing these activities as better left to local organizations. ER and Kellogg hired a bevy of New Dealers to spearhead her community work. La Guardia insisted that social defense had to be subordinated to strictly military needs. Ordinary Americans, ER declared in a letter to La Guardia, had to "join together and do a job as everyday citizens in Civilian Defense." She set mid-January as the date for her division to be running at full speed. The fascist threat represented the greatest challenge to American democracy since Abraham Lincoln's time, and ER knew that her home defense work was hardly finished. She would ensure that grassroots participation in social defense roles was not sacrificed on the altar of La Guardia's single-minded quest to militarize America.[38]

9

We Can't All Run to Central Pk

[Mayor La Guardia is a] fat little bumptious character, clowning and screaming dictatorially . . . . [He] makes an average of 700 speeches a year, conducts an occasional orchestra, sits in on occasional Cabinet meetings, dashes to all the best fires, conducts a vast correspondence in the seven foreign languages he writes and cusses in, and fires one of his chief or petty assistants at least once daily.

—*Time*

La Guardia raised his home defense campaign to new heights in the fall of 1941. He led a series of war games that aimed to rouse the public from its stupor, foster a war psychology, and persuade civilians to join his ranks. His task was far from an easy sell. Nonetheless, contrary to journalistic accounts then and historical accounts since, La Guardia made significant headway that fall. He mobilized hundreds of thousands of Americans, drew positive notice for his drills, and taught much of the East Coast to cope with potential invasions, air raids, and sabotage, among other threats. While his antics became more and more polemical throughout the fall, he also forged alliances with the military, the FBI, some leaders in the administration, and mayors nationwide. He became a hero to some, but a threat to democracy in the eyes of critics of various ideological stripes.

La Guardia's goal was nothing less than to change what liberalism itself meant to the American people as the country inched closer to entering the Second World War. Liberal leadership, he felt, faced an unprecedented peril, and liberals had to prioritize the militarization of domestic life over the kinds of social defense programs that so enamored ER and on which he had largely built his reputation as the mayor of modern New York. While he never weighed in on the question of whether the nation should permanently militarize to handle the nature of the new threat environment, his oratory and policies strongly implied that in the age of existential threats to American democracy, liberalism's number one job was to keep civilians physically protected—to teach them how to defend themselves from air raids, fifth column bombs, and enemy propaganda, and to use government power to curb the forces that could lead to panic, riots, and revolution. La Guardia embodied a growing strain in the liberal temperament, and while he was more bombastic than most liberals in late 1941, his politics heralded a military-first orientation toward domestic government and a much more militarized view of government's core functions in national life than liberals had envisioned during the heyday of the New Deal in the early and mid-1930s.

At the same time in the fall of 1941, La Guardia's relationship with ER came close to coming unraveled. As each of them felt the war approaching U.S. shores, they brandished their contrasting philosophies and butted heads over matters small and big. By early December, their feud was defining the greater divide within liberalism itself. La Guardia's personality became both his great political asset and his chief defect. His flamboyance, eloquence, and bellicosity alienated not only conservative isolationists but also many social defense liberals. Yet his style and persona kept him going at an amazing pace that hardly any other American leader could match. His personality drew attention to his message, making him among the most tendentious and inspiring wartime leaders in the United States.

That fall, La Guardia helped forge a consensus about the nature of the threats facing the American people. In late September, he learned from Army leaders that the key areas to be protected included portions or all of twenty-five states and the capital. These target zones, the military concluded, ran from the West and East Coasts, the Gulf of Mexico, and the U.S.-Canadian border for three hundred miles inland; approximately fifty million Americans lived in these regions. La Guardia, therefore, had to focus on defending the fifty million residents whose lives were endangered.[1]

La Guardia launched his war games in New York City, a logical choice. He hoped to turn New York into a home defense model, and the city became his personal laboratory enabling him to run experiments and see which activities did or did not have the desired effect. He could test programs that the British had pioneered and sell the concept of defending America to a public still wary of saber-rattling by elected officials.

In September, he began transforming his city into just such a national inspiration. He signed three emergency orders, establishing fire and air raid units to defend New Yorkers from enemy aggression. His aide Lester Stone hailed city police and firefighters for giving eyewitness accounts of activities in London and recommending concrete steps for cities to take in defense of Americans. New Yorkers were pioneers, Stone bragged. La Guardia had lots of reasons to feel optimistic about the progress his city was making. His drills, large and raucous, forced New Yorkers to pay attention to his mission. On September 12, he led approximately twenty thousand civilians in a blackout drill near Port

Washington in downtown Manhattan, which drew positive publicity. Such drills elicited cooperation from apartment dwellers and business owners, who turned off their lights, and the city which turned off its street lamps. Drivers had to turn off the headlights on their cars and park, and only emergency vehicles were allowed to be driven on the streets. The job of wardens was to go door to door, street by street, ensuring that residents were complying with the blackout and that loiterers and onlookers were swept off the sidewalks. Wardens helped people who needed to find shelter, and some of them stood atop the city's sky-scrapers and scanned the skies for German bombers.[2]

La Guardia also saw signs across the country that Americans were real-izing that inaction was unacceptable and a threat to democracy. In Texas and Louisiana, war drills demonstrated that a mass movement was unfolding nation-wide; the numbers were impressive: Approximately 1,000 airplanes flew over-head, 12,000 wardens patrolled streets, 500,000 soldiers mobilized for war, and 800,000 phones were being used during the drills, suggesting a rising passion for La Guardia's mission. These drills marked "the greatest single test of" aircraft warning ever held, he boasted. Their goal was to shave a few minutes off the time it took home defenders to respond to an imminent air raid, because those pre-cious minutes would be the difference between a resilient nation and a country racked with fear, according to the Army.[3]

In the meantime, the war in the Atlantic had come to involve American war-ships, with Roosevelt trumping up an incident and telling the American people on September 11 that a Nazi submarine had launched "a brazen attack" on the U.S. destroyer *Greer*, which was bringing mail and supplies to marines stationed in Iceland. (In truth, it was a British plane that fired first on the German subma-rine, prompting the German ship to attack the *Greer*. The *Greer* returned fire, but the exchange missed the targets and neither of the boats suffered any harm.) Assailing Nazi subs and raiders as "the rattlesnakes of the Atlantic," Roosevelt adopted a policy allowing American planes and naval ships to shoot at any German or Italian war vessel as soon as it had been sighted in U.S. waters. Hitler was hoping to finish the invasion of the Soviet Union and avoid any further hos-tilities with the Americans in the Atlantic until at least mid-October. A German U-boat, however, torpedoed the U.S. destroyer *Kearny*, killing 11 Americans, on October 17, and Roosevelt again took to the radio to declare that Nazis had attacked America and that he had seen a "secret map" purporting to show a South America divvied up into "5 vassal states," a claim that he simply appeared to have concocted. On October 31, 115 U.S. sailors died when a German U-boat torpedoed the *USS Reuben James*, ratcheting up the tensions between the United States and the Nazi regime.[4]

Amid these losses, Americans increasingly appeared to adopt the views and embrace the policies of La Guardia's OCD. In New Mexico, leaders held a statewide blackout, in which homes, shops, and businesses extinguished their lights, plunging the population into darkness. Newton, Massachusetts, trained 1,500 air raid wardens, prompting the *Christian Science Monitor* to call the suburb "one of the best-developed civilian defense organizations" anywhere. In Syracuse, an official vowed that if the enemy attacked the city its home defenders would be standing ready to repel him. *Life* magazine affirmed the emerging consensus that enemy threats were indeed perilous and that home defense offered the hope of keeping the country intact and, in the long run, democracy alive. According to Gallup, by late September 70 percent of the public believed that defeating Germany was a more important priority than keeping out of the war, while nearly the same percentage supported Roosevelt's policy of letting American naval vessels shoot on sight in the Atlantic. In early October, Gallup found that 69 percent of the public thought that boys should be given military training in their high schools.[5]

Even though La Guardia believed that the momentum was with him, he also concluded that progress was not nearly sufficient and that much more remained to be achieved. Nonchalant attitudes, he felt, posed a grave underlying danger to his mission. Oratory—alarmist at times—was one strategy for arresting the public's complacency. In order to whip up Americans' fears, he disseminated graphic descriptions of the threat of air raids. On September 23, he told an estimated audience of twenty thousand New Yorkers who were attending the Fifth Annual Police Show in Madison Square Garden that the nation's cities badly needed more gas masks and more firefighting equipment. He and his colleagues delivered their message with visuals, too. Seven hundred volunteers partook in a drill that illustrated the effects of demolition and incendiary bomb explosions, while out of the Garden's loudspeakers came noises from an actual raid during the Blitz of London, a "dreadful, penetrating warble" that, *Time* reported, sounded like nothing else on earth. This La Guardia-led spectacle, the magazine added, had "scared the whey out of [New Yorkers]." La Guardia was not displeased.[6]

This kind of an event had some fairly big upsides and few downsides. If people felt scared, he reasoned, they would in turn feel motivated to join his movement. Spain, France, England, and China had demonstrated that in modern warfare nobody was safe from air power. La Guardia thought Americans needed to envision similar destruction in their own cities: fires raging, streets littered with glass and rubble, subways stopped, and social services sidelined. Then, hysteria, like a vise, would grip the public. He wanted them to see that, too. Then, and only then, would they be motivated to minimize the threat of mass panic. La Guardia's fall campaign to spread public fear had another advantage–his message might break the isolationist stranglehold on large swaths of the country, make people feel less calm about the war, and spur action.

Never one to curb his emotions in public, La Guardia used his instinct for drama to drive his message home. In what he called a "mock invasion of New York City" that required eight months of preparation, he wanted to test every person and agency who had to respond to an actual attack, and he wanted the public to be caught by surprise, too. The drill had an electric effect on reporters and home defenders alike. On October 10, 1,500 soldiers acting as invaders assaulted Fort Tilden in Rockaway, Queens. More than two dozen planes provided air cover for the invading forces. On the other side of this exercise 3,000 home defense troops carried radios, binoculars, and even scythes as they manned their posts. Six hundred women volunteers tracked enemy flight paths from the seventh floor of a steel-reinforced building in an undisclosed location. The test bore more than a passing resemblance to a real invasion of the United States, and it was hard for civilians to ignore the simulated attack on their city. The skies lit up with searchlights, while interceptor balloons and anti-aircraft guns were primed for action. City papers ran one photograph showing helmeted soldiers pointing their guns toward the sky in defense of Brooklyn's Marine Parkway Bridge and another one revealing a soldier on the ground using a parked car as cover as he pointed his rifle at the enemy. The war, these pictures suggested, was coming to New York, and New Yorkers had better be prepared for street-to-street combat in a concrete jungle.[7]

Along the East Coast, one drill begat others, and they kept getting larger and larger. One of them, coordinated by the Army and the OCD, positioned 40,000 air raid watchers at observation posts, including the sand dunes of Cape Cod and the Empire State Building's rooftop. Hundreds of planes streaked through the skies, as radio broadcasters, fearing a repeat of "the 'Martian invasion' episode," warned audiences not to panic because these were drills and nothing more. War games unfolded along the coastal waters, from Cape Ann, Massachusetts, to Cape Lookout, North Carolina; Georgia, Florida, and South Carolina were among the other states involved.[8]

Though La Guardia has often been accused of intentionally misrepresenting the threat and deceiving the American people, he absolutely believed that the threats were real. His men continued to send him confidential reports from their tours of London, and the U.S. military and intelligence officials peppered him with warnings that the chances of air raids on U.S. soil were increasing. He adopted the persona of a mid-twentieth-century version of Paul Revere, riding across the country, shouting that the enemy was coming. If he didn't warn people, he felt, Americans—like the French—would continue to think that the Nazis could never conquer such a mighty country as theirs. Such hubristic attitudes presented a dire peril, and La Guardia wanted to do his part to explode that mindset and the assumptions that underpinned it.

His missions to London—far from propagandistic ploys—were, in his mind, fact-finding visits. He directed his aides to study evacuation methods used in London and got advice on it from Britain's chief medical officer. La Guardia wanted to learn how American city officials should react during an eruption of hysteria in the midst of air raids. American advisors shared La Guardia's detailed interest in home defense policies, and they suggested some radical solutions. One aide proposed fingerprinting every American so they could be easily identified in the aftermath of an air raid. His New York housing advisor Harry Prince urged him to track people in the United States whom authorities deemed suspicious and proposed that La Guardia require every building with more than fifty occupants to adopt a self-defense plan. At times, La Guardia's aides were more militaristic than their boss. Some members of his police force who were on a tour of London proposed that La Guardia give police in the United States new "powers of arrest, search and seizure," and they suggested that the OCD conduct drills in which suspicious packages were left near defense plants.[9]

La Guardia echoed their concerns and championed their ideas. In a confidential letter to the chairman of the Federal Reserve's Board of Governors, La Guardia pointed out that "piers, docks, wharves, inland waterways, bridges, electric and steam power plants, telephone and telegraph plants, wireless stations, reservoirs, aqueducts, water mains, gas mains, manufacturing plants, warehouses, tunnels, terminals and other facilities of supply, production, storage, transportation and communication" hubs were all in the sights of the Axis Powers. From the very beginning, he informed James Forrestal, the Undersecretary of the Navy, of his concern that Southern California's ports were especially vulnerable to attack and ordered an aide to visit Los Angeles and work with local officials to strengthen port security.[10]

Despite his decision to seek a third term in City Hall, home defense remained one of La Guardia's principal concerns. Indeed, he saw his missions as indistinguishable from each other, and he threw out all manner of ideas aimed at securing the nation from the designs of its foes. He urged FDR to sign an executive order using federal resources to protect the nation's infrastructure. (Probably reluctant to arouse isolationist opposition, FDR refused.) He established a Civil Air Patrol and began to recruit thousands of pilots to use private planes to patrol the nation's coastal waters. More broadly, he tried to counter the country's passion for individual liberty by singing the praises of obedience to authority and to collective action in order to protect the public. Defending society trumped the contentment or idiosyncratic desires of any one individual. He spoke in favor of forging a disciplined army. If he had his way, his home front also had to assume the characteristics of a highly militarized society. He insisted that Congress and the White House allocate funds to procure and distribute more than 50 million gas masks including more than 2 million, some in the form of Mickey Mouse masks, for infants and children. Cities, he argued, needed more stretchers, hospital beds, and fire-fighting equipment. Mobilization was poised to develop on an unprecedented scale. The OCD calculated that in the 300-mile coastal target zones, home defense was responsible for protecting 500,000 blocks (including 1,228 in Honolulu). Further, the OCD proposed putting ladders, buckets, and water pumps on each of these streets. La Guardia estimated that these target zones needed a ratio of one warden for every 500 people and planned to create in just these zones a 3 million person army, accounting for 6 percent of the 50 million people living there.[11]

Forging close ties to the nation's military establishment, La Guardia and his aides also wanted the OCD to become, essentially, a fourth military branch. The OCD's leaders and the military's commanders had common interests and a shared mindset. The Army needed the OCD, as military planners wanted to free up the Army to plan for offensive operations rather than focus on defending the Western Hemisphere. The fears that roiled the military ranks were much the same as La Guardia's: if the Nazis bombed the United States, for example, civilians had to be resilient physically and psychologically. They had to keep their innermost demons in check and not become hysterical. Equally vital, they had to keep showing up to work in the factories that produced the bombs and tanks that would enable the military to win any wars it fought in Europe and Asia. When La Guardia wrote Secretary of War Henry Stimson that "bombing . . . , gassing, sabotage, and fifth-column activities" were all likely prospects in the United States, Stimson and his aides concurred. La Guardia requested that Stimson order Army reserves on active duty to volunteer in the OCD; "We should be able to get some excellent command material," La Guardia reasoned. For his part, Stimson praised La Guardia as a military asset, while Army leaders praised the OCD's war games for welding local officials and military leaders into a coordinated command structure. "We haven't a moment to lose," one military official reminded home defense leaders. Indeed, the brass was so enamored of home defense that one official suggested that the OCD emulate the Nazis' authoritarian style by inculcating greater discipline in America's home defense ranks.[12]

The FBI and the OCD forged a partnership based on a set of shared values and a united perspective. Like La Guardia, FBI Director J. Edgar Hoover looked to glean information on civil defense from the experience of Londoners. Some of his FBI agents toured the city to study police powers during and after air raids. La Guardia and Hoover collaborated in several areas where the U.S. home defense program needed to be enhanced. They established a training program for police departments, and La Guardia embraced an offer from a G-man to have Hoover's agents give the police insights on handling military crises at home. La Guardia lauded Hoover for devoting his considerable power to teaching America's policemen about defense of their cities during air raids. Hundreds of OCD-FBI schools were established by October, offering police short-term courses of six days to three weeks. One day soon, La Guardia and Hoover agreed, police departments would need to deal with people who panicked in the midst of air raids on their cities.[13]

Other FBI home defense proposals shed light on another aspect of the Hoover–La Guardia alliance: their shared desire to militarize the home front. La Guardia signed off on an FBI proposal that auxiliary police forces carry military-grade .38 caliber pistols made by Smith and Wesson. Together, the two agencies estimated that OCD volunteers in target zones required around a quarter of a million guns to defend against an invasion and keep law and order during and after air raids. Their "conservative" estimate for the Midwest and other non-target regions was that 300,000 guns had to be provided to defense volunteers for the protection of 77 million civilians. More broadly, a sense of impending doom gripped some of the OCD's personnel. "We are working in the *dark* as to how long we have and *must work fast*," one memo discussing the need for first aid announced.[14]

FDR had begun to sour on La Guardia's leadership, but the mayor was still a strong liberal ally and Roosevelt treated him as a member of his national security team. FDR also regarded him as politically helpful to the administration. Few public figures made the case for intervention in the war as forcefully and brilliantly as La Guardia, and from his perch at the OCD, La Guardia was drawing national notice for his pro-British, pro-FDR arguments. La Guardia's insistence that the United States was no longer a bastion of physical safety usefully countered the Charles Lindbergh isolationist narrative that Americans had nothing to fear. The more that isolationists blasted La Guardia as FDR's propagandist, the greater the alliance became between the two men. When the *Chicago Tribune* called La Guardia a war-monger who was doing the president's bidding, it strengthened La Guardia's standing in Roosevelt's view.[15]

Even La Guardia's bid for a third term in City Hall became a debate about the wisdom of FDR's foreign policy. La Guardia ran partly on a platform of support for FDR's program of sending aid to Great Britain, predicting that if the United States went to war, it would take thirteen months for the country to defeat its enemies. FDR, for his part, hailed La Guardia's leadership of New York as "the most honest and . . . most efficient municipal government of any within my recollection." Presidential advisors went out of their way to praise La Guardia and support his bid for a third term. When FDR announced that he had in his possession a map purporting to show the Nazis' plans for carving up Latin America, he gave a tacit nod to La Guardia's insistence that an invasion of the United States was not unthinkable and that home defense was the best bulwark.[16]

Although the two men shared a worldview and a political and policy agenda, they clashed over some of La Guardia's most tendentious oratory. FDR grew concerned that La Guardia's fear campaign would further antagonize and embolden the president's isolationist critics, and he tended to regard La Guardia's incessant warnings as overkill. As great an asset as La Guardia was to the administration, he was also becoming a liability, giving the New Deal's critics fodder for their oft-leveled charge that liberals had totalitarian tendencies and would use government to trample on individual rights. *Time* magazine captured this critique, calling La Guardia not just one of the world's busiest men but also "a fat little bumptious character, clowning and screaming dictatorially" as he toured the country, whipping up audiences into a lather. *Time* added that he "makes an average of 700 speeches a year, conducts an occasional orchestra, sits in on occasional Cabinet meetings, dashes to all the best fires, conducts a vast correspondence in the seven foreign languages he writes and cusses in, and fires one of his chief or petty assistants at least once daily." In short, he was an overstretched zealot whom even FDR could not contain. When La Guardia likened his critics to looters who during an earthquake sought to line their own pockets, not even his liberal allies considered his response responsible or politically savvy.[17]

La Guardia's focus was as scattered as ever. In addition to running for reelection, he kept working on militarizing the civilian population, preparing citizens to experience the terrors of urban warfare. During four consecutive days in October, La Guardia revealed that he was committed to mass mobilization. He held a meeting with his OCD aides, talked to ER about national defense, attended a White House Cabinet meeting, talked to officials about the OCD's budget, and spoke to FDR about the role of farmers in the defense program. He even found time to testify in front of the House Committee on Military Affairs, pleading with Congress to devote ample resources that would help cities procure equipment to fight fires caused by incendiary bombs. He inhabited his war role so thoroughly that aides investigated if it was possible to put a radio broadcast system in his home or car so he could talk to the public over all city radio channels during any emergency.[18]

Even if FDR had mixed feelings about his OCD chief, La Guardia had begun to build his own national constituency that seemingly supported his military objectives. Civilians endorsed his views and took action in response to his incessant pleas. The OCD leader was in demand that fall; Detroit, Springfield, Massachusetts, and Philadelphia officials invited him to address their residents on the topic of home defense. One admirer called

La Guardia's role in the OCD evidence of the mayor's "splendid cooperation with our Defence Program." His defense job, this correspondent enthused, made La Guardia "doubly valuable to both [New York] City and the Nation." "We can't 'all' run to Central Pk," another admirer advised him, proposing that New York police seize control of the basements of wealthy New Yorkers, turning them into shelters to be used by the public during air raids. Some reporters and editors depicted La Guardia as a savior of democracy, lauding him as "America's Home Defender" and "The Man Who'll Keep You Safe." He was, a magazine added, "one of the political miracles of his generation." The publication described him as a "short, swarthy, barrel-bodied man, who pounds and rants and swears" and still managed to get things done and generate public ardor for his preparedness crusade.[19]

A tension stood at the center of La Guardia's mission, however, and he never figured out how to resolve it. On the one hand, he had to deploy fear as a weapon in the struggle to mobilize complacent civilians and persuade them to join his ranks. On the other, as some of his colleagues in the administration argued, fear was an easily manipulated emotion, and too much of it would set the stage for panic and a breakdown in civil society. Even some of La Guardia's OCD advisors worried that large civil defense notices in newspapers along with radio talks and on-air dramas about air raids would spread public hysteria.[20]

La Guardia rejected those who urged restraint. The greater danger, he continued to believe, was a public unaware of the peril, oblivious to global realities. He seized on events overseas to demonstrate that the United States was in Hitler's crosshairs. When a U-boat sunk the Reuben James, La Guardia informed his audience at Brooklyn's Volunteer Defense Headquarters that the sinking of an American vessel was a sign that the war was shifting toward the Western Hemisphere. "When we started to make studies of defense measures in England," he explained, "the danger here was theoretical. Now this destroyer has been sunk. Don't you see how it is creeping up on us all the time?" Later in the day, he startled 1,500 women attending a home defense conference when he announced that the Reuben James was at the bottom of the Atlantic, and that 120 U.S. sailors had been aboard the destroyer. The sinking, he pointed out, brought all Americans "closer and closer to the terrible moment," and there was only one answer that they could give: "civilian training to protect our homes and our people."[21]

La Guardia took comfort in knowing that at least some segment of the public understood and sympathized with his point of view. According to one Roosevelt administration analysis, residents of Illinois had concluded that Lend-Lease and other assistance to Britain and Russia, which the Nazis had invaded in June, were smart strategies to keep Americans safe. A newspaper editor in Utah called on Washington to undertake a mission to gain control of Iceland so as to deprive the Nazis of air bases that they could use to attack Americancities. La Guardia, hoping that his rhetoric was effective but determined not to rest on his laurels, grew even more belligerent in the fall of 1941. His office sent priests and rabbis suggested language for a sermon to deliver on a national day of celebration, "Freedom Sunday," during Civilian Defense Week. Ostensibly, the day was intended to honor religious freedom; La Guardia's suggested sermon, which featured a–home defense message, affronted the clergy as a heavy-handed attempt by the government to trample on the sanctity of churches and temples. La Guardia, one critic charged, had just tried "to goose-step the priests, ministers and rabbis of this country," and the language of his sermon amounted to, said another, "an unspeakable insult." La Guardia replied that he was merely trying to pray "for the safety of the country" and "give thanks to God Almighty for our freedom," but his critics were not appeased.[22]

La Guardia's approach—critics cast it as fraught and blinkered—became another flashpoint in the debate about America's response to the Second World War. Some fellow liberals felt perturbed by his arrogant refusal to take their advice. When La Guardia asked Office of Facts and Figures director Archibald MacLeish to help him spread the OCD's message, MacLeish invited him to lunch to discuss some ideas, but La Guardia refused to meet with him. MacLeish stewed. Consultation, collaboration, soliciting input from his colleagues and aides: these traits were largely absent from La Guardia's stewardship of home defense. Rather than build alliances across the government, he barked orders to subordinates, insisting that aides follow his directives as if they were the word of God, or at least those of a commanding general, and he demanded utmost attention to all of his pronouncements. "NO COMMUNICATION, FORMAL OR INFORMAL OR OTHERWISE, CONCERNING CIVILAN AIR CORPS SHOULD BE SENT TO ANY PERSON, DEPARTMENT, BUREAU, COMMITTEE, BOARD, COUNCIL, OR ANYONE, ANYWHERE, WITHOUT MY PERSONAL SIGNATURE. HOLD EVERYTHING UP," he thundered to aides in one typical missive.[23]

He also lamented that in many regions progress toward defending America was too slow. He bemoaned the lax attitudes and programmatic delays that he believed hampered his mission and invited the enemy to attack America. In late November, his aides informed him that some sectors had lagged in recruiting firefighters and police, and La Guardia ordered fourteen of his aides to go into the field and send daily reports "to me personal, air mail, special delivery" to assess conditions and spur enrollments. He instructed his aides to "remain on duty until you are certain that actual enrollment and actual training has commenced in earnest." With the stakes so high and time running out, La Guardia dwelled on all of the things that were still unfinished.[24]

The picture in New England was particularly mixed. Aides told La Guardia that the region had made substantial headway, establishing more than 1,200 defense councils. In Boston 7,000 air raid wardens were taking training seminars; more than 2,000 volunteer firefighters and more than 5,000 first-aid workers were on duty. Other reports waxed optimistic about La Guardia's program. Massachusetts had recruited 80,000 air raid wardens, while Connecticut had established 50 emergency teams capable of performing surgery and nursing tasks to treat the injured.[25]

His aides reported that Vermont, Rhode Island, and New Hampshire viewed the federal role in home defense with skepticism and preferred to take charge of their own defense rather than follow orders given from Washington. Maine's railroad workers felt mistreated by the Roosevelt administration, which had used Canadian railroads for transporting goods instead of Maine's, making it harder to recruit them for home defense tasks. But even the less-compliant states had taken steps in the right direction. New Hampshire held an incendiary bomb demonstration that La Guardia's aides witnessed. The aides spoke to youth, urging them to volunteer, and more than 1,200 volunteers had already enrolled in New Hampshire's program. Vermont had approximately 1,500 volunteers on duty, and a former military officer who ran the state's program had launched effective training workshops for police and first-aid workers. Newport, Rhode Island, had set up training facilities so its wardens could learn how to handle chemical warfare.[26]

Still, New England also underscored the hurdles facing La Guardia's quest to militarize civilian life. New Hampshire still lacked the number of volunteers it needed to run a home defense effectively, while the Red Cross in Washington had rebuffed the OCD's recommendations for training volunteers. In late November, the OCD's T. S. Walmsley wrote to a colleague that there was "no time to lose" due to the imminent nature of the threat. But even one of the best regions, New England, was rife with complacency. In a survey conducted by Gallup from November 27 to December 1, 49 percent of West Coast residents and 45 percent of East Coast residents said their city might be bombed, while 40 and 44 percent said there was no chance. A majority of Americans said that if an air raid came they would either stay indoors or seek shelter in a large public building or in a basement, while 12 percent said a "street, park, field, or subway." Another 12 percent said they "would not know what to do." Though divisions remained, the public was more convinced that air raids were real threats and a vast majority had given at least some consideration to what they would do in case of attack.[27]

By December, the OCD had become a more influential force in national life than La Guardia's critics had acknowledged: the agency had a budget of $900,000 from FDR's emergency funds and a 300-person staff headquartered in Washington. Almost 1 million volunteers were actively training for service, including more than 200,000 air raid wardens, more than 200,000 firefighters, and almost 50,000 police. While La Guardia had not yet reached his target of recruiting 6 million civilians for home defense, he was on his way to achieving his goal. He accelerated other activities. He sought meetings with federal colleagues to evaluate the nation's evacuation procedures, and his agency looked to Seattle, which had adopted the Emergency Evacuation of Civilians and Property, as a model for the rest of America. La Guardia continued to urge Congress to give him the money to buy the millions of gas masks, steel helmets, shovels, and buckets that he insisted civilians in the target zones required. Criticism, such as the *Chicago Tribune*'s charge that he had irresponsibly "whip[ped] up a war fever," had little appreciable effect on La Guardia's faith in the rightness of his cause.[28]

He was more concerned in early December that a bipartisan effort in Congress, as Rep. Overton Brooks warned the OCD's Corrington Gill, would cut the OCD's appropriations. The OCD's leadership also faced continued congressional resistance to repeated funding requests for gas masks and other vital equipment in the coastal communities. La Guardia had to assuage the governors, who regarded him as hostile to their states' interests and filed complaints with the White House. Hoping to curb their hostility toward him, he made plans to meet with governors in Phoenix, Chicago, New Orleans, and Cincinnati in December. Isolationists, especially Midwesterners, continued to oppose La Guardia's vocal calls for expansive home defense, and Nebraska Governor Dwight Griswold wrote La Guardia that the OCD could not persuade Midwesterners "that they are about to be bombed." One Illinois resident scolded La Guardia that evacuation drills held in New York City's schools were idiotic. La Guardia was unfazed; Chicago and Detroit, he defiantly argued in early December, were susceptible to foreign enemy air raids and people there must not let their hubris lull them into a false sense of safety. But La Guardia was much more than just a lightning rod, as has frequently been suggested. Some members of the public revered him, and a Chicago architect spoke for other admirers when he wrote La Guardia that any person who simply "waited for the first air raid" was courting death. Put differently, he saw La Guardia as a prophet, crucified in his own times but a visionary who had power to see the future nonetheless.[29]

Just as Franklin Roosevelt was souring on the Little Flower, Eleanor Roosevelt increasingly chafed under his withering disdain for her social defense ideals. ER was, La Guardia thought, focused on soft activities such as basket weaving, which he felt had little relevance to a militarized home defense program. Their paths began to diverge, literally and figuratively. On December

2, he and ER had planned to discuss recruitment problems in Philadelphia, when La Guardia's flight to New York later that afternoon was suddenly cancelled. La Guardia did not wait around to see ER but instead rushed to the airport to catch an early plane, skipping their meeting. He handed his aide Corrington Gill a set of memos on the topic and asked him to deliver them to her when she arrived and send his regrets. If La Guardia hoped that ER was going to quit fighting for her ideals, he was badly mistaken. She promoted her agenda in stops along the East Coast: after meeting young people and viewing athletic performances in Philadelphia to mark the city's National Defense Week, she declared that Americans must have access to healthy diets and get plenty of exercise. She praised the pledges written for volunteers by poet Carl Sandburg, which reminded civilians of the value of self-discipline and the need to sacrifice in pursuit of freedom. "I pledge myself to do a little thinking every day about the need of discipline and how, in a time of national danger more than ever, my own rights as a citizen are tangled and interwoven with the rights of others and these rights always deserve a decent respect," Sandburg's second pledge said. When she arrived in New York City, she attended a conference on immigration, appeared at a benefit for the Women's Trade Union League, and held meetings with organizations representing nurses and the blind.[30]

Still, ER agreed with La Guardia that time was not on their side and that mass mobilization was proceeding too slowly. She asked Elinor Morgenthau to provide her with an updated account of the state of volunteer recruitment. She informed the country that soon she would expand the type of roles that individual volunteers could perform.[31]

As the first week of December 1941 came to a close, ER and La Guardia remained at loggerheads. On December 1, ER wrote La Guardia that she had made plans to discuss health and welfare issues with advocates. She planned to study how Alabama, Louisiana, and New York had advanced human security in their respective states. But she also upbraided him by reminding him that the executive order put social defense at the center of the mission and he could not simply ignore this pillar of the OCD's agenda. ER had developed her own parallel set of aides and operations within the OCD, and she used the White House to hold meetings on home defense. In the same week that she scolded La Guardia, she discussed her program with home defense aides Paul Kellogg and Justine Polier at the White House. Afterwards, she ushered them into a room, and they talked to the president. FDR informed them that "this son of man has just sent his final message to the Son of God," a reference to what the president considered his final attempt to avert war with Japan by sending a communiqué to Emperor Hirohito. Perhaps unwittingly, FDR was giving ER and her aides an alarming insight: U.S. involvement in the war may be closer than many Americans suspected. The home defense program, he seemed to suggest, had better be ready.[32]

10

A Man Must Be Protected

Democracy cannot be static. Whatever is static is dead.
—Eleanor Roosevelt, January 1942

Fiorello La Guardia and Eleanor Roosevelt had different reactions to the attack on Pearl Harbor as their country embarked on its great crusade to vanquish fascism. La Guardia saw Pearl Harbor as confirmation that liberalism had to adjust to the reality of wartime—or else America would be shattered. Adjustment, to him, meant an almost single-minded use of the government to keep civilians safe from enemy attacks of various kinds and to motivate, recruit, and instill in average Americans the desire to participate in quasi-military roles to defend their towns and cities. He envisioned millions of men and women, wearing steel helmets and armed with gas masks, organizing people so they switched off their lights, took shelter, and gave first aid to the injured during air raids. While he abhorred fascism, he also infused liberalism with a penchant for social order, mass discipline, and collective action in the hopes of militarizing the home front in order to keep people safe. In the days following Pearl Harbor, his reputation as a lightning rod soared. Blamed for having done too little to prepare the country for air raids, faulted for whipping up hysteria in ways that might induce civilians to panic, La Guardia became a toxic figure, even as his vision of military security began to find fertile roots in democratic soil in December 1941.

By contrast, the days following Pearl Harbor confirmed ER's belief that human security had to form a pillar of any home defense initiative. On December 8, more than one thousand Seattle residents rioted when some of their fellow citizens refused to turn out their store lights during a citywide blackout. One woman, whose husband was serving as a boiler technician aboard the USS Kane, pointedly asked rioters if they were just "going to stand by while these lights threaten the very life of our city?" "Break them!" she shouted. "Turn them out." Mass hysteria caused by rumors of enemy threats to both coasts strengthened ER's resolve to promote her vision of New Deal liberalism.[1]

If citizens rampaged through cities, panicked at any rumor, or despaired over the level of inequality and lack of access to economic opportunity, then they would refuse to heed FDR's call to turn America into the great arsenal of democracy. Citizens might turn on their government and fail to fight the Axis because they had little faith that democracy was the superior system and that it offered them the best hope for the future. The antidote to all of these fears was a robust social defense liberalism guided by the federal government in partnership with millions of citizens who best knew their own communities' needs and best understood how those needs should be met. By giving people a direct stake in their democracy, and by improving life for all regardless of race, creed, or religion, wartime liberalism, ER continued to argue, would turn the crisis into a great opportunity to build a better country and usher in a more prosperous and peaceful society. While her arguments were eloquent and forceful in the weeks following the attacks, opposition to enacting her reform vision soared. Social defense was beginning to take a backseat to military security, even as ER waged a rear-guard campaign through the OCD to enact, at last, her vision of a wartime New Deal.

La Guardia learned of the attack on Pearl Harbor while he was in his apartment on Fifth Avenue on the afternoon of December 7. He had long expected this moment, and he moved as quickly as possible to assert his control over home defense in his city. A police car whisked him to City Hall. He ordered city commissioners to implement their once-secret plans to defend skyscrapers, docks, and waterways. He talked to the White House, the FBI, and the Army and was so filled with adrenaline that he barked an order to New England's home defense head that he must hold a big parade in Boston the next day. "My men don't march," the regional director replied in exasperation. "They don't [even] know how to march."[2]

La Guardia felt few qualms about insinuating himself into virtually any aspect of home defense. He put a target on the back of Japanese living in the United States. Calling Japan's sneak attack part of the "Nazi technique of mass murder," La Guardia directed that all Japanese nationals and Japanese Americans must be barred from getting together for any meetings, and he ordered them confined to their homes "pending determination of their status by Federal authorities." La Guardia shut down Japanese restaurants and clubs in New York City, while FBI and local law enforcement agents rounded up scores of Japanese and Japanese Americans, detaining them on Ellis Island. La Guardia's words and deeds underscored the depth of his antipathy toward people of Japanese descent, demonstrating, in the words of one historian, "a malignant racism." Not satisfied to leave matters there, La Guardia turned on his longtime critics when he arrogantly vowed that "those who have been sneering and jeering at [home] defense activities and . . . placing obstacles in their path" would now enjoy the protections that La Guardia would see fit to provide for them. But any further dissent, he emphasized, would not be tolerated. This was a war, not "a pinochle party," he thundered, a dig at Eleanor Roosevelt's New Deal agenda, which he considered frivolous, like a card game. La Guardia contributed to the atmosphere of near-open panic in some quarters of the country. Riding through the capital in a police cruiser, he shouted into a loudspeaker, "Calm! Calm! Calm!" "We are not out of the danger zone by any means," he later warned over the radio.[3]

Eleanor Roosevelt was not surprised by the attack at Pearl Harbor and moved as quickly as La Guardia had to etch her own vision into the culture now that war had finally come to the United States. She had warned for years that Americans were not safe in their castles, and she felt a bit relieved that Americans at last knew exactly what they were going to have to face in the years ahead. Word of the attack on Pearl Harbor reached her as she stood in a hallway in the White House and noticed that aides were surrounding two phones and military officials were rushing past her. "The blow had fallen," she later reflected. "The clouds of uncertainty and anxiety" had given way to the knowledge that a total war on behalf of preserving democracy had been joined. When she found FDR in his study, she took inspiration from his calm focus on the steps he needed to take in response to the surprise attack.[4]

In the hours after Japan bombed Pearl Harbor, historian Steven Gillon has written, "intelligence was scarce and difficult to obtain." At first, the president did not know the size of the attack force or the extent of damage inflicted on the naval fleet. He worried that Japan was preparing to invade Hawaii. Over dinner, he discussed the possibility that if Japanese forces invaded the West Coast, they might be able to reach Chicago. Honolulu experienced the kind of shock and terror that ER and La Guardia had brooded about in European cities. Now the horror had come to an American territory and killed American civilians and servicemen. The bombings killed more than 2,400 Americans; wounded another 1,000 people; and left women and children dazed and storefronts in rubble. Eighteen U.S. ships and almost 300 U.S. planes had been destroyed or so badly damaged that they were put out of service. Concerns about a collapse of civic order and additional attacks on Hawaii led to a declaration of martial law on the territory within hours of the bombing, and military rule did not end until almost three years later, on October 24, 1944.[5]

Far from tabling her social agenda, the aftermath of Pearl Harbor confirmed to ER that social defense was needed more than ever. The first lady played multiple roles in the hours after the attack. Above all, she donned the mantle of the typical American woman. She declared that she felt the same fears that all American women were feeling, and she reminded mothers that she had a son on a destroyer and two children living in harm's way on the West Coast. Like them,

ER said, she could not, no matter how hard she tried, "escape a clutch of fear at your heart." She wore other hats, too. She urged a rapid military mobilization, but she believed that it was equally important to preserve the "New Deal social objectives that had fostered the spirit that would make it possible for us to fight the war." She deemed it critical "to give people the feeling that in fighting the war we were still really fighting for these same objectives." Americans needed to know that the war was being waged not just to defeat the Axis Powers militarily but also to better the health and well-being of all citizens. If FDR, Harry Hopkins, and other liberals saw military mobilization as the only thing that mattered after Pearl Harbor, Eleanor Roosevelt maintained that social defense was a pillar of national defense on which victory depended.[6]

ER's wartime leadership reveals that her version of New Deal liberalism had more active support among select liberals than historians have typically recognized. The shock of Pearl Harbor provided an impetus to her and other liberals to realize at least some of their objectives. While social liberalism was highly embattled in the weeks after December 7, 1941, and while it would be subordinated to the needs of the national security state, she kept the reform issue in the public eye, tying defense of democracy to a grassroots social movement improving the lives of all Americans.[7]

At 9 a.m. on December 8, ER walked into OCD's headquarters, held a meeting with her staff, and suspended the fourteen-women mission to London that she had been planning. The time for studying home defense had come and gone, she declared, and now Americans had to act fast to implement plans to defend civilians militarily and socially. Paul Kellogg drafted a statement for her that captured the outlook of social defense liberals in the hours after the attack. He wanted ER to announce her intention to initiate an agenda of "social engineering" to tackle community needs and benefit the lives of the American people.[8]

Less than twenty-four hours after the attack on Pearl Harbor, ER showed that she sided with Kellogg. She proposed giving every school-age child "Oslo Breakfasts" that were packed with nutrients and endorsed better access to medical care for youth and better day-care facilities for the children of workers in war industries.[9]

Pearl Harbor arguably turned ER into the most forceful New Deal advocate in the United States. No other American combined her expansive philosophy with her national following, bully pulpit, work ethic, and political power. She spoke forcefully about the grave dangers facing civilians from threats overseas. On December 8, she asked one OCD regional director to prepare his zone for enemy attacks; at her behest he wrote governors in his region to put their civil defense plans into motion immediately. She warned Americans that the fascist countries felt so desperate that they would "try things which seem foolhardy to more secure people." "If you are going to die anyway, you might as well die with a grand gesture," she explained, raising the prospect of suicide attacks inside the United States. She ordered an aide to buy blackout shades and drape them over windows in the White House, and she declared that any American who said civilians need not worry about attacks from overseas lived in a fantasy.[10]

The mundane trappings of her job in the OCD also belied her leading role in the struggle to enact a wartime New Deal. She had a non-descript office (listed on a sheet as room 931), and "Eleanor Roosevelt, Assistant Director" appeared as just one of dozens of names on a list of OCD employees. But her position, of course, was hardly a typical one; she had access to the inner sanctum of the White House and to inside information that nobody at her level in the administration would normally have. FDR told her that Japan had destroyed about one-third of the Navy's forces in the attack on Pearl Harbor and that the Japanese air force had the capacity to bomb the West Coast.[11]

In the hours after Pearl Harbor, as rumors of enemy activity in waters near San Francisco and bombers in midair streaking toward the West Coast ran rampant, ER came to a painful realization: she was going to have a hard time keeping the White House as a symbol of democratic openness, one of her longtime priorities. Pearl Harbor had turned 1600 Pennsylvania Avenue into a fortress bristling with Secret Service agents, special police details, and fences. After December 7, 1941, the White House truly ceased to be the "people's house," and the tug between openness and safety lurched in the direction of security.

This was a blow to the world she knew prior to Pearl Harbor. Few subscribed to the notion of an open White House more than Eleanor Roosevelt. In the 1930s, the first lady cast her new home as a democratic living room where Americans should come together for conversation and debate on big issues. Security was so lax that two high school students, on a dare, nonchalantly entered the White House on New Year's Eve in 1938, found FDR and the first lady, and requested their autographs. Both Roosevelts cultivated an informal air when they occupied the White House, a trademark of their political style and a symbol of their sympathy for ordinary citizens, who in turn felt that the couple understood their needs and treated them as friends. Using the White House to project their faith in "the common man," FDR and ER shook hands with 14,056 members of the public in the mansion in 1939 alone.[12]

Americans believed that the White House was their house, too. People wrote ER to ask her if they could stop in and pay her a visit. Four members of the public wanted to know whether she would permit them to see the White House's "swimming pool and recreation room" and said they would bring "our swim suits, just in case." One correspondent learned that he needed only to hand the letter he had received from the White House to the chief usher anytime from 10 a.m. to noon on the following day to gain admittance to the presidential mansion. During the Easter Egg Roll on the South Lawn, anybody could join in the fun as long as they had children under age thirteen with them. "You do not need an invitation to enter the grounds," one White House letter instructed.[13]

The bombs that fell on Pearl Harbor, more than the planes that struck on September 11, 2001, are responsible for changing the White House and Washington into a place where security trumped openness. Eleanor Roosevelt called the nation's capital "a completely changed world" in the wake of the attack. Days later, the Japanese Embassy had FBI agents and private detectives protecting it, lest "some fanatic attempt to bomb" it, one law enforcement officer said. Armed men defended Washington's bridges and power plants. The White House received a cache of submachine guns, FBI agents and plainclothes police officers patrolled nearby streets, and the *Washington Post* reported that a "special detail" with red lanterns was stationed on the mansion's perimeter, seeking to keep crowds away. The *Post* also warned Washingtonians to prepare for imminent air raids on the capital.[14]

Franklin and Eleanor found themselves unable to turn back the clock. The Easter Egg Roll was canceled. The White House closed its doors to the public, and it "will no doubt remain closed" until war's end, one correspondent learned. The Secret Service nixed ER's idea of hosting a White House tea for 350 foreign students. The Christmas tree was put not in Lafayette Park or on the Ellipse but on the White House grounds, where agents could check those who witnessed the lighting ceremony.[15]

ER resented the creeping paranoia she witnessed, yet she also accepted the new reality. On the one hand, she said in exasperation, according to an aide, perhaps security services should go so far as "to take down the Washington monument because an enemy could measure the distance between it and the White House," using the landmark to help target the residence. On the other, she resigned herself to the fact that intensified security was necessary. When a deranged woman bit a guard's thumb so badly that he required medical care, even ER concluded that the White House could no longer remain the people's house. "A man must be protected while he is the President of the United States," she said in her memoir, reflecting on the stepped-up security measures after Pearl Harbor.[16]

The transformation acquired its own momentum; security begat more and more security. The steps that the Secret Service took in the days after Pearl Harbor were extraordinary even by today's standards: no more members of the public were permitted to visit the White House's first floor; every staffer and White House resident was fingerprinted; employees were given gas masks and practiced air raid drills. The first family balked at putting Secret Service-sanctioned gun crews on the White House roof, but ER reasoned that the ban on flights over the White House at least gave her husband a better's night sleep.

Although FDR quashed a proposal to camouflage the White House so as to make it a more difficult target for enemy bombers, his Secret Service drilled hard with a stopwatch to spirit a wheelchair-bound man to a newly built bomb shelter in the Treasury Department. When Secret Service agents forced FDR to dine one night with his Cabinet in the mansion and not in a less secure hotel as originally planned, FDR deemed it "a wonderful opportunity . . . for Hitler." If the Germans bombed the White House, they could destroy the government, and "if all of us except Frances were killed we would have a woman president," FDR joked, referring to Labor Secretary Frances Perkins.[17]

If the White House could no longer remain open to all, the first lady was nonetheless bent on calming people's fears, preventing an outbreak of hysteria, and keeping civilians' eyes focused on military victory and the continuation of social progress. Despite the fears that now gripped the capital, La Guardia had concluded that the most immediate risk to the country was in the big cities on the West Coast. So he announced that he and ER would fly to the coast immediately, tour the cities, and help defend the home front against Japanese aggression. On the night of December 8, they boarded a plane and flew to Los Angeles.

The harrowing flight reminded them both that traveling in wartime brought a fresh set of fears. When the plane hit turbulence, passengers' drinks, dinners, and books flew all over the cabin, and ER bumped her head on the ceiling while milk spattered La Guardia's suit. The pilot received a report in the cockpit that San Francisco was under attack. After the pilot informed ER of the grim news, she awoke La Guardia, who was sleeping in his compartment. Her face ashen, she told him that they had a report of bombs falling on San Francisco. La Guardia reacted calmly and forcefully; if the rumor was true, he said, they would go straight to San Francisco. He instructed ER at their refueling stop in Nashville to phone officials in Washington for confirmation. She learned that the report was false, so the plane left Nashville and continued toward Los Angeles.[18]

ER enjoyed being around a leader as decisive and fearless as La Guardia; she said he displayed "real integrity and courage" in the midst of an unprecedented military crisis. Landing amid a light rain at Burbank Airport, ER found the climate to be eerie and disorienting. Most commercial flights had ceased after Pearl Harbor, and Burbank Airport was largely devoid of travelers. Governor Culbert Olson and Mayor Fletcher Bowron met the home defense leaders at the airport, but Bowron, ER soon realized, maintained contrary to all evidence that the threat to his city was virtually nil; his naïveté took ER by surprise. Fortunately, from her vantage point, other leaders in California had acknowledged that the dangers were real and they had already taken steps to mitigate the risks to civilians.[19]

California was not completely unprepared to handle an air raid. In the mid-1930s, the U.S. military held secret drills anticipating a foreign enemy attack against California. By 1939, mayors and police across the state practiced how to react if their cities were bombed. Governor Olson had partnered with the FBI to pursue the threat of fifth columnists. He had barred members of allegedly subversive organizations from joining the home guard. A few weeks prior to the attack on Pearl Harbor, Olson prevailed on the White House to tell the state "what we [Californians] may be up against" militarily. Now, Olson stationed National Guard troops to protect bridges and railroad stations, and he established volunteer recruitment centers in San Francisco and Los Angeles. ER asked state officials to tell her "what are the most helpful things we in Washington can do to help you."[20]

From the first leg of their tour on, ER's and La Guardia's views and agendas clashed in subtle but fundamental ways. They both believed that Japan had the ability to attack coastal cities. But they faced the question of how much fear they should engender—how much work they had to do to wake people up to the scope of the threat—and how much they should appeal to reason and calm people's already frayed nerves. There was no formula or handbook that could guide their answers. Their first stop was a public meeting on home defense in L.A.'s federal building. ER took a car with Bowron from the airport, while La Guardia rode with Olson. Ultimately, she worked to tamp fears down, and he fought to heighten them. She urged civilians to get a handle on their inner anxieties; he worried that civilian complacency would breed a lack of preparation— ultimately reaping death and destruction on an unprecedented scale. She viewed her number one job as to "calm people down"; he had to whip people up into an antifascist frenzy so they would acquire the military discipline to respond to air raids.[21]

In a room jammed with worried civilians, La Guardia began his mobilization campaign on the West Coast with stark words that served as a wake-up call. The war, he thundered, was coming closer to L.A. The Navy, he explained, had suffered big losses, and the odds that L.A. would be bombed had risen substantially. While ER praised La Guardia's fearlessness, she practiced a different kind of politics, seeking to reassure people that if they did what they were told, they, their city, and their country would be all right. She admitted that every person in the city felt afraid and she included herself in that group. But she beseeched all residents of the city to act "as though we're not afraid." She said that it was okay for them to pray, but she warned that prayer alone was insufficient; there could be no paralysis and everybody had to do jobs that benefited their communities.[22]

ER failed to calm people's fears in any lasting way. The *Los Angeles Times* warned that the city was a danger zone teeming with fifth columns looking to lead a coup and topple City Hall. Leaders at all levels—federal, state, and city— added to the impending sense of doom by sending fear-soaked messages to the people of California. State Attorney General Earl Warren urged residents to report any suspicious activity to their nearest FBI office. The Army banned almost all radio broadcasts from airing on the West Coast. Adding to the alarm, the FBI had begun to raid Japanese homes, padlock Japanese stores, and arrest Japanese Americans whom agents saw as trying to subvert the U.S. government.[23]

Residents lived in true fear of a Japanese invasion. Even though ER and La Guardia had come from Washington to impose some order on home defense in L.A., the city descended into chaos on the night of December 10. With the skies clear for the first time since the attack on Pearl Harbor, military officials received a report that planes were streaking toward L.A. The Army ordered the city to implement a blackout. Police cleared the streets of cars and pedestrians, while ER and La Guardia warned residents to stay away from public spaces. The air raid turned out to be a false alarm, but the alert set a pattern that would repeat itself across the country despite ER's and La Guardia's best efforts—rumors causing blackouts that shut down entire cities and exposed the flaws in the nation's air defenses.[24]

Fears of foreign enemy attacks inched up the West Coast like an airborne virus. The military conducted reconnaissance missions off coastal waters, adding to the sense of danger, and officials evacuated approximately 1,000 people from Carmel, Monterey, and Santa Cruz. In San Francisco, officials put sandbags around the Pacific Telephone & Telegraph Building, giving the city a somewhat militarized feel, and the FBI studied a homemade film of flashing lights near the bay because it was thought to show a signal system useful to enemy planes. Seattle residents were even more rattled. The mob that rioted on December 8 smashed store windows that emitted light, including red and green electric Christmas candles in a downtown jewelry store. At one point, rioters stopped to sing "God Bless America" and then resumed their rampage.[25]

The hysteria gave rise to conspiracy theories. Some Washington State residents pointed out that brush fires they had seen looked like an arrow giving bombers a map to follow in order to hit Seattle. Fears were so ubiquitous that officials came to see public events on the West Coast as too risky. They canceled Santa Anita's racing season, moved the Rose Bowl football game from Pasadena to Durham, North Carolina, and radio broadcasters urged station managers to refrain from any programming that had the potential to spread "horror."[26]

Brandishing distinct definitions of civil defense and wartime liberalism, ER and La Guardia agreed that they would leave L.A. and go their separate ways. He headed north; she went south. Each one was such a big personality bringing so much public cachet to the debate that they figured they could gain more attention for the mission by traveling separately. La Guardia arrived in San Francisco just after 9 a.m. on December 10, and he warned residents that they had frittered away "precious time" prior to Pearl Harbor and that they must expect that combat was going to reach their homes. La Guardia punctuated his message with a story: he had information, he said, that the vast majority of Americans did not have, and people had better listen to him closely and heed his commands. A few weeks prior to Pearl Harbor, he recounted, he had actually predicted that Hawaii was likely to be bombed and claimed that he had warned officials to prepare for just such an attack. He had not simply pulled this kind of information "out of my hat," he added. His tale had a moral: follow orders, and you might be able to spare your life and the lives of your loved ones.[27]

As La Guardia doused people's anxieties in verbal kerosene, ER arrived in San Diego disappointed by her brush with home defense in Los Angeles. While officials she had met in L.A. had plenty of plans committed to paper, they had failed to implement most of them. The city, she concluded, needed to acquire more medical supplies, set up more hospital beds, and train additional emergency medical teams. She also mocked as a recipe for panic the plan by the city to keep children locked up at school during an air raid, insisting that children (and their parents) would be far better off if they were sent home by the fastest route possible. And parents in the city, she informed OCD aide Corrington Gill in a confidential memo, must have access to "nursery schools and kindergartens . . . day nurseries in defense areas, and in certain sections where the parents have skills and can be called for by civilian defense." L.A. was lagging behind here, too.

For all of her frustration with Los Angeles officials, she found hope for home defense in San Diego. Updating her staff in Washington on her observations through a series of confidential memos, ER reported that a Mrs. Shreiner, one of her people in San Diego, had established eight volunteer recruitment centers while a team of able women filled in for Shreiner when she was away, creating a sound volunteer program overall. San Diego had also stockpiled medical supplies, trained doctors in emergency response, and set up a program to supply 1,000 hot meals and create 200 hospital beds in the immediate aftermath of any air raid. California as a whole was soon expected to have thousands of volunteers in a Women's Ambulance and Transport Corps.[28]

Pleased to see so much progress in San Diego's volunteer program, the first lady took a train to San Francisco (it was hard to travel by plane with so much air traffic grounded). While dining in L.A.'s train station during her trip north, ER heard over the loudspeaker that the Army had just ordered the West Coast to undergo a blackout. ER saw officials holding lanterns to light a path for travelers, as people calmly carried on their business.[29]

When she arrived in San Francisco, ER found possibly the worst leadership she would encounter on her week-long tour. The city's residents appeared to be enthusiastic about joining the OCD's ranks, but Mayor Angelo Rossi and the fire and police chiefs were prone to patriotic bluster that, in ER's eyes, mainly paid lip service to civil defense. During a public meeting, ER listened as local home defense leaders bragged and figuratively pounded their chests, although they had shortchanged key precepts of her social defense agenda and seemed incapable of shoring up the city's military defenses. When she informed San Francisco's fire chief that an infusion of federal funds for buying equipment was unlikely to happen any time soon, she found him lacking in the ingenuity that the city required to defend its residents from incendiary bombs. "Doing," she confided to her staff, discussing Rossi's hardly stellar team, "was different from saying!" She concluded something else during her time in San Francisco: La Guardia had failed to exert much in the way of visionary leadership. While his urgent remarks on threats facing residents inspired some military home defenders in the city, he had omitted any mention of the New Deal social objectives that she had been pushing, and she was dismayed by his oversight and nonchalance. He had failed to urge the city to change its policies so women could serve as air raid wardens (they were currently barred from doing so), and he had neglected to call attention to the need for more women volunteers in social welfare and public health positions.[30]

Her frustrations mounting, ER began to lean toward a more centralized, aggressive leadership from the OCD's Washington headquarters. Abhorring the parochialism she found in San Francisco, and displeased with La Guardia's blinkered vision of home defense, ER still paid tribute to the grassroots character of volunteer participation. But increasingly, she wanted Washington to direct the work. She asked that Morgenthau use federal funds to send into the field more "information on insignias and uniforms" for home defense and urged her Washington staff to take Red Cross training courses and volunteer as air raid wardens at night, thus setting a model of volunteerism for the American people. She continued to respect the diverse needs and politics of each community, but she also concluded that if home defense was going to thrive, then Washington had to have a strong coordination and policy role. In a memo to her staff, ER forecast that volunteers on a large scale would now enroll in social defense, but the grassroots enthusiasm was in and of itself insufficient. Her team had to cultivate partnerships between the OCD and liberal institutions including colleges, the League of Women Voters, and the YMCA—groups, she said, that wanted Washington's guidance.

These were not the only orders she issued to her colleagues at headquarters. She also asked them to step up efforts to assist local officials in answering people's questions regarding home defense; give people more access to nutrition and wartime consumer information; work with local communities to strengthen their "volunteer bureaus [and] information centers"; and, she added with a pat on her own back, "in every big city they have to have several sub-bureaus in different parts of the city which is exactly what I visualized originally." Uniformity, she said, trumped local autonomy. She talked to La Guardia about the need to make air raid alerts uniform across the country, and she argued that one of the core missions of air raid wardens had to become giving social services to their communities. The activity was so intense in Washington that Kellogg, as one colleague informed ER during her West Coast tour, was ready to implement the OCD's community action plan in states and cities across the country.[31]

Her next stop—the Pacific Northwest—gave her time to reflect on the sur-real sensation of traveling in wartime conditions. While on a train bound for Oregon, she marveled that at night the train had to be in motion with its lights turned off in order to avoid being seen from the air. She did not object to such measures, which she seemed to agree were necessary for her protection and the safety of her fellow passengers.[32]

In Portland, she met with officials in private, which she preferred to public meetings where posturing was the norm, and she received their honest assess-ment that if a disaster struck they were not yet prepared to handle it. Still, ER appreciated their candor and concluded that the city and state had taken strides in the right direction. In Washington State, she was pleased by the number of civilians volunteering for home defense roles, and she admired the resilience of Seattle's residents. Her daughter and granddaughter lived in the city nearest to Japan, she reported, yet her granddaughter was still getting dressed up to go to a dance—a triumph of normalcy over hysteria.[33]

In Seattle, ER was disturbed by the treatment of Japanese Americans and wrestled with herself about how this challenge should be handled. She denounced the "great hysteria [directed] against minority groups," publicly released a pic-ture of her standing next to Japanese Americans, and declared that the value of tolerance made American democracy a sharp contrast to the racism practiced by the Nazis. She explained to one correspondent that Americans had a moral responsibility to safeguard the rights of Japanese descendants. No citizen must be made to feel "that they have suddenly ceased to be Americans," ER warned. Anti-Semitism and racism damaged American democracy, which had to remain "the one real hope for the future," she added. The Japanese question was such a tough issue that her staff in Washington, D.C., opted to ask her to draft a personal reply to a correspondent who had asked for her views on the issue. Finally, she found pragmatic reasons to safeguard the rights of Japanese Americans. Japanese farmers, she wrote Secretary of the Treasury Henry Morgenthau, harvested 75 percent of the nation's winter vegetable crop, and there was simply no way for the country to replace the loss of so many vegetables if these farmers were detained.[34]

Despite her insistence that U.S. citizens from Germany, Italy, and Japan must receive equal treatment under the law, she was not immune to the pervasive fear of internal enemies that had begun to sweep the public. ER told civilians to report suspicious activity to the FBI and called the eruption of anti-Japanese sentiment a natural response to the attack on Pearl Harbor. She admitted that some people in fact had come to the United States to try to be helpful to the enemy and reassured the public that FBI agents were "rounding up as rapidly as possible all those that are suspect and there are a goodly number." Indeed, as part of a broader home defense campaign after Pearl Harbor, Hoover's FBI rounded up German and Italian enemy "aliens"; internal security was seen by those responsible for it to be fraught with peril, even though there were no documented cases of actual espionage. Facts were almost irrelevant. Rumor produced fear, and fear led to hysteria, and hysteria led to abuses.[35]

An even bigger problem for ER was the OCD's growing ties to the FBI. The rapid move toward this partnership helped create conditions that made the Japanese American internment camps politically popular. National security liberalism dispensed with constitutional protections, and the popular and elite conviction, without any evidence to support such claims, that Japanese Americans and Japanese immigrants were loyal to Hirohito and abetted the bombing of Pearl Harbor provided the context in which the camps could be established. In a New Year's Day radio address, La Guardia labeled his home defense critics "Japs" and "friends of Japs," provoking anti-Japanese feeling. When Oahu's Civilian Defense director offered his help to the FBI and praised the cooperation between the agencies, La Guardia informed Hoover that such collaboration did not surprise him, that he and Hoover made a good team, and that he had full faith in the FBI's ability to help meet the threats facing the American people.[36]

Despite her mixed record on the issue, ER came in for harsh criticism from her foes for her alleged sympathy for "aliens" from Axis-aligned nations. The *Los Angeles Times* called on ER "to retire from public life" because she had committed the sin of "bemoaning the plight of the treacherous snakes we call Japanese." The first lady concluded at the end of her trip that her presence helped "calm some of the rather hysterical fears" that were then spreading across the West Coast. But her tour of the region also invited the New Deal's opponents to attack her as soft on military security and incapable of leading an agency charged with protecting American lives.[37]

La Guardia had achieved more in home defense than his critics were willing to concede. His swagger and fearlessness inspired ER and countless other Americans. His ability to draw the nation's eyes to military defense gave his program vitality. One official called his idea of giving armbands to OCD volunteers brilliant. Even his flawed public relations drive had achieved some results when leading newspapers reprinted OCD bulletins informing civilians how to keep themselves safe during air raids. The White House released a picture of FDR sitting near La Guardia in a meeting of the war Cabinet, a sign that La Guardia had penetrated the inner sanctum. Few civilian and military officials disputed his long-standing belief that the most imperiled regions were the 300-mile zones running from the coasts inland, and that home defense should protect these zones first. Perhaps the greatest vindication of his (and ER's) movement was the surge of volunteers into the home defense program. Once mocked as wild-eyed, this program registered forcefully on the national conscience. New England alone had more than 1,250 defense councils; La Guardia won praise for having helped recruit thousands of air raid wardens in New York City prior to December 7, and he was now seeking to enlist 300,000 pilots in the OCD's Civil Air Patrol. One media report even said that La Guardia had asked the City Council chairman in New York to prepare to take over for him in case he decided to serve in home defense on a full-time basis.[38]

Even though Americans were filling La Guardia's ranks by the thousands, the White House had a different idea about his future. Despite the progress he had made, his own city came off as woefully unprepared to handle air raids while he was away on the West Coast. La Guardia's absence was only part of the problem in New York City. Army commanders were so jittery that when the Army base on Mitchel Field, Long Island, took a call from a member of the public inquiring about enemy bombers, they heard it as an actual air raid alarm and wrongly concluded that hundreds of enemy planes were racing toward Manhattan.

The Army alerted La Guardia's police that an air raid was coming, and the police alerted air raid wardens using radio signals and teletype communications. The city decided to order one million school children to go home for the day. The unruly mobilization transformed New York into a zone of chaos. Some children yelled and ran through Times Square. Workers in skyscrapers fled and poured into the streets, when they were supposed to shelter on a floor in the middle of the building. Commercial flights were canceled; most radio broadcasts in the region fell silent. Some New Yorkers stayed on the streets and gazed up at the sky in defiance of air raid orders, while Wall Street experienced its steepest loss since the day France fell in June of 1940.

The false alarm was a national debacle. The Army sought to pin the blame on La Guardia, upbraiding him for allowing his aides in City Hall to panic. La Guardia's standing plummeted because he was away from his city, and even after he had returned home, he came off as hot-headed, uncertain, and incapable of wresting order from the civic chaos. He met with senior aides in City Hall, who praised his firm leadership. But in a news conference, La Guardia projected an air of hubris and incompetence. Dressed in shirt sleeves with his tie loose around his neck, he leaned back in his chair, spread his arms wide, and announced that the Army was in charge of making all decisions regarding blackouts. Addressing the public's noncompliance during the recent false alarm, he warned that any

New Yorkers refusing to clear public spaces and take shelter risked their own lives and would face the full consequences of the law. All the same, La Guardia had trouble explaining simple procedures to New Yorkers. If they heard an alarm, he said, it meant that a blackout was coming, but even if they did not hear an alarm the city could still have a blackout.[39]

He ratcheted up his scare tactics. "We have never had war by a foreign power brought to the streets of our city and right into our homes," he declared. He described the terror of "glass . . . rain[ing] right down on the streets" and predicted that workers who panicked and fled from skyscrapers would be "crushed to death" at the exits. Subversives, he warned, might enter crowded subway stations and yell "Bombs!," while he recommended that Americans spy on suspicious Germans and Italians who lived in their neighborhoods. If New Yorkers defied his orders, they would sow what he termed "fear, disorder, confusion, and panic," and he signed a bill promising six months in jail and $500 fines for anybody who violated city air raid orders.[40]

La Guardia bore the brunt of the blame for home defense's woes. In fact, the Army both initiated and reinforced La Guardia's incendiary warnings. Secretary Henry Stimson wrote La Guardia that the U.S. military was responsible for ordering blackouts and halting radio broadcasts, as if such decisions were to become more frequent now that the war had begun. The Army even developed a color-coded air raid warning system: yellow was a confidential signal to home defense operators that enemy planes had been seen heading toward their city; blue informed civilians to prepare for an air raid; a red alert urged people to take shelter immediately due to the imminent air raid threat. Taking its cue from home defense officials, the *New York Times* observed that "both Atlantic and Pacific Coast cities will be bombed before we are through," thus affirming La Guardia's predictions.[41]

As the face of home defense, La Guardia came under fire for his hysterical oratory, his confused messages, and his inflammatory admonishments that civilians had better follow his prescriptions—or else risk death. Moreover, in the days following Pearl Harbor, the country was eager to find people to blame for the utter absence of defenses there, and La Guardia—even though he was not explicitly faulted for letting down the Navy's guard—became swept up in the sense that home defense had failed and that Americans had died in an attack the government had failed to anticipate. His tour of the West Coast, as his city experienced chaos, revived the charge that nobody could serve as mayor and home defense chief simultaneously. "We voted to keep you in N.Y.—not all over the nation," one correspondent berated La Guardia. Columnists described him as a frantic figure who had failed to prepare even his own city to cope with an air raid. Columnist Raymond Clapper blasted La Guardia's "part-time theatricals" and showy displays of bravado. Walter Lippmann faulted La Guardia's shrill oratory, which sowed public fears, and his churlish "desk-thumping." What Americans truly needed, Lippmann thundered, was limited martial law in the 300-mile coastal danger zones, a law requiring civilians to serve in military roles on the home front, and a new Assistant Secretary of War for Home Defense. (Lippmann also likened ER's "fads, fancies, homilies, and programs to the activities of an excited village improvement society.") One cartoon spoofed La Guardia as a band leader playing more instruments than he could handle and advised him to "stick to [his] drum," which was running his city. *Time* reported that while fewer than 2 percent of all New York buildings were equipped to handle air raids, La Guardia was frittering away his days by putting women in uniforms and having them salute him, which protected not a single New Yorker.[42]

La Guardia's own constituents hurled complaints at City Hall, denouncing home defense as an inept effort that did not go far enough. Thus, local reactions to home defense complicated the federal dynamic, as citizens experienced the program through their own eyes rather than the federal government's efforts to paint it in a flattering light. One typical letter chastised La Guardia because "we have no air raid shelters, no gas masks, no proper protection. . . . I am afraid to go to bed at night—we are targets for the Japs and Germans, who are at our shores . . . ," and P.S.: "This city is full of spies—so is Long Island." Another New Yorker vented that "not enough has been done for civilian defense . . . Why haven't we got gas masks? The possibility of bombings is very real now . . . why aren't there anti-aircraft guns on the bridge towers around New York? It seems to me that is a fundamental protection." It was not all hostile. Admirers celebrated home defense as a necessary protective step that also bound Americans to their communities and their country and respected individual rights. One New York tenants association praised the civil defense program for bringing "New Yorkers . . . together in neighborhood units. Notices calling tenant meetings in apartment houses are bringing out the crowd; and people, who never used to exchange the time of day in the elevators . . . are suddenly becoming neighbors" in defense of their communities. But at the grassroots, critics outgunned La Guardia's dwindling supporters.[43]

Congress turned against the Little Flower, too. Members came to regard him as an inept director with an authoritarian streak, a bluster-prone, out-of-control leader puffed up with his own importance and incapable of hardening the nation's defenses. The House voted in favor of having La Guardia fired from the OCD, expressing no confidence in America's home defense chief. The first lady worked behind the scenes to push La Guardia out of the director's chair. She held talks with Wayne Coy and Harold Smith, two White House aides, and they agreed that La Guardia had to quit. Coy and Smith asked FDR to discuss with them the need to rid the OCD of La Guardia. Their brief against view of

La Guardia was one that FDR now shared: Critics had called him ineffectual; he had unceremoniously fired aides, harmed employee morale, and had no business running both New York City and the OCD once the United States had officially entered the war. Aides told Roosevelt that the OCD had actually sent 18,000 posters to a town with a population of 6,000 people—one indication that nobody was minding the store. La Guardia had created other headaches for the president. FDR had grown tired of listening to the disputes pitting his wife against La Guardia. "Each one comes with a story; each one is right; each one comes to me. I cannot cope with it and I want you to try to keep them away from me and reconcile their differences," he instructed Anna Rosenberg.[44]

In mid-December, FDR informed La Guardia that his service as the OCD's director had put him in an impossible position and that henceforth he had to focus all of his energy on governing, and defending, New York. La Guardia was reluctant to leave a job he loved in a moment when the country desperately needed his leadership. He blamed the news media for his predicament and assured FDR that social and military defense programs were going to be better handled, but it was clear to any fair-minded observer that without ER's and FDR's backing he could not survive as home defense chief for much longer.[45]

His personality had invited any number of criticisms on the grounds that he was reckless, terrible to his staff, and fanned people's fears rather than soothed their anxieties. Another person in La Guardia's position would have almost surely been less controversial than him. At the same time, a lower-profile figure would also have probably made less headway, enlisted fewer citizens, and gained less attention to the mission. La Guardia's brand of liberalism represented both his greatest strength and his chief defect, drawing support from national security liberals who believed in government power to ensure social stability during emergencies, while antagonizing isolationists, social defense liberals, and citizens who found his orders an affront to their personal freedoms. It is hard to imagine anybody excelling in his job after Pearl Harbor, when the country was rife with so much fear and hysteria. But La Guardia lit a match to the flame and turned it into a conflagration.

With La Guardia being pushed out of the director's chair, on December 15, ER returned to Washington, D.C., eager to fill the void that his departure was sure to bring. The time was ripe for her volunteer, social defense vision of liberalism: she would move fast to bring it to communities nationwide. Within hours of her landing, Morgenthau and other aides updated her on the volunteer movement. Her clear goal, ER announced, was to build "a stronger community organization than we have ever had before in our country." While the days following Pearl Harbor are hardly seen as halcyon ones for New Deal liberalism, ER was flush with progressive excitement, calling social welfare a cornerstone of defense. Jane

Seaver stepped up OCD's efforts to recruit young people. ER worked to help single women who had just moved to Washington adjust to their new lives far from their homes. "The proof of the pudding will be in the eating," she said of her agenda, meaning that if more Americans had better lives as a result of her activities, then social defense would have proven its worth. After a decade of economic depression, Americans, the first lady maintained, knew that national defense meant not only protection from physical harm but also secure communities rooted in economic prosperity, good health, access to the arts, and a vibrant civic life. Air raid wardens must do their part to "meet the needs of each and every person . . . who is not able to meet them himself," she said. "Some people have an idea that this has nothing to do with defense. They say it is really only a way of putting over on an unsuspecting community, in the guise of defense, some of the very bad things which go by the name of 'New Deal Measures.' These people, I am afraid, are putting the cart before the horse. If there had never been a New Deal, we would have had to accept this conception of defense. We have learned from London that it is the [socially] insecure who rush in large numbers to congregate together in air raid shelters. They must be given security or their fears run riot."[46]

Liberals showcased ER as the brave leader of a movement that appeared poised to fulfill the promises of the First and Second World Wars–namely, that war presented a chance to strengthen liberalism and improve the lives of all citizens. One staff member wrote in a memo that ER must be the "prime interpreter" of social defense to the rest of the country and that her "imagination and initiative" gave her the ability to understand people's needs in this moment of mass hysteria. ER logged eighteen-hour days, read every document in her briefcase, and recruited experts to join her cause. She spent Christmas Day singing carols; visiting the Salvation Army; going to a conference on British relief; and dining with Winston Churchill, who was visiting Washington to discuss the war with FDR.[47]

News from the front in the Pacific was grim. In December, Japanese forces had captured Hong Kong, Guam, and Wake Island, and when they invaded the Philippines, General Douglas MacArthur's forces in the Far East were undermanned, undersupplied, and had to retreat to the Corregidor island in the Bataan peninsula. Despite these defeats, ER's hopes for the New Year were understandably high. She believed with some justification that many Americans agreed with her that moral, spiritual, and economic advances had to accompany military mobilization—and she envisioned Washington partnering with city and state leaders and countless individuals to achieve this social revolution. In late December, she indicated that she intended to stay in the OCD and fight. She discussed the OCD's budget for 1942 with administration officials, and she announced that she still felt that she was contributing to the home defense mission and that she planned to stay on as assistant director until she knew that her brand of New Deal liberalism was firmly ensconced in communities across America.[48]

11

Fair Game

> Freedom from actual want, freedom to do a job, freedom to have a part
> in your government, freedom to say what you think . . . are what has
> made this country give hope to people. I think we have to continue
> doing this as a part of civilian defense in every community.
> —Eleanor Roosevelt, January 1942

In the first two months of 1942, ER began to realize some aspects of her vision.
Americans flocked to join her home defense movement as volunteers fulfilling
their responsibility to each other and democracy, giving themselves a greater
stake in the outcome of the war against fascism. The home defense volunteer
forces also provided a lift to national morale, as concrete steps, such as rescuing
victims during natural disasters and assisting women factory workers with child
care, made Americans feel more secure in their lives in communities nationwide. Finally, the volunteer corps conducted tasks such as feeding Americans
in need, growing vegetables for healthier diets, leading physical fitness activities,
and ensuring access to health care for those without it. As La Guardia lost his
credibility in the wake of Pearl Harbor, ER stepped up her campaign to redefine
New Deal liberalism along the lines of mass mobilization, morale building, and
spreading social equality to more and more Americans through a federal-grass-
roots partnership. But a rise in the public's hysteria, a growing hostility toward
New Deal liberals in power during wartime, and grim news from East Asia combined to help subordinate social defense liberalism to national security needs.
All of these developments formed the backdrop for a national scandal that led to
Eleanor Roosevelt's resignation and dealt a blow to her effort to keep New Deal
liberalism on equal footing with national security liberalism.[1]

Time was running out for La Guardia. In early 1942, critics continued to pum-
mel him: he had neglected his work as mayor, and his inflammatory rhetoric
did more to stoke mass fears of enemy attacks than unite the public behind a
sensible war strategy. He had fomented a kind of paranoia across much of the

United States. In Washington, FDR directed Federal Works Agency administrator Philip Fleming, Carmody's successor, to work with the OCD to strengthen the protection of the Capitol Building, the Treasury, and the Smithsonian. FDR wanted to put the nation's cultural treasures in bomb shelters. Over at the OCD's headquarters, the fears that La Guardia had provoked reached a high pitch. T. S. Walmsley, the OCD's deputy director, wanted La Guardia to recruit clergymen to a program aimed at tending to injured civilians in the wake of air raids. When L. D. Gasser, who led the OCD's Protection Division, learned that a lot of air raid wardens were bringing guns with them when they reported for duty, he urged them to refrain from engaging the enemy in combat; fearing that wardens might become vigilantes, Walmsley told colleagues that arming them was unwise at this time.[2]

Civilians offered their own ideas for home defense. Some of them were outlandish and did not reflect the reality of the actual threat. One New Orleans man suggested that the OCD establish a "National Civilian Suicide Squad of America," which would recruit thirty-five- to fifty-five-year-old men to carry out suicide attacks on internal enemies. Gasser forwarded the man's idea to some of his colleagues and thanked him for his enthusiasm. Even Eleanor Roosevelt predicted that air raids on the United States were not a question of if but when. She urged the government to camouflage its vital infrastructure to hide buildings from enemy pilots. She felt that bad weather had thus far helped protect Americans from air raids, but she warned that civil air patrols were perhaps "the only thing that stands between us and the raids next spring."[3]

As fear engulfed the home defense debate, FDR concluded that his only option was to fire La Guardia. La Guardia refused to go quietly. In mid-December, La Guardia had met with FDR in the White House, where the president told him that no person could possibly serve as both mayor and OCD director simultaneously. La Guardia protested that his critics were driven by their political agenda and that the newspapers had unfairly made him into an object of ridicule. FDR was not persuaded. He and ER both supported Harvard Law School Dean James M. Landis as La Guardia's replacement. As former chairman of the Securities and Exchange Commission, Landis had earned a reputation as a skilled administrator with strong New Deal ties. As home defense director for New England, he had transformed his region into a much-praised model of physical protection, with tens of thousands of trained air raid wardens, firefighters, and police drilling hard for war. Beyond that feather in his cap, Landis seemed to ER more receptive to her social ideals than the single-minded La Guardia.[4]

On January 2, FDR asked Landis to assume La Guardia's responsibilities. The next day, Landis talked to La Guardia. He informed FDR that they intended to discuss the transition with the president soon. Meantime, La Guardia was still seeking to ingratiate himself with ER. He sent her a nutrition pamphlet that included a bit of humor: "The Director of Civilian Defense was so impressed with this pamphlet that the Mayor of the City of New York is getting out that he thought you would like to see it." ER praised the pamphlet and promised to give it to her Nutrition Committee.[5]

The warm exchange belied their increasingly frosty relationship, however. La Guardia's policies and attitude toward home defense continued to rankle. As columnists Drew Pearson and Jack Anderson reported, La Guardia had repeatedly rebuffed ER's reforms. And she took exception to his plan to have only petite women march down Fifth Avenue in designer uniforms and salute him as they passed by in a parade. The average woman could not afford such uniforms, ER pointed out, which meant that the poor would be barred from joining the volunteer ranks.[6]

La Guardia had antagonized his colleagues in Washington and had become an object of ridicule to his one-time allies in the administration. Ickes confided to his diary that the mayor was "on the way out." On January 9, Landis assumed control of the OCD's daily operations, and La Guardia said he intended to spend more time "in the field." It was a face-saving remark by a defeated man. La Guardia had stopped attending Cabinet meetings (he had loved doing so), the news media continued to criticize him, and he admitted to New Yorkers that he intended to resign from the OCD soon. The *Newark Evening News* captured his precarious position, publishing a cartoon that depicted La Guardia hanging on with his fingertips to a plane in mid-flight; "When Will He Let Go," the caption asked. By early January La Guardia had become a figurehead who was no longer in charge of the OCD.[7]

ER rushed to fill the void. She hoped to showcase America as the world's one truly robust democracy. While La Guardia's reputation plummeted, ER's climbed to new heights. She sharpened her message, asserting that social defense offered a prime means to realize FDR's Four Freedoms. After the war, she said, Americans must live "more decently and happily together" and share in the fruits of economic security. She also watched as some of the initiatives she and La Guardia had taken prior to Pearl Harbor began to reap dividends. The volunteer movement burst into the nation's conscience, and the surge of people into home defense was, ER said, "a wonderful thing." In the three weeks following Pearl Harbor, according to her office, more than 2.5 million Americans registered in the volunteer program, nearly tripling the ranks of volunteers. In January alone, more than two million additional volunteers registered for service, bringing the total volunteer number to more than 5.6 million. (In contrast, the Armed Forces had fewer than 4 million people on active duty.) The number of volunteers in the physical protection and social defense programs both experienced explosive growth. Military defense volunteers increased their ranks by 600,000 in January alone, while social defense rose by approximately 250,000 volunteers. ER took heart; the movement she had helped launch had morphed into a grassroots juggernaut.[8]

By February's end, home defense had nearly 2,000 volunteer centers located in city halls, firehouses, and the offices of the Red Cross. Between mid-December and mid-January, about 10,000 Americans applied to join the OCD's Civil Air Patrol, while state-level activity also ramped up. In Louisiana, authorities reported a surge of volunteer sign-ups, while Pennsylvania had 617 local defense councils statewide by early 1942. Veterans, workers, and municipal employees tended to populate the ranks of the military defense services, while housewives, members of civic groups, and New Deal agency employees tended to join the social defense program.[9]

Volunteers undertook a variety of socially beneficial tasks. They provided information to consumers about making smart purchases, trained workers in industries that needed skilled labor, conducted salvage campaigns, sought to make local transit more efficient so rubber needed to make tires could be preserved for military uses, sold defense bonds and stamps, built day-care centers for mothers working in defense factories, planted and promoted Victory Gardens, taught principles of nutrition, and sought to organize doctors and nurses to improve the health of all people in a given community. ER's program relied on face-to-face meetings and conferences, letters, phone calls, and partnerships between government, industry, civic groups, and local and state officials. Baltimore offered a microcosm of ER's robust effort to transform the life of the average civilian. The city's social defense program, led by a bank president, a landscape architect, a manufacturer, and other established members of the city, helped draw 1,000 women volunteers to a single meeting, where they pledged themselves to recruiting hundreds of additional women volunteers. Baltimore's social defenders mounted a public health campaign to stamp out the city's rat infestation; gave fellow residents information about cooking nutritious meals, planting victory gardens, and conserving vital materials; and set up a center where mothers could swap old kids' shoes for newer ones. Block leaders styled themselves as jack-of-all-trades social helpers, able to tackle any problem that might arise in their neighborhoods to keep morale up among the people. The OCD's Volunteer Talents Section used writers and artists to spread the volunteer mission to people, and the agency distributed thousands of posters, handbooks, and pamphlets urging "all able-bodied, responsible persons in the community—men and women, housewives, laborers, business and professional people" to join the ranks "for the mutual protection of all."[10]

As La Guardia moved to the margins of the debate, ER reorganized her programs to make them more cohesive. She changed the name of her division; the Division of Volunteer Participation became the Division of Community

Planning, stressing the local thrust of social planning. Seeking to spread her influence, she installed allies in key OCD posts. Judge Justine Polier took charge of community affairs, Eloise Davison covered morale building and social welfare, Wilma Shields coordinated volunteers, Jane Seaver led a youth initiative, Crystal Fauset ran African American affairs, while Betty Lindley and Elinor Morgenthau served as trusted lieutenants who helped put ER's plans into action. Paul Kellogg gained control of daily OCD operations. ER also sought approval to hire more staff in the regions so they could recruit more volunteers.[11]

ER's office hummed with the energy of a wartime agency in the midst of combat conditions. Her aides drafted radio scripts for the OCD, distributed training manuals to civilians, and established recruitment offices. ER had six clerks and a more senior aide whose mission was to help ER respond to her piles of mail. ER herself also buzzed with conviction and desire. She pushed her team hard. She wanted better intelligence about community needs and improved relations with local leaders. She asked an aide to find "an average American family" whom the OCD could use to publicize the benefits of social defense. She was so devoted to raising the OCD's profile and spreading her gospel that she wanted to know if television, a fresh tool for reaching the masses then under experiment in New York City, might help with this mission.[12]

As the country faced the reality of a long war, ER also concluded that her dream of building a women's civilian volunteer army was misguided and that men and women had to be recruited into the same program. Otherwise, she fretted, home defense might become a ghetto that restricted women to lesser roles. She explained her reasoning to Corrington Gill, deputy director in charge of Operations: "If the whole responsibility of organizing volunteers is given over to [the local women's director], it becomes a thing only for women." And if "the women's activities compete with other activities . . . , that is bad." Recruit the men, too, she commanded.

She also took up the fight to make civil rights a cornerstone of home defense. She lobbied for the appointment of an African American on the Volunteer Participation Committee. African Americans, she argued, must have the chance to work in the defense industry. And she urged the regional directors to strike from volunteer forms any questions regarding race and religion in order to curb the chances of discrimination. She made a point of celebrating the tradition of African Americans' contributing to the nation in wartime. Yet, despite her public pleas, progress on the question of race was slow. A colleague sent ER a memo describing how an OCD official predicted "a riot in the Army" if African Americans were suddenly allowed to become blood donors. The NAACP's Washington, D.C. branch reported to the OCD that African American morale in the city had hit bottom, a result of local police abuse and the persistence of Jim

Crow in home defense. ER was helpless to change such entrenched conditions through an agency that had few enforcement tools at its disposal.[13]

She also campaigned to mobilize young people. Working with Jane Seaver, she sent pamphlets and bulletins to raise awareness of home defense on college campuses and inside youth organizations. She gave radio talks about the role of youth in home defense, yet, here, too, her efforts yielded mixed results. The White House meddled in ER's public relations efforts, complicating their outreach to young people.[14]

It was easy for the first lady to immerse herself in social defense in the early weeks of 1942. After all, the survival of democracy, she felt, was at stake. The United States was now a combatant, and she had a key role in the struggle against fascism. She became the nation's most effective advocate for mass mobilization, publicizing the volunteer movement, fighting to keep people's spirits up, preparing civilians physically and psychologically to handle air raids on their homes, and strengthening democracy's foundation. She fed off the enthusiasm Americans felt for her cause. Thousands of letters poured into her office. She enjoyed receiving letters from Americans from all walks of life. A shipbuilder eager to volunteer in her program wrote: "You have a grate [sic] reputation." An expert on childhood education wrote that he badly wanted to serve in her movement, while a Seattle resident informed her that he wanted to assist with morale building. A Missouri woman asked ER to help her daughter find a job in home defense. ER was delighted by the public's affection and found strength in their faith in her mission; the relationship between her and her admirers was symbiotic. The people's "patriotism and enthusiasm" for social defense "is a constant inspiration to me in my work as Assistant Director," she assured one correspondent. She was so eager to write to her fans that on a four-hour train ride she dictated enough letters that one of her secretaries had a full day's worth of work as a result.[15]

The first lady offered an alternative vision to Nazi totalitarianism. She gave women a public purpose in total war, and she prioritized social action and community concerns over individual needs, stressing the importance of the collective good rather than the wants of individuals. She sought to humanize democratic capitalism through the social defense experiment. Meeting with labor leaders in the White House, a portrait of Abraham Lincoln hanging over her head, she declared that the nation must achieve freedom from want, freedom to think, and freedom to participate in their representative government.[16]

Still, even as the volunteer ranks dramatically expanded, ER never resolved the core tension plaguing the home defense mission: what was Washington's role in mass mobilization? She spoke the language of grassroots, voluntary participation. Social change, she argued, had to emerge partly from the bottom up; after all, local communities knew their own needs better than remote Washington, and neighbors were best positioned to help neighbors in the struggle for social justice. She called OCD's headquarters "a nice little ivory tower" where plans were hatched, but the real work, she said, must unfold in the communities. Ordinary people imbued with the "confidence and ability to meet attack on every front" had to take charge of this campaign. Nonetheless, a locally oriented home defense movement could easily become unfocused and chaotic. Without a firm guiding hand, communities had forged a potpourri of programs. One idea behind much of the New Deal was that the federal government, in times of crisis, must do for communities and individuals what they could not do for themselves. Without specific direction from the OCD, local rules, norms, and values would prevail over national policies.[17]

The first lady never found an answer to this most elemental of dilemmas in the mass mobilization program. She had largely given up on passing national legislation to expand Social Security, enacting greater legal protections for organized labor, and establishing new relief and economic recovery agencies. She recognized that Congress no longer had an appetite for such reforms. Even FDR and his aides had cooled to the idea of anything that hinted at a new New Deal. She also had trouble reconciling divergent civilian views of home defense and what it meant to people's lives. Was it hunters, veterans, and farmers who owned their own guns serving in the vanguard of military defense, as one Portland, Oregon, man questioned, or was it planting gardens, feeding neighbors, and housing soldiers, as others asked.[18]

As Landis found his footing in the OCD, ER understood that her presence posed unique and uncomfortable challenges for him. "Being the President's wife would make it pretty awkward for a good many people if I were to" lead an interdepartmental committee, as somebody had proposed, she wrote him. She tacitly acknowledged that he was in charge, not she. When the two of them met, she insisted on climbing one flight of stairs to see him in his office rather than have him come down to hers. But, in fact, she was much better known than Landis, and she was not shy about using her role as first lady to win people to her cause. Landis said that her presence put him in an impossible position because she had ties to "the President considerably closer than mine!" If she took a stand on an issue, it automatically involved the president of the United States. By offering to stay on in civilian defense, Ickes concurred, ER was putting "a hell of a proposition up to Landis."[19]

Having the first lady in the OCD also redounded to Landis's benefit. He put her to work. He asked that she focus on educating consumers. Her job, he explained, was to help the country enact the four freedoms. In signing Administrative Order No. 22, Landis also put her in charge of a new Community and Volunteer Participation Branch, which was designed to cope with social and economic problems and promote the rights of youth and workers. The first lady

seemed to bond with Landis. One night, after participating in a series of meetings, ER and Landis went to a play together, a sign of a burgeoning professional
relationship that augured well for her future in the OCD.[20]

She assured reporters that as long as the agency's leaders wanted her, she
intended to remain on the job. She also wrote Landis that she wanted to stay in
her job, although if they found a viable successor, she would consider stepping
down. But she hated the thought of giving up on her great purpose in public
life—strengthening democracy for all its citizens. When MacLeish warned that
ER's "intensive drive to bring about widespread participation in [social defense]
activities may create the suspicion that it is all a propaganda device for New Deal
objectives, with resulting disunity and friction in the community," she dismissed
his comment as unenlightened. On her core mission, there could be no back-
sliding. During the first days of February, ER's schedule was as busy as ever. She
toured home defense initiatives in the Midwest and South, discussed African
American women's roles in Pensacola, Florida, and observed the training of air
raid wardens. Poised to weave social defense into people's lives, she could not
have known that she was about to be ensnared in the first major national scandal
of World War II.[21]

ER had long considered exercise as more than simply an individual choice to
fine-tune one's body and nurture one's spirit. In wartime, all Americans, she felt,
had to be physically fit. She cited countless benefits: more young men eligible
to fight in the Army, a healthier workforce producing more guns and tanks, and
resilience in case of air raids. She led by example. She organized lunch and afternoon calisthenics and square dancing sessions for staff on the roof of OCD's
headquarters. To her, liberalism meant not only economic opportunity for
workers and poor people; it also featured the arts, entertainment, and physical
fitness, a holistic philosophy that built a democratic culture, cultivated creative
thought, and tended to the masses' psychological well-being. Such thinking was
hardly radical in the context of the times. As one correspondent complained to
her, too many people "go to movies, bingo games, or some café where they are
onlookers" and are not engaged in physical activity. "Rest, good food and wholesome recreation," noted a physiologist in the *Journal of the American Medical
Association*, were keys to winning the war. Dancing, a Californian wrote ER, was
a balm to the spirit; entertainment, an Oklahoma man insisted, helped children
who were forced to hunker in caves cope with the shock of air raids.[22]

Against this backdrop, ER made a fateful decision. In early 1942, she hired two
friends to advance the arts and exercise agendas of the OCD. Hollywood film
star Melvyn Douglas agreed to run an arts council dedicated to recruiting artists
and writers as volunteers to promote home defense. Although the media later
reported that Douglas received a hefty sum in his new job, he was hired without

pay. His volunteers were going to write radio scripts, draft speeches, and produce films promoting the war effort. Douglas wanted to help win the war, and he complained that his fellow Californians too often refused to see the acute threat the Axis posed to their way of life. Not only Ickes but also MacLeish supported this arts program, and Douglas came aboard with a goal of recruiting twenty thousand writers, actors, musicians, and playwrights, a back-door attempt to revive the now-defunct Federal Theatre Project and find a positive role for America's artists in lifting the spirits of an angst-ridden public.[23]

Second, even more sensationally, she hired dancer Mayris Chaney at a salary of $4,600 a year to lead a dance program aimed at building children's morale. ER viewed Chaney, who was a close friend of hers, as an inspired pick. She had hosted Chaney at the White House and the family estate in Hyde Park, and Chaney had honored the first lady by inventing a dance called The "Eleanor Glide," which she demonstrated in front of ER during a preview in New York City. Chaney shared ER's ardor for women's equality, even seeking to open doors to women who wanted to train in a home defense school for men. ER believed that Chaney knew how to teach "appropriate activities that could be carried on in the confined space of a bomb shelter" akin to what the British had done. Plus, there was a principle at stake: women, ER believed, deserved to earn as much as men. Chaney had earned more in her career at various times, and, after all, ER had 17 staff members who earned more than $2,600 a year, putting Chaney's salary in line with the money paid to her colleagues. Fewer than 75 people on her staff earned any salary, but ER saw nothing wrong with some hard-working senior leaders receiving government compensation. Still, the typical Army soldier earned $21 a week, or $252 a year, while Chaney was making more than what even an Army colonel made annually.[24]

ER's heart was in the right place. It is hard to imagine a more disastrous choice than Chaney, however. For one thing, Chaney had once performed in a night club as a "fan," or seminude, dancer. She was also one of ER's old friends, which opened the OCD to charges of wartime cronyism. Worse, Chaney's salary affronted Americans who were being bombarded with calls to sacrifice their time (and, in some cases, risk their lives) in defense of their democracy for little or no pay. On February 5, Ickes wrote in his diary: today, "Hell broke loose."[25]

He wasn't being hyperbolic. Leading newspapers and members of Congress almost simultaneously began to report the news that ER had put her friends, Douglas and Chaney, on the government payroll at $4,600 a year each. Almost overnight, ER became, as one columnist wrote, the "most discussed [person] in" America as "the propriety of what the president's wife is doing and saying about civilian defense and particularly her belief that it extends to various social welfare activities that ordinarily would [not] be associated with civilian defense" had rocketed into the national consciousness. The controversy touched several third rails in American politics: what constituted ethical conduct in wartime; how the government should raise national morale; what roles should women have in a total war; and was ER as first lady "fair game," as one of her critics asserted, or was she off limits? The scandal blindsided ER. But even the dance professionals were miffed. One Drake University dance expert wrote the first lady that in her view Chaney was a cipher within the professional dance world. Chaney's image as a nightclub performer rubbed salt in ER's self-inflicted wound. Seminude dancing, one admirer scolded, was amoral. Chaney replied to the uproar by saying that her goal was to etch rhythm into children's lives; her remark hardly inspired public confidence.[26]

The timing of the controversy could hardly have been worse for the administration. In February, Japanese forces conquered Singapore, invaded Burma, and turned toward India. Allied defeats in the Pacific deepened anxiety among those Americans on the coasts who already suspected that their lives were under threat. At home, the scandal gave the New Deal's critics an opening, and they seized on the chance to discredit social liberalism and FDR's war leadership. Conservative Southern Democrats and Republicans in Congress decried ER's use of taxpayer dollars to enrich her friends. They trashed the New Deal itself as a corrupt boondoggle that retarded the defense campaign. On February 5, Rep. Leland Ford excoriated the 17 staff members in ER's division who earned salaries as high as $5,600 a year. While the critics aimed their fire at all of ER's liberal hires, they found such high salaries for women particularly galling. Ford called dancing and singing "ballyhoo" and declared that Americans were shedding blood and treasure for democracy, not "for the purpose of social gatherings, a great playtime and a Roman holiday." ER's actions threatened the Allied cause, Ford complained, and Congress ought to launch a formal investigation. Other members blasted ER for paying Chaney twice as much as a captain who had died in combat. Here was evidence of a "bundles for Eleanor campaign" enabling her cronies to profit off the fighting. Republican Rep. R. B. Wigglesworth called her aide Paul Kellogg a fifth columnist, while Texas Democratic Rep. Martin Dies, who chaired the House Committee on Un-American Activities, predicted that in the next six months the country was going to be invaded from both coasts and said that frivolities in Washington made Americans less safe. The House approved a bill barring the OCD from spending money on "physical fitness by dancers, for fan-dancing, street shows, theatrical performances or other public entertainment," even though the bill included $100 million for gas masks and other equipment. Congress, gossip columnist Walter Winchell quipped, had declared war on Eleanor Roosevelt, even if it had voted for "War on the Axis."[27]

Newspapers—one of the most vibrant sources of information at the time—stirred the outrage against the first lady that reached a crescendo in communities nationwide. ER had never had such bad press, one of her friends remarked. Indeed, anti-New Deal pundits had struck gold. Right-wing columnist Frank Kent accused ER of seeking millions of dollars for her wartime New Deal and insinuating herself in national politics even though she held no elected post. She "covers . . . more territory than anyone else in the country," he complained. Columnist Westbrook Pegler charged that her communist sympathies guided her leadership of the OCD. Beyond her typical anti-New Deal nemeses, some pro-New Deal scribes also complained bitterly about ER's blindness. Pundit Raymond Clapper used consecutive articles to liken ER's OCD to a "personal parking lot for pets and protégés." Editorials, cartoons, and news reporters piled on. The *Sacramento Bee* editorialized that ER's actions recalled World War I-era officials seeking self-enrichment at the public trough; Chaney was "a grave handicap" to defense, and ER's mail was running heavily against her, the *Bee* reported. FDR had even started editing his wife's columns, the *Bee* alleged.[28]

Other newspapers saw the hires as the clearest evidence to date that Washington had prioritized social engineering ahead of military victory. According to Charlottesville's unfriendly newspaper, the *Daily Progress*, ER had turned the OCD into a "social laboratory of that group of theorists that believes the citizens must always be directed in every phase of living by agents of the Federal Government"—a step toward dictatorship by elites scheming "at some Washington, Philadelphia, or New York tea party." The *Boston Herald* denounced ER's division as a "vast uplift enterprise." Newspapers published devastating pictures that showed Chaney powdering her face as she looked into a mirror with captions calling her ER's protégé. The *Kansas City Times* showed an image of Chaney as she did the "Eleanor Glide," lifting one arm in the air while her other held on to her skirt. One cartoon depicted a line of dancers, artists, and musicians—assorted "nuts and cranks"—waiting to receive their check from the OCD's pay window.[29]

The scandal not only tarnished the OCD's reputation but also called FDR's leadership into question. Its repercussions were so toxic that even a close FDR ally like Ickes worried that he too would be swept up in it; he had prevailed on La Guardia to hire one of his friends, which would smell "fishy" if the news leaked. Landis believed that in spite of her good heart, ER had harmed the OCD, and she had to go. The public outrage sealed the first lady's fate. While ER retained some pockets of public support, thousands of Americans fumed that she had paid a hefty sum to her liberal friend for a program with the thinnest of connections, in their eyes, to wartime readiness.[30]

The outrage spread not just via media reports but also by word of mouth. One volunteer from Terre Haute, Indiana, wrote to ER that her son was making $21 a month while stationed at a base in Hawaii, doing an actual war job, in contrast to arts and dance lessons. Lansing, Michigan residents wrote ER that they were so upset that they refused to buy any more war bonds. Pittsburgh's residents reacted to the scandal by reducing their purchase of defense stamps by 25,000.[31]

The letters flowing in to ER's office were, for the most part, scathing. Her staff put the missives into positive, unfavorable, and abusive categories; one tally described 238 letters as vitriolic, 106 as negative, and only 62 supportive of the first lady's actions. Some conservative Democrats and Republicans, who had long been hostile to the New Deal, argued that liberals had used the crisis as an opportunity to conduct social experiments. Citing Chaney's hiring as evidence of malfeasance, they protested that liberals at last had to abandon the New Deal if the Allies were to have a chance of winning the war; social liberalism and wartime mobilization were simply incompatible forces, these critics said. They added that ER had misused taxpayer dollars, abused the public trust, and harmed national morale. A Pennsylvania mother whose son had died at Pearl Harbor observed that Chaney's employment made her want to retch.[32]

ER, still other critics insisted, was divorced from the real needs of the common man. An Ohio woman scolded: "People aren't giving up their sons, working long hours, buying defense bonds . . . to have you making a Roman holiday with a Communist movie actor and a dancer, at salaries that are ridiculous." The hires offended "middle class white collar workers" struggling to put furniture in their homes, another correspondent charged. How could ER deign to ask women to volunteer their time while she paid a dancer so much money, another woman wondered.[33]

ER was also accused of using the government to promote immoral behavior among an unsuspecting populace: one Reverend scolded her to recall that "Hell is full of the fruits of dancing." Equally disturbing, ER had upset gender roles and family values, and her critics saw a woman's place as in the home and not in the political arena. "Voters place a man in office," a California woman reminded ER. "Go home and sew for the Red Cross," thundered a Michigan woman. "You better spend your time in the kitchen . . . and leave a man's job to a man," a West Virginian warned her. "Stick to your knitting," huffed another critic. And, another woman added, ER had no business using "our money" to support her "colored and radical friends."[34]

The New Deal's defenders tried to rebut some of these charges, and ER, in spite of the terrible press, retained a good deal of support from her adoring public. Beyond personal affection for her, some liberals remained wedded to her vision of revolutionizing social affairs in the midst of war. Perhaps her most popular idea, the one that gained the most loyal national following, was that neighbors had to come together in support of their fellow neighbors. Although the Civil Air Patrol was La Guardia's idea, it ultimately took a form that reflected ER's vision every bit as much as it embodied his. Tens of thousands of pilots not only patrolled the swamps of Georgia looking for saboteurs and played the role of targets during anti-aircraft battery drills in Illinois, but they also battled forest fires in the west, transported freight across Pennsylvania, and monitored ice breakups in the Great Lakes as a way of protecting domestic shipping. Civil defense volunteers fulfilled ER's vision when they led relief and rescue efforts in the wake of an accidental blast in an explosives factory that injured and killed dozens of workers in Maryland. When more than 15,000 volunteers, responding to floods, helped evacuate residents in Indiana and Oklahoma, they adopted the kind of community action that she had repeatedly lauded. CD wardens became the first rescuers to arrive at the scene of a terrible railroad disaster that killed scores of people near Philadelphia. Giving first aid and carrying the injured into ambulances, the volunteers confirmed ER's view that organized civilians could help their fellow Americans during unanticipated emergencies. Two women volunteers established a casualty station near the scene of a mining disaster in Montana, winning kudos for their rapid, well-organized reaction. From Pittsburgh to San Diego, home defenders reportedly saved children and elderly who were caught in fires; CD volunteers saved residents' lives during tornadoes in Cleveland, reported the *Cleveland Plain Dealer*, and nationally they became known for heroically helping the innocent and rescuing the injured from floods, fires, and other natural disasters and man-made accidents. The *Washington Star* called the collective volunteer effort in response to a nightclub fire in Boston "the classic example of CD in time of disaster." CD volunteers even helped find the motorist who killed a person while driving and then sped away from the scene in Kansas City, Missouri. Volunteers were doing work that was going to continue to reap benefits once the war had ended, observed the *Star*, stressing the long-term benefits for postwar democracy.[35]

Support for ER's activities permeated the culture, and one sympathetic columnist even suggested that she drop the pretense of holding a ceremonial role and actually run for governor of New York. After all, her 1940 Democratic Convention address outshone all the rest, he reasoned, and it was not unprecedented for women to seek and win elective office. Another admirer called her a true friend to the downtrodden: "No other First Lady has ever been so democratic and helpful and made the great masses of common people feel so completely that the White House was not something set aside for austere and aristocratic rulers, far removed from the sympathetic interest and understanding of the plain people, but a really democratic home, provided by the people for those whom they had honored with their trust and confidence—as their leaders, protectors, defenders and friends. For so much that you have done untold numbers of our people are deeply grateful."[36]

Some cultural leaders and ordinary citizens defended ER as a decent person and true national hero. Her critics had sown disunity in wartime, making

Hitler's job easier, they insisted. Children's author Dr. Seuss had a cartoon in *PM* magazine that depicted Hitler rejoicing at Americans' "Cheap Gunning for Eleanor Roosevelt." *Common Sense*'s editor Selden Rodman wrote ER that she was "doing a great job," urged her to keep it, and vowed in his next issue to run two pro-ER articles. Other admirers praised her devotion to "enlightened New Deal control" in the OCD, vowed to implement ER's vision with or without her, and castigated the right's "hatred of the last eight years, of the galling march of social change." Some supporters saw the attacks as thinly veiled swipes at her sex. The *San Francisco News* said ER had become "the object of resentful comments" because she was a woman in a position of power, and "other women in the same position" had to endure similar criticisms. An Akron, Ohio, resident blasted the men in Congress for smearing somebody who was so important to the nation's women. Her defenders castigated Congress as a place filled with "pot bellied," "old" men of "low caliber"; they were "muckleheads," one supporter wrote. Congress's behavior was so outrageous that one of ER's fans urged a "Tea Party at the polls" to kick out the incumbents who had treated her so badly.[37]

But the voices of her critics drowned out her defenders, and ER came across as defensive. She described members of Congress as Victorian-era prudes who disliked dancing. Although she tried to refocus on her work, the scandal made it almost impossible for her to do so. She continued with her daily OCD activities, discussing home defense with high schoolers and lunching with newspaper boys selling defense stamps; Paul Kellogg even sent her a memo proposing the use of movies and exhibits to show the benefits of home defense to average citizens. Chaney also had pockets of support, but these were comparatively small and politically ineffective. Chaney's hometown supporters in San Francisco countered the scandal mongering by portraying Chaney as a fifth-generation American and a patriot.[38]

ER's news conference on February 9 before a packed group of reporters on the OCD's thirteenth floor sealed the first lady's fate. Wearing a black dress with white trim that suggested a high-stakes occasion, she appeared prepped for battle. Her performance was a disappointment. Seated around a long conference table next to Malvina Thompson and J. S. Helm, her trusted secretaries and confidantes, ER permitted both men and women reporters to stay, even though her typical press conferences were limited to women. She wanted to answer her critics, defend Chaney's and Douglas's reputations, and explain her decisions. She vowed to meet with congressmen face to face to give them the truth. She insisted that physical fitness was a military necessity, citing the fact that 60 percent of all men who had been drafted into the military in North Carolina had failed their physicals. Still, she didn't persuade those who were already hostile to her. Columnist Helen Essary thought that ER appeared nervous and had hoped that she would dispense with the talk "about folk dancing and pageants" and instead focus "on practical ways of saving your life and mine if the enemy comes."[39]

Historians often dismiss the entire controversy in a handful of pages as an unfortunate episode in ER's impressive career, without pausing to understand the context of how the first national political scandal after Pearl Harbor erupted or what it meant politically. While ER's decision making was deeply flawed and invited a wave of national criticism (much of it justified), the reaction to the scandal also illustrated the animosity toward women in positions of power; the complexity of giving any first lady a formal role in her husband's administration; and the fierce reaction not only from anti-New Deal conservative Republicans and southern Democrats but also from some pro-New Deal liberals who ridiculed ER's efforts to infuse social reform into the war program. The scandal demonstrates the extent to which New Dealers were ready to relinquish their social ideals. And it also sidelined ER at the moment when hysteria was peaking, diminishing a potential voice of dissent in the debate about interning Japanese Americans in concentration camps.

In the context of a war that was going poorly and a public that was feeling skittish, FDR officially accepted La Guardia's resignation on February 10 and gave Landis complete control over the OCD. When reporters asked the president about ER's future with the agency, he punted, replying that Landis had full power as the new director. FDR knew that ER's days were numbered; the Chaney scandal was a debacle for him, too. The revelations had emboldened FDR's anti-New Deal critics and sowed doubts about his competence as commander-in-chief. ER reluctantly understood that her time was up, and she began to prepare to hand over her division to a trusted ally. She wrote Landis that Jonathan Daniels should replace her, and Landis concurred that Daniels was a good choice who should serve "in the capacity that you suggest." Speaking to students at Cornell University, ER said that she was going to resign soon, acknowledging how unwise it was "for a vulnerable person like myself to try a government job."[40]

Her departure was more than a mere formality. ER left a big void, and her allies and admirers deeply mourned her loss as a collective blow to their shared vision of a better democratic future for all Americans. Her staff called her resignation "a deep . . . personal loss." On February 18, she made it official, writing Landis that she was leaving the OCD because she felt confident that there would be "completely competent people in charge." If she remained in her post, she added, conservative critics would continue to use her as a lightning rod to ruin the OCD's reputation. At the same time, she expressed her appreciation for La Guardia. He had allowed her to tackle "a part of the work in which you did not believe." She thanked him for his patience "because you must have wanted to stop a great many things."[41]

On February 20, she held some wrap-up meetings with Landis and her staff. Then, there was one last party. At headquarters, she shook hands with every staff member who approached her. She felt a kinship with the OCD's employees, and her colleagues rued the loss of her brave leadership on social issues. As ER prepared to depart, so too did Morgenthau, Lindley, and Polier.[42]

In the end, ER waxed defiant, denouncing her critics. She derided the news media's penchant for sensationalism, saying the headlines splashed across front pages "puffed [me] up with importance!" She told the *New York Times* that simply "to know me is a terrible thing," suggesting that any of her friends and coworkers were fair game simply because they associated with the likes of Eleanor Roosevelt. She lauded the role of dancers and artists in any civilized society, vilified her detractors as arrogant defenders of the wealthiest interests, and in a letter to Kellogg described her foes as "the same people who have fought NYA, CCC, WPA, [and] Farm Security." She had capitulated only out of fear that staying would diminish the OCD's effectiveness. As for Mayris Chaney, she defended her as a first-rate dancer who had the skills and background to run a great morale-building program. (ER also noted that Chaney had made more money in prior jobs.) Whatever one thought of Chaney, the issue of dancing was a red herring, she argued; it was such a good form of exercise that she wanted the federal government to make it a permanent social program. Social defense had made significant strides, she concluded, and now was no time for New Deal liberals to retreat.[43]

A good many liberals lamented her ouster and embraced her message. They planned to forge ahead with social defense even if she no longer led the OCD's program. Kellogg praised ER's brilliant leadership for having shone a light on joblessness, housing, and access to medical care caused by the wrenching transition to a defense economy. The Director of the Selective Service John Langston complained to ER that her critics had unfairly "hurled barbs" instead of "strewing flowers" on her, while sympathetic writer Marquis Childs called it an anti-ER witch hunt. Mrs. Gifford Pinchot, a member of the OCD's Volunteer Participation Committee, assured ER that the hatred for her reflected her effective devotion to a vital strain of democratic liberalism. Pinchot lamented how "this hater group has managed to catch the ear of the public (frightened and confused as it has been in the last few weeks by the distressing war picture and Fifth Column propaganda), and so has been able to capitalize on the situation." Even Harold Ickes, who wanted ER to depart, admitted that the enemies of liberalism were clearly bent on causing as much trouble as possible. For his part, Landis praised ER's service and the considerable progress she had made toward achieving her goals. Other defenders assured ER that her cause was not lost: she had left her "mark in the pages of a grateful future," one correspondent wrote. The New Deal "still means as much to us as it ever did," a volunteer from Washington,

D.C. announced. George Plugmire, a state senator from Idaho, let ER know that in spite of the Chaney scandal, he and his family retained their faith in her wartime New Deal. He wrote that "My wife and baby and I feel that we know you and the President as we have never before been priviledged [*sic*] to know any previous official family at the White House," and "you seem to know just the things that trouble us. . . . We are hurt and grieved to think that Americans could be so mean as to thwart the good work you were so unselfishly carrying on. . . . We admire your courage Mrs. Roosevelt and are grateful to have such a real American Mother as our First Lady. May God bless you and our great President during these hours of extreme trial."[44]

In the wake of her departure, ER urged liberals to stand their ground. But she, too, mourned the loss of one aspect of her bold experiment. She called valid the criticism that a first lady must not hold an official position in the administration. "People can gradually be brought to understand that an individual, even if she is a President's wife, may have independent views and must be allowed the expression of an opinion," she wrote in her "My Day" column on February 23. "But actual participation in the work of the Government, we are not yet able to accept." Seven decades later, the public remains wary of any first lady who inserts herself too forcefully into the politics and policy debates of her times. Nonetheless, while ER's position was no longer tenable, her vision remained alive within the OCD—and among millions of volunteers who continued to flock to its ranks.[45]

The Liberal Approach

Civilian defense stands out as probably the greatest example of mass mobilization . . . ever undertaken voluntarily by citizens of a democratic nation.

—Confidential Report, "Defense Against Enemy Action Directed at Civilians," U.S. Provost Marshal General, April 30, 1946

In 1942, New Deal liberalism became subordinated to the search for physical safety. The OCD raised hopes among some liberals that the New Deal could be protected even after the country had entered the war. Other liberals, however, abandoned social defense and clamored for military action on the home front, which, they said, would protect citizens from fascist threats. When La Guardia, followed by Eleanor Roosevelt, resigned from the OCD in February 1942, FDR put the agency in good liberal hands, a decision that gratified ER. A New Dealer who also shared La Guardia's bent toward militarization, James M. Landis, the dean of Harvard Law School, ran the Office of Civilian Defense with drive, zeal, and verve until his resignation in August 1943. His tenure brought the shifting character of wartime liberalism, as well as its growing philosophical divisions, into sharp relief.[1]

Under Landis, the first lady's vision of social defense came second to the national security state and national surveillance needs. Landis's warnings verged on hysteria, but they were hardly disingenuous. Rather, they were genuine expressions of liberal anxiety. During the mid-1930s, some liberals had concluded that the nascent use of aerial bombing during World War I, the targeting of civilians as a pillar of fascist war strategy (as demonstrated in Spain, Poland, France, and Britain), and the rapid and unpredictable advances in military technologies exposed Americans for the first time to the terrors of air war (among other forms of attack on the home front). The national security calculus had been upended; events once thought unthinkable had become plausible, even likely, in the eyes of some liberals. The absence of any large-scale attacks subsequent to Pearl Harbor does not necessarily mean that liberal leaders knew that the home front would not be attacked. In the context of the times, their fears, though hyperbolic and misplaced with the benefit of hindsight, were also real and hardly a simple propaganda ploy to build pro-war public opinion.

Yet, it is also true, liberal internationalists reaped a clear strategic advantage from their incessant warnings. By showcasing the ways in which civilians were exposed militarily, liberals could more easily press their case that the nation had to embrace military preparedness. After Pearl Harbor, reminding Americans that their lives were endangered served the purpose of uniting people behind the fledgling war effort, persuading citizens to "do their part," preparing the public for a long war rather than a swift military triumph. Partly as a result of the fears whipped up by liberals such as Landis, citizens volunteered in home defense, joined the armed forces, found jobs in defense factories, and were more likely to accept restrictions on personal liberties, including the need to conserve food, gas, and metals as well as adhering to dimout and blackout instructions (not to mention interning their fellow Americans). Ultimately, promoting and hyping the threat served both the political needs and policy ends of mobilizing a skeptical nation for war. It also reflected the intellectual commitments and hard-earned convictions of the liberal purveyors of alarm.

In response to these currents, Landis and his colleagues adopted a version of home defense that featured the use of government power to conduct surveillance of citizens, inculcate discipline as the citizen's most laudable trait, spread fear in order to achieve a commitment to community rather than individualism from the man and woman on the street, and protect people from military threats rather than economic insecurities. Elected and unelected progressives rather than military leaders in early World War II were most responsible for erecting the architecture of the national security state that would go far to shape the ideas, attitudes, and direction of liberals in the postwar world.

Although Landis argued that the country should not be forced to choose, as he put it, "between guns and butter," he quickly decided that the severity of the home threat required him to prioritize national security as his chief goal and largely delay significant action on social defense until another day. Landis cast aside the New Deal's focus on economic protections and social reforms in favor of steps designed to protect people from physical harm. He also argued that volunteerism from the bottom up was the thing that distinguished America's civil defense program from totalitarian societies. Citizens working with Washington to defend their communities would be the key to achieving an acceptable level of civil defense. Struggling to figure out how to achieve national security without sacrificing democratic values during the age of total war, Landis sought to balance the need for public safety with social goals.

But the former trumped the latter. He concluded that the lives of 130 million Americans and the survival of the republic rested on his slim shoulders. He bore the full weight of this awesome responsibility, believing that he alone was saddled with the task of ensuring that Americans were prepared to "fight [the enemy] with our bare hands," as he urged in 1942. He had what one reporter deemed the hardest job in wartime Washington. He believed that military intelligence and media reports about grave dangers were accurate, and his warnings to the American public were hardly propaganda aimed at achieving ulterior goals. Rather, his fears were real, rooted in the rough consensus among liberals that the nation had become, like the proverbial sitting duck, easy prey, waiting for a predator to strike. In February, even FDR told reporters that Detroit and New York City could both be bombed within the next 48 hours, summing up liberals' bleak view of military conditions in early 1942.[2]

The surge in the OCD's ranks that occurred in 1942 also suggested that Landis's message was beginning to resonate across a broad swath of the population. Participation rates were exploding in a direction that favored home defense as a civilian's highest calling aside from direct military service. By February 1, 5.6 million Americans were enrolled as home defense volunteers and nearly 8,500 defense councils were in operation. By the end of 1942, 10 million Americans had volunteered for home defense. An estimated 7 to 8 million people served as air raid wardens, firefighters, and auxiliary police. Some 3 million citizens held social defense posts in which they fed the hungry, provided medical care to the sick, built nursery schools, expanded access to housing, aided communities facing natural disasters, and served as block wardens, ensuring that neighbors' basic needs for food, shelter, and clothing were being adequately met. During World War II, 17 million citizens worked in war industries, and more than 16 million served in the armed forces. But the 10 million volunteers in home defense demonstrated that under Landis the federal government had achieved the kind of civilian-run mass army that both La Guardia and ER had sought.[3]

How did a New Deal stalwart become the leader of the drive to militarize American society in the early months of World War II? The *New York Times* wrote that Landis had the "eyes . . . , face . . . , [and] ideas of a reformer who believes that . . . leader[s] in a democracy . . . tell people how to make their lives better." Reporters called him a "human barbed wire fence" whose wiry frame could not contain his "abundance of nervous energy." He had a face that said, "Don't step on me." Forty-three years old in 1942, he bristled with zeal and intensity. He came to work early, ate brief lunches of sandwiches and apples, and held two-hour meetings on Saturday mornings. Born in 1899 in Japan, he was the son of American missionaries who had moved overseas to seek converts to Christianity. Landis was fluent in Japanese, attended Princeton, graduated at the top of his class, and received the Fay Medal, awarded to the graduate with the brightest future. Landis lived up to expectations. He graduated from Harvard Law School with highest honors in 1924 and served as a law clerk to Supreme Court Justice Louis Brandeis, where he subscribed to Brandeis's belief that citizens had to participate in the life of their democracy for it to flourish.[4]

After his clerkship, Landis became a professor of law at Harvard specializing in administrative and labor law. In 1933, he joined the group of brilliant young Americans who were drawn to Washington to work on Roosevelt's New Deal. He made his greatest mark by helping draft the Securities and Exchange Act and then serving as Securities and Exchange Commission Chairman Joseph P. Kennedy's senior aide, where he drafted most of the SEC's major early decisions. In 1935, Roosevelt made him Kennedy's replacement. Landis regarded the New Deal as a defense "against the inevitable wants of age, and the economic accident of unemployment." He came to regard New Deal agencies as "tribunes of the common man," democratic bastions that ensured Americans basic economic protections from unrestrained industrial capitalism.[5]

Roosevelt admired Landis as a scholar whose expertise had contributed to the smooth functioning of democracy. Landis hailed the president as a great leader who had met the needs of the common man, assuaged economic distempers, and averted a collapse of society. Shortly after Roosevelt's second inauguration, Landis returned to Harvard to become dean of the Law School. Although he published two books on the law, Landis continued to be drawn to public service rather than simply scholarship and university administration. He built a distinguished record at Harvard nonetheless: he revised the school's curriculum, wrote personal letters to his students and their parents about their performance, and placed Harvard's brightest graduates in the nation's most coveted legal jobs.[6]

At the same time, he relished his public roles during Roosevelt's second term. Most controversially, he defended labor leader Harry Bridges, who had led strikes of longshoremen in San Francisco, against ultimately unsuccessful government attempts to deport him for alleged ties to radicals. (The case prompted conservatives to charge that Landis was a communist; Landis replied that he could not in a million years explode "all the lies that have been told about me.") Ironically, Landis also subordinated economic reforms during the early war years that favored labor to the nation's military needs.[7]

In 1940, he wrote that Roosevelt needed to win a third term because he was the only candidate qualified to save the American people from the growing threat of fascist dictatorship. He maintained that government was responsible for directing social forces in ways that improved the daily lives of ordinary citizens. He was so civic minded that in a poem his students had written, they poked fun at his penchant for stretching his interests far beyond the confines of Harvard Yard: "Jim Landis runs the Law School—(or so the saying goes),/But what this creature looks like—nobody present knows./He fixes up the railroads—in

Washington, D.C. [serving on Roosevelt's Railroad Commission]/And off in never, never land he fixes up 'Plan E' [a plan to strengthen local government]".[8]

In 1940, Landis turned away from New Deal economic reforms to the problems of national security and home defense. He argued that liberals needed to lead the country in a period of adjustment to meet war needs, a gradual shift that reflected what he called "the basic tenet of the liberal approach." Beginning in December 1940, he began going to Washington on a regular basis to serve as an advisor to the Defense Commission. The next month, he helped lead an American Defense organization based in Harvard that sought to build support for Roosevelt's foreign policy.[9]

Torn between New Deal reform and national security, Landis began to liken the vulnerabilities confronting Americans to the defenseless British position after Neville Chamberlain proclaimed an age of peace following the debacle at Munich. Landis wrote of Nazi planes filled with "a carload of bombs" able to fly great distances to attack the United States. Home defense, Landis's biographer has written, "was an old cause of his." During World War I, he won a prize in high school for an essay portraying citizens as duty bound to prepare the country to go to war. In 1941, having been named director of New England's home defense region, he envisioned "a place in the ranks" for everybody. As director, he came to view national security, rather than social reform, as liberalism's highest priority. He promoted home defense with single-minded determination. He wanted to recruit 100,000 people to scan the skies for enemy bombers; he tripled the number of firefighters in his region; and he urged civilians to hang together so they could function as "an army, not a mob." His leadership of the region earned plaudits as the most disciplined and best-organized example of home defense in the country.[10]

By the time Landis assumed full control of the OCD in late February 1942, he was facing a set of cultural pressures and political tests. He tackled them with alacrity. First, he had to repair the OCD's battered public image; the agency, noted the *Christian Science Monitor,* was the object of more vitriol than any other agency in the administration. Americans lampooned the OCD as the home of fan dancer Mayris Chaney, Eleanor Roosevelt's "pet." Even though Landis had fired Chaney and transferred the physical fitness division to another federal agency, critics vilified the OCD for teaching people how to play the "ancient game of Mumbledy-Peg" and hiring a "co-ordinator for crap-shooting, ... pinochle playing, ... elephant riding, [and] doughnut-dunking." Landis fired some of the ex-mayors whom he regarded as cronies of La Guardia's, promising Roosevelt that he would undertake a honest study of the OCD's staff, activities, and organization. The OCD was going to become disciplined and efficient, he assured Roosevelt, and military protection was going to draw the lion's share of his focus and energy.[11]

ER and La Guardia had left Landis with other headaches. He had to repair relations between Washington and state capitals, which, Landis said, were "as intricate . . . as any [problems] that I have seen." He thought the volunteers under him were lacking in discipline. Some critics wanted the OCD to establish a police state and impose martial law because it was insufficiently aggressive in defending the country. More broadly, Landis faced charges from dissenters on one side who said his agency had been militarized and from other protesters who argued that home defense had become a Trojan Horse for social engineering rather than an organization for military protection. Landis announced his intention to prepare Americans "to deal with whatever the swiftly-moving future may have in store." "Battlegrounds," he warned, "shift fast." Militarily, he cited the enormous benefits that a robust program would produce, cutting, he claimed, the casualty rate of an attack by 90 percent, resulting in "tragedies but not massacres, fires but not conflagrations." West Coast ports, he wrote the War and Navy Secretaries, needed to be ready to take in evacuees. The OCD's primary mission, he argued, was the protection of lives and property. He notified Under Secretary of War Robert Patterson that "continuous bombardment" of the United States would grow more likely if the enemy were to establish bases near American shores and cited a need to camouflage factories. In his private estimation, the West Coast was in the greatest peril, followed by northeastern cities, and then centers of war industry such as Detroit and Chicago. He had to prepare 50 million civilians in the target zones to resist air raids and other forms of attacks. These fears were not entirely irrational. In September 1942, Japanese submarines shelled the coast near Santa Barbara, California, provoking speculation in the media that the war had inched closer to civilian lives.[12]

Yet Landis was more than merely trafficking in fear to enact some prearranged agenda. He not only believed that the threats were legitimate, multidimensional, and imminent; he also felt it his mission to make people see the threats as directly impinging on their lives. He wanted to strike a balance between combating complacent attitudes toward the threats while being careful not to provoke citizens into a state of panic. This balancing act proved to be impossible.

As the United States entered its third month of fighting in February, the setbacks overseas provoked an outbreak of hysteria on the West and East Coasts. More than 2,000 Americans had died at Pearl Harbor, and part of the Navy lay at the bottom of the Pacific. Japan had won victories in Hong Kong, Manila, and Singapore. Military commanders were predicting that the country was to be attacked again, while in March almost two-thirds of citizens said Americans were not taking the war with the gravity it required. The chief of staff of the Army warned of attacks on Oahu by air, sea, and ground. Army commanders were so concerned about Hawaii that they stationed more than 45,000 combat troops in defense of the territory, with plans to put 100,000 soldiers there.[13]

Landis's assumption of his job coincided with a U.S. military command that despite its own stated wishes found itself inexorably being dragged into the defense of the home front. Shortly after midnight on February 25, U.S. military radar detected an object in the sky about 120 miles to the west of Los Angeles. The Navy issued a Green alert, calling gunners to their batteries. Then, for unknown reasons, a colonel issued a report that more than two dozen planes were approaching Long Beach, just south of Los Angeles, at about 12,000 feet altitude. The Navy ordered a blackout of the entire city of Los Angeles. Shortly after 3 a.m. in Santa Monica, a suspicious object (which proved to be a balloon carrying a flare) drew fire from anti-aircraft guns, and other batteries began to fire, discharging more than 1,400 rounds. Amid the commotion one person had a heart attack and died. Several other people died in traffic accidents sown by the chaos. Daylight brought little clarity to what occurred overnight. The Army claimed that at least one and perhaps as many as five planes had probed the air space above the city. Secretary of the Navy Knox, however, said that there were no planes, and the *New York Times* called the entire episode a case "of expensive incompetence and jitters" and pointedly asked why the guns on the ground were so utterly ineffective, and why American planes failed to "go up to engage" the attacking aircraft. The event came to be known as the "Battle of Los Angeles."[14]

Now that the war had actually begun, the years of campaigning by FDR and La Guardia were coming to fruition. It was as if all the pent-up fears—from the bombing of Spain to the fall of France, from Murrow's reports during the Blitz to the attack on Pearl Harbor—came to the surface and spawned more and more public fear. An Army captain warned that the Nazis were planning to spread disease among people in the northeastern states, which would be "difficult to combat." One resident of San Francisco cited the Battle of Los Angeles as a wake-up call to the nation's politicians. A resident of Connecticut worried that there was no way to combat poison gas. Defense factories in Schenectady, New York, were said to be on Hitler's target list. When news of the fall of Singapore reached a woman from Lexington, Kentucky, she asked Landis if he intended to wait for days "before the fall of California—and the West Coast—before we build air-raid shelters?" A former pilot in Britain's Royal Air Force warned Pennsylvanians that they were not "too far away" to suffer the brunt of an attack. The enemy, he assured them, was working on bombers that could fly 8,000 miles, meaning bases in Bordeaux, France, directly imperiled American lives. Maine's home-defense director announced that Nazi spies had just landed on the state's coast with a mission to "dynamite and burn" their targets.[15]

The hysteria had a way of feeding on itself, with a consensus forming that involvement in the war would bring death and destruction to America. The OCD made a secret estimate that a single bomber could cause up to one hundred fires in fifteen minutes. Landis heard from a senior staff member that they needed to quickly distribute helmets and gas masks to fend off a likely chemical attack. OCD's Chief Medical Officer George Baehr considered giving guidance to morticians on handling mass casualties, filed a request for "colored prints showing the effects of gas" on humans (he wanted to display them at an upcoming American Medical Association conference), and informed one doctor that only trained physicians should treat bombing victims who had "crushing injuries of the abdomen, chest or spine." The lack of knowledge about how best to camouflage buildings weighed on Landis. He also worried that panic could hamper war production by, leading to spontaneous unwarranted evacuations of people.

Above all, though, Landis outdid La Guardia in using his seat of power to forge the home front into aspects of a police state. Amid the pressures of his post, he put a premium on militarizing civilians as democracy's answer to the challenge of total war. Civil liberties were sacrificed, and elements of a surveillance state became commonplace. Landis expanded the OCD's ties to the military, drawing crucial intelligence from Army officers, keeping majors and colonels in key roles in the agency, and employing some sixty Army officers in the regions at work on home defense. He struck a deal with the American Legion to train its members as air raid wardens. Some of his aides conducted "character investigation[s]" of volunteers. His agency joined eighteen other federal agencies in defending the nation's airports, railways, and communication lines, militarizing national infrastructure. He considered distributing more than ten million dog tags to children ages one through thirteen (in case they were to die in attacks), while FDR issued an executive order reimbursing any hospital $3.75 for every day that civilians wounded by enemy fire were treated there. In Maine, residents were urged to tell the police of any suspect individuals because "it only takes a minute to blow up a bridge or sink a ship."[16]

Meanwhile, although the hysteria did not necessarily improve national morale, it did alert civilians to the threats they faced, making them seem real and imminent, breeding in some a need for action. Still, the widespread rumors— and Landis kept tabs on them—were so absurd that they raised questions: could the United States actually win the war? Did it have the wherewithal to withstand the siege that was about to take place? In California, there was talk of a plot by Japan to spread typhus by releasing diseased fleas; others in the country spoke of Nazi efforts to poison drinking water (causing "huge boils" followed by death). A factory worker in Illinois was said to have punctured gas masks, while some in New Jersey heard that a handful of enemy bombers had been shot down over New York's Mitchel Air Field one day after the attack on Pearl Harbor and that the enemy action had been kept out of the news. These were hardly isolated instances of conspiratorial thinking by a handful of citizens; even the OCD's Major Reed Landis reported to the country that spies had painted signs "on rooftops, in cornfields . . . woods and . . . fences," telling bombers where to find their targets, but he failed to provide people with any evidence. With the enemy so potent, and so ubiquitous, and with even Landis and the OCD fostering a sense of paranoia, national vulnerability became a focal point of people's lives, a terrible truth with which they had to reckon.[17]

In this climate of suspicion and fear Landis and his agency played a contributing role in the decision to establish camps interning Japanese nationals and Japanese Americans, most of whom resided on the West Coast. Although the internments have been portrayed as the outgrowth of racism that burst forth following Japan's bombing of Pearl Harbor, the apparatus and political climate that helped make the camps possible were established months earlier. The camps came to life inside of the civil defense debate. Liberal Democrats and Republicans had joined conservatives in raising the specter of fifth columnists during the late 1930s. Despite a lack of any evidence, La Guardia and Landis had both claimed that spies and saboteurs menaced the internal security of the country, fostering suspicions that made the public more receptive to arguments that the Japanese population was the greatest threat facing them after Pearl Harbor. Landis was among those who described the West Coast as the nation's most inviting target. Ultimately, the camps were seen by numerous residents as a fair step to protect their lives. Citizens who helped trample the rights of other citizens won support and legitimacy from Landis and his colleagues in Washington.[18]

Led by Lt. General John DeWitt and an entity named the War Relocation Authority set up under the Interior Department, the camps emerged in part from the civil defense debate and were spurred in part due to the active involvement of the Office of Civilian Defense. The Army endorsed steps to detain and neutralize what the brass and much of the public, ignoring all evidence to the contrary, considered a dangerous population. The Joint Chiefs and military leaders feared "inimical action" on Hawaii from "approximately 100,000 residents of Japanese origin," and in the days after Pearl Harbor asked that the most dangerous 20,000 people be taken to "a concentration camp" on the continental United States. In February, California Governor Culbert Olson falsely claimed that he knew that "Japanese residents of California" had begun to prepare "for fifth column activities," while L.A. Mayor Fletcher Bowron (again, without evidence) announced that "Right here in our own city are those who may spring to action at an appointed time in accordance with a prearranged plan wherein each of our little Japanese friends will know his part in the event of any possible attempted invasion or air raid . . . We cannot run the risk of another Pearl Harbor episode in Southern California." FDR agreed with the consensus among most of his advisors and signed Executive Order 9066 on February 19, authorizing civilian and military leaders to round up tens of thousands of citizens and Japanese nationals living in the United States. The Army's job was to remove people from their homes and transport them to the camps, and the War Relocation Authority would take over once people reached assembly centers. While the Federal Reserve seized the assets of those being interned, and the Federal Security Agency was in charge of public health and welfare in the camps, Landis's OCD was a voice in support of internment and even recruited volunteers to assist in the process.[19]

On March 2, the Army leaders asked the OCD's West Coast region (based in San Francisco) to help it with the "removal of aliens." James Sheppard, the regional director, informed Landis that the Army's request "was sprung upon us last night" but he added that home defense officials in the region had already conducted surveys related to the internments and had been hard at work "on the [Japanese] problem." (Sheppard also anticipated an imminent declaration of martial law, which home defense would help enforce; "We will have to be thinking about this," too, he wrote Landis.)[20]

The years-long campaign against the threat of fifth columnists fostered the atmosphere that made the internments politically permissible and culturally acceptable. The OCD had joined forces with the Department of Justice's Alien Enemy Control Unit and the FBI to defend the nation's roads, water, power, and defense plants against the threat of the saboteur, and the term "alien enemies" had become embedded in the lexicon of the times. One home defense manual urged wardens to scrutinize enemy "alien[s]" in order to combat the threat of fifth columnists. The city of San Francisco established restrictions on Japanese, Italian, and German immigrants from visiting sensitive areas of the city, and volunteers in home defense were asked to send their supervisors intelligence on people whom they suspected of subversion. Landis prohibited citizens from enemy nations from becoming members of the OCD's Citizen Defense Corps, which protected infrastructure, and informed Attorney General Biddle that the members' loyalty had to be nothing short of ironclad.[21]

Landis endorsed the internment camps and sought information from the attorney general about Japanese nationals working, for instance, for the Utah Copper Company. His officials on the West Coast were gratified that the internments had gone smoothly. By championing the camps, Landis was able to show his agency's military significance and its role in defending America. When DeWitt requested that the OCD assume responsibility for a program giving "aliens" from Germany and Italy permits so they could be temporarily exempted from travel and other restrictions on their movement, Landis vowed that home defense would be "eager . . . to assume the common burdens of war." He pledged his assistance to the internment program. Volunteers swore an oath and served as "Alien Permit Officers" as Sheppard enjoined his men to perform any job "within the definition of civilian defense . . . at a moment's notice." Sheppard also updated Landis about the status of the permit program, and two home defense officials on the West Coast during a phone call discussed how the program was going "to continue indefinitely, unless there are orders for evacuation of the Germans and Italians." By the summer, the West Coast had 237 "alien permit officers" under the home defense program, many of whom had a professional background in law enforcement. "If the Japanese . . . should be released within this region," Sheppard informed Landis, lawless activities would spike and law enforcement agents' burden would become even greater.[22]

Under Landis, the OCD joined the FBI in a campaign to train volunteer police in such topics as fifth columnists, fascism and communism, and unspecified information about the internments. The OCD's leadership adopted an investigatory mindset, keeping tabs on those the government suspected of subversion. This contributed to the atmosphere in which the camps were established, and they lent momentum to the cause of mass mobilization. There was a growing conviction that peril was a fact of life for at least fifty million coastal residents. The ascendance of national security liberalism in 1942 accelerated due to Landis's collaboration with J. Edgar Hoover. Landis worked with Hoover to identify communist infiltrators in local defense groups, while Hoover sent the OCD confidential tidbits about a potential Nazi sympathizer in charge of the defense council in Seaside Park, New Jersey, and urged the agency to take action against fascists directing defense activities around the country. The OCD also asked the War Department to investigate Nazi ties to a New Jersey golf course. In New York City, an air raid warden alleged that La Guardia's police had threatened to purge from the ranks any wardens who dared to criticize the mayor's leadership. Ultimately, Landis opted for the discipline of military command over the chaos that he felt came with civilian control. Adhere to the military's orders and turn civilians into a branch of the Army, Landis commanded Colonel Walter Metcalf, who was directing the OCD's Second Corps Region. By the end of February, Landis boasted of almost 85,000 police volunteers in four states and the District of Columbia and predicted that in coming weeks tens of thousands more were likely to join the ranks.[23]

No region of the country was more on edge than the West Coast, and officials at all levels were eager to keep fanning regional fears—in effect, rallying the country around a shared imminent threat. When a few residents of Los Angeles requested evacuation advice from the federal government, OCD officials urged them to consider relocating to "the Eastern side of the Rocky Mountains." Los Angeles, a fire warden told a meeting of home defenders at the Biltmore Hotel, needed to be ready to battle 1,400 fires in the Hollywood Hills, all lit within three minutes. By early April, L.A. County had prepared 180 first aid stations and 4,500 hospital beds, and the sheriff announced that its experience with floods, earthquakes, and the St. Francis Dam disaster in 1928 was going to be invaluable. But the intermittent declaration that the coast was prepared was offset by an ever-present sense of panic, which, fueled by years of public warnings from newspapers to city halls, trumped any appeals for calm. Although he vowed that residents were going to wage "total war without complete military domination of every civilian effort" (distinguishing democratic civil defense from the Nazi program), James Sheppard, the West Coast's regional director, also described the coast as "a combat zone" and quoted a Pearl Harbor survivor who warned that without civil defense "fires, casualties, and . . . other catastrophes" were going to reap chaos and destroy America. Be prepared to combat "the inculcation of fear" spread through rumors, Sheppard warned, hyping the threat of chaos. When the city of Los Angeles lit explosives in an air raid demonstration, residents called police stations and newsrooms seeking information in sometimes desperate tones.[24]

When Landis took over the OCD he quickly learned that coastal residents were filled with fear while Midwesterners tended to be hostile to home defense instructions given by the federal government. As one report from the OCD indicated, field visits to twenty-seven states yielded regional distinctions in attitudes toward Landis's agenda. Coastal residents tended to see wardens (armed with whistles, white hats, and armbands) as "solemn symbols" of national defense; Midwesterners tended to denounce home defense as yet "another irritating example of how 'They' in Washington fail to grasp that different regions have different needs and conditions." Some interior residents said air raids were not all that likely to happen in their region, and OCD officials observed that Coloradans agreed that if the enemy bombed Denver, the United States might as well surrender on the spot.

Notwithstanding these voices of dissent, in the spring of 1942 the country's interior regions also manifested fears of attack, though the coastal populations were understandably the most anxiety ridden. On April 19, Harold Ickes wrote in his diary of "appalling" losses of oil tankers in the Atlantic that could doom England; in May, he observed that Hawaii was on alert because military leaders believed another attack was coming. An air raid on San Diego, warned the commander of California's Women's Ambulance and Transport Corps, would destroy the city. Landis viewed these fears as useful in expanding civilian defense, and he added to the public's anxieties in appearances at town hall meetings and war rallies. He warned that the country faced a threat of unimaginable proportions. "Stay and take it," he thundered in May to residents of Los Angeles during a meeting there. Reasoning that the Pacific Coast was easily accessible to Japan's military and that war production made coastal cities inviting targets, Landis announced, "We knew the Japanese had aircraft carriers, and we are beginning to suspect they may have more than we at first thought they had."[25]

"We ought to have the guts to fight [the enemy] with our bare hands," he urged Southern Californians. He exhorted civilians to "drill and drill and drill" and raised chemical weapons as a plausible type of attack and urged civilians to board up their homes and take cover on upper floors to avoid the gas during such an assault. Landis toured the country with his message. His voice soft, he told eight thousand volunteers at a rally in the Cotton Bowl in Dallas that fascist bombers were breeders of "terror," that U.S. cities could soon resemble Rotterdam and London, and that Americans had to prepare to experience "the grime and dirt and the tragedy of bombing." Lights flashed, sounds of an actual air raid from England played on the loudspeakers, and members of the Texas home guards bayoneted dummies in the image of Hitler and Mussolini and shredded them before the crowd. The next night in Cleveland, Landis addressed a rally attended by twelve thousand, some of whom had to stand because there were too few seats. After firefighters demonstrated how they would fight incendiary bombs, Landis warned that the Nazis could fly "from Iceland or Greenland to the rich industrial area of the Great Lakes" in about the time it would take people in Cleveland to fly to New York. He described Cleveland as another potential Bataan, where American and Filipino forces had surrendered to Japan, or like a city in subjugated France, and he declared that all citizens had better "think war, sleep war, and eat war" before it was too late.[26]

That spring, Landis also led air raid drills, underscoring how his pro-volunteer movement had grown in size, stature, and discipline, and the militant characteristics of the drills (most of them were blackouts) gratified him. The drills drew positive notice from the public, raised Landis's profile, and transformed the OCD in the eyes of some Americans into a skilled and essential war agency. A new narrative of Landis as an aggressive, indefatigable administrator of the first rank took hold. In addition, Landis and liberals in general came to be indelibly associated with guardians of the nation's physical (as opposed to spiritual, economic, or social) defense. The popularity of Landis's program, and the support he engendered, suggested that the shift of liberalism toward national security struck a chord with the American people in the first months of World War II. The *New York Times* praised Landis's agency as ready "for instant action" and showed Landis sitting at his desk, pursuing policies that were saving lives. The *Times* asserted that Landis had "one of the most important jobs in the war program."[27]

Embarrassments still marred Landis's mission, however, and criticism of him dovetailed with broadsides that critics had long leveled against Roosevelt's liberal policies. Some of the dissent centered on the ineptitude of the Roosevelt administration, a byproduct of big government, said critics. That spring, when Landis toured Washington, D.C., in a plane to observe the city during a blackout, the media marveled that his own headquarters remained a blaze of lights, proof that ineptitude in federal operations bedeviled the OCD. The drills also occasionally were the cause of death, such as when a woman startled by the alarms fell from her apartment's fourth floor, and the *Washington Post* chastised residents who had gazed skyward during the drill for courting "mutilation and death." A false alarm in New York City lasted but a minute (the Army had reported a bomber heading to the city), yet one air raid warden died, as did another person who tripped on stairs in his home; an off-duty police officer who tried to arrest two men because they refused to take shelter was left with a fractured skull and near death. Landis's national security orders, dissenters argued, had failed to achieve universal compliance while crucial drills cost people their lives. Charges of incompetence and intrusion leveled at a leviathan government found a target in the emerging national security state.[28]

Public anxieties—some rooted in government inaction; some focused on big-brother directions from wardens and other home defense representatives—fueled a rise in anger toward the liberal elites populating the capital. Critics lauded the individualist ethos and described Landis as a typical liberal bent on trampling the rights of the people through his insinuation of government into their lives. Others complained that New Dealers in charge of home defense behaved as if Washington knew how best to protect them, rather than ordinary Americans fending for themselves, responsible for their own safety. One critic—scoffing at "obscuration of illumination," the term used by the OCD to describe a blackout—mocked Landis's "manly Hahvagh [Harvard, said with a snobbish accent] effort" to talk to the masses and begged him to return to Cambridge. Landis, conservatives charged, was "pink." Other critics shared their fears that authorities had failed to tell them how they should behave during an air raid. The OCD, in their view, was doing too little to protect them, and liberalism had not given civilians a sufficient level of military defense. A woman from Brooklyn said she planned to "grab the baby and run" if Nazis dropped bombs on her borough. Another woman expressed the mood of uncertainty and dread, saying that she was not quite sure what to do in response to a Nazi invasion. The government, they implied, had given them insufficient guidance.[29]

In spite of the criticism of government overreach and Washington's timidity in protecting the public, Landis had gone far to defuse some of the most fundamental charges leveled against the agency. He stated that boondoggling was unacceptable, abolished the Youth Activities and Physical Fitness programs, and told members of Congress that he had saved money by firing his predecessors' cronies. He had distributed more than 50,000 helmets and armbands (a modest step forward), and he had $74 million in his coffers to be used on gas masks, firefighting equipment, and medical supplies. An April executive order issued by FDR expanded Landis's authority, declaring that Landis was in charge of "a war agency." If people violated codes for wearing OCD insignia, they were now subject to federal criminal charges. Any community that took equipment from the OCD had to take orders from Landis, who also had the power to fire members of a Citizens Defense Corps and to give insignia to civilians who had met federal training standards. Power, Landis felt, was there for him to use to protect the public militarily, and that spring he wielded it.[30]

La Guardia's establishment of the Civil Air Patrol became an emblem of citizen participation guided by the sure hand of liberalism. La Guardia had established CAP one week before the bombing of Pearl Harbor, and CAP's pilots, flying private planes, had become an actual military force. Under Landis, they located enemy submarines off the coasts and guided bombers so they could hit their targets. Some 30,000 people served as volunteer pilots with a fleet of 12,500 planes, which equaled around half of all private planes in the country.[31]

The drills of the spring marked a moment of triumph for Landis's vision of national security. Despite the sense of dread pervading the public, confidence that the country was finally getting prepared to cope with war on the home front generated praise for Landis's leadership. A reporter for the *New York Times* perched on top of the Empire State Building hailed the "remarkable spectacle" of a completely darkened lower Manhattan during a twenty-minute blackout drill. After zipping through the city in his "war car" (a smaller, speedier version of his peacetime limousine), La Guardia praised "the lower East Side [for] spit[ting] right in the face of the sixth columnists. The obstructionists, the appeasers, those unfriendly to the successful prosecution of the war, had anticipated and wished the drill would be a complete flop. Instead it was 100 percent successful." Fifty-five hundred lights on the streets went dark, 3,000 police were deployed, and 9,000 wardens—the *Times* called them "heroes"—helped keep apartments dark. "The teeming old-law flats of the lower East Side, as well as the great developments like Knickerbocker Village, the settlement houses ... the two and three story buildings overlooking Chinatown's crooked little elbow, the dingy bars and unique tattoo shops of the Bowery—all went dark," the *Times* reported. New York also held a surprise drill on June 5 when La Guardia warned police graduates that "the Oberschwein and the yellow dog are not going to give us much notice." In eight hours he would completely black out the city, and the mayor then watched from the 103rd floor of the Empire State Building as seven million people seemingly complied, and the city went dark. Wardens carried whistles and patrolled parks and streets, the lights of Broadway were turned off, 400 police removed people from Times Square, residents of tenements on Manhattan's West Side burst out in "God Bless America," and the city's newspapers called the drill "close to perfection."[32]

The drills burnished Landis's reputation as a decisive administrator, a liberal lion in command of his quasi-military operation. On April 9, fifty miles of Los Angeles became almost completely dark, and an aide to Landis praised the exercise as an example of civilian discipline coming to life on a mass scale. (Nonetheless, one warden fell off a building, and five people died from heart attacks during the blackout.) Washington, D.C.'s first drill during the daytime on June 2 drew positive coverage, as well. The White House, a symbol of democracy and among the enemy's leading targets, swiftly shut its gates, deployed armed soldiers, and distributed gas masks to staff. Three Cabinet members broke off their meeting to seek shelter, and ambulances raced to the Roosevelts' residence. The *Washington Post* and *Washington Times-Herald* reported that approximately 55,000 civilians found shelter, 98 out of 99 office buildings adhered to the restrictions, 16,000 wardens patrolled streets, and bus service came to a standstill. In a second drill in the capital, "a huge civilian defense army" of 30,000 volunteers fanned out across the city, searching for violators who could be punished with three months in jail. Here, too, was more evidence that Landis had succeeded in militarizing the home front, prepping the country to handle the horrors of war in its own backyard.[33]

Just as the New Deal coalition gave Roosevelt popular political support in the 1930s, a national security coalition that took shape in the spring of 1942 drew civilians into the quasi-military ranks of Landis's organization. In June, Japanese submarines surfaced and managed to shell a town on Oregon's coast, and there were sporadic reports of fifth columnists being discovered in the country. But, for the most part, the intensity, scale, and hysteria of the drills far outpaced the number and size of enemy attacks that occurred. The drills had a doctrinaire quality about them, spreading across the country as exercises in civilian self-discipline and expressions of patriotism. But they also showed the public's ardor to join in active defense of the homeland. During one drill, three million Bostonians seemed to get off the streets "as if by magic" and made downtown "a deserted city," the Associated Press reported, and a photo of Washington Street, newspaper row, showed no pedestrians or moving cars, the center of a bustling city that had been rendered lifeless. Seattle involved more than 50,000 volunteers in an air raid drill (the city was a mere eight hours by plane from the Japanese-occupied Aleutian Islands, the AP explained), people smeared in lipstick and catsup played victims of parachute bombs in Springfield, Massachusetts, and soldiers guarded railways and post offices in Philadelphia. Even the Midwest took on a militarized cast in support of Landis's home defense vision. The sixteen-story Otis Building in downtown Chicago's Loop required its 2,000 workers to be fingerprinted, photographed, and to show proof of citizenship, all of which was then sent to the FBI.[34]

Even when spirits rose in the United States after American naval forces won the battle of Midway in June 1942, Landis remained true to his message of imminent catastrophe facing civilian communities. He used updated intelligence on advances in Axis weapons to tell a House subcommittee that there was a "grave possibility of bombardment" on both coasts. When a committee member asked the director if Americans were likely to panic during air raids, Landis said they would "stand up" and endure. Lt. Barry Bingham, a top aide to Landis, warned that when California was hit with air raids, "all of Washington will be blamed" for making false assumptions. From Seattle to San Diego, the coast felt like a war zone, and it was widely considered the most vulnerable region in the country: balloons dotted the skies to stop planes from bombing civilians; San Francisco had drills almost every night, and visiting the city in late May Landis said the chances of air raids were "greater here than anywhere else" and promised that equipment to defend against chemical attacks was due to arrive soon. When Japan bombed Dutch Harbor in Alaska in early June, fears that the West Coast was next on the list again increased. A few days later, a boy sold newspapers on Sansome Street in downtown San Francisco by screaming "Stimson [Secretary of War] says we get it today."[35]

The news media willingly spread the OCD's message of national security as the preeminent role for wartime civilians; Landis's aides used newspapers almost as if they were in-house propaganda organs. Editors reprinted official OCD notices and published some of the OCD's articles and other instructions. "The Pittsburgh newspapers have cooperated wholeheartedly" with the OCD's PR campaign. One agency official advised a *New York Times* journalist that "in whatever you write, it is important to emphasize that Volunteer Nurses' Aides will be needed in increasing numbers and needed quickly in cases of . . . sabotage or direct enemy action." He praised a surge in training nurses since "Jap Sunday."[36]

But the new liberal vision led to excesses in the public square. There was enough confidential intelligence and public signs that the home front was endangered to maintain a siege mentality among the public throughout the second half of 1942. In response, Americans sought to form their own paramilitary outfits, requesting that the president permit, for example, citizens to form a group that armed its members with revolvers and shotguns to down parachute troops. Another proposal arrived in Washington that local police track "at all times the exact location of all undesirable citizens." One man in Idaho asked if the president would allow him to set up a band of guerrilla fighters to guard the coast. If such displays of hyper-militarism worried officials such as Landis, they were equally concerned that too many civilians refused to take the threat with the necessary gravity. Some businesses prioritized profits over safety, with the majority of hotels on Miami Beach defying orders to blackout windows with special shades.[37]

The stress exacted a toll on Landis; *Time* magazine described him as haggard and worn down by his monumental effort to prepare the home front for war. When he engaged with La Guardia in a public spat about the best methods for dousing incendiary bomb fires, two of the nation's liberal leaders, each responsible for protecting millions of citizens, were battling not over economic security but over quasi-military home defense techniques. The dispute underscored the shift in the debate among liberals. The issues that most mattered to them and the country were no longer ER's vision of ensuring social justice, but rather stopping the spread of fires.[38]

But, as *Time* summed up the issue, Landis had made great strides in less than a year at the helm of home defense. His militarism was paying dividends. He was moving to supply cities with 100,000 firefighting uniforms, 108,000 pairs of rubber boots, and millions of pieces of medical equipment. Five million gas masks were being manufactured for purposes of home defense, air raid warnings had been made more uniform and reliable, and *Time* reported that the Civil Air Patrol was logging half a million miles each week "on courier and scouting work." The ranks of the civilian army were heading toward the 10 million mark, and under Landis the OCD was "functioning up to the full measure of its authority." Despite the passage of months with no major attack since Pearl Harbor, the absence of bombing did not persuade people that the peril had subsided. In September, Lt. Gen. DeWitt reported that a Japanese seaplane had bombed a forest in Oregon (the only time the continental United States was bombed during the war). Americans, Landis said in Chicago, had "barely felt war's touch . . . but they will, and very shortly, too." He cautioned "that upon the success or failure of Rommell's campaign in Egypt, the remoteness or nearness of enemy bombers over the land hinges. Should Alexandria fall, and the Mediterranean become controlled by the axis, and the African coast fall into their hands, the American mainland will surely feel the weight of axis bombs." Raising the specter of France ("Who . . . thought that France could fall within 60 days?"), Landis warned that the Nazis could acquire bases near enough to put Chicago in danger before anybody even knew it. Jabbing the air with his cigarette, he predicted that the war "is going to get tougher!" He warned that "some planes [always] get through." Stepping into a meeting room at Los Angeles's Biltmore Hotel, he tossed his wrinkled hat on a mantle and, "hawk-faced, thin-haired and intense," in the words of the *Los Angeles Times*, assured people that the war was going to be long and criticized people's leisure habits as inimical to self-defense. Peppering his remarks with such words as "ain't" and "swell," Landis and the OCD, one volunteer later wrote him, "had . . . improved immeasurably in stature" since the spring. The *Pasadena Star-News* published a photo showing Landis and two of his colleagues studying emergency plans on a desk. Although dressed in a jacket and tie, Landis, lips pursed, embodied grit and military defiance—liberalism for a new age.[39]

His reputation as a different kind of reformer from his New Deal days received an additional boost from his launch of the "dimout" campaign on the Eastern and Western Seaboards, arguably his most tangible military achievement of the war. In 1942, Nazi U-Boats were using the silhouettes cast by coastal lights to sink U.S. merchant marines and their cargo. Scores of ships had been sunk, and scores of sailors had died. New York City gave off so much light that a ship could be spotted fifty miles out to sea. There was "danger in the glow," the *Times* warned. The government refused to restrict ships to daytime travel, lest they cut in half the cargo heading for the Allies. The Department of War and OCD initiated an effort to curb the glow of lights from coastal cities. In late February, Landis ordered that lights on the West Coast emitted by cars, shops, piers, signs and homes be dimmed, and a month later, the State of New York agreed to dim its entire coastline. The "dimouts" were volunteer participation at its best.[40]

The rollout of the campaign was anything but smooth. Few people understood who was responsible for keeping their lights dimmed. "Dim-out regul[ation]s have been worked out in Conn," Landis wrote a resident of Connecticut who had complained about the inconsistencies in the campaign. "They will no doubt get into smooth operation soon." To some critics the notion that Washington had ordered homes, cars, and businesses to curb the level of lighting they used exhibited government meddling in people's private lives. Landis's campaign also triggered tensions between economic profits and national security. Florida officials worried that a blackout on the state's East Coast could ruin the local economy. Atlantic City refused to dim its lights lest it kill its tourist trade. Rather than taking steps to bolster the economy as they had done during the thirties, liberals in Washington were prioritizing public safety over jobs and economic progress. The lack of night lights not only interfered with economic activity but also led to inquiries about whether the dimouts had caused automobile accidents, increased crimes, and slowed industrial production. Landis dismissed these concerns as secondary to national security.[41]

By May, Landis had made significant gains in arranging dimouts. Executive Order 9066 was used by officials to force stores, amusement parks, and operators of street lamps located within three miles of the New England shore to darken their lights. The dimouts changed the tenor and flow of life in New York City. Ebbets Field, home to the Brooklyn Dodgers, and the Polo Grounds, home to the New York Giants, stopped holding night baseball games. When dark fell, parks in the city were closed, and Coney Island shut down. On the West Coast, James Sheppard enforced the rules through a Regional Illuminating Engineer; patrols policed violators on beaches, cars were diverted from coastal roads, and shades came down on windows along the shoreline.[42]

Mobilizing millions of individuals and business owners to respect the restrictions represented a major challenge. Landis and the military grew impatient with the occasional lack of compliance. Concerns about public safety persuaded them to impose elements of martial law on civilians. In August, Lt. Gen. DeWitt issued a proclamation (endorsed by Landis) that asked the OCD to enforce dimout rules, and by mid-September, DeWitt, dissatisfied with the results, established a confidential program to impose "legal sanctions" on violators. Landis agreed to send reports of violations to the U.S. attorney for possible prosecution. DeWitt vowed that people who defied the rules would be expelled from the coastal zones and charged with the crime of defying military orders. In the OCD, some leaders believed that the dimout regulations "might have some legal effect under the common law of military necessity, but we were never very confident about it," the regional counsel for the West Coast told Landis.[43]

Despite a stream of complaints that the lighting restrictions were authoritarian, much of the public rallied behind the cause. "Street lights should be eliminated," Charlotte Winter of Manhattan wrote FDR. "Our ships and sons out there come first!" Wardens knocked on doors, checking on people's lights. One judge in Suffolk County fined a business $25.00 for refusing to abide by the restrictions. (Penalties carried a maximum fine of $5,000 and a year in jail.) By mid-August, the campaign had curbed the lighting from 74,000 of 113,000 streetlights in the New England dim-out zone, and Landis praised the military and local police for their "splendid cooperation." Over ten days in October, police in Los Angeles arrested at least 32 people who had allegedly violated lighting restrictions ("bright lights"; "lights very bright," the charges read). Over two weeks in December 1942, police arrested 25 violators a night on average on San Francisco's Bay Bridge and listed in a report nearly 4,000 violations over the same two-week period. From December 15 to January 15, officials levied more than 3,000 fines (ranging from $25 to $250), and one Appellate court upheld the conviction of a businessman whose store's neon sign remained lit. "We are engaged in war," the court wrote, and "public safety" trumped individual liberty as well as economic activity that did not further the war effort. A culture of compliance backed by an enthused public took root. An engineer who studied the matter reported that more than 90 percent of restricted residential and commercial lights had been dimmed, while motor vehicles complied at a rate of around 95 percent. The West Coast, Sheppard wrote Landis, was "the best in the country."[44]

Civilians endorsed the dimout as a step toward a safer homeland. A Hackensack, New Jersey, resident wrote home defense leaders that the Henry Hudson Parkway and a nearby freight yard should go dark as precautions "now that we are at WAR." One Virginian informed Washington that local dances at nearby hotels clogged roads and generated a blaze of lights, imperiling "the safety of my wife and family, . . . [and] my country . . . I cannot understand the gross negligence." One Brooklyn resident warned the president, "If there is a

landing of japs in our hemisphere . . . or bombing of n.y.," city lights could function as "a compass directing enemy aeroplanes to vital defense areas" and had to
be dimmed. Highway 101, a California resident complained, looked like a "wall
of cars" at night, "lit up for our enemy." By the fall, the Gulf Coast had joined the
West and East Coasts in enacting restrictions, and the OCD's close collaboration
with the military militarized daily life, with security restrictions taking priority
over the individual's right to live without interference from Washington.[45]

By September 1942, Landis told a West Virginia audience that the odds of
attacks had risen greatly and declared that Ambassador Grew, former envoy to
Tokyo, "has warned us that the Japanese firmly intend to dictate the peace from
the White House. This boast may sound fantastic, but many Japanese believe
it will become reality. I have lived in Japan, and you can believe me when I say
that it will serve no useful purpose to underrate the Japanese—particularly as
soldiers." His job, he said, was to keep civilians ready to serve in their quasi-
military roles and not become paralyzed "during those long hours of the dawn
watch." Despite the grim tone and urgent warnings, Landis by the fall felt that
he had made progress in ensuring national defense. He believed that national
morale had improved, equipment had begun to reach OCD volunteers, operations centers were functioning well, and coordination with the Army had grown
stronger. By late October, the OCD had 9.5 million Americans serving as volunteers, defending more than three-fourths of the total population. Best of all, the
country was receiving some of the protections that Landis had long promised
if people took home defense seriously. Civil Air Patrol pilots were forcing Nazi
submarines to move further away from the coast, while bombing enemy ships
and protecting U.S. ships from U-boats. More than a dozen pilots had died, and
sixty planes had been lost, sure signs that Landis's army was engaged in actual
combat. Moreover, volunteers fed, comforted, and treated wounded survivors
of a boat that had been torpedoed near Provincetown, Massachusetts. (Landis
called the episode a "story of greatness" and victims, tears running down their
faces, thanked those who had saved them.)[46]

Other dramatic episodes underscored the militarized facets of Landis's civilian army; it was the fulfillment of La Guardia's vision. When a train crashed
in Maryland, volunteers, bands around their arms, helped rescue victims and
recover the bodies of the eleven people who had died in the accident. When four
prisoners who had served in Rommel's Africa Corps found a way to escape their
jailers and jump off a train in Altamont, California, two members of the Civilian
Defense Auxiliary Police discovered one of the escapees sleeping in a car, and
home defense activists helped capture all four of the Nazis prisoners. Home
defenders fought fires in Connecticut, and an estimated one hundred thousand volunteers established canteens, patrolled streets, directed traffic, and kept

industrial production going after a massive flood jeopardized coal and steel production in Pittsburgh. The media reported that two women volunteers doused
a fire at a Washington, D.C., training school even before firemen could reach the
site. Volunteers also helped people cope with a flood in Ohio, a nightclub fire in
Boston, and a rare blizzard in Seattle. Civil defense volunteers helped cope with
floods in Virginia that left fifteen people dead and two thousand homeless.[47]

Landis had helped take liberalism on a new path toward public order and
physical safety. He defined home defense, and, by extension, liberal leadership
in domestic society, by demanding compliance with federal, state, and local war
regulations, putting community well-being above individual rights and business
interests, using fear of attacks to persuade civilians to support national defense,
and defining citizen participation largely on military grounds. He continued to
give his support to a wartime New Deal, but in the dimouts, the war rallies, and
internments, his true passion as a national security liberal in the scary days of
1942 was being brought most vividly to life.

13

All These Rights Spell Security

The one supreme objective for the future, which we discussed for each
Nation individually, and for all the United Nations, can be summed
up in one word: Security. And that means not only physical security
which provides safety from attacks by aggressors. It means also economic security, social security, moral security—in a family of Nations.
—Franklin Delano Roosevelt, January 11, 1944

With James Landis firmly in charge of the OCD, Eleanor Roosevelt's succes-
sors continued to make social reform a major part of home defense. Although
military defense remained Landis's top priority, he, too, fought to keep the New
Deal alive, at least as an idea on the margins of the national discourse. His public
oratory appropriated some of Eleanor Roosevelt's themes from her days in the
OCD and presaged the ideas that would form the crux of FDR's January 1944
fireside chat in which he called on Congress to enact a second "economic bill of
rights."

Liberalism's approach to domestic reform was also continuing to shift, and
Landis and his colleagues looked to the grassroots to work as partners with
Washington in a burst of volunteer participation that would improve living conditions in every community and give Americans a greater stake in the outcome
of the war. The bottom-up character of home defense enabled Landis to define
his program as a fundamentally democratic approach that sharply contrasted
with totalitarian models run by and for the state with zero deviation based on
local needs. In 1942 Landis adopted Eleanor Roosevelt's argument that social
defense was needed to raise the morale of the people and make democracy more
worth defending as a positive alternative to the nightmare of citizenry under Nazi
subjugation. In brief, the increasingly militarized bent of liberalism and home
defense still had a place, albeit small, for such concepts as the pursuit of social
justice, economic rights, and community action, defining them as essential to
the very idea of "security" in wartime America. By 1943, as the Allies defeated
the Japanese at Guadalcanal, forced a quarter-million German and Italian troops
to surrender in North Africa, and invaded Sicily (Europe's "soft underbelly," said

Churchill), the threat of military attacks against America receded from the concerns of most Americans. But Landis argued that social defense justified the continuing need for the Office of Civilian Defense.[1]

The Mayris Chaney scandal set back but did not derail entirely the quest for social reform through the OCD. At the first staff meeting after the first lady's resignation, her successor, Jonathan Daniels, told his colleagues, "We are [going] to move forward, not losing the spirit of Mrs. Roosevelt." "Reactionaries," he argued, ought not to be permitted to halt the march of progress for citizens who needed help. Daniels, the assistant director of the OCD's Civilian Mobilization Branch (which replaced ER's Community and Volunteer Participation Division), continued to recruit volunteers who would address needs stemming from dislocations created by the war, assisting consumers, industrial workers, soldiers and their families, and giving a boost to the national morale. Wilmer Shields, an ally of the first lady who also remained, went so far as to revive ER's controversial concept of mandating national service for every woman in the United States. (There is no evidence that this plan went anywhere.)[2]

Eleanor lobbied Franklin to put Landis in charge of the OCD because she saw in him a New Dealer who would sympathize with her vision of a wartime reform agenda. After she had left the OCD, however, she soured on his leadership, pitying "poor Jonathan Daniels," who, she wrote, "is up against an impossible situation . . . —Landis is proving like LaGuardia & I know what he is going through." Given the militarized direction in which Landis was taking home defense, ER's disappointment had a basis in reality, yet she shortchanged the ways that Landis was also subtly pursuing her agenda. Early in his tenure, Landis said that community needs had to be met in order for democratic society to flourish during the war. He agreed with the first lady that gale-force winds were threatening to destroy the foundation of democracy in the world, and he cited poverty and hunger as evils akin to the Nazi military, imperiling America's war effort and peacetime social order. In late February 1942, he urged a colleague in Massachusetts to find a tough-as-nails liberal to help run things there, somebody who would champion the cause of social defense but manage to "keep out the 'lunatic fringe,'" a tendency among liberals to join hands with far-left activists "which you and I frequently don't see but which do[es] disturb a lot of people."[3]

Landis continued to call on volunteers to fulfill "the promises of American life for which we now are fighting" and "bring order quickly out of this enforced chaos" precipitated by the war. Americans had to concern themselves with winning the peace, which meant advancing all of the goals and more that the New Deal was designed to address. Landis, for example, ordered his staff early in his tenure to ensure that the volunteer movement provided African Americans with a fuller chance to participate than they previously had.[4]

The OCD also began to see some signs of concrete progress in achieving ER's vision. The evidence came in bits and pieces, but taken together it revealed that nonmilitary conceptions of home defense were gaining pockets of support around the nation. By March, nearly 2,000 centers to recruit volunteers to home defense had been established in city halls, firehouses, and Red Cross offices, covering just about every major population center in the United States. The surge of volunteers in the OCD that occurred under Landis reflected more than just a desire among Americans to serve in military roles. The Civil Air Patrol received approximately 10,000 applications in a single month, and some of the pilots did nonmilitary tasks. On the whole, members of civic leagues, house-wives, and workers in New Deal agencies were the most likely to sign up for roles in social defense, whereas veterans, union members, and city workers tended to populate the ranks of military defenders. The volunteer surge in the states also reflected the mass appeal of home defense, even if the idea of a wartime New Deal took a backseat to military security. Louisiana reported a massive wave of enrollees, while 617 defense councils in Pennsylvania were running by early 1942. Volunteers did a wealth of tasks in social defense aimed at improv-ing access to economic opportunity and giving people a feel of social stability in their daily lives. Volunteers provided consumers with information about their rights, trained civilians in skills that the war industry needed (to help people land good jobs, too), mounted salvage campaigns, bolstered transit systems, built and ran day care centers, planted Victory Gardens to feed their own fami-lies (the Gardens were a joint program between the OCD and Department of Agriculture designed to bolster the national well-being and make it possible for farms to devote more of their crops to feed soldiers in the field), provided women with more information about nutritious diets, and mobilized doctors and nurses who gave medical care to patients in communities in need. One of ER's supporters argued that "a positive, progressive purpose" was necessary to guide the labor of the OCD's volunteers, and some three million Americans dur-ing the war were fulfilling this vision as wartime New Dealers had defined it. The American Association of University Women set up nursery schools in Mobile, Alabama, as part of the home defense volunteer movement, while Seattle resi-dents offered to let their homes double as day care centers, and an estimated 100 women in the city were trained as specialists in childcare.[5]

In the OCD's training literature for volunteers, air raid wardens were depicted as selfless gods bursting with patriotic virtues, and one manual, written by the WPA, characterized the typical "John Doe" volunteer as socially conscientious and neighborly, a friend to the disabled who provided first aid during emergen-cies. Wardens possessed "coolness and courage," tamping down the anxieties of fellow citizens to keep the ever-present threat of panic in check.[6]

The OCD, Landis argued in 1942, had to be more than simply "a one-winged bird." It could not be restricted solely to "the protective phase" of civilian defense. He described how his "own efforts go mainly into the field of protection and I have been hard at work in the last few weeks getting helmets and masks and other equipment off the production line," while simultaneously asserting that providing social services and improving people's lives through home defense "is not the folderol which some people have tried to call it." When Landis discovered that wartime conversion in New York was going to put three hundred thousand workers out of their jobs, he offered a proposal to retrain them so that they could find other work in the rapidly shifting national economy.[7]

Landis understood that at least part of the public wanted roles in the volunteer services that were not confined to military defense. The OCD, he explained, had received numerous letters from Americans eager to aid in the war effort, and he warned Senator Millard Tydings that the administration and Congress would "be foolish to say to those Americans who are unable to work in the protective services, 'You have no place in this war.'" Landis tasked regional directors with mobilizing volunteers to bolster people's well-being by improving social conditions, while the nine regional headquarters analyzed and reported to Washington on their area's most urgent needs, including child care for women working in defense plants. Such assistance was designed to reduce the amount of work that women had to miss and benefit the children who received such care. Sickness and poor health were like fifth columnists, Landis argued, and he estimated that such woes had combined to hinder industrial production, depriving the war economy of 448 bombers and 3,200 tanks. Foster care, day care, and after-school programs led by volunteers were part of their civic duty, Landis announced, pointing out that 4.5 million women were expected to enter the defense workforce within 2 years. Democracy, he argued, benefited from social defense in another respect: by enlisting more volunteers to tackle jobs useful to their communities, America's volunteer participation would stand in stark contrast to the Nazis' top-down agenda. Home defense in America had to be built "on a foundation of individual initiative and cooperation with the guidance of the government," said Landis.[8]

During one meeting, Landis bragged to his colleagues that cultural resistance to social defense was mostly melting away across the country. That was an oversimplification. By mid-1942, Jonathan Daniels had resigned, and "the dream of the OCD as a 'people's movement' ended," one of the first lady's biographers argued. But the first lady's spirit was brought to life in the form of projects such as Landis's "Block Plan." The plan called on block wardens to visit homes in their neighborhoods and give their neighbors easier access to "many federal programs upon which success in this war so largely depends," as Landis described it. As well, every home, Landis declared, had to become "an outpost of battle, of glory and, at last, triumph," and social services beneficial to the lives of the common man had to be, he urged, as "carefully planned as our protective services." The range of activities was almost as broad as the needs of the wartime nation. While racial questions were largely ignored or overlooked, social defense was able to provide aid to farmers in the Midwest, promote nutrition and physical fitness to an often receptive public, establish day care centers for children nationwide, and make a dent in such problems as illiteracy, recreation, malnutrition, and family security. In field surveys conducted by OCD officials, citizens expressed some enthusiasm for social defense programs, with Iowa and North Dakota among the states that seemed unlikely to be bombed or invaded where residents instead desired more social services to stem disruptions caused by the mobilization.[9]

Under Landis, in fulfillment of one of the first lady's precepts for social defense, hundreds of thousands of women across America participated in the program. A woman named Harriet Jack graduated from the Massachusetts Women's Defense School, a training program for women in home defense, and captured the mood among some of the volunteers when she expressed her commitment to feeding Americans who were displaced during any wartime emergency. Women had a prominent role in some key local programs. They comprised 20,000 of the capital's 33,000 home defense volunteers and headed three-quarters of the city's volunteer centers. About half of Detroit's 20,000 volunteers were women. In 1942, when the government asked thousands of Americans if they were doing anything to advance the war effort, more than 25 percent of women responded that they were serving as volunteers in home defense, while only about 12 percent of men said they contributed through volunteering. By making the volunteer movement hospitable to women, the first lady had hoped that they would learn skills that facilitated their entrance into professions and industrial trades. The goal was to establish a more level playing field among men and women in the economic life of the country. One woman admonished FDR to "let us girls and women learn to work for our country." In the OCD, that request was being answered in the affirmative.[10]

The broad intensity and growing level of mass interest in Landis's volunteer initiative represented another victory for liberals who had championed the cause of social defense prior to Pearl Harbor. In February 1942, the Office of Facts and Figures found in a confidential survey of more than 4,500 citizens that 80 percent believed they had ample opportunity to participate in the defense program, while 70 percent said they felt as if they were already contributing to the war effort. According to a poll conducted later that year, 78 percent of civilians judged the home defense program functioning "very well" or "fairly well" in their area and only 8 percent described local defense in their community as "poor." (Fourteen percent had no opinion.)[11]

To be sure, many volunteers continued to cast their gaze on the threat of bombs. The American public was increasingly split on how severe the threat to their lives was and whether or not home defense was even still necessary. One air raid warden captured this rift in mass opinion when he informed Landis that when an air raid siren began to blow in downtown Los Angeles, shoppers continued with their business nonchalantly. "Had a bombing occurred at Seventh and Broadway, there would have been a horrible massacre of citizens," he warned Landis, adding that he was "concerned for the lives of myself and all those around me."[12]

Nevertheless, Landis's efforts helped give social defense a legitimacy and respectability in a time when the war's outcome was far from certain and military concerns were foremost in the minds of most Americans. During the summer of 1942, Landis urged Americans to join OCD's Citizens Service Corps, an elite program for volunteers who had performed 50 or more hours of community service and wanted to work in socially useful fields, including public health, social welfare, and recreational activities. In 1943, Landis bestowed an award on some volunteers in Seattle who had established such strong facilities to care for children of mothers doing war work that they were seen as preparing future generations of citizens to prosper in postwar America. Landis set up volunteer organizations targeting elementary and high school students, tapped thousands of Boy Scouts and others to lead salvage campaigns, and assigned OCD's Labor Division to ensure that union members, a cornerstone of the New Deal coalition, had prominent roles in home defense programs. Addressing 13,000 industrial workers at a war rally in Cincinnati, Landis declared that the home defense movement had to earn "the whole-hearted support of the labor movement." To minimize the chances of manpower shortages, the OCD worked to ensure that the nation's farms and factories had a steady supply of skilled and unskilled labor. In Ohio, nearly 10,000 residents turned out in response to a defense council's call for workers in war industries, and approximately 1,000 railroad workers in Missouri voluntarily grew oat and wheat on farms after finishing their shifts— "real war work," Landis called it.[13]

The director enlisted Rotarians, Kiwanis, and other members of civic clubs to combat anti-New Deal screeds appearing in the news media. In reply to a letter from Anna Boettiger, Eleanor Roosevelt's daughter, Landis pressured Seattle's wardens to address social needs, something that they had failed to do thus far.[14]

Despite the strides made by the OCD in 1942, Landis's agency still failed to spur the kind of social transformation that Eleanor Roosevelt had envisioned. The OCD's greatest strengths were also its gravest defects. Empowering local authorities and stressing community needs enabled officials to stress the democratic character of home defense and dance around the criticism of the OCD as big-footed interference from liberal elites in the capital. But, by empowering local officials, Washington in numerous instances deprived itself of the tools to make the program cohesive and enabled individuals to apply to home defense virtually any definition they pleased. Should home defense, as an Indiana activist argued, be organized around the goal of making the United States into "the strongest *Christian* nation in the world?" Should the OCD, as a Los Angeles resident pleaded, attack the problem of vehicular accidents, the worst threat to his city? Or was the main goal of the endeavor to ensure that the four-year-old child of a Pittsburgh mom had access to his diabetes medications? While military safety enjoyed a modicum of clarity in terms of its purpose, human security was such an amorphous goal that agreed-upon definitions were elusive. Even Landis could not clearly define what he meant by the term.[15]

He claimed that home defense was advancing physical (and social) security. But in fact, it was also costing some civilians their lives. Dimouts, said some critics, were behind rising rates of auto accidents and spikes in crime rates and slowed the output of the war industries. The Greater New York Safety Council reported that the dimouts had contributed in 1942 to the deaths of 857 New Yorkers from traffic and other accidents, prompting the Council to declare, "Death lurks in the dimout." According to another 1942 study, car accidents had killed 27,800 Americans, and the dimouts were thought to have played a role.[16]

As some liberals clearly realized from the New Deal experience, paying deference to mores and laws passed by cities and states was a recipe for inaction on racial progress. Although the New Deal has rightly been criticized by historians for largely omitting from its agenda the cause of racial equality, Eleanor Roosevelt and Landis were eager to use the OCD to give African Americans opportunities to join as equals the ranks of home defense. Regarded as a loyal constituency by ER and Landis, African Americans were nevertheless for the most part shut out of the volunteer movement. Only 5 percent of the African American population felt that they were able to join or contribute to home defense, and a woman in New Orleans captured the strength of resistance to racial progress when she wrote Landis that New Orleans's reactionary men refused to believe that "the Civil War is over." White residents, she observed, were so wedded "to the old idea of 'ordering a nigger around' that we can't get anywhere" in bringing African Americans more fully into the volunteer program. One OCD aide replied that Washington had no power to compel a community to admit groups of people that the community did not want to admit. (The city had also prohibited women from joining the ranks of air raid wardens; Washington was helpless to redress this problem.)[17]

By the second half of 1942, some volunteers had become critical of the OCD's mission. They complained that the OCD had nothing concrete for them to do that contributed to national defense. In New York, one government report concluded, some of the volunteers who signed up under the "first flush of enthusiasm" following Pearl Harbor "after a while found nothing to do, became disgusted, and dropped out." In Indiana, citizens were divided over the value of the OCD. Twenty-five percent of residents did not think that they were vulnerable to air raids; others, however, said that "war industries here are not absolutely safe." Many months after Pearl Harbor, internecine political conflict dogged the home defense program. Republicans hostile to the New Deal ran home defense in Iowa, where they complained about OCD directives. The Texas program was described as "a hellish jumble of loose ends," while Wisconsin's volunteers complained of a shortage of funds for defense. Nor was the OCD proving to be the engine of immediate economic progress for the poor and uneducated that some New Dealers foresaw. It was mainly the well-educated and well-off who volunteered for duties. Whatever economic benefits came from serving in the OCD, it was typically not the poor who received them.[18]

By 1943, having seen minor and mostly harmless attacks on U.S. soil (sightings of enemy submarines; sporadic shelling of coastal lands far from population centers; the capture of hapless Nazi spies), the American public was growing more skeptical of the claim that the home front was in grave peril. There were differences of opinion, as well as confusion and a human desire to believe that things would be okay. *Time* and *Newsweek* observed that doubts about national vulnerability had begun to crest. La Guardia, followed by Landis, had warned of imminent raids for so long that the country had grown less inclined to believe such warnings.

As a consequence, Landis's campaign to mobilize Americans became more graphic and strident. When Joseph Goebbels boasted that the Nazis were going to bomb New York, Boston, and Washington, Landis replied "that we must be ready" because Hitler "wants pictures of burning American cities to show his people." In the spring of 1943, following Allied victories in North Africa, however, Americans became more confident about the war's outcome and less receptive to Landis's message. The public's turn away from home defense moved Landis to consider asking "Congress to consider legislation making it mandatory for civilians to devote a certain number of hours a week as air raid wardens, auxiliary policemen or fire watchers." (But his plan for compulsory national service, like so many others, never gained traction.) He also published "Get Ready to Be Bombed" in *The American Magazine* in May 1943. Elsewhere, the director cited military experts who had persuaded him that by the end of the year "air-raid sirens may blow in earnest in at least a few, and maybe many, American cities." He specified the air routes by which the Axis would attack six U.S. cities: The Nazis, he predicted, would use bases in Norway to send planes on missions to bomb Detroit. Their long-range planes were capable of bombing Philadelphia from their bases in France; Greenland could serve as their refueling stop. Aircraft carriers posed a new menace, Landis wrote, and Japanese bases on the Aleutian Islands put raiders within striking distance of Duluth, Minnesota. Landis described how a giant bomber had recently crossed the Atlantic before flying over an unnamed "eastern state without being once spotted by observers or picked up on our listening apparatus." Japan had dropped incendiary bombs near the Oregon–California border, he reminded Americans, ending his argument with an exclamation point.[19]

Landis's allies echoed his plea that Americans had to remain on high alert. Lt. Gen. DeWitt told Americans that "a shrewd enemy takes advantage of a public state of lethargy." Major General Ulysses Grant III, the grandson of the Civil War general and president, warned the public of a "Pearl Harbor on the continental United States." The OCD's chief medical officer, Dr. George Baehr, predicted that Japan was going to attack America with poison gas. James Sheppard warned West Coast residents that air raids were probable and that the enemy "will strike hardest where the attack is least expected." Complacency, FDR insisted, posed the greatest obstacle to achieving victory in the war.[20]

Landis struggled to find ways to keep his program relevant. The army had asked the OCD to provide stability to communities surrounding military bases, and Landis asserted that the dislocations due to mobilization required the government to aid affected communities, such as Norfolk, Virginia. He pointed out that factory fires, sabotage, and industrial accidents accounted for 400 deaths and over 2,000 injuries a week in 1942, totaling $1 billion in lost national output. "In the interest of national safety," Landis urged capital, labor, and home defense volunteers to launch a concerted attack on industrial problems.[21]

Popular support for home defense remained generally strong through much of the year, though some signs indicated that officials were having a harder time persuading the public of the danger. Despite a growing confidence in 1943 that the U.S. military was at last beginning to win the war, much of the public remained on edge, hoping for safety, yet conditioned by years of warnings from politicians and military commanders to expect terror to strike in their once-peaceful communities. Some Americans doubted that their lives were really safe; others concluded that the fears were overblown, and that geography still protected citizens from the ravages of modern war. On the ground, however, city leaders and volunteers reinforced the message of danger with vivid displays of drama and spectacle. On a Sunday night in June, 30,000 people jammed the University of Washington's football stadium to attend a war show. P-38 fighter planes buzzed over the crowd, dropping fake bombs and firing fake bullets that incinerated a fake bar, beauty salon, and grocery store. This scale of destruction and horror is "what we may expect when we are raided by the enemy," warned Seattle's mayor. The mock explosions literally rocked the stadium, and thousands of white-helmeted, armband-clad volunteers, anti-aircraft gunners, firefighters, and rescue dogs showed off the civilian army that now bristled at full strength. The *Seattle Post-Intelligencer* reported that "the audience paid special attention to a pair of good-looking girls who stripped down to bathing suits," lending a risqué touch to a macabre show.[22]

Much of the news media also remained persuaded that the nation was still in significant danger in 1943. One report issued by the OCD found that of 239 newspaper articles and editorials published between March 21 and May 15, 210 of them described air raids as a real threat. (Thirteen of the articles also praised the OCD for its role in assisting people during natural and other nonmilitary disasters.) The media deepened the public's sense of siege by publicizing, for example, German threats to use French bases to launch Heinkel-177 planes and bomb New York.[23]

By mid-1943, Landis admitted to a member of Congress that his job in the OCD had given him more "headaches" than any other position he had held. The stress of his work was showing in his treatment of aides; he berated one of them for failing to track the OCD's news coverage. That task "seems to me your job, not mine," he scolded, calling the aide's lapse "a serious matter." Republicans in Congress had drastically cut his Victory Speakers program, a decision, Landis lamented, that eliminated "our community war information work," including the education of citizens about the rationing system, for example. The program, Landis wrote Rep. Louis Ludlow, his ally on the Appropriations Committee, had rendered important service to African Americans, "bringing Negroes into the work of local Defense Councils" and into the "general field of civilian defense." Its death dealt a blow to the drive for social equality. Other bureaucratic defeats added to his woes as the OCD's director. The War Department took control of the Civil Air Patrol, shrinking Landis's portfolio. By the summer of 1943, some defense councils were also shrinking in size; enrollments in Washington, D.C., for example, fell by more than 20,000, prompting FDR to warn citizens that they must not relax "our efforts anywhere in the field of home defense until our enemies have been brought to their knees in unconditional surrender." But successful sea and land campaigns in the Pacific and Atlantic theaters made it difficult to sustain earlier fears of attack. Even the Secretary of the Navy, Frank Knox, contradicted Landis's (and Roosevelt's) message, telling more than 1,500 people in California that the threat of enemy raids on the Pacific Coast had waned substantially. "How, in the name of the Lord, do you expect us to maintain an efficient Civilian Defense organization if the Secretary of the Navy creates the impression that there is no danger of enemy attack on this coast!," Stockon's city manager asked Landis.[24]

In 1943, the OCD was also a victim of its own achievements. Landis's "dimouts" had saved the lives of merchant marines and their cargo, and reduced the impact of submarine attacks. Landis informed the Secretary of the Navy that public complacency was intensifying alongside the public's resistance to compliance with dimout rules. Rumors about the fate of Landis's agency became commonplace that summer. The State Department asked Landis if he was open to an appointment as minister for economic affairs in the Middle East. If FDR agreed to the transfer, Landis replied, he would accept the post. FDR wrote, "I want to see Jim Landis for ten minutes about this." Eager to enter into the war fray more directly, Landis had concluded that growing public indifference to home defense had turned his post into a thankless task. He even recommended that the Budget Bureau cut the OCD's funding. (Worried that gutting a war agency would "cause a great let-down in the war effort," speechwriter and advisor Samuel Rosenman prevailed on Roosevelt to keep the OCD's resources intact.) Landis, said Jonathan Daniels, "got depressed" when he realized that his mission was no longer central to the campaign to win the war militarily.[25]

On September 10, Landis's tenure came to a close with little fanfare. FDR announced that he was resigning to become American director of Economic Operations in the Middle East. Landis expressed "gratitude for having been permitted to serve my country in this significant post for over a year and a half," he wrote the president. "I have now contributed to that office as much as I can give." Home defense, he added, had "been close to my heart for more than two years. I have believed in it not only as a means for affording protection at home but as a means for effectively mobilizing the manpower of our communities for the countless tasks that war demands. I know that you have recognized its significance in these ways and that over the tomorrows that stretch between now and peace your insistence upon the devotion of America's millions to the discharge of their responsibilities at home will continue to inspire that loyalty and that tireless energy that this war for freedom demands."

Landis, FDR declared, had performed a "fine job under great difficulties." And, FDR added, it was not time yet to declare victory and abolish the OCD: "At home, as abroad, we dare not let down in this effort to enable everyone to play his part, large or small, in the waging of this war. The role of Civilian Defense in mobilizing our American communities to this end cannot be overestimated, for it affords the means for welding our people into one army that will continue to do battle in the many ways that war demands on every front that they can find. That battle can never be over here at home until victory abroad is assured."[26]

John Martin, a Rhodes Scholar and New Deal lawyer who had served as one of Landis's assistant directors, replaced Landis. By late 1943, however, despite White House rhetoric about the OCD's continuing importance, the agency had lost much of its appeal. The military progress overseas had largely persuaded the public that attacks were less likely than ever, and the incessant warnings of recent years now seemed hollow. The predictions of Armageddon were harder for officials to sustain with the same force they once packed. But FDR still refused to abolish the program; demobilizing the volunteer army before victory had been achieved, he felt, endangered the entire war effort.[27]

In the New Year, ill with the flu after having participated in the Tehran Conferences, Roosevelt sent his annual message to Congress in writing and then read portions of it over a national radio broadcast the night of January 11, 1944. Landis and ER were long gone from the home defense program, but their imprint on the debate about the role of government and civilians on the home front was still being heard and felt. Roosevelt's address famously urged Congress to pass a second "economic bill of rights," setting, as one historian has written, "the liberal agenda for the postwar period." Historians have typically portrayed Roosevelt's address as the last hurrah of the New Deal. While FDR announced in his talk his support for a GI Bill of Rights, which Congress ultimately passed, the other elements of his reform package died in Congress, foundering on the shoals of a conservative Congress and the nation's focus on winning the war. Nonetheless, Roosevelt's vision was nurtured in the wartime debate between La Guardia and Eleanor Roosevelt about the proper meaning of "security" and government's role in ensuring that all citizens had it. The argument for social reform served as a bridge between the heyday of the New Deal and Roosevelt's 1944 economic rights speech. Franklin echoed Eleanor when he declared that "the one supreme objective for the future" was not only "physical security which provides safety from attacks by aggressors" but also "economic security, social security, moral security." He called "overconfidence and complacency . . . our deadliest enemies" and announced support for a law that would require every adult citizen to perform national service during the war emergency. His vision of mobilizing the grassroots to wage total war against social and military threats alike encapsulated Eleanor's Roosevelt's vision for social defense.[28]

The president declared that "without economic security and independence" Americans could not experience the fruits of "true individual freedom." These new rights, as he enunciated them, included the right to a living wage, adequate shelter, health care, education, and "protection from the economic fears of old age, sickness, accident, and unemployment." Roosevelt summed up his argument when he said that "all these rights spell security" both for Americans and for the people of the world.[29]

On April 12, 1945, Roosevelt died from a cerebral hemorrhage while he was vacationing in Warm Springs, Georgia. His fourth term was in its infancy. In 1945, Harry Truman, who succeeded Roosevelt, issued an executive order that abolished the Office of Civilian Defense, but this step by then was less substantive than symbolic, a statement that the war had finally ended. Once Landis had departed from the OCD, the public lost much of its appetite for the volunteer program, yet the ideas underpinning the home defense debate remained forces that would shape the direction of postwar liberalism.

Would government provide economic and social security to the American people at the same time that it thwarted physical threats to the nation's security? How would democratic governments define "national security" in an age when nuclear weapons threatened the lives of millions of people? Postwar liberals, and the United States more generally, would continue to grapple with these questions among others long after the Roosevelt years had passed. Prior to and during the war, liberalism had shifted its focus to waging total war. But the idea of liberalism also involved a commitment to bringing economic security and social benefits to more Americans, and this idea never died. The competition between military defense and human security would remain a tension in postwar liberalism as vital as when it commanded so much attention during the Roosevelt years. From the Cold War to the War on Terror, this debate about liberalism's creed—the ideas that gave it energy and definition—remains fundamental to the character of American democracy.

Conclusion

National Security Liberalism

From whence shall we expect the approach of danger? Shall some
trans-Atlantic military giant step the earth and crush us at a blow?
Never. All the armies of Europe and Asia . . . could not by force take
a drink from the Ohio River or make a track on the Blue Ridge in the
trial of a thousand years. No, if destruction be our lot we must ourselves
be its author and finisher. As a nation of free men we will live forever
or die by suicide.

—Abraham Lincoln, 1838

Recognizing that fascism posed a threat to America earlier than most citizens
did, Eleanor Roosevelt lobbied pacifists, isolationists, and antiwar liberals to
endorse FDR's defense mobilization as the only sane response to fascist aggression. But she never tired of highlighting the problems—including poverty, malnutrition, racial and gender inequality—that the New Deal and society had not
yet solved. In both regards, ER became a principal architect of liberalism as "a
fighting faith." She insisted that social and economic problems had to remain
at the center of the debate about democracy in wartime. She helped forge the
liberal tradition of projecting America's values to the world while also pushing
Americans to live up to their founding principles. The United States, ER argued,
had to show other people why democracy was superior to totalitarian regimes.
As a proponent of "national greatness," she further insisted that Jim Crow and
economic injustice at home prevented America from winning hearts worldwide
and made it more difficult for the United States to conquer dictatorships.

During World War II, the choices made by liberals had immediate consequences for liberalism and the country. Social defense was ultimately subordinated to the needs of national security. As home defense evolved, what "defense"
and "security" even meant narrowed in wartime society to connote military preparedness rather than "human security."

After her ouster from the Office of Civilian Defense, ER did not stand on the sidelines of the great domestic debates. An American Legion commander proposed that she keep "quiet for the [war's] duration," after she had upset him by questioning whether the country was adequately meeting the needs of GIs. Giving a press conference, ER replied that staying silent was not part of her plan. Between 1942 and 1945, she continued to defend the rights of youth, women, African Americans, the poor, workers, and American soldiers. She forwarded to General George Marshall so many letters filled with complaints from GIs and their families that Marshall assigned two aides to investigate and fix the problems. Visiting wounded GIs in virtually every hospital on the West Coast, she lifted their spirits. She toured factories, hospitals, and bombed buildings in London's East End and talked to British firefighters and police about the importance of home defense during a visit to England in October 1942. As Allied victory neared, she urged the country to pursue full employment and ensure that women had access to policy-making roles.[1]

La Guardia, for his part, returned to his New Deal roots. After leaving the OCD for good, he stayed in New York's City Hall on a full-time basis. Although he longed to "get into uniform" and have a direct impact on the war overseas, Secretary of War Henry Stimson blocked FDR's plan to appoint La Guardia as a Brigadier General who would be in charge of Allied-occupied Italy. (La Guardia, Stimson felt, was too political for the role.) Rather than serving as a uniformed officer in the European theater, La Guardia made his mark on wartime liberalism in his third term as mayor launching experiments in New York City that aimed to make it the world's great center of commerce and culture during the war and beyond. One historian writes that he became the "leading voice in the nation for a postwar public works program," and the mayor even proposed a progressive public health insurance plan to provide health care to New Yorkers.[2]

The fates of ER, La Guardia, and Landis's ideas reflect some of the trajectories and conflicts within liberalism in the postwar world. ER's vision influenced aspects of postwar liberalism in ways that often are not well understood. FDR, Harry Truman, George Kennan, Adlai Stevenson, Arthur Schlesinger Jr., John F. Kennedy, and Lyndon B. Johnson have received the lion's share of credit (and derision) as the fathers of postwar liberalism. But elements of ER's social defense ideals were expressed in Harry Truman's Fair Deal, John F. Kennedy's New Frontier, and Lyndon Johnson's Great Society, all of which rested in part on the notion that without achieving social democracy at home, the United States would be ill-equipped to project its values—freedom, opportunity, human rights—effectively overseas. Just as ER had envisioned a grassroots wartime movement to improve life for all at the local level and bring the fruits of democracy to more Americans, JFK's and LBJ's programs, especially the Peace Corps and the War on Poverty, similarly asked citizens to get engaged in the issues of their time and take responsibility for their country's future. ER, JFK, and LBJ all emphasized the role of youth in achieving progressive social reforms.[3]

After 1945, as the country became more conservative, ER's vision of bringing African Americans into the mainstream of American life and providing better housing and child and health care to all citizens took a backseat to combating the communist threat. Truman instituted loyalty oaths, established the Department of Defense, aided Greece and Turkey in the struggle against Communism, and waged a war on the Korean Peninsula. It would take roughly twenty years from the end of World War II before the country experienced a new wave of social liberalism that culminated in civil rights, Medicare, and the war on poverty.[4]

ER continued her campaign for progressive reforms during the early Cold War and became the conscience of liberalism even though it was in retreat. In order to win the peace, New Deal liberalism, she argued, not only had to spread democratic values abroad but also enact the unfinished agenda of the New Deal in the United States. Taking a post as a delegate to the United Nations between 1945 and 1952, ER tried to live up to her creed. She led efforts to assist refugees, promoted the UN's Commission on Human Rights, and helped draft the Universal Declaration of Human Rights—seeking to translate the sacrifices of World War II into tangible benefits for more of the world's peoples.[5]

She also remained a force in domestic politics, inspiring liberals to move more quickly and aggressively to guarantee that wartime sacrifices were not squandered. Befriending and advising two-time Democratic presidential nominee Adlai Stevenson, ER became increasingly outspoken on issues of racial and social justice during a decade when progressives were on the defensive. Carrying the banner of New Deal liberalism in directions far different from the reforms passed at the height of the 1930s economic crisis, she was one of a number of prominent reformers who helped lay the predicate for the movements for social justice that ultimately flourished during the 1960s. Criticizing the Democratic Party's incremental approach to racial justice, she befriended civil rights leaders; joined the Congress on Racial Equality's and the NAACP's boards; and, as a result, the KKK threatened to kill her. As her biographer Allida Black has argued, ER saw "racial injustice [as] the biggest threat to democracy" in postwar America. She supported sit-ins and endorsed direct action to force an end to racial segregation and even raised money for activists who had been jailed in the early sixties for protesting Jim Crow.

Her devotion to civil liberties also deepened during the postwar years. She became the first well-known liberal to denounce Sen. Joseph McCarthy's anticommunist crusade, declaring it an affront to individuals' freedom. Combating gender inequality, she lobbied the Kennedy administration to appoint more women to government posts. JFK ultimately made her chair of the President's Commission on the Status of Women. She then testified before Congress and helped win passage of the Equal Pay Act guaranteeing equal pay to women who held the same jobs as men. (She also served on the board of the Peace Corps.) On November 7, 1962, at the age of seventy-eight, she died from tuberculosis, aplastic anemia, and heart failure, just as the nation was on the verge of a new burst of social liberalism that would have heartened her had she lived.[6]

La Guardia was also active in the postwar world, but he had little time left. After his departure from City Hall in 1945, he became a pundit, writing and speaking out on federal health reform and social justice, and he led a United Nations effort to assist refugees displaced by the war. In 1947, at the age of sixty-four, he died of pancreatic cancer. Fiorello La Guardia's vision for home defense found arguably even more resonance in the culture of 1950s America than ER's. His idea to prioritize militarism ahead of other national concerns gained traction among some liberals during the Cold War. The communist threat and the rise of government surveillance and military spending crowded out liberals' passion for attacking problems of poverty, slums, civil rights, and civil liberties.[7]

James Landis, also eager to shape the peace, decided to give up his tenured post at Harvard in order to accept Truman's request that he chair the Civil Aeronautics Board. Returning to his early roots as an economic regulator, Landis's aggressive efforts as chairman antagonized the airline industry, and, under pressure from industry leaders, Truman fired Landis in late 1947. Landis later agreed to serve as a lawyer and counselor to Joseph P. Kennedy (for whom he had worked at the SEC). In 1950, he delivered an address drawing on his experiences in home defense and outlining his view of home defense in the nuclear age. He argued that "the central problem of civil defense" was Washington's inability to require individuals, cities, and states to follow civil defense rules and regulations. The federal government had also failed to fund state and local programs, imposing an unfunded mandate on cities and states. In spite of his warnings, however, the Cold War program continued to be plagued by the same problems.[8]

His ending was tragic. In 1961, Landis joined the Kennedy administration as a special assistant in charge of reforming economic regulations. But when the Internal Revenue Service investigated him for failing to pay his income taxes over several years, he was forced to resign. Sentenced to thirty days in prison, he was disbarred, and soon thereafter, he died a broken man.[9]

As numerous historians have shown, civil defense, which was reconstituted by Truman in 1950, represented a triumph for national security liberals. Gone from the program was any talk of Eleanor Roosevelt's social defense agenda. Liberals fretted about communists infiltrating American government and society, and many of them stood by as redbaiting Senator Joseph McCarthy launched a hunt for traitors in the State Department, Army, and elsewhere. During the Cold War, civil defense abandoned New Deal liberalism's commitment to social and economic security. Truman's first civil defense director, Millard Caldwell, a former governor of Florida, was a segregationist, thus ensuring that ER's (and Landis's) idea of promoting racial equality through civil defense was doomed, even though Truman did support civil rights.

While home defense in London during the Blitz gave the notion of civil defense credibility in the United States (it seemed to be saving lives and keeping morale intact), home defense during the Cold War became something of a farce, directing schoolchildren to practice duck-and-cover drills in case of a nuclear attack; urging citizens to construct private shelters in their basements; and teaching Americans how to evacuate on the nation's highways if Soviet missiles were fired at U.S. cities. Most of these strategies rested on the concept of "self-help." But the federal government refused to fund the civil defense program, recruited only 4 million civil defense volunteers (the goal was 15 to 17 million), and oversaw the building of just 1,500 private shelters in 35 states by 1960—roughly one for every 100,000 citizens. An orgy of propaganda films and advertisements suffused the culture of 1950s America, but there was scant support among the public or, really, the federal government, for the civil defense program. Self-help was simply too unrealistic in the face of the threat of nuclear weapons.

More than any single development, Pearl Harbor shattered the assumption that Americans were insulated from the world's conflicts. The attack ushered in the age when the country felt vulnerable to threats originating from abroad. While liberal anticommunists became entrusted with national security for much of the early Cold War, New Deal liberalism remained a powerful idea in some quarters, even though it wasn't drastically expanded during the early Cold War.[10]

By the time terrorists attacked America on September 11, 2001, few Democrats identified themselves as New Deal liberals. Yet the tension between guns and butter, on vivid display during World War II and the Cold War, has remained a feature of debates about politics and policy in the twenty-first century. Liberals argue with conservatives and among themselves about the proper balance between individual freedom and national security. The number of resources that should be funneled into the Department of Homeland Security, the CIA, and the U.S. military for war-fighting purposes and defense against terrorist attacks has provoked sharp dissent. Some liberals argue that "nation-building right here at home," as President Barack Obama argued in 2012, is more important than spilling blood and treasure to stabilize the Middle East.

These debates are traceable to the struggle among liberals to alert citizens to the war on "two fronts"—at home and abroad—during the Roosevelt years. As long as the United States has enemies overseas and threats from within, the fight over the best balance between guns and butter will remain central to America's national identity—an enduring legacy of the campaign by liberals in World War II to liberate Americans from the grip of fear.

NOTES

Abbreviations

New York City Municipal Archives: NYCMA; Fiorello H. La Guardia Papers: LG
National Archives and Records Administration, College Park, MD: NARA; Records of the Office
of Civilian Defense, Record Group: RG, Entry: E
Franklin Delano Roosevelt Library: FDRL
    Franklin D. Roosevelt Papers: FDRL
    Eleanor Roosevelt Papers: ERP, FDRL
    Harry Hopkins Papers: Hopkins Papers, FDRL
Library of Congress (LoC), Manuscript Division, Washington, D.C.:
    James McCauley Landis Papers: Landis Papers.
    Archibald MacLeish Papers, 1907–1981: Archibald MacLeish Papers
    Harold Ickes Diary: Ickes Diary

Introduction

1. For an account of the demonstrations in Prague, see Walter B. Kerr, "Czechs Surrender Sudetenland to Hitler; Angry Throngs in Prague Shout for War; Poland in Ultimatum Demands Its Share," *New York Herald Tribune*, Sept. 22, 1938.
2. Robert J. Brown, *Manipulating the Ether: The Power of Broadcast Radio in Thirties America* (Jefferson, NC: McFarland & Company,1998), 207, 213. "Excerpts from the 'War' Broadcast," *New York Times*, Nov. 1, 1938.
3. For a revisionist view that the media greatly exaggerated the panic, see W. Joseph Campbell's *Getting It Wrong: Ten of the Greatest Misreported Stories in American Journalism* (Berkeley: University of California Press, 2010), ch. 2, as well as http://www.slate.com/articles/arts/history/2013/10/orson_welles_war_of_the_worlds_panic_myth_the_infamous_radio_broadcast_did.2.html; and Jefferson Pooley and Michael Socolow, in Joy Elizabeth Hayes, Kathleen Battles, and Wendy Hilton-Morrow, eds., *War of the Worlds to Social Media: Mediated Communication in Times of Crisis* (New York: Peter Lang Publishing, 2013). Estimates—both of the number of listeners and the percentage of those who panicked—are unreliable and have often been exaggerated. See http://paleofuture.gizmodo.com/did-the-war-of-the-worlds-radio-broadcast-really-cause-1453582944 and http://www.radiolab.org/story/91622-war-of-the-worlds/. As the recent scholarship makes clear, key aspects of the panic were also almost certainly hyped by the media. But some of the revisionist scholarship makes it sound like the newspapers almost completely fabricated the panic for purposes of discrediting radio. However, it's hard to imagine all of those newspapers conspiring simultaneously and falsifying the record just to launch a coordinated attack on radio. Most importantly, the revisionist scholarship tends to shortchange the context of October 1938—the

265

hysterical tone of the newspaper coverage, the warnings about fascism from elected leaders, the radio broadcasts about fascist terror including Hitler's annexation of Czechoslovakia's
Sudetenland, which suffused the culture in the late thirties. So even if the revisionist view was
right about the paucity of panic after "War of the Worlds," the episode still begs for an expla-
nation about why the country was paying such rapt, almost panicked attention to Nazi military
advances in Europe. The reaction to the "War of the Worlds" was ultimately about concerns about
Nazi advances in Europe, as Hadley Cantril suggested in *The Invasion from Mars: A Study in the
Psychology of Panic* (Princeton: Princeton University Press, 1940). My arguments also draw on
David Greenberg's *Republic of Spin: An Inside History of the American Presidency* (New York: W.
W. Norton, 2016), ch. 22, in which Greenberg argues that "hysterical New Jerseyans weren't listening to their radios in a vacuum . . . their responses were shaped by the escalating international
hostilities of late 1938 . . . they were thus already caught up in a vexed debate about their own
preparedness to meet a foreign threat, not from outer space but from the Axis powers." See 209.

4. Marshall Andrews, "Monsters of Mars on a Meteor Stampede Radiotic America," *Washington Post*, Oct. 31, 1938. "Radio Listeners in Panic, Taking War Drama as Fact," *New York Times*, Oct. 31, 1938.
5. Brown, *Manipulating the Ether*, 205, 217. Bruce Lenthall, *Radio's America: The Great Depression and the Rise of Modern Mass Culture* (Chicago: University of Chicago Press, 2007), 2.
6. Marshall Andrews, "Monsters of Mars on a Meteor Stampede Radiotic America," *Washington Post*, Oct. 31, 1938. "Radio Listeners in Panic, Taking War Drama as Fact," *New York Times*, Oct. 31, 1938.
7. U.P.I., "Radio Story of Mars Raid Causes Panic," *Los Angeles Times*, Oct. 31, 1938. James D. Secrest, "Martian Invasion by Radio 'Regrettable,' Says McNinch," *Washington Post*, Nov. 1, 1938, xi. "Radio 'Scare' Program Brings Censor Demands," Staff Correspondent, *Christian Science Monitor*, Oct. 31, 1938. Editorial, "Tower Views by Clearway," *Christian Science Monitor*.
8. AP, "H. G. Wells Explains," in *Christian Science Monitor*, Oct. 31, 1938. "Radio Listeners in Panic, Taking War Drama as Fact," *New York Times*, Oct. 31, 1938. U.P.I., "Radio Story," *Los Angeles Times*, Oct. 31, 1938.
9. Editorial, "Great American Jitters," *Washington Post*, Nov. 1, 1938. "Raid Panic Laid to Nerves," *Los Angeles Times*, Nov. 7, 1938, A3. Dorothy Thompson, "Mr. Welles and Mass Delusion," *Washington Post*, Nov. 2, 1938, X9.
10. "Radio: Boo!" *Time*, Nov. 7, 1938. "Radio Listeners in Panic," *New York Times*, Oct. 31, 1938. For an overview of the U.S. reaction to the Munich Agreement, see David M. Kennedy, *Freedom from Fear: The American People in Depression and War, 1929–1945* (New York: Oxford University Press, 1999), 418–421. Morton Jerome Jacobs, "The Real 'Monsters,'" *Washington Post*, Nov. 10, 1938, 11. Brown, *Manipulating the Ether*, 200.
11. http://www.poetryfoundation.org/bio/archibald-macleish. Brown, *Manipulating the Ether*, 190, 215. Albert D. Hughes, "Radio Scare: Boston Misses 'Martian Raid,'" *Christian Science Monitor*, Nov. 1, 1938.
12. ER, *This I Remember* (New York: Harper & Brothers, 1949), 233.
13. For FDR's day of infamy speech, see http://www.archives.gov/publications/prologue/2001/winter/crafting-day-of-infamy-speech.html. For La Guardia quote, see Jan Jarboe Russell, *The Train to Crystal City: FDR's Secret Prisoner Exchange and America's Only Family Internment Camp During World War II* (New York: Scribner, 2015), 19.
14. Doris Kearns Goodwin, *No Ordinary Time: Franklin and Eleanor Roosevelt: The Home-Front in World War II* (New York: Simon and Schuster, 1994), 295–299.
15. For Bullitt, see "U.S. Not Aroused, Bullitt Warns," *Utica Daily Press*, Oct. 20, 1940, http://ns2.fultonhistory.com/Process%20small/Newspapers/Utica%20NY%20Daily%20Press/Utica%20NY%20Daily%20Press%201940.pdf/Utica%20NY%20Daily%20Press%201940%20-%204302.PDF. For figures on the Blitz, see Anton Rippon, *How Britain Kept Calm and Carried On: Real-Life Stories from the Home Front* (London: Michael O'Mara Books Limited, 2014), under section "Put That Light Out!"
16. Lady Stella Reading to ER, Feb. 17, 1941; see also Reading to ER, May 6, 1941, ER 100: Personal Letters, ERP, FDRL, http://www.fdrlibrary.marist.edu/_resources/images/ersel/ersel079.pdf.

17. For a strong synopsis of the OCD's origins, see Patrick S. Roberts, "The Forgotten Lessons of Civil Defense Federalism for the Homeland Security Era," 354–383, *Journal of Policy History*, Vol. 26, No. 3, 2014. For FDR's executive order, see "Franklin D. Roosevelt: Executive Order 8757 Establishing the Office of Civilian Defense," May 20, 1941, http://www.presidency. ucsb.edu/ws/?pid=16117. "La Guardia Is Dead; City Pays Homage to 3-Time Mayor," *New York Times*, Sept. 21, 1947. For an overview of civil defense in the United States, see David M. Kennedy, ed., Margaret E. Wagner, Linda Barrett Osborne, Susan Reyburn, and Staff of Library of Congress, *The Library of Congress World War II Companion* (New York: Simon and Schuster, 2007), 176–178. For an astute, in-depth analysis of La Guardia's life and career, see Thomas A. Kessner, *Fiorello H. La Guardia and the Making of Modern New York* (New York: McGraw-Hill, 1989).

18. The idea of La Guardia as a champion of national security liberalism during WWII draws on Anne Kornhauser's *Debating the American State: Liberal Anxieties and the New Leviathan, 1930–1970* (Philadelphia: University of Pennsylvania Press, 2015). See 3–4: "Statist liberalism," Kornhauser writes, " . . . abided as well a more repressive national security state, which was prefigured in World War II and fully developed during the immediate postwar years." She adds that "the concept of statist liberalism acknowledges modern liberalism's admiration for state power in various forms, even as the uses of that power changed over time and undermined many of the policies and priorities of the early New Deal." La Guardia's views of state power also shifted over time in response to his perception of the greatest threats facing urban America. The notion of La Guardia's national security liberalism also builds on Alan Brinkley's *The End of Reform: New Deal Liberalism in Recession and War* (New York: Knopf, 1995). Brinkley argues that some New Deal liberals embraced a liberalism that largely rejected centralized economic planning and sought to accommodate a consumer-oriented economy through pro-growth economic policies. La Guardia's brand of liberalism offers yet another example of how New Deal liberals diverged in their views of federal power in the post-1937 period—that the state must be most responsible for inspiring and instructing citizens in order to defend them against physical harm. "The new liberalism that evolved in response to this changing [post-1937] world wrapped itself in the mantle of the New Deal, but bore only a partial resemblance to the ideas that had shaped the original New Deal," Brinkley writes (p. 4). Matthew Dallek, "Civic Security," *Democracy: A Journal of Ideas*, Issue #7, Winter 2008.

19. Dee Garrison, *Bracing for Armageddon: Why Civil Defense Never Worked* (New York: Oxford University Press, 2006), 33. Kessner, *Fiorello H. La Guardia*, 495–496.

20. For a description of La Guardia wearing his Stetson hats, see Joseph Heller, *Now and Then: From Coney Island to Here* (New York: Alfred A. Knopf, 1998), 61. "La Guardia Is Dead; City Pays Homage to 3-Time Mayor," *New York Times*, Sept. 21, 1947.

21. The Eleanor Roosevelt Papers Project, https://www.gwu.edu/~erpapers/teachinger/q-and-a/q8-newsarticle.cfm.

22. For ER's height, see "Biography of Eleanor Roosevelt," http://www.fdrlibrary.marist.edu/ education/resources/bio_er.html. "What the men . . . " quoted in Blanche Wiesen Cook, *Eleanor Roosevelt, 1884-1933: Volume I* (New York: Penguin Books, 1992), 162–167, 233. ER, "Because the War Idea Is Obsolete," from *Why Wars Must Cease*, ed. Rose Young (New York: Macmillan, 1935), 20–29, in Black, *What I Hope to Leave Behind*, 496.

23. Blanche Wiesen Cook, *Eleanor Roosevelt, Volume 2: The Defining Years, 1933–1938* (New York: Penguin Books, 1999), 539.

24. The best accounts of ER's life and career include Blanche Wiesen Cook's superb multivolume life of ER; Allida M. Black's first-rate *Casting Her Own Shadow: Eleanor Roosevelt and the Shaping of Postwar Liberalism* (New York: Columbia University Press, 1996). Lois Scharf's incisive, brief biography, *Eleanor Roosevelt: First Lady of American Liberalism* (Boston: Twayne Publishers, 1987); Doris Kearns Goodwin's engaging account, *No Ordinary Time*; and Maurine Beasley's astute *Eleanor Roosevelt: Transformative First Lady* (Lawrence: University Press of Kansas, 2010). Brigid O'Farrell's *She Was One of Us: Eleanor Roosevelt and the American Worker* (Ithaca, NY: Cornell University Press, 2010) explores ER's connection to labor unions and the American working class. "Franklin, I think . . . " quoted in "What New Deal Policies Did Eleanor Roosevelt Influence?" The Eleanor Roosevelt Papers Project, http://www.gwu.edu/~erpapers/teachinger/q-and-a/q20.cfm.

25. Franklin D. Roosevelt, Annual Message to Congress, Jan. 4, 1939, http://www.presidency.ucsb.edu/ws/index.php?pid=15684. "Gases and airplanes," Eleanor Roosevelt, *This Troubled World* (New York: H.C. Kinsey and Co., Inc., 1938), 41. Cook, *ER Vol. 2*, 562.
26. No Author, "First Lady Backs Billion for Defense," *Washington Post*, May 17, 1940. No Author, "First Lady's Plea Ignored by Youth," *New York Times*, May 27, 1940. Joseph Lash, *Eleanor and Franklin: The Story of Their Relationship Based on Eleanor Roosevelt's Private Papers* (New York: W. W. Norton & Company Inc., 1971), 632–633.
27. ER, "My Day," May 22, 1940. ER, "My Day," May 17, 1940.
28. AP, "Women Defense Training Urged," *Los Angeles Times*, Jan. 2, 1941, E7. Florence Kerr, "Volunteer Mobilization of Women"; "*This Is the Home Defense Program Prepared by Mrs. Florence Kerr at the Request of the President,*" undated, F: "1941 Kerr, Florence 1/1–2/28," ER 70: Correspondence with Government Departments, 1941 I-Kerr, Florence, ERP, FDRL.
29. See "The Published and Recorded Works of Eleanor Roosevelt," The Eleanor Roosevelt Papers Project, https://www.gwu.edu/~erpapers/abouteleanor/erbibliography.cfm. Timeline of Polling History: People Who Shaped the United States and the World, http://www.gallup.com/poll/9964/timeline-polling-history-people-shaped-united-states-world.aspx. Franklin D. Roosevelt, State of the Union Message to Congress, Jan. 6, 1941, http://www.fdrlibrary.marist.edu/pdfs/fftext.pdf. Franklin D. Roosevelt, State of the Union Message to Congress, Jan. 11, 1944, http://www.fdrlibrary.marist.edu/archives/address_text.html.
30. Hillary Clinton became the second first lady to hold an official appointed position when she chaired the Health Care Task Force under President Bill Clinton, in 1993. The ten million-plus volunteer figure is the most widely cited number. See, for example, Wilbur R. Miller, *The Social History of Crime and Punishment in America: An Encyclopedia* (Thousand Oaks, CA: Sage, 2012), 2282. See Robert Miller, *The War That Never Came* (dissertation), 12. Patrick S. Roberts, *Disasters and the American State: How Politicians, Bureaucrats, and the Public Prepare for the Unexpected* (Cambridge: Cambridge University Press, 2013), 45.
31. See Goodwin, *No Ordinary Time*, 323–326.
32. Blanche Wiesen Cook's first two volumes of ER's life have only come up to 1938 as of this writing. ER's leadership of home defense is skipped over in Black's *Casting Her Own Shadow*. Lois Scharf's biography, *Eleanor Roosevelt*, devotes a mere four pages to her tenure as OCD's assistant director. Goodwin's engaging account, *No Ordinary Time*, similarly moves quickly past ER's home defense movement. As the title implies, Hazel Rowley's *Franklin and Eleanor: An Extraordinary Marriage* (New York: Farrar, Straus, & Giroux, 2011) dwells on the first couple's relationship, while Beasley's *Eleanor Roosevelt* briefly situates the episode in the larger arc of ER's fascinating political career. Brigid O'Farrell's *She Was One of Us* explores ER's connection to labor unions and the American working class.
33. The best account of James Landis's life is Donald A. Ritchie, *James M. Landis: Dean of the Regulators* (Cambridge, MA: Harvard University Press, 1980). On p. 3 of Ritchie, Landis described himself as devoted to upholding the capitalist system. "I've been called everything, including a Socialist and a Communist," he explained, "but my theory is a simple one. My desire was to take this system of capitalism and make it live up to its pretensions. Certainly not to overturn it." For the OCD's activities, see Ritchie, *James M. Landis*, 108; and Richard R. Lingeman, *Don't You Know There's a War On?, The American Home Front, 1941–1945* (New York: G.P. Putnam's Sons, 1970), 44-5. For Landis's nonmilitary activities, see Dallek, "Civic Security," in *Democracy: A Journal of Ideas* 7, Winter 2008. For "think war" quote, see George Z. Griswold, "Landis Tells 12,000: Sleep and Eat War," *Cleveland Plain Dealer*, Apr. 1, 1942, RG171, E: 185, B: 6, F: 7-A-1: Statements or Speeches by Landis.
34. For FDR's fireside chat, see Franklin D. Roosevelt, Fireside Chat I: On the Banking Crisis, March 12, 1933, http://millercenter.org/president/fdroosevelt/speeches/speech-3298. My book draws on Michael Sherry's idea that prior to the nuclear age, the United States witnessed the "creation of an apocalyptic mentality, consisting of expectations of ultimate danger and destruction." Sherry argues that expectations of Armageddon were actually rooted not in the Cold War but in the first half of the twentieth century and the advent of aerial bombers, long predating nuclear weapons. My book sifts how what Sherry calls the "attitudes and practices" of air war shaped the politics and culture of the debate about home defense during World War II. See Michael S. Sherry, *The Rise of American Air Power: The Creation of Armageddon,*

ix–x (New Haven, CT: Yale University Press, 1987). Further, it draws on Sherry's definition of "militarization," which included any activities, politics, or policies that supported military affairs in domestic American life.

35. For "world has grown . . . ," see Franklin D. Roosevelt, Annual Message to Congress, Jan. 4, 1939, http://www.presidency.ucsb.edu/ws/index.php?pid=15684.

36. Some twentieth-century historians have begun to locate the origins of a lot of Cold War tendencies in the WWII experience. For example, Wendy Wall, in *Inventing the American Way: The Politics of Consensus from the New Deal to the Civil Rights Movement* (New York: Oxford University Press, 2008), describes how the "consensus" often attributed to the Cold War had roots in the FDR era. Kim Phillips-Fein does something similar with a certain strain of conservatism. My own book seeks to add to the historiographical trend, arguing that more traditional studies of mid-twentieth-century America have overdone the significance of the Cold War and neglected the importance of WWII. The politics of the World War II period were less a break from what lay ahead than a link to the Cold War era. Historians have examined the self-help strategy during the 1950s, civil defense's portrayal in the mass media and popular culture, and its prescriptive shortcomings and propagandistic excesses. For a strong analysis of the Cold War's self-help policy in the United States, see Laura McEnaney, *Civil Defense Begins at Home: Militarization Meets Everyday Life in the Fifties* (Princeton, NJ: Princeton University Press, 2000); for a classic study of the Cold War, family life, and American culture, see Elaine May, *Homeward Bound: American Families in the Cold War Era* (New York: Basic Books, 1988); for the failure of civil defense policy, see Dee Garrison, *Bracing for Armageddon;* for civil defense as a propaganda tool, see Guy Oakes, *The Imaginary War: Civil Defense and American Cold War Culture* (New York: Oxford University Press, 1994).

37. Elwyn A. Mauck, "Civilian Defense in the United States, 1940–1945,"(Unpublished Manuscript by the Historical Officer of the Office of Civilian Defense) chs. XIII-IX, 48, RG171, E: 231–232, B: 1, F: Narrative Account. . . . In his 1942 year-end report, Landis announced that more than ten million volunteers had registered for home defense roles. The areas of the United States considered "strategic" or "target" zones include areas along the Pacific, Atlantic, and Gulf coasts, each spanning around 300 miles inland. There were approximately 50 million American living in these areas. See La Guardia to FDR, Sept. 23, 1941, and attached Legislative Proposal (Exhibits A, B, C), RG171, E: 10, B: 109, F: 500-Civilian Protection. Henry Stimson and Ralph Bard to La Guardia, Sept. 29, 1941, RG389, E: 468, B: 1939, F: Civil Defense Training. Thomas Hamilton, "OCD Goes Into Action Against New Air Peril," *New York Times*, Dec. 14, 1941, E7.

38. My book builds on James Sparrow's argument that the "warfare state" grew in ways that far exceeded the growth of the New Deal state during the 1930s. At the same time, my book stresses that individuals and New Deal critics made home defense on their own terms, resisting directions from Washington, defying quasi-military leaders, and engaging in roles that they deemed most valuable to their communities. The OCD made no dent in the entrenched system of Jim Crow racism, as Southern officials effectively sidestepped efforts by Washington to integrate African Americans into a united home defense campaign. See Sparrow, *Warfare State: World War II Americans and the Age of Big Government* (New York: Oxford University Press, 2011), introduction. For Southern resistance to efforts to mitigate Jim Crow during the long New Deal years, see Ira Katznelson, *Fear Itself: The New Deal and the Origins of Our Time* (New York: W. W. Norton & Company, 2014). As Mason B. Williams argues, the crises of the Great Depression and World War II "forced Americans to search for new means of collective action," and within this search, the struggle over home defense unfolded, pitting individual liberties against government authority. And while Americans politics was indeed "undergoing a process of nationalization" during the Roosevelt years, my book argues that the resistance among city governments and individuals was also robust and that the "age of 'federal cooperatism' " was buffeted by long-standing forces hostile to state power and centralized control. See Williams, *City of Ambition: FDR, La Guardia, and the Making of Modern New York* (New York: W. W. Norton & Company, 2013), xii–xiii.

39. "War of the Worlds: The Script," http://www.radioheardhere.com/waroftheworlds/.

Chapter 1

1. While the Dies Committee and its predecessor enjoyed some popular support, a number of liberals, especially political leaders, saw these committees as overzealous and irresponsible. See Frederick Barkley, "DIES INQUIRY WINS OUT WITH POPULAR SUPPORT," *New York Times,* Jan. 28, 1940, E6; "Civil Liberties Union, Teachers Flay Dies Probe," *Washington Post,* Jan. 15, 1940, 7; "15,000 HEAR ATTACK ON 'GAG RULE' TREND," *New York Times,* Apr. 4, 1935, 3.

2. Eleanor Roosevelt, "Keepers of Democracy," *Virginia Quarterly Review* 15 (Jan. 1939). Blanche Wiesen Cook, *Eleanor Roosevelt: Volume 2: The Defining Years 1933–1938* (New York: Penguin, 2000), 571–576.

3. The predecessor to the Dies Committee, the McCormack-Dickstein Committee was formed in 1934. While it investigated both fascist and communist propaganda, its primary focus was on fascists. Ironically, while the McCormack-Dickstein Committee was chaired by a New Dealer (John McCormack), angry Republicans and Southern Democrats used its successor to attack and undermine many of FDR's policies as "communist." See Richard M. Fried, *Nightmare in Red: The McCarthy Era in Perspective* (New York: Oxford University Press, 1990), 46–49. United States House of Representatives, History, Art & Archives, The Permanent Standing House Committee on Un-American Activities, http://history.house.gov/Historical-Highlights/1901-1950/The-permanent-standing-House-Committee-on-Un-American-Activities/.

4. While home defense covered a range of social and military activities such as air raid precautions and defense of the public health (to cite two), social defense, as it was used in World War II America, referred to the idea of making all Americans secure in their basic needs including food, shelter, health, and living-wage jobs. The term had a military connotation (namely, that a more prosperous, just America would be better able to defend itself from acts of total aggression), but it was used by liberals to evoke the imperative of communities' addressing unmet needs in wartime in order to counter the lure of fascist ideology and ensure a brighter postwar economic and social future for democracy and its citizens. Eleanor Roosevelt, "Keepers of Democracy," 1–5. Cook, *ER Vol. 2,* 574–576.

5. Barbara Somervill, *Eleanor Roosevelt: First Lady of the World* (Minneapolis: Compass Point Books, 2006), 37. Joseph P. Lash, *Eleanor and Franklin* (New York: W. W. Norton & Co., 2014), 633–637.

6. ER, *This Is My Story* (New York: Harper & Brothers, 1937), 199–203. See chapter 10 for her description of her life in Washington as the wife of the assistant secretary of the Navy.

7. ER, *This Is My Story,* 232, 244–247. Woodrow Wilson, "Address to a Joint Session of Congress Requesting a Declaration of War Against Germany," Apr. 2, 1917, http://www.presidency.ucsb.edu/ws/?pid=65366. Jeremy Black, *The Great War and the Making of the Modern World* (New York: Continuum International Publishing Group, 2011), 131–132.

8. ER, *This Is My Story,* 253–258, 266–268.

9. Ibid., 256–260.

10. Ibid., 269–271. Between 1906 and 1916, ER and FDR had six children, but one of them died from the flu shortly after his birth in 1909.

11. ER, *This Is My Story,* 287–289.

12. David M. Kennedy, *Over Here: The First World War and American Society* (New York: Oxford University Press, 2004), 290–295; Kennedy called the government-led crackdown an "antiradical frenzy." Kennedy persuasively argues that some historians have overstated the depth of progressive disillusionment in the postwar United States. Yet, as he also points out, Robert La Follette's 1924 progressive presidential campaign "arose . . . from the ashes to which the post-Armistice period had reduced progressive hopes."

13. ER, "Because the War Idea Is Obsolete," from *Why Wars Must Cease,* ed. Rose Young (New York: Macmillan, 1935), 20–29, in Allida M. Black, *What I Hope to Leave Behind: The Essential Essays of Eleanor Roosevelt* (Brooklyn, NY: Carlson Publishing, Inc., 1995), 493–496. ER's essay was based on a talk she delivered at an anniversary celebration of the National Committee on the Cause and Cure of War. See Cook, *ER Vol. 2,* 238. Black, *What I Hope to Leave Behind,* xxvii. By 1938, ER's attitude about war was gradually shifting. She published *This Troubled World,* which pointed out the League of Nations' mistakes in the post-World

War I years and urged the American people to pursue a course of global peace. But she also issued stronger antifascist statements and lobbied government officials and the public to see Hitler as a direct danger to the United States.

14. William E. Leuchtenburg, *Franklin D. Roosevelt and the New Deal, 1932–1940* (New York: Harper & Row, 1963), 279.

15. Adam J. Berinsky, Eleanor Neff Powell, Erick Schickler, Ian Brett Yohai, "Revisiting Public Opinion in the 1930s and 1940s." The authors report that FDR's late 1939 approval ratings stood at around 60 percent. http://web.mit.edu/berinsky/www/files/3040.pdf. Cook, *ER Vol. 2,* 555.

16. Leuchtenburg, *FDR and the New Deal,* 271–274.

17. ER, "Good Manners," *Ladies' Home Journal* 56 (June 1939): 21, 116–117, in Black, *What I Hope to Leave Behind,* 27. Also see Black, *What I Hope to Leave Behind,* xvii.

18. Lash, *Eleanor and Franklin,* 561–562.

19. For discussion of Freud, see Karen L. Levenback, *Virginia Woolf and the Great War* (Syracuse: Syracuse University Press, 1999), 124–125. For Douhet, see Kennedy, *Freedom from Fear,* 602.

20. Haile Selassie quotes come from Robert A. Pape, *Bombing to Win: Air Power and Coercion in War* (Ithaca, NY: Cornell University Press, 1996), 335. Robert Mackay, *Half the Battle: Civilian Morale in Britain during the Second World War* (Manchester: University of Manchester Press, 2002), 20. See Mackay's Introduction for the shifting definition of "morale" in wartime England.

21. ER, *This Troubled World,* in Black, *What I Hope to Leave Behind,* 477–490. Special to the *New York Times,* "More Arms Needed, Mrs. Roosevelt Says, As 'Force' Alone Moves 'Certain Groups,'" *New York Times,* Feb. 15, 1938. Lash, *Eleanor and Franklin,* 556.

22. "Unpreparedness . . . " quoted in Lash, *Eleanor and Franklin,* 566–567. " . . . what is happening in Spain . . . " from ER, "My Day," June 1, 1937, quoted in Lash, *Eleanor and Franklin,* 567. Japan invaded Manchuria in 1931 and had threatened other regions in Asia prior to its 1937 invasion of China. Lash, *Eleanor and Franklin,* 568.

23. Quoted in Lash, *Eleanor and Franklin,* 569–575.

24. ER, *This Troubled World,* in Black, *What I Hope to Leave Behind,* 477–490.

25. ER, "My Day," Sept. 24, 1938.

26. ER quoted in Cook, *ER Vol. 2,* 539–542.

27. For Hurricane reports, see Cook, *ER Vol. 2,* 545. ER quoted in Cook, *ER Vol. 2,* 547.

28. Cook, *ER Vol. 2,* 556–557, 564–571. For her anti-Semitism, see James MacGregor Burns and Susan Dunn, *The Three Roosevelts: Patrician Leaders who Transformed America* (New York: Grove Press, 2001), 512.

29. For the royal visits, see ER, *This I Remember,* 182–184. Teaching Eleanor Roosevelt Glossary, Marie Souvestre (1830–1905), the Eleanor Roosevelt Papers Project, https://www.gwu.edu/~erpapers/teachinger/glossary/souvestre-marie.cfm.

30. ER quoted in Lash, *Eleanor and Franklin,* 572. ER, *This Troubled World,* in Black, *What I Hope to Leave Behind,* 477–490.

31. "our country . . . " It. Orig. ER, "Mobilization for Human Needs," *The Democratic Digest* 8:, no. 11 (Nov. 1933): 1, in Black, *What I Hope to Leave Behind,* 59. Allida M. Black, *Casting Her Own Shadow: E.R. and the Shaping of Postwar Liberalism* (New York: Columbia University Press, 1996), 42–43. Cook, *ER Vol. 2,* 565.

32. Cook, *ER Vol. 2,* xviii–xx. " . . . as individuals . . . " ER quoted in Black, *Casting Her Own Shadow,* 27–29. ER, "Race, Religion and Prejudice," *New Republic* 106 (May 11, 1942): 630, published in Black, *What I Hope to Leave Behind,* 159–160.

33. ER, "Are We Overlooking the Pursuit of Happiness?" *The Parents' Magazine* 11 (Sept. 1936): 21, 67, in Black, *What I Hope to Leave Behind,* 61–63. Questions and Answers about Eleanor Roosevelt, The Eleanor Roosevelt Papers Project, http://www.gwu.edu/~erpapers/teachinger/q-and-a/q25.cfm. For more on Neibuhr's conversion, see Burns and Dunn, *The Three Roosevelts,* 433; and "On Being with Krista Tippett," Oct. 25, 2007, http://www.onbeing.org/program/moral-man-and-immoral-society-rediscovering-reinhold-niebuhr/extra/reinhold-niebuhr-timeli-1. ER's ideas were her own, even as pacifists-turned-interventionists such as theologian Reinhold Niebuhr influenced her. ER wrote

her own speeches, columns, and books and, unlike FDR, had no team of speechwriters on her staff.

34. American Youth Conference quotes from Leuchtenburg, *FDR and the New Deal*, 347–348. "If we hope . . . " ER, *This Troubled World*, in Black, *What I Hope to Leave Behind*, 477–490.

35. Cook, *ER Vol. 2*, 522–526.

36. Black, *Casting Her Own Shadow*, 41–43.

37. ER to Abner Larned, Aug. 6, 1940; Larned to ER, July 31, 1940; and Larned to Kerr, July 20, 1940, F: "WH Correspondence, 1933–45,"and F: "LA 1940," ER100: Personal Letters, Kellog-Lapee, ERP, FDRL. ER's Secretary to La Guardia, Jan. 3, 1939; Stanley Howe to ER, Aug. 31, 1939, F: "La 1939," ER70: Correspondence with Government Departments, ERP, FDRL. Kerr to Malvina Thompson, Feb. 2, 1939, F: "Kerr, Florence June–Aug. 1939," ER70: Correspondence with Government Departments, ERP, FDRL.

38. Kerr to ER, Jan. 26, 1939, F: "Kerr, Florence June–Aug. 1939," ER70: Correspondence with Government Departments, ERP, FDRL.

39. ER Secretary to Kerr, Nov. 25, 1939; ER Secretary to Kerr, Dec. 15, 1939, F: "Kerr, Florence Sept.–Dec. 1939," ER70: Correspondence with Government Departments, ERP, FDRL. ER Secretary to Kerr, Apr. 7, 1939; ER Secretary to Kerr, May 4, 1939, F: "Kerr, Florence June–Aug. 1939," ER70: Correspondence with Government Departments, ERP, FDRL.

40. Kerr to ER, Apr. 13, 1939, F: "Kerr, Florence June–Aug. 1939," ER70: Correspondence with Government Departments, ERP, FDRL.

41. "Report on the Handling of Mrs. Roosevelt's Mail," from Feb. 1 to Mar. 31, 1939, F: "Kerr, Florence June–Aug. 1939," ER70: Correspondence with Government Departments, ERP, FDRL. Kerr to Thompson, Nov. 18, 1939, F: "Kerr, Florence Sept.–Dec. 1939," ER70: Correspondence with Government Departments, ERP, FDRL. WPA official Florence Kerr informed the first lady's secretary Malvina Thompson, for instance, that the WPA had reassigned a woman named Carlotta Holtz to the Tariff Commission after she had been terminated. Kerr provided ER's office with the start date of Holtz's new job and the hope that Holtz's salary would ultimately return to its previous level.

42. ER to Kerr, Dec. 2, 1939, F: "Kerr, Florence Sept.–Dec. 1939," ER70: Correspondence with Government Departments, ERP, FDRL. ER Secretary to Kerr, Feb. 21, 1939, F: "Kerr, Florence June–Aug. 1939," ER70: Correspondence with Government Departments, ERP, FDRL. See Susan Ware, *Beyond Suffrage: Women in the New Deal* (Cambridge, MA: Harvard University Press, 1987) for ER's record of appointing women.

43. Franklin D. Roosevelt, Public Papers of the President, "Annual Message to Congress," Jan. 4, 1939, http://www.presidency.ucsb.edu/ws/index.php?pid=15684&st=&st1=#axzz1 oM0Os0Vt. Franklin D. Roosevelt, Public Papers of the President, "Radio Address for the Mobilization of Human Needs," Mar. 11, 1938. " . . . no intention of neglecting . . . " quote from Lowell Mellett to Lauchlin Currie, June 5, 1940, summary of memos and letters between McNutt, Pepper, Townsend, and the president, F: "Federal Security Agency," OF 3700: Federal Security Agency, FDRL.

44. Memo, Louis Johnson to FDR, May 8, 1939, F: "Federal Security Agency 1939," OF 3700: Federal Security Agency, FDRL. For analysis of the formation of the FSA, see Mariano-Florentino Cuéllar, "'Securing' the Nation: Law, Politics, and Organization at the Federal Security Agency, 1939–1953," *University of Chicago Law Review* 76 (Jan.): 587.

45. Letter, Lucy R. Mason to FDR, June 30, 1939, F: "Federal Security Agency, Endorsements 1939–45," OF 3700a: Federal Security Agency, Endorsements, FDRL. Cross-file sheet, Budget Director, from unknown, July 5, 1939; Memo, from unknown author to General Watson, Nov. 9, 1939, F: "Federal Security Agency, 1939," OF 3700: Federal Security Agency, FDRL.

46. Letter, McNutt to FDR, Mar. 25, 1941; Memo, to FDR from unknown author, July 28, 1939, F: "Federal Security Agency 1941," OF 3700: Federal Security Agency, FDRL. When McNutt was invited to address the National Young Democrats Convention, he told FDR that he would like to address the topics of the "Liberalism of youth" and "Social Security," and the president wrote "*OK*" by hand next to McNutt's proposal. Letter, McNutt to Landis, Sept. 30, 1940, JML, LoC, Harvard File, B 22 F: "1937–45 Civilian Conservation Corps Jan. 1940–Mar.

1941." Also see Memo, FDR to McNutt, Sept. 18, 1940, F: "Federal Security Agency," OF 3700: Federal Security Agency, FDRL. Black, *Casting Her Own Shadow*, 30–31.

47. Memo, McNutt to FDR, Aug. 26, 1940, F: "Federal Security Agency," OF 3700: Federal Security Agency, FDRL.

48. Memo, FDR to Sec. of Agriculture, Sec. of Labor, and McNutt, Sept. 28, 1939, Cross-File Sheet, to McNutt, Sept. 29, 1939, F: "Federal Security Agency 1939," OF 3700: Federal Security Agency, FDRL. For background on Brownlow and his reorganization proposal, see William D. Pederson, ed., *A Companion to Franklin D. Roosevelt* (Malden, MA: Wiley-Blackwell, 2011); Rodney Grimes, ch. 19, "The Institutional Presidency." Cross-Reference Sheet, to Lauchlin Currie, Oct. 25, 1939, F: "Federal Security Agency, 1939," OF 3700: Federal Security Agency, FDRL.

49. Lash, *Eleanor and Franklin*, 583–584. She appreciated the power of radio "because one can actually hear these leaders make their speeches."

50. Black, *What I Hope to Leave Behind*, xxvii.

Chapter 2

1. Williams, *City of Ambition*, xiv. Stetson Conn, Rose C. Engelman, and Byron Fairchild, *United States Army in World War II: Guarding the United States and Its Outposts*, vol. 2 (Washington, D.C.: U.S. Government Printing, 1960), 4. Franklin D. Roosevelt, Public Papers of the President, "An Appeal to Great Britain, France, Italy, Germany and Poland to Refrain from Air Bombing of Civilians," Sept. 1, 1939, http://www.presidency.ucsb.edu/ws/index.php?pid=1 5797&st=&st1=#axzz1oM0Os0Vt David M. Kennedy, *Freedom from Fear*, 426–427. Charles Lindbergh, "America and European Wars," Sept. 15, 1939, http://www.charleslindbergh. com/pdf/9_15_39.pdf. Quoting Lindbergh, "Appeal to Isolationism," in Kennedy, *Freedom from Fear*, 433.

2. Gaddis Smith, *The Last Years of the Monroe Doctrine, 1945–1993* (New York: Hill and Wang, 1994), 3–5. FDR quoted in Robert Dallek, *Franklin D. Roosevelt and American Foreign Policy, 1932–1945* (New York: Oxford University Press, 1979), 39, 43. For a discussion of FDR's "good neighbor" policy, see 38–39. Monroe proclaimed that any European effort to infiltrate "any portion of this hemisphere [was] dangerous to our peace and safety."

3. Kennedy, *Freedom from Fear*, 325, 385–399. Lynne Olson, *Those Angry Days: Roosevelt, Lindbergh, and America's Fight over World War II, 1939–1941* (New York: Random House, 2013), 436. Lawrence S. Kaplan, *The Conversion of Senator Arthur H. Vandenberg: From Isolation to International Engagement* (Lexington: University Press of Kentucky, 2015), ch. 3. Justus D. Doenecke, *Storm on the Horizon: The Challenge to American Intervention, 1939–1941* (Lanham, MD: Roman & Littlefield, 2000), 165. Burns and Dunn, *The Three Roosevelts: Patrician Leaders Who Transformed America*, 347.

4. "Tribute to Fliers Paid at City Hall," *New York Times*, July 16, 1938, 3. W. H. Auden, ed. Edward Mendelson, *The English Auden: Poems, Essays and Dramatic Writings 1927–1939* (London: Faber and Faber, 1977), Sept. 1, 1939, 245.

5. Kessner, *Fiorello La Guardia*, ch. 1.

6. Kessner, *Fiorello La Guardia*, 48. Fiorello H. La Guardia, *The Making of An Insurgent, An Autobiography: 1882–1919* (Philadelphia: J. B. Lippincott Company, 1948), 162–163.

7. La Guardia, *The Making of An Insurgent*, 170, 173, 176, 183. Also see Kessner, *Fiorello La Guardia*, 53–56. La Guardia's military service was not without controversy, however. Thousands of New Yorkers opposed to the war signed a petition asking the House of Representatives to declare La Guardia's seat vacant, so New York could have a congressman who was doing only one job focused entirely on his constituents. See La Guardia, *Making of An Insurgent*, 196.

8. Kessner, *Fiorello La Guardia*, 47–53, 468. La Guardia, *The Making of An Insurgent*, 185–186.

9. "The Blue Cross Defence League," n.d., flier, NYCMA, LG, B: 4176, F: "03 OCD Corr (1) 1941/11." La Guardia quoted in Kessner, *Fiorello La Guardia*, 468, 57, 63–64. For La Guardia's take on profiteers, see La Guardia, *The Making of An Insurgent*, 199–200.

10. Kessner, *Fiorello La Guardia*, 246–248.

11. Robert Miller, "The War that Never Came: Civilian Defense, Mobilization, and Morale During World War II" (Ph.D. dissertation, University of Cincinnati, 1991), 42–44. Kessner, *Fiorello H. La Guardia*, caption under photo next to p. 364. Williams, *City of Ambition*, 135. Don Whitehead, "LaGuardia, Home Defense Boss, 'Little Man Who's Everywhere,'" May 28, 1941, *New Orleans State Special News Service*. NYCMA, LG, B: 4171, F: 04 OCD: Correspondence #131 (4) 1941/05. "LaGuardia Offers City's Aid in Flood," *New York Times*, Jan. 28, 1937, 16.

12. Letter, La Guardia to FDR, Aug. 22, 1935, F: "U.S. Conference of Mayors," PPF 782: U.S. Conference of Mayors, FDRL. The Constitution of the United States Conference of Mayors," n.d., Ibid. Letter, Betters to Early, Sept. 11, 1933, Ibid.

13. Kessner, *Fiorello La Guardia*, 339. Report, The United States Conference of Mayors, "100 American Cities . . . " March 12, 1936, F: "U.S. Conference of Mayors," PPF 782: U.S. Conference of Mayors, FDRL.

14. Letter, FDR to La Guardia, May 10, 1939, F: "U.S. Conference of Mayors," PPF 782: U.S. Conference of Mayors, FDRL. Press Release, FDR, Nov. 16, 1936, Ibid.

15. Franklin D. Roosevelt, Public Papers of the President, "Excerpts from the Press Conference," Nov. 5, 1938, http://www.presidency.ucsb.edu/ws/index.php?pid=15572.

16. Sherry, *The Rise of American Air Power*, x–xii. See Richard Lingeman, *Don't You Know There's a War On? The American Home Front, 1941–1945* (New York: G. P. Putnam's Sons, 1970). In John Morton Blum's *V Was for Victory: Politics and American Culture During World War II* (New York: Harcourt Brace Jovanovich, 1976), the OCD is described through the lens of Eleanor Roosevelt's scandal, and little attention is paid to the era's cultural fears of airplanes being used to kill and maim Americans in large numbers. See 224. In *Days of Sadness, Years of Triumph: The American People 1939–1945* (Madison: University of Wisconsin Press, 1985), Geoffrey Perrett argues that "aviation was not yet an integral and integrating part of daily life," but to the extent that planes represented a threat, it was passengers flying commercial planes who felt threatened, rather than civilians on city streets, 139–142.

17. The classic account of a "moral panic" can be found in Stanley Cohen, *Folk Devils and Moral Panics* (London: MacGiben and Kee Ltd, 1972). Also see Roos Pijpers, "'Help! The Poles Are Coming': Narrating a Contemporary Moral Panic," *Human Geography* 88:1 (2006): 91–103. For Twain quote, see *Ten Books in One*, "A Connecticut Yankee in King Arthur's Court" (Shoes and Ships and Sealing Wax, 2008), 488. See also David Ketterer, "Epoch-Eclipse and Apocalypse: 'Special Effects' in a Connecticut Yankee," *PMLA* 88:5 (Oct. 1973): 1104–1114. For Donnelly quote, see Steven Trimble and Donald E. Winters, "Warnings from the Past: Ceasar's Column and 1984," *Minnesota History* (Fall 1984): 112, http://collections.mnhs.org/MNHistoryMagazine/articles/49/v49i03p109-114.pdf. For Polish expert, see Lee Kennett, *The First Air War: 1914–1918* (New York: The Free Press, 1991), 1. The most thoughtful analysis of pre-1930s fears of air war can be found in Sherry, *In the Shadow of War*, Prologue. Sherry quoted on 3–4. Brett Holman, *The Next War in the Air: Britain's Fear of the Bomber, 1908–1941* (Burlington, VT: Ashgate Publishing, 2014), 221–223.

18. Hanson W. Baldwin, "The Fear of Flying Death Darkens," *New York Times*, Sept. 26, 1937. Rader Winger, "All Britain Strains to Perfect Defenses Against Air Attacks," *Washington Post*, Feb. 27, 1938.

19. No Author, "War Clouds Darken European Skies as Hitler Marches On," *Washington Post*, Mar. 20, 1938. Barnet Nover, "The Air Threat," *Washington Post*, June 2, 1938.

20. For gas mask quote, see Herbert Marder, *The Measure of Life: Virginia Woolf's Last Years* (Ithaca: Cornell University Press, 2000), 263. Cook, *ER Vol. 2*, 538–542.

21. AP, "U.S. Is Held Ideal for Air Defense," *New York Times*, Apr. 7, 1937. No Author, "Gas Attack on America Seen as Civilian Danger," *Los Angeles Times*, June 8, 1937. J. Gilbert Norris, "Gas Will Have Important Role in Next War, Say Experts—on the Battlefield," *Washington Post*, May 14, 1939. No Author, "Among the Magazines," *Washington Post*, Feb. 13, 1938.

22. Walter Lippmann, "Today and Tomorrow: The Doors of America," *Washington Post*, Jan. 12, 1939. Dorothy Thompson, "Defense Against Terrorization," *Washington Post*, Jan. 20, 1939. Westbrook Pegler, "Fair Enough," *Washington Post*, Oct. 10, 1938.

23. No Author, "Bombing Raids Can Be Halted, Expert Claims," *Washington Post*, Oct. 17, 1937. Special to *New York Times*, "Hits Exaggeration of War Gas Peril," *New York Times*, Dec. 27, 1937. Miller, "The War That Never Came," 17, citation in B. Franklin Cooling, "United States Army Support of Civil Defense: Formative Years, 1935–1942," *Military Affairs* (Feb. 1971): 7–8. C. R. Roberts to Paul McNutt, Jan. 10, 1942. RG171, E: 10, B: 4, F: 020, Jan. 22–31, 1942. Wall Street Journal Washington Bureau, "Says Large Bombing Planes Only Defense for Air Raids," *Wall Street Journal*, Oct. 26, 1937. AP, "Andrews Fears European Air Raids on U.S." *Washington Post*, Jan. 17, 1939. Frederick P. Graham, "We Rate 5th in Air, Says Gen. Andrews," *New York Times*, Jan. 17, 1939.

24. Stetson Conn and Byron Fairchild, *United States Army in World War II: The Western Hemisphere*, The Framework of Hemisphere Defense, Vol I, (Washington, D.C.: U.S. Government Printing Office, 1960), 15. Barry Sullivan, "Efficiency of Planes Encouraging to Staff," *Washington Post*, May 22, 1938. Handson W. Baldwin, "Air Defense Lacks Attack Solutions," *New York Times*, Oct. 12, 1938.

25. Conn and Fairchild, *United States Army in World War II: The Western Hemisphere*, Vol. I, 3, 8-9. Memo, Harry Woodring to FDR, June 15, 1940. Hopkins Papers, Book 2-National Defense—Isolationists, FDRL; Sherwood Collection; Box 301, F: "Book 2: National Defense Program, 1940–41, Part I." The War Department told Roosevelt in mid-1940 that "the protection of the civil population from air attack has been considered for some time by the War Department."

26. Letter, Randolph to FDR, Mar. 30, 1936. F: "Council of National Defense, 1933–39," OF 813: Council of National Defense, FDRL. Memo, Chief of Naval Operations to FDR, Mar. 16, 1938, F: "OF 3163 Air Defense League, 1937–1939," OF 3163: Air Defense League, FDRL. "Air Defense League, Application for Membership," Ibid. "Why should I join the Air Defense League?" Flier, Ibid. Letter, Kern Dodge to FDR, Mar. 2, 1938. Ibid., Letter, Dodge to McIntyre, Mar. 15, 1938, Ibid. In 1938, League president Kern Dodge told FDR that presidential inaction with respect to air power had actually endangered the civil population. FDR issued a defensive reply. "Precise bombing on a maneuvering target from any considerable altitude is inherently extremely difficult," he scolded Dodge. Dodge, he added, lacked access to secret studies conducted by the Army and the Navy. He asked that the League be investigated. Letter, FDR to Dodge, n.d. Ibid.

27. Ickes Diary, 5527–5529, May 25, 1941, LoC, MSS, Reel 4 July 5, 1940–Dec. 27, 1941 Shelf No. DM16, 142. For background on Seversky, see "Pioneer Profile," https://www.aiaa.org/SecondaryTwoColumn.aspx?id=15185. John Q. Barrett, ed., Robert Jackson, *That Man: An Insider's Portrait of Franklin D. Roosevelt* (New York: Oxford University Press, 2004), 81.

28. La Guardia to Miss Le Hand, Apr. 11, 1938, and Speech Transcript, Press Release, Office of the Mayor, Apr. 11th, 1938, F: "La Guardia, Fiorello, 1933–1939," PPF 1376: La Guardia, Fiorello, FDRL. United Press, "'Quarantine' of Nazis Asked by LaGuardia," *Washington Post*, Nov. 20, 1938, 12.

29. "Plan to Widen South America Trade Drafted," *St. Petersburg Times*, Apr. 12, 1938. "LA GUARDIA OFFERS A RECOVERY PLAN," *New York Times*, Apr. 12, 1938, 1. See Kessner, *Fiorello H. La Guardia*, 464–465.

30. Franklin D. Roosevelt, Public Papers of the President, "Message to Congress Recommending Increased Defense Appropriations," Jan. 29, 1938. http://www.presidency.ucsb.edu/ws/index.php?pid=15573&st=&st1=#axzz1oM0Os0Vt

31. Conn and Fairchild, *United States Army in World War II: The Western Hemisphere*, Vol. I, 3–4. Anne O'Hare McCormick, "As He Sees Himself," *New York Times Magazine*, Oct. 16, 1938, 19. Transcript of FDR's Congressional Message, "Defense Gives U.S. Only Safety," *Washington Post*, Jan. 5, 1939.

32. "Problems Caused by War To Be Topic of Mayors," *New York Times*, Sept. 16, 1939, 4. Memo, Aug. 16, 1940, La Guardia to Hull, Sept. 5, 1939, F: "La Guardia, Fiorello, 1933–1939," PPF 1376: La Guardia, Fiorello, FDRL.E.M.W. to FDR, Sept. 28, 1939, F: "La Guardia, Fiorello, 1933–1939," Ibid. La Guardia to FDR, Feb. 1, 1938; La Guardia to LeHand, Feb. 1, 1938, FDR to La Guardia, Feb. 4, 1938, F: "President's Secretary's File Subject File La Guardia, Fiorello H. Box 141," PSF: 141, FDRL.

33. Map, RG171, E:10, B: 39, F: 095-Committee to Defend America. Conn and Fairchild, *The Framework of Hemisphere Defense: The Western Hemisphere*, Vol. I, 12–13. Special to *New York Times*, "President Urges Needs of Defense," *New York Times*, Mar. 5, 1939.

34. Leuchtenburg, *FDR and the New Deal*, 287. Franklin D. Roosevelt, *Public Papers of the President*, "An Appeal to Great Britain, France, Italy, Germany and Poland to Refrain from Air Bombing of Civilians," Sept. 1, 1939. For the Message to president from "His Majesty's Government," Sept. 1, 1939, see http://www.forgottenbooks.com/readbook_text/Department_of_State_Bulletin_1940_v1_1000514818/193.

35. "Events in Europe Summarized," *Washington Post*, Aug. 24, 1939. Conn and Fairchild, *The Framework of Hemisphere Defense: The Western Hemisphere*, Vol. I, 7.

36. Leuchtenburg, *FDR and the New Deal*, 293. AP, "Modern Warfare Destroys Normal Order of Civilian Life," *Los Angeles Times*, Sept. 14, 1939. No author, "War on Civilians," *Washington Post*, Sept. 16, 1939.

37. Franklin D. Roosevelt, Public Papers of the President, "Fireside Chat," Sept. 3, 1939.

38. William V. Nessly, "President Launches Vast Program to Keep America at Peace," *Washington Post*, Sept. 10, 1939. Charles Lindbergh, "America and European Wars," Sept. 15, 1939, http://www.charleslindbergh.com/pdf/9_15_39.pdf. Quoting Lindbergh, "Appeal to Isolationism," in Kennedy, *Freedom from Fear*, 433. Editorial, "Mr. Fish as Symbol," *Washington Post*, Aug. 17, 1939.

39. John G. Norris, "Congressmen Says U.S. Lags in Air Defense," *Washington Post*, Dec. 15, 1939. Memo, Stettinius to FDR, Sept. 25, 1940. Weekly Operations Progress Report of Oct. 3, 1940, Industrial Materials Division, F: "Subject File Council of National Defense Sept. 1940–May 1941," PSF: 128, Council of National Defense, FDRL. Memo, F.D.R. to Stettinius, July 1, 1940, F: "June–Aug. 1940," OF 813-a: Advisory Commission to the Council of National Defense: Reports, 1940-1941, FDRL. Stettinius to FDR, July 17, 1940, F: "Council of National Defense Apr.–Aug. 1940," PSF: 128, Council of National Defense, FDRL. "Report on Underground Tankage for Aviation Gasoline from the Engineers' Committee on Oil Storage, Oct. 1940," F: "President's Secretary's File Subject File Council of National Defense Oct. 1940: Report to the President," PSF: 128, Council of National Defense, FDRL. Memo, Stettinius to FDR, Nov. 26, 1940, F: "Council of National Defense Oct. 1940: Report to the President," PSF: 128, Council of National Defense, FDRL. For a take on the storing of missiles in the Great Plains during the Cold War, see Gretchen Heefner, *The Missile Next Door: The Minuteman in the American Heartland* (Cambridge, MA: Harvard University Press, 2012).

40. Dr. George Gallup, The Gallup Poll: "U.S. to Stay Out of War, Bare Majority Says; Fewer Voters Think We'll be Drawn In," *Washington Post*, Oct. 25, 1939.

41. Leuchtenburg, *FDR and the New Deal*, 297. Quoted in *Time*, "It Shall Come to Pass" Jan. 1, 1940.

Chapter 3

1. Secretary to ER to Elizabeth Eagan, Jan. 29, 1940, and four questions with ER's handwritten answers. F: "40.1 Messages Sent 1940 A-H," ER 40.1: Messages sent by Mrs. Roosevelt, ERP, FDRL. FDR, "State of the Union Message to Congress," Jan. 11, 1944, http://docs.fdrlibrary.marist.edu/011144.html.

2. ER's two-front campaign is a little-examined aspect of her wartime leadership. Blanche Wiesen Cook's excellent multivolume biography of ER has only gone up to 1938 as of this writing, while other biographies of the first lady either skip over ER's 1940 mobilization campaign or focus on her years as a postwar liberal. For examples, see Black, *Casting Her Own Shadow*; Scharf, *First Lady of American Liberalism*; and Beasley, *Eleanor Roosevelt: Transformative First Lady*. Susan Ware, *Beyond Suffrage: Women in the New Deal*, (Cambridge, MA: Harvard University Press, 1981), 2. Ware's landmark study is mostly restricted to New Deal liberalism during the 1930s. In "Eleanor Roosevelt and Women in the New Deal: A Network of Friends," Frances M. Seeber focuses on ER's role in building that network during the 1930s. See Seeber, *Presidential Studies Quarterly*, Vol. 20, No. 4, Modern First Ladies White House Organization (Fall 1990), 707–717.

3. ER, "Fear is the Enemy," *The Nation* 150 (Feb. 10, 1940): 173, in Black, *What I Hope to Leave Behind*, 499. ER, "The Moral Basis of Democracy," (New York: Howell, Soskin & Co., 1940), in Black, *What I Hope to Leave Behind*, 69–89.

4. ER, "The Moral Basis of Democracy," in Black, *What I Hope to Leave Behind*, 80. Report on the Organization Meeting of the Consumer Interests Committee, New Jersey State Council of Defense, Oct. 31, 1940, F: "70 ER Correspond. w/Gov't Depts 1941 Elliott, Dr. Harriet, 2 of 2."; and "Report of Consumer Division Organization and Activity, June 1940–Jan. 1941," F: "70ER Correspond. w/Gov't Depts 1941 Elliott, Dr. Harriet, 2 of 2," ER 70: Correspondence with Government Departments, ERP, FDRL.

5. Dorothy Thompson, "On The Record: To The Intolerant!" *Washington Post*, Feb 22, 1939, 9. ER, "The Moral Basis of Democracy," in Black, *What I Hope to Leave Behind*, 69–89. ER, "Intolerance," *Cosmopolitan* (Feb. 1940): 24, 102–103, in Black, *What I Hope to Leave Behind*, 155–157.

6. "Eleanor Roosevelt: The World's First Lady," Women's Leadership in American History, CUNY, https://www1.cuny.edu/portal_ur/content/womens_leadership/eleanor.html. The Eleanor Roosevelt Papers Project, "Arthurdale," https://www.gwu.edu/~erpapers/teach-inger/glossary/arthurdale.cfm. Even though Arthurdale was eventually sold to private interests in 1941, ER was proud of the program for having improved workers' lives.

7. ER, "My Day," Jan. 4, 1940.

8. ER, "My Day," Apr. 23.

9. ER, "My Day," May 17.

10. Kennedy, *Freedom From Fear*, 28, 438–441. A. N. Wilson, *Hitler* (New York: Basic Books, 2012), 135.

11. "The United States Committee for the Care of European Children," The Eleanor Roosevelt Papers Project, https://www.gwu.edu/~erpapers/teachinger/glossary/uscom.cfm. Lash, *Eleanor and Franklin*, 633–637. ER, "Insuring Democracy," *Collier's* 105 (June 15, 1940): 70, 87–88, in Black, *What I Hope to Leave Behind*, 91–95. James H. Rowe to FDR, June 15, 1940, F: "Political Refugees, June 1938–June 1940," OF 3186: Political Refugees, FDRL, http://fdrlibraryvirtualtour.org/graphics/07-28/7.3_Prelude%20to_the_Holocaust.pdf.

12. Katznelson, *Fear Itself*, Introduction. On 24–25, Katznelson astutely writes that "the South exercised its critical position to affect decisions concerning global power, national security, civil liberty, unions, and the character of capitalism." No Author, "First Lady Backs Billion for Defense," *Washington Post*, May 17, 1940.

13. No Author, "First Lady's Plea Ignored by Youth," May 27, 1940, *New York Times*.

14. ER, "My Day," May 17, 1940. Special to the *New York Times*, "First Lady Scores Forced Enlisting," *New York Times*, June 14, 1940. No Author, "First Lady Says War Perils U.S.," *Washington Post*, Jan. 17, 1940.

15. Richard Moe, *Roosevelt's Second Act: The Election of 1940 and the Politics of War* (New York: Oxford University Press, 2013). Moe shows how Roosevelt worked to preserve the gains of the New Deal during the election year. FDR, "Address Delivered by President Roosevelt at Charlottesville, Virginia," 6/10/40, https://www.mtholyoke.edu/acad/intrel/WorldWar2/fdr19.htm

16. George R. I. to FDR, June 22, 1940, F: "Great Britain Jan.–Sept. 1940," PSF: 33, Diplomatic Correspondence, FDRL. FDR, Address to White House Conference on Children in a Democracy, Jan. 19, 1940, F: "National Conference on Nutrition for Defense, 1941–42," OF 4389, FDRL. Cross-Reference Sheet, Edward O'Neal, Aug. 2, 1940, F: "Council of National Defense Reports June-Aug. 1940," OF 813a: Advisory Commission to the Council of National Defense, Reports, 1940–1941, Miscellaneous and Special Folders, FDRL. Mpk to the Advisory Commission to the Council of National Defense, Aug. 30, 1940, Ibid. Cross-Reference Sheet, Sept. 19, 1940, Rep. Robert F. Rich, Sept. 19, 1940, F: "Council of National Defense Reports Sept.–Dec. 1940," OF 813a: Advisory Commission to the Council of National Defense, Reports, 1940–1941, Miscellaneous and Special Folders, FDRL. His administration also feared that the migration of workers in high-demand areas would produce a shortage of workers in defense areas.

17. For ER-Perkins conversation, see Burns and Dunn, *The Three Roosevelts*, 432–433.

18. For a description of ER–FDR's political relationship, see Burns and Dunn, *The Three Roosevelts*, 265–276.

19. Agnes Reynolds to ER, June 10, 1940, F: "Re 1940," ER 100: Personal Letters, ERP, FDRL. Lash to ER, n.d., F: "LA 1940," ER 100: Personal Letters, ERP, FDRL. Lash added how much he enjoyed going to City College with the First Lady. Roosevelt's visit to his mother "was the proudest moment in her life."

20. E.R. to FDR, n.d. and Sydney Markey to Aubrey Williams, Aug. 14, 1940, F: "ER70 (1940) Corresp. w/Gov't Depts La," ER 70: Correspondence with Government Departments, ERP, FDRL.

21. ER, "I Want You to Write to Me," *Woman's Home Companion* 60 (August 1933): 4, in Black, *What I Hope to Leave Behind*, 13. Letter, Secretary to ER to Virginia Potter, Feb. 17, 1941, F: "40.1 Messages Sent 1941 L-R," ER 40.1: Messages sent by Mrs. Roosevelt, ERP, FDRL. Secretary to ER to La Guardia, March 27, 1940; Elizabeth Rathbone to ER, Monday, n.d.; letter, Secretary to ER to Constance Lagan, Sept. 9, 1940, F: "ER70 (1940) Corresp. w/ Gov't Depts La.," ER 70: Correspondence with Government Departments, ERP, FDRL. ER to La Guardia, Feb. 9, 1940, F: "1940 LaGuardia, Fiorello," ER 100: Personal Letters, ERP, FDRL. Secretary to ER to William Lawson, July 30, 1940, F: "ER70 (1940) Corresp. w/Gov't Depts La.," ER70: Correspondence with Government Departments, ERP, FDRL. Letter, ER's Secretary to John Lyons, Jan. 25, 1940, F: "70 ER Corresp. With Gov't Depts 1940 Li-Ly," ER 70: Correspondence with Government Departments, ERP, FDRL. Cross-reference sheet, Tressie C. Daniel, Dec. 30, 1940, F: "Council of National Defense Reports 1941," OF 813a: Advisory Commission to the Council of National Defense, Reports, 1940-1941, ERP, FDRL. While her office cited the 600 to 700 per day figure, other sources estimate that she received around 150,000 letters total during 1940.

22. Thompson to Evelyn Miller Crowell, Oct. 21, 1940, F: "40.1 Messages Sent 1940 A-H," ER 40.1: Messages sent by Mrs. Roosevelt, ERP, FDRL. Letter, ER to Mr. Rickel, Sept. 20, 1940, F: "1940 RL-Ri," ER 100: Personal Letters, ERP, FDRL. Secretary to ER to Helen Dunn, March 7, 1940, F: "40.1 Messages Sent 1940 A-H," ER 40.1: Messages sent by Mrs. Roosevelt, ERP, FDRL.

23. Memo, Elliott to FDR, Nov. 8, 1940; Jay Nash to ER, Nov. 15, 1940; Jay Nash to FDR, Nov. 13, 1940; John Carmody to FDR, Nov. 19, 1940, F: "OF813a 1940 A Physical Training Program," OF 813a: Advisory Commission to the Council of National Defense, Reports, 1940–1941; OF 813e: Coordinator of Health, Welfare and Related Defense Activities, 1940–1941; OF 828: Sterling, Frederick A., FDRL. ER, "My Day," Nov. 8, 1939; Aug. 20, 1941.

24. ER to Miss Rhoades, n.d., Rhodes et al., to ER, July 12, 1940, F: "Re 1940," ER 100: Personal Letters, ERP, FDRL. "First Lady Urges Compulsory Youth Duty for Defense," July 11, 1940, clip in ER files without newspaper name. F: "1940 RL-Ri," ER 100: Personal Letters, ERP, FDRL. No author, "First Lady Favors Defense Training For Women, Too" *Washington Post*, July 1 1940. President Truman and the entire military establishment would push for universal military training in the late 1940s, and visions of such plans have surfaced now and again. No author, "First Lady's Training Proposal Questioned," *Washington Post*, June 4, 1940. Frank Kent, "The Great Game of Politics," *Los Angeles Times*, July 9, 1940, ER, "My Day," Oct. 23 and Nov. 8, 1939. William Aspray, George Royer, Melissa G. Ocepek, Formal and Informal Approaches to Food Policy, (New York: Springer, 2014), 109.

25. MacLeish to Hopkins, June 24, 1940; Hopkins to MacLeish, July 25, 1940, F: "Book 2: National Defense Program-1940–41 Part II," Hopkins Papers, Sherwood Collection Book 2: National Defense-Isolationists, FDRL. Hopkins to Lowell Mellett, June 29, 1940, F: "Book 2: National Defense Program-1940–41 Part I," Hopkins Papers, Sherwood Collection Book 2: National Defense-Isolationists, FDRL.

26. Underline orig., Selden Rodman to ER, July 12, 1940, F: "40.4 Requests for Interviews, 1934–41 O-Z," ER 40.3: Requests for Information about the White House, ERP, FDRL. The National Defense Advisory Commission, "Functions and Activities," Dec. 28, 1940, RG171, B: 95, F: 380-Council on Nat'l Defense. Press Release, FDR Message, "To the Congress of the United States," Sept. 13, 1940, F: "OF813a Sept.–Dec. 1940 Council of National Defense Reports," OF 813a: Advisory Commission to the Council of National Defense, Reports, 1940–1941, FDRL.

27. "Advisory Commission to the Council of National Defense," May 28, 1940, F: "813a June-Aug. 1940," OF 813a: Advisory Commission to the Council of National Defense, Reports, 1940-1941, FDRL. The National Defense Advisory Commission, "Functions and Activities," Dec. 28, 1940, RG171, B: 95, F: 380-Council on Nat'l Defense. Mark Sullivan, "Defense Board Make-Up Found Not What New Dealers Wanted," *New York Herald Tribune*, Dec. 24, 1940, F: "OF813a Sept.–Dec. 1940 Council of National Defense Reports," OF813a: Advisory Commission to the Council of National Defense, Reports, 1940–1941, FDRL. Ellen Woodward to FDR, May 29, 1940; Elliott to FDR, June 1, 1940, F: "813a June–Aug. 1940," OF 813a: Advisory Commission to the Council of National Defense, Reports, 1940–1941, FDRL. The National Defense Advisory Commission, Functions and Activities, Booklet, Dec. 28, 1940, LoC, Landis Papers, Harvard File, B: 21, F: "1937–45 Boston News Bureau." Letter, Elliott to ER, Jan. 15, 1941, F: "70ER Correspond. w/Gov't Depts 1941 Elliott, Dr. Harriet, 2 of 2," ER 70: Correspondence with Government Departments, ERP, FDRL. "Office of Consumer Adviser, Defense Commission," Outline of program, F: "Book 2: National Defense Program 1940–41 Part I," Hopkins Papers, Book 2-National Defense Isolationists Sherwood Collection, FDRL. "Preliminary Analysis of Economic Problems with which the Consumer Adviser is concerned, and Types of Information Needed," n.d. F: "Reports July–Aug. 1940," OF 813a: Advisory Commission to the Council of National Defense, Reports, 1940–1941, FDRL. Elliott to Hopkins, June 25, 1940, F: "Book 2: National Defense Program 1940–41 Part I," Hopkins Papers, Book 2-National Defense Isolationists Sherwood Collection, FDRL.
28. Memo, Elliott to FDR, July 11, 1940, F: "OF813a June–Aug. 1940 Council of National Defense Reports," OF 813a: Advisory Commission to the Council of National Defense, Reports, 1940–1941, FDRL. M. L. Wilson, "Nutrition and Defense," USDA Extension Service, Oct. 21, 1940, Report on the Organization Meeting of the Consumer Interests Committee, New Jersey State Council of Defense, Oct. 31, 1940; "Report of Consumer Division Organization and Activity, June 1940–Jan. 1941;" Harriet Elliott to ER, Jan. 2, 1941; Secretary to ER to Elliott, Jan. 21, 1941, F: "70ER Correspond. w/Gov't Depts 1941 Elliott, Dr. Harriet, 2 of 2," ER 70: Correspondence with Government Departments, ERP, FDRL. AP, "First Lady Says Religion Aids Defense," *Washington Post*, Aug. 2, 1940. Consumer Division, Aug. 7, 1940, and press release, Harriet Elliott, Aug. 2, 1940, F: "Reports July–Aug. 1940," OF 813a: Advisory Commission to the Council of National Defense, Reports, 1940–1941, FDRL.
29. Report on the Organization Meeting of the Consumer Interests Committee, New Jersey State Council of Defense, Oct. 31, 1940, F: "70ER Corresp. w/Gov't Depts 1941, Elliott, Dr. Harriet, 2 of 2," ER 70: Correspondence with Government Departments, ERP, FDRL. Ellen Woodward asserted that those who criticized unemployment assistance were giving "comfort to the enemy." Woodward to ER, n.d. Monday, F: "ER 70 (1940) Corresp. w/Gov't Depts Woodward, Ellen S," ER 70: Correspondence with Government Departments, ERP, FDRL. For more on Woodward's life and career, see Martha H. Swain, *Ellen S. Woodward: New Deal Advocate for Women* (Jackson: University Press of Mississippi, 1995).
30. Memo, Roberta to General Watson, July 30, 1940, F: "OF813a June–Aug. 1940 Council of National Defense Reports," OF 813a: Advisory Commission to the Council of National Defense, Reports, 1940–1941, FDRL. AP, "Women Defense Training Urged," *Los Angeles Times*, Jan. 2, 1941, E7.
31. Oral history interview with Florence Kerr, 1963 Oct. 18–Oct. 31, Archives of American Art, Smithsonian Institution.
32. No author, "WPA is Aloof to Army But Will Keep in Step," *Christian Science Monitor*, Aug. 17, 1940. "W.P.A. Praised by Woman Aide," *Los Angeles Times*, Oct. 23, 1940.
33. James Rowe to Elliott, Aug. 14, 1940, F: "Council of National Defense Reports June-Aug 1940," OF 813a: Advisory Commission to the Council of National Defense, Reports, 1940–1941, FDRL. Suzanne, "Madame Chairman," *Washington Post*, Aug. 4, 1940. Memo, Lenroot to Perkins, Dec. 16, 1940, F: "Book 2: National Defense Program 1940–41 Part II," Hopkins Papers, Sherwood Collection, Book 2-National Defense-Isolationists, FDRL. "Biography, Dr. Martha May Eliot," NIH, http://www.nlm.nih.gov/changingthefaceofmedicine/physicians/biography_99.html. Memo, Martha Eliot to Harriet Elliott, June 11, 1940, F: "Book 2: National Defense Program 1940–41 Part I," Hopkins Papers, Book 2-National Defense

Isolationists Sherwood Collection, FDRL. Eliot's report, *Civil Defense Measures for the Protection of Children*, appeared in 1942.

34. Letter, Fred Hoehler to Hopkins, June 10, 1940, and attached, undated memo; Hopkins to Hoehler, June 30, 1940, F: "Book 2: National Defense Program 1940–41 Part II," Hopkins Papers, Sherwood Collection, Book 2-National Defense-Isolationists, FDRL. The National Defense Advisory Commission, "Functions and Activities," Dec. 28, 1940, RG171, B: 95, F: 380-Council on Nat'l Defense. FDR, Campaign Address at Boston, Mass, Oct. 30, 1940. http://www.presidency.ucsb.edu/ws/?pid=15887.

35. For books that counter the standard narrative about the waning of the New Deal, see Katznelson, *Fear Itself*; Nelson Lichtenstein, *State of the Union: A Century of American Labor* (Princeton, NJ: Princeton University Press, 2002); and Meg Jacobs, *Pocketbook Politics: Economic Citizenship in Twentieth-Century America* (Princeton, NJ: Princeton University Press, 2006). Eddy to ER, Oct. 7, 1940, F: "Reports-A Physical Training Program," OF 813-a: Advisory Commission to the Council of National Defense, Reports, 1940–1941, FDRL. ER, Address to 1940 Democratic Convention, *New York Times*, July 19, 1940, 5, in Black, *What I Hope to Leave Behind*, 373. Special to the New York Times, "Wallace Speaks to Farmers' Group," *New York Times*, July 25, 1940. Wallace assured an audience of 5,000 people attending Chicago's American Negro Exposition that racism posed a threat to democracy equal to Hitler's army and warned that African Americans (and other minorities) would not "defend a system which has no place for them." United Press, "Wallace Calls Jobless Threat to Democracy," *Los Angeles Times*, Sept. 3, 1940.

36. FDR, Address to White House Conference on Children in a Democracy, Jan. 19, 1940, F: "National Conference on Nutrition for Defense, 1941–42," OF 4389: National Conference on Nutrition for Defense, FDRL. Memo, McNutt to FDR, Aug. 26, 1940; Cross-Reference Sheet, to the Federal Security Administrator, Jan. 19, 1940; Cross-Reference Sheet, to Director of the Budget, June 1, 1940, F: "Federal Security Agency," OF 3700: Federal Security Agency. FDRL. See Cathro Kidwell to FDR, Nov. 30, 1940; and Bishop Auxiliary of N.Y. to FDR, Nov. 27, 1940, F: "Reports, A Physical Training Program," OF 813a: Advisory Commission to the Council of National Defense: Reports, 1940–1941, FDRL. Memo, FDR to ER, July 29, 1940, F: "Council of National Defense 1940," OF 813: Council of National Defense, FDRL. Memo, Elliott to FDR, Nov. 8, 1940, F: "Reports-A Physical Training Program," OF 813-a: Advisory Commission to the Council of National Defense: Reports, 1940–1941, FDRL.

37. For 1940 election results, see Susan Dunn, *1940: FDR, Willkie, Lindbergh, Hitler—the Election Amid the Storm* (New Haven, CT: Yale University Press, 2013), 264. ER, "My Day," May 17, 1940; May 22, 1940.

38. Murray Latimer to Lauchlin Currie, Nov. 30, 1940; also see memo to FDR, from unknown, Dec. 2, 1940, Currie to FDR, Dec. 2, 1940, F: "Speech Material: Annual Message to Congress 1941," PPF 1820: Speech Materials and Suggestions; Transcripts of President's Speeches, FDRL.

39. "Draft of Language for Message on Job Training and Security Program," Dec. 2, 1940; Frederic Delano to FDR, Dec. 3, 1940; "The Development of Public Responsibility for Work Security and Relief Needs," n.d., Ibid.

40. Christopher Capozzola, *Uncle Sam Wants You: World War I and the Making of the Modern American Citizen* (New York: Oxford University Press, 2008), 7. "Progressives," Capozzola writes, "dreamed of a new era of shared sacrifice," while countless Americans joined voluntary civic associations to meet their political obligations during the war crisis. Also see Nancy Gentile Ford, *The Great War and America: Civil-Military Relations During World War I* (Westport, CT: Praeger Security International, 2008), 52.

41. Paul McNutt to FDR, Jan. 3, 1941; memo, Wayne Coy to FDR, Dec. 26, 1940, F: "Speech Materials and Suggestions 1940 Oct-Dec.," PPF 1820: Speech Materials and Suggestions; Transcripts of President's Speeches, FDRL.

42. Paul McNutt to FDR, Jan. 3, 1941, Ibid. For a biography of McNutt, see Dean J. Kotlowski, *Paul V. McNutt and the Age of FDR* (Bloomington: Indiana University Press, 2015). See 5–6 in particular: like ER, McNutt took an expansive view of the meaning of "security." "It is difficult to find a single word which more nearly epitomizes the longings of the human spirit than the

word 'security,'" he said. "Implied here are those decencies of civilization which we regard as essential to the good life—economic security, political security, intellectual and spiritual security."

43. ER, "My Day," Dec. 10, 1940. Cross-Reference Sheet, to Director of Budget, Dec. 31, 1940, F: Federal Security Agency, OF 3700: Federal Security Agency, FDRL. Coy to ER, Dec. 23, 1940, F: "70 ER Corr. W Gov't Depts. 1941 Cot-Coy;" Ellen Woodward to ER, Dec. 6, 1940, F: "ER 70 (1940) Corresp. w/Gov't Depts Woodward, Ellen S," ER 70: Correspondence with Government Departments, ERP, FDRL. Liberals beyond Washington both imbibed and deepened Eleanor Roosevelt's message, seeking to influence FDR's agenda. In the aftermath of FDR's election, advice flowed liberally. One professor requested a meeting with the president to talk about improving living conditions and recreation facilities in military towns. The Friends of the New York State Soldiers and Sailors sought new ways to aid the families of drafted men, while the National United Welfare Committee for Defense hoped to discuss with FDR ways they could aid soldiers and factory workers. Cross-Reference Sheet, Memo for Paul McNutt, Dec. 26, 1940; for the Hobby Federation, see McIntyre note, Dec. 7, 1940; for the druggist, see Watson referral, Dec. 7, 1940; for "Friends" committee, see William Hassett to Wayne Coy, Dec. 10, 1940; for National United Welfare offer, see Harper Sibley, et. al. to FDR, Nov. 23, 1940, and FDR to Early, Dec. 18, 1940; for offer to entertain soldiers, see Early to Al Jolson, Jan. 8, 1941, F: "Coordinator of Health, Welfare and Related Defense Activities, 1940–41," OF 813e: Coordinator of Health, Welfare and Related Defense Activities, 1940–41, FDRL.

44. FDR, Annual Message to Congress on the State of the Union, Jan. 6, 1941. For descriptions of the crafting of the speech and various drafts, see Samuel I. Rosenman, *Working with Roosevelt* (New York: Harper & Brothers, 1952), 262–264; and http://www.fdrlibrary.marist.edu/ pdfs/ffdrafts.pdf; http://www.fdrlibrary.marist.edu/fourfreedoms.

Chapter 4

1. "An Ordinance Creating a Local Defense Council and Prescribing Its Duties and Responsibilities," May 28, 1940, Sample Ordinance, RG171, E: 10, B: 104, F: 410: State Defense Leg., thru Oct. 1940.

2. William Fulton, "Dewey Demands Immediate Home Defense Action," *Chicago Daily Tribune*, June 18, 1940. Dewey's speech is reprinted after the article. For an overview, see Leuchtenburg, *FDR and the New Deal*, 312–313.

3. Barnet Nover, "We Know Now: America's Defense Problem," *Washington Post*, May 20, 1940. "War & Peace: Reaction," *Time*, May 27, 1940. Memo, Division of Press Intelligence, Editorial Reaction Toward Aid for the Allies, June 10, 1940, F: "National Emergency council 1940," OF 788: National Emergency Council, FDRL. Walter Lippmann, "Today and Tomorrow: The Weakest Link in American Defense," *Los Angeles Times*, June 11, 1940.

4. George Gallup, "50% Favor Compulsory Military Training," *Washington Post*, June 2, 1940. "War & Peace: Reaction," *Time*, May 27, 1940.

5. Editorial, "Spawn of the Trojan Horse," *Oregonian*, May 18, 1940, F: "Fifth Column 1940," OF 1661a: Espionage: Fifth Column, FDRL. W. Karl Lations to Chairman, National Defense Commission, Aug. 21, 1940; and Lations, "Uniform Civilian War-Plan Needed," n.d., RG171, E: 11, B: 5, F: 381: Region I: MA, L.C., to 12/31/41.

6. Dallek, *Franklin D. Roosevelt and American Foreign Policy*, 225–227. In Chicago, for instance, the number of members in the pro-Nazi German-American Bund movement was negligible; see Klaus P. Fischer, *Hitler and America* (Philadelphia: University of Pennsylvania Press, 2011), 94–96. For an interpretation of Hitler's split views of the United States as both a morally deviant nation and an industrial powerhouse, see Fischer, *Hitler and America*, Introduction. For more on the debate about Hitler's European versus his global military ambitions, see Jochen Theis, *Hitler's Plans for Global Domination: Nazi Architecture and Ultimate War Aims* (New York: Berghahn Books, 2012), foreword by Volker Berghahn, xiii.

7. Russell B. Porter, "Nazi Agents Found Busy in Mexico; Viewed as Threat to U.S. Defense," Aug. 28, 1940, F: "Fifth Column 1940," OF 1661a: Espionage: Fifth Column, FDRL.

8. Cross-Reference Sheet, Herman Moore, Sept. 6, 1939; H. M. Kannee to Eleanor Bumgardner, Sept. 16, 1939; Cross Reference Sheet, rlv, Memo for the President, Dec. 7, 1939, F: "Espionage 1933–4," OF 1661: Espionage, FDRL. *Time*, "Intolerance: Boo!" May 29, 1939. Letter, Martin Dies to FDR, et al., June 1, 1940; FDR to Dies, June 10, 1940; Cross-Reference Sheet, William McReynolds, June 8, 1940, F: "Fifth Column 1940," OF 1661a: Espionage: Fifth Column, FDRL. Gallup Poll, Interviewing Date 8/2-7/40, Survey #204-K, Question #6b. Also cited in George Gallup, "The Gallup Poll: Four of 10 Americans Believe Nazis Would Attack U.S. if Britain Is Beaten," *Washington Post*, Sept. 14 1940, 2. Henderson to FDR, Oct. 14, 1940, FDR to General Watson, Oct. 22, 1940, F: "Sept.–Dec. 1940 Council of National Defense," OF 813: Council of National Defense, FDRL. In *Franklin D. Roosevelt and American Foreign Policy, 1932–1945*, Robert Dallek argues that the actual threat to the country was, on balance, minimal, and that the Nazis made little headway in their efforts to subvert America's industrial capacity and dampen public confidence in the U.S. government. See 226–227.

9. FDR, Address Delivered to Congress, May 16, 1940, https://www.mtholyoke.edu/acad/intrel/WorldWar2/fdr16.htm.

10. Hon. Claude Pepper, "Defense of America," Radio Address, Congressional Record, May 25, 1940, LoC, Landis Papers, Harvard file, B: 25, F: "1937–45 Pepper, Claude."

11. Jackson, *That Man*, 86.

12. HLH Memo, no recipient, Aug. 15, 1940, F: "Book 2: Ideas for Defense Effort," Hopkins Papers, Book 2-National Defense-Isolationists Sherwood Collection, FDRL.

13. Miller, "The War That Never Came," diss., 18. In Cooling, "United States Army Support of Civil Defense: Formative Years, 1935,-1942," *Military Affairs* (February 1971): 7–8; and Conn, Engleman, Fairchild, *United States Army in World War II: The Western Hemisphere*, 45–79.

14. Cross Reference Sheet, John Carmody, June 21, 1940, F: "Council of National Defense Reports June–Aug. 1940;" Cross-Reference Sheet, John Carmody, June 21, 1940, F: "OF813a June–Aug. 1940 Council of National Defense Reports," OF 813a: Advisory Commission to the Council of National Defense: Reports, 1940–1941, FDRL. Lauchlin Currie to FDR, June 7, 1940, F: "Book 2: National Defense Program 1940–41 Part I," Hopkins Papers, Book 2-National Defense-Isolationists Sherwood Collection, FDRL.

15. Harry Woodring to FDR, June 15, 1940; Cross-Reference Sheet, Lauchlin Currie, June 14, 1940, F: "Book 2: National Defense Program 1940-41 Part I," Hopkins Papers, Book 2-National Defense-Isolationists Sherwood Collection, FDRL. See Lee Kennett, *For the Duration: The United States Goes to War—Pearl Harbor—1942* (New York: Scribner, 1985), 28.

16. Memo, Betters to La Guardia, June 20, 1940; letter, Betters to "Mayor," June 24, 1940, RG171, E: 10, B: 70, F: 095-US Conference of Mayors. Memo, Paul Betters to La Guardia, June 30, 1940; and memo, FDR to McReynolds, n.d., F: "Book 2: National Defense Program 1940–41 Part I," Hopkins Papers, Book 2: National Defense, Isolations Sherwood Collection, FDRL. Cross-Reference Sheet, Paul Betters, June 20, 1940, F: "OF813a June–Aug. 1940 Council of National Defense Reports," OF 813a: Advisory Commission to the Council of National Defense: Reports, 1940–1941, FDRL.

17. Letter, Betters to "Mayor," June 24, 1940, RG171, E: 10, B: 70, F: 095-US Conference of Mayors.

18. Letter, Maury Maverick to Harry Hopkins, June 26, 1940; and Maverick to Paul Betters, June 26, 1940, F: "Book 2: National Defense Program 1940-41 Part I," Hopkins Papers, Book 2: National Defense, Isolations Sherwood Collection, FDRL.

19. United States Conference of Mayors in Convention, Letter, Betters to International Municipal Signal Association, and attached transcript, n.d., RG171, E: 10, B: 124, F: 520-Fire Protection, thru Nov. 30, 1940.

20. Watson to Minton, Aug. 31, 1940; Minton to Watson, Aug. 10, 1940, and attached "Ruthjane, Press Conference Aug. 6, 1940," F: "Home Defense Misc. 1940-1941," OF 4249: Home Defense, FDRL. Also see FDRL's Franklin catalog, "Press Conferences of President Franklin D. Roosevelt, 1933–1945," Series 1: 662–667, July 23, 1940–Aug. 6, 1940, 95. Online Biography of Frank Bane, "A Guide to the Papers of Frank Bane," Special Collections, University of Virginia Library, http://ead.lib.virginia.edu/vivaxtf/view?docId=uva-sc/viu03469.xml. The National Defense Advisory Commission, Functions and Activities,

Booklet, Dec. 28, 1940, LoC, Landis Papers, Harvard File, B: 21, F: "1937–45 Boston News Bureau."

21. Online Biography of Frank Bane, "A Guide to the Papers of Frank Bane," Special Collections, University of Virginia Library, http://ead.lib.virginia.edu/vivaxtf/view?docId=uva-sc/viu03469.xml. The National Defense Advisory Commission, Functions and Activities, Booklet, Dec. 28, 1940, LoC, JML Papers, Harvard File, B: 21, F: "1937–45 Boston News Bureau."

22. Memo of Conference with Mayor La Guardia Aug, 14, 1940, Summary dated Aug. 15, 1940. No Name. RG171, E: 10, B: 70, F: 095-US Conference of Mayors. Luther Evans to Thomas Baldwin, Oct. 16, 1940; and "State Laws of Interest in Relation to the Home Guard Provisions of the National Defense Act," Nov 3, 1940, RG171, E: 10, B: 104, F: 410: State Defense Leg., thru Oct. 1940. Press Release, Governor Saltonstall's office, Aug. 5, 1940, RG171, E: 11, B: 5, F: 381: Region I: MA, S.C., to 12/31/41. Bane to H.E. Strasser, Dec. 10, 1940, RG171, E: 11, B: 75, F: 520: Region IX: CA, thru 7/17/41. Confidential memo, Howard Gardner to Bane, Jan. 3, 1941, re: "State and Local Defense Councils in California," RG171, E: 11, B: 71, F: 381; Region IX: CA, S.C., 1/1-12/31/41. Lydell Peck to "all California Fire Chiefs," June 14, 1940, RG171, E: 11, B: 75, F: 520: Region IX: CA, thru 7/17/41. Lydell Peck, "Report of a Conference on the Problem of Developing a Training Program for Fire Department Personnel in Fire Investigations, Sabotage and Kindred Crimes," July 1940; and Peck, "Report of Conference for the Purpose of Suggesting a Plan for Organization of Industrial Plants and Key Industries against Sabotage by Fire," Bulletin #2, July 1, 1940, RG171, E: 11, B: 75, F: 520: Region IX: CA, thru 7/17/41.

23. FDR to Harold Stassen, Aug. 14, 1940; Edwin Watson to no name, Aug. 7, 1940; Stassen to FDR, Aug. 7, 1940; Cross-Reference Sheet, Attorney General, June 13, 1940; regarding Minnesota's forces, FDR replied vaguely that he "hoped that the international situation will not necessitate the use of such forces," F: "Home Defense Misc. 1940–1941," OF 4249: Home Defense, FDRL. "Wisconsin Council of National Defense" and other one-page descriptions of state councils across the country, n.d. RG171, E: 10, B: 90, F: 317-Reports thru Dec. 31, 1941.

24. Division of State and Local Cooperation, "Weekly Operations Progress Reports," Oct. 23, 1940, F: "Council of National Defense Reports Sept-Dec. 1940," OF 813a: Advisory Commission to the Council of National Defense: Reports, 1940--941, FDRL.

25. Edgar Freed to Addison Foster, June 28, 1940, Sprague to Bane, Aug 20, 1940, RG171, E: 11, B: 77, F: 381: Region IX: OR, S.C. *Daily Capital Journal*, Oct. 26, 1938, https://www.news-papers.com/newspage/94757696/. Confidential Memo, Howard Gardner to Bane, Jan. 24, 1941, RG171, E: 11, B: 77, F: 317: Region IX: OR. Sprague to Bane, Feb. 11, 1941, RG171, E: 11, B: 77, F: 381: Region IX: OR, S.C. Letter, Herman Kehrli to Bane, Oct. 31, 1940; Kehrli to "Mayors, Police Chiefs, Fire Chiefs, and Municipal Utility Superintendents," Oct. 28, 1940; and attached Memo, "Protecting Cities Against Sabotage" published by League of Oregon Cities, Oct. 23, 1940, RG171, E: 11, B: 77, F: 000: Region IX: OR.

26. "Minutes of the Meeting of the Washington State Defense Council," Darwin Meisnest, Secretary, Aug. 29, 1940. RG171, E: 11, B: 78, F: 381: Region IX: WA, S.C. "Washington, Digest of Material," Feb. 20, 1941, RG171, E: 11, B: 78, F: 381: Region IX: WA, S. C. Langlie was quoted in an editorial in the *Spokane Spokesman-Review*. Memo, Howard Gardner to Bane, Feb. 1, 1941, RG171, E: 11, B: 79, F: 317: Region IX: WA. Frances Hays to no name, Feb. 14, 1941, RG171, E: 11, B: 78, F: 400: Region IX, WA, L.C. A handwritten note reads: " . . . gave Gardner copy of this request." "Washington, Digest of Material," Feb. 20, 1941, RG171, E: 11, B: 78, F: 381: Region IX: WA, S.C. "Minutes of the Meeting of the Washington State Defense Council," Darwin Meisnest, Secretary, Aug. 29, 1940. RG171, E: 11, B: 78, F: 381: Region IX: WA, S.C. Memo, Howard Gardner to Bane, Feb. 1, 1941, RG171, E: 11, B: 79, F: 317: Region IX: WA.

27. Gallup Poll, 9/15, Interview Date Aug. 24–29, 1940, Survey #207-K, Question #3a. Also cited in George Gallup, "The Gallup Poll: Four of 10 Americans Believe Nazis Would Attack U.S. if Britain Is Beaten," *Washington Post*, Sept. 14 1940, 2. Cross-Reference Sheet, Memorandum for General Watson, May 21, 1940; letter, James Rowe to Attorney General, June 1, 1940, F: "Espionage 1933–45," OF 1661: Espionage, FDRL. Rowe to R.J.

Taylor, July 2, 1940, F: "813a June–Aug. 1940," FDRL, OF 813a: Advisory Commission to the Council of National Defense: Reports, 1940–1941, FDRL. Lydell Peck, "Report of a Conference on the Problem of Developing a Training Program for Fire Department Personnel in Fire Investigations, Sabotage and Kindred Crimes," July 1940; and Peck, "Report of Conference for the Purpose of Suggesting a Plan for Organization of Industrial Plants and Key Industries against Sabotage by Fire," Bulletin #2, July 1, 1940, RG171, E: 11, B: 75, F: 520: Region IX: CA, thru July 17, 1941. Barry Sullivan, "The Spy Scare," *Washington Post*, Apr. 9, 1939.

28. Memo of Conference with Mayor La Guardia Aug. 14, 1940, Summary dated Aug. 15, 1940, RG171, E: 10, B: 70, F: 095-US Conference of Mayors. W. H. McReynolds to FDR, Aug. 8, 1940; FDR to McReynolds, Aug. 12, 1940, F: "OF 813a June–Aug. 1940, Council of National Defense Reports," OF 813a: Advisory Commission to the Council of National Defense: Reports, 1940–1941, FDRL.

29. La Guardia to FDR, Apr. 5, 1940; FDR to La Guardia, Mar. 27, 1940, F: "La Guardia, Fiorello 1940–1945," PPF 1376: La Guardia, Fiorello, FDRL. Times World Wide, "Air Academy Stone is Laid by Mayor," *New York Times*, Aug. 7, 1940. La Guardia to Edwin Watson, June 10, 1940; La Guardia to FDR, June 28, 1940; Press Release from Stephen T. Early, Secretary to the President, Aug. 22, 1940, F: "La Guardia, Fiorello 1940–1945," PPF 1376: La Guardia, Fiorello, FDRL. Kessner, *Fiorello H. La Guardia*, 468–469, 480. Williams, *City of Ambition*, 282.

30. See Independent Committee for Roosevelt and Wallace, http://www.gwu.edu/~erpapers/teachinger/glossary/indcom-for-fdr-wallace.cfm. La Guardia to FDR, July 18, 1940, F: "La Guardia, Fiorello 1940-1945," PPF 1376: La Guardia, Fiorello, FDRL. Kessner, *Fiorello H. La Guardia*, 480. Jackson, *That Man*, 16.

31. Edwin Watson to FDR, Oct. 1, 1940; La Guardia to Flynn, Oct. 25, 1940; Langdon P. Marvin to La Guardia, May 20, 1940; and FDR to La Guardia, June 15, 1940, F: "La Guardia, Fiorello 1940–1945," PPF 1376: La Guardia, Fiorello, FDRL. "Harvard men, like other business men, have, of course, criticized F.D. during these years and they are rather an independent crowd," the Chairman of the Associated Harvard Clubs wrote to La Guardia. FDR's reference was to this line in Marvin's letter.

32. Special to the New York Times, "La Guardia Scores Campaign of 'Fear,'" *New York Times*, Oct. 30, 1940, 16. Kessner, *Fiorello H. La Guardia*, 480–481.

33. Harry Woodring to FDR, June 15, 1940, F: "Book 2: National Defense Program 1940-41 Part I," Hopkins Papers, Book 2-National Defense-Isolationists Sherwood Collection, FDRL. See Kennett, *For the Duration: The United States Goes to War*, 28. William Conklin, "Jackson Bids Cities Unify Our Defense," *New York Times*, Sept. 20, 1940, 14.

34. Hearings before the Committee on Military Affairs, U.S. Senate, on S. 4175, Sept. 5, 1940, RG171, E: 10, B: 111, F: 502-Home Guards, May 1–31, 1941.

35. FDR to La Guardia, Sept. 12, 1940, RG171, E: 10, B: 70, F: "095-US Conference of Mayors."

36. William Conklin, "Jackson Bids Cities Unify Our Defense," *New York Times*, Sept. 20, 1940, 14. AP, "Nazis Watched, Says Jackson," *Los Angeles Times*, Sept. 20, 1940, 10. United States Conference of Mayors, 1940 Annual Conference, Program, RG171, E: 10, B: 70, F: 095-US Conference of Mayors. Letter, La Guardia to FDR, Sept. 7, 1940; memo, Stephen Early to Bill Hassett, Sept. 6, 1940, F: "U.S. Conference of Mayors," PPF 782: U.S. Conference of Mayors, FDRL. "Mayors Will Meet Here on Defense," *New York Times*, Sept. 19, 1940, 10.

37. WM. D. Lilly to FDR, Nov. 18, 1940, F: "Council of National Defense Reports, Sept.–Dec. 1940," OF 813a: Advisory Commission to the Council of National Defense: Reports, 1940–1941, FDRL. Fred M. Davenport to FDR, Dec. 17, 1940; and FDR to Davenport, Dec. 19, 1940, F: "La Guardia, Fiorello 1940–1945," PPF 1376: La Guardia, Fiorello, FDRL. Cross-Reference Sheet, William Bell, Jr., Nov. 19, 1940, F: "OF813a Sept.–Dec. 1940 Council of National Defense Reports," OF 813a: Advisory Commission to the Council of National Defense: Reports, 1940–1941, FDRL. The reference most likely refers to La Guardia's role leading the U.S. side of the joint U.S.-Canadian Defense Commission. James Meade to FDR, Dec. 20, 1940; Stephen Early to General Meade, Dec. 23, 1940, F: "Council of National Defense Reports Sept.–Dec. 1940," OF 813a: Advisory Commission to the Council of National Defense: Reports, 1940-1941, FDRL. Kessner, *Fiorello H. La Guardia*, 484–485.

38. Letter, Sidney Sherwood to FDR, Nov. 26, 1940, F: "Subject File Council of National Defense Sept. 1940–May 1941," PSF:128: Council of National Defense, FDRL. Gallup, Interviewing Date Dec. 18–23, 1940, Survey #226-K, Question #3, 261; also see George Gallup, "Republican and Democratic Voters found in Substantial Agreement on Defense Program," *Washington Post*, Jan. 15, 1941, 3.
39. Defense Training for Public Employees, The Status of In-Service Training Programs, Report No. 144, American Municipal Association, Dec. 1940, RG171, E: 10, B: 107, F: 455-Training, thru June 1941. *Defense*, page 1, Jan. 7, 1941, Vol. 2, No. 1, in RG171, E: 10, B: 97, F: 380–385: Progress Report to FDR Feb. 26, 1941. *Defense*, Jan. 7, 1941, Vol. 2, No. 1, 1.
40. "Washington Prepares for Civilian Defense," *Washington Post*, May 25, 1941, B3.

Chapter 5

1. For some standard books in the literature on the New Deal, see Leuchtenburg, *Franklin D. Roosevelt and the New Deal*; Anthony J. Badger, *The New Deal* (New York: Farrar, Straus and Giroux, 1989); Arthur M. Schlesinger Jr., *The Age of Roosevelt* (Boston: Houghton Mifflin, 3 vols., 1956–1960); Aaron D. Purcell, ed., *The New Deal and the Great Depression* (Kent, OH: The Kent State University Press, 2014); Wilbur J. Cohen, ed., *The New Deal: Fifty Years After, A Historical Assessment* (Austin: Lyndon Baines Johnson Library, Lyndon B. Johnson School of Public Affairs, 1984); Alonzo L. Hamby, ed., *The New Deal: Analysis and Interpretation* (New York: Longman, Inc., 1981).
2. See Brinkley, *The End of Reform*, in which he argues that the idea of New Deal liberalism slowly evolved after 1938 to include an economic growth-oriented liberalism that departed from state economic planning and focused on the needs of a consumer-oriented society. See Jacobs, *Pocketbook Politics*, 3. James T. Sparrow, in *Warfare State: World War II Americans and the Age of Big Government* (New York: Oxford University Press, 2011), sees the war rather than the New Deal as the moment when the federal government began to touch the lives of Americans in more pervasive ways. Jordan A. Schwarz, in *The New Dealers: Power Politics in the Age of Roosevelt* (New York: Knopf, 1993), sees the New Deal shaping politics on a global scale in the postwar era. ER's role in the Office of Civilian Defense is overlooked in Joan Hoff-Wilson and Marjorie Lightman, eds., *Without Precedent: The Life and Career of Eleanor Roosevelt* (Bloomington: Indiana University Press, 1984).
3. Eleanor Roosevelt, "Workers Should Join Trade Unions," *American Federationist* 48 (Mar. 1941): 14–15, in Black, ed., *What I Hope to Leave Behind*, 387.
4. See Eleanor Roosevelt Papers Project, "Wendell Willkie," (1892–1944), http://www.gwu. edu/~erpapers/teachinger/glossary/willkie-wendell.cfm. ER to Dr. R. M. Nicholson, Jan. 16, 1941, F: "Ni-O," ER 100: Personal Letters, FDRL. Lash, *Eleanor and Franklin*, 633–637.
5. Robyn Muncy, *Creating a Female Dominion in American Reform, 1890–1935* (New York: Oxford University Press, 1991), 93–99. John Dewey, "The Social Possibilities of War," http://teach-ingamericanhistory.org/library/document/the-social-possibilities-of-war-2/.
6. AP, "Home Mobilization of Women Is Asked," *New York Times*, Jan. 2, 1941, 7. Eleanor Roosevelt, "Workers Should Join Trade Unions," *American Federationist* 48 (March 1941): 14–15, in Black, ed., *What I Hope to Leave Behind*, 387. Lash, *Eleanor and Franklin*, 637–639. Kerr to ER, Jan. 27, 1941, F: "Home Defense 1940–1941," OF 4249: Home Defense, ERP, FDRL. The ER/Kerr proposals framed home defense as a program "which makes every woman and child, as well as every man, an indispensable unit in Home Defense." While their focus was on recruiting women (and girls) above all others, their home defense plans envisioned a place in the ranks for every citizen.
7. Florence Kerr, "VOLUNTEER MOBILIZATION OF WOMEN;" "THIS IS THE HOME DEFENSE PROGRAM PREPARED BY MRS. FLORENCE KERR AT THE REQUEST OF THE PRESI-DENT," undated., F: "1941 Kerr, Florence Jan. 1–Feb. 28," ER 70: Correspondence with Government Departments, ERP, FDRL. For the most authoritative account of FDR's court-packing plan, see Jeff Shesol, *Supreme Power: Franklin Roosevelt vs. The Supreme Court* (New York: W. W. Norton, 2010). AP, "Women Defense Training Urged," *Los Angeles Times*, Jan. 2, 1941, E7.

8. Florence Kerr, "VOLUNTEER MOBILIZATION OF WOMEN;" *"THIS IS THE HOME DEFENSE PROGRAM PREPARED BY MRS. FLORENCE KERR AT THE REQUEST OF THE PRESIDENT,"* undated, F: "1941 Kerr, Florence Jan. 1–Feb. 28," ER 70: Correspondence with Government Departments, ERP, FDRL. No Author, "Mrs. Miller Talks on WPA Aid to Defense," *Washington Post*, Feb. 1, 1941, 11. ER had abandoned her idea of forcing all citizens to do a term of national service. She bowed to critics who said her plan reeked of fascism, and she knew that FDR was opposed to her idea, too.

9. "Tentative Plan for—American Social Defense Administration," undated, included in exchange of correspondence between ER, Kerr, and FDR, F: "1941 Kerr, Florence Jan. 1–Feb. 28," ER 70: Correspondence with Government Departments, ERP, FDRL.

10. Memo, Mollie Somerville to Miss Thompson, Jan. 7, 1941; for the meeting's purpose, see Kerr to Mrs. Henry Morgenthau, Jan. 16, 1941, F: "1941 Kerr, Florence Jan. 1–Feb. 28," ER 70: Correspondence with Government Departments, ERP, FDRL. Marcia Winn, "Map Mobilization of Women," *Chicago Daily Tribune*, Mar. 6, 1941, 1.

11. Florence Kerr, "VOLUNTEER MOBILIZATION OF WOMEN;" *"THIS IS THE HOME DEFENSE PROGRAM PREPARED BY MRS. FLORENCE KERR AT THE REQUEST OF THE PRESIDENT,"* undated, F: "1941 Kerr, Florence Jan. 1–Feb. 28," ER 70: Correspondence with Government Departments, ERP, FDRL. Kerr to FDR, Jan. 8, 1941, F: "Home Defense 1940–1941," OF 4249: Home Defense, FDRL. Kerr also concerned herself with less weighty matters. On January 10, she asked Malvina Thompson, ER's secretary, about getting tickets for the third inauguration, seats with the best views of the inaugural parade, and getting to the White House for the inaugural lunch. "Sorry to be so dumb but this is my first Third Inaugural," Kerr deadpanned. The next day, Thompson provided Kerr with the run-down of the day's logistics. See Kerr to Malvina Thompson, Jan. 10, 1941; Thompson to Kerr, Jan. 11, 1941, F: "1941 Kerr, Florence C. Jan. 1 to Feb. 28," ER 70: Correspondence with Government Departments, ERP, FDRL.

12. Kerr to ER, Jan. 10, 1941; Kerr to FDR, Jan. 10, 1941; Kerr to Malvina Thompson, undated, F: "1941 Kerr, Florence, Jan. 1–Feb. 281," ER 70: Correspondence with Government Departments, ERP, FDRL.

13. Quotes and story about mother-in-law from Lash, *Franklin and Eleanor*, 637–639. The Measurement and Behavior of Unemployment, 216, http://www.nber.org/chapters/c2644.pdf.

14. Special to the *New York Times*, "President Drafts Home Guard Plan," *New York Times*, Jan. 15, 1941, 10. FDR to General Watson, Jan. 11, 1941, "F: Council of National Defense Reports 1941," OF 813a: Advisory Commission to the Council of National Defense, 1941, FDRL.

15. Kerr to FDR, Jan. 14, 1941, F: "Home Defense 1940–1941," OF 4249: Home Defense, FDRL. Oral history interview with Florence Kerr, Oct. 18–31, 1963, Archives of American Art, Smithsonian Institution. E.M.W. to FDR, Jan. 16, 1941, E.M.W. to FDR, memo and attached comments, Jan. 16, 1941, F: "Home Defense 1940–1941," OF 4249: Home Defense, FDRL.

16. Kerr to Mrs. Henry Morgenthau, Jan. 16, 1941; Kerr to FDR, Jan. 14, 1941, F: "Home Defense 1940–1941," OF 4249: Home Defense, FDRL.

17. Oral history interview with Florence Kerr, Oct. 18–31, 1963, Archives of American Art, Smithsonian Institution. Paul McNutt, "Comments with regard to Plan for 'Home Defense Commission,'" n.d.; also see John Carmody to FDR, Jan. 16, 1941, F: "Home Defense 1940–1941," OF 4249: Home Defense, FDRL.

18. Kerr to Thompson, Feb, 13, 1941, Ibid. Virginia Nowell to ER, Jan. 23, 1941; ER to Nowell, Feb. 4, 1941, F: "Ni-O," ER 100: Personal Letters, ERP, FDRL. Roosevelt scrawled on top of Nowell's letter, "I have no idea unless it is that I know of military preparation for women being considered." One of her secretaries presumably revised her handwritten note and added the language quoted in the text. "National Defense and Social Welfare," no author, n.d. RG171, E: 10, B: 40, F: 095-Council of State Governments. C.D. Jackson to ER, Feb. 27, 1941; Kerr to ER, undated, F: "1941 I-Ja," ER 70: Correspondence with Government Departments, ERP, FDRL.

19. Kerr to Malvina Thompson, Jan. 30, 1941; Kerr to ER, Feb. 6, 1941; Kerr to ER, Feb. 24, 1941, F: "1941 I-Ja," ER 70: Correspondence with Government Departments, ERP, FDRL.

20. Mary Norton to ER, Jan. 21, 1941, F: "President's Secretary's File Subject File Congress: 1941–44," PSF: 127, FDRL. FDR to McNutt, Kerr et. al., Jan. 24, 1941, F: "Council of National Defense Reports 1941," OF 813a: Advisory Commission to the Council of National Defense: Reports, 1940–1941, FDRL.
21. Kerr to ER, Jan. 27, 1941, F: "Home Defense 1940–1941," OF 4249: Home Defense, FDRL.
22. Katharine Graham, "American Women Mobilizing by Hundreds of Thousands for Defense Work," *Washington Post*, Mar. 9, 1941, B3.
23. No Author, "Dr. Hazen Hits Social Disease Control in D.C.," *Washington Post*, Feb. 6, 1941, 7. Marguerite Wells to Malvina Thompson, Jan. 15, 1941. Thompson to Kerr, Jan. 16, 1941; Kerr to "Welles" (*sic*), undated; Kerr to Thompson, Jan. 23, 1941, F: "1941 Kerr, Florence C. Jan. 1 to Feb. 28."ER 70: Correspondence with Government Departments, ERP, FDRL. Dorothy Overlook to FDR, Feb. 21, 1941, F: "Home Defense 1940–1941." OF 4249: Home Defense, FDRL. Jesse Ash Arndt, "First Lady Receives Board Of G.F.W.C. at White House," *Washington Post*, Jan. 16, 1941.
24. American Embassy, London, Confidential Report on "Women's War Work in Great Britain," Section V *Women's Voluntary Services*, Feb. 2, 1942, RG171, E: 12, B: 7, F: Women: Report on Women's War Work in Great Britain (3 of 3). Also see Helen Cumming, "Victoria Would Be Surprised," *New York Times*, July 13, 1941, SM6.
25. Richard Overy, *The Bombing War: Europe, 1939–1945* (London: Penguin Books, 2013), see ch. 3. Peter Doyle, *ARP and Civil Defence in the Second World War* (Oxford: Shire Publications, 2010), 59–63. Olson, *Citizens of London*, 82–83, which includes a smart, succinct summary of the WVS' wartime activities and impact. Dispersal was done through appeals to reason and persuasion, not through the force of law. (You could not legally or ethically force mothers to send their children away if they refused to do so, former London County Council Chairman, Albert Davis, told New York home defense officials.) Pregnant women, the elderly, and disabled were also on the evacuation list. Parents of evacuated children could pay what they could to care for their children, and the state would pick up the remaining costs. Ideally, parents with some means would cover 60 percent of the costs and the national government would cover 40 percent. John O'Ryan to All Chairmen, Jan. 9, 1942, NYCMA, LG, B: 4181 F: 02, OCD: Press Releases (1) 1942/01. Anne Stewart Higham, "Women in Defense of Britain: An Informal Report," Journal of Educational Sociology, Vol. 15, No. 5, Women in National Defense, (Jan. 1942), 293–300. "Women's Voluntary Services for Civil Defence," The Bulletin, Sept. 1941, No. 23, 1, RG171, E: 12, B: 7, F: "Women: Report on Women's War Work in Great Britain (1 of 3)."
26. Olson, *Citizens of London*, 82-83. Murrow, *This is London*, 170–176. One woman described how in one shelter she found people in shock after a direct hit. One man saw a bomb crash through another shelter, killing everybody inside. "A cheap high-heeled shoe and a man's oily cloth cap" were visible from the rubble. Murrow—most renowned for his eyewitness accounts of the blitz—suggested that fear had draped the city like one of its trademark fogs, class rifts plagued Londoners, and chaos and order vied for supremacy. He described civilians lying on "hard wooden benches" with only a canvas curtain protecting them, while retired colonels, European royalty, and cosmopolitans swirled Scotch and soda and socialized "with the right sort of people" in posh hotel lobbies. Meantime, the government had to aid the "homeless . . . from the fire-blackened East End. They must be cared for, they must be moved, they must be fed, and they must be sheltered . . . . If morale is to be maintained at its present high level, there must be no distinction between the troops living in the various sections of London." British home defense forces struggled to defend the poor from diseases, winter weather, and the bombs raining down on them nightly. "Upon the success of their efforts all else depends," he said, a tone of uncertainty creeping into his confidence. Anne Stewart Higham, "Women in Defense of Britain: An Informal Report," *Journal of Educational Sociology*, Vol. 15, No. 5, Women in National Defense. (Jan. 1942), 293–300. Katharine Graham, "American Women Mobilizing by Hundreds of Thousands for Defense Work," *Washington Post*, March 9, 1941, B3. "Women's Voluntary Services for Civil Defence," The Bulletin, p.1, Sept. 1941, No. 23, RG171, E: 12, B: 7, F: Women: Report on Women's War Work in Great Britain (1 of 3).
27. Reading to ER, Oct. 23, 1941, Ibid.
28. See Olson, *Citizens of London*, 82. Cook, *Eleanor Roosevelt, Vol. 2*, 356, 375.

29. *Washington Post,* "The Post Radio Time Table," Oct. 29, 1940, 28. *Christian Science Monitor,* "Over Editor's Desk," Dec. 14, 1940, WM15. Helen Cumming, "Victoria Would Be Surprised," *New York Times,* July 13, 1941, 20. James Landis to Lady Reading, June 10, 1942, F: "ER OCD General Correspondence 1942 J-Z," ER 71: Office of Civil Defense, ERP, FDRL. Reading originally sent the materials to Eleanor Roosevelt, who forwarded the information to the Office of Civilian Defense. Reading to ER, Jan. 15, 1941; Reading to ER, Feb. 17, 1941, F: "1941 Reading, Lady Stella," ER 100: Personal Letters, ERP, FDRL.
30. Reading to ER, May 6, 1941, Ibid.
31. ER to Reading, Mar. 17, 1941; Reading to ER, Sept. 17, 1941; ER to Reading, Aug. 9, 1941, Ibid.
32. Special to *New York Times,* "Mission Develops U.S. Civil Defense," Feb. 14, 1941, 6. *New York Times,* "Plea for Doctors Made for Britain," Mar. 11, 1941, 25.
33. Eric Biddle, "The Transition to Total Defense," Review of "British Cities at War," by James Sundquist, in *Public Administration Review,* Vol. 1, No. 5 (Autumn 1941) 493–497. Averill Harriman to FDR, May 7, 1941, F: "Great Britain, Harriman, Averill," PSF: 47, FDRL.
34. Marcia Winn, "Deny, Confirm Home Defense Unit for Women," *Chicago Daily Tribune,* Mar. 7, 1941, 9.
35. No Author, "Storm in House over Scheme to Mobilize Women," *Chicago Daily Tribune,* Mar. 8, 1941, 5.
36. For information on McCormick, see *New York Times,* "Debates Swirled About McCormick," Apr. 1, 1955. Marcia Winn, "Map Mobilization of Women," *Chicago Daily Tribune,* Mar. 6, 1941, 1. Editorial, "Mrs. Roosevelt's Frauenfront," *Chicago Daily Tribune,* Mar. 7, 1941, 10.
37. Eva Mae Isaacs to ER, Mar. 24, 1941, F: "1941 I-Ja," ER 70: Correspondence with Government Departments, ERP, FDRL. See ER Secretary to Sophie Janota, Mar. 21, 1941, F: "Ni-O," ER 100: Personal Letters, ERP, FDRL. And see ER Administrative Officer for Social Correspondence to Jane Inch, Apr. 25, 1941; and Administrative Officer to Eva Isaacs, Mar. 27, 1941, F: "1941 I-Ja," ER 70: Correspondence with Government Departments, ERP, FDRL.
38. Eleanor Roosevelt, "Social Gains & Defense," *Common Sense* 10 (March 1941): 71–72, in Black, ed., *What I Hope to Leave Behind,* 389–391.
39. Secretary to ER to Kerr, Feb. 5, 1941; FDR to ER, Feb. 4, 1941; Kerr to ER, Feb. 12, 1941, F: "1941 Kerr, Florence C. Jan. 1 to Feb. 28," ER 70: Correspondence with Government Departments, ERP, FDRL. "Mrs. Kerr Says Defense Means More Than Arms," *Washington Post,* Mar. 19, 1941, 12.
40. Jessie Ash Arndt, "First Lady Addresses 74th Club," *Washington Post,* Apr. 17, 1941.
41. Helen Gahagan Douglas to ER, May 27, 1941 Helen Gahagan Douglas to ER, Mar. 31, 1941, F: "1941 Gahagan, Helen," ER 100: Personal Letters, ERP, FDRL.

Chapter 6

1. For description of the first attack on London and "animals" quote, see Olson, *Citizens of London,* 43–44. For timber yards on fire, see Bill Killick, WW2 People's War, BBC, Disclaimer: "WW2 People's War is an online archive of wartime memories contributed by members of the public and gathered by the BBC. The archive can be found at bbc.co.uk/ww2peopleswar." http://www. bbc.co.uk/history/ww2peopleswar/stories/16/a2396216.shtml. See Office of Government Reports, "Information Digest," Oct. 30, 1941. The War Department sent "military observers" to England with the goal of assigning them to the Army Aircraft Warning Service when they returned to America. NYCMA, LG, box 4175, folder 14, OCD, Press Releases 1941/10. *Washington Times-Herald,* "N.Y. Firemen Visit London and Praise It," Oct. 30, 1940, RG171, E: 10, B: 124, F: 520-Fire Protection, thru Nov. 30, 1940. J. P. Brander to La Guardia, May 1941, RG171, "National Headquarters General Correspondence 1940–42," 091 to 091, E: 10, B: 26, F: "England to Oct. 31, 1941."
2. For a strong analysis of the Cold War's self-help policy in the United States, see McEnaney, *Civil Defense Begins at Home;* for a classic study of the Cold War, family life, and American culture, see Elaine May, *Homeward Bound;* for the failure of civil defense policy, see Dee Garrison, *Bracing for Armageddon;* for civil defense as a propaganda tool, see Guy Oakes, *The Imaginary*

War. For some overviews of the U.S. response to the Blitz in the literature, see David M. Kennedy's Pulitzer Prize–winning *Freedom from Fear;* John Morton Blum, *V Was for Victory: Politics and American Culture During World War II* (San Diego: Harcourt Brace & Co., 1976); and David Kaiser, *No End Save Victory: How FDR Led the Nation into War* (New York: Basic Books, 2014).

3. Daniel T. Rodgers, *Atlantic Crossings: Social Politics in a Progressive Age* (Cambridge, MA: Harvard University Press, 1998), 1. For La Guardia's incendiary rhetoric and hyperbole, see Kessner, *Fiorello H. La Guardia.* "Americans were just too confident that a mainland attack was an unlikely possibility to take his hyperactivity seriously," Kessner argues (494). For a description of the absurdities of civil defense in World War II, see Lingeman, *Don't You Know There's a War On?.*

4. Royal Daniel Sloan Jr., "The Politics of Civil Defense: Great Britain and the United States" (PhD diss., University of Chicago, 1958), 35–38.

5. See Philip Seib, *Broadcasts from the Blitz: How Edward R. Murrow Helped Lead America into War* (Washington, D.C.: Potomac Books, 2006), 41–54, 69–99. For more information, see Ferdinand Kuhn Jr., "British Unyielding," *New York Times,* Aug. 29, 1939, 1; Chicago Tribune Press Service, "British Minister of War Reveals Defense Flaws," *Chicago Daily Tribune,* Nov. 4, 1938; and *Los Angeles Times,* "Prof. Offers to Test Air Raid Shelters," Aug. 27, 1939, A5.

6. Ibid., 69–99. For Churchill quote, see Richard Titmuss, *History of the Second World War: Problems of Social Policy,* United Kingdom Civil Series, 1950. Roger Parkinson, *Summer, 1940: The Battle of Britain* (New York: David McKay Co., 1977), 24–27, 192–193. Richard Overy, *The Battle of Britain: The Myth and the Reality* (New York: Penguin, 2000), 99–100. John O'Ryan to "All Chairmen," Jan. 9, 1942, NYCMA, LG, B: 4181, F: 02, OCD: Press Releases (1) 1942/01. Ministry of Information, Issued for the Ministry of Home Security, "Front Line, 1940–41: The Official Story of Civil Defence of Britain" (London: His Majesty's Stationery Office, 1942), 7–8. See Ronan Thomas, "The Blitz," http://www.westendatwar. org.uk/page_id__152_path__0p2p.aspx.

7. Albert Lepawsky, "The London Region: A Metropolitan Community in Crisis," *American Journal of Sociology* 46, no. 6 (May 1941): 827–829. Editorial, "Current Comment," *Los Angeles Times,* Sept. 19, 1940, A4.

8. *New York Times,* Obituary, "Edward R. Murrow, Broadcaster and Ex-Chief of U.S.I.A., Dies," Apr. 28, 1965. Archibald MacLeish, "A Superstition Is Destroyed," Dec. 2, 1941, in "In honor of a man and an ideal. . . . Three Talks on Freedom," in LoC, Archibald MacLeish Papers, B: 46, F: Speeches and Lectures: Speeches: "A Superstition Is Destroyed," dinner in honor of Edward R. Murrow, Dec. 2, 1941. Ibid., 160–161; Gerd Horten, *Radio Goes to War: The Cultural Politics of Propaganda During World War II* (Berkeley: University of California Press, 2002), 37; A. M. Sperber, *Murrow, His Life and Times* (New York: Fordham University Press, 1986), 168; Seib, 16. Edward R. Murrow, *This Is London: Witnesses to War* (New York: Schocken 1989), 162–163, 178–182, 201.

9. Ibid., 166–169, 199–201, 229–230.

10. Quotes from Robert Post, "Havoc in 'The City,'" *New York Times,* Dec. 31, 1940, 1. See also United Press, "Nazis Blast London After Yuletide Truce," *Los Angeles Times,* Dec. 1, 1940.

11. "Britain Under Fire: More Personal Experiences," letter from a London social worker printed in *Christian Science Monitor,* Oct. 9, 1940, 22. "News from Europe—Uncensored," *New York Times,* Oct. 13, 1940, 47. For other letters, see "Letters from Britain Describe Plans for Safety in Air Raids," *New York Times,* Nov. 10, 1940, 52; and "Letters from Britain Say Bombings Fail to Spread Terror," *New York Times,* Dec. 7, 1940, 23.

12. Peter Paul, "Could Los Angeles Take It?" *Los Angeles Times,* Nov. 3, 1940, 3. William McGaffin, "French Panic Teaches British Fear Itself Is Thing to Fear," *Washington Post,* Jan. 7, 1941, 9.

13. James Wilkinson to John Erhardt, Nov. 15, 1940, F: "Nov. 1940," PSF: 34, FDRL.

14. Rene Kraus, *The Men Around Churchill* (Philadelphia: Lippincott, 1941), see biographical essay, "Lord of London: Herbert Morrison," 144, 152–167.

15. Hugh Wagnon, "Britain's Policeman: Herbert Morrison Is Responsible for Civil Defense," *Washington Post,* Mar. 9, 1941, B5. Kraus, *The Men Around Churchill,* 144–146, 152–167. "His voice is the echo of the streets he represents," Kraus wrote.

16. For an illuminating discussion of American federalism in the World War II–era civilian defense program, see Patrick S. Roberts, "The Lessons of Civil Defense Federalism for the Homeland Security Era," *Journal of Policy History* 26, no. 3 (2014). Harry Prince, "Summary Report of Civilian Defense Studies in England," July 16 to Aug. 15, 1941, 1–3. NYCMA, LG, B: 4175, F: 07, OCD: Civilian Defense Studies in England, 1941/09/15. AP, "Speeding of Shelters Pledged by British Home Secretary," *Christian Science Monitor*, Oct. 10, 1940, 6.

17. Ibid., 56–64. United Press, "London Shelter Red Tape Cut," *Los Angeles Times*, Oct. 7, 1940, 2.

18. Special Cable to the *New York Times*, "War Aim Statement Expected in London," *New York Times*, Dec. 12, 1940, 3. David Anderson, "British Expected to Define War Aims Early Next Year," *Washington Post*, Dec. 12, 1940, 2. AP, "'We'll Hold On,' Britons Are Told," *Christian Science Monitor*, Nov. 1, 1940, 9.

19. A. H. Raskin, "Green Tells A.F.L. Roosevelt Wants Parleys with C.I.O. Resumed—Stimson Warns Labor Must Share Sacrifices," *New York Times*, Nov. 19, 1940, 1. Harold Laski, "Britain's Labor Ministers," *Washington Post*, Jan. 4, 1941, 7. Larry Rue, "Britons to Quiz Cabinet on War in House Session," *Chicago Daily Tribune*, Jan. 20, 1941, 6. Special Cable to the *New York Times*, "Britain to Compel All to Fight Fires," *New York Times*, Jan. 1, 1941, 3. Larry Rue, "British 'Social Revolution' Put Closer to Goal," *Chicago Tribune*, Mar. 20, 1941, 30.

20. "N.Y. Firemen Visit London and Praise It," *Washington Times-Herald*, Oct. 30, 1940, RG171, E: 10, B: 124, F: 520-Fire Protection, through Nov. 30, 1940. See also Cross-Reference Sheet, C. L. Frederic to Betters, May 1, 1941, RG171, E: 10, B: 124, F: 520–Fire Protection, Apr. 1–June 19, 1941. Their report would be published in 1941.

21. Letter, George Richardson to FDR, Sept. 26, 1940, RG171, E: 10, B: 124, F: 520–Fire Protection, through Nov. 30, 1940.

22. The American Municipal Association also published reports on Britain's program. See Roy Owsley to General L. D. Gasser, June 16, 1941, RG171, E: 10, B: 30, F: 095-AMA, 1/1–6/20/41. For the police proposal, see Captain Donald Leonard to Frank Bane, May 5, 1941, RG171, E: 10, B: 48, F: 095-1ACP. See "Police Chiefs' Newsletter," vol. 8, no. 3, March 1941, starting with "Scotland Yard Asks U.S. Police to Clear Inquiries Through FBI." RG171, E: 10, B: 48, F: 095-1ACP. J. Edgar Hoover to James M. Landis, Feb. 18, 1942, RG171, E: 12, B: 1, F: Loose, No. 7. See also memo, Assistant Chief Inspector of New York City Police Department to Chief Inspector, Aug. 25, 1941. In the summer of 1941, the New York police met with FBI Assistant Director Hugh Clegg and asked if the FBI would provide the police with copies of the FBI's London reports "for a few days" so they could examine the reports and apply their lessons to their own police operations. The FBI had already sent La Guardia copies of its reports. NYCMA, LG, B: 4174, F: 10 OCD: Corr (2) 1941/09.

23. Major Ernest Brown to Frank Bane, May 24, 1941, RG171, E: 10, B: 110, F: 501-Police Cooperation. Captain Donald Leonard to La Guardia, July 22, 1941, RG171, E: 12, B: 1, F: Confidential: 000. See also Lester Stone to W. W. Chaplin, Oct. 4, 1941, NYCMA, LG, B: 4175, F: 09, OCD: Corr (1) 1941/10.

24. "3 U.S. Officers Fly Atlantic to Study Bombings," *Chicago Daily Tribune*, Oct. 11, 1940, 1. Special to the *New York Times*, "Legion Head to Survey Civilian Role in England," *New York Times*, Jan. 19, 1941. Lydell Peck to Frank Bane, Feb. 14, 1941, RG171, E: 10, B: 124, F: 520-Fire Protection, Apr. 1–June 19, 1941. Cross-Reference Sheet, Harold Sinton, Federal Housing Administration, Mar. 4,1942, OF 4422: Office of Civilian Defense, FDRL. See also "Separate Battalion, Fort Devens—July 1940," announcement addressed to "Battalion Attention!" from Joseph Walker Jr., May 1, 1941, NYCMA, LG, B: 4171, F: 04, OCD: Corr #131 (4) 1941/05.

25. "Mayor Will Set Up Defense Unit; He Hints He May Not Finish Term," *New York Times*, Jan. 9, 1941, 1.

26. Quoted in Robert E. Miller, "The War That Never Came: Civilian Defense, Mobilization, and Morale" (PhD diss., University of Cincinnati, 1990), 33.

27. La Guardia, "Preliminary Report for Civil Defense Organization and Administration in the United States," Jan. 31, 1941, http://memory.loc.gov/service/gdc/scd0001/2008/20081009006pr/20081009006pr.pdf. See also Warren Francis, "Mayors Urge National Civil Defense System," *Los Angeles Times*, Feb. 2, 1941, 10.

28. AP, "Mayors Urge Air Defense Plan for Cities," *Washington Post*, Feb. 2, 1941, 7.

29. David M. Kennedy, *Over Here: The First World War and American Society* (New York: Oxford University Press, 1980), 114–117. See also McEnaney, *Civil Defense Begins at Home*, 23; and Garrison, *Bracing for Armageddon*, 32. For an excellent discussion of the Woman's Committee of the Council of National Defense and its efforts to tie social uplift to war mobilization, see Muncy, *Creating a Female Dominion in American Reform*, 96–101.

30. Lydell Peck, "Report of a Conference on the Problem of Developing a Training Program for Fire Department Personnel in Fire Investigations, Sabotage and Kindred Crimes," July 1940, RG171, E: 11, B: 75, F: 520: Region IX: CA, thru 7/17/41. Lydell Peck, "Report of Conference for the Purpose of Suggesting a Plan for Organization of Industrial Plants and Key Industries against Sabotage by Fire," Bulletin no. 2, July 1, 1940, in ibid.

31. La Guardia, "Preliminary Report for Civil Defense Organization and Administration in the United States," Jan. 31, 1941, http://memory.loc.gov/service/gdc/scd0001/2008/20081009006pr/20081009006pr.pdf. Charles Hurd, "Mayors Call for Civil Defense Plan, Telling President of Air Raid Needs," *New York Times*, Feb. 2, 1941, 1. "Text of Plea by the Conference of Mayors to President Roosevelt for Civil Defense Plan," *New York Times*, Feb. 2, 1941, 39.

32. La Guardia, "Preliminary Report for Civil Defense Organization and Administration in the United States," Jan. 31, 1941, http://memory.loc.gov/service/gdc/scd0001/2008/20081009006pr/20081009006pr.pdf. Warren Francis, "Mayors Urge National Civil Defense System," *Los Angeles Times*, Feb. 2, 1941, 10. Editorial, "The Exploding Petals of The Little Flower," *Chicago Daily Tribune*, Feb. 4, 1941, 14. If bombs had fallen on the United States in late 1940 or early 1941, there would have likely been panic and chaos, and it's unclear if home defense such as it existed then could have saved many lives.

33. AP, "La Guardia Warns Cities of Air War," *New York Times*, Feb. 21, 1941, 6.

34. http://www.library.georgetown.edu/dept/speccoll/hopbio.htm; for Ickes, see The Eleanor Roosevet Papers Project, http://www.gwu.edu/~erpapers/teachinger/glossary/ickes-harold.cfm. Cross-Reference Sheet, ARB and JB to "Missy," n.d. A note says that the original memo was dated Jan. 24, 1941, F: "LaGuardia, Fiorello Cross-References." PPF 1376: La Guardia, Fiorello, FDRL. FDR advised Ickes to find somebody to handle publicity for La Guardia's committee, but whether that pressure was applied was unclear.

35. See Miller, *The War That Never Came*, 33–35.

36. Frank Bane to William McReynolds, Feb. 6, 1941; Harold Smith to FDR, Feb. 13, 1941. See also attached handwritten note, "McReynolds and Bane," n.d., and "Wm. McReynolds," Feb. 20, F: "Reports-Division of State and Local Cooperation 1941," OF 813a: Advisory Commission to the Council of National Defense: Reports, 1940–1941, FDRL. Cross-Reference Sheet, ARB and JB to "Missy," n.d. A note says that the original memo was dated Jan. 24, 1941, F: "LaGuardia, Fiorello Cross-References," PPF 1376: La Guardia, Fiorello, FDRL.

37. "Citizens Urge D.C. to Prepare Against Air War," *Washington Post*, Jan. 5, 1941, 1. "Air Raids' in East Start 4-Day Test," *New York Times*, Jan. 22, 1941, 12. Lawlor Hart, Letter to the Editor, "Training Offered to Civilians," *New York Times*, Feb. 12, 1941, 20. Dr. George Gallup, "The Gallup Poll: Many Easterners Found Leaning Toward Idea of Trial 'Blackouts,'" *Washington Post*, Feb. 15, 1941, 3.

38. "City Defense Group Plans for Air Raids," *New York Times*, Jan. 16, 1941, 1. Major General, The Adjutant General to Frank Bane, Mar. 6, 1941; and attached, "Civil Defense Basic Organization, prepared by the War Department with the Assistance and Advice of Other Federal Agencies," Washington, D.C., 1941, RG171, E: 12, B: 1, F: 020. The department declared that a "study of recent events in Europe shows the dangers to which a civilian population is subjected during war." Press Release, Office for Emergency Management Division of State and Local Cooperation, Apr. 29, 1941, RG171, E: 10, B: 119, F: 515-Air Raid Shelters, thru November 1941.

39. See Charles Short to Frank Bain [*sic*], Dec. 2, 1940; and attached "Preliminary Outline Suggestion for *Defense Constabulary*," revised Nov. 28, 1940, RG171, E: 10, B: 110, F: 501-Police Cooperation. See also Alvin Roseman to Frank Bane, Oct. 16, 1940; Daniel Hoan to Bane and Roseman, Dec. 11, 1940, RG171, E: 10, B: 110, F: 501-Police Cooperation. See

Willard Day, "Comments on Police Mobilization Plan by Bruce Smith," Dec. 13, 1940. Miller, *The War That Never Came*, 32–33. Hoan also feared that setting up a civil defense program too soon would "spread hysteria."

40. See Pa Watson to FDR, Apr. 22, 1941, and Watson to FDR, Apr. 21, 1941, F: "LaGuardia, Fiorello, 1940–1945," PPF 1376: La Guardia, Fiorello, FDRL. Press Release, statement by La Guardia, Apr. 20, 1941, City of New York, Office of the Mayor, RG171, E: 10, B: 70, F: 095-US Conference of Mayors. See also Cross-Reference Sheet, C. L. Frederic to Betters, May 1, 1941; Betters to Hoan, Apr. 29, 1941, RG171, E: 10, B: 124, F: 520-Fire Protection, Apr. 1–June 19, 1941. New York City Fire Department, "Wartime Fire Defense in London: The Organization, General Plan and Methods Used by the London Fire Brigade to Control Fires Resulting from Incendiary Bombing as Observed by Members of the New York City Fire Department Assigned to London from October 22, 1940 to January 14, 1941" (Washington, D.C., 1941). Press Release, Office for Emergency Management, Division of State and Local Cooperation, Apr. 3, 1941, RG171, E: 10, B: 124, F: 520-Fire Protection, Apr. 1–July 19, 1941. "Mayor Assails Grumbling in Defense Crisis," Mayor Edward Kelly statement, reprinted in *Chicago Daily Times*, Apr. 25, 1941, F: "Speech Materials and Suggestions 1941 Jan–Apr," PPF 1820: Speech Material and Suggests; Transcripts of President's Speeches, FDRL.

41. Colonel Joseph A. Baer, "U.S. Home Defense Gaining Headway," *New York Times*, Apr. 13, 1941, 35. "The U.S. v. Bombs," *Time*, Apr. 21, 1941, 30.

Chapter 7

1. "The U.S. v. Bombs," *Time*, Apr. 21, 1941. Memo, Chief of Naval Operations H. R. Stark to All Bureaus and Offices, Navy Department et al., June 11, 1941, RG171, E: 10, B: 11, F: 045, to July 31, 1941.

2. Eugene Casey to FDR, May 23, 1941, F: "Speech Materials and Suggestions 1941 May"; Eugene Casey to FDR, May 8, 1941, PPF 1820: Speech Materials, FDRL. See Ickes diary, 406–408. La Guardia to FDR, Apr. 25, 1941, F: "PSF Office of Civilian Defense: 1941," PSF: 145, FDRL. Hadley Cantril to Anna Rosenberg, Mar. 20, 1941, F: "Speech Materials and Suggestions 1941 Jun–Apr.," PPF 1820: Speech Materials, FDRL.

3. FDR to Harold Smith, April 7, 1941, F: "Home Defense 1940–1941," OF 4249: Home Defense, FDRL. Edward Folliard, "Washington Prepares for Civilian Defense," *Washington Post*, May 25, 1941, B3.

4. AP, "Civil Defense Order Ready," *Los Angeles Times*, April 20, 1941, 8.

5. See H. T. Hunter to FDR, May 14, 1941; Alfred Collins to FDR, May 23, 1941; Bishop John Ward to FDR, May 13, 1941, F: "OF 4426 National Emergency 1941," OF 4426: National Emergency, FDRL. Col. Edmund Burke to Stephen Early, March 14, 1941; C. H. Williams and Harold Miller to FDR, Sept. 19, 1940, F: "Home Defense 1940–1941," OF 4249: Home Defense, FDRL. See Frank L. Hayes, "New Home Guard Being Set up by Men 35 to 45," and other articles; *Chicago Daily News*, June 20, 1940. C. H. Williams to FDR, Nov. 25, 1940; C. H. Williams to FDR, Dec. 30, 1940, W. J. Lacroix to FDR, Mar. 25, 1941, iF: "Home Defense 1940–1941," OF 4249: Home Defense, FDRL. Lash, *Eleanor and Franklin*, 639.

6. FDR to Smith, May 21, 1941, F: "Office of Civilian Defense April–July 1941," OF 4422: Office of Civilian Defense, FDRL. Miller, *The War That Never Came*, 34–38. See Ickes diary, 406–408.

7. Edward Folliard, "Washington Prepares for Civilian Defense," *Washington Post*, May 25, 1941, B3.

8. La Guardia to FDR, Apr. 25, 1941, F: "President's Secretary's File Subject File Office of Civilian Defense: 1941 Box 145," PSF: 145, FDRL.

9. Harry Hopkins to Miss Tully, May 15, 1941, F: "Home Defense 1940–1941," OF 4249: Home Defense, FDRL. Harold Smith to FDR, May 17, 1941, F: "Office of Civilian Defense Apr.–July 1941," OF 4422: Office of Civilian Defense, FDRL. FDR Executive Order, "Establishing the Office of Civilian Defense in the Office for Emergency Management of the Executive Office of the President," May 20, 1941, Ibid. See Ickes diary, 406–408.

10. M. H. McIntyre to Harold Smith, May 20, 1941, F: "Office of Civilian Defense Apr.–July 1941," OF 4422: Office of Civilian Defense, FDRL.

11. John O'Neill to FDR, April 23, 1941, F: "Home Defense 1940–1941," OF 4249: Home Defense, FDRL. Lash, *Eleanor and Franklin*, 640. Ickes said La Guardia was likely to "run all over the field with the ball" and couldn't do both jobs simultaneously. ER, "My Day," May 14, 1941. Ernest Lindley, "LaGuardia and the Civil Defense Program," *Washington Post*, May 25, 1941, B5.

12. Frank Bane, advocates for him said, knew local and state officials, studied volunteer efforts already underway, and helped the territories of Hawaii, Alaska, and Puerto Rico set up home defense programs to defend against invasion. Leona Graham to Frank Bane, Apr. 25, 1941, RG171, E: 10, B: 27, F: 092-Territories. Ernest Lindley, "LaGuardia and the Civil Defense Program," *Washington Post*, May 25, 1941, B5. Miller, *The War That Never Came*, 38–40. See Ickes diary, 406–408.

13. "Mayor is Noncommital," *New York Times*, May 18, 1941, 33. John O'Neill to FDR, Apr. 23, 1941, F: "Home Defense 1940–1941," OF 4249: Home Defense, FDRL. "LaGuardia to Head Home Defense; He Sees President About Program," *New York Times*, May 20, 1941, 1.

14. Cross-Reference Sheet, La Guardia, Aug. 12, 1936; Cross-Reference Sheet, La Guardia, Sept. 13, 1939; Cross-Reference Sheet, La Guardia, May 5, 1939; FDR to La Guardia, June 10, 1935, F: "La Guardia, Fiorello Cross-References," PPF 1376: La Guardia, Fiorello, FDRL. Cross-Reference Sheet, Ray Spear, June 11, 1941, F: "Office of Civilian Defense Apr.–July 1941," OF 4422: Office of Civilian Defense, FDRL. Lash, *Eleanor and Franklin*, 640. Ernest Lindley, "LaGuardia and the Civil Defense Program," *Washington Post*, May 25, 1941, B5.

15. Kessner, *Fiorello La Guardia*, 490–491. Kessner is especially strong at describing the back-and-forth between FDR and La Guardia in early 1941. Don Whitehead, "LaGuardia, Home Defense Boss, 'Little Man Who's Everywhere,'" May 28, 1941, New Orleans State Special News Service, NYCMA, LG, B: 4171, F: 04 OCD: Correspondence #131 (4) 1941/05. Cross-Reference Sheet, La Guardia, May 19, 1941, F: "Office of Civilian Defense Apr.–July 1941," OF 4422: Office of Civilian Defense, FDRL. Cross-Reference Sheet, "for memo. To Mr. Forster . . . " Ibid. FDR asked La Guardia to respond to one person who wanted the administration to stop the Nazis from holding a rally at Madison Square Garden.

16. "Defense Task Put to Port Authority," *New York Times*, May 1, 1941, 16. Allegations of a plot to assassinate FDR and La Guardia surfaced, prompting the Secret Service to investigate.

17. Cross-Reference Sheet, Memo for The Attorney General et al., Dec. 29, 1939, F: "LaGuardia, Fiorello Cross-References," PPF 1376: La Guardia, Fiorello, FDRL. First Deputy Commissioner to Lester Stoner, May 29, 1941, NYCMA, LG, B: 4171, F: 04 OCD: Correspondence #131 (4) 1941/05. "Chief of Our Home Defense Volunteers . . . ," May 30, 1941, *The United States News*, NYCMA, LG, B: 4171, F: 04 OCD: Correspondence #131 (4) 1941/05. FDR to La Guardia, Jan. 29, 1941, F: "President's Secretary's File La Guardia, Fiorello H. B 141," PSF: 141, FDRL. Cross-Reference Sheet, Presidential Memo for La Guardia, May 19, 1941; Cross-Reference Sheet, Director of Budget, June 12, 1941, F: "Office of Civilian Defense Apr.–July 1941," OF 4422: Office of Civilian Defense, FDRL.

18. La Guardia to General Edwin Watson, May 1, 1941, F: "LaGuardia, Fiorello 1940–1945," PPF 1376: La Guardia, Fiorello, FDRL. AP, "Draft Boards Are Assailed by LaGuardia," *Washington Post*, May 5, 1941, 7.

19. "Mayor in New Role Bids Aides Assure City Food Supply," *New York Times*, May 21, 1941, 1. AP, "Mrs. Roosevelt Asked to Quit," *Los Angeles Times*, Feb. 11, 1942, 1. In his press conference announcing La Guardia's resignation in February 1942, FDR acknowledged that La Guardia's position had never been formalized due to questions about whether or not such an appointment would violate the state's constitution. Chicago Tribune Press Service, "LaGuardia's New Job Believed to Stir War Fever," *Chicago Daily Tribune*, May 21, 1941, 6. UP, "Civil 'Army' Plans Shaped," *Los Angeles Times*, May 23, 1941, 5. Ernest Lindley, "LaGuardia and the Civil Defense Program," *Washington Post*, May 25, 1941, B5.

20. "Babies" quoted in Miller, *The War That Never Came*, 47–48. Chicago Tribune Press Service, "LaGuardia's New Job Believed to Stir War Fever," *Chicago Daily Tribune*, May 21, 1941, 6. AP, "Million Men Wanted for Home Guards," *Los Angeles Times*, May 21, 1941, 1. UP, "Civil 'Army' Plans Shaped," *Los Angeles Times*, May 23, 1941, 5. Harold Smith to FDR, May 20, 1941; FDR to Smith, May 21, 1941, F: "Office of Civilian Defense Apr.–July 1941," OF 4422: Office of Civilian Defense, FDRL. FDR wanted to "speed up any careful exploration of

the role of exemptees" in home defense. FDR to Frank Knox, May 20, 1941, Ibid. Presidential Proclamation, draft; Proclamation, May 27, 1941; memo, Watson to FDR, May 28, 1941; FDR to Henry Stimson, May 20, 1941; FDR to Robert Jackson, May 20, 1941. Ibid.

21. *The Daily Missoulian,* May 31, 1941, RG171, E: 10, B: 8, F: 032.1-R. Chicago Tribune Press Service, "LaGuardia's New Job Believed to Stir War Fever," *Chicago Daily Tribune,* May 21, 1941, 6. H. I. Phillips, "The Once Over," *Washington Post,* May 24, 1941, 7. Edward Folliard, "Washington Prepares for Civilian Defense," *Washington Post,* May 25, 1941, B3.

22. Special to the *New York Times,* "La Guardia to Head Home Defense; He Sees President about Program," *New York Times,* May 20, 1941, 1. AP, "Million Men Wanted for Home Guards," *Los Angeles Times,* May 21, 1941, 1. UP, "Civil 'Army' Plans Shaped," *Los Angeles Times,* May 23, 1941, 5. "New Agency for Civilian Defense: Editors' Views," May 30, 1941, no publication, NYCMA, LG, B: 4171, F: 04 OCD: Correspondence #131 (4) 1941/05. Editorial, "Our Country Calls," *West End Press,* May 23, 1941, NYCMA, LG, B: 4171, F: 04 OCD: Correspondence #131 (4) 1941/05. John Higgins to La Guardia, May 21, 1941, NYCMA, LG, B: 4171, F: 04, OCD: Correspondence #131 (4) 1941/05. Joseph Carson Jr., to FDR, May 26, 1941, Ibid. Press Release, City of New York, Office of the Mayor, May 22, 1941, NYCMA, LG, B: 4171, F: 04 OCD: Correspondence #131 (4) 1941/05. Norman November to La Guardia, May 21, 1941; John Morris to La Guardia, May 21, 1941; Frank Novak Jr., to La Guardia, May 29, 1941, RG171, E: 10, B: 111, F: 502-Home Guard, May 1–31, 1941. A. Philip Randolph to La Guardia, May 29, 1941, NYCMA, LG, B: 4171, F: 04 OCD: Correspondence #131 (4) 1941/05. Telegram, Florence Kerr to La Guardia, May 22, 1941; for Kerr pressuring La Guardia to hire Roosevelt, see letter, Kerr to La Guardia, May 22, 1941, RG171, E: 10, B: 92, F: 321: La Guardia, F. H.

23. *Time* "National Affairs: LaGuardia's Job," May 26, 1941. "Civilian Defense is Full-Time Job Run on Part-Time Basis," *Washington Post,* Sept. 6, 1941, 1. *Time* called the headquarters "a commandeered apartment house in Washington." "Confused & Unprepared," *Time,* Dec. 19, 1941, 13. Miller, "The War That Never Came," 47–48. AP, "Broader Registration Will Be Considered," *Washington Post,* May 22, 1941, 3. La Guardia to Bernard Shientag, May 27, 1941; La Guardia to Dennis Mahoney, May 27, 1941, NYCMA, LG, B: 4171, F: 04 OCD: Correspondence #131 (4) 1941/05. UP, "Civil 'Army' Plans Shaped," *Los Angeles Times,* May 23, 1941, 5. "The Nation," *New York Times,* June 1, 1941, E2.

24. Special Dispatch to the Sun, "LaGuardia Dares Nazis to Action," *The Sun,* May 29, 1941. Lawrence Davies, "La Guardia Warns of Aid to Enemy by Lack of Unity," *New York Times,* May 29, 1941, 1.

25. Edward T. Folliard, "Washington Prepares for Civilian Defense," *Washington Post,* May 25, 1941, B3.Lowell H. Brown to La Guardia, June 17, 1941, NYCMA, LG B: 4176, F: 10, OCD Report: Background Story for Civilian Defense Week 1941/11. Brown browbeat La Guardia to get Washington to assure "an adequate air fleet" in case Nazis bombed New York. La Guardia's secretary replied that the mayor knew America's military was ready to defend New York, but he was not at liberty to divulge the secret defense plans.

26. See "LaGuardia Checks on Hub Defense," *Boston Evening American Photo,* RG171, E: 10, B: 92, F: 321: La Guardia: Diary, 1st Corps Area. "Mayor LaGuardia's Diary-June 4, 1941," RG171, E: 10, B: 92, F: 321: La Guardia, Diary, 1st Corps Area. "Air-Raid Wardens Start Enrolling in City Today," *New York Times,* June 20, 1941, 1. La Guardia Address, "Massachusetts Committee on Public Safety Luncheon," June 3, 1941, RG171, E: 10, B: 92, F: 321: La Guardia; Diary: 1st Corps Area. La Guardia Address, "Before the City Defense Commission," Boston, June 3, 1941, Ibid. La Guardia Address, "Mayors' Conference, Hotel Statler, Boston Mass." June 4, 1941, Ibid. June 7, 1941, City Hall, Columbus, Ohio, Ibid. La Guardia to George Field, June 30, 1941, Ibid.

27. La Guardia Address, "Massachusetts Committee on Public Safety Luncheon," June 3, 1941, RG171, E: 10, B: 92, F: 321: La Guardia; Diary: 1st Corps Area. He wanted to train women by exposing them to "mangled bod[ies]" in hospital emergency rooms so they acquired greater "fortitude." La Guardia Address, June 4, 1941, The Mayor's Conference, Hotel Statler, Boston, RG171, E: 10, B: 92, F: La Guardia, Diary, 1st Corps Area. La Guardia needed fewer firefighters in lower Manhattan due to the dense concentration of "fire-proof skyscrapers" and more of them in the Bronx, Coney Island, and Brighton Beach where abundant wood-frame homes

were highly flammable. "You will have to meet your own local situation as it exists," he warned Boston. La Guardia Address, June 7, 1941, City Hall, Columbus, Ohio, RG171, E: 10, B: 92, F: 321: La Guardia, Diary: 5th Corps Area. Mary Mahoney, "'Pray for Me,' Pleads LaGuardia, Tackling Big Home Defense Job," *Boston Globe*, June 4, 1941, NYCMA, LG, B: 4171, F: 04 OCD: Correspondence #131 (4) 1941/05.

28. "Mayor LaGuardia's Diary," June 6, 1941, RG171, E: 10, B: 92, F: 321: La Guardia Diary, 3rd Corps Area. "Mayor LaGuardia's Diary," June 7, 1941, RG 171, E: 10, B: 92, F: 321: La Guardia, Diary, 5th Corps Area. Telegram, to La Guardia, June 20, 1941; La Guardia to Charles Mann, June 25, 1941, RG171, E: 10, B: 2, F: "Criticisms-Protests through January 14, 1942." "Air-Raid Wardens Start Enrolling in City Today," *New York Times*, June 20, 1941, 1. La Guardia Address, June 7, 1941, City Hall, Columbus, Ohio, RG171, E: 10, B: 92, F: 321: La Guardia, Diary: 5th Corps Area. He announced that the government was planning to put any evacuees in rural areas and not in Midwestern cities.

29. La Guardia to Secretary of the Navy, June 11, 1941, RG171, E: 10, B: 10, F: 045, Mar. 1, 1942-. Sherman Miles to La Guardia, Aug. 21, 1941, and attached memo from Miles to La Guardia, Aug. 21, 1941, RG171, E: 12, B; 2, F: Confidential: 020: June 17–Nov. 22, 1941.

30. Sumner Welles to La Guardia, July 8, 1941; and memo, La Guardia to Cordell Hull, n.d. RG171, E: 10, B: 27, F: 091-Foreign Countries. One La Guardia aide wanted to launch a counter-propaganda effort across Central America; another saw PR benefits from using "our OCD symbols" in the region and hoped La Guardia "will have an opportunity to exercise his leadership in this important field." George Saunders to no name, Aug. 9, 1941, RG171, E: 10, B: 104, F: 381-9: Commercial/Cultural Relationship—Americas. George Saunders to Mayor Walmsley, Aug. 30, 1941, RG171, E: 10, B: 104, F: 381-9: Commercial and Cultural Relationship between Americas. George Saunders to Mayor Walmsley, Sept. 19, 1941, Ibid. J. Edgar Hoover to Assistant Chief of Staff, War Department, Aug. 28, 1941; La Guardia to Franklin D'Olier, Sept. 4, 1941; D'Olier to La Guardia, Sept. 8, 1941, RG171, E: 12, B; 1, F: Loose, No. 3. AP, "Finger Printing of All Population is Recommended," *Christian Science Monitor*, Aug. 29, 1941, 3. James Kirby to Duncan Cassidy, July 30, 1941, RG171, B: 26, F: "England to Oct. 31, 1941." La Guardia to Secretary of the Navy, June 12, 1941. The letter also went out to Secretaries of War, Interior and other Departments. RG171, E: 10, B: 11, F: 045, to July 31, 1941. Quoted in Lash, *Eleanor and Franklin*, 645. International News Service, "LaGuardia Gets Talent from Agencies by Lend-Lease Process," *Washington Post*, Sept. 28, 1941, 10.

31. G. K. Donald to Secretary of State Hull, "Strictly Confidential," June 14, 1941, RG171, E: 10, B: 27, F: 091, Canada to 9/30/41. "Information Secured in England by American Observers," 2, 3, 5, 7–14. Also see memo, Leo Seybold to F. Lloyd Eno, June 3, 1941, RG171, B: 26, F: "England to Oct. 31, 1941." As one U.S. summary said, women excelled at navigating "the worst type of 'blitz.'" The report condescendingly added that "with their minds unoccupied," women became "very jittery." La Guardia to FDR, June 12, 1941, F: "President's Secretary's File Subject File Office of Civilian Defense: 1941," PSF: 145, FDRL. La Guardia to J. Edward Rogers, June 30, 1941. Ibid. La Guardia to The Viscount Halifax, K. G., June 18, 1941; La Guardia to Cordell Hull, Sept. 3, 1941, RG171, E: 10, B: 25, F: 091-British Mission, Bingham. "England Promises Help to La Guardia," *New York Times*, May 25, 1941, 12. Herbert Morrison to La Guardia, July 18, 1941, RG171, B: 26, F: "England to Oct. 31, 1941." Herbert Morrison to La Guardia, Aug. 18, 1941, RG171, E: 10, B: 25, F: 091-British Mission. La Guardia to Edward J. Kelly, June 5, 1941, RG171, E: 10, B: 110, F: 501-Police Cooperation.

32. Edwin Watson to John Kelly, June 26, 1941, F: "Office of Civilian Defense Apr.–July 1941," OF 4422: Office of Civilian Defense, FDRL. For a summary of Rosenberg's career, see "Rosenberg, Anna Marie Lederer," by Elisabeth Israels Perry, in *Notable American Women: A Biographical Dictionary, Completing the Twentieth Century*, ed., Susan Ware (Cambridge, MA: Harvard University Press, 2004). "Office of Facts and Figures," Sept. 23, 1943, LoC: Archibald MacLeish Papers, B: 52, F: Subject File: OFF: "History of the Office of Facts and Figures."

33. FDR to La Guardia, July 14, 1941, F: "Office of Civilian Defense Apr.–July 1941," OF 4422: Office of Civilian Defense, FDRL. "Air-Raid Wardens Start Enrolling in City Today,"

New York Times, June 20, 1941, 1. La Guardia to FDR, June 12, 1941, F: "President's Secretary's File Subject File Office of Civilian Defense: 1941," PSF: 145, FDRL.

34. Adlai Stevenson to La Guardia, Aug. 4, 1941; and attached memo, "Proposed Organization," drafted by Stevenson, RG171, E: 10, B: 10, F: 045, Aug. 1–Oct. 31, 1941.

35. *New York Times*, "Air-Raid Wardens Start Enrolling in City Today," June 20, 1941, 1. John Mitchell, "If the Bombers Come to Us," *The Living Age*, Aug. 1941; 360, 4499; APS Online, 532.

36. La Guardia, "If Enemy Bombers Come … " *Los Angeles Times*, Aug. 17, 1941, H8. John Mitchell, "If the Bombers Come to Us," *The Living Age*, Aug. 1941; 360, 4499; APS Online, 532. "Air-Raid Wardens Start Enrolling in City Today," *New York Times*, June 20, 1941, 1. Report attached to La Guardia's dear Colleague letter, June 18, 1941, "Emergency Fire Defense: Plan to Provide Adequate Protection Immediately," RG171, E: 10, B: 124, F: 520-Fire Protection, Apr. 1–June 19, 1941. Cross-Reference Sheet, June 10, 1941, La Guardia, F: "Office of Civilian Defense Apr.–July 1941," OF 4422: Office of Civilian Defense, FDRL. Miller, *The War that Never Came*, 49–50. George Field to La Guardia, May 26, 1941; La Guardia to George Field, June 30, 1941; Cross-Reference Sheet, Mrs. William Pouch, June 4, 1941, RG171, E: 10, B: 39, F: 095—Committee to Defend America.

37. "Office of Facts and Figures," Sept. 23, 1943, LoC: Archibald MacLeish Papers, B: 52, F: Subject File: OFF: "History of the Office of Facts and Figures." L. W. Hutchins to Marvin McIntyre, June 9, 1941, F: "Office of Civilian Defense Apr.–July 1941," OF 4422: Office of Civilian Defense, FDRL. John Mitchell, "If the Bombers Come to Us," *The Living Age*, Aug. 1941; 360, 4499; APS Online, 532.

38. "Transcript of Telephone Conversation with Mayor LaGuardia," May 29, 1941, RG171, E: 10, B: 51, F: 095: L.

39. "Civilian Defense is Full-Time Job Run on Part-Time Basis," *Washington Post*, Sept. 6, 1941, 1. Sumner Welles to La Guardia, July 8, 1941; and memo, La Guardia to Cordell Hull, n.d., RG171, E: 10, B: 27, F: 091-Foreign Countries. Cross-Reference Sheet, M .C. Hazen, July 12, 1941, Ibid. International News Service, "The President's Day," *Washington Post*, July 19, 1941, 2. La Guardia to Frank Dixon, Aug. 4, 1941, RG171, E: 10, B: 124, F: 520-Fire Protection, 6/20-8/31/41. La Guardia to Percy Bugbee, July 3, 1941, Ibid. L. D. Gasser to the Chief of Staff, June 20, 1941, RG171, E: 10, B: 126, F: 525-Gas Defense, thru Feb. 15, 1942. La Guardia to W. Cooper Green, Mayor of Birmingham, July 24, 1941, RG171, E: 10, B: 104, F: 420.2. Telegram, Harold Stassen to La Guardia, Aug. 1, 1941, RG171, E: 11, B: 51, F: 520: Region VI, IL. Quoted in Lash, *Eleanor and Franklin*, 641. W. L. to FDR, June 26, 1941; J. Edgar Hoover to La Guardia, Nov. 22, 1941, and attached FBI Report made by J. R. McCulloch, Oct. 1, 1941. RG171, E: 12, B: 1, F: Loose, No. 3.

40. La Guardia, "If Enemy Bombers Come … " *Los Angeles Times*, Aug. 17, 1941, H8.

Chapter 8

1. "Suggestions for the Agenda of the Volunteer Participation Committee" and "Notes on the Proposed Agenda," n.d., RG171, E: 10, B: 83, F: 200 "Volunteer Participation, -Dec. 15, 1941." Lash, *Eleanor and Franklin*, 640–642.

2. ER, "My Day," Apr. 2 and Apr. 14, 1941.

3. ER, "My Day," Apr. 16, Apr. 22, Apr. 30, July 30, and July 31, 1941. ER, "What's Wrong with the Draft," *Look* 5 (July 15, 1941): 23–25, in Black, 395–397.

4. ER, My Day, June 28 and Sept. 23, 1941. ER to Myrtle Reeves, May 12, 1941, F: "Re 1941," ER 100: Personal Letters 1941 Pi-Ri, ERP, FDRL.

5. For an excellent discussion of the invasion of Russia and diplomatic tensions in the Pacific, see Kennedy, *Freedom from Fear, Part II*, 83–87. *Defense*, 8, 10, 12, 13, "State and Local Cooperation … "; "Health and Welfare … " "Consumer Division," Mar. 11, 1941, Vol. 2, No. 10, F: "Council of National Defense Reports 1941," OF 813a: Council of National Defense, FDRL. ER, "My Day," Nov. 19, 1941.

6. ER, "My Day," June 11, 1941. ER distinguished her idea for national service from her husband's agenda, pointing out that her proposal was hers alone and not the president's. ER, "My Day," Nov. 19, May 8, May 9, Apr. 19, Aug. 28, Aug. 29, June 21, June 23, 1941. *Defense*, 8, 10,

12, 13, "State and Local Cooperation . . . "; "Health and Welfare . . . " "Consumer Division," Mar. 11, 1941, Vol. 2, No. 10, F: "Council of National Defense Reports 1941," OF 813a: Council of National Defense, FDRL. William Fulton, "Women Alarmed by Drift Toward Regimentation," *Chicago Daily Tribune*, Nov. 12, 1941, 5. Eleanor Roosevelt, "Defense and Girls," *Ladies' Home Journal* 58 (May 1941): 25, 54, in Black, *What I Hope to Leave Behind*, 501–503. If she subscribed to many of the gender roles of her day, she also envisioned women as fuller participants in the nation's economic life. When she saw ten women in an NYA Boston program making truck parts, she hailed their "physical ability." ER, "What's the Matter with Women?" *Liberty* 18 (May 3, 1941): 12–13, in Black, *What I Hope to Leave Behind*, 265–267.

7. ER, "My Day," May 17, 1941. William Fulton, "Women Alarmed by Drift Toward Regimentation," *Chicago Daily Tribune*, Nov. 12, 1941, 5. "Defense and Girls," *Ladies' Home Journal* 58 (May 1941): 25, 54, in Black, *What I Hope to Leave Behind*, 501–503. Memo, draft, anonymous to ER, Apr. 28, 1941, RG171, E: 12, B: 3, F: Confidential: 200.

8. Cross-Reference Sheet, Florence Kerr, May 22, 1941, F: "Office of Civilian Defense Endorsements 1941–42," OF 4422: Office of Civilian Defense, FDRL. Telegram, Florence Kerr to La Guardia, May 22, 1941; for Kerr pressuring La Guardia to hire Eleanor Roosevelt, see letter, Kerr to La Guardia, May 22, 1941, RG171, E: 10, B: 92, F: 321: La Guardia. La Guardia agreed to meet with Kerr and representatives of the Volunteer Women of America to discuss the home defense issue. But there's no evidence that anything significant came of their conversation. "Schedule of Appointments," May 23, 1941, NYCMA, LG, B: 4171, F: 04 OCD: Correspondence #131 (4) 1941/05. Cross-Reference Sheet, Harriet Elliott, May 22, 1941, F: "Office of Civilian Defense Endorsements 1941–42," OF 4422: Office of Civilian Defense, FDRL.

9. Lash, *Eleanor and Franklin*, 640–641. ER, "My Day," June 18, 1941. Eleanor Roosevelt praised the opportunities that New York's NYA program afforded almost 3,000 African Americans in La Guardia's city. ER, "My Day," May 29, 1941.

10. ER, "My Day," July 30, July 31, 1941. Secretary to ER, May 21, 1941, F: "1941 I-Ja," ER 70: Correspondence with Government Departments, ERP, FDRL. Samuel Grafton, "I'd Rather Be Right," May 9, 1941, *Philadelphia Record*, F: "40.2 Messages Refused 1941 M," ER40.2: Messages Refused, ERP, FDRL. M.H. McIntyre to Marion Ripy, June 10, 1941, Ibid. Jeannette Rankin to La Guardia, June 5, 1941, RG171, E: 10, B: 8, F: 032.1-R. Cross Reference Sheet, to Paul McNutt, Apr. 14, 1941, F: "Federal Security Agency 1941," OF 3700: Federal Security Agency, FDRL. FDR to ER, June 6, 1941, F: "Office of Civilian Defense April-July 1941," OF 4422: Office of Civilian Defense, FDRL. Florence Kerr to ER, May 26, 1941, F: "Mar.–Aug.1941 Kerr, Florence," ER70: Correspondence with Government Departments, ERP, FDRL. FDR, Fireside Chat, Dec. 29, 1940, UCSB, the American Presidency Project, http://www.presidency.ucsb.edu/ws/?pid=15917.

11. Williams, *City of Ambition*, 308–312. Lash, *Eleanor and Franklin*, 640–641.

12. No Author, "LaGuardia Bars Civil Defense Registration," *Washington Post*, June 19, 1941, 4. ER to Florence Kerr, July 22, 1941, F: "Mar.–Aug. 1941 Kerr, Florence," ER 70: Correspondence with Government Departments, ERP, FDRL. Anna Rosenberg to La Guardia, Aug. 22, 1941; T. S. Walmsley to Eloise Davison, Aug. 30, 1941, RG171, E: 10, B: 83, F: 200 "Volunteer Participation, -Dec. 15, 1941." ER, "My Day," July 8, July 9, and July 24, 1941. Secretary to ER to Mrs. Harry Rogers Pratt, Sept. 3, 1941, F: "1940–44, K-R," ER 40.3: Messages Requested-White House, ERP, FRDL. Other requests for White House visits from people around the country appear in these folders. ER, "My Day," Aug. 30, Sept. 1, and Sept. 9, 1941. Cross-Reference Sheet, La Guardia, July 8, 1941, F: "Office of Civilian Defense Apr.–July 1941," OF 4422: Office of Civilian Defense, FDRL.

13. For a list of Committee members, see "Civilian Defense: Volunteer Office," United States Office of Civilian Defense, Washington, D.C., https://archive.org/stream/ ACivilianDefenseVolunteerOffice/ACivilianDefenseVolunteerOffice_djvu.txt. Quoted in Lash, *Eleanor and Franklin*, 641.

14. Press Release, "Informal Remarks of the President to Members of the Volunteer Participation Committee," July 24, 1941, F: "1941–42," OF 4422c: Office of Civilian Defense Volunteer Participation, FDRL. He called women "as important in the defense of Britain as men on a

destroyer." "Civilian Defense is Full-Time Job Run on Part-Time Basis," *Washington Post*, Sept. 6, 1941, 1. Lash, *Eleanor and Franklin*, 641.

15. "Civilian Defense is Full-Time Job Run on Part-Time Basis," *Washington Post*, Sept. 6, 1941, 1. "Need for More Child Centers Stressed as Aid to Mothers Taking Defense Jobs," *New York Times*, Oct. 15, 1941, 16. San Diego considered a plan to fingerprint all children. "Appointees, Civilian Participation Program, Fourth Civilian Defense Area," n.d., RG171 E:10, B:83, F: 200 "Volunteer Participation, -Dec. 15, 1941. "Daily Information Digest of the Medical Division," Sept. 3; Sept. 8; Sept. 16; Oct. 8; Oct. 9; Oct. 23, 1941, RG171, E: 10, B: 101, F: 380-101: Daily Info Digest, 10/31, 41; Nov. 24; Dec. 1; Dec. 9, 1941, Dec. 11, 1941, Nov. 1–Dec. 31, 1941. Cornelia Bryce Pinchot to ER, Sept. 13, 1941, F: "1941 Pinchot, Gifford & Mrs.," ER 100: Personal Letters 1941 Pi-Ri, ERP, FDRL. Chapman, Oscar, OH, Harry S. Truman Library, http://www.trumanlibrary.org/oralhist/chapman.htm#subjects.

16. Kerr quoted in Lash, *Eleanor and Franklin*, 641. *Washington Post*, "Civilian Defense is Full-Time Job Run on Part-Time Basis," Sept. 6, 1941, 1. Albert Gailord Hart to Charles Friley, Aug. 30, 1941, RG171, E: 10, B: 2, F: "Criticisms-Protests through January 14, 1942." Copyright by New York Times, "Volunteer Civil Defense Board Created," *Washington Post*, Sept. 14, 1941, 8. ER quoted in Lash, *Eleanor and Franklin*, 641–642.

17. Ernest Lindley, "The OCD Flounders," *Washington Post*, Sept. 5, 1941, 11. Other critics continued to charge that the mayor had "too many irons in the fire" and neglected civilian participation, as one letter to the *Washington Post* asserted. ER, "My Day," Sept. 3, 1941. ER quoted in Lash, *Eleanor and Franklin*, 642.

18. Lash, *Eleanor and Franklin*, 640–642 (Rosenberg quoted on 642). ER, "My Day," Sept. 15, 1941. Helen Gahagan to ER, Sept. 15, 1941; ER to Helen Gahagan, Sept. 16, 1941, F: "1941 Gahagan, Helen," ER 100: Personal Letters 1941 Go-Her, ERP, FDRL. Blanche Stover to ER, Sept. 30, 1941, and attached draft essay, "The objectives of . . . ," n.d., F: "1941 L-R," ER40.1: Messages Sent, ERP, FDRL. Frank Kluckhohn, "Public Morale Viewed as a Defense Problem," *New York Times*, Aug. 31, 1941. E8

19. Quotes come from Lash, *Eleanor and Franklin*, 641–642.

20. ER to Cornelia Bryce Pinchot, Sept. 19, 1941; Malvina Thompson to Cornelia Bryce Pinchot, Sept. 24, 1941, F: "1941 Pinchot, Gifford & Mrs." ER100: Personal Letters, ERP, FDRL. Lash, *Eleanor and Franklin*, 643. Helen Gahagan to ER, Sept. 15, 1941; ER to Helen Gahagan, Sept. 16, 1941, F: "1941 Gahagan, Helen," ER100: Personal Letters 1941 Go-Her, ERP, FDRL. Blanche Stover to ER, Sept. 30, 1941, and attached draft essay, "The objectives of . . . ," n.d., F: "1941 L-R," ER40.1: Messages Sent, ERP, FDRL. ER quotes on Hall and mother-in-law come from Goodwin, *No Ordinary Time*, 279–280. ER, "My Day," Sept. 11, Sept. 15, Sept. 26, 1941.

21. ER, "My Day," Sept. 17, Sept. 19, Sept. 30, 1941. See Goodwin, *No Ordinary Time*, 280, for discussion of the unprecedented nature of her appointment. Dallas Dort to ER, Sept. 20, 1941; ER to Helen Gahagan, Sept. 16, 1941, F: "1941 Gahagan, Helen," ER100: Personal Letters 1941 Go-Her, ERP, FDRL. On October 23, an office manager in home defense headquarters sent her the official appointment letter. "List of Employees of the Office of Civilian Defense," Sept. 17, 1941, NYCMA, LG B: 4174, F: 12 OCD: Corr (4) 1941/09.

22. Tommy quoted in Goodwin, *No Ordinary Time*, 280. ER, "My Day," Sept. 17, Sept. 19, Sept. 30, 1941.

23. Lash, *Eleanor and Franklin*, 644. ER, "My Day," Sept. 16, 1941. For description of Seaver, see "Confused & Unprepared," *Time*, Dec. 19, 1941, 13.

24. Anna Rosenberg to ER, Sept. 27, 1941, and attached letter dated Sept. 17 1941, RG171, E: 10, B: 83, F: 200 "Volunteer Participation, -Dec. 15, 1941." Lash, *Eleanor and Franklin*, 643–644. Also see Goodwin, *No Ordinary Time*, 281. Mayor's Schedule, Sept. 17 to Oct. 5, RG171, E: 10, B: 92, F: 321: La Guardia, F.H. Appointments. ER, "My Day," Sept. 24, Sept. 30, Oct. 7, 1941.

25. La Guardia to "all Members of Volunteer Participation Committee," Oct. 4, 1941. RG171, E: 10, B: 83, F: 200 "Volunteer Participation, -Dec. 15, 1941." ER, *This I Remember*, 231–232. Goodwin, *No Ordinary Time*, 279–280. Lash, *Eleanor and Franklin*, 644–645. ER, My Day, Sept. 11, Sept. 25, Sept. 26, Oct. 6, Oct. 20, Nov. 1, Nov. 3, James Landis to T. Semmes

Walmsley, Sept. 26, 1941, RG171, E: 10, B: 83, F: 200 "Volunteer Participation, -Dec. 15, 1941."

26. Lee Geyer to La Guardia, Sept. 26, 1941, RG171, E: 10, B: 2, F: "Criticisms-Protests through January 14, 1942." "Reports from the Regional Directors in response to Wire . . . ," Sept. 27, 1941, RG171, E: 10, B: 83, F: 200 "Volunteer Participation, -Dec. 15, 1941. T.S. Walmsley to ER, Oct. 8, 1941; T.S. Walmsley to ER, Sept. 30, 1941, Ibid.

27. Trumbull Marshall, Letter to the Times, *New York Times*, Oct. 4, 1941, 14. Goodwin, *No Ordinary Time*, 281. Paul Kellogg to Raymond Clapper, Feb. 9, 1942; ER to Corrington Gill, Oct. 24, 1941, F: "1942 Kellogg, Paul," ER 100: Personal Letters 1942 Ilma, Viola-Ke, ERP, FDRL. For Polier's background, see memo to ER on Justine Wise Polier; and memo on Polier, both dated Feb. 9, 1942, F: "ER O.C.D. Offers of Service 1942 P-R.," ER 71: Office of Civil Defense, ERP, FDRL. On Dec. 1, Polier received a paid position at the OCD, although she was only making about 50 percent of the salary she earned as a judge. Polier and Eleanor worked together to come up with recommendations to improve the national welfare. Lash, *Eleanor and Franklin*, 644–646. Wilmer Shields to ER, Oct. 23, 1941, RG171, E: 10, B: 83, F: 200 "Volunteer Participation, -Dec. 15, 1941." Mrs. J.M. Helm to Eloise Davison, Oct. 22, 1941, RG171, E: 10, B: 99, F: 380-10: OCD, Aug. 1, 1941–June 30, 1942. ER, "My Day," Oct. 1, Oct. 7, Nov. 8, 1941.

28. Press Release, Oct. 2, 1941, Transcript of ER's Remarks, Office of Civilian Defense, RG171, E: 10, B: 124, F: 520-Fire Protection, Oct. 1–30, 1941. ER, "My Day," Oct. 2, Oct. 3, Oct. 23, Nov. 8, 1941. Edith Haspel to ER, Oct. 14, 1941; Eloise Davison to Mrs. Joseph Haspel, Nov. 8, 1941; La Guardia to Jane Seaver, Nov. 1, 1941, RG171, E: 10, B: 83, F: 200 "Volunteer Participation, -Dec. 15, 1941." Davison replied on the first lady's behalf that female citizens would get their chance to volunteer, which would make women more " 'crisis conscious' " and "less neurotic." William J. A. Glancy to ER, Nov. 24, 1941, RG171, E: 10, B: 83, F: "Women in Defense, Nov. 1–Nov. 30, 1941."

29. George H. Lyon to ER, Oct. 2, 1941, RG171, E: 10, B: 83, F: 200 "Volunteer Participation, -Dec. 15, 1941."

30. Elinor Morgenthau to ER, Oct. 27, 1941, RG171, E: 10, B: 83, F: 200 "Volunteer Participation, -Dec. 15, 1941." It's unclear if ER and her team ever found reporters who actually carried out Morgenthau's proposed agenda. But the fact that they were seriously entertaining this suggests that they saw the press as an ally immobilizing the country to endorse a wartime New Deal.

31. "Suggestions for the Agenda of the Volunteer Participation Committee" and "Notes on the Proposed Agenda," n.d., "Suggestions for Agenda to be used for the meeting of the Volunteer Participation Committee," n.d., RG171, E: 10, B: 83, F: 200 "Volunteer Participation, -Dec. 15, 1941." La Guardia to "All Members of Volunteer Participation Committee," Oct. 18, 1941, Ibid.

32. Ray Tucker, "The Man Who'll Keep You Safe," n.d., no publication, in NYCMA, LG B: 4176, F: 03 OCD: Corr (1) 1941/11. La Guardia to Mrs. John Boettiger, Oct. 11, 1941, RG171, E: 10, B: 101, F: 380-102: Volunteer Participation Committee, thru 3/31/42. La Guardia to "All Members of Volunteer Participation Committee," Oct. 18, 1941, Ibid. La Guardia to "Dear Mrs . . . ," NYCMA, LG, B: 4175, F: 10 OCD: Corr (2) 1941/10. Office of Civilian Defense, Press Release, n.d. NYCMA, LG, B: 4176, F: 10, OCD: Report: Background Story for Civilian Defense Week 1941/11. La Guardia to Jane Seaver, Oct. 25, 1941, RG171, E: 10, B: 101, F: 380-102: Volunteer Participation Committee, thru 3/31/42. La Guardia to Jane Seaver, Nov. 1, 1941, RG171, E: 10, B: 101, F: 380-102: Volunteer Participation Committee, thru July 31, 1942. ER, *This I Remember*, 230–231.

33. ER, My Day, Oct. 15, Oct. 16, Oct. 17, Oct. 22, Oct. 30, Oct. 31, 1941 Barry Bingham to ER, Oct. 25, 1941, RG171, E: 10, B: 101, F: 380-102: Volunteer Participation Committee, thru 3/31/42. ER to T.S. Walmsley, Oct. 27, 1941; T. S. Walmsley to ER, Oct. 25, 1941, RG171, E: 10, B: 83, F: 200 "Volunteer Participation, -Dec. 15, 1941." Christine Sadler, "Civilian Defense Office 'Digs In'-Housekeeping Registrants Unresponsive," *Washington Post*, Nov. 8, 1941, 10. Anna Rosenberg to ER, Oct. 11, 1941, RG171, E: 10, B: 83, F: 200 "Volunteer Participation, -Dec. 15, 1941." H. H. Dudley to ER, n.d. RG171, E: 10, B: 85, F: 230-Veterans' Participation

thru Jan. 31, 1942. La Guardia to "members of the Volunteer Participation Committee," Nov. 15, 1941, RG171, E: 10, B: 83, F: 200 "Volunteer Participation, -Dec. 15, 1941."

34. Eloise Davison to Emily Barringer, Nov. 27, 1941; Anna Rosenberg to La Guardia, Nov. 7, 1941; J.S. Deutschle to Corrington Gill, Nov. 5, 1941, RG171, E: 10, B: 83, F: "Women in Defense, Nov. 1–Nov. 30, 1941." "Verbatim Transcript of Proceedings, Archibald MacLeish's Speech," Nov. 8, 1941, RG171, E: 10, B: 99, F: OFF. Eloise Davison to Archibald MacLeish, Oct. 31, 1941, and attached Conference agenda, and notes for MacLeish on "November 8 Meeting," RG171, E: 10, B: 99, F: OFF. Eloise Davison to ER, Nov. 7, 1941; Mrs. Roy C. F. Weagly to ER, Nov. 28, 1941; Grace Frysinger to Eloise Davison, Nov. 14, 1941, RG171, E: 10, B: 83, F: "Women in Defense, Nov. 1–Nov. 30, 1941." The conference, about one dozen women in the federal government informed Davison, raised "many fine points." Elisabeth von Hesse to ER, Nov. 14, 1941, Ibid. Not everybody found the conference satisfactory. Three of the women there longed for a franker dialogue. "We paid our own expenses . . . traveled long distances . . . [and] only hear[d] from the Civilian Defense heads whose speeches we read in the papers every week," one woman upbraided the first lady. Instead of hearing like-minded women discuss how they used their skills to advance social defense, the audience was fed a diet of threadbare ideas; this critic vowed to submit "a very unsatisfactory report" to her board. ER, "My Day," Nov. 7, Nov. 10, 1941.

35. "Civil Defense Week Activity Set at Schools," *Washington Post*, Nov. 9, 1941, 5. "Newcomers Urged to Join D.C. Defense," *Washington Post*, Nov. 13, 1941, 15. ER, "My Day," Nov. 13, Nov. 15, 1941. Papers of ER, Document 213, Broadcast, Nov. 16, 1941, George Washington University Gelman Library.

36. Alice Drake to ER, Nov. 19, 1941; ER to Drake, Nov. 25, 1941, RG171, E: 10, B: 83, F: "Women in Defense, Nov. 1–Nov. 30, 1941." La Guardia to All Members of the Volunteer Participation Committee, Nov. 8, 1941, RG171, B: 101, F: 380-101: Volunteer Participation Committee, Mar. 31, 1942. Speech Draft attached to letter from Elisabeth von Hesse to ER, Nov. 14, 1941, RG171, E: 10, B: 83, F: "Women in Defense, Nov. 1-Nov. 30, 1941." Tom Cushing to Adjutant General, Nov. 8, 1941; and Eloise Davison to Cushing, Nov. 22, 1941. RG171, E: 10, B: 83, F: "Women in Defense, Nov. 1–Nov. 30, 1941." Cross Reference Sheet, La Guardia to Zeidler, Nov. 15, 1941; Zeidler to La Guardia, Oct. 29, 1941, RG171, E: 10, B: 83, F: "Women in Defense, Nov. 1–Nov. 30, 1941."

37. ER to La Guardia, Nov. 22, 1941, RG171, E: 10, B: 83, F: "Women in Defense, Nov. 1-Nov. 30, 1941." ER, "My Day," Nov. 20, Nov. 22, 1941. ER to La Guardia, Nov. 25, 1941; La Guardia to ER, Nov. 26, 1941, NYCMA, LG B: 4176, F: 05, OCD: Corr (3) 1941/11. Office of Civilian Defense, Press Release, Nov. 29, 1941, RG171, E: 10, B: 83, F: "Women in Defense, Nov. 1–Nov. 30, 1941."

38. ER to Mrs. Anthony Drexel Biddle, Jr., Nov. 25, 1941, RG171, E: 10, B: 83, F: "Women in Defense, Nov. 1–Nov. 30, 1941." ER to La Guardia, Nov. 27, 1941; Justine Wise Polier to ER, Nov. 28, 1941; Paul Kellogg to Judge Justine Wise Polier, n.d.; ER to La Guardia, Nov. 29, 1941, Ibid.

Chapter 9

1. Henry Stimson and Ralph Bard to La Guardia, Sept. 29, 1941, RG389, E: 468, B: 1939, F: Civil Defense Training.

2. Lester Stone to W. W. Chaplin, Oct. 4, 1941; and Chaplin to La Guardia, Sept. 26, 1941. NYCMA, LG, B: 4175, F: 09, OCD: Corr (1) 1941/10. Franklin D'Olier to La Guardia, Sept. 10, 1941, NYCMA, LG B: 4174, F: 11 OCD: Corr (3) 1941/09. From no name to La Guardia, Sept. 10, 1941, Ibid.

3. Office of Civilian Defense, press release, Sept. 14, 1941, NYCMA, LG, B: 4174, F: 12, OCD: Corr (4) 1941/09. OCD, *Daily Information Digest*, Sept. 4, 1941, RG171, E: 10, B: 101, F: 380-101: *Daily Info Digest*, Oct. 31, 1941. Press Release, "Air Force Combat Command to Hold Interceptor Exercises in October," Sept. 3, 1941, RG171, E: 10, B; 99, F: 380-10: OCD, May 1–July 31, 1941. And see T. Semmes Walmsley to Directors, Civilian Defense Regional Offices, Sept. 12, 1941, RG171, E: 10, B; 99, F: 380-10: OCD, 5/1–7/31/41. Press Release,

"Details of Interceptor Exercises on Eastern Seaboard During October," Sept. 18, 1941, War Department, RG171, E: 10, B: 99, F: 380-10: OCD, May 1–July 31, 1941.

4. See Kennedy, *Freedom From Fear*, 497–500.

5. La Guardia, Office of Civilian Defense, Informational Bulletin, Sept. 20, 1941, RG171, E: 46, B: 4, F: 020-War Dept. (4 of 4). T. S. Walmsley to La Guardia, Sept. 11, 1941, RG171, E: 10, B: 99, F: 380-10: OCD, 8/1/41–6/31/42. La Guardia to Military Attache, Sept. 27, 1941, RG171, E: 10, B: 26, F: England to Oct. 31, 1941. "Peaceful Newton Has Elaborately Trained Civil Defense Groups," *Christian Science Monitor*, Oct. 31, 1941, 16. Staff Correspondent, "Syracuse High in Civilian Defense Work," *Christian Science Monitor*, Oct. 16, 1941, 17. "First Aid: It is Citizen's Big Civilian Defense Job"; Margaret Leech, "Wartime Washington," NYCMA, LG, B: 4175, F: 02, OCD: Magazine (2) 1941/09/29. Interviewing Date Sept. 19–24, 1941, Survey #248-K Question #4a; Interviewing Date Sept. 19–24, 1941, Survey #248-K Question #6; Interviewing Date Oct. 3–8, 1941, Survey #249 Question #1, http://ibiblio.org/pha/Gallup/Gallup%201941.htm.

6. Press Release, Office of the Mayor City of New York, Sept. 23, 1941, NYCMA, LG B: 4174, F: 13, OCD: Corr (5). "Home Front: Terrible Bombings," *Time*, Oct. 6, 1941.

7. "'Raid' Soon to Test Harbor's Defense," *New York Times*, Oct. 4, 1941, 8. "Police War Plans Get First Big Test," *New York Times*, Oct. 11, 1941, 6. "AIR: Wings Over Manhattan," *Time*, Oct. 20, 1941.

8. "'Raid' Soon to Test Harbor's Defense," *New York Times*, Oct. 4, 1941, 8. "'Invasion' of City Part of Mock War," *New York Times*, Oct. 7, 1941, 17.

9. La Guardia to Sir R. I. Campbell, Sept. 5, 1941; "Reference Memorandum," Conference with Sir Wilson Jameson, Oct. 18, 1941, RG171, E: 10, B: 26, F: "England to Oct. 31, 1941." Harry Prince to La Guardia, Sept. 15, 1941, and attached Summary Report of Civilian Defense Studies in England, July 16 to Aug. 15, 1941, NYCMA, LG, B: 4175, F: 07, OCD: Civilian Defense Studies in England, Sept. 15, 1941. Donald Leonard and Arthur Wallander to La Guardia, Sept. 23, 1941, and attached report on "Police Civilian Defense," NYCMA, LG, B: 4175, F: 08, OCD: Report, Duties of Police in Civilian Defense," Sept. 23, 1941.

10. La Guardia to Marriner Eccles, Sept. 5, 1941, RG171, E: 12, B: 3, F: Confidential: 400. James Forrestal to La Guardia, Sept. 9, 1941; La Guardia to Forrestal, Sept. 11, 1941, RG171, E: 12, B: 1, F: Confidential, 000.

11. La Guardia to Frank Knox, Sept. 29, 1941, RG171, E: 12, B: 1, F: Confidential: CAP: Chronological. La Guardia to FDR, Sept. 23, 1941, and Attached Legislative Proposal (Exhibits A, B, C), RG171, E: 10, B: 109, F: 500-Civilian Protection. One memo estimated costs of more than $57 million for auxiliary firefighting equipment and more than $26 million for gas masks; these were by far the two most expensive items in the proposed budget. See memo for "The Board for Civilian Protection," n.d., Ibid. Chicago Tribune Press Service, "Plans for National Policemen Hinted," *Los Angeles Times*, Oct. 2, 1941, 1.

12. Henry Stimson to La Guardia, Nov. 3, 1941, and attached memo to "All officers," n.d., RG171, E: 10, B: 5, F: 020, Nov. 1–17, 1941. La Guardia to Jane Seaver, Nov. 22, RG171, E: 10, B: 101, E: 380-102: Volunteer Participation Committee, thru May 31, 1942. John Dick to Corrington Gill, Oct. 31, 1941, RG171, E: 10, B: 125, F: 520.1-Fire School, Oct. 1–Dec. 31, 1941.

13. J. Edgar Hoover to James Landis, Feb. 18, 1942, "Personal and Confidential," RG171, E: 12, B: 1, F: Loose, No. 7. La Guardia to Roy LeCraw, Oct. 23, 1941, RG171, E: 10, B: 110, F: 501-Police Cooperation.

14. Colonel Burn to General Gasser, Oct. 31, 1941, RG171, E: 10, B: 103, F: 381-6: OPM, 7/1-12/31/41. Also see L. D. Gasser to V. Clair, Nov. 10, 1941, RG171, E: 10, B: 103, F: 381-6: OPM, July 1–Dec. 31, 1941. "First Aid for Civilian Defense Units," n.d., RG171, E: 10, B: 131, F: 729: First Aid, thru Nov. 30, 1941.

15. Editorial, "Please, Fiorello, No Air Raid Wardens," *Chicago Daily Tribune*, Sept. 10, 1941, 14.

16. Memo for The Press Conference, Oct. 24, 1941; La Guardia to FDR, Oct. 24, 1941, F: "La Guardia, Fiorello 1940–1945," PPF 1376: La Guardia, Fiorello, FDRL. "La Guardia Gets New Deal Blessing," *New York Times*, Oct. 3, 1941, 16. "Priorities Urged on Transit Needs," *New York Times*, Oct. 3, 1941, 47. "Weekly Analysis of Press Reaction," Nov. 14, 1941, F: "National Emergency Council 1941," OF 788: National Emergency Council, 1938–Feb. 1942, FDRL.

17. "Mayor Sees U.S. on Brink of War," *New York Times*, Nov. 1, 1941, 4. "New York: Tigers Have Nine Lives," *Time*, Oct. 27, 1941.
18. Memo, J. S. Steiner to Captain James Harten, Oct. 3, 1941, RG171, E: 10, B: 92, F: 321: La Guardia, F. H. L. D. Gasser to John McKenzie, Oct. 9, 1941, RG171, E: 10, B: 127, F: 530-Defense Communication Systems.
19. Daniel Sweeney to Major Reed Landis, Nov. 25, 1941, NYCMA, LG B: 4176, F: 05, OCD: Corr (3) 1941/11. Dave H. Morris to Harold Moskovit, Oct. 20, 1941, F: "President's Secretary's File La Guardia, Fiorello H., B 141," PSF: 141, FDRL. Rosalind Mordecai to La Guardia, Oct. 10, 1941, NYCMA, LG, B: 4175, F: 11, OCD: Corr (3) 1941/10. La Guardia's secretary John Slocum assured Mordecai that a building's middle floors were safer than basements, which were vulnerable to gas leaks and direct hits, as the British had learned. New York's police agreed that the city's subways, basements, and other underground structures imperiled civilian lives in air raids. John Slocum to Rosalind Mordecai, Oct. 24, 1941; also see William Turk to John Slocum, Oct. 21, 1941, Ibid. Ray Tucker, "The Man Who'll Keep You Safe," n.d., no publication, in NYCMA, LG B: 4176, F: 03 OCD: Corr (1) 1941/11.
20. John Slocum to Rosalind Mordecai, Oct. 24, 1941; William Turk to John Slocum, Oct. 21, 1941, NYCMA, LG, B: 4175, F: 11, OCD: Corr (3) 1941/10.
21. "Women Urge Repeal of Neutrality Act; Law is Called 'Farcical and Outdated,' *New York Times*, Nov. 1, 1941, 18. "Mayor Sees U.S. on Brink of War," *New York Times*, Nov. 1, 1941, 4.
22. Lowell Mellett to FDR, Oct. 20, 1941, F: "National Emergency Council 1941," OF 788: National Emergency Council, 1938–February 1942, FDRL. S. Howard Evans to Archibald MacLeish, Nov. 5, 1941, RG171, E: 10, B: 99, F: OFF. AP, "La Guardia Replies to Critics of Mailed Sermon Outline," *Los Angeles Times*, Nov. 10, 1941, 1.
23. La Guardia to Archibald MacLeish, Nov. 8, 1941, RG171, E: 10, B: 99, F: OFF. La Guardia to T.S. Walmsley, Nov. 25, 1941, NYCMA, LG B: 4176, F: 05, OCD: Corr (3) 1941/11. Caps Orig. Henry Lambert to La Guardia, Nov. 22, 1941, Ibid. Lambert acknowledged the mayor's letter "authorizing us to manufacture the Volunteer Participants insignia, as designed by yourself."
24. T. S. Walmsley to Dean James Landis, Nov. 18, 1941, RG171, E: 10, B: 1, F: "Region I 317–Dec. 31, 1941. La Guardia to General Gasser et al., Nov. 17, 1941, RG171, E: 10, B: 99, F: 380-10: OCD, Aug. 1, 1941–June 30, 1942.
25. James Landis to T. Semmes Walmsley, Sept. 16, 1941, RG171, E: 10, B: 2, F: "Criticisms-Protests through January 14, 1942." Donald Leonard to La Guardia, Nov. 25, 1941, RG171, E: 10, B: 1, F: "Region I 317–Dec. 31, 1941. James Landis, Area Report for November 11, 1941 Roll Call (All Information as of Oct. 31, 9141), Nov. 6, 1941, RG171, E: 10, B: 2, F: "Criticisms-Protests through January 14, 1942."
26. Mayor Walmsley to Major Landis, Nov. 27, 1941; Major Landis to Mayor Walmsley, Nov. 27, 1941, RG171, E: 10, B: 1, F: "Region I 317–Dec. 31, 1941." Major Brewer to La Guardia, Nov. 26, 1941; Major Brewer to La Guardia, Second Report, n.d.; Major Brewer to La Guardia, Nov. 28, 1941; Donald Leonard to La Guardia, Nov. 28, 1941; Major Brewer to Mayor Walmsley, Dec. 5, 1941, Ibid. Maine was a mixed bag. The Roosevelt administration had opted to route airport construction materials through Canada, bypassing Maine and infuriating 1,500 Maine railroad workers who now "rais[ed] hell" against any military program connected to Washington, including home defense.
27. Major Landis to Mayor Walmsley, Nov. 27, 1941;Major Brewer to La Guardia, Nov. 26, 1941; Major Brewer to La Guardia, Second Report, n.d.; Major Brewer to La Guardia, Nov. 28, 1941;T. S. Walmsley to Major Brewer, Nov. 28, 1941, Ibid. La Guardia to Governor Frank Dixon, Nov. 29, 1941, RG171, E: 10, B: 86, F: 250-Nationall Unity, Sept. 10–Nov. 30, 1941. He intended, he explained, to raise people's spirits by hosting "simultaneous Christmas parties in every city, town, and village in the United States on Saturday evening, December 27." Gallup Poll, Nov. 27–Dec. 1, 1941, Survey #254-K, http://ibiblio.org/pha/Gallup/Gallup%201941.htm.
28. Paul McNutt to La Guardia, Dec. 2, 1941, RG171, E: 10, B: 98, F: 380-6: Welfare, Nov. 26–Dec. 31, 1941. H. H. Kelly to Mr. Fredenhagen, Nov. 26, 1941, RG171, E: 10, B: 128, F: 571-Central Transportation Committee. Thomas Hamilton, "OCD Goes Into Action

Against New Air Peril," Dec. 14, 1941, *New York Times*, E7. Jacob Lewis to Director of Civilian Defense, Dec. 1, 1941; "Civilian Defense," *Chicago Daily Tribune*, Dec. 1, 1942, RG171, E: 10, B: 2, F: "Criticisms-Protests through January 14, 1942."

29. Corrington Gill to La Guardia, Nov. 27, 1941, RG171, E: 10, B: 99, F: 380-10: OCD, Aug. 1, 1941–June 30, 1942. La Guardia to Henry Stimson, Nov. 28, 1941, RG171, E: 10, B: 5, F: 020, Nov. 18–30, 1941. T. S. Walmsley to Captain Harten, Oct. 20, 1941, NYCMA, LG, B: 4175, F: 10, OCD: Corr (2) 1941/10. La Guardia to Grace Sparks, Nov. 14, 1941, RG171, E: 10, B: 92, F: 321: La Guardia, F. H. Ray Hueburt to La Guardia, Nov. 14, 1941, RG171, E: 10, B: 2, F: "Criticisms-Protests through January 14, 1942." "La Guardia Finds Midwest Cool on Civil Defense," *Washington Post*, Dec. 2, 1941, 27. Jacob Lewis to Director of O.C.D., Dec. 1, 1941, RG171, E: 10, B: 2, F: 000.3, -Jan. 14, 1942.

30. For the exchange of memos and notes between ER and La Guardia, see Corrington Gill to ER, Dec. 2, 1941; ER to La Guardia, Dec. 2, 1941; La Guardia to ER, Dec. 2, 1941; ER to La Guardia, Dec. 1, 1941 re: Olin Dows; ER to La Guardia re: Selective Service, Dec. 1, 1941; ER to La Guardia, Dec. 1, 1941, "These are a few points . . ."; ER to La Guardia, Nov. 28, 1941, RG171, E: 10, B: 99, F: 380-10: OCD, 8/1/41–6/31/42. ER, "My Day," Dec. 3, Dec. 4, 1941.

31. ER, "My Day," Dec. 4, Dec. 6, 1941.

32. For the exchange of memos and notes between ER and La Guardia, see Corrington Gill to ER, Dec. 2, 1941; ER to La Guardia, Dec. 2, 1941; La Guardia to ER, Dec. 2, 1941; ER to La Guardia, Dec. 1, 1941 re: Olin Dows; ER to La Guardia re: Selective Service, Dec. 1, 1941; ER to La Guardia, Dec. 1, 1941, "These are a few points . . ."; ER to La Guardia, Nov. 28, 1941, RG171, E: 10, B: 99, F: 380-10: OCD, Aug. 1, 1941–June 30, 1942. For memos, see ER to Morgenthau, Dec. 5, 1941; and ER to Wilmer Shields, Dec. 5, 1941. RG171, B: 83, GC, F: 203 Reports-Volunteer Participation." Lash, *Eleanor and Franklin*, 646. FDR's quote is from Lash.

Chapter 10

1. HistoryLink.org, HistoryLink File 10649, "Crowd Smashes Store Windows and Lights in Seattle Blackout Riot on December 8, 1941," http://www.historylink.org/_content/printer_friendly/pf_output.cfm?file_id=10649. Also see "Glass-smashing Mob Blacking Out Lights," *Seattle Times*, December 9, 1941, 1.

2. Quotes from the conversation with La Guardia come from Lash, *Eleanor and Franklin*, 647. Ritchie, *James M. Landis*, 107.

3. "La Guardia Acts to Guard Cities," *New York Times*, Dec. 8, 1941, 3. Goodwin, *No Ordinary Time*, 295. For an earlier example of La Guardia's wartime rhetoric, see "Air-Raid Wardens Start Enrolling in City Today," *New York Times*, June 20, 1941, 1. Williams, *City of Ambition*, 321–324. William Manchester, *The Glory and the Dream: A Narrative History of America, 1932–1972* (RosettaBooks LLC, Electronic Edition, 2013), see ch. 8.

4. ER, "My Day," Dec. 8, 1941. ER, *This I Remember*, 232–233.

5. Steven M. Gillon, *Pearl Harbor: FDR Leads the Nation Into War* (New York: Basic Books, 2011), X–XV. Barbara Maranzani, "Five Facts about Pearl Harbor and the USS Arizona," Dec. 7, 2011, http://www.history.com/news/5-facts-about-pearl-harbor-and-the-uss-arizona. Conn, Engelman, and Fairchild, *Guarding the United States and Its Outposts*, 199–201. Also see ER, *This I Remember*, 232–233.

6. ER, *This I Remember*, 238–239. ER's Remarks, Pan American Coffee Bureau (ER's regular weekly radio broadcast), Dec. 7, 1941, The Eleanor Roosevelt Papers Project, https://www.gwu.edu/~erpapers/teachinger/q-and-a/q21-pearl-harbor-address.cfm.

7. FDR's wartime leadership is among the most analyzed issues in the historical literature on World War II. By comparison, ER's wartime leadership has revealed relatively scant attention. For studies of FDR's role, see biographies such as Alonzo Hamby, *Man of Destiny: FDR and the Making of the American Century* (New York: Basic Books, 2015), which stresses Vice President Henry Wallace's role in keeping New Deal liberalism afloat; and James MacGregor Burns, *Roosevelt: The Soldier of Freedom* (New York: Harcourt Brace Jovanovich Inc., 1970). Other studies of FDR's wartime leadership include David Kaiser, *No End Save Victory: How FDR Led the Nation into War* (New York: Basic Books, 2014); Dallek, *Franklin D. Roosevelt*

and American Foreign Policy; Goodwin, _No Ordinary Time_; Kennedy, _Freedom from Fear_. For a broad overview of national security leadership in the twentieth century, see Julian Zelizer, _Arsenal of Democracy: The Politics of National Security—from World War II to the War on Terror_ (New York: Basic Books, 2010).

8. Justine Wise Polier to ER, Dec. 8, 1941, and attached document, "Possible points and framework for _Statement by Mrs. Roosevelt_ . . . " RG171, E: 10, B: 83, F: 22 "Volunteer Participation, -Dec. 15, 1941."

9. ER, "What Must We Do to Improve the Health and Well-Being of the American People?" _Town Meeting_ 7, no. 8 (Dec. 8, 1941): 13–15, in Black, ed., _What I Hope to Leave Behind_, 403–404. ER, "My Day," Dec. 8, 1941.

10. ER, _This I Remember_, 234–237. Bert Murphy to Elinor Morgenthau, Dec. 9, 1941, RG171, E: 10, B: 105, F: 435: Building and Plant Protection thru 12/31/41. "FDR's Pearl Harbor Address to the Nation," Dec. 8, 1941, http://www.americanrhetoric.com/speeches/fdrpearl-harbor.htm.

11. List of OCD Employee office numbers and phone numbers, n.d., NYCMA, LG B: 4177, F: 01 OCD: Corr (3) 1941/12. Lash, _Eleanor and Franklin_, 647.

12. For the number of White House visitors who shook hands with FDR and ER, see Stephen Early to Julian Fromer, Mar. 9, 1940, F: "1940-44, A-D," ER 40.3: Messages Requested-White House, ERP, FDRL. AP, "Gate Crashers at White House Get Past Guard," _Chicago Daily Tribune_, Jan. 3, 1939, 2.

13. Lt. Jimmy Snyder et al., to ER, Apr. 30, 1941, F: "1940-44 S-Z," ER 40.3: Messages Requested-White House, ERP, FDRL. Secretary to ER to Edna Arnwine, Mar. 19, 1941; Administrative Officer to Noah Bass, Apr. 26, 1940, F: "1940-44 A-D," ER 40.3: Messages Requested-White House, ERP, FDRL.

14. "Heavy Guard Thrown Around Capital's Most Vital Spots," _Washington Post_, Dec. 8, 1941, 3. Editorial, "Defend the District," _Washington Post_, Dec. 11, 1941, 18. ER to Lorena Hickok, in Rodger Streitmatter, ed., _Empty Without You: The Intimate Letters of Eleanor Roosevelt and Lorena Hickok_, (Boston: Da Capo Press, 1998), 240.

15. Harold Wessel to ER, Dec. 6, 1941; Administrative Officer Social Correspondence to Harold Wessel, Dec. 10, 1941, F: "1940-44 S-Z," ER 40.3: Messages Requested-White House, ERP, FDRL. Wessel had met the first lady on a flight to Chicago from Salt Lake City around 1937, and Wessel recalled "with delight" their conversation as they each ate breakfast. Upon landing he introduced his mother to the first lady, who radiated warmth and kindness. "If you had not been the most gracious lady I had ever met, I would not think of taking such a liberty as this," Wessel wrote. Goodwin, _No Ordinary Time_, 298–299.

16. ER, "My Day," Dec. 9, 1941. Goodwin, _No Ordinary Time_, 298–299, 305. ER, _This I Remember_, 248–249.

17. Stephen Early to Julian Fromer, Mar. 9, 1940; Secretary to ER to Dagne Nordholm, June 16, 1942; Secretary to ER to Verona Lawton, Aug. 11, 1942, F: "1940-44 K-R," ER 40.3: Messages Requested-White House, ERP, FDRL. Goodwin, _No Ordinary Time_, 298–299, 305. The Secret Service prevailed on FDR to move the tree to the White House complex so agents could control the space around it, although agents feared that the lights might become a beacon for enemy bombers. For FDR quote to Morgenthau and information about gas masks and air raid drills, see ER, _This I Remember_, 237, 248–249.

18. Lash, _Eleanor and Franklin_, 647. The genesis of the false alarm, two theories held, were that the Army had failed to tell San Francisco leaders about blackout drills it was holding, spiking their fears, or that watchers had mistakenly thought they heard planes approaching and notified the chain of command.

19. ER, _This I Remember_, 236–237.

20. "Air Raid Test Plan Explained to Sheriffs by Army Officers," _Los Angeles Times_, June 15, 1939, A2. "A Plan for the Tentative Organization of a State Home Defense Force," Submitted by R. C. Olson of California, and page 2 of untitled statement submitted by Olson, undated, RG171, E: 11, B: 71, F: 381: Region IX: CA, S.C., thru July 31, 1940. Culbert Olson to FDR, Nov. 21, 1941, RG171, E: 10, B: 2, F: Criticisms-Protests through January 14, 1942. Roy Martin to Corrington Gill, Dec. 10, 1941; FDR to Wayne Coy, Nov. 27, 1941, RG171, E: 10, B: 2, F: Criticisms-Protests through Jan. 14, 1942. Frank Bane to Semmes Walmsley, Dec. 9,

1941, and attached summary of New Orleans meeting of southern governors and defense officials, RG171 E: 11, B: 71, F: 381-Region IX: CA, S.C., Jan. 1–Dec. 31, 1941. In response to Olson's complaints, La Guardia held a meeting with governors in New Orleans on November 24. He pledged his desire to work with them in the wake of an "actual attack" and urged them to stop complaining. AP, "No Token Attack: LaGuardia Sees War Closer to Home," *Washington Post*, Dec. 10, 1941, 8. ER to Corrington Gill, n.d (Dec. 1941), RG171 E: 11, B: 71, F: 381-Region IX: CA, S.C., Jan. 1–Dec. 31, 1941. Goodwin, *No Ordinary Time*, 296.

21. ER, *This I Remember*, 236–237.
22. AP, "No Token Attack: LaGuardia Sees War Closer to Home," *Washington Post*, Dec. 10, 1941, 8. ER, *This I Remember*, 236–237.
23. AP, "No Token Attack: LaGuardia Sees War Closer to Home," *Washington Post*, Dec. 10, 1941, 8. "Civilians Urged to Keep Calm," *Los Angeles Times*, Dec. 8, 1941, 1F. Goodwin, *No Ordinary Time*, 295–297.
24. The brilliant Stephen Spielberg movie *1941* captures these fears and the panic mentality that gripped the West Coast. Foster Hailey, "Los Angeles Dark 3 Hours in Alarm," *New York Times*, Dec. 11, 1941, 20
25. "Flares a Puzzle in San Francisco," Dec. 11, 1941, *New York Times*, 20. HistoryLink File 10649, "Crowd Smashes Store Windows and Lights in Seattle Blackout Riot on December 8, 1941," http://www.historylink.org/_content/printer_friendly/pf_output.cfm?file_id=10649. Also see "Glass-smashing Mob Blacking Out Lights," *Seattle Times*, Dec. 9, 1941, 1.
26. "Radio: Home Front," *Time*, Dec. 22, 1941.
27. "Flares a Puzzle in San Francisco," Dec. 11, 1941, *New York Times*, 20.
28. ER, *This I Remember*, 237. ER to Elinor Morgenthau, Dec. 12, 1941; Dec. 11, 1941; Dec. 10, 1941, RG171 E: 11, B: 71, F: 381-Region IX: CA, S.C., Jan. 1–Dec. 31, 1941. Julia Dowell to Ed Isac, Apr. 6, 1942, RG171, E: 47, B: 49, F: Region IX: 310, Jan.–May 1942.
29. ER, "My Day," Dec. 12, 1941.
30. Lash, *Eleanor and Franklin*, 648. For a description of her day in San Francisco, see ER, "My Day," Dec. 13, 1941. ER to Elinor Morgenthau, Dec. 12, 1941; Dec. 11, 1941; Dec. 10, 1941; ER to Mr. Gill, n.d.; ER to Dr. Baehr, n.d. (Dec. 1941), RG171 E: 11, B: 71, F: 381-Region IX: CA, S.C., Jan. 1–Dec. 31, 1941.
31. Lash, *Eleanor and Franklin*, 648. For a description of her day in San Francisco, see ER, "My Day," Dec. 13, 1941. Justine Wise Polier to ER, Dec. 12, 1941, RG171 E: 11, B: 71, F: 381-Region IX: CA, S.C., Jan. 1–Dec. 31, 1941. For a description of her day in San Francisco, see ER, "My Day," Dec. 13, 1941. ER to Elinor Morgenthau, Dec. 12, 1941; Dec. 11, 1941; Dec. 10, 1941; ER to Mr. Gill, n.d.; ER to Dr. Baehr, n.d. (Dec. 1941), RG171 E: 11, B: 71, F: 381-Region IX: CA, S.C., Jan. 1–Dec. 31, 1941. Concerned, as always, about youth, ER wanted the National Student Federation and International Student Service to ramp up their mobilization efforts.
32. ER, *This I Remember*, 237.
33. Wilmer Shields to ER, Dec. 10, 1941, RG171, E: 10, B: 83, F: 200 Volunteer Participation, -Dec. 15, 1941. ER to Shields, Dec. 14, 1941, Ibid. Goodwin, *No Ordinary Time*, 296–297. ER, "My Day," Dec. 15, 1941.
34. Goodwin, *No Ordinary Time*, pp. 296–297. L. J. Shafer to ER, Dec. 10, 1941; S. Howard Evans to E. M. Knight, Dec. 16, 1941; ER to Shafer, Dec. 18, 1941, RG171, E: 10, B: 2, F: "Criticisms-Protests through January 14, 1942." J. L. Shafer to La Guardia, Dec. 10, 1941, RG171, E: 10, B: 2, F: "Criticisms-Protests through January 14, 1942." ER, "My Day," Dec. 16, 1941. ER to Elinor Morgenthau, Dec. 12, 1941; Dec. 11, 1941; Dec. 10, 1941; ER to Mr. Gill, n.d.; ER to Dr. Baehr, n.d. (Dec. 1941), RG171 E: 11, B: 71, F: 381-Region IX: CA, S.C., Jan. 1–Dec. 31, 1941.
35. ER to Elinor Morgenthau, Dec. 12, 1941; Dec. 11, 1941; Dec. 10, 1941; ER to Mr. Gill, n.d. (Dec. 1941); ER to Dr. Baehr, n.d. RG171 E: 11, B: 71, F: 381-Region IX: CA, S.C., Jan. 1–Dec. 31, 1941. Wilmer Shields to ER, Dec. 26, 1941, and attached suggested memo on Civilian Mobilization, RG171, E: 10, B: 83, F: Women in Defense, Nov. 1–Nov. 30, 1941. ER, "My Day," Dec. 16, 1941. Hoover sent FDR a memo in mid-1942 claiming the FBI had apprehended nearly 9,000 Japanese, German, and Italian subversives; see Michael Dobbs, *Saboteurs: The Nazi Raid on America* (New York: Knopf, 2004), 134.

36. L. J. Shafer to La Guardia, Dec. 10, 1941; ER to Shafer, Dec. 18, 1941, RG171, E: 10, B: 2, F: 000.3, -Jan. 14, 1942. L. J. Shafer to ER, Dec. 10, 1941; S. Howard Evans to E. M. Knight, Dec. 16, 1941; ER to Shafer, Dec. 18, 1941, RG171, E: 10, B: 2, F: "Criticisms-Protests through January 14, 1942." J. L. Shafer to La Guardia, Dec. 10, 1941, RG171, E: 10, B: 2, F: "Criticisms-Protests through January 14, 1942." T.G.S. Walker to Robert Shivers, Dec. 23, 1941; J. Edgar Hoover to La Guardia, Dec. 30, 1941; La Guardia to Hoover, Jan. 9, 1942, RG171, E: 10, B: 28, F: 092-Hawaii, 11/1/41. Kessner, *Fiorello H. La Guardia*, 504.
37. Goodwin, *No Ordinary Time*, 297–299. See ER, *This I Remember*, 232, 237.
38. Memo for the Mayor, Dec. 20, 1941; La Guardia to James Landis, Dec. 22, 1941, NYCMA, LG, B: 4177, F: 06, OCD: Corr (8) 1941/12. "Navy Sets Up Plans to Train College Men," see accompanying photo and caption, *Washington Post*, Dec. 21, 1941, 6. Thomas Hamilton, "OCD Goes Into Action Against New Air Peril," *New York Times*, Dec. 14, 1941, E7. "To Meet the Improbable," *Time*, Dec. 22, 1941. AP, "La Guardia Hints He Will Quit as New York Mayor," *Chicago Daily Tribune*, Dec. 24, 1941, 18. La Guardia, went the rumor, told New York City Council President Newbold Morris to prepare to assume the mayor's office.
39. "2 False Air 'Raids' Upset New Yorkers," *New York Times*, Dec. 10, 1941, 1. T. S. Walmsley to La Guardia, Dec. 9, 1941, RG171, E: 10, B: 5, F: 020, Dec. 1–15, 1941. "Mayor Confers on City's Defense," *New York Times*, Dec. 14, 1941, 64. "Text of Mayor La Guardia's Radio 'Chat' on War Front at Home," *New York Times*, Dec. 15, 1941, 14.
40. "Text of Mayor La Guardia's Radio 'Chat' on War Front at Home," *New York Times*, Dec. 15, 1941, 14. He admitted that his instructions—what to do during alarms versus blackouts—were "confusing" and interjected to his audience that "if you hear hammering or noise, it's the carpenters outside" where he was talking live on the radio. He interrupted himself to note that he needed bigger "offices to assume all of these activities." He resumed his talk: "Anyhow, I was telling you about our troubles in street lighting." "City Air Raid Bill is Signed by Mayor," Dec. 23, 1941, *New York Times*, 1.
41. Henry Stimson to La Guardia, Dec. 12, 1941, RG171, E: 10, B: 5, F: 020, Dec. 1–15, 1941. "Air-Raid Blackouts Solely Up to Army," *New York Times*, Dec. 14, 1941, 1. But the claim of science-based signaling was absurd; even the general admitted that the Army's various alerts meant only that "something may happen" not that something would happen. Thomas Hamilton, "OCD Goes Into Action Against New Air Peril," *New York Times*, Dec. 14, 1941, E7. If the raids were likely to bring 70 to 80 bombers launched from aircraft carriers, they probably would be smaller than those on London—hardly reassuring to Americans in the cities. Indeed, the authorities cited aircraft carriers as the greatest source of a likely air raid.
42. Unnamed to La Guardia, Dec. 16, 1941, NYCMA, LG, B: 4177, F: 03, OCD: Corr (5) 1941/12. Mary Hornaday, "Intimate Message: Washington," no paper, n.d. in NYCMA, LG, B: 4177, F: 05 OCD: Corr (7) 1941/12. Hornaday added that ER's interest in nutrition and school lunches had undercut popular support for the home defense program. Raymond Clapper, "What OCD Needs," Jan. 16, 1942, in RG171, E: 10, B: 2, F: Criticisms-Protests through Jan. 14, 1942. Walter Lippmann, "Today and Tomorrow: Mayor LaGuardia and Mrs. Roosevelt," *Washington Post*, Dec. 16, 1941, 19. "Too Big a Straddle," n.d. no paper title, in NYCMA, LG, B: 4177, F: 09 OCD: Corr (11) 1941/12. Cartoon, "La Guardia One-Man Band," NYCMA, LG, B: 4177, F: 09, OCD: Corr (11) 1941/12. "Confused & Unprepared," *Time*, Dec. 29, 1941, 13.
43. "Mother" to La Guardia, Feb. 17, 1942 (stamped "rec'd"), NYCMA, LG, B: 4182, F: 10, OCD Correspondence (17). Hilda Schilling to La Guardia, Feb. 15, 1942, NYCMA, LG, B: 4182, F: 08 OCD Correspondence (15). Marian Greenberg, "Lavanburg Tenants Organize for Defense," NYCMA, LG B: 4181 F: 8 OCD Report: Levanburg Tenants Organize for Defense (5).
44. Robert De Vore, "Group Favors Civil Defense Under Army," *Washington Post*, Jan. 7, 1942, 1, RG171, E: 10, B: 2, F: Criticisms-Protests through Jan. 14, 1942. Hamilton Swinburne, Letter to the Editor, "Congressional Leadership," *Washington Post*, Jan. 14, 1942, X8. "LaGuardia Given Priorities for Civil Defense Material," *Washington Post*, Jan. 20, 1942, 14. Lash, *Eleanor and Franklin*, 648. Mrs. Rafler to Mrs. Lindley, Dec. 13, 1941, RG171, E: 10, B: 2,

F: Criticisms-Protests through Jan. 14, 1942. Editorial, "Free-for-All Civilian Defense," n.d., no publication, in RG171, E: 10, B: 2, F: Criticisms-Protests through Jan. 14, 1942. FDR quoted in Goodwin, *No Ordinary Time*, 324.

45. Goodwin, *No Ordinary Time*, 324. Lash, *Eleanor and Franklin*, 648. Raymond Clapper, "What OCD Needs," Jan. 16, 1942, in RG171, E: 10, B: 2, F: Criticisms-Protests through Jan. 14, 1942.

46. ER, *This I Remember*, 237–238, 240. ER, "My Day," Dec. 17, Dec. 18, 1941.

47. Wilmer Shields to ER, Dec. 26, 1941, and attached suggested memo on Civilian Mobilization, RG171, E: 10, B: 83, F: Women in Defense, Nov. 1–Nov. 30, 1941. No name to Justine Polier, Dec. 15, 1941, RG171, E: 10, B: 83, F: 200 Volunteer Participation,—Dec. 15, 1941. ER, "My Day," Dec. 19, Dec. 23, Dec. 24, Dec. 25, 1941.

48. Eleanor Roosevelt, "Let Us Have Faith in Democracy," *Land Policy Review* 5 (Jan. 1942): 20–23, in Black, ed., *What I Hope to Leave Behind*, 97–99. For an excellent synopsis of the War in the Pacific, see Kennedy, *Freedom From Fear*, 526–529. ER, "My Day," Dec. 29 and 30, 1941.

Chapter 11

1. The quote at the top comes from a letter in which ER is quoted: No name to Jane Seaver, Jan. 31, 1942, RG171, E: 10, B: 101, F: 380-102, Volunteer Participation Committee, thru 3/31/42.

2. FDR to Philip Fleming, Jan. 12, 1942, RG171, E: 10, B: 6, F: 031, President, 8/1/1941-. Gasser to Kirby, Jan. 6, 1942; T.S. Walmsley to La Guardia, Jan. 15, 1942, RG171, E: 10, B: 117, F: 514.1-Air Raid Warning System, Jan. 1-16, 1942. And at bottom of Jan. 6 memo, see Walmsley to Gasser, Jan. 7, 1942.

3. Alvin Cobb to Cordell Hull, Jan. 11, 1942; Gasser to Cobb, Feb. 12, 1942, RG171, E: 10, B; 115, F: 513-Rescue Squads. ER, "My Day," Jan. 27, 1942.

4. Paul Kellogg to Raymond Clapper, Feb. 9, 1942, F: "1942 Kellogg, Paul," ER 100: Personal Letters 1942 Ilma, Viola-Ke, ERP, FDRL. For a description of La Guardia's ouster, see Williams, City of Ambition, 320–324.

5. Cross-Reference Sheet, Landis, Jan. 2, 1942; Landis, Jan. 4, 1942, F: "Landis, James M," PPF 4858: Landis, James M, FDRL. La Guardia to ER, Jan. 6, 1942; ER to La Guardia, Jan. 16, 1942, RG171, E: 12, B: 3, F: Confidential: 200.

6. Drew Pearson and Robert Allen, "Fiorello Flops: LaGuardia's a Good Mayor, But is Too Busy, Too Bossy to Handle Defense Job," Washington Merry Go-Round, *Minneapolis Star-Journal*, Jan. 3, 1942, F: "Federal Security Agency Endorsements 1939-45," OF 3700: Federal Security Agency, FDRL.

7. Nona Baldwin, "La Guardia Hints He May Quit OCD," *New York Times*, Jan. 23, 1942, NYCMA, LG, B: 4182 F: 2, OCD: Corr (9) 1942/02/09. Cartoon, "When Will He Let Go?" *Newark Evening News*, Feb. 5, 1942, NYCMA, LG, B: 4181, F: 17, OCD: Corr (5) 1942/ 02/05. Press Release, Office of Civilian Defense, Jan. 9, 1942, NYCMA, LG, B: 4181 F: 02, OCD: Press Releases (1) 1942/01. Harold Ickes Diaries, Jan. 25, 1942, 6266–6267, LoC, Reel 4, July 5, 1940-Dec. 27, 1941, Shelf No. DM16 142. La Guardia to FDR, Feb. 10, 1942, NYCMA, LG, B: 4182, F: 03, OCD: Corr. (10) 1942/02/10.

8. ER, "My Day," Jan. 10, Jan. 28, 1942. News Release, O.C.D., Jan. 9, 1942, NYCMA, LG, B: 4181, F: 02, OCD: Press Releases (1) 1942/01. http://www.nationalww2museum.org/ learn/education/for-students/ww2-history/ww2-by-the-numbers/us-military.html

9. The volunteer numbers appear in a memo, Wilmer Shields to Mr. Jackson, Mar. 12, 1942; the volunteer office numbers are in a memo, Shields to Jackson, Mar. 26, 1942, RG171, E: 10, B: 83, F: 203 Reports-Volunteer Participation. "Volunteer Code," Feb. 5, 1942, RG171, E: 10, B: 83, F: 200 Volunteer Participation, Dec. 16, 1941-. La Guardia to Jane Seaver, Jan. 17, 1942, RG171, E: 10, B: 101, F: 380-102: Volunteer Participation Committee, thru. 3/31/42. See Wilmer Shields to Mr. Jackson, Mar. 10, 1942 for the different cities; Shields to Jonathan Daniels, Mar. 10, 1942, for USO and other groups, RG171, E: 10, B: 83, F: 203 Reports-Volunteer Participation.

10. Landis to "Dear Mr.," Apr. 7, 1942, RG171, E: 46, B: 27, F: 380.1-OCD. Betty Eckhardt May to Molly Flynn, Apr. 11, 1942; Jonathan Daniels to Josephine Roche, Apr. 10, 1942;

Daniels to Thomas Sharp, Apr. 3, 1942, RG171, E: 10, B: 83, F: 200 Volunteer Participation Dec. 16, 1941-. Jonathan Daniels to Mr. Sheridan, Mar., 23, 1942, RG171, E: 10, B: 83, F: 200 Volunteer Participation Dec. 16, 1941-. "District's OCD Home Program Leaderless; Baltimore Shows What Can Be Done," *Washington Star*, May 2, 1943, A-2, RG171, E: 46, B: 28, F: 380.104-Civilian War Services. Jonathan Daniels, Summary Report of the Civilian Mobilization Branch, May 1942, RG171, E: 46, B: 26, F: 330-Civilian Defense Board. Quote from handbook comes from "Civilian Defense on the Home Front, 1942," The Gilder Lehrman Institute of American History, http://www.gilderlehrman.org/history-by-era/world-war-ii/resources/civilian-defense-home-front-1942.

11. ER to "All Heads of Divisions," Jan. 2, 1942, RG171, E: 10, B: 83, F: 200 Volunteer Participation, Dec. 16, 1941-. ER to Landis, Jan. 9, 1942, RG171, E: 10, B: 92, F: 321: Landis: Landis, James M. Mary Louise Alexander to ER, Jan. 16, 1942, RG171, E: 10, B: 99, F: 380-10: OCD, 8/1/41-6/31/42. Alexander proposed sending ER a weekly update about each section's activities. Mary Louise Alexander to Landis, copy ER, Jan. 19, 1942, RG171, E: 10, B:" 83, F: 220 Women in Defense, Jan. 1, 1942-. Mary Louise Alexander to Miss Davison, Jan. 10, 1942, RG171, E: 10, B: 83, F: 220 Women in Defense, Jan. 1, 1942-. Wilmer Shields to Landis, Jan. 19, 1942, RG171, E: 46, B: 27, F: 380.1-OCD. ER made plans to hire an associate chief of staff (a slot, for reasons that were unclear, reserved for a man). Betty Lindley to Landis, Jan. 19, 1942, RG171, E: 46, B: 27, F: 380.1-OCD.

12. Mary Louise Alexander to ER, Jan. 16, 1942, RG171, E: 10, B: 99, F: 380-10: OCD, 8/1/41-6/31/42. Mary Louise Alexander to Landis, copy ER, Jan. 19, 1942, RG171, E: 10, B: 83, F: 220 Women in Defense, Jan. 1, 1942-. Mary Louise Alexander to Miss Davison, Jan. 10, 1942, Ibid. "Civilian Defense," Jan. 13, 1942, article attached to Selma Hirsh to Landis, Feb. 21, 1942, RG171, E: 46, B: 27, F: 380.1-OCD. Betty Lindley to Landis, Jan. 19, 1942, Ibid. ER to Martin Jones, Feb. 2, 1942; Col Burn to ER, Jan. 29, 1942, RG171, E: 10, B: 107, F: 455-Training, Feb. 1, 1942-. ER vowed to "personally watch the development of this system in New York City."

13. ER to Corrington Gill, Jan. 3, 1942. RG171, B: 83, E: 10, F: "220 Women in Defense, Jan. 1, 1942-." ER to Corrington Gill, Jan. 6, 1942, Ibid. ER to Mrs. Arthur Gilder, Jan. 7, 1942, Ibid. ER to Dr. Robert Weaver, Jan. 5, 1942. RG171, E: 10, B: 90, F: 280-Negroes in Defense. "Memorandum on Civilian Morale Among Negroes in the District of Columbia," Jan. 14, 1942, Ibid. ER, "My Day," Jan. 13, 1942. Justine Wise Polier to ER, Jan. 26, 1942, RG171, E: 10, B: 90, F: 317-Reports, Jan. 1, 1942.

14. ER, "My Day," Jan. 10, 1942. Jane Seaver to Landis, Jan. 19, 1942, RG171, E: 46, B: 27, F: 380.1-OCD. Seaver complained that three or four of her aides had to squeeze into a single office and that the paucity of OCD meetings hindered the free flow of information.

15. Aracelio Hernandez to ER, Jan. 17, 1942, F: "ER O.C.D. Offers of Service 1942 Go-He," ER 71: O.C.D. Offers of Service, ERP, FDRL. For Seattle man, see Carl Gregory to ER, Jan. 14, 1942; no author to ER, Jan. 12, 1942, F: "O.C.D. Offers of Service 1942 Me-O," ER 71: O.C.D. Offers of Service, ERP, FDRL. Mrs. E.B. Mobley to ER, n.d., and Helm to Mobley, Feb. 21, 1942, F: "O.C.D. Offers of Service 1942 Me-O," ER 71: O.C.D. Offers of Service, ERP, FDRL. ER, "My Day," Jan. 16, Jan. 20, Jan. 22, 1942. Mrs. J.M. Helm to Abraham Goldfeld, Feb. 9, 1942; ER to Frederick Guggenheimer, Jan. 30, 1942, F: "O.C.D. Offers of Service 1942 Go-He," ER 71: O.C.D. Offers of Service, ERP, FDRL. Mrs. J. M. Helm to Charles Crabb, Feb. 13, 1942, F: "O.C.D. Offers of Service 1942 Ci-D," ER 71: O.C.D. Offers of Service, ERP, FDRL.

16. ER to Frederick Guggenheimer, Jan. 30, 1942, F: "O.C.D. Offers of Service 1942 Go-He," ER71: O.C.D. Offers of Service, ERP, FDRL. ER, "My Day," Jan. 24, 1942. The quote is from a letter, No name to Jane Seaver, Jan. 31, 1942, RG171, E: 10, B: 101, F: 380-102, Volunteer Participation Committee, thru 3/31/42.

17. Mrs. David Paine to ER, Jan. 18, 1942; ER to Paine, Jan. 28, 1942, F: "O.C.D. Offers of Service 1942 P-R," ER 71: O.C.D. Offers of Service, ERP, FDRL.ER, "My Day," Jan. 23, Jan. 26, 1942. Mary Louise Alexander to ER, Jan. 16, 1942, RG171, E: 10, B: 99, F: 380-10: OCD, 8/1/41-6/31/42. Mary Louise Alexander to Landis, copy ER, Jan. 19, 1942, RG171, E: 10, B:" 83, F: "220 Women in Defense, Jan. 1, 1942-." Mary Louise Alexander to Miss Davison, Jan. 10, 1942, RG171, E: 10, B:" 83, F: 220 Women in Defense, Jan. 1, 1942-.

18. Louis Heuer to ER, Jan. 16, 1942, F: "ER O.C.D. Offers of Service 1942 Go-He," ER 71: O.C.D. Offers of Service, ERP, FDRL.
19. Mrs. J.M. Helm to Marion Haviland, Feb. 9, 1942, F: "ER O.C.D. Offers of Service 1942 Go-He," ER 71: O.C.D. Offers of Service, ERP, FDRL. Quotes from Lash, *Eleanor and Franklin*, 652. Harold Ickes Diaries, Jan. 25, 1942, 6266–6267. LoC. Reel 4, July 5, 1940-Dec. 27, 1941 Shelf No. DM16 142.
20. Landis to ER, Jan. 19, 1942, RG171, E: 10, B: 83, F: 220 Women in Defense, Jan. 1, 1942-. Landis, Administrative Order No. 22, Establishment and Organization of Community and Volunteer Participation Branch, Feb. 5, 1942, RG171, E: 10, B: 99, F: 380-10: OCD, Feb. 1, 1942. ER, "My Day," Jan. 19, Jan. 21, 1942.
21. Harold Ickes Diaries, Jan. 25, 1942, 6266–6267, LoC. Reel 4, July 5, 1940-Dec. 27, 1941 Shelf No. DM16 142. Mrs. J.M. Helms to Dorothy Goldberg, Feb. 2, 1942, F: "ER O.C.D. Offers of Service 1942 Go-He," ER 71: O.C.D. Offers of Service, ERP, FDRL. "Civilian Participation Activities of O.C.D.;" Archibald MacLeish to ER, Jan. 16, 1942; Landis to ER, Jan. 23, 1942; ER to Landis, Jan. 21, 1942, RG171, E: 10, B: 83, F: 200 Volunteer Participation, Dec. 16, 1941-. ER, "My Day," Jan. 6, Feb. 4, Feb. 5, Feb. 6, 1942.
22. Mrs. Knight to All Employees in the Washington Office of O.C.D., Dec., 20, 1941, RG171, E: 10, B: 93, F: 321: Roosevelt, ER. Howard Murray to ER, Jan. 24, 1942; Helm to Murray, Feb. 3, 1942, F: "ER O.C.D. Offers of Service 1942 Me-O," ER 71: O.C.D. Offers of Service, ERP, FDRL. Marks Shaine to ER, Feb. 25, 1942, and summary of attached article in Journal of the American Medical Association, Vol. 118, No. 8, Feb. 21, 1942, F: "ER Correspond. OCD Re: Douglas-Chaney Appt.—Favorable 1942 R-Z," ER 71: O.C.D. 1942 Administrative Douglas-Chaney Appointments, ERP, FDRL.Va. Stewart to ER, Feb. 24, 1942; Frank Welker to ER, Feb. 12, 1942, Ibid. Robert Goodwin to Wilmer Shields, Jan. 5, 1942, and enclosed report, Fourth Meeting of the Regional Federal Council of the Office of Defense Health and Welfare Services, Dec. 4 and 5, 1941, RG171 E: 10, B: 98, F: 380-8: Price Administration and Civilian Supply. ER, "My Day," Jan. 20, 1942.
23. Selma Hirsh to Landis, Feb. 21, 1942, RG171, E: 46, B: 27, F: 380.1-OCD. MacLeish to ER, Jan. 17, 1942; ER to MacLeish, Jan. 20, 1942, RG171, E: 10, B: 99, F: OFF. MacLeish to Landis, Jan. 26, 1942; and attached "War Council of Arts," Jan. 5, 1942, RG171, E: 10, B: 99, F: OFF. Olin Dows to Joseph Lilly, Feb. 6, 1942, NYCMA, LG, B: 4181 F: 15, OCD: Corr (3), 1942/02/03.
24. E.M. Knight to ER, Jan. 23, 1942, RG171, E: 10, B: 125, F: 520.1-Fire School, 1/1-2/28/42. ER, *This I Remember*, 231–232. Mrs. Kester Enders to ER, Feb. 5, 1942; and attached article, AP, "Mayris Chaney, Dancer, Gets $4,600 Defense Job," F: "ER OCD re: Douglas-Chaney Apptments-Unfavorable 1942 Feb.-Mar C-E," ER 71: O.C.D. 1942 Administrative Douglas-Chaney Appointments, ERP, FDRL. Four people on ER's staff made at least $5,600 including chief of staff Betty Lindley and her aide Jonathan Daniels, who reportedly earned $8,000. Quotes come from Lash, *Eleanor and Franklin*, 649.
25. "Civilian Defense Office Needs Radical Operation"; "Decline," n.d., *Sacramento Bee*, F: "ER OCD re: Douglas-Chaney Apptments-Unfavorable 1942 Feb-Mar C-E," ER 71: O.C.D. 1942 Administrative Douglas-Chaney Appointments, ERP, FDRL. ER, *This I Remember*, 244. United Press, "Miss Chaney's O.C.D. Job Stirs Call for Inquiry," Feb. 6, 1942, in F: "ER OCD Douglas/Chaney Apptments Unfavorable 1942 F-Ha," ER 71: O.C.D. 1942 Administrative Douglas-Chaney Appointments, ERP, FDRL. Harold Ickes Diaries, Feb. 7, 1942, 6333–6335, LoC. Reel 4, July 5, 1940-Dec. 27, 1941 Shelf No. DM16 142.
26. David Lawrence, "Washington Today," n.d., no paper, in F: "ER Correspond. OCD Re: Douglas-Chaney Appt.—Favorable 1942 L-P," ER 71: O.C.D. 1942 Administrative Douglas-Chaney Appointments, ERP, FDRL. Mary Carroll Hillis to ER, Feb. 6, 1942, F: "ER OCD Douglas/Chaney Apptments-Unfavorable 1942 He-K," ER 71: O.C.D. 1942 Administrative Douglas-Chaney Appointments, ERP, FDRL. Chaney's name didn't appear in *Dance, Educational Dance*, and *Dance Observer*, three insiders' magazines. Amy Ransome to ER, Feb. 28, 1942, F: "ER Correspond. OCD Re: Douglas-Chaney Appt.—Favorable 1942 R-Z," ER 71: O.C.D. 1942 Administrative Douglas-Chaney Appointments, ERP, FDRL. Chaney is quoted in Seymour Schlussel to ER, Feb. 7, 1942, F: "ER OCD Re: Douglas-Chaney Apptments-Unfavorable 1942 Feb-Mar S," ER 71: O.C.D. 1942 Administrative

Douglas-Chaney Appointments, ERP, FDRL. ER to Paul Kellogg, Feb. 10, 1942, F: "1942 Kellogg, Paul," ER 100: Personal Letters 1942 Ilma, Viola-Ke, ERP, FDRL. Other Americans framed the attacks as political: "I regret exceedingly the unjust publicity being hurled at your worthy head" by the same farmers "who used to jeer me for wearing a Roosevelt button," one Pittsburgh man wrote the first lady.

27. Dallek, *Franklin D. Roosevelt and American Foreign Policy*, 325. United Press, "Miss Chaney's O.C.D. Job Stirs Call for Inquiry," Feb. 6, 1942, F: "ER OCD Douglas/Chaney Apptments Unfavorable 1942 F-Ha," ER 71: O.C.D. 1942 Administrative Douglas-Chaney Appointments, ERP, FDRL. C.J.L., "Sacramento," n.d., F: "OCD re: Douglas-Chaney Apptments-Unfavorable 1942 Feb.-Mar C-E," ER 71: O.C.D. 1942 Administrative Douglas-Chaney Appointments, ERP, FDRL. "Just Why Should This Youth Get a Commission?" *Sacramento Bee*, n.d. F: "ER OCD re: Douglas-Chaney Apptments-Unfavorable 1942 Feb-Mar C-E," ER 71: O.C.D. 1942 Administrative Douglas-Chaney Appointments, ERP, FDRL. Editorial, "The Criticism of Mrs. Roosevelt," enclosed in letter to ER, F: "ER OCD Douglas/Chaney Apptments Unfavorable 1942 F-Ha," ER 71: O.C.D. 1942 Administrative Douglas-Chaney Appointments, ERP, FDRL. Kellogg to R.B. Wigglesworth, Feb. 22, 1942; and memo, Kellogg to Wigglesworth, Feb. 22, 1942; Kellogg to ER, Feb. 23, 1942, F: "1942 Kellogg, Paul," ER 100: Personal Letters 1942 Ilma, Viola-Ke, ERP, FDRL. Radio Broadcast, Bob Shuler, KMTR, Feb. 15, 1942, F: "ER OCD Douglas/Chaney Apptments Unfavorable 1942 S," ER 71: O.C.D. 1942 Administrative Douglas-Chaney Appointments, ERP, FDRL. Lash, *Eleanor and Franklin*, 649–651.

28. Lash, *Eleanor and Franklin*, 651. For information on Byrd's Committee, see "Saga of the OCD," Feb. 12, 1942, *Roanoke World-News*, F: "ER Correspond. OCD Re: Douglas-Chaney Appt.— Favorable 1942 L-P," ER 71: O.C.D. 1942 Administrative Douglas-Chaney Appointments, ERP, FDRL. Frank Kent, "Kent Deplores Mrs. Roosevelt's Defense of Her Recent Activities in O.C.D.-Bad Feeling Created," n.d. *Baltimore Sun*, F: "ER OCD Re: Douglas-Chaney Appts. (Favorable) 1942 A-E," ER 71: O.C.D. 1942 Administrative Douglas-Chaney Appointments, ERP, FDRL. Westbrook Pegler, "Criticizing First Lady," Feb. 11, 1942, no paper, F: "ER OCD re: Douglas-Chaney Apptments Unfavorable 1942 Feb-Mar A-B," ER 71: O.C.D. 1942 Administrative Douglas-Chaney Appointments, ERP, FDRL. Westbrook Pegler, "Personal Attack on Mrs. F.R.," n.d., attached to letter to ER, "No woman ever merited . . . " F: "ER OCD re: Douglas-Chaney Apptments-Unfavorable 1942 Feb-Mar C-E," ER 71: O.C.D. 1942 Administrative Douglas-Chaney Appointments, ERP, FDRL. Raymond Clapper, "Too Many Teacher's Pets in the OCD," no paper, n.d.; and "No Place for Rhythmic Dancing in the OCD," Feb. 9, 1942, *Oregon Forward*, attached to letter from Mrs. Ray Baker, n.d; also see, Raymond Clapper, "Clapper's Washington," Feb. 6, 1942, *Boston Traveler*. His first piece appeared on Friday, F: "ER OCD re: Douglas-Chaney Apptments-Unfavorable 1942 Feb-Mar C-E," ER 71: O.C.D. 1942 Administrative Douglas-Chaney Appointments, ERP, FDRL. Attached newspaper articles and letters to the editor in Anderson to Ford letter, n.d., including one titled, "Good Example," F: "ER OCD re: Douglas-Chaney Apptments Unfavorable 1942 Feb-Mar A-B," ER 71: O.C.D. 1942 Administrative Douglas-Chaney Appointments, ERP, FDRL. "Civilian Defense Office Needs Radical Operation"; "Decline," n.d. *Sacramento Bee*, F: "ER OCD re: Douglas-Chaney Apptments-Unfavorable 1942 Feb-Mar C-E," ER 71: O.C.D. 1942 Administrative Douglas-Chaney Appointments, ERP, FDRL.

29. "Defensedoggling," *Daily Progress*, Feb. 10, 1942, F: "ER OCD Douglas/Chaney Apptments Unfavorable 1942 S," ER 71: O.C.D. 1942 Administrative Douglas-Chaney Appointments, ERP, FDRL. "Eleanor the Good," *Boston Herald*, Feb. 6, 1942, attached to J.C. Bray to ER, Feb. 6, 1942, F: "ER OCD re: Douglas-Chaney Apptments Unfavorable 1942 Feb-Mar A-B," ER 71: O.C.D. 1942 Administrative Douglas-Chaney Appointments, ERP, FDRL. See photo in newspaper, n.d., "Congressmen Object," F: "ER OCD re: Douglas-Chaney Apptments Unfavorable 1942 Feb-Mar A-B," ER 71: O.C.D. 1942 Administrative Douglas-Chaney Appointments, ERP, FDRL. "Today in Washington," n.d., no paper, F: "ER OCD Douglas/Chaney Apptments-Unfavorable 1942 He-K," ER 71: O.C.D. 1942 Administrative Douglas-Chaney Appointments, ERP, FDRL. AP, "Protégé to $4,600 Job," *Morning Kansas City Times*, Feb. 5, 1942, F: "ER OCD Douglas/Chaney Apptments Unfavorable 1942 F-Ha," ER 71: O.C.D. 1942 Administrative Douglas-Chaney Appointments, ERP, FDRL.

Cartoon, stamped Edw. H. Beier, Scranton, PA, F: "ER OCD re: Douglas-Chaney Apptments Unfavorable 1942 Feb-Mar A-B," ER 71: O.C.D. 1942 Administrative Douglas-Chaney Appointments, ERP, FDRL.

30. Harold Ickes Diaries, Feb. 7, 1942, 6333–6335, LoC. Reel 4, July 5, 1940-Dec. 27, 1941 Shelf No. DM16 142. Quote from Landis in Lash, *Eleanor and Franklin*, 650.

31. Mrs. Kester Enders to ER, Feb. 5, 1942; and attached article, AP, "Mayris Chaney, Dancer, Gets $4,600 Defense Job," F: "ER OCD re: Douglas-Chaney Apptments-Unfavorable 1942 Feb.-Mar C-E," ER 71: O.C.D. 1942 Administrative Douglas-Chaney Appointments, ERP, FDRL. J.A. Boice to ER, Feb. 6, 1942, and attached AP, "Probe Asked after Dancer Gets OCD Job," Feb. 5, 1942, F: "ER OCD re: Douglas-Chaney Apptments Unfavorable 1942 Feb-Mar A-B," ER 71: O.C.D. 1942 Administrative Douglas-Chaney Appointments, ERP, FDRL. *Pittsburgh Press*, "Note to Mrs. Roosevelt," n.d. clipping attached to Nellie Frank to ER letter, F: "ER OCD Douglas/Chaney Apptments Unfavorable 1942 F-Ha," ER 71: O.C.D. 1942 Administrative Douglas-Chaney Appointments, ERP, FDRL.

32. Memo, no from or to; n.d.; "I have separated . . . ," F: "ER OCD Re: Douglas-Chaney Appts. (Favorable) 1942 A-E," ER 71: O.C.D. 1942 Administrative Douglas-Chaney Appointments, ERP, FDRL. More than half of them were classified as "abusive." Lash, *Eleanor and Franklin*, 651. Mrs. Lewis Gray to ER, n.d., F: "ER OCD Douglas/Chaney Apptments Unfavorable 1942 F-Ha," ER 71: O.C.D. 1942 Administrative Douglas-Chaney Appointments, ERP, FDRL.

33. Mary Kibbe Allen to "the editor of . . . ," ER 71, B: 428, F: "ER OCD re: Douglas-Chaney Apptments Unfavorable 1942 Feb-Mar A-B," ER 71: O.C.D. 1942 Administrative Douglas-Chaney Appointments, ERP, FDRL. Nellie Frank to ER, Feb. 14, 1942, F: "ER OCD Douglas/Chaney Apptments Unfavorable 1942 F-Ha," ER 71: O.C.D. 1942 Administrative Douglas-Chaney Appointments, ERP, FDRL. Genevieve Burke to ER, Feb. 6, 1942, F: "ER OCD re: Douglas-Chaney Apptments Unfavorable 1942 Feb-Mar A-B," ER 71: O.C.D. 1942 Administrative Douglas-Chaney Appointments, ERP, FDRL. Dillon to ER, Feb. 9, 1942, F: "ER OCD re: Douglas-Chaney Apptments-Unfavorable 1942 Feb.-Mar C-E," ER 71: O.C.D. 1942 Administrative Douglas-Chaney Appointments, ERP, FDRL. Sylvia Becker to ER, Feb. 9, 1942, F: "ER OCD re: Douglas-Chaney Apptments Unfavorable 1942 Feb-Mar A-B," ER 71: O.C.D. 1942 Administrative Douglas-Chaney Appointments, ERP, FDRL.

34. Rev. Zed Hopeful Copp to ER, Feb. 10, 1942, F: "OCD re: Douglas-Chaney Apptments-Unfavorable 1942 Feb.-Mar C-E," ER 71: O.C.D. 1942 Administrative Douglas-Chaney Appointments, ERP, FDRL. Mrs. A.E. Curtenius to ER, Feb. 11, 1942, Ibid. William Barrett to ER, Feb. 10, 1942; attached newspaper articles and letters to the editor in Anderson to Ford letter, n.d., including one titled "Good Example," Ibid. M.W. Chapman to ER, Feb. 12, 1942; M.H. Cogan to ER, Feb. 9, 1942: "Tend to your own knitting," Cogan wrote ER, F: "ER OCD re: Douglas-Chaney Apptments-Unfavorable 1942 Feb-Mar C-E," ER 71: O.C.D. 1942 Administrative Douglas-Chaney Appointments, ERP, FDRL. Mary Cohen to ER, Feb. 9, 1942, Ibid.

35. Landis, "Two Years of OCD," *New York Times Magazine*, May 30, 1943, 10, RG171, E: 185, B: 14, F: 9-A-1: Landis: Statements & Speeches. "AIR: Civilian Pilots," *Time*, May 4, 1942. "Explosives Blast Kills 13, Hurts 60," *New York Times*, May 5, 1943, 24. AP, "Seven Dead as Floods Sweep Five States; Thousands Homeless," *Washington Star*, May 19, 1943, 1; Telegram, May 20, 1943, "OCD Director Landis . . .," RG171, E: 185, B: 12, F: Emergencies . . . 7/6/42-7/1/43. "Kearny Squads Hunt Four Still Missing in Blast," *New York Herald Tribune*, Aug. 21, 1943, 7; International News Service, "50 Feared Dead in N.J. Factory Explosion," *Washington Post*, Aug. 20, 1943, 1-A. AP, "Death Toll May Reach 100 in Wreck of Congressional Limited; Scores Hurt," *Washington Post*, Sept. 7, 1943, 1. Eric Cudd, "Victims of Train Wreck Strewn Along Tracks," *Philadelphia Inquirer*, Sept. 7, 1943, 1. "Air Raid Wardens and Fire Guards Fight Fire," La. OCD, Baton Rouge, La, Nov. 1943, 7. "CD Fireman Rescues Three from Flames," Pittsburgh, Pa, Nov. 18, 1943, 2. "Air Raid Warden Cited by Chief for Risk During Fire," *The Defender*, Dec. 27, 1943, 2. James Sheppard to Landis, Mar. 8, 1943, RG171, E: 47, B: 48, F: Region IX: 100 (1 of 2). Analysis of Attitudes Toward Civilian Protection, Newspaper Clippings, 3/21-5/15/43; 6/1/43. Report Analysis and Statistics Division, RG171, E: 185, B: 31, F: 14, Misc. (2 of 3).

36. David Lawrence, "Washington Today," n.d., no paper, F: "ER Correspond. OCD Re: Douglas-Chaney Appt.—Favorable 1942 L-P," ER 71: O.C.D. 1942 Administrative Douglas-Chaney Appointments, ERP, FDRL. Dodson to ER, Feb. 12, 1942, F: "ER OCD re: Douglas-Chaney Apptments-Unfavorable 1942 Feb.-Mar C-E," ER71:O.C.D. 1942 Administrative Douglas-Chaney Appointments, ERP, FDRL.

37. *PM*, Cartoon, Feb. 11, 1942, sent by Jesse Gordon, F: "ER Correspond. OCD Re: Douglas-Chaney Appt.—Favorable 1942 F-K," ER71:O.C.D. 1942 Administrative Douglas-Chaney Appointments, ERP, FDRL. Selden Rodman to ER, Feb. 14, 1942, F: "ER Correspond. OCD Re: Douglas-Chaney Appt.—Favorable 1942 R-Z," ER71:O.C.D. 1942 Administrative Douglas-Chaney Appointments, ERP, FDRL. Eloise Tudor to ER, Feb. 11, 1942; Emma Vellani to ER, Feb. 23, 1942, Ibid. Grafton quote from Lash, *Eleanor and Franklin*, 650. John Barry, "Ways of the World: Eleanor Roosevelt," *San Francisco News*, Feb. 26, 1942, F: "ER OCD Re: Douglas-Chaney Appts. (Favorable) 1942 A-E," ER71:O.C.D. 1942 Administrative Douglas-Chaney Appointments, ERP, FDRL. Baird to ER, Feb. 7, 1942, Ibid. Belinda Jelliffe to ER, Feb. 12, 1942, F: "ER Correspond. OCD Re: Douglas-Chaney Appt.—Favorable 1942 F-K," ER71:O.C.D. 1942 Administrative Douglas-Chaney Appointments, ERP, FDRL. Florence Macavoy to ER, Feb. 9, 1942, F: "ER Correspond. OCD Re: Douglas-Chaney Appt.—Favorable 1942 L-P," ER 71: O.C.D. 1942 Administrative Douglas-Chaney Appointments, ERP, FDRL. Samuel Cleland to ER, Feb. 11, 1942, F: "ER OCD Re: Douglas-Chaney Appts. (Favorable) 1942 A-E," ER71:O.C.D. 1942 Administrative Douglas-Chaney Appointments, ERP, FDRL. Charles Belous to ER, Feb. 24; and Ralph Ingersoll, "Enemies of the Republic," Feb. 20, 1942, Ibid. Clara Watson to ER, Feb. 25, 1942, F: "ER Correspond. OCD Re: Douglas-Chaney Appt.—Favorable 1942 R-Z," ER 71: O.C.D. 1942 Administrative Douglas-Chaney Appointments, ERP, FDRL. Dorothy Amrhein to ER, Feb. 24, 1942, F: "ER OCD Re: Douglas-Chaney Appts. (Favorable) 1942 A-E," ER 71: O.C.D. 1942 Administrative Douglas-Chaney Appointments, ERP, FDRL. Lyde Ramsey Arrott to ER, Feb. 13, 1942, Ibid. Cornelia Baerthlein to ER, Feb. 14, 1942, Ibid. Mary Kennedy to ER, Feb. 13, 1942, F: "ER Correspond. OCD Re: Douglas-Chaney Appt.—Favorable 1942 F-K," ER 71: O.C.D. 1942 Administrative Douglas-Chaney Appointments, ERP, FDRL.

38. ER, *This I Remember*, 231–232. Mr. Jackson to ER, Feb. 7, 1942, RG171, E: 10, B: 83, F: 200 Volunteer Participation, Dec. 16, 1941-. Paul Kellogg to ER, Feb. 8, 1942, F: "1942 Kellogg, Paul," ER 100: Personal Letters 1942 Ilma Viola-Ke, ERP, FDRL. Opal Hadley to ER, Feb. 7, 1942, F: "ER Correspond. OCD Re: Douglas-Chaney Appt.—Favorable 1942 F-K," ER 71: O.C.D. 1942 Administrative Douglas-Chaney Appointments, ERP, FDRL. "S.F. Friends Rallying to Support of Mayris Chaney," n.d., from unnamed local evening San Francisco paper, attached to letter from John Friel to ER, Feb. 11, 1942, F: "ER OCD Douglas/Chaney Apptments Unfavorable 1942 F-Ha," ER 71: O.C.D. 1942 Administrative Douglas-Chaney Appointments, ERP, FDRL. Grady to ER, Feb. 7, 1942, F: "ER Correspond. OCD Re: Douglas-Chaney Appt.—Favorable 1942 F-K," ER 71: O.C.D. 1942 Administrative Douglas-Chaney Appointments, ERP, FDRL. Marguerite Davis to ER, Feb. 14, 1942, F: "ER OCD Re: Douglas-Chaney Appts. (Favorable) 1942 A-E," ER 71: O.C.D. 1942 Administrative Douglas-Chaney Appointments, ERP, FDRL. Lillian Amos to ER, Feb. 12, 1942, Ibid. Ethel Manning to ER, Feb. 10, 1942, F: "ER Correspond. OCD Re: Douglas-Chaney Appt.—Favorable 1942 L-P," ER 71: O.C.D. 1942 Administrative Douglas-Chaney Appointments, ERP, FDRL.

39. ER, "My Day," Jan. 14, Feb. 9, 1942. Jesse Cottrell, "Mrs. Roosevelt Replies to Congressional Critics," *Raleigh News and Observer*, Feb. 9, 1942, F: "ER OCD Douglas/Chaney Apptments Unfavorable 1942 F-Ha," ER 71: O.C.D. 1942 Administrative Douglas-Chaney Appointments, ERP, FDRL. Helen Essary, "Dear Washington," Feb. 9, 1942, no paper, in NYCMA, LG, B: 4182, F: 02, OCD: Correspondence (9) 1942/02/09.

40. Mrs. J.M. Helms to Dorothy Goldberg, Feb. 2, 1942, F: "ER O.C.D. Offers of Service 1942 Go-He," ER 71: O.C.D. 1942 Administrative Douglas-Chaney Appointments, ERP, FDRL. Landis to ER, Feb. 9, 1942, RG171, E: 10, B: 83, F: 200 Volunteer Participation, Dec. 16, 1941-. Lash, *Eleanor and Franklin*, 652.

41. ER to La Guardia, Feb. 18, 1942, F: "1942 LaGuardia, Fiorello," ER 100: Personal Letter 1942 Ki-La, ERP, FDRL. ER to Landis, Feb. 18, 1942, F: "1942 Landis, James," ER 100: Personal Letter 1942 Ki-La, ERP, FDRL. Lash, *Eleanor and Franklin*, 652.

42. ER, "My Day," Feb. 21, 1942. Charles Murchison to ER, Feb. 25, 1942, F: "ER Correspond. OCD Re: Douglas-Chaney Appt.—Favorable 1942 L-P," ER 71: O.C.D. 1942 Administrative Douglas-Chaney Appointments, ERP, FDRL.

43. Lash, *Eleanor and Franklin*, 651–652. ER, *This I Remember*, 240. "Saga of the OCD," Feb. 12, 1942, *Roanoke World-News*, F: "ER Correspond. OCD Re: Douglas-Chaney Appt.—Favorable 1942 L-P," ER 71: O.C.D. 1942 Administrative Douglas-Chaney Appointments, ERP, FDRL. Frank Kent, "Kent Deplores Mrs. Roosevelt's Defense of Her Recent Activities in O.C.D.-Bad Feeling Created," n.d. *Baltimore Sun*, F: "ER OCD Re: Douglas-Chaney Appts. (Favorable) 1942 A-E," ER 71: O.C.D. 1942 Administrative Douglas-Chaney Appointments, ERP, FDRL. ER to Louis Binns, Feb. 10, 1942, F: "1942, Bi-Bl," ER 100: Personal Letters, 1942 Ba-Bl, ERP, FDRL. ER, "My Day," Feb. 10, Feb. 11, Feb. 13, Feb. 14, Feb. 16, Feb. 17, 1942.

44. Paul Kellogg to ER, Feb. 9, 1942, F: "1942 Kellogg, Paul," ER 100: Personal Letters 1942 Ilma, Viola-Ke, ERP, FDRL. Paul Kellogg to Raymond Clapper, Feb. 9, 1942, Ibid. Kellogg also asserted that Chaney had come aboard prior to ER's arrival; there is no evidence that this was true. John Langston to ER, Feb. 18, 1942. F: "ER Correspond. OCD Re: Douglas-Chaney Appt.—Favorable 1942 L-P," ER 71: O.C.D. 1942 Administrative Douglas-Chaney Appointments, ERP, FDRL. Childs quote in Goodwin, *No Ordinary Time*, 325. ER, "My Day," Feb. 21, 1942. Mrs. Gifford Pinchot to ER, Feb. 20, 1942, F: "1942 Pinchot, Mrs. Gifford," ER 100: Personal Letters 1942 Pe-Re, ERP, FDRL. Harold Ickes Diaries, Feb. 22, 1942, 6356, LoC. Reel 4, July 5, 1940-Dec. 27, 1941 Shelf No. DM16 142. AP, "Mrs. Roosevelt Defended," Feb. 16, NYCMA, LG, B: 4182, F: 11, OCD: Corresp (18) 1942/02/18. Arthur Clarendon Smith to Editor, *Washington Post*, Feb. 17, 1942, F: "ER Correspond. OCD Re: Douglas-Chaney Appt.—Favorable 1942 R-Z," ER 100: Personal Letters 1942 Pe-Re, ERP, FDRL. Douglas Speech, Feb. 16, 1942, RG171, E: 46, B: 14, F: 120.1: Speeches (2 of 3). "With Complete Authority," *Kansas City Star*, Feb. 12, 1942, F: "ER OCD Douglas/Chaney Apptments Unfavorable 1942 S," ER71:O.C.D. 1942 Administrative Douglas-Chaney Appointments, ERP, FDRL. Dominic Mascio to ER, Feb. 23, 1942, F: "ER Correspond. OCD Re: Douglas-Chaney Appt.—Favorable 1942 L-P," ER 71 O.C.D. 1942 Administrative Douglas-Chaney Appointments, ERP, FDRL. Thomas Dyett to ER, Feb. 17, 1942, F: "ER OCD Re: Douglas-Chaney Appts. (Favorable) 1942 A-E," ER 71: O.C.D. 1942 Administrative Douglas-Chaney Appointments, ERP, FDRL. Agnes Spencer to ER, Feb. 14, 1942, F: "ER Correspond. OCD Re: Douglas-Chaney Appt.—Favorable 1942 R-Z," ER 71: O.C.D. 1942 Administrative Douglas-Chaney Appointments, ERP, FDRL. George Pugmire to ER, Feb. 23, 1942, F: "ER Correspond. OCD Re: Douglas-Chaney Appt.—Favorable 1942 L-P," ER 71: O.C.D. 1942 Administrative Douglas-Chaney Appointments, ERP, FDRL.

45. ER to Landis, Feb. 18, 1942, F: "1942 Landis, James," ER 100: Personal Letter 1942 Ki-La, ERP, FDRL. ER to Kerr quoted in Goodwin, *No Ordinary Time*, 325-326. Lash, *Eleanor and Franklin*, 653. ER, "My Day," Feb. 23, 1942. For an insightful account of Hillary Clinton's role in health care reform in 1993, see Theda Skocpol, *Boomerang: Health Care Reform and the Turn against Government* (New York: W. W. Norton, 1996). Also see Shawn J. Parry-Giles, *Hillary Clinton in the News: Gender and Authenticity in American Politics* (Champaign: University of Illinois Press, 2014) 63. ER, *This I Remember*, 232, 249–250.

Chapter 12

1. Prepared under the supervision of The Provost Marshal General, "Defense Against Enemy Action Directed at Civilians," Apr. 30, 1946, RG389, E: 468, B: 1940, F: Study 3b-1. A. A. Hoehling, *Home-Front, U.S.A.* (New York: Thomas Y. Crowell Company, 1966), 46.

2. Franklin D. Roosevelt, Press Conference, Feb. 17, 1942, The American Presidency Project, http://www.presidency.ucsb.edu/ws/index.php?pid=16223. "They can come in and shell New York tomorrow night, under certain conditions. They can probably, so far as that goes, drop bombs on Detroit tomorrow night, under certain conditions," the president announced.

3. Paul Durrie to Alex Miller, Mar. 12,1942, RG171, E: 10, B: 85, F: 230-Veterans' Participation, Feb. 1, 1942-. For the most part, children helped sell defense stamps, led conservation campaigns, and readied homes in case of fire, among other tasks. C. Brooks Peters, "The OCD,

Under James M. Landis, Is Now Geared for Instant Action," *New York Times*, May 3, 1942, RG171, E: 185, B: 6, F: 7-A-1: Statements and Speeches, Landis. "Stay and Take It, Landis Urges Coast on Bombing," *Los Angeles Times*, May, 29, 1942, Ibid. L. D. Gasser to Malcolm Jones, Mar. 28, 1942, RG171, E: 10, B: 115, F: 514-Air Raid Precautions, Mar. 21–Apr. 14, 1942. Sparrow, *Warfare State*, 6. More than 3,000 people in Des Moines enrolled in civil defense training schools in the schools' opening week.

4. Luther Huston, "Barbed-Wire Boss of the OCD," *New York Times*, May 31, 1942, 11, RG171, E: 185, B: 14, F: 9-A: Landis. No Author, "OCD Chief Urges Truth Be Told Of War Losses," *Chicago Tribune*, Sept. 7, 1942, RG171, E: 185, B: 6, F: 7-A-1: Statements & Speeches by Landis. "Army & Navy: OCD Reports," *Time*, Aug. 10, 1942.

5. FDR to James Conant, Jan. 5, 1936, LoC, Landis Papers, B: 13, F: "1935–37 Roosevelt, F. D." Landis, "Law and the New Liberties," *Current Legal Thought*, Abstracted from 4 *Missouri Law Review* 105, April 1939, in Vol. V, July–Aug., 1939, No. 9, 519–522, LoC, Landis Papers, B: 163, Speech, Article and Book File, F: "Law and the New Liberties," Feb. 7, 1939. Landis, "Liberty as an Evolutionary Idea," *Vital Speeches of the Day*, Apr. 27, 1938, LoC, Landis Papers, B: 163, Speech, Article and Book File, F: "Liberty as an Evolutionary Idea, Apr. 27, 1938." Landis to Stanley Fuld, Nov. 29, 1948, LoC, Landis Papers, B: 181, Miscellany, F: "Biographical Material, Unarranged."

6. Landis to Miss Le Hand, Jan. 13,1937; Landis to FDR, Jan. 13,1937; Landis to FDR, handwritten note, Jan. 13, 1937; Landis to FDR, press release, Sept. 14, 1937, F: "Landis, James M," PPF 4858: Landis, James M, FDRL. FDR to Landis, Sept. 14, 1937, Ibid.

7. Luther Huston, "Barbed-Wire Boss of the OCD," *New York Times*, May 31,1942, 11, RG171, E: 185, B: 14, F: 9-A: Landis. Mrs. DT Basttie to Landis, Feb. 10, 1942, RG171, E: 46, B: 1, F: 000.3: Criticisms/Protests (folder 3 of 4). "If you lived to be a thousand years of age, you could never, never live [down] your 'whitewash' of Bridges," a Kansas woman scolded Landis. Landis said he would never be able to counter "the lies that have been told about me." Landis to Josiah Stryker, Nov. 3, 1939, LoC, Landis Papers, B: 15, No Folder title.

8. Landis to Miss S.P. Breckinridge, Aug. 6, 1940, LoC, Landis Papers, Harvard File, B: 21, F: "1937–45, 'B.'" Landis to Sarah McDonough, Sept. 27,1940, LoC, Landis Papers, B: 17, Landis Chron file, F: "1940, Sept. 15–30." "Libelous Lyrics Written on Several Laughable Occasions," Christmas, 1938, LoC, Landis Papers, B: 181, Miscellany, F: "Biographical Material, Unarranged." Landis to John Lynch, Sept. 13, 1940, LoC, Landis Papers, B: 17, Landis, F: "1940, Sept. 1–15." Landis to F. A. Saunders, Nov. 20 1939, LoC, Landis Papers, B: 15, No folder title. While he continued to immerse himself in minor details of academic life (he sought to make a traffic crossing less perilous and chastised one student because he had entered the stacks with an expired library card), he also inquired in 1940 if one second-year law student could join a Harvard-based artillery unit in order to finish his schooling without violating the new selective service law. Landis to S. Herbert Dorfman, Dec. 19,1939; Landis to Bernard Rubenstein, Dec. 19, 1939, LoC, Landis Papers, B: 15, No folder title. Landis, "Economic Change and the Dynamics of Law," Draft Speech, LoC, Landis Papers, B: 163 Speech, Article & Book File, F: "1939, June 5 Economic Change + the Dynamics of Law." Secretary to the Dean to R. H. Phelps, Apr. 20, 1940, LoC, Landis Papers, B: 17, Landis, F: "1940, Aug. 15–30." Also see Landis to Chester Sargent, Sept. 4, 1940, LoC, Landis Papers, B: 17, Landis, F: "1940, Sept. 1–14." Landis to Felix Frankfurter, Aug. 21, 1940, LoC, Landis Papers, B: 17, Landis, F: "1940, Aug. 15–30." Landis to Edward Rowe, Sept. 27, 1940, LoC, Landis Papers, B: 17, Landis Chron file, F: "1940, Sept. 15–30." Landis to Thomas Corcoran, Oct. 15, 1940; Landis to Ed Whitley, Oct. 16, 1940, LoC, Landis Papers, B: 17, Landis Chron File, F: "Oct. 1–Nov. 30, 1940." "Plan E Carries City by Margin of 7,500 Votes," *Cambridge Sun*, Nov. 7, 1940, LoC, Landis Papers, Harvard File, B: 26, F: "Plan E Pamphlets." Landis to Charles Gross, Sept. 30, 1940, LoC, Landis Papers, B: 17, Landis Chron File, F: "1940, Sept. 15–30."

9. Landis to Sylvester Gates, Oct. 18, 1940, LoC, Landis Papers, B: 17, Landis Chron file, F: "Oct. 1–Nov. 30, 1940." Landis to Harold Laski, Oct. 28, 1940, LoC, Landis Papers, B: 17, Landis Chron file, F: "Oct. 1–Nov. 30, 1940." Landis to A. Julius Freiberg, Nov. 1, 1940, LoC, Landis Papers, B: 17, Landis Chron File, F: "Oct. 1–Nov. 30, 1940." Landis to Charlie Murchison, Nov. 12, 1940, LoC, Landis Papers, B: 17, Landis Chron File,

F: "Oct. 1–Nov. 30, 1940." Landis to P. A. O'Connell, Dec. 28, 1940, LoC, Landis Papers, B: 18, Chron File. Landis to John Baker, Nov. 26, 1940, LoC, Landis Papers, B: 17, Landis Chron File, F: "Oct. 1–Nov. 30, 1940." "Telegram," to FDR, Jan. 9, 1941, from American Defense, Harvard Group; Landis to Sam Rayburn, Jan. 9, 1941, LoC, Landis Papers, B: 18, Chron File.

10. Landis, "Organized Civilian Defense," Dec. 1941, Speech to Boston National Convention, see LoC, Landis Papers, B: 170, Speech, Article and Book File, F: "'Organized Civilian Defense,' *Postmasters Gazette*, Dec 1941." Donald Ritchie, *James M. Landis*, 102. Landis, "Morale and Civilian Defense," *American Journal of Sociology*, Vol. 47, No. 3 (Nov. 1941): 331–339.

11. Staff Correspondent, "Reorganized Civilian Defense Now Under Landis Led Board," *Christian Science Monitor*, Apr. 16, 1942, 8. W. P. Clark to Sen. Walter George, Mar. 4, 1942, RG171, E: 46, B: 1, F: 000.3: Criticisms/Protests (folder 1 of 4). During World War I, Landis had written an article "The Duty of a Private Citizen in the Matter of National Preparedness" that suggested his long-standing devotion to mobilization from the bottom up. Oscar Newbridge to Landis, Mar. 18, 1942; Landis to Newbridge, Mar. 20, 1942, RG171, E: 10, B: 2, F: 000.3, Jan. 15, 1942. Clarence Baender, Mar. 14, 1942; no name to Landis, Mar. 16, 1942, RG171, E: 10, B: 2, F: 000.3, Jan. 15, 1942-. Luther Huston, "Barbed-Wire Boss of the OCD," *New York Times*, May 31, 1942, 11, RG171, E: 185, B: 14, F: 9-A: Landis. Landis to FDR, Feb. 10, 1942, and attached "A Summary of The Immediate Objectives to Be Pursued by the Office of Civilian Defense," RG171, E: 46, B:27, F:380.1—OCD.

12. Landis to Judge Stanley Fuld, Nov. 29, 1948, LoC, Landis Papers, B: 181, Miscellany, F: "Biographical Material, Unarranged." Landis, "The Need for Civilian Protection," Jan. 17, 1942, Vital Speeches of the Day, Vol. 8, Issue 10, 319–320. Landis to Florence Struve, Mar. 21, 1942, RG171, E: 10, B: 115, F: 514-Air Raid Precautions, Mar. 21–Apr. 9, 1942. Landis to Robert Patterson, Jan. 30, 1942, RG171, E: 10, B: 4, F: 020, Jan. 22–31, 1942. L. D. Gasser to Maury Maverick, Jan. 7, 1942, RG171, E: 10, B: 102, F: 381: War Production Board, Jan. 1–Mar. 31, 1942. AP, "Japanese Fire-Bomb Attack on Oregon Timber Suspected," *Baltimore Sun*, Sept. 15, 1942, 1. The attacks near Santa Barbara caused hardly any damage.

13. Eliot Robinson to Landis, Jan. 12, 1942, and attached, "Another Monstrosity," *New Bedford Standard Times*, Jan. 10, 1942, RG171, E: 10, B: 92, F: 321: Landis, James M. "Minutes of the First Meeting of the Civilian Defense Board," Apr. 24, 1942, RG171, E: 46, B: 26, F: 330-Civilian Defense Board. "Intelligence Report: Trends in American Public Opinion Since Pearl Harbor," Sept. 11, 1942, RG44, E: 165, B: 1806, F: Intelligence Report: Trends in American Public Opinion Since Pearl Harbor. By March, the sentiment was virtually unchanged with 29 percent predicting war's end by February 1944. For an analysis of the home front following Pearl Harbor, see David Kennedy, *Freedom from Fear*, ch. 8. Joint U.S. Chiefs of Staff, Hawaiian Defense Forces, Feb. 12, 1942; Situation in Hawaiian Islands Regarding Japanese Population, F: "Confidential File Hawaii," PSF: 7, FDRL.

14. Wesley Frank Craven, James Lea Cate, eds., *The Army Air Forces in World War II*, v. 1, 277–286 (Washington, DC: Office of Air Force History: For Sale by the Supt. Of Docs., U.S. G.P.O., 1983). www.sfmuseum.org/hist9/aaf2.html. L. D. Gasser to Landis, Apr. 20, 1942, RG171, E: 10, B: 126, F: 525.1-Gas Masks, Apr. 1–30, 1942. The warnings were hardly propaganda aimed just at whipping up prowar sentiment. War Department leaders asked Landis to send "baby protectors and Mickey Mouse [gas] masks" to children in Hawaii, Alaska, Puerto Rico, and other endangered places.

15. Michael Sullivan to ER, Jan. 13, 1942; George Baehr to Sullivan, Jan. 17, 1942, RG171, E: 10, B: 131, F: 720-Health. Officials assured the captain that they had planned for this eventuality. E. V. Burnett to R. Walmsley, Feb. 25, 1942, RG171, E: 46, B: 1, F: 000.3: Criticisms/Protests (folder 1 of 4). John Danaher to Office of Civilian Defense, Dec. 23, 1941, RG171, E: 10, B: 127, F: 525.1-Gas Masks, Jan. 1–15, 1942. UP, "Civilians Warned of Raids, Told to Make Own Fight," Feb. 18, 1942, *New York Journal American* (according to letter), RG171, E: 10, B: 109, F: 500-Civilian Protection. A woman from Flushing, Long Island, wrote President Roosevelt that she had "voted for you every time you ran for office and believed in you and still will if you see that something is done to protect us." Frank Crowther to C. H. Woodward, Jan. 10, 1942, RG171, E: 10, B: 105, F: 435-Building and Plant Protection, Jan. 1–31, 1942. Mrs. George Connell to Landis, Feb. 20, 1942, RG171, E: 10, B: 118, F: 515-Air

Raid Shelters, Mar. 1-16, 1942. "British RAF Pilot Criticizes Critics of OCD," article in local paper, sent by Mose Leibowitz to ER, Mar. 5, 1942, F: "ER Correspond. OCD Re: Douglas-Chaney Appt.—Favorable 1942 L-P," ER 71: Office of Civilian Defense, ERP, FDRL.

16. James Kirby to James Haswell, Feb. 20, 1942, RG171, E: 10, B: 110, F: 501-1: Aux. Police Force. L. D. Gasser to Frank Matthews, Jan. 12, 1942, RG171, E: 10, B: 127, F: 525.1-Gas Masks, Jan. 1–15, 1942. Gasser to Adolph Bergman, Jan. 30, 1942, RG171, E: 10, B: 127, F: 525.1-Gas Masks, Jan. 16–31, 1942. Gasser to Landios, Feb. 4, 1942, RG171, E: 10, B: 126, F: 525-Gas Defense, thru Feb. 15, 1942. Gasser to Lindsey Humphreys, Feb.18, 1942, RG171, E: 10, B: 126, F: 525-Gas Defense, Feb. 16–Mar 9, 1942. George Baehr to Maynard Weller, Feb. 10, 1942, RG171, E: 10, B: 129, F: 700, Medicine, Etc., Feb. 1–28, 1942. George Baehr to British Library of Information, March 25, 1942, RG171, E: 10, B: 129, F: 700-Medicines, etc., Mar. 1, 1942-. Albert Cinelli M.D., to George Baehr, Feb. 27, 1942; Baehr to Cinelli, Mar. 5, 1942, RG171, E: 10, B: 131, F: 729: First Aid, Mar. 1, 1942-. Dr. Mould to Dr. Baehr, "Courses for Physicians on Medical Aspects of Chemical Warfare, Apr. 28, 1942, RG171, E: 10, B: 129, F: 700-Medicine, etc., Mar. 1, 1942-. One training school asked Baehr to send it a film showing the impact of chemical gas on animals. Landis to Arthur Hardy, Feb. 7, 1942, RG171, E: 10, B: 120, F: 516-Camo.Feb. 1–March 15, 1942. Landis to Paul McNutt, Feb. 1, 1942, RG171, E: 10, B: 98, F: 380-6: Welfare, Jan. 1, 1942. L.D. Gasser to Landis, Apr. 20, 1942, RG171, E: 10, B: 127, F: 540-Evacuation, Apr. 1, 1942-. UP, "Landis Cites Bomb Danger in Detroit," Mar. 28, 1942, RG171, E: 46, B: 1, F: 000.3: Criticisms/Protests (folder 1 of 4). Landis to R. Bradley, Mar. 26, 1942, RG171, E: 10, B: 2, F: 000.3, Nov. 21, 1942-. E. A. Seridan to John Hartman, Mar. 19, 1942, RG171, E: 10, B: 2, F: 000.3, Jan. 15, 1942-. Henry Dudley to Paul Harvey, Mar. 17, 1942, RG171, E: 10, B: 85, F: 230-Veterans' Participation, Feb. 1, 1942-. L. D. Gasser to Malcolm Jones, Mar. 28, 1942, RG171, E: 10, B: 115, F: 514-Air Raid Precautions, Mar. 21-April 14, 1942. L. D. Gasser to Maury Maverick, Jan. 28, 1942, RG171, E: 10, B: 102, F: 381: War Production Board, Jan. 1–Mar. 31, 1942. "Notice of Agreement between the Federal Security Agency and the Office of Civilian Defense," signed by Landis, Feb. 26, 1942, RG171, E: 10, B: 130, F: 710-Hospitals, May-Dec. 1941. Francis Farnum, "Help Spot the Spies and Saboteurs"; AP, "Spies Land in Maine," *Boston American,* May 22, 1942; "Axis Agents Land in Maine—State on Alert," *Boston Monitor,* May 22, 1942, RG171, E: 46, B: 30, F: 000: Region I.

17. At the same time that he was sowing hysteria with much of his public commentary, Landis also commanded aides to keep certain signals (so-called yellow and blue alerts) confidential to avoid outbreaks of public panic, and the OCD refused to urge mass vaccinations for typhoid and tetanus lest they sow hysteria about germ warfare coming to the United States. He never managed to strike a consistent balance, as he veered between hysteria on the one hand and withholding information from the public on the other. Landis to Robert Knapp, Oct. 23, 1942, "Rumors Current in the United States," Sept. 1–30, 1942, by Robert Knapp, RG171 E: 47, B: 32, F: Region I: MA, S.C. 381. United Press, "Warn Enemy Bombs May be Here Soon," *New York Times,* Jan.13, 1942, 2. George Baehr to Thomas Uniker, Feb. 7, 1942, RG171, E: 10, B: 131, F: 720-Health. Landis to Regional Directors, Instructional Letter No. 33, May 5, 1942, RG171, E: 46, B: 25, F: 330: Civilian Defense Board. Landis feared that "simply by sending up successive flights of planes sufficiently close to require a warning" the enemy could sow panic, mass flight, and chaos in communications.

18. For examples in the literature that stress racial animus toward Japanese Americans as a root cause of the camps, see Roger Daniels, *Prisoners without Trial: Japanese Americans in World War II* (New York: Hill and Wang, revised edition, 2004); and John W. Dower, *War Without Mercy: Race and Power in the Pacific War* (New York: Pantheon, 1993). Eric L. Muller, *American Inquisition: The Hunt for Japanese American Disloyalty in World War II* (Chapel Hill: University of North Carolina Press, 2007) demonstrates how midlevel federal bureaucrats conducted tests assessing the loyalty of Japanese Americans. The OCD had created a network of alliances with the FBI, the White House, the military, the American Legion, and law enforcement agencies focused on disrupting plots imperiling the country.

19. For a smart, concise history of the internment camp, see Daniels, *Prisoners without Trial.* Daniels points out that even those considered liberal titans hyped the internal Japanese threat, ignoring the reality that there was no evidence linking Japanese Americans to subversive

activities within the United States. Two months after Pearl Harbor, California's Attorney General Earl Warren assured a congressional committee that "the fifth column activities that we are to get, are timed, just like the invasion of France, and of Norway . . . I believe that we are just being lulled into a false sense of security . . . Our day of reckoning is bound to come." Edward R. Murrow repeated the false rumor that Japanese American graduates of prominent West Coast colleges and universities were seeking to attack the U.S. home front. In January, he said in Seattle that "if Seattle ever does get bombed, you will be able to look up and see some University of Washington sweaters on the boys doing the bombing!" Olson and Bowron quotes from Daniels, *Prisoners without Trial*, 42–43. Joint U.S. Chiefs of Staff, Hawaiian Defense Forces, Feb. 12, 1942; Situation in Hawaiian Islands Regarding Japanese Population, F: "Confidential File Hawaii," PSF: 7, FDRL. See Daniels, 37–38. For FDR's decision to intern Japanese Americans, also see Greg Robinson, *By Order of the President: FDR and the Internment of Japanese Americans* (Cambridge, MA: Harvard University Press, 2001), ch. 3. General Regional Advisory Council Region XII, Minutes of Meeting, May 1, 1942, RG171, E: 47, B: 50, F: Region IX: 330.1.

20. James Sheppard to Landis, Mar. 3, 1942, RG171, E: 47, B: 49, F: Region IX: 317.
21. C. E. Groninger to Paul McNutt, Mar. 26, 1942; McNutt to Groninger, Apr. 6, 1942, RG171, E: 46, B: 3, F: 001-Aliens. "Restrictions Applying to Enemy Nationalities," memo by Nat Schmulowitz, Mar. 9, 1942, RG171, E: 10, B: 117, F: 514.1-Air Raid Warning System, Mar. 21, 1942-. Landis to Regional Directors, Mar. 20, 1942, draft; Landis to Regional Directors, n.d. RG171, E: 46, B: 3, F: 001: Aliens." Noncitizens were allowed to register for volunteer service, but the Defense Corps was off-limits to immigrants from nations deemed hostile to the United States. Landis to Francis Biddle, Apr. 8, 1942, RG171, E: 46, B: 3, F: 001: Aliens. "Aliens of enemy nationality should [not] be permitted to engage in any of the protective activities connected with Civilian Defense," Landis wrote Biddle on April 8. "We cannot afford to rely upon hairline decisions on the question of loyalty" when citizens' lives were at stake. Home defense, he added, should have the same eligibility requirements as the armed services. Landis and his team viewed all "enemy aliens" as possible subversives. Landis helped establish byzantine rules for judging the loyalty of "enemy aliens" led by a Board of Inquiry that could differentiate the loyal from the disloyal would-be volunteers. Stanley Gewirtz to John Martin, Mar. 4, 1942, RG171, E: 46, B: 3, F: 001: Aliens. Landis to Regional Directors, Mar.20, 1942, draft; Landis to Regional Directors, n.d. RG171, E: 46, B: 3, F: 001: Aliens. Edward Ennis to Landis, Apr. 29, 1942; Landis to Ennis, May 6, 1942, RG171, E: 46, B: 3, F: 001: Aliens.
22. General Regional Advisory Council Region XII, Minutes of Meeting, May 1, 1942, RG171, E: 47, B: 50, F: Region IX: 330.1. Edward Ennis to Landis, Apr. 29, 1941; Landis to Ennis, May 6, 1941, RG171, E: 46, B: 3, F: 001: Aliens. Landis to James Sheppard, Aug. 19, 1942; Landis to George Levison, Aug. 21, 1942, RG171, E: 47, B: 48, F: Region IX: 001. Landis agreed with DeWitt that the OCD needed to assign a liaison to the Wartime Civil Control Administration, which was overseeing the camps from an office in San Francisco's Whitcomb Hotel. John Martin to John Richardson, Aug. 25, 1942, RG171, E: 47, B: 48, F: Region IX: 001. James Sheppard to Landis, Aug. 24, 1942; Western Defense Command and Fourth Army Wartime Civil Control Administration, Aug. 19, 1942; J.L. DeWitt to Sheppard, Aug. 19, 1942; and attached memos from Sheppard, Aug. 24, 1942, RG171, E: 47, B: 48, F: Region IX: 001. "Telephone Conversation between Mr. John B. Martin and Mr. George Levison, San Francisco, California," Aug. 24, 1942, RG171, E: 47, B: 48, F: Region IX: 001. In late August, the OCD's John Martin and regional deputy director George Levison discussed the internment camps by phone. The permit program, Levison assured Martin, "is to continue indefinitely, unless there are orders for evacuation of the Germans and Italians." Martin wanted all potential permit officers to undergo background investigations because some applicants may not be "desirable." To Levison, however, speed was paramount; "it's Monday and this thing has got to be in operation Thursday," Levison replied. By late August, the West Coast's 250-plus defense councils had hired 237 "alien permit officers," nearly a third of them having a law enforcement background. Local councils, Sheppard told DeWitt, "are willing to undertake any assignment." In September and October, one officer granted more than 750 travel permits to "German Aliens" while rejecting requests from scores of others. By year's end, however,

DeWitt abolished the program. Staff Meeting, Ninth Regional Office of Civilian Defense, Sept. 21, 1942, RG171, E: 47, B: 50, F: Region IX: 330.1. James Sheppard to J. L. DeWitt, Aug. 27, 1942, RG171, E: 47, B: 48, F: Region IX: 001. "Travel and Curfew Report," Oct. 3, Oct. 10, Oct. 31, 1942, Richard J. Wilson, RG171, E: 47, B: 48, F: Region IX: 001. George Levison to Landis, Dec. 26, 1942, RG171, E: 47, B: 48, F: Region IX: 001. James Sheppard to Landis, June 11, 1943, RG171, E: 47, B: 49, F: Region IX: 330-Civilian Defense Board.

23. "Training for Emergency Police Work," file date, Feb. 20, 1942, RG171, E: 10, B: 110, F: 501-Police Cooperation. Hoover to La Guardia, Jan. 21, 1942, and attached memo, n.d., Hoover to Landis, Jan. 28, 1942, RG171, E: 12, B: 1, F: Loose, No. 1. "*PERSONAL AND CONFIDENTIAL*," Hoover labeled one memo excoriating the state of home defense conditions on Hawaii. J. Edgar Hoover to La Guardia, Feb. 5, 1942, RG171, E: 12, B: 2, F: Confidential: 020: 12/1/41. Thomas Dignan to La Guardia, Feb. 13, 1942, RG171, E: 12, B: 1, F: Loose, No. 3. J. Edgar Hoover to La Guardia, n.d., RG171, E: 12, B: 1, F: Loose, No. 1. L.D. Gasser to Adjutant General, Jan. 16, 1942, RG171, E: 12, B: 2, F: Confidential: 020: 12/1/41-. Walter Sandt to FDR, Mar. 23, 1942, RG171, E: 10, B: 2, F: 000.3, Mar. 21, 1942-. Landis to Walter Metcalf, May 18. 1942, RG171, E: 47, B: 33, F: Region II: 500. James Kirby to James Haswell, Feb. 20, 1942, RG171, E: 10, B: 110, F: 501-1: Aux. Police Force.

24. Miss L. Fredrickson to U.S. War Department, Apr. 15, 1942; L.D. Gasser to Fredrickson, May 1, 1942, RG171, E: 10, B: 109, F: 500-Civilian Protection. "County Making Gains in Air Raid Protection," *Los Angeles Times*, Apr. 7, 1942, A1. Address by James Sheppard, Apr. 21, 1942, RG171, E: 47, B: 48, F: Region IX: 100 (2 of 2). Sheppard called home defense the military's "strong right arm," denounced militarized efforts that harmed "individual freedom," and promised that "we can take anything," despite the naysaying from "wise-cracking columnists and soothsayers." James Sheppard to Landis, Mar. 3, 1942, RG171, E: 47, B: 49, F: Region IX: 317. AP, "Raid Drill on Coast Mistaken for Attack," *Washington Star*, Aug. 8, 1942, 2A, RG171, E: 185, B: 8, F: 8-G: Practice Air Raids, Aug. 1, 1942.

25. Special Services Division to R. Keith Kane, Memo, "OCD-A Good Program that Could be Made Better," Oct. 30, 1942, RG171, E: 46, B: 27, F: 380.1-OCD. Harold Ickes, Diary, Apr. 19, 1942, 6548; May 24, 1942, 6632-3, LoC. Julia Dowell to Ed Isac, Apr. 6, 1942, RG171, E: 47, B: 49, F: Region IX: 310, Jan.–May 1942.

26. "Stay and Take It, Landis Urges Coast on Bombing," *Los Angeles Times* May 29, 1942, RG171, E: 185, B: 6, F: 7-A-1: Statements/Speeches, Landis. Lloyd Price, "Be Ready, Dallas Told Bombings Will Come," *Dallas Morning News*, May 31, 1942, RG171, E: 185, B: 6, F: 7-A-1: Statements and Speeches, Landis. George Z. Griswold, "Landis Tells 12,000: Sleep and Eat War," *Cleveland Plain Dealer*, Apr. 1, 1942, RG171, E: 185, B: 6, F: 7-A-1: Statements or Speeches by Landis. Landis also called social workers caring for children of women factory laborers "war workers"; he hailed millions of Americans who in their daily lives were "responding magnificently" to the home front threat.

27. "CIVILIAN DEFENSE READY FOR ACTION: Landis Extends His Control Over the Local Units," *New York Times*, May, 3, 1942.

28. Landis to All Members of Washington Staff, Mar. 24, 1942, RG171, E: 10, B: 112, F: 512-Blackouts, Mar. 24–31, 1942. "4-Story Fall Kills Woman in Raid Test," *Washington Post*, July, 31, 1942, RG171, E: 185, B: 8, F: 8-G: Practice Air Raids, thru July 1942. Minutes of The East Coast Conference of State Defense Directors, Sept. 30, 1942, RG171, E: 46, B: 26, F: 330.1: Conferences (2 of 2). "Mayor Oks Alarm Result; 2 Die 5 Hurt in Confusion," *PM*, New York City, Sept. 8, 1942, 20, RG171, E:185, B:8, F: 8-G, Practice Air Raids Aug. 1, 1942-.

29. FDR to Landis, July 13, 1942, F: "Landis, James M," PPF 4858: Landis, James M, FDRL. Landis to FDR, July, 14, 1942, RG171, E: 46, B: 4: F: 031. FDR mocked Landis at a press conference and even kidded him in a letter: "To your dying day, you will be kidded about a certain famous letter on the subject of turning out the light!" Landis "richly deserve[d]" FDR's ridicule, he replied. "At least there is no blackout on your part these days of humor and kindliness." Interviews by Raymond Abrashkin, "What'll You Do If New York is Bombed?" *PM*, Aug. 23, 1942, 14, RG171, E: 185, B: 8, F: 8-G, Practice Air Raids, Aug. 1, 1942-.

30. Landis to Harry Byrd, Apr. 24, 1942, RG171, E: 12, B: 7, F: Organization, 1 to 3. Landis transferred the entire Physical Fitness Division to the Office of Defense Health and Welfare

Services. McNutt then abolished the Physical Fitness Division that he had inherited from the OCD in the wake of the Chaney scandal. McNutt fired directors in charge of "bowling, ping pong, tennis, horseshoe pitching and other sports," according to one newspaper. "Minutes of the First Meeting of the Civilian Defense Board," Apr. 24, 1942, RG171, E: 46, B: 26, F: 330-Civilian Defense Board. "Office of Civilian Defense," Apr. 16, 1942, RG171, E: 46, B: 27, F: 380.1-OCD. C. Brooks Peters, "The OCD, Under James M. Landis, Is Now Geared for Instant Action," *New York Times*, May 3, 1942, RG171, E: 185, B: 6, F: 7-A-1: Statements and Speeches, Landis.

31. "AIR: Civilian Pilots," *Time*, May 4, 1942.

32. Milton Bracker, "Tip of Manhattan in First Blackout; 100%, Says Mayor," *New York Times*, Mar. 26, 1942, 1. "Whole of City Blacked Out for First Time," *New York Herald Tribune*, June 6, 1942; Meyer Berger, "First City-Wide Blackout Darkens 320 Square Miles," *New York Times*, June 6, 1942, RG171, E: 185, B: 8, F: 8-G: Practice Raids (thru July 7, 1942). At the mayor's press conference, borough presidents shouted at La Guardia to tell the public that their borough performed the best; "with such splendid rivalry, how can we go wrong," La Guardia said.

33. Landis to L. D. Gasser, Apr. 16, 1942; George Levison to unknown, n.d., RG171, E: 47, B: 31, F: Region I: 500. John Maynard, "Capital's First Daylight Alert Proves Success," *Washington Times Herald*, June 3, 1942; Christine Sadler, "D.C.'s 1st Real Day Raid Drill is Successful," *Washington Post*, June 3, 1942, RG171, E: 185, B: 8, F: 8-G: Practice Raids (thru July 1942). "Planes Lend Realism to Full Blackout," *Washington Times-Herald*, June 18, 1942, RG171, E: 185, B: 8, F: 8-G: Practice Air Raids (thru July 1942).

34. AP, "Japanese Fire-Bomb Attack on Oregon Timber Suspected," *Baltimore Sun*, Sept. 15, 1942, 1. AP, "Daylight Sirens Halt Boston Life," *New York Times*, June 23, 1942, RG171, E: 185, B: 8, F: 8-G: Practice Raids (thru July 1942). AP, "Seattle Raid Defense Clicks Almost 100%," *Baltimore Sun*, Aug. 3, 1942, RG171, E: 185, B: 8, F: 8-G: Practice Raids Aug. 1, 1942-. "Scores 'Killed' in Springfield Air Raid Test," *Boston Herald*, Sept. 21, 1942, 2, RG171, E: 185, B: 8, F: 8-G: Practice Air Raids, Aug. 1, 1942-. "Mid-Morning Raid Drill Called Nearly Perfect, 'Better Than in London,'" *Philadelphia Inquirer*, Nov. 17, 1942, 14, RG171, E: 185, B: 8, F: 8-G, Practice Air Raids (Oct. 9–Dec. 18, 1942). Jerry Lynn, "Chicago Mobilizes! Otis Building Workers Know What To Do If Air Raid Strikes Loop," *Daily Times, Chicago*, Feb. 17, 1942, RG171, E: 10, B: 115, F: 514-Air Raid Precautions, Mar. 1–20, 1942.

35. Harold Ickes Diary, June 14, 1942, 6705, LoC. AP, "Landis Thinks Coasts Might Have Bombing," *Baltimore Sun*, June 30, 1942, 3, RG171, E: 185, B: 6, F: 7-A-1: Statements & Speeches by Landis. Minutes of Second Meeting of the Civilian Defense Board, June 12, 1942, RG171, E: 46, B: 26, F: 330: Civilian Defense Board. Board Meeting, June 8, 1942. Archibald MacLeish Papers, LoC, B: 52, F: Subject File: Off: Minutes of Meetings. "Landis Warns City of Great Defense Lag," *San Francisco Chronicle*, May 26, 1942, RG171, E: 185, B: 6, F: 7-A-1: Speeches/Statements by Landis. Lawrence E. Davies, "West Coast Expects Bombs," *New York Times*, June 7, 1942, RG171, E: 185, B: 13, F: 5. Enemy Air Raids.

36. George Baehr to Waldemar Kaempffert, Jan. 21, 1941, RG171, E: 10, B: 129, F: 700-Medicine, etc., Jan. 15–31, 1942. L. D. Gasser to James Roy, May 1, 1942, RG171, E: 10, B; 115, F: 514-Air Raid Precautions, Apr. 5, 1942.

37. L.B. Griffin to FDR, Apr. 29, 1942, RG171, E: 10, B: 110, F: 502-Home Guard, 3/1/42. Ivar Johnson to FDR, Dec. 20, 1941; Gasser to Johnson, Jan. 14, 1942, RG171, E: 10, B: 110, F: 501-Police Cooperation. Grant Riesland to FDR, Feb. 24, 1942, RG171, E: 10, B: 110, F: 502-Home Guards, Mar. 1, 1942. Thomas Cheesborough to Jonathan Daniels, Feb. 28, 1942; L. D. Gasser to Cheesborough, Mar. 25, 1942, RG171, E: 10, B: 112, F: 512-Blackouts, Mar. 24–31, 1942. W. P. Carlile to Office of Civilian Defense, Apr. 20, 1942; L. D. Gasser to Carlile, May 2, 1942, RG171, E: 10, B: 110, F: 501.1-Aux. Police Force. Lester Stone to Elizabeth Thomson, Jan. 26, 1942, and attachment, RG171, E: 10, B: 92, F: 321: La Guardia, F. H. Other businesses smelled an opportunity, asking Washington to buy their sandbags, alarms, and clocks for home defense.

38. "Army & Navy: OCD Reports," *Time*, Aug. 10, 1942. "Landis Assails Failure of Surprise Blackout," Unnamed Newspaper, July 22, 1942, 3, RG171, E: 185, B: 6, F: 7-A-1: Statements &

Speeches, Landis. "La Guardia Invited By Landis to See Bomb Demonstration," *Washington Star*, July 30, 1942, 17A, RG171, E: 185, B: 6, F: 7-A-1: Statements/Speeches by Landis.

39. "Army & Navy: OCD Reports," *Time*, Aug. 10, 1942, AP, "Japanese Fire-Bomb Attack on Oregon Timber Suspected," *Baltimore Sun*, Sept. 15, 1942, 1. "OCD Chief Urges Truth Be Told of War Losses," *Chicago Tribune*, Sept. 7, 1942, RG171, E: 185, B: 6, F: 7-A-1: Statements & Speeches by Landis. "Home Front War To Get Tougher, Landis' Warning," *Chicago Sun*, Sept. 7, 1942, RG171, E: 185, B: 6, F: 7-A-1: Statements/Speeches, by Landis. Special Services Division to R. Keith Kane, Memo, "OCD-A Good Program that Could be Made Better," Oct. 30, 1942, RG171, E: 46, B: 27, F: 380.1-OCD. "Landis Lauds Civil Defense Strides; Warns Danger of Attack Remains," *Los Angeles Times*, Sept. 23, 1942, RG171, E: 185, B: 6, F: 7-A-1, Statements/Speeches, Landis. Fred Carver to Landis, Sept. 26, 1942, and attached, C. P. Corliss, "Landis Urges OCD Legal Backing," *Pasadena Star-News*, Sept. 23, 1942, RG171, E: 47, B: 48, F: Region IX: 100 (1 of 2).

40. Report by Committee of Illuminating Engineers, n.d., RG171, E: 16, B: 42, F: Dimouts: Coastal, thru Oct. 10, 1942. James Sheppard to Commanding General, Western Defense Command and Fourth Army, Presidio of San Francisco, Mar. 20, 1942, RG171, E: 16, B: 42, F: Dimouts: Coastal, thru Oct. 10, 1942. Joseph Loughlin to U.S. Grant, 3rd, Aug. 10, 1942, RG171, E: 16, B: 42, F: Dimouts, thru Aug. 31, 1942. In contrast to blackouts, "dimouts" were typically partial blackouts in which only certain homes, businesses, and roads needed to be darkened because they were close enough to the coast to illuminate ships at sea. In other cases, people were allowed to dim their lights, rather than turn them off, theoretically enabling them to go about their business. "GLOW OF CITIES STILL AIDS U-BOATS," *New York Times*, May 24, 1942, E10.

41. Bernard Branner to Landis, May 6, 1942, RG171, E: 16, B: 42, F: Dimouts, thru Aug. 31, 1942. L. D. Gasser to John P. Smith, May 18, 1942, RG171, E: 46, B: 4, F: 020-War Dept (3 of 4). T. J. Davis to Gasser, Apr. 20, 1942, RG171, E: 16, B: 42, F: Dimouts: Coastal, thru Oct. 10, 1942. Ralph Melbourne to Office of Civilian Defense, May 5, 1942, RG171, E: 16, B: 42, F: Dimouts: Coastal, thru Oct. 10, 1942. Richard Carpenter to James Sheppard, May 28, 1942, RG171, E: 47, B: 50, F: Region IX: 512. M. C. Mapes to Lt. Colonel Kephart, n.d., RG171, E: 16, B: 42, F: Dimouts, Jan. 1–31, 1943. Landis to J. Edgar Hoover, Apr. 12, 1943, RG171, E: 16, B: 40, Dimouts: Apr. 1–30, 1943. In 1943, Landis asked J. Edgar Hoover to send his office an FBI analysis of the charge that crime in restricted lighting zones had risen.

42. Marc Peter, Jr. to State Defense Councils, Apr. 29, 1942, RG171, E: 16, B: 42, F: Dimouts: Coastal Lighting thru Oct. 19, 42. Headquarters First Corps Area Regulations Governing the Control of Seacoast Lighting in Maine, New Hampshire, Massachusetts, Rhode Island and Connecticut, May 2, 1942, RG171, E: 16, B: 42, F: Dimouts: Coastal, thru Oct. 19, 1942. L. D. Gasser to Brutus Gundlach, May 11, 1942, RG171, E: 16, B: 42, F: Dimouts: Coastal, thru Oct. 10, 1942. James Sheppard, Regional Regulations No. 1, May 11, 1942, RG171, E: 16, B: 42, F: Dimouts: Coastal, thru Oct. 10, 1942. Report by Committee of Illuminating Engineers, n.d., RG171, E: 16, B: 42, F: Dimouts: Coastal, thru Oct. 10, 1942. The OCD partnered with Pacific Gas and Electric, Southern California Edison, and Pugent Sound Power and Light to make the campaign effective.

43. Report by Committee of Illuminating Engineers, n.d., RG171, E: 16, B: 42, F: Dimouts: Coastal, thru Oct. 10, 1942. Minutes of the Meeting of the Regional Civilian Defense Board, June 25, 1942, RG171, E: 12, B: 7, F: Meetings 1 to 5. Press Release, Office of Civilian Defense, Aug. 5, 1942, RG171, E: 46, B: 4, F: 020: War Dept. (Folder 2 of 4). James Sheppard to Landis, Sept. 14, 1942, RG171, E: 47, B: 50, F: Region IX: 512. "Meeting of Executive Committee Ninth Regional Civilian Defense Board," Sept. 24, 1942, RG171, E: 47, B: 50, F: Region IX: 330.1. J.L. DeWitt, Public Proclamation No. 12, Oct. 10, 1942, RG171, E: 47, B: 48, F: Region IX: 310. Lloyd Smith to Landis, Dec. 30, 1942, RG171, E: 16, B: 42, F: Dimouts, Jan.1–31, 1943.

44. Charlotte Winter to "Commander in Chief," May 25, 1942; and attached article by George Barrett, "Glow of Cities Still Aids U-Boats," *New York Times*, May 24, 1942, RG171, E: 16, B: 42, F: Dimouts: Coastal, thru Oct. 10, 1942. "The Year After Pearl Harbor: A Resume of Civilian Defense Activities in the Town of Islip, 1942," RG171, E: 47, B: 33, F: Region II: NY: 381, L .C. Joseph Loughlin to U.S. Grant, 3rd, Aug. 10, 1942, RG171, E: 16, B: 42,

F: Dimouts, thru Aug. 31, 1942. Landis to John T. Smith, Sept. 4, 1942, RG171, E: 16, B: 42, F: Dimouts, Sept. 1–Oct. 10, 1942. Landis to Sherman Miles, July 3, 1942, RG171, E: 46, B: 4, F: 022-War Dept. (3 of 4). Landis to Hugh Drum, June 29, 1942, RG171, E: 46, B: 4, F: 020-War Dept. (3 of 4). "Reports of Violations of Public Proclamation No. 10," Nov. 1–15, 1942, by C. B. Horrall, RG171, E: 47, B: 50, F: Loose, "Light Control." The round-up involved men (police arrested only one woman) between the ages of 24 and 60. Violators had committed "2-A" infractions and courts often set bail at $5.00. "Analysis & Control Sheet" of Reports: From OCD Oct. 10–12, 1942, RG171, E: 47, B: 50, F: Loose, "Light Control." Richard Wilson to James Sheppard, Jan. 12, 1943, RG171, E: 16, B: 42, F: Dimouts, Jan. 1-31, 1943. "Breakdown by Sectors—Dimout Reports," Dec. 15, 1942–Jan. 15, 1943, RG171, E: 47, B: 50, F: Loose, "Light Control." OCD, Ninth Civilian Defense Region to Commanding General, Western Defense Command, Dec. 16, 1942, RG171, E: 16, B: 42, F: Dimouts, Oct. 28–Dec. 30, 1942. Lloyd Smith to Landis, Jan. 6, 1943, Ibid. Also see, Memorandum Opinion, Superior Court No. CR A 1933, "City Dim-Out Violation Affirmed on Appeal," n.d., RG171, E: 16, B: 42, F: Dimouts, Jan. 1–31, 1943. Charles Jones and W. T. Hudnell, Jr., to Commanding General, I Fighter Command, Aug. 26, 1942, RG171, E: 12, B: 5, F: Blackouts, 1 to 4. Pilots flying 7,000 feet above New York City observed Queens, Staten Island, and the West Bronx almost completely dark; they found only scattered lights south of Manhattan's Central Park and East Side Drive. Frank Hansen to James Sheppard, Sept. 5, 1942, and attached reports, RG171, E: 47, B: 50, F: Region IX: 512. James Sheppard to Landis, Oct. 9, 1942, RG171, E: 47, B: 50, F: Region IX: 512.

45. Jack Barrett to Civil Defense Board, Sept. 29, 1942, RG171, E: 16, B: 42, F: Dimouts, Sept. 1–Oct. 10, 1942. A Resident to the Officer in Charge, Office of Civilian Defense, June 10, 1942, RG171, E: 16, B: 42, F: Dimouts, thru Aug. 31, 1942. Leon Adler to FDR, n.d., RG171, E: 16, B: 42, F: Dimouts, thru Aug. 31, 1942. John Conover to FDR, July 4, 1942, RG171, E: 16, B: 42, F: Dimouts, thru Aug. 31, 1942. Jerrold Owen to Landis, June 30, 1942, RG171, E: 47, B: 52, F: Region IX: OR. After receiving a telegram from a Navy vice admiral that Oregon and Washington faced an imminent threat and had to dim coastal lights immediately, Oregon's home defense leader—unable to reach the governor and acting governor during the governor's absence from Oregon—ordered counties to dim their lights. "When the lives and property of our citizens are threatened and we receive an order from the Admiral in command of the Northwest Sea Frontier, we are going to do our best to comply with it even though it does not follow the customary channels and even if we cannot obtain definite approval from higher authority in the OCD," coordinator Jerrold Owen wrote Landis. The vice admiral, for his part, cited "States Rights," saying governors and not Washington had the power to decide home defense questions. Unnamed OCD official to Admiral Edward Jones, June 25, 1942, RG171, E: 47, B: 50, F: Region IX: 512.

46. AP, "Landis Says Danger of Raids in United States Has Grown," *Christian Science Monitor*, Sept. 29, 1942, 5, RG171, E: 185, B: 6, F: 7-A-1: Statements & Speeches, Landis. Minutes of Meeting of the Civilian Defense Board, Oct. 9, 1942, RG171, E: 46, B: 25, F: 330: Civilian Defense Board. "Morale and the OCD," *Newsweek*, Feb. 22, 1943, 37, RG171, E: 185, B: 14, F: 9-A: Landis. "Tip of Cape Wins Honor," *Boston Herald*, July 14, 1942, 1; AP, "War Emergency Met By Local Defense," *New York Times*, July 5, 1942, 28, RG171, E: 185, B: 12, F: Emergencies . . . , July 6, 1942–July 1, 1943.

47. "Men with Picks, Afraid to Dig," *Washington News*, Sept. 25, 1942, 5, RG171, E: 185, B: 12, F: Emergencies . . . July 6, 1942–July 1, 1943. AP, "4 Nazi Soldiers Flee Prison Train," *New York Times*, Nov. 26, 1942, 24. "Civilians Recapture German Prisoners," *Washington Daily News*, Nov. 26, 1942, 31, RG171, E: 185, B: 12, F: Emergencies . . . July 6, 1942–July 1, 1943. "Stamford Combats Worst Fire 9 Hours," *New York Times*, Jan. 2, 1943, 14, RG171, E: 185, B: 12, F: Emergencies . . . July 6, 1942–July 1, 1943. "Catastrophe: War and High Water," *Time*, Jan. 11, 1943, 17, RG171, E:185, B:12, F: Emergencies. . .July 6, 1942–July 1, 1943. "Lady Wardens Beat Firemen to Punch," *Washington Times-Herald*, Mar. 21, 1943, 4-A, RG171, E: 185, B: 12, F: Emergencies . . . July 6, 2942–July 1, 1943. "15 Die; Property Loss Mounts Into Millions," *Washington News*, Oct. 17, 1942, 4, RG171, E: 185, B: 12, F: Emergencies . . . July 6, 1942–July 1, 1943.

Chapter 13

1. For Churchill quote, see Neil Midgley, "Why Churchill Thought Attacking Italy Could Win Him World War Two," *Telegraph*, Oct. 14, 2012. FDR, State of the Union Message to Congress, Jan. 11, 1944, http://docs.fdrlibrary.marist.edu/011144.html.

2. Landis to Jane Seaver, Mar. 7, 1942, RG171, E: 10, B: 101, F: 380-102: Volunteer Participation Committee, thru Mar. 31, 1942. Wilmer Shields to Mr. Jackson, Mar. 25, 1942, RG171, E: 10, B: 83, F: 220 Women in Defense, June 1, 1942-. Daniels quote from Dr. Robert McElroy, "Narrative Account of the Office of Civilian Defense," ch. 8, 7, RG171: Entries 231–232: Box 1, F: "Narrative Account," chapters VIII–IX.

3. ER quote in Lash, *Franklin and Eleanor*, 653. Landis to Robert Dechert, Feb. 3, 1942, RG171, E: 10, B: 109, F: 500-Civilian Protection. Landis to "Mike," Feb. 24, 1942, RG171, E: 47, B: 32, F: Region I: MA, S.C., 381.

4. Landis, "The Need for Civilian Protection," Jan. 17, 1942, Vital Speeches of the Day, Vol. 8, Issue 10, 319–320. Dr. Robert McElroy, "Narrative Account of the Office of Civilian Defense," ch. 8, 7–8, RG171: Entries 231–232: Box 1, F: "Narrative Account," chapters VIII–IX.

5. The volunteer numbers appear in a memo, Wilmer Shields to Mr. Jackson, Mar. 12, 1942; the volunteer office numbers are in a memo, Shields to Jackson, Mar. 26, 1942, RG171, E: 10, B: 83, F: 203 Reports-Volunteer Participation. "Public Attitudes Toward Civilian Defense," Feb. 21, 1942, RG44, E: 164, B: 1796, F: Polling Division Report No. 5. Wilmer Shields to Marguerite Zapoleon, Mar. 28, 1942, RG171, E: 10, B: 83, F: 220 Women in Defense, June 1, 1942-. "Volunteer Code," Feb. 5, 1942, RG171, E: 10, B: 83, F: 200 Volunteer Participation, Dec. 16, 1941-. La Guardia to Jane Seaver, Jan. 17, 1942, RG171, E: 10, B: 101, F: 380-102: Volunteer Participation Committee, thru Mar. 31, 1942. See Wilmer Shields to Mr. Jackson, Mar. 10, 1942, for the different cities; Shields to Jonathan Daniels, Mar. 10, 1942, for USO and other groups, RG171, E: 10, B: 83, F: 203 Reports-Volunteer Participation. For information on the victory gardens, see Miller, "The War that Never Came," 209–211. "Food," declared Landis in 1943, "can and will shorten the war," quoted in Miller, 212. Landis to "Dear Mr.," Apr. 7, 1942, RG171, E: 46, B: 27, F: 380.1-OCD. Betty Eckhardt May to Molly Flynn, Apr. 11, 1942; Jonathan Daniels to Josephine Roche, Apr. 10, 1942; Daniels to Thomas Sharp, Apr. 3, 1942, RG171, E: 10, B: 83, F: 200 Volunteer Participation Dec. 16, 1941-. Jonathan Daniels to Mr. Sheridan, Mar. 23, 1942, RG171, E: 10, B: 83, F: 200 Volunteer Participation Dec. 16, 1941-. For information about child care and the role of the regions, see Miller, *The War That Never Came*, 213–215.

6. "Lecture Manual for Air Raid Warden Instructors," Milton Polissar, RG171, E: 10, B: 117, F: 514.1-Air Raid Warning System, Mar. 21, 1942-.

7. Wm. L. Powers to Landis, Mar. 16, 1942; Landis to Powers, Apr. 13, 1942, RG171, E: 10, B; 2, F: 000.3, Mar. 21, 1942. Landis to Sidney Hillman, Feb. 17, 1942; Hillman to Landis, Mar. 26, 1942, RG171, E: 10, B: 102, F: 381: WPM, April 1, 1942. Hillman was skeptical, claiming that training that many workers just wasn't feasible.

8. Landis to Millard Tydings, Apr. 3, 1942, RG171, E: 46, B: 27, F: 380.1-OCD. Landis to "Dear Mr.," Apr. 7, 1942, RG171, E: 46, B: 27, F: 380.1-OCD. Landis, "Victory Forum," *Boston Globe*, Aug. 27, 1942, RG171, E: 185, B: 6, F: 7-A-1: Statements/Speeches by Landis. Landis to Clarence Little, Mar. 5, 1942, RG171, E: 10, B: 83, F: 200 Volunteer Participation Dec. 16, 1941-. Landis to Regional Directors, Apr. 6, 1942, RG171, E: 10, B: 101, F: 381: Civilian Defense.

9. Minutes of Meeting of the Civilian Defense Board, Oct. 9, 1942, RG171, E: 46, B: 25, F: 330: Civilian Defense Board. Lash, *Franklin and Eleanor*, 653. Minutes of Meeting of the Civilian Defense Board, Oct. 9, 1942, RG171, E: 46, B: 25, F: 330: Civilian Defense Board. Landis's quote comes from Miller, *The War That Never Came*, 233. Special Services Division to R. Keith Kane, memo, "OCD-A Good Program That Could Be Made Better," Oct. 30, 1942, RG171, E: 46, B: 27, F: 380.1-OCD. Jonathan Daniels to Margaret Shotwell, Mar. 17, 1942, RG171, E: 10, B: 83, F: 220 Women in Defense, June 1, 1942-. Landis, "Avenging Pearl Harbor: Civilian Defense Setup Progresses," *Washington Daily News*, Dec. 7, 1942, 8. RG171, E: 185, B: 14, F: 9-A-1: Landis: Statements & Speeches.

10. Harriet Jack to Landis, Jan. 12, 1942, RG171, E: 10, B: 85, F: 223-Emergency Feeding. Wilmer Shields to Marguerite Zapoleon, Mar. 28, 1942, RG171, E: 10, B: 83, F: 220 Women in Defense, June 1, 1942-. "Preliminary Report on Attitudes Toward Civilian Defense, Feb. 18, 1942, RG44, E: 164, B: 1796, F: Polling Division Report No. 5, Public Attitudes Toward Civilian Defense, Feb. 18, 1942.

11. "Public Attitudes Toward Civilian Defense," Feb. 21, 1942, RG44, E: 164, B: 1796, F: Polling Division Report No. 5. "Preliminary Report on Attitudes Toward Civilian Defense, Feb. 18, 1942, RG44, E: 164, B: 1796, F: "Polling Division Report No. 5, Public Attitudes Toward Civilian Defense, Feb. 18, 1942." Dr. Robert McElroy, "Narrative Account of the Office of Civilian Defense," chs. 5, 9, RG171: Entries 231–232: Box 1, F: "CD in the US . . ." chapters. I–VIII.

12. Vernon Hunt to Landis, Mar. 18, 1943, RG171, E: 47, B: 51, F: Region XI: CA, L.C. 381.

13. Miller, *The War That Never Came*, 209, 217, 220–227. Miller writes that Newman Jeffrey, a leader of the Amalgamated Clothing Workers of America union, ran the OCD's Labor Division. Landis wanted local defense councils to reflect the interests of "business, professional, social, and consumer groups," adding "that labor's right to representation on *every* defense council is just as fundamental, if not more so."

14. Cross-Reference Sheet, Anderson, Cong. Clinton P., Mar. 19, 1942, F: "Daniels, Jonathan," PPF 1020: Daniels, Jonathan, FDRL. FDR relied on Landis to defend the New Deal, asking him to draft a response to Congressman Clinton Anderson's telegram, which warned of newspaper attacks on progressive reforms including the forty-hour work week. But, when Landis learned of Republican home defenders in Connecticut organizing a drill to coincide with a major FDR speech, Landis complained "that C.D. activities should be associated with politics." Landis to Malvina Thompson, Jan. 1, 1943, "From Mrs. John Boettiger," Dec. 24, 1942, RG171, E: 47, B: 48, F: Region IX: 310. ER to Landis, May 9, 1942, F: "1942 Landis, James," ER 100: Personal Letters 1942 Ki-La, ERP, FDRL.

15. Mrs. A. L. Spohn to ER, Dec. 23, 1941, RG171, E: 10, B:" 83, F: "220 Women in Defense, Jan. 1, 1942-." C. D. Cornett to ER, Dec. 10, 1941, and see attached article, "Los Angeles third in traffic deaths," Nov. 13, 1941, RG171, E: 10, B: 2, F: "Criticisms-Protests through January 14, 1942." Los Angeles had the third highest number of car fatalities of any city in 1941—402 dead. M. B. Cameron, "Telegram Phoned in by Mrs. Thompson from Washington," Dec. 20, 1941; Shirley Wimberly to La Guardia, Dec. 16, 1941, RG171, E: 10, B: 2, F: "Criticisms-Protests through January 14, 1942." Mrs. C. Kenneth Coty to La Guardia, Dec. 15, 1941, RG171, E: 10, B: 2, F: "Criticisms-Protests through January 14, 1942."

16. Dudley Diggs to Stanley McCandless, Jan. 19, 1943, RG171, E: 16, B: 40, F: Dimouts, Feb. 1-Mar. 31, 1943. "City of New York (Manhattan Only)," RG171, E: 16, B: 40, F: Dimouts, Feb. 1-March 31, 1943. Landis to National Safety Council, Feb. 2, 1943, RG171, E: 16, B: 40, F: Dimouts, Feb. 1–Mar. 31, 19443. Edwin Vennard, "Wartime Lighting and Safety," n.d., RG171 E:16, B:40, F: Dimouts, July 1–Sept. 30, 1943. While the article states that some of these deaths were probably due to dimouts, it acknowledges that "the extent to which lighting was a contributing factor is not definitely known."

17. "Public Attitudes Toward Civilian Defense," Feb. 21, 1942, RG44, E: 164, B: 1796, F: Polling Division Report No. 5. "Preliminary Report on Attitudes Toward Civilian Defense, Feb. 18, 1942, RG44, E: 164, B: 1796, F: "Polling Division Report No. 5, Public Attitudes Toward Civilian Defense, Feb. 18, 1942." Lou Wylie (Mrs. Howard Van Sicklen) to Landis, Mar. 28, 1942; Gasser to Van Sicklen, Apr. 4, 19/42, RG171, E: 10, B: 83, F: 220 Women in Defense, June 1, 1942-.

18. Special Services Division to R. Keith Kane, memo, "OCD-A Good Program that Could Be Made Better," Oct. 30, 1942, RG171, E: 46, B: 27, F: 380.1-OCD. "Public Attitudes Toward Civilian Defense," Feb. 21, 1942, RG44, E: 164, B: 1796, F: Polling Division Report No. 5. "Preliminary Report on Attitudes Toward Civilian Defense," Feb. 18, 1942, RG44, E: 164, B: 1796, F: Polling Division Report No. 5, Public Attitudes Toward Civilian Defense, Feb. 18, 1942.

19. Landis to Leslie Allen, Mar. 13, 1943, RG171, E: 47, B: 33, F: Region II: NY, 381. L.C. International News Service, "Goebbels' Threat of Raids Called Sop to Home Front," *Washington Post*, Mar. 3, 1943, 1; "Landis Warns D.C. to Expect Raids by German Bombers,"

Washington Times Herald, Mar. 3, 1943, 3, RG171, E: 185, B: 13, F: 5, Enemy Air Raids. "Axis Can Raid U.S. From Coast to Coast," *Washington Daily News,* May 4, 1943. LoC, Landis Papers, F: "Family Papers, Landis, Dorothy Purdy Brown, Clippings," B: 194.

20. "Army, OCD Leaders Agree Pacific Coast Menaced," Mar. 15, 1943, Ninth Civilian Defense Region Newsletter, vol. 2, no. 2., RG171, E: 185, B: 13, F: 5, Enemy Air Raids.

21. Landis to Harold Smith, Apr. 10, 1943, RG171, E: 46, B: 25, F: 330: Civilian Defense Board. Landis to Industrial Protection Council of the U.S. Office of Civilian Defense, Feb. 25, 1943, RG171, E: 46, B: 25, F: 330: Advisory Council for Industrial Plants.

22. William Schulze, "Realistic Big War Show Thrills and Warns Seattle," *Seattle Post-Intelligencer,* June 14, 1943, Seattlepi.com, "Seattle History: The Bombing of Seattle." The event had a raucous, chaotic feel. Police rounded up the boys on the field and brought them back to the stands. When an eight-year-old got separated from his father, the emcee interrupted the extravaganza to tell the boy to go to his father waiting for him at a popcorn stand.

23. Analysis of Attitudes Toward Civilian Protection, Newspaper Clippings, Mar. 21–May 15, 1943; June 1, 1943. Report Analysis and Statistics Division, RG171, E: 185, B: 31, F: 14, Misc. (2 of 3).

24. Landis to Mr. Sheridan, June 26, 1943, RG171, E: 46, B: 28, B: 380.108: Public Advice & Counsel. Donald Hayworth to Landis, June 29, 1943, Landis to Hayworth, July 8, 1943, Landis to Louis Rabaut, July 9, 1943, RG171, E: 46, B: 28, F: 380.104: Civilian War Services. Landis to Louis Ludlow, July 10, 1943, RG171, E: 46, B: 28, F: 380.104: Civilian War Services. Cross-Reference Sheet, Francis Biddle, Apr. 20, 1943, F: "Daniels, Jonathan 1935–1943," OF 5230: Daniels, Jonathan, FRDL. Miller, *The War that Never Came,* FDR quote comes from 239. W. B. Hogan to Landis, July 7, 1943, RG171, E: 47, B: 5, F: Region IX: CA, L.C. 381.

25. Landis to Secretary of the Navy, July 28, 1943, RG171, E: 16, B: 42, F: Dimouts: Lighting. Thomas Devine to Landis, Aug. 10, 1943, RG171, E: 46, B: 28, F: 380.104: Civilian War Services. Cordell Hull to FDR, July 16, 1943; FDR to General Watson, July 21, 1943, F: "Landis, James M," PPF 4858: Landis, James M, FDRL. Miller, *The War That Never Came,* 240–243.

26. Landis to FDR; FDR to Landis; Press Release, Sept. 10, 1943, F: "Landis, James, M," PPF 4858: Landis, James M, FDRL.

27. For details about Martin, see *Chicago Tribune,* "Rhodes Scholar Bids for Senate on G.O.P. Ticket," July 25, 1951.

28. Sparrow, *Warfare State,* 3.

29. The American Presidency Project, 1944 State of the Union Message: FDR's Second Bill of RightsSpeech, Jan. 11, 1944, http://www.presidency.ucsb.edu/ws/?pid=16518.

Conclusion

1. The Eleanor Roosevelt Papers Project, "Question: What Did ER Do at the United Nations?," http://www.gwu.edu/~erpapers/teachinger/q-and-a/q29.cfm. Lash, *Franklin and Eleanor,* 654–663, 701–707.

2. Quotes and information comes from Williams, *City of Ambition,* 354–361, 373, see ch. 10, Epilogue.

3. See Barack Obama acceptance speech, Democratic National Convention, Sept. 6, 2012. Retrieved from http://www.washingtonpost.com/wp-dyn/articles/A19751-2004Jul27.html.

4. For the idea of progressivism in retreat during the 1950s, see Robyn Muncy's *Relentless Reformer: Josephine Roche and Progressivism in Twentieth Century America* (Princeton, NJ: Princeton University Press, 2014). For an insightful study of the ADA, see Steven M. Gillon, *Politics and Vision: the ADA and American Liberalism, 1947–1985* (New York: Oxford University Press, 1987).

5. The Eleanor Roosevelt Papers Project, "Question: What Did ER Do at the United Nations?," http://www.gwu.edu/~erpapers/teachinger/q-and-a/q29.cfm.

6. Ibid., Allida M. Black, "Biography of Anna Eleanor Roosevelt," http://www.gwu.edu/~erpa-pers/abouteleanor/erbiography.cfm. Also see "Biography of Eleanor Roosevelt," http://www.fdrlibrary.marist.edu/education/resources/bio_er.html.

7. Mason, *City of Ambition*, 354–361, ch. 10, Epilogue. See Kessner, *Fiorello H. La Guardia*, 591–592. "La Guardia is Dead; City Pays Homage to 3-Time Mayor," *New York Times*, Sept. 21, 1947.

8. Patrick S. Roberts, "Disasters and the American State: How Politicians, Bureaucrats, and the Public Prepare for the Unexpected," *Journal of Policy History* (Cambridge: Cambridge University Press, 2013), 59.

9. For a full life of James Landis, see Donald Ritchie's thoughtful *James M. Landis: Dean of the Regulators*. In the *Triumph, Tragedy, and Lost Legacy of James M. Landis: A Life on Fire* (Oxford: Bloombsury Press, 2014), Justin O'Brien focuses on Landis's legacy as a regulator of financial markets. In "The Legacy of James Landis," a talk commemorating the seventi-eth anniversary of the 1934 Securities and Exchange Act, Ritchie argues that Landis's failure to file income tax returns stemmed from "a psychological failing" rather than from a willful deception. http://3197d6d14b5f19f2f440-5e13d29c4c016cf96cbbfd197c579b45.r81.cf1.rackcdn.com/collection/oral-histories/landis120804Transcript.pdf. For another portrait of Landis as a regulator, see Thomas K. McCraw, *Prophets of Regulation: Charles Francis Adams, Louis D. Brandeis, James M. Landis, Alfred E. Kahn* (Cambridge, MA: Harvard University Press, 1984).

10. For an analysis of Pearl Harbor's place in the nation's collective memory, see Emily S. Rosenberg, *A Date Which Will Live: Pearl Harbor in American Memory* (Durham, NC: Duke University Press, 2003). For various takes on the civil defense program's shortcomings during the Cold War, see Kregg Michael Fehr, *Sheltering Society: Civil Defense in the United States, 1945–1963*, (Ph.D. dissertation, Texas Tech University, 1999); Oakes, *The Imaginary War*; and Andrew Grossman, *Neither Dead Nor Red: Civil Defense and American Political Development during the Early Cold War* (New York: Routledge, 2001).

INDEX

Africa, 44, 47, 73, 131, 245, 252
African Americans, 17, 21, 66, 87, 157,
    246, 254
  defense industry, 209
  ER and, 8–9, 29, 31, 55, 58, 61, 66, 88, 90,
    209, 260–261, 297n9
  home defense or OCD and, 166, 209–210,
    251, 254, 269n38
  La Guardia and, 39, 58, 124, 127–128
  morale of, 210
  women, 212
air bases, 42, 44–45, 47, 73, 179
Air Defense League, 45, 275n26
Air Raid Precautions Act or Department,
    105, 108
air raids, 29, 71, 74, 83, 112–115, 123,
    185, 270n4
  army or navy and, 120, 199
  deaths in, 140, 236
  defenses against, 4, 14, 43–45, 49, 81,
    107–110, 120, 129, 135
  drills (see drills)
  FBI and, 110, 175–176
  feasibility or odds of, 14, 41–42, 44, 46, 107,
    129, 173, 181, 206, 234, 252–254
  London or Great Britain, 25, 42–43, 95,
    103–105, 108–109, 135, 235
  mass media or novels on, 4, 41–43, 83, 103,
    107, 190, 200, 254
  morale during, 210, 212
  noncompliance, 130, 199, 250
  oceans as defense against (see United
    States: ocean buffer for)
  panic or riots during, 3, 23, 35, 40, 42–43,
    77–78, 103, 105, 111, 117, 129–130, 151,
    174, 176, 202, 234, 239
  police and, 133, 175–176, 178

  routes for, 72–73, 252–253
  shelters, 95, 105, 108, 111–113, 178, 180, 200,
    202, 229
  sirens, alarms, or false alarms, 76, 111, 158,
    193, 196, 198–199, 236, 240, 250, 252
  Spain, 24, 43
  tips for civilians, 132–133, 198, 236
  volunteers, 94–95, 105
  warnings or concern about, 9, 14, 35–37,
    39–43, 45, 119–120, 173, 178 (see also
    fears: attacks by air)
  watch posts or patrol centers, 77, 166, 173
  watchers, 95, 105, 115, 133, 173
  weather and, 206
  WWI, 104
air war, 4, 20, 23, 42–43, 45, 71, 223,
    268n34, 274n17
aircraft carriers, 42, 45, 234, 253, 306n41
airports, 36, 45, 75, 129, 182, 191–192,
    230, 302n26
Alabama, 2, 83, 154, 182, 247
Alaska, 44, 73, 131, 239, 292n12, 315n14
Aleutian Islands, 238, 253
"alien enemies," 197, 232, 317n21
Allies, 48, 113, 216, 241, 245
  aid for, 9, 14, 47, 59, 120, 132–133
ambulances, 2, 95, 166, 194, 217, 238
America First (Committee), 92, 128, 132
American Association of University Women,
    61, 247
American Legion, 32, 76, 110, 115, 128, 230,
    260, 316n18
American Social Defense Administration, 10,
    88–89, 155
American Women's Voluntary Services (AWVS),
    94–97, 165, 287
Anderson, Marian, 8, 29

anti-aircraft batteries or guns, 25, 45–46, 49, 107, 173, 200
antifascists, 3, 64, 192
   ER and, 8, 24, 26–29, 31, 34, 52–55, 59, 64–65, 101, 138, 153, 166–167, 185, 189, 259, 271n13
   La Guardia and, 79–80, 113, 119, 122, 125–126, 128, 130–132, 138, 153, 185, 192
   Spain, 24
anti-Semitism, 26, 196, 271n28
antiwar activists or organizations, 14, 36–37, 49, 70, 87, 92, 112, 114, 128, 259
   ER and, 9–10, 19–24, 29, 33, 86
appeasement, 9, 25, 54, 86, 158, 162, 179, 237
Arizona, 38, 162, 181
Arkansas, 93, 162
Armageddon, 3, 17–18, 52, 255, 268n34
Armistice, 21, 39, 270n12
Atlanta, 31, 82
Austria, 37, 39, 44
aviation technology, 37, 41–45, 223, *see also* military technology
Axis, 28, 51, 121, 186, 188, 197, 214
   agents in US, 116
   bombing by or planes, 15, 130, 152, 239, 252
   threat to US, 15, 47, 130, 152, 174, 213, 239, 252, 266n3

Baltimore, 82, 130, 208
Bane, Frank, 76–79, 114–116, 124, 133, 292n12
Bataan, 202, 235
Belgium, 54, 134
Berkeley, 265, 289
Bermuda, 47, 72
Betters, Paul, 75–76
Biddle, Eric, 97–98, 232
biological or germ warfare, 13, 44, 112, 130, 144, *see also* chemical warfare or weapons
Birmingham, 2, 29, 296
blackouts, 113, 172, 194, 235–238
   Army or Navy role in, 199, 229, 304n18
   compliance with, 171, 185, 199, 224, 239
   drills, 6, 78, 113, 115, 122, 170, 235, 237, 304n18
   Florida, 239, 241
   New York City, 170–171, 237
   Seattle, 78, 185
   support for, 115, 128
   Washington or White House, 122, 189, 235
   West Coast, 193–194, 229
Blitz, 95, 109–110, 295n31
   blitzkrieg, 53, 70
   England, 63, 97, 104
   evacuations during, 63
   France, 76, 126
   Great Britain, 96, 137
   London, as target of, 103–107, 172, 263
   morale during, 105

   Murrow on, 5, 106, 229, 287n26
   US views of, 70, 76, 97, 103–107, 110, 116–117, 124, 288n2
Boston, 40, 63, 217, 238, 244, 297n6
   attacks on, 117, 130, 252,
   home defense in, 180, 186
   Marathon bombing, 15,
   meetings in, 129
   newspapers, 130, 215
Bowron, Fletcher, 191, 231
Brandeis, Louis, 12, 226
Brazil, 47, 73, 131
bridges, 36, 81, 85, 173–174, 190, 192, 200, 230, 242
Britain, *see* Great Britain
Bullitt, William C., 5, 26, 29, 122, 128

California, 112, 160–161, 213, 229, 243
   air raids in, 192–194, 234, 239
   attacks by foreign enemy, 193, 254
   attacks by Japanese, 71, 192–193, 228, 230, 253
   defense factories in, 56, 77
   drills in, 192, 235, 239, 304n18
   ER and La Guardia in, 191–194
   evacuations in, 193
   fear or riots in, 192–193
   fifth columnists in, 192, 231, 316n19
   home defense in, 83, 111, 191
   Japanese Americans in, 193, 231–232
   social defense in, 92, 100
   Southern, 174, 231, 235
   state defense agency, 77
Canada, 41, 70, 72, 112, 116, 133, 170, 180, 302n26
   Permanent Joint Board on Defense, 80, 127
Carmody, John, 59, 74, 92
CBS, 1, 3, 106, 132
Chamberlain, Neville, 1, 53, 105, 227
Chaney, Mayris, 148, 213–216, 218–221, 227, 246, 309n26, 318n30
chemical warfare or weapons, 6, 44, 106, 130, 144, 180, 230, 235, 239
Chicago, 81, 105, 117, 164, 228, 238, 240, 281n6
   air raids or enemy attacks in, 181, 187, 240
   defenses in, 110, 121, 150
   Democratic National Convention in, 63
   New Deal or WPA in, 62
Chicago Tribune, 98, 109, 114, 176, 181
children, 30, 61–62, 95, 165, 194, 198, 217, 263, 297n15, 313n3
   aid for or welfare of, 66, 87, 92–93, 99–100, 139, 155, 163, 188, 210, 251
   care of, 11, 139, 205, 247–250, 261, 318n26, 322n5
   dancing, 148, 212–214
   Easter Egg Roll, 136, 190
   in Europe or Asia, 45, 54, 58

evacuation of or safe passage for, 24, 63, 287n25
gas masks or dog tags for, 175, 230, 315n14
labor laws, 21
Roosevelts', 19–20, 154, 187, 196, 270n10
social defense and, 11
women and, 3, 11, 23–24, 43, 48, 87, 119, 129, 163, 187, 285n6
China, 22–24, 29, 36, 43, 45, 172, 271n22
Christian Science Monitor, 4, 95, 107, 172, 227
Churchill, Winston, 54, 73, 98, 105, 109, 202, 246
cities, 4, 52, 80–83, 88, 91, 113, 177, 193, 262–263
air raids or bombing of, 13, 18, 23, 35–36, 43, 48, 81, 83–84, 96, 98, 107, 109, 114, 117, 119, 123, 129–130, 172, 176, 179, 189, 192, 235, 252, 306n41
British, 96, 98, 103, 105, 108
defense of, 7, 69, 75–76, 79, 81, 111–112, 126, 128, 170, 175, 185
East Coast, 199, 228, 241 (*see also* East Coast)
European, 43, 172, 187, 235
evacuation of, 74, 295n28
fascist or pro-Nazi sentiments in, 70
Great Depression or New Deal in, 30, 32, 40–41, 103
leaflets dropped on, 117
mayors of, 40–41, 47, 69, 75, 79, 82–83, 111, 114, 116, 192
New Deal in, 30, 32, 40–41, 85
panic or riots in, 2, 172, 176, 186
police or FBI and, 83, 121, 172, 176, 192
vulnerable, 4, 6, 112–114
West Coast, 189, 191–192, 199, 234, 241 (*see also* West Coast)
Civil Air Patrol, 13, 174, 198, 206, 208, 216, 237, 240, 243, 247, 254
civil defense, 14, 44, 75, 82, 98, 104, 131, 144, 150, 178, 231, 234, 262, 267n17, 269n36, 288n2, 289n3, 291n39
see also home defense
Britain, 97, 104–105, 108, 110, 175, 263
classes, 83, 313n3
Cold War, 14, 325n10
ER and, 147, 158, 160, 188, 193, 195
funding for, 263
New York, 200
Truman and, 262–263
volunteers, 217, 224, 244, 263
Civil Defense Board, 112–113
Civilian Conservation Corps (CCC), 11, 22, 32, 92, 220
civilian defense, 45, 60, 172, 200, 232
army, 76, 133, 238
ER on, 97, 122, 163, 165, 194
FDR on, 255
La Guardia on, 110, 114, 128
police, 243
see also home defense, civil defense, or Office of Civilian Defense

Civilian Defense Week, 165, 179
civilians
army or defense force, 7, 69, 76, 126–127, 130, 133, 158, 175, 209, 225, 238, 240, 243, 254–256
defense training of, 45
military targets, 5, 9, 13–14, 23, 27, 29, 37, 39, 42–44, 47–48
morale (*see* morale)
protection of, 35–36, 41–42
civil liberties, 18, 20, 27, 52, 230, 261–262, 277n12
civil rights, 20, 26, 29, 31, 55, 82, 157, 209, 261–263
Cold War, 10, 14, 257, 261–263, 268n34, 269n36, 276n39, 288n2, 325n10
Colorado, 121
Committee to Defend America by Aiding the Allies, 47, 133
communications, 3, 57, 76, 110–111, 123–124, 198
communism or communists, 17–18, 69–70, 215–216, 226, 233, 261–263, 270n3
Connecticut, 42, 45, 180, 229, 241, 243
Council of National Defense, 78, 112
Coy, Wayne, 64–67, 122, 124, 201
Cuba, 38, 73
Currie, Lauchlin, 64–65, 67, 74
Czechoslovakia, 1, 5, 8, 25–26, 36, 43, 48, 66, 266n3

Daniels, Jonathan, 158, 219, 246, 248, 255, 309n24
Daughters of the American Revolution, 8, 29, 133
Davison, Eloise, 161–162, 164–166, 209
defense, 8, *see* civil defense; home defense; military defense; national defense; social defense
democracy
American, 9–10, 13, 18, 27–29, 35, 37, 52, 54, 67, 99, 167, 196, 257
bigotry and, 29, 196, 280n35
civil defense and, 158, 160
fascism or totalitarianism vs., 4, 8–10, 13, 25, 28–29, 34, 54–55, 65, 113, 167
Mann on, 25
threats to, 24, 27, 35, 169
tolerance and, 196
Democrats, 78, 217, 261
1938 election, 22, 85
antiwar or isolationist, 9, 14, 37
congressional, 3, 22, 37, 214
conservative, 214, 216, 231
corrupt, 39
FDR allies, 73, 124
liberal, 73, 119, 231, 263
pro-intervention, 9, 122
segregationists, 54
southern, 22, 214, 219, 270n3
Stevenson, 261

Denmark, 44, 53, 66, 105
Detroit, 81, 152, 177, 181, 225, 228, 249,
    252, 313n2
Dewey, John, 85, 87
DeWitt, John, 231–232, 240, 242, 253, 317n22
Dies, Martin, 18, 72, 214, 270n1, 270n3
dimouts, 224, 241–242, 244, 251, 254–255,
    320n40, 323n16
Division of State and Local Cooperation, 76–77,
    83, 124, 133
draft, 63, 77, 80, 83, 87, 111, 120, 123, 126,
    133, 218
drills
    air raid, 44–45, 115, 145–146, 171, 191, 235,
        238, 304n17
    anti-aircraft battery, 217
    blackout (*see* blackouts)
    California, 192, 235, 239, 304n18
    deaths during, 236, 238
    defense plants, 174
    duck-and-cover, 14, 263
    East Coast or Atlantic seaboard, 45, 115,
        169, 173
    emergency, 4
    evacuation, 181
    La Guardia's, 113, 145–146, 169–173,
        181, 237
    Landis's, 235, 237
    New England, 115, 206, 238
    OCD and, 174, 235
    Seattle, 78, 238
    support for, 115, 171, 238
    war, 171, 173
    Washington or White House, 122, 191, 238
Dunkirk, 20, 54

East Coast, 1, 6, 26, 42, 115, 169–170, 173, 182,
    see also cities; drills
electric grid, *see* power stations or grid
Eliot, Martha, 62–63, 165
Elliott, Harriet, 60–61, 91, 156, 161, 165
England, 54, 234, 260
    bombing or Blitz, 43, 63, 104–105, 107, 109,
        131, 137, 172, 235
    declares war on Germany, 33
    history, 104–105
    defeat of, 56
    ER and, 26, 96–97, 166, 260
    France and (*see* France)
    model for USA, 5, 49, 97, 103, 109–111, 113,
        116, 166, 178, 288n1
    US ally, 48, 73
    WWI, 43, 104
    see also Great Britain
Ethiopia, 23, 36
evacuations, 14, 48, 76, 95, 113, 174, 181, 233

factories, 174, 260
    accidents or fires in, 130, 217, 253
    aircraft, 45
    arms or explosives, 78, 217
    day care near, 10
    defense, 58, 70, 76–77, 123, 175
    employees in defense, 11, 56, 77, 121, 139,
        208, 224, 248
    employees in other, 130, 175, 205, 208, 217,
        230, 250, 281n43
    guards or protection for, 6, 113, 126, 174, 232
    military targets, 23, 45, 77, 103, 120, 174,
        228–230
    productivity in, 86, 112
Fair Employment Practices Committee
    (FEPC), 157
Fair Labor Standards Act, 21–22
fascism or fascists, 15, 23, 31, 74, 205
    bomb civilians, 37, 43, 223, 235
    communism and, 17, 233, 270n3
    democracy vs., 4, 8–10, 13, 18, 26, 28, 34, 54,
        80, 86, 108, 113, 128, 166–167
    dictators, 119, 226
    economy and, 108
    FBI vs., 233
    growth or appeal of, 4, 22, 28, 92, 270n4
    Hitler or Nazi, 25–26, 116
    ideology, 18, 27, 34, 53, 86, 88, 270n4
    mass media on, 5
    threat, 8, 14, 22, 24, 27, 29, 36, 57, 66,
        113–114, 117, 125–126, 129–132, 167,
        223, 235, 259, 266n3
    threat downplayed, 23
    in USA or Western Hemisphere, 17, 29, 44,
        46, 70, 82, 92, 104
    see also antifascists
FBI, 76, 83, 131, 169, 186, 190, 193, 238
    agents visit London, 103, 110, 175, 290n22
    home defense or OCD and, 121, 175–176,
        197, 232–233, 316n18
    Hoover as director (*see* Hoover)
    investigates fifth columnists or alleged Nazi
        sympathizers, 72, 125, 192, 233
fears
    Armageddon, 3, 52
    attacks by air, 3, 7, 13, 18, 35, 41–45, 103–104,
        107, 112, 154, 172, 236, 239, 274n16–17
    attacks by foreign enemies, 4–5, 15, 193,
        205, 234
    attacks by land, 45, 116
    attacks by sea, 25
    attacks by space aliens, 1–2, 17, 35, 114, 135, 173
    attacks on home front, 5, 13–14, 47, 50, 61, 224
    biological or chemical weapons, 13, 44
    collective, mass, or public, 5, 105, 117, 185,
        200, 205, 229

diminished, 253–254
ER or FDR and, 17–18, 50, 52, 68, 71, 165,
    187–188, 191–192, 197, 202, 206, 229, 256
fascism, 57
fifth columnists or internal enemies, 5, 13, 58,
    70–72, 197
freedom from, 11, 13, 68, 165, 263
Hitler, 3, 13
invasion, 3, 17, 49, 71, 193
La Guardia and, 7, 112, 125, 128–129, 134,
    172, 177–178, 181, 185, 187, 192–193,
    199–201, 206, 229
Landis and, 13, 224–225, 228, 231, 234, 244
mass media and, 1–3, 5, 42–45, 70, 106–107
Nazis, 14, 18, 71, 129
regional, 233–234
rumors or anecdotes and, 70, 185, 193, 197
social defense and, 186, 202
Federal Security Agency (FSA), 32, 66, 91, 147,
    163, 232
fifth columnists, 82, 91, 120, 157, 214, 220,
    231–233, 238, 316n19
    California, 77, 192
    fears of, 13, 58, 70–72
    Japanese Americans viewed as, 231–233
    La Guardia on, 47, 128, 169, 175, 233
    Landis on, 233, 248
    Oregon, 78
    special police force for, 116
    Texas, 76
firefighters or fire officials
    California, 112, 195, 233
    equipment, 111, 114, 134, 172, 175, 177,
        236, 240
    home or civil defense and, 6, 13, 77, 83, 100,
        111, 113, 115–117, 130, 152, 208, 217, 225,
        233–235, 243, 260
    London or British, 5, 103, 105, 108–111, 115,
        170, 260
    New England, 206, 227
    New York or La Guardia and, 6–7, 39–40,
        113–114, 116, 123, 125, 127, 130, 134, 164,
        169–170, 177
    pilots, 217
    volunteer, 130, 179–181, 225, 244,
        252–253
Fish, Hamilton, 49, 122, 154
Florida, 44, 49, 73, 76–77, 158, 162, 173, 212,
    241, 263
France, 48, 66, 73, 76, 84, 104, 235,
    252, 316n19
    bombing of, 172, 223
    England or Great Britain and, 33, 48, 54, 73,
        84, 105
    fall of, 5, 74, 78, 105, 109, 126, 198, 229, 240
Franco, Francisco, 24, 36, 43, 48

freedom(s)
    British, 109
    economic or from want, 18, 68, 205, 210
    ER on, 18, 59, 153, 156, 205
    FDR on or four, 11, 13, 67–68, 207, 211
    "Freedom Sunday," 179
    La Guardia on, 113, 179
    limits on or individual, 98, 150, 201, 256,
        261, 263
    religious, 68, 179
    speech, 52, 67–68, 205

gardens, 11, 157, 166, 208, 247
gas masks, 6, 115, 122, 172, 185, 200, 236,
    240, 248
    distribution of, 6, 25, 43, 108, 130, 190, 230,
        238, 315n14
    funds for, 134, 175, 181, 214, 301n11
    London, 25, 43, 108
Georgia, 19, 30, 166, 173, 217, 256
Germany
    army or military, 37, 73
    bases, 42, 44, 254
    bombing or air raids by, 5, 23, 36, 42–44, 48,
        104, 106–108, 110, 171, 191, 254
    chemical warfare by, 112
    defeat of, 172, 245
    diplomatic relations with US, 19
    invades Balkans, 126
    invades Poland, 33, 48
    Luftwaffe or air force, 5, 36, 42, 48, 54, 73,
        105–106, 109
    naval power, 49, 73, 171
    threat to USA, 9, 55, 71, 115, 120, 191,
        200, 254
    WWI and, 19, 23, 42, 54
Gill, Corrington, 181–182, 194, 209
Great Britain, 1–2, 55, 95–98, 103–117, 223
    aid for, 9–10, 48, 54, 80, 96, 113–114, 120,
        157, 176, 178, 202
    air raids or Blitz, 5, 23, 42–43, 96, 103–109,
        117, 137
    army or navy, 49, 54, 110, 129, 154
    civil or home defense or home security, 97–98,
        103–105, 107–111, 131, 166, 287n26
    declares war on Germany, 48
    Empire or territories, 47, 95
    ER and, 26, 54, 95–96, 202
    firefighters, 5, 103, 105, 108–111, 115, 170, 260
    France and (*see* France)
    history, 104–105
    Home Office, 104–105
    Lend-Lease program (*see* Lend-Lease)
    as model for USA, 109, 116–117, 131, 134,
        170, 174, 213
    morale in (*see* morale)

Great Britain (*Cont.*)
   Munich Conference, 1, 25
   Royal Air Force, 73, 171, 229
   social welfare programs, 66, 97, 113
   USA and, 2, 29, 66, 70, 79, 83, 104, 106–107,
      120, 227
   WWI, 42, 104, 108
   see also England
Great Depression, 2, 13, 27, 62, 65–66, 85, 91,
      120, 132, 202, 269n38
   cities during, 40, 104
   New Deal to end, 14, 113
Greenland, 44, 72, 131, 235, 252

Harriman, Averell, 95, 98
Hawaii, 194, 292n12, 315n14
   bases in, 44, 216
   Japanese internments, 231
   Japanese invasion of, 187, 228
   military rule or troops in, 187, 228
health care, 11, 28, 33, 53, 86–87, 98–99, 119,
      163, 165, 205, 256, 260–261, 313n45
Hitler, Adolf, 98–99, 116–117, 218, 235
   air raids or Blitz and, 106–109, 111
   anti-Semitism of, 26, 29
   appeasement of, 25
   democracy vs., 4, 24–25, 35
   ER or FDR on, 1, 8, 24–29, 33, 36–37, 46,
      55–56, 191
   La Guardia on, 35–37, 46, 79–80, 125, 129,
      134, 178
   military aggression or victories of, 1, 3–4,
      25–26, 30, 37, 48, 53–54, 69, 71, 74, 78,
      109, 121, 154, 171
   speeches, 8, 25, 33
   threat to USA, 70–72, 107, 109, 111, 120, 125,
      128–129, 131, 164, 178, 229, 252
   US views of, 1, 3, 13, 35, 69–70, 120
Holland, 54, 109, 134
Hollywood, 166, 212, 233
home defense
   agencies or organizations, 104, 111
   arts and exercise and, 212–213, 218, 227
   British, 97–98, 103–105, 107–111, 131, 166,
      260, 263, 287n26
   cities, 69, 75–76, 79, 81–83, 113
   civil liberties, 15, 230
   civil rights and, 209–210, 251
   civilian or popular views of, 206, 211, 242,
      248, 253
   Cold War, 14, 262–263
   costs of, 108, 114, 134
   defined or scope of, 5, 14, 69, 76, 89, 121, 244,
      251, 259, 270n4
   ER and, 1, 4, 7, 11–12, 15, 61, 93–94, 122,
      143, 156–158, 164–167, 181–183, 185,
      188, 192–195, 203, 205, 207, 209–212,
      245–246, 256, 260, 262

   FBI and, 176, 197
   FDR and, 14, 37, 46, 68–69, 73–76, 79, 83, 91,
      98, 114, 119–122, 125, 157, 183, 254
   fear and, 172
   federal coordination or control of, 7, 15, 69,
      75, 81–84, 91, 113–114, 120–121, 180,
      195, 210, 234, 236
   Great Britain, England, or London, 5, 49, 97
   human security and, 185
   internments and, 232–233
   La Guardia and, 4, 6–7, 14, 35, 37, 69, 75–76,
      79–81, 111–113, 157, 119, 122–128,
      130–133, 156–157, 164, 167, 169–170,
      172–175, 177–181, 186, 192–193, 195,
      197–201, 205–207, 262
   Landis and, 12, 206, 224–225, 227, 238, 240,
      243–246, 248, 250, 252–253, 255–256, 262
   local or neighborhood, 69, 91, 112, 121, 166,
      200, 211, 245, 248
   military, militarized, or soldiers and, 7, 14, 74,
      130–131, 166, 175, 181, 240, 246
   morale and (*see* morale)
   national defense and, 61, 82–83
   policies, 174
   politics of or debates over, 98, 114–116, 122,
      151, 206, 252, 256–257
   propaganda, 7, 112, 179
   regions or regional directors, 12, 158, 162,
      198, 212, 227, 234
   social defense and, 89–92, 122, 228,
      245–247, 250
   states, 77–79, 83, 91, 113, 166, 180, 208
   statistics (*see* statistics)
   target zones for, 15, 170, 175–176, 181,
      198, 200
   views of, 15, 69–70, 172
   volunteers, 6, 12, 15, 69, 74, 83, 104, 121, 132,
      164–165, 180, 196, 205, 207–208, 217,
      224–225, 247–249, 253
   West Coast, 232–233
   WWII and WWI compared, 112–113, 129
   see also civil, or civilian, defense
Home Defense Commission, 89–91, 93
home front, 27, 59, 65–66, 76, 88, 97, 99, 156,
      200, 224, 237
   bombing of, 104, 223
   defense of, 4, 69, 73, 83, 100, 123, 1127, 128,
      131, 175, 191, 229, 239
   fears of attacks on (*see* fears)
   militarized, 7, 12, 104, 119, 123, 167,
      174–176, 180, 185, 230, 238
   morale on, 91, 100
   natural disasters threaten, 12
   social defense of, 97–98
   threats to, 13–14, 50, 72, 125, 239, 252,
      316n19, 318n26
   views of, 96, 98, 159, 256
home guards, 75, 81, 111, 121, 132, 192, 235

homeland security, 15, 263
Hoover, J. Edgar, 7, 110, 125, 175–176, 197, 233,
    305n35, 317n23, 320n41
Hopkins, Harry, 57, 59–60, 62–63, 67, 73, 96,
    114, 164, 188
hospitals, 2, 6, 8, 20, 33, 64, 95, 97, 111, 260
House Un-American Activities Committee
    (HUAC), 18, 72
Hull, Cordell, 47, 131
human rights, 8, 29
human security or defense, 28, 51–56, 58, 61–65,
    82, 89, 97, 113, 119, 121, 182
    definition of, 51, 251, 259
    military or national defense vs., 12, 55, 59–60,
        257, 259
    part of military or national defense, 15, 31,
        51–52, 155, 185
    see also social defense

Iceland, 44, 131, 171, 178, 235
Ickes, Harold, 33, 91, 213, 234, 291n34, 292n11
    home defense or OCD and, 114, 123, 207,
        211, 215, 220
    Secretary of the Interior, 45–46, 114
    social defense and, 122
Idaho, 162, 221, 239
Illinois, 178, 181, 217, 230
immigrants, 79, 87–88, 232, 317n21
    ER and, 29–30, 52, 182
    German, 125, 197, 199, 232
    Italian, 125, 197, 199, 232
    Japanese, 197, 232
    La Guardia and, 35, 37–39, 199
    Palmer Raids, 21
incendiary bombs, 6, 76–77, 111, 114, 123, 177,
    195, 240
    demonstrations, 146, 172, 180, 235
    London, 103, 105
Indiana, 32, 66, 215, 217, 251–252
industrial plants, *see* factories
internal security, 125, 197, 231
internment camps, 197, 231–232, 244
Iowa, 62, 249, 252
isolationists, 23–24, 48, 83, 98, 114, 201
    American, 15, 18, 36–37, 41, 122, 173
    conservative, 70, 113, 122, 134, 701
    Democrats (*see* Democrats: antiwar or
        isolationist)
    ER on, 9, 25, 27, 86, 154, 259
    FDR opposed by, 120, 127–128, 174, 176–177
    home defense and, 7, 14
    left-wing, 154
    Midwest, 15, 64, 99, 115, 132, 181
    post-WWI, 36, 49
    Republican (*see* Republicans: antiwar
        or isolationist)
Italian Americans, 7, *see also* immigrants: Italian
Italy, 23, 35, 38, 48, 260

Jackson, Robert, 46, 73, 80, 82, 122
Japan, 183, 191, 196, 230, 235
    air raids or bombing by, 36, 42, 234,
        238–240, 253
    Alaska or Aleutian Islands and, 131,
        238–239, 253
    China and, 3, 24, 29, 36, 271n22
    defeat of, 245
    embargo, 154
    Germany and, 71
    Hawaii and, 187
    Landis and, 225, 243, 253
    in Pacific or SE Asia, 202, 214, 228
    Pearl Harbor (*see* Pearl Harbor)
    West Coast bombing or invasion, 4–5, 131,
        187, 189, 192–193, 196–197, 228, 231,
        234, 238–240
Japanese Americans, 142, 186, 193, 196–197,
    219, 231–233
Jews, 17, 26, 29
Jim Crow, 29, 210, 259, 261, 269n38
Johnson, Lyndon B., 260–261

Kansas City, 73, 215, 217
Kellogg, Paul, 162, 166–167, 182, 188, 196, 209,
    214, 218, 220
Kennedy Sr., Joseph P., 29, 226, 262,
Kennedy, David M., 112, 270n12, 288n2
Kennedy, John F., 260–262
Kentucky, 229
Kerr, Florence, 11, 62, 87–94, 98–100, 128,
    155–158, 272n41, 285n6, 286n11, 297n8
Knox, Frank, 229, 254

La Guardia, Fiorello, 169–182
    accomplishments, 197–198
    aides or staff, 163, 174, 179, 201
    antifascist (*see* antifascists: La Guardia and)
    authoritarian, 175, 200
    biography, 6–7, 35, 37–39, 260, 262
    Civil Air Patrol and, 216, 237
    critics of, 7, 113, 123–124, 127, 133–134, 153,
        158–160, 177, 179, 181, 187, 199–201,
        205–208, 233
    on democracy, 35
    ER and, 4–5, 7–8, 11–12, 52, 58, 70, 124,
        138, 156–160, 164, 167, 170, 181–182,
        191–196, 201, 207, 215, 219, 256
    FDR or New Deal and, 6, 12, 14, 35–37,
        39–41, 44, 46–50, 69, 75–76, 79–82, 84,
        111, 122, 124–125, 176–177, 181, 201,
        206, 229, 256
    fears or hysteria and (*see* fears: La Guardia and)
    fire-fighting, 6–7, 39–40
    home defense or home front and, 35, 47, 50,
        68–69, 75–76, 79–84, 107–117, 124, 128
    Hoover or FBI and, 175–176
    Japanese or Japanese Americans and, 186, 197

La Guardia, Fiorello (*Cont.*)
  Permanent Joint Board on Defense, 80, 127
  Landis and, 206, 219, 225, 227–228, 230–231,
    240, 243, 246, 252
  as liberal, 80, 119, 124, 127, 129, 160,
    169–170
  Morrison and 103, 107–110, 127, 132, 138
  national security and, 36
  as New York mayor, 4, 6, 35–36, 39–40, 75,
    79, 81, 124–127, 134, 169, 174, 176, 260
  Office of Civilian Defense (OCD) and,
    12, 119–120, 122–134, 137, 155–167,
    201, 207
  ousted from OCD, 201, 206–207, 219, 223
  Pearl Harbor and, 185–187, 194, 205
  as pilot, 38–39
  on threats, 13, 42, 46, 111, 173, 252
  U.S. Conference of Mayors and, 40
  war games, 170, 173, 175
  West Coast tour (*see* West Coast)
Landis, James, 13, 149, 223–256
  biography, 12, 225–226, 262–263
  ER and, 211–212, 215, 219–220, 228, 246
  at Harvard Law School, 226, 236, 262
  Hoover and, 233
  Japan, Japanese, or Japanese Americans and,
    225, 231–234, 243, 253
  La Guardia and (*see* La Guardia)
  militarization by, 228, 230, 232–233, 238,
    243, 246
  New Deal or social defense and, 224,
    226–227, 245–250
  New England home defense and, 206, 227
  as OCD director, 12, 147, 206–207, 211–212,
    215, 219–220, 223–225, 227–255
  OCD resignation, 255–256
  SEC and, 206
  warnings from, 223–224, 228, 231, 235, 238,
    240, 243, 252–253
Larned, Abner, 29–30
Lash, Joseph, 11, 57, 88
Latin America, 36, 45–47, 71, 73, 88, 131, 177
League of Nations, 20–21, 270n13
League of Women Voters, 61, 94, 195
Lend-Lease, 63, 91, 93, 98–99, 111, 120,
    125, 178
liberal internationalists, 47, 73, 106, 119, 122,
    125, 224
liberals
  camps or types of, 53, 55, 86, 119, 170
  "the liberals," 114
  see also national security liberalism; New Deal
    liberalism; military defense liberalism
Lindbergh, Charles, 23, 37, 48, 70, 128,
    132, 176
Lindley, Betty, 209, 220, 309n24
Lippmann, Walter, 44, 70, 200

London, 25, 29, 54
  bombing or Blitz of, 5, 23, 43, 103–107, 111,
    172, 263, 287n26
  East End, 95, 108, 260, 287n26
  evacuations from, 48, 95, 174
  home defense programs, 108–110, 114–115,
    131, 135, 175, 263
  model for USA, 5, 43, 97, 103–104, 106–111,
    114, 131, 170, 173–175, 188, 202, 235, 263
  Underground, 108, 116
  US delegations or missions to, 5
  WVS in, 95–97
  WWI or "Zeppelin" raids, 23, 42–43
Long Island, 38, 44, 198, 200
Los Angeles, 3, 162, 234, 251
  air raids or bombing of, 107, 193, 250
  "Battle of," 229
  blackouts, 238, 242
  ER and/or La Guardia in, 4, 154, 191–194
  port security in, 174
  rumors or false alarms, 193
  threats to, 191–192, 233
Los Angeles Times, 43, 106–107, 127, 134, 192,
    197, 240
Louisiana, 171, 182, 208, 247
Luftwaffe, 5, 48, 54, 105–106, 109

MacLeish, Archibald, 59–60, 106, 120, 165, 179,
    212–213
  "Air Raid," 4, 42
  "Fall of the City," 3
magazines, 11, 43–44, 51, 54, 60, 172, 178, 218,
    252, *see also* Time
Maine, 77, 154, 180, 229–230
Marshall, George, 74, 82, 260
Massachusetts, 77, 111, 172–173, 177, 180, 238,
    243, 246, 249
Maverick, Maury, 75–76
McCarthy, Joseph, 261–262
McCormack-Dickstein Committee, 270n3
McNutt, Paul, 32–33, 66, 91, 94
McReynolds, William, 63, 79, 114–115
Mellett, Lowell, 60, 114
Mexico, 19, 44, 71, 73, 76–77, 79, 112, 170–171
Michigan, 216
Midwest, 2, 30, 62, 70, 79, 114, 130, 249, 295n28
  home defense in, 158, 176, 181, 212, 234, 238
  isolationist, 15, 64, 99, 115, 132, 181
militarization
  civilians or daily life, 13, 69, 129–130, 177,
    180, 230
  defined, 269n34
  home defense, 77, 107, 111, 113, 121, 238,
    245–246
  home front, 7, 12, 104, 119, 167, 175, 179,
    185, 238
  of infrastructure, 230

La Guardia and, 14, 69, 107, 111, 119, 129–130, 167, 169–170, 176–177, 180, 185, 223
Landis and, 13, 223, 225, 228, 238, 243, 246
liberalism, 245
social reform and, 51, 169
military defense, 9–10, 83, 112, 156, 195, 197, 211, 236, 245, 248
human security and, 12, 89, 257
liberals or liberalism, 53, 56, 61
social and, 11, 51, 65–66, 109, 201, 208, 247
volunteers, 207–208, 247
military technology, 23, 37, 125, 223, *see also* aviation technology
Minnesota, 25, 77, 164, 253
Missouri, 210, 217, 250
mobilization, 33, 80, 82, 224, 241, 247, 256
civilian, 6, 246
democracy and, 60
ER and, 18, 28, 31, 35–36, 51, 86, 94, 96, 162–164, 182, 188, 205, 210–211
FDR and, 31, 77, 259
home defense, 89, 91
industry, 32
Landis and, 252–253, 255
La Guardia and, 35–36, 116, 119, 128, 133, 177, 192, 198
mass, 6, 50, 62, 98, 115, 150, 163, 177, 182, 205, 210–211, 223, 233
military or war, 13, 18, 31, 35–36, 51–55, 57, 60–61, 63–65, 112, 154, 156, 161, 188, 203, 216, 249, 259
National Guard, 83
New Deal and, 86
social reform, social defense, or human security and, 18, 35, 52–53, 63–65, 94, 162
social, 94
volunteers, 115, 155, 248
women, 31, 62, 94–95, 98, 161, 165
youth, 210
Monroe Doctrine, 36, 70, 273n2
Montana, 127, 156, 217
morale, 23, 208–211, 213–214
British or English, 23, 105–106, 116, 271n20, 287n26
civilian, public, or national, 5, 23, 27, 31, 37, 59, 95, 155, 157, 214, 230, 243, 246
ER and, 7, 9–10, 12, 27, 53, 91, 100, 157, 162, 164, 205, 210–211, 245
home defense or OCD and, 14, 69, 74, 91, 100, 113–114, 123, 126, 157, 205, 209, 263
New Deal and, 32–33
social defense and, 158, 209, 245
Morgenthau, Elinor, 11, 89, 157, 161, 163–164, 182, 202, 209, 220, 299n30
Morgenthau, Henry, 95, 195–196
Morrison, Herbert, 103, 107–110, 127, 132, 137–138

Munich, 1, 25, 56, 227
Murrow, Edward R., 5, 106, 229, 287n26, 316n19
Mussolini, Benito, 23–24, 36, 48, 79, 235

NAACP, 157, 209, 261
national defense
Advisory Commission, 60
citizens' roles in, 59
ER on, 24–25, 27, 31, 33, 51
FDR on, 31
home defense and, 61
policies, 37
social welfare or social defense and, 18, 31, 33, 51
volunteers, 121
National Guard, 76–77, 83, 192
national security liberalism, 51, 197, 201, 205, 233, 235, 244, 262–263
defined, 6
La Guardia's, 11–12, 70, 130, 155, 267n18
Landis's, 13
national security, 14–15, 36, 114, 188, 224, 227, 236, 239, 241
advisors or officials, 69, 104, 110, 176
air war and, 45
cities, 82
coalition, 238
defined, 257
politics, 98, 101, 126, 263
social reform, human defense, or human security and, 12, 31, 61, 66, 91, 157, 205, 227, 259
state, 188, 223–224, 236
views of, 7–8, 45, 36, 237
national service, 59, 99, 155, 246, 252, 256, 286n8, 296n6
National Youth Administration (NYA), 8, 11, 22, 32, 53, 57–58, 65, 92, 155, 220
natural disasters, 12–13, 40, 205, 217, 225
earthquakes, 43, 233
fires, 13
floods, 13, 40, 43, 100, 217, 233, 244
Nazis, 43, 66, 96, 98–99, 134, 165, 243, 246, 248
air raids, bombing, or Blitz, 106–108, 129, 175, 179, 227
appeasement of, 25, 54, 86
bases, 47, 129, 131, 179, 240, 252
Czechoslovakia, 1, 26
democracy vs., 157, 245
fascism or totalitarianism of, 26, 34, 210
germ warfare, 131, 229–230
Japan and, 186
Jews and, 26
Latin or South America, 45–47, 70–71, 131, 171, 176–177
parachutists, 126

Nazis (*Cont.*)
  propaganda, 47, 71
  racism, 196
  Russia, 178
  submarines (*see* submarines; U-boats)
  sympathizers or spies in USA, 52, 69, 79, 86,
    116, 229, 233, 252
  threat to bomb USA, 43, 47, 175, 179, 227,
    235–236, 252
  threat to USA or Western Hemisphere, 5,
    44–47, 57, 70–73, 79, 103, 111, 119–120,
    154, 173, 240
  victories, 53
Nazism, 18, 25, 46, 54
Nebraska, 80, 181
Neutrality Acts, 24, 36
New Deal, 2, 6–11, 85, 259–260
  coalition, 18, 31, 56, 61, 63, 90, 238, 250
  critics or opponents, 12, 22, 28, 44, 69–70, 98,
    150, 159, 165, 177, 215, 219, 250, 252
  end of, 85
  ER or FDR and (*see* Roosevelt, Eleanor;
    Roosevelt, Franklin D.)
  military and, 9–10, 85–86
  programs or agencies, 8, 10–11, 53, 57–59
  wartime, 7, 14, 18, 27, 31–33, 35, 51–52,
    62–63, 65, 86, 161, 186, 189, 215, 221, 244,
    247, 299n30
New Deal liberalism, 36–37, 85–86, 153, 185,
    188, 202–203, 205, 223, 261–263, 267n18,
    276n2, 285n2
  ER and, 8–9, 12, 28
  as national security philosophy, 36
  Wallace and, 303n7
New England, 12, 72, 129, 162, 180, 186, 198,
    241–242
  drills, 115, 206, 238
  Landis as home defense director of, 12,
    206, 227
New Hampshire, 77, 180
New Jersey, 1, 3, 45, 69, 77, 230, 233, 242, 266n3
New Mexico, 171–172
New Orleans, 19, 127, 181, 206, 251
New York City, 55, 58, 70, 105, 233
  air raids or bomb threats, 7, 35, 40, 47, 81,
    109, 115, 152, 170, 178, 198–200, 225, 252,
    254, 302n19
  blackouts or dimouts, 170–171, 237, 241,
    251, 321n44
  Brooklyn, 80, 127, 173, 178, 236, 241–242
  Bronx, 129, 321n44
  corruption in, 36, 38–39
  defense of, 5, 49, 81, 109–111, 114–115,
    132–133, 144, 170, 198, 201
  drills (*see* drills: La Guardia's)
  evacuation plans, 77

home defense modeled on England or
    London's, 5, 49, 109–110
Japanese, German, and/or Italians in, 186, 199
La Guardia as mayor of (*see* La Guardia)
landmarks, 81, 115
Manhattan, 2, 115, 117, 146, 171, 198, 237,
    242, 294n27, 321n44
panic or riots in, 103, 198–199
police, 2, 40, 82, 110, 125, 133, 178
Queens, 58, 80, 173, 321n44
rumors or false alarms about attacks in,
    198–199, 230, 236
subway, 7, 40, 116, 199
threats to, 111, 116, 125
"War of the Worlds," 1–3
WPA in, 40
New York State, 69, 77, 83, 112, 120, 163, 217,
    229, 241
New York Times, 2–3, 20, 29, 43, 45, 71, 117, 199,
    220, 229, 237, 239
  on Blitz or London, 95, 97, 106
  on La Guardia, 6, 39, 127
  on Landis, 225, 235
Newfoundland, 72, 131
newspapers, 49, 237, 254, 323n14
  on ER, 213, 215
  on La Guardia, 127, 160, 176, 178, 206
  radio and, 5, 41, 178
  on war in Europe, 26, 41, 70, 107
  on "War of the Worlds," 1–2, 265–266n3
  warnings in, 43, 70–71, 106, 178, 198,
    234, 239
9/11, 15, 263
North Carolina, 2, 60, 154–155, 173, 193, 218
Norton, Mary, 89, 93
Norway, 53, 66, 252
nuclear war or weapons, 14–15, 257,
    262–263, 268n34

Obama, Barack, 263
Office of Civilian Defense (OCD)
  abolishment of, 256
  budget or size of, 128, 180–181, 203
  ER as asst. director of, 4, 11, 138, 153, 156,
    160–161, 189, 203, 211, 213
  ER leaves, 12, 147, 260
  establishment of, 6, 117, 119, 123, 153
  internment camps and, 231
  La Guardia and (*see* La Guardia)
  Landis as director, 147, 223, 234, 246, 248,
    254, 256
  Martin as director, 255, 317n22
  public relations, 161, 163–164
  regions or regional directors, 163, 165, 186,
    188, 197, 209, 232–234, 242, 248
  social defense and, 122, 126, 155–156, 182, 246

Ohio, 2, 130, 181, 216, 218, 244, 250, 259
Oklahoma, 2, 13, 212, 217
Olson, Culbert, 77, 191–192, 231
Omaha, 73, 114
Oregon, 78, 196, 211, 238, 240, 253

pacifists, 8–9, 19, 21–23, 25, 35–36, 39, 55–56,
    108, 259
Panama, 45, 48, 71
parachutists, 70, 126, 238–239
Paris, 5, 8, 20, 29, 117
Pasadena, 92, 193, 240
patriotism, 9, 21, 82, 94, 98, 154, 210, 238
Pearl Harbor, 7, 15, 32, 193, 209, 229–230, 234,
    252–253, 263
  blame for, 185, 199
  ER and, 142, 185, 187–188, 197, 202
  FDR and, 4, 187–188
  Japanese Americans or immigrants following,
    142, 197, 231
  La Guardia and, 185–187, 194, 205, 237
  no major attacks after, 223–224, 240
  losses, 140, 187, 189, 192, 216, 228
  racism increases after, 231
  security increases after, 189–191, 197
Peck, Lydell, 77, 111
Pegler, Westbrook, 44, 215
Pennsylvania, 31, 70, 121, 162, 189, 208,
    216–217, 229, 247
Perkins, Frances, 33, 57, 89, 122, 191
Philadelphia, 105, 114, 119, 128, 137, 156, 177,
    182, 215, 217, 238, 252
Pinchot, Mrs. Gifford, 158, 220
Pittsburgh, 216–217, 239, 244, 251
Poland, 33, 48, 109, 134, 223
police, 2, 5, 42, 69, 76, 83, 110–111, 172, 193, 243
Polier, Justine, 182, 209, 220, 299n27
Portland, 73, 196, 211
power stations or grid, 72, 78, 81–82, 113, 131,
    174, 232
Progressive era, 52, 54
progressives, 27, 62–63, 66, 79, 83, 85, 87, 104,
    161, 224
  antiwar or pacifism and, 20–21
  ER and, 53, 58, 86, 97, 202, 261
  organizations or movement, 31, 87
  youths and, 29, 261
propaganda, 92, 104, 112, 121, 169, 212, 220,
    224–225, 239, 263
  anti-American, 72
  "Freedom Sunday" campaign, 7, 179
  Nazi, 46–47
public health, 32, 39, 58–59, 61, 74, 76, 77, 83,
    87–88, 93, 121, 126, 161, 195, 232, 260
  social defense or OCD and, 10, 208, 250
Puerto Rico, 44, 48, 292n12, 315n14

racism, 29, 54, 77, 186, 196, 231, 269n38, 280n35
radio, 1–5, 26, 41, 48, 90, 124, 173, 178, 193, 256
Reading, Stella, 5–6, 95–97
Red Cross, 95, 208, 216, 247
  ER and, 19–20, 58, 94
  in Europe, 54
  training, 180, 195
refugees, 8, 26, 29, 54, 71, 261–262
Republicans, 14, 35, 60, 64, 78, 154, 285, 323n14
  anti–New Deal, 22, 69, 78, 216, 219, 252
  antiwar or isolationist, 9, 98
  congressional, 154, 214, 254
  conservative, 22, 154, 214, 216, 219, 231
  Dewey, 69
  ER vs., 22, 53, 154
  FDR vs., 22, 63
  La Guardia as, 6, 35, 38, 80–81
  liberal, 119, 231
  pro-intervention, 122
  Willkie, 64, 81
Revolutionary War, 17, 104
Rhode Island, 2, 180
Roche, Josephine, 32–33
Rockefeller, Nelson, 71, 88
Rodman, Selden, 60, 99, 218
Roosevelt, Eleanor (ER)
  American Social Defense Administration and,
    10, 88–89, 155
  antifascist (*see* antifascists: ER as)
  antiwar or pacifism and, 8, 19, 21, 23–24
  biography, 7–9, 18, 26, 261–262
  charity by, 58, 101
  civil rights and, 8, 29, 54–55, 88, 90, 209,
    260–261, 297n9
  correspondence, 11, 29–31, 54, 58, 210
  criticism of, 12, 24, 59, 98–99, 155
  on democracy, 27, 29, 35
  FDR and, 4, 7–9, 11, 31, 54, 56–61, 88–91,
    156–159, 165, 201, 214–215, 219
  as first lady, 10–11, 22, 51
  influence of, 9–11, 54, 57, 61, 66–67
  international views, 9, 23–27, 54, 86
  Japan or Japanese Americans, 24, 29, 142,
    196–197
  Jews and, 26, 29
  La Guardia and (*see* La Guardia)
  "My Day," 10–11, 53, 159
  New Deal or New Deal liberalism and, 8–11,
    28, 30, 32, 51–54, 61, 63, 86, 90, 153–154
  Office of Civilian Defense (*see* Office of
    Civilian Defense)
  Reading and, 5–6, 95–97
  social defense and (*see* social defense: ER on)
  speeches, 27–28, 54–55, 63, 217
  Theodore Roosevelt and, 7
  WWI and interwar period, 18–21

Roosevelt, Franklin D. (FDR)
  air attacks or forces and, 41–42, 44–46, 225
  allies or supporters, 8, 32, 47–48, 80–81
  antifascist, 82, 125, 226
  asst. secretary of navy, 8, 19
  court-packing plan, 21, 85, 88, 285n7
  criticism of or opposition to, 13, 18, 21–22,
    28, 36, 55, 66, 69, 75, 80, 177, 219
  fireside chats or speeches, 4, 11, 13, 17, 31, 48,
    64–67, 72, 74, 90, 245, 256
  GI Bill of Rights, 256
  home defense and (*see* home defense)
  international or foreign policy views, 36, 41,
    44, 46–48, 73, 79, 81, 176, 183
  internment camp order, 231
  La Guardia and (*see* La Guardia)
  Landis and, 12, 236, 255
  military and, 18, 22, 31–32, 48, 55–56, 63–66,
    72, 74, 83, 111, 188, 259
  national security or defense and, 9, 31,
    36–37, 60, 74
  New Deal and, 2, 11, 13–14, 18, 22, 28, 31–33,
    40–41, 53, 56–57, 61, 63–65, 85–86, 90,
    154, 211
  OCD and (*see* Office of Civilian Defense)
  on Pearl Harbor, 4, 187–189
  postwar liberalism and, 260
  social defense, social welfare, or human
    security and, 10, 13–14, 31, 33, 53, 64–65
  term #1 (1933–1937), 18, 52
  term #2 (1937–1941), 1, 8, 11, 18, 21–22,
    25, 41, 56
  term #3 (1941–1945), 4, 11, 63–65, 75, 80,
    82–83, 87, 153
  term #4 (1945) and death, 256
Rosenberg, Anna, 132, 159
  buffer between La Guardia and ER or FDR,
    134, 201
  public relations role, 132, 158, 161, 165
Rosenman, Samuel, 67, 124, 255
Royal Air Force, 73, 229
rumor, 2, 4, 98, 124, 185–186, 189, 191, 193,
  197, 230, 234, 255

sabotage, 14, 49, 71, 112, 120, 134, 169, 175,
  232, 239, 253
San Antonio, 75–76
San Diego, 194, 234, 239
San Francisco, 43, 58, 189, 226, 229
  dimouts or drills, 239, 242, 304n18
  ER and/or La Guardia in, 191, 193–195
  false alarms or rumors of attacks in, 5, 189,
    191, 304n18
  home defense in, 158, 192–195
  OCD's West Coast headquarters, 232
  restricts immigrants, 232
  newspapers, 218, 239
Seattle, 70, 73, 196, 210, 239, 244, 247

blackouts, 78, 185
  drills or war show, 78, 238, 253–254
  evacuation plans, 181
  riot in, 185, 193
  child care in, 247, 250
Seaver, Jane, 161, 202, 209–210
self defense, 6–7, 14, 24, 104, 240
Sheppard, James, 232–234, 241–242, 253
Sherry, Michael, 42, 268–269n34, 274n17
skyscrapers, 81, 115, 125, 130, 171, 186, 198–199
Smith, Harold, 91, 115, 122–123, 201
social defense liberalism, 8, 11, 13, 57, 61, 119,
    132, 170, 186, 188, 201, 214, 216, 236, 250,
    261–262
  critics of, 98–99
  defined, 10, 89, 270n4
  ER and, 10–13, 18, 24–25, 27, 35, 51, 66–67,
    88–101, 122–123, 153, 155–158, 162,
    164–167, 181–182, 186–188, 195, 201–202,
    207, 209–210, 212, 220, 223, 247, 256, 262
  military or military security and, 10–11, 35,
    51, 63, 65, 67, 97, 169, 186, 256
  national defense or security and, 18, 31, 91,
    188, 202, 223, 259
  New Deal and, 212, 220, 223
  in postwar era, 260, 262
  morale and, 245
  OCD and, 246–247, 249
  volunteers, 207–208, 225, 247–248
  see also American Social Defense
    Administration
Social Security, 10, 22, 32–33, 61, 65–66, 132
South America, 47, 70–71, 73, 171
South Carolina, 56, 77, 173
Soviet Union, 14, 154, 171
Spain, 22–23, 45, 104, 172, 223, 229
  Civil War, 3, 24, 36, 43, 48
  Guernica, 5, 43
spies, 71–72, 79, 98, 108, 116, 200,
  229–231, 252
state defense councils or efforts, 69, 75, 77–79,
  83, *see also* home defense: states
statistics, 108, 218, 265n3, 315n13
  active duty military, 207, 228
  African Americans, 251
  air raids or bombing, 7, 104, 114, 129, 133,
    173, 180, 200, 252
  Blitz casualties, 5, 23, 43, 103, 105
  civil defense, 263
  drills, 115, 128, 171, 238, 242
  ER correspondence, 278n21
  FDR approval ratings, 22, 83, 172, 271n15
  Gallup polls, 36, 49, 70, 72, 78–79, 83,
    172, 180
  home defense, 15, 95, 104, 108, 112, 115, 128,
    132, 158, 165–166, 176, 180, 207, 225, 227,
    240, 249–250, 254
  Japanese Americans, 196, 231

OCD, 11, 166, 173, 175, 180–181, 198, 208, 236–237, 247
unemployment, New Deal, or social defense, 91, 40, 65–66, 100
Stevenson, Adlai, 132, 260–261
Stimson, Henry, 109–110, 175, 199, 239, 260
submarines, 13, 19, 171, 228, 237–238, 243, 252, 254
Sudetenland, 1, 8, 25, 265n1, 266n3
Supreme Court, U.S., 12, 21, 89, 120, 125, 226

Tacoma, 73, 78, 142–143
Texas, 77, 79, 171, 214, 235, 252
Thompson, Dorothy, 3, 44,
Thompson, Malvina, 162, 218, 272n41, 286n11
Time magazine, 3, 49, 70, 117, 128, 169, 172, 177, 200, 239
Tokyo, 47, 243
total war, 7, 9, 14, 23, 51, 62, 129, 187, 224, 230, 234, 256–257
age of, 12, 14, 42, 48, 134
practice of, 21, 97
threat or fears of, 23, 27
"total defense" for, 62
women's role in, 210, 214
totalitarianism, 24–25, 27, 29, 31, 52, 59, 65–66, 177, 210, 224, 245, 259
U.S. politicians accused of, 12, 21
Truman, Harry S. 256, 260–263

U-boats, 19, 171, 178, 241, 243, *see also* submarines
unemployment, 28, 51–52, 56, 61–62, 91, 124, 164, 226, 256
benefits, 32, 53, 64–67
mass, 37, 40
uniforms, 89, 123, 127, 157, 165, 195, 200, 207, 240
unions, 21, 32, 57, 70, 247, 250, 277n12
ER and, 165, 267n24, 268n32
La Guardia and, 82, 119, 132–133
United States: attacks on, 1–2
coasts of, 6, 9, 15, 24, 45–46, 69, 170, 181, 185, 200 (*see also* East Coast; home defense: target zones for; West Coast)
enters WWI, 19
enters WWII, 4
European war and, 3–5, 24, 36–38, 44, 48–49, 56, 154
fears about attacks on (*see* fears)
ocean buffer for, 2, 14, 25, 37, 41, 49, 72
United Veterans of Foreign Wars, 76
U.S. Armed Forces, 9, 58, 63, 109, 155, 207, 224–225
U.S. Conference of Mayors, 40–41, 47, 75, 79, 82, 111, 116
U.S. Air Force, 48–49, 63

U.S. Army, 32, 38, 112, 131, 155, 186
African Americans and, 87, 209
bases or camps, 9, 44, 121, 123, 166, 198, 253
blackouts and, 193–194, 199, 304n18
defense against air attacks, 15, 39, 44–45, 171, 198, 229, 236
defense against invasion, 25, 48, 175
disaster relief by, 40
drills by, 44, 115, 171, 173, 304n18
home defense or OCD and, 74, 81, 120, 170, 175, 199, 230–233, 243, 253
internment camps, 231–232
McCarthy seeks traitors in, 262
Secretary of, 228
size of, 18, 24, 33, 39, 63
soldiers, 86, 90, 212–213
warnings by officers, 117, 131, 228–229
U.S. Army Air Corps or Service, 38, 44
U.S. Committee for the Care of European Children, 54, 58
U.S. Navy, 24–25, 47–48, 63, 112, 154, 171–172, 238, 321n45
"Battle of Los Angeles," 229
FDR as asst. secretary of, 8, 18–19
home defense and, 120, 126, 131–132
Pearl Harbor's impact on, 187, 189, 192, 199, 228
Secretary of, 131, 174, 228–229, 254–255
USS Kearny, 171
USS Reuben James, 171, 178
Utah, 178, 232

Vermont, 69, 180
Virginia, 49, 56, 244, 253
Volunteer Participation Committee, 156–157, 163, 209, 211, 220, 246
Volunteer Women of America, 297n8

Wallace, Henry, 63, 80, 122
War Department, 32, 78, 81, 93, 103, 116, 126, 233, 275n25, 288n1, 315n14
home defense and, 74, 254
"War of the Worlds," 1–4, 17, 35, 41–43, 45, 48, 265–266n3
air raids and, 111
Kirby cartoon, 135
radio medium and, 3
War Relocation Authority, 231–232
wardens, 6, 122, 130, 132–133, 171, 175, 236, 242
air raid, 139, 146, 172, 180–181, 195–196, 198, 202, 206, 212, 225, 230, 233, 236, 247, 250–252
anti-spy activities, 232
block, 248
civil defense, 217
fire, 233

wardens (*Cont.*)
  New York, 198, 233, 236–238
  Seattle, 250
  statistics, 225
  training or training literature, 212, 247
  views of, 234
  Washington, D.C., 238
  women or minorities as, 251
Washington Post, 3, 55, 106, 109
  on air attacks, 3, 43, 83, 122, 129, 190
  on drills, 236, 238
  on La Guardia, 124, 127, 159
  public opinion influenced by, 44
  on women's mobilization, 62, 94–95, 165
Washington, D.C., 3, 6, 8, 36, 38, 206
  African American congregation in, 9, 55
  air raids in, 190
  defense of, 115, 165
  drills in, 122
  ER in or on, 18–21, 55, 190
  landmarks or monuments, 122, 190
  spies in, 79
Washington State, 73, 78, 99, 193
water reservoirs or supply, 6, 77–78, 81–82, 113,
    130, 174, 230, 232
Watson, Edwin "Pa," 91, 116
Wehrmacht, 48, 53–54
Welles, Orson, 1, 3–4, 16, 35, 42, 70, 111, 114,
    116–117, 265n2
  "Fall of the City," 3
  see also "War of the Worlds"
West Coast, 2, 6
  air raids or bombing, 180, 189
  ER and La Guardia's tour of, 142, 191,
    198–199
  Japanese invasion of, 4–5, 71, 131, 187
  public events canceled, 193
West Virginia, 243
Western Hemisphere, 36, 45–48, 125, 128, 175
White House, 29, 136, 141, 163, 182,
    189–191, 304n17
Willkie, Wendell, 9, 64, 81, 83, 86, 124
Wilson, Woodrow, 19–20, 165
Wisconsin, 77, 252
women
  ambulance or transport drivers, 95, 166,
    194, 234
  British, 95–98, 156, 164, 166, 297n14
  ER and, 10, 30–31, 51, 61–62, 86–89, 155,
    165, 261–262
  factory workers, 130, 139, 205, 208,
    248, 318n26
  home defense roles, 77–78, 156–157, 163,
    165–166, 178, 209, 249
  knitting, 19, 60, 123, 129
  mobilized, 31, 62, 94–95, 165
  organizations or committees, 61, 87, 182

New Deal, 31–32, 51, 62–63
  rights for, 31, 39, 62
  social defense and, 10, 88–92, 100, 162
  suffrage, 87, 165
  training or jobs for, 10–11, 57–58, 61–62,
    87–88, 155, 249
  volunteers, 10, 19, 60–62, 86–89, 94, 155,
    158, 163–166, 195, 249
Women's (Royal) Voluntary Services (Britain),
    5–6, 95–98
Wood, Robert, 36, 132
Woodring, Harry, 74–75, 81–82
Woodward, Ellen, 60–61, 67, 89, 91, 158
Woolf, Virginia, 43, 135
Works Progress Administration (WPA), 11, 58,
    59, 67, 87, 92–93, 128, 220, 247
  artists or writers, 57
  criticism of, 40–41
  end of, 11
  ER and, 29–31
  Harrington and, 30
  head, staff, or supervisors, 29–31, 59, 61–62
  New York City, 40
  recreation programs, 59
World War I, 11, 18–19, 21, 23, 35–36, 46, 61,
    79, 108, 215, 227
  air raids in, 42–43, 104, 130, 223
  Armistice, 21, 39, 270n12
  ER in, 8, 19–20, 87, 161
  Germany in, 54
  isolationism following, 36, 49
  La Guardia in, 6, 38
  lessons learned from, 112
  veterans, 45
  women during, 165
  WWII compared to, 23, 112–113, 129
World War II, 10, 123, 129, 259
  battle of Midway, 238
  civil defense during, 104
  early years of, 224–225, 235
  ER views of, 34
  home defense during, 14–15, 104, 113, 225
  mass media and, 42
  sabotage during, 112
  US entry into, 4
  women and, 165

Young Men's Christian Association
    (YMCA), 195
Young Women's Christian Association
    (YWCA), 29, 31
youths, 59, 61, 64, 67, 88, 90, 159, 188, 236, 209,
    212, 260–261
  conferences or groups, 8–9, 28–29, 55,
    210, 305n31
  OCD or home defense and, 161, 180, 210
  training for, 59, 65